Women's Issues for a New Generation

WOMEN'S ISSUES FOR

OXFORD
UNIVERSITY PRESS

A NEW GENERATION

A Social Work Perspective

GAIL UKOCKIS, PHD, LSW

OXFORD
UNIVERSITY PRESS

Oxford University Press is a department of the University of Oxford. It furthers
the University's objective of excellence in research, scholarship, and education
by publishing worldwide. Oxford is a registered trade mark of Oxford University
Press in the UK and certain other countries.

Published in the United States of America by Oxford University Press
198 Madison Avenue, New York, NY 10016, United States of America.

Library of Congress Cataloging-in-Publication Data
Names: Ukockis, Gail L., 1962– author.
Title: Women's issues for a new generation : a social work perspective /Gail Ukockis, PhD, LSW.
Description: Oxford ; New York : Oxford University Press, [2016] | Includes bibliographical
references and index.
Identifiers: LCCN 2015043338 | ISBN 9780190239398 (alk. paper)
Subjects: LCSH: Social work with women. | Women—Social conditions. | Feminism. | Social service.
Classification: LCC HV1444 .U46 2016 | DDC 362.83/53—dc23
LC record available at http://lccn.loc.gov/2015043338

This book is dedicated to the memory of my sister Carol, who loved books even more than me.

When I was a kid, she would read about esoteric topics like the Epic of Gilgamesh and tell me all about it. She was a great teacher and a great friend.

Contents

PART 3 Women in the International Context

Preface

WRITING THIS BOOK has been a joy not only because I care so much about the subject, but because I see a resurgent interest in women's issues. Just last night (August 6, 2015), a presidential candidate at a debate had to account for the derogatory statements he had made about women. Only last week, Congress considered defunding Planned Parenthood—a source of vital health services for millions of women. A once-loved comedian, accused of drugging and raping dozens of women, has lost the protection of his celebrity status because the alleged victims were finally taken seriously. On a daily basis, the issues discussed in this book are front-page news.

This time period, then, is an ideal time to reconsider "women's liberation" (second-wave feminism) for the new generation. Whether you are an instructor, student, or general reader, you have the unique opportunity to apply concepts from this book to your own life and your social setting. You may consider yourself a feminist or traditionalist or any label. No matter your belief system, though, we should all share the same basic knowledge of history and other contexts of women's issues. We need this common knowledge for constructive dialogues about social action.

In one way, this book is a form of activism. The first step for any type of activism is education not only about the specific issue (e.g., racist stereotypes) but the wider framework of that issue. I wrote this book to generate in-depth discussions about the realities of being a woman in the United States and in other countries. When I was teaching a women's-issues class and a student would tell me that she or he had talked about one of the topics with a roommate or parent, I felt a warm glow. Obviously, this book has no answers to the complex problems of gender inequality but, hopefully, it will be a catalyst for finding those answers.

Since this book has adopted the famous "the personal is the political" creed of the second-wave movement, I have added Author's Notes to some chapters. I encourage the readers to apply items in the book to their own lives so they can see the connection between the personal and the political.

I was not born a feminist, but I have vivid memories of when "women's lib" burst into the public arena when I was around eight or nine. Going to a Catholic school, I was disappointed by the fact that my brothers could serve as altar boys but I could not be an altar girl. I was too young, though, to understand words such as "patriarchy." As the youngest of seven kids, I wanted to be like my brothers because they seemed to have more fun than my sisters. It did not occur to me that society had imposed a different set of rules for females. My mother lived a tragic life as an alcoholic and battered wife. Not until many years later did we realize that the words *domestic violence* applied to our own troubled family.

My childhood vow was that no matter what, I was going to be strong and independent and not get beat up by any man. This motivation certainly did not mean that I disliked or distrusted most males. Many good, kind men have influenced me since I was a child. It did mean, though, that I could not comprehend the idea of submission to a dominant man (father, husband, etc.). I did not know of any male who was morally or intellectually superior to me. This may sound arrogant and I certainly did not voice this idea to my parish priest, but I simply believed in my own talents and brains above any possible male authority.

When did I identify myself as a feminist? This is a tricky question because the "f word" still evokes some negative reactions. Recently, I even heard a domestic violence advocate say, "I'm not a feminist, but … ." When the feminist movement became popular in the early 1970s, I was a tween who wanted to be pretty. Women leaders, though, had to live with bitter criticisms and sneering contempt. The media portrayed them as angry, big-mouthed, and ugly. Very ugly! Way too ugly to get a man. That was why these women were protesting—they could not get a man, so they were punishing the rest of us.

I grew up, then, thinking that the feminist leaders were ugly. Yes, I agreed with them about equal pay but did I want to be lumped in with these pathetic, repellant creatures? I wanted to be pretty. Why did I have to choose between feminism and being pretty?

Fast forward to 1983, when I had just graduated from college. Gloria Steinem had just published her book of essays (*Outrageous Acts and Everyday Rebellions*) and I went to the bookstore for the book signing. As I approached the table, I was speechless. She was not ugly at all! In fact, she was lovely. Truly beautiful. She must have thought I was a moron when I could barely say a word.

Another hesitation to my claiming the name of "feminist" was the fear of being seen as a lesbian. Homophobia made me hesitate in identifying with a movement that included some women who were lesbians and even more shocking, bisexuals. Not until I spent a few months living in a lesbian mecca (Northampton, Massachusetts) did I get cured of this fear. Who cares if anyone thinks I'm a lesbian? Now that fear seems ludicrous, and I hope it no longer exists with the younger generation.

The eternally controversial topic of abortion also complicated the advancement of feminist goals. Does being a feminist mean you *have* to support legalized abortion? Later, I met several women who had had abortions and began to shift my position toward the pro-choice camp. Abortion, though, remains a wedge issue that antifeminists use to undermine all the other causes related to equal rights.

Despite these concerns about being called a feminist, I still accepted that label because I could not imagine obeying any male authority. As a teenager, I briefly attended a conservative evangelical church. I remember expressing shock when a grown woman told of how she would follow her father's authority until she got married. Another woman turned to me and chided, "Why do you have to be such a feminist?" I was flabbergasted. How could my opinion that adults should make decisions for themselves be considered un-Christian in any way? Not surprisingly, I did not last long at that church.

Not until I started teaching a women's issues class in 2003, though, did the *feminist* label become strongly associated with me. Some people expected me to be a hairy-legged man hater who was determined to brainwash my gullible female students into joining a lesbian/moon-worshipping/vegetarian cult. Despite this stereotype, I still shave my legs and enjoy romantic comedies.

This class and book have given me a fuller understanding of feminism's multifaceted aspects. Somebody once told me when I was in my twenties that a woman is not truly a feminist until she hits forty. I was deeply insulted by that statement, but now I somewhat agree with it. Now I see the ingrained patterns of oppression instead of isolated cases of put-downs. I used to cringe at the idea of being a radical feminist (or any other type of radical) because I would rather be a moderate centrist. But new dimensions of misogyny have emerged, from Internet threats to feminist bloggers to blatant ridicule of female leaders. The older I get, the more I want to fight back.

Hopeful signs are appearing, though, such as younger women claiming their right to be taken seriously and younger men fighting the hypermasculine command to "be a man." When I had taught this class, I often had male students who were taking the class not because of personal interest but because they needed the seminar credit. The anxiety of these male students usually appeared on the first day of class, since they were not sure that they would be welcome in this class. Was I a male-basher out to emasculate any man foolish enough to sign up for this class? This experience of teaching males in a "women's issues" class has made me realize even more that compartmentalizing these issues as important to only women was both foolish and counterproductive. For example, fathers could be just as concerned about affordable day care as the mothers because parenting is a joint effort.

I extend a full invitation, then, to women, men, and those who cross the gender line (e.g., transgender persons.) Rejecting the idea that somebody has to be born with a female body to be considered a real woman, I accept each person's self-definition of gender. This book is intended to be inclusive.

Although I had taught this class for eleven years, I never tired of the topics. As a social worker, I emphasize the person-in-environment perspective of daily realities such as street harassment and inadequate day care. The term *women's issues* is used deliberately, then, because I define "women's studies" as more theoretical and conceptual.

Hopefully, this book will encourage some readers to explore women's studies with its intellectually gifted writers.

One feature of this book is its companion webpage, which includes bonus readings that will be updated. This book, written for a one-semester class, could not completely cover the wide range of topics and opinions that deserve further reading. Also included on the website are study guides and other helpful information.

Besides encouraging outside readings, another goal of this book is to encourage critical thinking. Discussion questions and case studies, either in class or as homework, are intended to sharpen readers' analytical skills. Related to critical thinking is the need for a sociological imagination, to consider what it would be like in another person's shoes. This book will expose you to several perspectives, some of which may be familiar but some may be foreign and even threatening to your worldview. You are not expected to agree with every reading, but to use your sociological imagination to understand the person's point of view. For example, why would marriage be equated with prostitution in the nineteenth century? If the facts about a woman's limited employment options and subsequent economic dependence were known, the comparison would make more sense to the modern reader.

Some of these topics may arouse anger and even depression, such as the rape epidemic in South Africa. But this book is also about activism—being positive, being effective, becoming a voice for the voiceless. Social injustice is not inevitable. Hopefully, you will feel inspired to pick a cause and learn how to advocate on behalf of others. Self-advocacy is also a powerful tool against injustice. Speak out for yourself, speak out for others, and speak in the name of social justice.

Lastly, a sense of joy resonates throughout the book. Yes, women have faced repression in the past and many still face it today. But despite the hardships, women (with their male allies) have defied the rules and changed them. There is still much more work to be done, but do not forget the triumphs.

Acknowledgments

WHEN I FIRST held the book contract in my hands, I was overjoyed. A few days later, though, panic seized me when I realized the extent of this project. Fortunately, several people have assisted me through the months of research, revisions, and fast food.

Jill Anderson, a former student who worked as my research assistant, is destined to flourish in her career in sociology. Through my years of teaching, I had many bright students like her who inspired me to keep on going.

Deb Sabo gave me a crash course in feminist theology, besides recommending some solid sources for the chapter on the Bible. Two other former colleagues, Julie Hart and Anjel Stough-Hunter, provided some keen insights. Annie Davis enhanced the domestic violence chapter with her suggestions and personal essay.

My proofreading friends helped me to avoid embarrassing mistakes: Britt Luarde, Cara Iacovetta, Maria Leland, Jonathon Cassell, and Miriam Potocky. The writing group at the Delaware Library, led by Vicky Schmarr, gave me useful suggestions to make the chapters more readable.

While finishing up this project, I was fortunate to work at the Central Ohio Area Agency on Aging with Darryl Miller and other great coworkers. At Oxford University Press, the editors Dana Bliss and Andrew Dominello have been wonderful.

Since I was a little girl, I have delighted in my trips to the library. The Columbus Public Library system, especially the Whetstone Branch, is outstanding in their collection of nonacademic books. Also, my history studies from the 1980s provided the intellectual foundation of this book, so kudos to all liberal-arts instructors. Your efforts to encourage good writing are critical in this age of texting.

My family cheered me on, especially my brother Frank and my aunt Sister Celine. Others who deserve recognition are my pool buddies (especially Jeri and Nacrina), my writing groups, Rochelle Lavens, Ellen and Jim MacDonald, Valerie and Dave Dorsky, Chris Houari, Fred Boerger, and of course my two cats Henry and Freddy. No longer does anyone have to ask me how the book is going (or beg to be fed, as did my cats).

Although Janet Snively has recently passed, I will always appreciate her encouraging words. I would read chapters out loud to my 90-year-old friend and she would burst out, "Young people need to know this! Get this book published!" I am happy that I did not let her down.

Through mentoring Autumn Perry and others, I have developed great hope for the future. It is hard to be pessimistic when you meet kids with the right stuff.

It is with true humility that I recognize the hard work of activists such as Celia Williamson (human trafficking) and Michel Coconis (social justice). I grew up in Denver while Representative Pat Schroeder was in office, which left a deep imprint on my life. Without the achievements of feminists and other progressive advocates, we would be living in a darker world. Writing the book has made me truly realize the legacy of suffragettes and others who defied injustice. I am not standing on the shoulders of giants, I am standing on the shoulders of giantesses.

Women's Issues for a New Generation

1

Women in the United States

1

Introduction

What Is a Feminist?

So what is a feminist? Would you call yourself one? If so, is there a therapy or cure for your condition? This famous quote is one good place to start the discussion.

> I myself have never been able to find out precisely what feminism is: I only know that people call me a feminist whenever I express sentiments that differentiate me from a doormat. (Rebecca West, 1913, cited on www.brainyquote.com/quotes/authors/r/rebecca_west.html)

The demand for respect, then, is one striking feature of feminism. For instance, women often face stigma for menstruation as if this natural function was somehow shameful. Being told that she has PMS (premenstrual syndrome) or is "on the rag" is one way for a woman to feel dismissed. Pregnancy has also provoked scorn if the mother is unmarried, and people may criticize a married woman for having too many babies. A young woman who dresses modestly may be told to look more feminine, but any woman showing her cleavage may have to deal with unwanted comments.

Respect is related to equality for many marginalized groups, including women who have demanded equal access to education, jobs, political power, and other rights. When I was working on this book, I would tell an older woman about it and she would tell me that she was not allowed to take a class because she was a woman. Another would tell me of sexual harassment that never was seen as a problem, and others told me of careers that they were not even allowed to consider. Not so long ago, then, women had to battle against restrictions that limited their full potential.

Feminism also presents a new way of looking at the world and into one's inner self. It is a way to develop a new value system that honors the dignity and worth of all persons. For centuries, religions and other ideologies have taught people to respect others and even love them. Feminism is one way to fulfill these idealistic goals.

Men can be feminists, too. As mentioned in the Preface, I have written this book to include males in the discussion. I believe that every women's issue is really everybody's issue. For instance, sexual assault happens to both males and females. Men (not just little boys) can be raped, too. The recent use of the word *bitch* to denote a prison sex slave (e.g., a man joking that "he's my bitch now" in a hostile encounter in a movie or TV show) illustrates that it is socially acceptable to laugh at males as rape victims. Also, men are often friends, boyfriends, or brothers of a female rape victim. The shock waves of a sexual assault affect not only the victim herself, but those who love her.

Besides inclusion of males into the discussion, the book also stresses critical thinking. Consider popular culture, which contains images that degrade not only women, but also men in a different sense. One example is Kanye West's song "Gold Digger," which glamorizes the idea of a rich man paying for sex. The video portrays a well-dressed man in contrast to the barely dressed women in provocative, open-legged poses. The lyrics demand that the woman kneel before her man to service him—" Get down girl go head get down" —a demand that some may find disturbing (Lyrics found on http://www. songlyrics.com/kanye-west-jamie-foxx/gold-digger-lyrics/). The song also belittles men because it implies that the only worthwhile man is one who can afford to buy a "gold digger" to kneel before him. In this context, a man who would want an honest, mutually satisfying relationship with a woman would probably be deemed as not very manly. The social pressures exerted by popular culture, then, can be destructive to both men and women.

The preceding example demonstrates that to think like a feminist is to examine what is right in front of you in a new way. Some people may claim that the women in the United States have already achieved full equality and that songs about gold diggers are irrelevant. Society may no longer need feminists, since they are as obsolete as VCR machines. This book argues otherwise by presenting numerous examples of inequality that are entrenched instead of incidental. After reading this book, do you agree or disagree that women all over the world still need feminism? Through research and observations, confirm or contradict that assertion. To think like a feminist, then, also involves questioning authority—even this book's author.

Social Work and Feminism

A strong link exists between social work and feminism. Besides the social work value of honoring the dignity and worth of all persons, two other themes stand out: social justice and cultural competence. According to the Social Work Code of Ethics, "Social workers pursue social change, particularly with and on behalf of vulnerable and oppressed individuals and groups of people" (full text available on the website www.socialworkers.

org). Feminist thought also encourages cultural competence not only regarding race and ethnicity, but also age, class, and other factors.

The issue briefing called "Social Work and Women's Issues" from the National Association of Social Workers states that:

> The majority of both the U.S. population and the clients that social workers serve are women. Attention to women's issues is essential because of the discrimination women continue to face in many aspects of their lives. Women perform the majority of the world's work, but control a disproportionately small share of its resources. In much of the world, economic, political, social, and cultural forces operate unfavorably for women and girls. As a result, women are adversely affected in the areas of education; health care, including reproductive and mental health; crime, especially as victims of violence; employment; and social welfare, especially income maintenance programs. The well-being of women and their families is negatively impacted at all stages of the life cycle, from girlhood through old age. (Document available on: http://socialworkers. org/advocacy/briefing/WomensIssuesBriefingPaper.pdf)

The Council on Social Work Education (CSWE) also stresses the importance of women's issues through committees on feminist scholarship and the status of female social work professors. Despite these two organizations' stances on women's rights, though, social work textbooks seldom focus on feminism. The author reviewed sixteen undergraduate textbooks and found only brief mentions of women's issues.

Since women were the primary founders of the social work profession, many common themes emerge between social work and women's issues. One concept in feminist thought is biological determinism, which would deem women as natural helpers. Like teachers and nurses, social workers appear as women merely extending their maternal role to the larger society. For instance, an article on the history of nursing notes that "women actively embraced the gendered meaning of nursing for the ease with which it allowed them to create work identities that remained connected with their personal identities despite their formal relationship" to their employers (D'Antonio, 1999, p. 271). Society, then, allowed women to be nurses without forcing them into a role conflict about their womanliness.

Since these nurturing women are only acting out their "natural" roles, the social norm is to pay them less than men in "real" jobs. Guy and Newman (2004) link lower pay to the female-dominated occupations that require emotional labor. "Simply stated, acts that grease the wheels so that people cooperate … are essential for job completion, but they are rewarded more with a pat on the back than with money" (Guy & Newman, 2004, p. 289).

Discussion Questions

1. How would you verify the author's assertion that most social work textbooks do not focus on women's issues? Design a systematic way to review the books available, and if possible conduct the review.
2. Write the best argument for and against this statement: Emotional labor should be paid less than other types of labor.

Figure 1.1 *Young woman facing choices (Photo courtesy of OUP)*

Structure of the Book

This book discusses feminism in the context of real-life issues that affect our daily lives: our jobs, our families, and ourselves. Each topic richly deserves at least two or three books on its own, but this book is only an introductory text. The three parts are: women in the United States, diversity, and women in the international context. I taught this class with the first half of the semester focusing on women in the United States and the second half on the international context. The middle section on diversity is intended to be self-study instead of lecture-based. Instructors may want to assign one diversity chapter (e.g., Chapter 16, Native Americans) to a student or group for a presentation and/or paper.

Part One: Women in the United States

This part begins with a brief summary of the challenges faced by women in history. The title of Chapter 2, A Proud History: Women's Lives Before Women's Lib, indicates the strengths of countless women who survived—and thrived—in difficult circumstances. Women's history includes two themes: women as weaker vessels (stress on their subordinate status) and warrior queens such as Elizabeth I of England. The dark story of the European witch hunts is related to the misogyny in today's society. Mary Wollstonecraft and others who questioned male authority, though, are bright lights that lit the way toward the U.S. suffrage movement of the early twentieth century.

Moving into the 1960s, Chapter 3 reclaims the term *women's lib* in its discussion of second-wave feminism. This turning point defied the traditional restrictions on women, such as male-only universities. Consciousness raising and legal battles created a new reality for most American women, but a backlash developed in the 1970s when anti-feminists successfully defeated the ERA (Equal Rights Amendment. A brief discussion of third-wave (and fourth-wave) feminism ends this chapter.

No women's studies book is complete without a chapter about gender, so Chapter 4 focuses on persons who cross the gender line between male and female: intersexed persons, transgender persons, and others. Gender has many levels: biological, psychological, and social. Arguing that gender is a spectrum instead of a male/female binary, this chapter also presents historical and cultural perspectives on this complex topic.

Lesbians and bisexual women, who also must confront the gender line, are the topic of Chapter 5. For lesbians, life before Stonewall (1969 protests, when the gay-rights movement first gained national attention) was often one of secrecy. Even when the women's lib movement began, lesbians were called the "Lavender menace" because heterosexual feminists were afraid of being discredited. The chapter also covers topics such as internalized homophobia and motherhood. (For purposes of this book, I will use the shortened version of LGBT with the understanding that it is not the full acronym LGBTIQA—Lesbian, Gay, Bisexual, Transgender, Intersex, Queer/Questioning, and Asexual, This acronym can be changeable, such as including TS for Two Spirits and P for Pansexual. I have even seen a new version: QUILTBAG—Queer, Intersex, Lesbian, Transgender, Bisexual, Asexual, and Gay.)

Besides LGBT rights, another controversy is whether the beauty standard is a feminist issue as explicated in Chapter 6. Fat-shaming can lead to eating disorders, and other body-image issues can affect women's lives. The last section stresses how society is producing a new beauty standard for men.

Males are also included in the discussion of rape and sexual assault in Chapter 7 because it is definitely not just a women's issue. Rape culture includes joking about rape, diminishing the status of victims (e.g., "she asked for it"), and even threatening women over the Internet. The chapter stresses that sex without consent is now considered rape, and that acquaintance rapes are more common than stranger rapes.

Chapter 8 also involves threats against women: domestic violence/intimate-partner violence. This chapter explains how somebody could be drawn into an abusive relationship. A script on verbal abuse then illustrates the manipulations an abuser uses even before the first physical encounter. Control is the key element of abuse, which impedes a person's ability to leave the relationship.

The next chapter, Chapter 9, Sex and Consequences, elucidates another concern for both women and men. Preventing unwanted pregnancies has been the goal of couples for centuries. The history of birth control, besides a description of the abortion controversy, illustrates the political and ethical dimensions of reproductive health.

Modern birth control has enabled women to work outside the home on a more consistent basis. Chapter 10, The Politics of Work and Motherhood, explains how women in the workplace often have to deal with sexual harassment and inequality. Mothers are typically underpaid compared to their peers, which is one cause of the feminization of poverty. The chapter also focuses on both women and social workers making positive changes in the political arena.

Careers and motherhood are not the only challenges confronting women. The end of Part One is a unique version of the human-behavior-in-the-social-environment emphasis in social work education. Chapter 11, From Teens to Crones: A Lifespan Perspective, discusses women in four stages: adolescence, higher education, nurturing, and old age. This lifespan-view chapter has a different structure than the rest of the book because it does not focus on any specific issue or group. Instead, the chapter illuminates topics that are common for most women. Although not all women attend college, the higher education section should be relevant to most readers.

Part Two: Diversity

Diversity and Intersectionality, Chapter 12, opens this part with an introductory note on how different aspects of a person (e.g., race, class, and body size) may intersect to create a matrix of domination. Incarcerated women exemplify this concept of intersectionality, since these women are less likely to be educated or wealthy but are more likely to be women of color with a history of abuse (either childhood or domestic). I highly recommend this chapter to all readers.

The next five chapters, though, may be considered optional lectures by an instructor facing time constraints. As mentioned earlier, I intended these chapters to be self-study. Chapter 13, Latinas in the United States, focuses on a fast-growing population with great potential for economic and political power. African Americans, the topic of Chapter 14, face similar challenges such as racism and poverty. Another concern is the number of police killings and vigilante-style shootings of young Black men, since some African-American mothers have to raise their sons in a hostile environment. In contrast are Asian Americans (Chapter 15), who have to cope with the "Model Minority" label and the high expectations of parents. Native Americans (Chapter 16) also struggle with stereotypes based on ignorance of their cultures. The last diversity chapter explicates the discrimination encountered by women with disabilities (Chapter 17). Like racism, ableism assumes that one group is superior to another. Hopefully, these chapters will motivate readers to learn more about each group.

Part Three: Women in the International Context

Chapter 18, Global Feminism, the first chapter in this part, begins with the dilemma of the West is Best mentality (i.e., ethnocentric beliefs) in relation to the universal rights ideal. This dilemma appears in the debates over international treaties such as the Convention on the Elimination of Discrimination Against Women (CEDAW). Global violence against women include war and nationalism, whereas gender imbalance threatens the well-being of women in many countries.

Chapter 19 shifts focus to women in developing nations in the age of globalization. After a brief history of the women-in-development movements, the chapter discusses how family planning, microcredit loans, and educational opportunities can drastically improve a woman's life.

Another aspect of global feminism is the split between modernism and tradition, as evident in Chapter 20, Women in Muslim Countries. Despite the popular conception of Muslim women hidden in veils and oppressed by men, many of these women provide feminist perspectives in the Islamic context. Religious fundamentalists do threaten the health and autonomy of Muslim women in some countries. However, other countries provide women with a wide range of empowering opportunities.

Complex realities also appear in Chapter 21, Women in Latin America. These women sometimes live in the political contexts of repressive governments and civil wars. The economic contexts of maquila factories, tomato farms, and working overseas also affect women who are fighting their way to equality.

Chapter 22 is Women in China. Like Latin America, China is transitioning from traditional values to modern ideals. Before Mao Zedong came into power in 1949, some families did not even bother to name their daughters because they were so little valued. As China lurched through the rapid changes imposed by the communist state, women's rights were sometimes sidelined. Now China is converting to a capitalist economy but has not fully rejected the legacy of honoring sons over daughters.

Chapter 23 moves to a topic that affects women in all countries: prostitution and the Sex Trade. This multibillion industry is based on both traditional practices and modern technology. The chapter also explores the motivations of the customers. Sometimes sex work is voluntary, but sex trafficking forces both children and adults into a heartbreaking existence. The chapter ends with ideas on how to fight human trafficking.

The connection between the sex trade and HIV/AIDS is an obvious one. Chapter 24 describes the other gender aspects of the HIV/AIDS pandemic, including women's lack of economic power and their exposure to violence. Because women of color are disproportionately affected by HIV/AIDS in the United States, the chapter also discusses the risk factors for this population.

Despite all the struggles fought by women all over the world, the book concludes on an optimistic note: Chapter 25, A Proud Future. After stressing that feminism benefits all genders, the conclusion provides examples of how activists have confronted anti-women practices. The struggles are far from over, but we are learning from each other how to build up the dignity of women.

Notes on the "Gold-Digger" Song

If you have not yet watched the "Gold Digger" video on the YouTube website, you still have another chance. How would this example of popular culture be connected to this book? The "Gold Digger" song is related to the history chapter, since the lyrics perpetuate the concept of a woman needing a man for economic survival. The beauty standard chapter also applies to this video, which is obvious with the voluptuous but flat-tummied women with perfect make-up and hair. A gold-digger's boyfriend/husband may or may not be violent. If he is abusive, then the chapter on domestic violence/intimate-partner violence may explain the dynamics of their relationship. If he believes that he has the right to have sex with her anytime he wants because he paid for it, then the chapter on rape/sexual assault also applies to this situation. The women in the video are African American, which is related to the racist stereotype of the hypersexual Jezebel as discussed in the diversity chapter.

Watching and critiquing this one video and its song lyrics, then, could initiate a feminist inquiry. The next step would be to examine other videos and related examples of popular culture, since the "Gold-Digger" song could be just an isolated example of sexism. What should be the third step of this inquiry?

Key Concepts in Book

Throughout the textbook, these concepts will appear as common themes. This section is meant as a reference guide for when the reader is asked to apply the terms to specific examples.

List of Concepts

Patriarchy
Misogyny, including the silencing of women and diminishing their talents and accomplishments
Objectification
Oppression
Male privilege
Public and private spheres
Invisibility of women's work
Essentialism and social constructionism
Intersectionality
War on Women

Patriarchy

Patriarchy, which literally means rule by the father, is the term used to describe a male-dominated society. According to Hebrew Scriptures, God said to Moses: "I am the God of your father, the God of Abraham, the God of Isaac and the God of Jacob" (Exodus 3:6, New International Version). In a patriarchal society, males are dominant and females are often invisible. By holding most of the power (economic, political, etc.), male leaders ridicule or even punish women who challenge their authority. Such a society values their sons and regards their daughters as disappointments who do not count in a family. Females raised in this setting must obey their fathers, husbands, brothers, and/or sons because independent women are seen as dangerous to the social order.

Obedience to the higher authority of males is often associated with religion, as in the case of the Quiverfull movement made famous by a TV show featuring the Duggar ("Twenty Kids and Counting") family. A Biblical reference to children being like arrows in a quiver (Psalm 127) has inspired some Christians to denounce birth control and to promote as many births as possible.

At the forefront of evangelical opposition to feminism is a group of self-described "patriarchy" advocates, who have reclaimed the term from women's studies curricula to advocate a strict "complementarian" theology of wives and daughters being submissive to their husbands and fathers (and) embrace these traditional gender roles (Joyce, K., 2009a). "

The counterpart to patriarchy, of course, is matriarchy—a society ruled by women. Sanday (2002) provides one example in Indonesia in which women are the decision makers and are honored for their wisdom. However, patriarchal societies are much more common in both historical and current times. As recently as 2014 Jody Hice, a Georgia pastor and politician, was asked about his opinion of a female candidate running for office and said, "If the woman's within the authority of her husband, I don't see a problem." (Marcotte, A., 2014b))

Misogyny

Misogyny (hatred of women) seemed to be a musty, archaic word used only in academia. Then in May of 2014, the Internet exploded with thousands of postings by women reclaiming this word. The trigger for this revived discussion was the Elliot Rodgers' video rant against women before he went on a shooting spree in California. Feeling rejected by women, he promised to "slaughter every single spoiled, stuck-up, blond slut I see." (Valenti, 2014). Hashtag activists in the "#yesallwomen" forum wrote reactions such as these: "because when a girl is harassed or even groped by a stranger in public, we're told to 'take it as a compliment'" and "Girls grow up knowing that it's safer to give a fake phone number than to turn a guy down."

Do these women's voices even matter? Should society grant them the same respect as the voices of men? The *silencing of women* is one striking aspect of misogyny that still occurs today. In the Middle Ages, some women faced a severe punishment for being a "scold" (i.e., "bitch" in today's terminology.) If a husband or authority figure considered a woman to be loud, opinionated, and/or disrespectful, she had to wear a metal contraption called the scold's bridle (Figure 1.2). Sometimes the authorities paraded her through town to complete her humiliation. (Fraser, 1984)

Are there any modern equivalents to the scold's bridle? In the 1970s sitcom *All in the Family,* Archie Bunker would yell at his wife: "Stifle!" Today, name-calling of outspoken women can be a powerful silencer, while fear of retaliation can be effective. On the "#yesallwomen" site was this comment: "Because when I want to call out somebody for making a sexist joke or comment online, I worry I'll burn professional bridges."

Ridicule is another weapon against "scolds." For example, the columnist George Will ridiculed the survivors of campus rape by stating that rape would "make victimhood a coveted status that confers privileges, victims proliferate," (Mirkinson, 2014) Inherent in his comments was the message: how dare those women take center stage on such an important issue?

Besides trying to silence women (see Figure 1.3), misogynists also *diminish women's accomplishments and talents.* The insult that "you throw like a girl" implies that everything a female does is always inferior to a male's attempts. History contains many tragic stories of women being denied their rightful places in athletics, academia, and other venues. For example, the fossil hunter Mary Anning revolutionized scientific thought in the nineteenth century. Because of her meticulous research, the scientific community made great advances in geology and paleontology.

Figure 1.2 *Scold's bridle (By Joel Dorman Steele and Esther Baker Steele [Public domain], via Wikimedia Commons)*

Figure 1.3 *Silencing of women (Photo source: Entofolio)*

Figure 1.4 *Objectification of the female body (Photo source: Entofolio)*

However, no woman could attend meetings at the Geologic Society of London or enter the doors of the Royal Society—much less receive full credit for her work. She faced financial struggles and public censure because it was so odd for a woman to spend days on the beach looking for fossils. In 2010, though, the Royal Society did recognize her as one of the ten most influential British women in the history of science. (royalsociety.org). Without the contributions of Anning and numerous other women, the world would be a much different place.

Objectification

Besides dismissing women as less than men, misogynists also objectify females instead of seeing their inner dignity. *Objectification* and sexual exploitation are related concepts because the media sometimes portrays women as nothing but a collection of breasts, buttocks, and other body parts (see Figure 1.4). One writer defines objectification as "disregard(ing) the humanness of any person for any purpose of self-satisfaction" (Rockler-Gladen, 2013).

On a deeper level, though, objectification also implies ownership and entitlement. A car owner has the full right to kick the tires or just let the car rust. Since he paid for the car, he can do anything he wants with it. A john (customer of a prostitute) who has paid for temporary ownership of a person exemplifies this aspect of objectification because he has the same sense of entitlement.

Oppression

Oppression is another key term in women's issues. "Vast and deep injustices" (Young, 2009, p. 56) occur when any population endures oppression. One example is when a traditional society reduces or completely removes the property rights of women. William Blackstone, author of *Commentaries on the Laws of England*, wrote in 1765 that married women had no separate legal identity from their husbands because "By marriage, the husband and wife are one person in law: that is, the very being or legal existence of the woman is suspended during the marriage, or at least is incorporated and consolidated into that of the husband ..." (cited in Lewis, no date) This meant that wives had absolutely no property rights including the inability to keep any salary or obtain an education without the husband's permission. A more recent example appears in Kenya, where widows are often deprived of their rightful inheritance (Ezer, 2012) and divorced women are left impoverished (Munyoro, 2015) Lack of property rights is not an abstract legal issue, but a matter of sheer survival for women.

Male Privilege

The other side of the oppression of women is *male privilege*, which Case (2007) defines as men having "more opportunies in employment and education" than women (Case, 2007, p. 427) Throughout history, most females did not receive the same level of education (or any at all) even if they were princesses. King James I of England, for example, did not want his daughter to learn Latin because "To make women learned and foxes had the same effect: to make them more cunning" (Fraser, 1984, p 122).

Although traditional societies usually deny females equal access to education, women now outnumber men in U.S. colleges (Goldin, Katz, & Kuziemko, 2006). However, the. major criteria for American women to obtain scholarships is still physical appearance and not academic merit—the Miss America contest is the greatest provider of scholarship money for women. In her comment about this fact and Miley Cyrus' famous transformation from wholesome Hannah Montana to the provocatively dressed twerker, Steinem made a compelling point:

> I wish we didn't have to be nude to be noticed ... But that's the way the culture is. I think that we need to change the culture, not blame the people that are playing the only game that exists (Decoste, 2013).

Male privilege also involves economic advantages (e.g., the pay gap) and social benefits. For instance, a woman regarded as sexually active is called a "slut," "whore," "skank," "tramp," and many other names. A man often receives praise for his sexual exploits, basking in the complimentary term of "player." When a woman refuses sex with a man, he may resent her because society has taught him that men are entitled to their bodies. Defenders of male privilege can be found on the websites of Men's Rights Activists/ Movement, Red Pill, and Pick Up Artists.

Discussing the concept of male privilege has nothing to do with denigrating men (i.e., "male bashing") but everything to do with a better awareness of inequalities. The term *white privilege* parallels the idea that not all whites are racists but they still benefit from a racially biased system. One example would be the different treatment a police officer shows toward a white, middle-aged college professor and an African-American youth wearing a hoodie. Feminists use the concept of male privilege, then, to critique a gender-biased system that benefits men.

Public and Private Spheres

One benefit that men have had for centuries is better access to the public sphere. The split between the *private and public spheres* meant that society often locked women into the "kinder, kirche, kuche" (children, church, and kitchen) sphere. Women should stay pure and unpolluted by the dirty, corrupt world. Although modern societies have mostly accepted women into the rough-and-tumble world of politics and big business, other societies still see the public sphere as dangerous to a female's morality. Recently, an Indonesian city government tried to impose "virginity tests" on high school senior girls to combat adultery and prostitution. Public opposition persuaded the officials to drop the idea (Nelson, 2014).

Invisibility of Women's Work

Within the private sphere is real work—raising children, keeping house, caring for the sick or elderly, and other labors. Because this type of labor does not involve a paycheck, though, it does not count in the modern market economy. This results in the *invisibility of women's work*, which adds to the diminishment of women's status. Kitchen gardens, for instance, are vital to feeding families in most developing countries. However, these women gardeners are doing sustenance farming instead of producing cash crops that can be sold—so kitchen gardening does not count as work.

Essentialism and Social Constructionism

After considering these destructive effects of misogyny, it is critical to review the major justification of patriarchal thought: *essentialism as opposed to social constructionism*. If somebody believes that women are essentially nurturing and men are essentially aggressive because of their biology, for instance, then supporting traditional gender roles seems logical. If women are weaker than men and need their protection, then it is best for society to keep women at home. A natural woman should only want a strong husband and several children.

Essentialism can also be related to racial/ethnic prejudice (e.g., "Latinos are essentially lazy") and other assumptions. How much of a person's identity is based on nature (as Lady Gaga would sing, "Born this way") and how much is based on nurture (environmental factors)? Are women essentially softer than men or were they socialized to act that way? Think of how a young girl reacts to the girly-girl trinkets at a Claire's store—is there a biological basis for her desire for that barrette, or was she socialized to like it? A little boy may want to go into that store because of the bright sparkly items, but would be admonished by his parent that stores like that are only for girls. Those who believe that socialization outweighs biological traits would state that gender is a social construct that can vary from culture to culture.

The nature/nurture argument, then, emerges in the debates between essentialism and social constructionists. Biological realities such as ovaries and estrogen obviously affect a person's identity, but the debate is over how much biology determines one's destiny. Simply put, a traditionalist would support the essentialist view, whereas a feminist would stress that gender is more of an artificial creation than a solid reality.

Intersectionality

Gender is but one aspect of a person's identity, which leads to the concept of *intersectionality*. Each person has a multiplicity of identities that interrelate to each other: race/ ethnicity, class, religion, and other differences (Yuval-Davis, 2006). These differences can amplify each other to a positive degree such as being young, rich, and beautiful. The stereotype of welfare queens, though, offers a vivid example of when identities intersect to create a stigmatized population. In her book *The Politics of Disgust: The Public Identity of the Welfare Queen*, Hancock (2004) discusses how the Congressional hearings on welfare reform in 1996 did not include a single welfare recipient. Instead, one Congressman told the story of one woman whose life was chaotic and messy because she was not like "us." Although most welfare recipients are white/Caucasian, the welfare queen stereotype usually assumes that she is African American. References to "black mothers' hyperfertility and laziness" (Hancock, 2004, p. 21) and welfare recipients as "brood mares" (p. 119) confirm that the author's use of the word "disgust" in her book title was appropriate.

Why do some people hate welfare queens so much? Racism is one reason, since racial minorities are more likely to be poor in the United States. Urban poverty in the ghetto is much more visible than rural poverty, which may include more white/Caucasians. On a website called "black women suck," which unfortunately is not a satire, this comment demonstrates the hostility toward these women:

> Every time I look at the taxes withheld from my paycheck I think about all the Black Women banging down the welfare office doors getting our money. They sit in there a few hours in their leather coats and hip hop attire including the stupid Baby Phat boots. (http://blackwomensuck.blogspot.com/)

Class prejudice is another reason for the stigmatization, since the term *white trash* indicates that poor people are the losers in a competitive society. To some people, poverty is less about economic need and more about moral superiority. Financially secure people must be more hard-working and mature than their poorer counterparts. (To confirm this observation, use the terms *white trash, trailer trash,* and *welfare Barbie* on a search engine such as Google Images. Describe the pictures—what do the liquor bottles and halter tops symbolize?)

Besides racism and classism, fat-shaming is another facet of this stereotype. The media often portrays low-income women as overweight. (To confirm this observation, use the term "gross Walmart shoppers" on a search engine such as Google Images. Do these images imply the insult of "fat lazy slob" or something else?) Poverty is a risk factor for obesity because of less access to healthy foods and exercise options. Gender is related to fat-shaming, since another shameful aspect of these women is the perceived uncontrolled sexuality and fertility. Poor women often face condemnation for having too much sex and having too many children (despite the fact that welfare recipients have the same fertility rate as other women.) Apparently, welfare recipients deserve punishment because they are women.

War on Women

The *war-on-women* theme, which Democrats started using in 2010 to criticize Republican policies, is a controversial topic. The People for the American Way, a liberal group, defines the War on Woman as attacking access to reproductive health (both abortion and birth control), defunding the Violence Against Women Act, blaming women for their poverty, and opposing equal pay legislation. "The tried-and-true right-wing attacks on mythical 'welfare queens' have a new meaning in an era when Republican politicians are desperately trying to roll back access to contraception. A cynical economic scapegoating strategy has become inextricably tied up with Religious Right attacks on women's autonomy" (People for the American Way, no date).

For example, politicians who cut the budgets of social services, on which women disproportionately rely. These conservatives would defend their actions because poor women were just ripping off the system. Another aspect of this "war" is the opposition to equal-pay legislation. The opponents stated that either the pay gap did not exist or women chose to accept lower pay.

The most contentious aspect of this "war" has been the politics of women's sexuality (reproductive health) that could override the medical needs of women. The Personhood Amendment, which would deem every fertilized egg to be a person even before implantation in the womb, would effectively outlaw hormonal birth control. The Pill (oral contraceptive) and the IUD (intra-uterine device) would be illegal even if the woman needed them for noncontraceptive reasons. One legal scholar writes about the proposed amendment in Mississippi:

> "Personhood amendments," which would define legal personhood as beginning at fertilization, appear to to gaining momentum in the United States.... The (Mississippi) Amendment sounds extreme, and its potential consequences are indeed far reaching ... the wording of the amendment reaches far beyond abortion, describing all fertilized human eggs as persons (Borgmann, 2011, pp. 115–118).

As of 2014, no state has passed the Personhood Amendment. However, in 2012 one Congressional hearing on birth control coverage invited only males to testify before the committee. When Sandra Fluke, a law student at a Catholic university, appeared before an unoffical hearing to testify about the expense of birth control, the radio commentator

Rush Limbaugh called her a "slut." A controversy raged between those who believe that birth control is a medical necessity and those who oppose it on moral grounds. The first part of a journal article's title about Rush Limbaugh said, "He sounded like a vile, disgusting pervert." That indicates the reactions of those who did not appreciate his request to watch Fluke have sex (Legge DiSanza, Gribas, & Shiffler, 2012). The controversies related to women's health and other aspects of the War on Women, then, show no sign of abating soon.

Critical Thinking Exercise: Stereotypes Yesterday and Today

Part One: The Shrew

1. Historically, assertive women were called: shrews, viragos, fishwives, nags, and jezebels. She is henpecking her husband; she is wearing the trousers in the family. Today, the most common term is probably "bitch." Are there any other derogatory terms used in your social group toward this type of woman?
2. Find three examples of a "bitch" in popular media. For instance, the girlfriend in the first *Hangover* movie deserves to be dumped because of her behavior. Are there any advertisements or TV/movie roles that reinforce this stereotype?

Figure 1.5 *The sweet delights of love (Undated photo courtesy of Library of Congress)*

Part Two: The Ugly Suffragette

1. Why were attacks on the physical appearance of these early feminists so important to the opponents? If you were a suffragette, would you have backed away from the movement for fear of being called ugly?

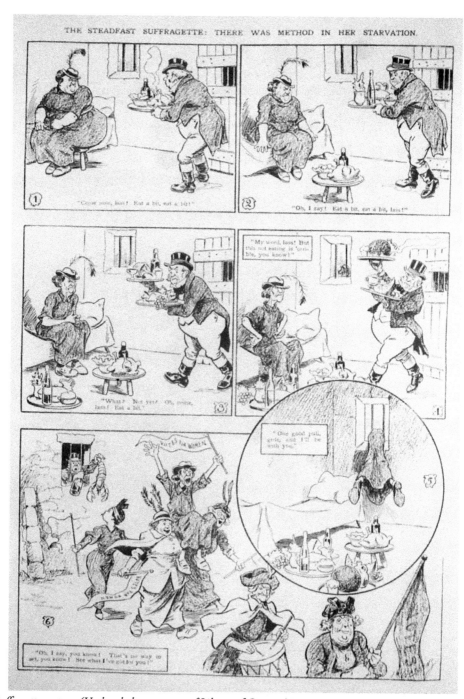

Figure 1.6 *Suffragette cartoon (Undated photo courtesy of Library of Congress)*

2. Suffragettes went on hunger strikes in jail, a civil disobedience action mocked by the cartoonist. Do you think that this cartoon succeeded in belittling the women?
3. Find three examples of a feminist being deemed ugly (either in pictures or words). A good place to start would be using the search term "ugly feminist."

Part Three: The Exotic and Sexy Latina

1. Use the search term *Latina dating websites* and *Mexican dating websites*. Compare this picture to the contemporary descriptions of Latinas. What pictures and images are used?
2. Use the search term *Latina* and click on the Images tab. How many of these images are respectful and how many are sexualized like Figure 1.7?
3. What could be the impact of this stereotype not just on Latinas but all women of color?

Figure 1.7 *Stereotype of Latina (Undated photo courtesy of Library of Congress)*

Figure 1.8 *Racist cartoon (Undated photo courtesy of Library of Congress)*

Part Four: Racist Portrayal of Black Women

1. In the 1960s, the "Black is Beautiful" movement fought against the type of racism you see in Figure 1.8. Have you seen any similar portrayals in the mainstream media?
2. Conduct a systematic review of pictures of models and young actresses from the mainstream media. How many are women of color? Out of these women, how many have lighter skin or other features that fit the white European beauty ideal?
3. Find a picture of a darker-skinned model. Is she portrayed in a standard way or in an exotic setting that stresses that she is the "Other?" How long did it take you to find this picture?

2

A Proud History: Women's Lives
Before Women's Lib

TO compress the history of women's lives into a single chapter seems foolhardy at best.
Hopefully, those who read this chapter will be motivated to read further about these fascinating topics.

Weaker Vessels or Warrior Queens?

The titles of A. Fraser's books, *The Weaker Vessel: Women in 17th-Century England (1984)* and *The Warrior Queens: From Britain's Boadicea to Elizabeth I* (1989), typify two approaches to women's history. The first book, which focuses on the lives of British women in the seventeenth century, stresses the barriers faced in a patriarchal society. Although viewing women as the fair or "softer sex" (Fraser, 1984, p. 4), society also considered them to be "weaker vessels" than men as stated in this quote from the King James Bible: "Likewise, ye husbands, dwell with *them* according to knowledge, giving honour unto the wife, as unto the weaker vessel, and as being heirs together of the grace of life; that your prayers be not hindered." (1 Peter 3:7) Women were "weaker vessels" because of:

- Moral weakness, since these descendants of Eve were allegedly more likely to sin than men. Some writers even questioned whether women had souls like men. Because of their propensity to promiscuity, women were easy targets for Satan to tempt into sin and even witchcraft.
- Physical weakness, since the high mortality rate of mothers giving birth signified that that women could not even handle the basic function of childbirth.

- Intellectual weakness, since women were supposedly disabled by having wombs and less substantial brains.
- Legal weakness, since women usually had to obey their fathers or husbands. For example, one father was angry that his 14-year-old daughter would not agree to a marriage so he had her "tied to the Bedposts and whipped" until she agreed (Fraser, 1984, p. 15).

One advantage to this approach would be the linkage between historic oppression and modern controversies, such as laws that have roots in patriarchal times. Rape laws, for instance, historically favored the male defendant over the female victim. However, emphasizing oppression may result in seeing women as passive victims instead of active players.

In contrast to this emphasis on oppression and women's attempts to overcome it, the Warrior Queens approach discusses the outstanding women who are the opposite of submissive females. For example, Queen Elizabeth I courageously led her English subjects to fight foreign armies. "I know I have the body of a weak and feeble woman, but I have the heart and stomach of a King, and of a King of England too, and think foul scorn that Parma or Spain or any Prince of Europe should invade the borders of my realm ..." (Fraser, 1989, p. 224). Another example would be the Trung sisters, two Vietnamese warriors who fought against Chinese invaders two thousand years ago (29 CE). When her brother urged her to stop fighting, Trung Au told him, "I want to rail against wind and tide, kill the whales in the ocean, sweep the whole country to save people from slavery, and I have no desire to take abuse" (Fraser, 1989, p. 237).

Discussion Question

The female protagonists in movies such as *The Hunger Games* and *Divergent* are modern versions of the Warrior Queen. They do not flinch from committing violence and can compete with any male fighter. However, are these heroines merely acting as honorary males like Queen Elizabeth? Discuss whether acting out this violently is a positive step for women or just conforming to social norms set by men.

Life in the Middle Ages in Europe

Women had few legal rights, but they worked hard. They processed food: vegetables from the garden, eggs from the hens, and milk from the cows. They made cheese, butter, beer, cider, and cured meats. In this preindustrial context, women were coproducers with men in managing the households. Paychecks did not exist for either men or women, so women's work was regarded as equal value to the men's contributions. Unlike today, there was no split between the public (work outside the home) or private (confined to home) spheres. The household was the site of the workplace, and men and women worked side by side (Ehrenreich & English, 1978).

Also, many women were experts in using herbs for healing since doctors were not available. In fact, many women even practiced medicine and wrote medical texts. Some women ran shops with or without husbands. The last name "Baxter," in fact, is the female version of "Baker" because so many women ran bakeries. (Ehrenreich & English, 1978).

Higher-born women had even more power than their common counterparts. When their husbands were absent for months or years, noblewomen ran manors that were as big as small towns. They directed the food supplies and defended the castles against attacks. However, women were often forced into marriage and lost any legal rights to their husbands. Avoidance of marriage was one reason why joining a convent was such an attractive option. Besides given the opportunity to be educated beyond a rudimentary level, nuns could advance to the high position of abbesses and direct church facilities (Anderson & Zinsser, 1988).

Education, then, was a rare privilege for these women. Medieval thinkers such as St. Thomas Aquinas opposed most education for women because it was the "seed-bed of impurity" Aquinas cited in www.cpp.edu article, "The Education of Medieval Women"). In the male-dominated society, both church and state had no place for well-educated women except in the convents. The only purpose for educating females was to teach them the sacred teachings and ensure that they would be better wives and mothers. They should lead "regular, chaste, and religious lives and to devote all their time to female labors" (Aquinas, no date). Aquinas based his thinking on this sentiment: "The woman is subject to man on account of the weakness of her nature … Man is the beginning of woman and her end, just as God is the beginning and end of every creature. Children ought to love their Father more than they love their mother" (Aquinas, no date.).

Some women, though, broke out of this stranglehold to flourish as intellectuals. Christina de Pizan gained international attention and royal acclaim for her work in the 1390s. As a court writer, she wrote books for kings and dukes. Her ability to overcome the traditional barriers to female success inspired her to write that "from the female, I became male … Formerly, I was a women; now I am a man, I do not lie, My stride demonstrates it well enough" (Anderson & Zinsser, 1988, p. 91).

Paradoxically, she advocated for the rights of women in forceful tones. She argued against the condemnation of women as weak and sinful, stating that most women were virtuous. The men "posed these false images [of women] out of jealousy, out of rage at pleasures lost to them, out of physical and moral impotence" (Anderson & Zinssner, 1988, p. 93). Only lack of education made women inferior. Women should claim their history because without it, they were "abandoned … exposed like a field without a surrounding hedge, without finding a champion to afford them an adequate defense" like a strong city wall (Kerber & DeHart, 1991, p. 3). In 1405, she also urges women to avoid men because of their base intents:

> In brief, all women—whether noble, bourgeois, or lower-class—be well-informed in all things and cautious in defending your honor and chastity against your enemies! My ladies, see how these men accuse you of so many vices in everything. Make liars of them all by showing forth your virtue, and prove their attacks by acting well.…gRemember, dear ladies, how these men call you frail, unserious, and easily influenced but yet try hard, using all kinds of strange and deceptive tricks, to catch you, just as one lays traps for wild animals. Flee, flee, my ladies, and avoid their company—under these smiles

are hidden deadly and painful poisons. And so may it please you, my most respected ladies, to cultivate virtue ... and to rejoice and act well. (De Pizan, 2007, p. 9)

Another remarkable woman in medieval history was Margery Kempe, who dictated her autobiography to a priest in the fifteenth century (Collis, 1964). She was a mayor's daughter who married a merchant. Despite having fourteen children, she still had the energy to set up two businesses (a tavern and a mill) that failed. Prone to mystical visions, she even preached to priests and monks about holiness.

She also told her husband that God wanted her to be chaste. John Kempe had been a background figure in her memoirs until she discussed his reaction to her message from God. Though threatened with instant death from supernatural causes if he didn't desist, he continued to make love to her. The children mounted up to the number of fourteen. One night when he approached her, she cried out to Jesus and "his manhood died away....'He had no power to towche (touch) hir at that tyme in that wyse'" (Collis, 1964, p. 35).

Later, she left her family to travel from England to Jerusalem on a pilgrimage that took years. When she returned, she was even more likely to preach to others to mend their ways. When she entered a bishop's hall, for instance, she saw gorgeous silks and other extravagances. She called the bishop the Devil and his contingent the Devil's men.

> They were very angry and swore at her, not seeing why they should be lectured like this by a stray woman pilgrim. She was told to shut up and mind her own business ... (others) were more receptive. These she continued to exhort, in the name of God, and obtained some response; they thanked her politely afterwards. (Collis, 1964, p. 184)

It is impossible to find out how many women in the Middle Ages had as much strength of character as de Pizan and Kempe. However, their stories indicate that not all women in pre-industrial Europe were either famous queens or faceless peasants. Women's history contains many such stories of bold women who outraged some but inspired others.

Gynocide: The Witch Hunts

Historians estimate that at least 40,000 persons (and up to 100,000) were executed as witches in Europe from the 1400s until the 1700s. At least three-fourths of the victims were women, thus prompting scholars to call this event a "gynocide"—the mass killing of women.

The causes of these attacks on women in the late medieval period include:

- Christianity's stress on stamping out any traces of paganism (pre-Christian religion), such as love spells and nature worship.

- The Biblical instruction that "Thou shalt not suffer (let) a witch to live" in Exodus 22:18.
- Suspicion of unmarried women, including widows, who had no male protectors.
- Hostility toward midwives, who had so much power in the birthing process.
- Fear of the "devil's mark" such as a birthmark that was seen as proof that a woman was in league with Satan.
- Religious persecution of heretics and others who defied the Catholic or Protestant authority.
- Any hint of sexual misconduct by women could inspire an accusation.
- Malicious neighbors who used the accusation of witchcraft as a way to punish an enemy.
- Conspiracy theories, such as believing that a witch had caused a village to get the plague.
- Fear of women in general (Ehrenreich & English, 1978; Durschmied, 2005).

In his book that places the Holocaust in a historical context, Katz (1994) compares the persecution of women to medieval antisemitism.

> The medieval conception of women shares much with the corresponding medieval conception of Jews. In both cases, a perennial attribution of secret, bountiful, malicious "power," is made. Women are anathematized and cast as witches because of the enduring grotesque fears they generate in respect of their putative abilities to control men and thereby coerce, for their own ends, male-dominated Christian society. Whatever the social and psychological determinants operative in this abiding obsession, there can be no denying the consequential reality of such anxiety in medieval Christendom. Linked to theological traditions of Eve and Lilith, women are perceived as embodiments of inexhaustible negativity. Though not quite quasi-literal incarnations of the Devil as were Jews, women are, rather, their ontological "first cousins" who, like the Jews, emerge from the "left" or sinister side of being. (Katz, 1994, p. 435)

Another author (Durschmied, 2005) describes the guidebook on fighting witchcraft, called *Malleus maleficarum (The Hammer of Witches)*. The Pope had appointed Jakob Sprenger to write this influential document.

> The book, in four volumes, went into the minutest detail. From midwives held responsible for stillborn children, archers who shot their arrows on Fridays, to half-demented sexual maniacs who used the devil as their excuse to fulfill their private fantasies, everything was discussed, and the dangers spelt out. One of the more astounding facets the *Malleus* points to is the role of women. Sprenger explained that the Latin name for female, *femina*, was actually made up of *fe* and *minus*, or "without faith." Therefore women had no faith, and became easy pretty for the devil's evil ways. They also had no virtue, and their carnal desires were insatiable—they *were* sex, and their entire thought process turned around the satisfaction of their sexual urges. This was in line with the clerical myth of the lascivious woman. (Durschmied, 205, p. 55)

Figure 2.1 *Traditional witch stereotype (Photo source: Entofolio)*

Discussion Questions: Why the Witch Hunt Still Matters

1. Men may have been in authority during the European Witch Hunts, but women participated in this tragedy by testifying against "witches." In fact, one historian (Dianne Purkiss) notes that midwives often brought charges against other women. In studying any injustice against women, then, the role of women as perpetrators deserves recognition.

   Can you think of any examples of women hurting other women as a social phenomenon?

2. The portrayal of unmarried childless women, especially older women, can be mean-spirited. Consider the examples from Walt Disney. The witch poisons her stepdaughter in *Snow White*, the mean sea creature made Ariel a mermaid, and Gothel steals youth from her kidnap victim in *Tangled*. Cruella de Ville even kills Dalmatians for their fur. Comment on this theme of demonizing older women as related to the European witch-hunts.

During the Enlightenment of the eighteenth century, great thinkers challenged the divine right of kings and other "natural" facts. Who says it is natural for kings to rule over nations simply based on birth? Why are the nobility able to live so luxuriously just because they had inherited this privilege?

Although these thinkers attacked social injustices, they failed to notice that the women's status was based on the traditional view of male superiority. Voltaire, for instance, wrote *Candide* (1759) about a young man going through many misadventures. Although he bluntly describes rape and other abuses of the females in the book, his writings show no indication that he supported the equality of women (e.g., Knapp, 2000). Another example of this blind spot is from Rousseau, who wrote in 1762:

> Men and women are made for each other, but their mutual dependence is not equal. We could survive without them better than they could without us. They are dependent on our feelings, on the price we put on their merits, on the value we set on their attractions and on their virtues. Thus women's entire education should be planned in relation to men. To please men, to be useful to them, to win their love and respect, to raise them as children, to care for them as adults, counsel and console them, make their lives sweet and pleasant. (Watkins, Rueda, & Rodriguez, 2001, p. 11)

In his novel *Emile,* Rousseau rejects the possibility of women being mature adults in his utopian vision. Instead, he considers them to be too promiscuous—too close to natural abandon and too far from rational thought—to be worthy of equality. "Women's desire is seen by Rousseau as both regressive and disruptive of the new social order he proposed; women's emancipation would mean a step backward for rational and egalitarian progress" (Kaplan, 2002, p. 352).

Not until Mary Wollstonecraft (Figure 2.2), then, did the Enlightenment principles emerge as an intellectual weapon against women's subordination to men. This brilliant thinker made two great contributions to history: she wrote the *Vindication of the Rights of Women* in 1792, and she gave birth to Mary Shelley, author of *Frankenstein.* (Unfortunately, she died during childbirth so her daughter never got to meet her.) She applied the ideas of the Enlightenment to women: "Surely the domestic tyranny of men over women is as bad as the royal tyranny of kings over their subjects?" (cited in Watkins, Rueda, & Rodriguez, 2001, p. 15).

She stated that femininity was a social construct, based on external standards and not from nature. Based on her belief system, she noted that women had the rights to independent work, education, and political action.

Following are some quotes from the *Vindication*, 1792:

- "She is brought up to be the toy of a man, his rattle and must jingle in his ears whenever, dismissing reasons chooses to be amused." (Wollstonecraft, 1792, p. 16).

Figure 2.2 *Mary Wollstonecraft (Undated photo courtesy of Library of Congress)*

- Wives are kept at home, "Confined in cages, like the feathered race. It is true that they are provided with food and raiment, for which they neither toil nor spin; but health, liberty and virtue are given in exchange" (Wollstonecraft, 1792, p. 16).
- Marriage is "legal prostitution" because the wives depended on their husbands for money (Wollstonecraft, 1792, p. 16).
- "Women may study the art of healing and be physicians as well as nurses. They might also study politics and businesses of all kinds, if they were educated in a more orderly manner. How many women thus waste life away, who might have practised as much as physician, regulated a farm, managed a shop, and stood erect supported by their own industry, instead of hanging their heads?" (Wollstonecraft, 1792, p. 17).
- "I do earnestly wish to see the distinction of sex abolished altogether ... save where love is concerned!" (Wollenstonecraft, 1792, p. 17).

Discussion on Wollstonecraft

1. Wollstonecraft is famous for stating that femininity is a social construct. She fought "conventional feminine stereotypes (that) confine and imprison us" (Walters, 2002, p. 269). Find three examples in the mainstream media of how women are still being socialized to be "feminine." Is this socialization still harmful in today's world?

2. Out of the preceding quotes, which do you think is the most significant? Why?

French Revolution

After the Enlightenment shook up French society with its challenges to kings and nobility, the American Revolution became another cause of the French Revolution. Women played a critical role in bringing down the monarchy. For instance, the Revolutionary Republican Women Citizens wore red and white uniforms, besides liberty bonnets. They also demanded the women's right to vote and hold political offices (Landes, 1988).

However, those who rallied for liberty, equality and fraternity turned a blind eye to the unequal status of women. One woman who spoke out for women's rights was stoned by the crowd and locked up in an asylum. The revolutionaries' Declaration of the Rights of Men did not mention women, so Olympe de Gouges declared the Declaration of the Rights of Women in 1791.

> Women awake! The tocsin (alarm bell) of reason is being heard throughout the whole universe: discover your rights! The powerful empire of nature is no longer surrounded by prejudice, fanaticism, superstition and lies. Courageously oppose the force of reason to the empty pretensions of superiority, unite yourselves. Oh women, deploy all the energy of your character and you will soon see these haughty men. Not groveling at your feet as servile adorers but proud to share the treasure of the Supreme Being! (cited in Watkins, Rueda, & Rodriguez, 2001, p. 24).

Olympe was sent to the guillotine for speaking out on behalf of women. As she walked to the guillotine, she cried out, "Scaffolds and executioners—are these then the results of the Revolution that should have been the glory of France, spreading without distinction over the two sexes and serving as a model to the universe?" (Watkins, Rueda, & Rodriguez, 2001, p. 25). The history of feminism, then, is not just about peaceful change but about violent retributions.

Industrialization (1700s and 1800s)

As Europe and the United States shifted from agricultural to industrial economies, the status of women also shifted. Before factories created a mass workforce that required formal discipline and payments, the household-based mode of production dominated.

There had been no split between the public sphere (workplace) and private sphere (home). Then paychecks became one of the dividing lines between men and women. Men "brought home the bacon" and women "took care of the house." This ideal only applied to the middle class, of course, since lower-income families have always included women who worked outside the home.

Collins (2003) describes the split between men and women in the early 1800s, which even included holidays:

> Men's and women's lives operated on separate tracks, even in society. At many dinner parties, the sexes were actually seated at opposite ends of the table. After they had finished eating, the men always left the ladies and retired to smoke and drink brandy. In the business districts, men lived in a growing alternate universe of restaurants and clubs and theaters, while women kept to their parlors and sewing rooms. Frances Trollope reported from Cincinnati that husbands even did the marketing. If it weren't for church services, she said, "all the ladies … would be in danger of becoming perfect recluses." Women were so cut out of the public life that even the holidays went on without them. The Fourth of July, with its military maneuvers and all-male parades, was the biggest occasion of the year.… As the nation got closer to midcentury, women gradually became the audience, clustering in yards and balconies to wave handkerchiefs, or perhaps sitting on special stands along the parade route. (Collins, 2003, p. 89)

Industrialization, then, enabled the invention of the Victorian ideal of the housewife (now called stay-at-home moms). The "Angel of the House" tried to stay pure by keeping away from the public sphere because it was now a manly place. For instance, the roughness of political campaigns should be no place for a woman. As the breadwinners, men had to go into the public sphere every day and fight to make a living. They wanted to go home and find peace and quiet with their wives, who were economically dependent on them (Rowbotham, 1989).

However, industrialization damaged the status of women because there was much less dignity in their domestic lives. No longer were their soap-making skills needed, since it was easy to buy soap in the store. No longer were their healing skills valued, since modern doctors were taking over the medical establishment. Housewives had only two requirements: look pretty and bear many children, preferably sons (Ehrenreich & English, 1978).

Two reactions emerged from this shift. The rationalists wanted to admit women into modern society by allowing them an equal footing with men. In a way, this meant letting women be "honorary men." Wollstonecraft's position, which is now classified as liberal modernism, was related to this reaction (Badowska, 1998). The romantics, however, saw the home as a refuge from the brutal world, and so women should just dress up in hoops and remain innocent of the world. This split between the rationalists and romantics still affects the modern discussion of women's rights today. Traditionalists still emphasize the "Angel of the House" ideal, while reformers stress the rationalist or an even stronger position.

Another split was between the economic man and the romantic woman (Ehrenreich & English, 1978). The economic man represented rational thought, competitive behavior, self-interested goals, and hard work. In contrast, the romantic woman was too irrational to make wise decisions. Instead, she was tender and submissive to her husband to the point of finding rapture in her obedience. Self-effacing, she was not supposed to call attention to herself or display any special talents. Instead, she was an ornamental object that replaced the hard-working women of the past.

Women who found it difficult to conform to this ideal because of boredom or frustration were often diagnosed with "nervous disorders" and ordered six weeks of bed rest. (The word *hysteria* came from the belief that the uterus caused emotional excess in women (see King, 1993). Some doctors even prohibited access to books during the bed rest, since thinking was seen as too agitating. These were the same doctors who urged women not to pursue higher education because it would affect their uteri and prevent pregnancies (Ehrenreich & English, 1993).

Housekeeping has been a priority for women for centuries, of course. Even with the technological advances of the Industrial Revolution, it was still hard drudgery to cook a meal or clean house. Women had to deal with outdoor privies, bugs, and other vermin, and cooking on hot stoves. Even in the 1800s, many mothers did not bother to wash their babies' diapers because doing laundry was so labor-intensive (fetching and heating up the water, etc.) "Most simply left the wet napkin by the fire to dry, then put it back on.... Some women actually regarded wet diapers as a wholesome device for hardening the baby's constitution ..." (Collins, 2003, p. 63) Women's magazines and housekeeping books, though, emerged as instruction manuals that raised the standards of cleanliness.

Abolitionism and Early Feminism

Even for the families of freed black slaves before the Civil War, the housewife ideal had little to do with most African-American women. Female slaves were raped by their masters or overseers to breed more slaves, and savage whippings took place.

One of the bright spots of the history of slavery in the United States is the Underground Railroad, in which heroines such as Harriet Tubman risked her life and led hundreds to freedom. Sojourner Truth spoke out about the double standard of white women (treated as pure, helpless creatures) and black women (treated as property) in this 1851speech, "Ain't I a Woman?"

> That man over there say women need to be helped into carriages and lifted over ditches—and ain't I a woman? I could work as much as a man and bear the lash as well—and ain't I a woman? I have borne five children and seen them almost all off into slavery and when I cried out with a woman's grief, none but Jesus hear—and ain't I a woman? (cited on www.feminist.com/resources)

The abolitionist movement not only led to the eventual emancipation of slaves but set the foundation of the early feminist movement (also called irst-Wave Feminism.) Many times, women were not allowed to speak at abolitionist meetings. This repression was a reminder of how wives were in a similar legal situation as slaves. For example, husbands could legally beat, rape, or lock up their wives. Divorce was rare because it was so difficult to obtain and the fathers were usually granted custody of the children. (Collins, 2003)

In this setting, it is remarkable that women such as Elizabeth Cady Stanton (Figure 2.3) were able to break out from the social repressions. This first-wave feminist described growing up female in a patriarchal household. When she was four, her little sister was born.

She heard so many of her parents' friends saying "What a pity it is she's a girl!" that she felt sorry for the baby. "True," she wrote, "our family consisted of five girls and only one boy, but I did not understand at that time that girls were considered an inferior order of beings." (Rogers, 2002, p. iii)

Figure 2.3 *Elizabeth Cady Stanton (Undated photo courtesy of Library of Congress)*

Later when her only brother died, she approached her father when he was sitting by the coffin. He embraced her and said, "Oh, my daughter, I wish you were a boy!" and she responded by saying that she would "try to be all my brother was." She tried her best to get her father to say one day, "Well, a girl is as good as a boy, after all" but he never did. Despite her academic achievements, he would only say, "Ah, you should have been a boy!" (Rogers, 2002, p. iv)

Like most women of her era, Stanton got married. Fortunately, her husband was a fellow abolitionist and agreed to delete the word *obey* from their wedding vows. Even for a happy marriage, though, being a wife had its drawbacks. Marriage took away a wife's property rights, so technically she did not even own the clothes on her back. If she had earned a paycheck, the employer would have paid the husband. According to Stanton, a young law student lectured to her when she showed him some jewelry she had been given as a Christmas present. "If you were my wife, these would be mine, and you'd wear them only with my permission. I could even exchange them for a cigar and you could watch them evaporate in smoke!" (Watkins, Rueda, & Rodriguez, 2001, p. 41). Although this man was a bit obnoxious, he was also correct.

Seneca Falls Convention of 1848

As mentioned earlier, first-wave feminism emerged from the abolitionist movement as women who opposed slavery began to see the parallels to their own oppression. At the Seneca Falls Convention of 1848, Stanton gave a speech excerpted here:

> But we are assembled to protest against a form of government existing without the consent of the governed—to declare our right to be free as man is free, to be represented in the government which we are taxed to support, to have such disgraceful laws as give man the power to chastise and imprison his wife, to take the wages which she earns, the property which she inherits, and, in case of separation, the children of her love; laws which make her the mere dependent on his bounty. It is to protest against such unjust laws as these that we are assembled today, and to have them, if possible, forever erased from our statute books, deeming them a shame and a disgrace to a Christian republic in the nineteenth century. We have met
> To uplift woman's fallen divinity
> Upon an even pedestal with man's. (Stanton, 1848)

Stanton also co-wrote the Seneca Falls Declaration, which was inspired by the Declaration of Independence. This document set the stage for the first wave of feminism in the United States. Whereas the Declaration of Independence describes the King's abuses of power, the Seneca Falls Declaration describes men's abuses of power:

- Women did not have the right to vote.
- Women had to obey laws although they had no political voice.

- Women were denied the most basic rights that even the lowest man had.
- Women had no political representation at all.
- Women became "civilly dead" when they got married, since they lost so many rights.
- Wives did not have any property rights, even the wages they earned.
- Wives had no independent moral authority apart from their husbands, their masters who could chastise the wives whenever they wanted.
- In divorce cases, men had the upper hand—especially regarding custody of the children.
- Single women who held property still had to pay taxes on it even though they had no political voice.
- All profitable careers were closed to women, so they were left with only low-paying jobs because they could not be professors or doctors.
- Women could not go to college (although a few women's colleges did exist in 1848, it was impossible for most women).
- Women are only allowed subordinate positions in church.
- A "different code of morals for men and women" could mean exclusion for women from society, whereas men were not held accountable (which probably applies to the sexual double standard).
- Men have "usurped the prerogative of Jehovah himself, claiming it as his right to assign for her a sphere of action, when that belongs to her conscience and to her God."
- Man "has endeavored, in every way that he could, to destroy her confidence in her own powers, to lessen her self-respect, and to make her willing to lead a dependent and abject life."

The Seneca Falls Declaration ends on a strong note:

Now, in view of this entire disfranchisement of one-half the people of this country, their social and religious degradation--in view of the unjust laws above mentioned, and because women do feel themselves aggrieved, oppressed, and fraudulently deprived of their most sacred rights, we insist that they have immediate admission to all the rights and privileges which belong to them as citizens of the United States (Stanton & Mott, 1848).

Discussion Questions

1. In your opinion, which of the abuses listed in the Declaration is the most compelling? Discuss its significance.
2. Do any of these abuses apply today?
3. When viewing the success of women today (e.g, the right to vote and the high rate of college attendance), what impact has it made on your life?

Figure 2.4 *Cartoon of suffragettes (Undated photo courtesy of Library of Congress)*

Suffrage Movement

The right to vote can be both a symbol of full citizenship and a tool for social change. As the first-wave feminists shifted from the abolitionist movement toward the suffrage movement, women found freedom in different ways. The bicycle, which became popular in the 1890s, allowed women to leave the house and explore the world. Another technological innovation was the typewriter, which gave thousands of women the chance to work in an office in a "respectable" occupation (Rainey, 2010).

Education was another avenue toward the pursuit of independence in the pre-suffrage era. One devoted teacher, Mamie Garvin Fields, considered her career to be a way to serve her fellow African Americans. When applying for a job, she refused to go through the back door for the interview.

> However, I said to myself, "You mean to tell me I got my education and still have to go through the kitchen? Never!" That was one of my words, "never!" My old aunts and uncles of the early days had race pride. Although slaves, they stood up. (Fields, 1989, p. 52)

Walking to her new school on a half-wild island, Fields had to walk across a log over a gully filled with frogs, lizards, and other creatures. The weed-covered school held several snakes but no blackboard or books—only a bell and attendance book. Despite so many obstacles, she taught hundreds of students through the years.

Although women like Fields could not vote until 1920, they still made valuable contributions to society. The suffrage movement gained movement after the Civil War as middle-class women spoke out for equality. However, the working class also influenced the suffrage movement. In 1903, the British women launched their suffrage movement and soon inspired their American counterparts (Ziarek, 2008). Also in 1903, the Women's Trade Union League of New York emerged as a powerful voice for working women (Martens, 2009).

Working conditions for low-skill women were often harsh and the pay was often much lower than male salaries. In the South, African American women could only find work as servants, farm laborers, or laundry workers. Laundries in the cities often employed immigrant women, which caused back pain and burnt feet. Sweatshops usually paid piecework rates (paid by the number of completed items) and charged for use of the machines (Hapke, 2004). Workers needed labor unions and political power to gain some economic justice.

One example of empowered women appeared in the 1912 labor strike by the Lawrence, Massachusetts workers. Around 20,000 workers (mostly women) faced hostile authorities in their quest for decent wages. The mortality rate for children under six was 50 percent, since the living conditions and food were so bad. During the strike, parents sent their children to New York City as the " 'Children of Lawrence' were paraded through the streets. Dirty-faced, malnourished, bewildered, they were housed by sympathetic families who gave them their first decent meals in a month and took them to the zoo...." (Watson, 2005, p. 3). The workers briefly won the battle for "Bread and Roses"—wages not just for bare survival, but for a dignified life.

Suffragists also spent decades fighting for dignity and recognition as full equals. Not until 1920, though, were women in the United States allowed to vote. For decades, women such as Susan B. Anthony (Figure 2.5) and Alice Paul (Figure 2.6) fought hard for this most basic right. One writer described how the suffragists lobbied the Congressmen:

Here was an army of young Amazons who looked them straight in the eye, who were absolutely informed, who knew their rights, who were not to be frightened by bluster, put off by rudeness, or thwarted either by delay or political trickery. They never lost their tempers and they never gave up ... They were young and they believed they could do the impossible ... (Kerber & De Hart. p. 333).

Unfortunately, many activists endured much worse during their fight. Alice Paul, for instance, had decided to call herself a "suffragette" instead of "suffragist" because her British counterparts were more militant. She wrote, "The difference between the suffragists and the suffragette militants who have excited so much criticism is that they are the ones who have really brought their question to the fore. They chained themselves to a grill in the parliament and went up in a balloon" (Baker, 2005, p. 196). Paul and other women were jailed for their street protests and went on a hunger strike in 1917 because of the brutal conditions.

However gaily you start out in prison to keep up a rebellious protest, it is nevertheless a terribly difficult thing to do in the face of the constant cold and hunger of undernourishment. Bread and water, and occasional molasses, is not a diet destined to sustain rebellion long. And soon weakness overtook us.

Figure 2.5 *Susan B. Anthony (Undated photo courtesy of Library of Congress)*

Figure 2.6 *Alice Paul, author of the Equal Rights Amendment that never got ratified (Undated photo courtesy of Library of Congress)*

Box 2.1 Was the Suffrage Movement Racist?

For decades, African-American organizations such as the National Association of Colored Women (NACW) fought for suffrage on a separate track from the white organizations. "African American women's work was invisible only in the sense that most whites had direct contact with their servants and were largely unaware of and generally indifferent to the world blacks inhabited" (Collier-Thomas, 2010, p. 275). Although it was dangerous for any blacks to be politically active in the South, women held rallies to encourage the vote.

Figure 2.7 *Cartoon titled "First parade of The New Woman's Society in Possumville" (Undated photo courtesy of Library of Congress)*

Southern suffragists, unfortunately, insisted on segregation and would not work with blacks. One light-skinned woman, Adella Hunt Logan, "passed" for white at their meetings so she could report to NACW. In the northern states, however, black suffragists could work more openly with their fellow activists. Black churches were often the meeting sites for suffragists. One African Methodist Episcopal (AME) Zion Church activist, May M. Brown, stated that women advised their husbands and even their churches on political matters. " 'We seldom go into the pulpits, but we often speak through the mouth of the preacher' " (Collier-Thomas, 2010, p. 280).

Figure 2.8 *"Well, Missy! Heah we is!" cartoon (Undated photo courtesy of Library of Congress)*

At the end of two weeks of solitary confinement, without any exercise, without going outside of our cells, some of the prisoners were released....

(In the hospital) we decided upon the hunger strike, as the ultimate form of protest left us—the strongest weapon left with which to continue within the prison our battle against the Administration....

From the moment we undertook the hunger strike, a policy of unremitting intimidation began (Paul, 1976, p. 153).

The authorities responded by first placing her in a psychiatric ward, then later force feeding her. This method consisted of using a metal clamp to force her mouth open for the tube, thus prompting the name for her: Iron-Jawed Angel. She still continued the hunger strike for weeks (Ford, 1991).

Of course, not everyone fighting for women's suffrage was white. Box 2.1 discusses the racial aspects of this social movement. After women won the right to vote, they faced another challenge: the Great Depression of the 1930s, which is described in Box 2.2.

Box 2.2 The Forgotten Decade of the 1930s

When the Great Depression started in 1929, high unemployment rates affected both men and women. Hunger marches by women holding signs such as "We March Against Starvation" (Mitchell, 1985, p. 105) expressed the desperate need felt by millions. In Atlanta, a mother and her baby were found on a hotel bed. Both had been poisoned, but the mother survived to "testify that she had poisoned the baby and herself because she was destitute...." (Blackwelder, 1977, p. 112).

Despite the desperate plight of women, most labor unions excluded women because they were seen as taking jobs away from men. The unions opposed the "feminist agitation" shown by the female workers (Hapke, 1995, p. xvi). As President Roosevelt developed the New Deal to pull the U.S. out of the Depression, he did not consider equality for women (see Figure 2.9).

In sum, from stenographers to assembly-liners to college teachers, women were denied equal pay for equal work under the provisions of the National Recovery Administration (NRA) code; if married, forbidden from government and other employment by a section of the Federal Economy Act; and similarly restricted by the agenda of mainstream periodical articles with titles such as "Do You Need Your Job?" They were accused of emasculation, promiscuity, or both if they resisted these constraints but praised if they complied with the dictates of the back-to-the-home movement (Hapke, 1995, p. xvii).

Figure 2.9 *"Forgotten women," unemployed and single, in job demand parade (Undated photo courtesy of Library of Congress)*

Discussion Question

What is the significance of studying the 1930s from the women's perspective, especially government policies?

Key Terms

Weaker vessels
Warrior queens
Patriarchy
Gynocide
Rationalism
Economic Man and Romanic Woman
Abolitionist movement
Seneca Falls Convention
Suffrage movement

A Proud History

43

3

Women's Lib (Second-Wave Feminism) and the Backlash

UNLIKE the first wave of feminism, the women's liberation movement that started in the late 1960s still stirs up debate. Some commentators regard modern feminism as unnecessary, while others simply dismiss it as completely negative. A new wave of feminists has responded to the backlash since the second wave, as every succeeding generation must defy the traditional view that women belong only in the private sphere.

From Rosie the Riveter to Betty Friedan

During the Great Depression of the 1930s, poverty and unemployment dominated so many lives that feminist goals seemed less important. Then during World War II, the U.S. faced an opposite problem: a shortage of workers because so many men were fighting overseas. Factories and other workplaces were begging for workers, so a government propaganda campaign persuaded many women that it was patriotic to take a "man's job."

The campaign worked very well, as the number of women working outside the home rose from twelve million to eighteen million. One-third of the nation's workforce during World War II was female—the United States could not have won the war without these workers. Many of these women exposed to the opportunities of "men's work" were excited about the pay and educational options. Women made bombs, became supervisors, and took classes in drafting. Although the public perception of Rosie the Riveter (see Figure 3.1) was of a "plucky housewife" who left her home only for the war effort, two-thirds of these female workers had already been working outside the home (Frank, Ziebarth, & Field, 1984, p. 75).

Figure 3.1 *Two women drilling holes on a dive bomber (Undated photo courtesy of Library of Congress)*

Unfortunately, the war's end meant that the demobilized soldiers needed jobs when they came home. Most women were either demoted or fired to free up the positions. In 1945, there was no such thing as an Equal Employment Opportunity Act to protect a worker from being fired based on gender or race (Honey, 1984).

The 1950s, then, saw the resurgence of the housewife ideal for middle-class women. As usual, many lower-class women (many of them women of color) had to work outside of the home but were mostly invisible. Girls were supposed to grow up both pretty and virginal, then marry their high school sweethearts (hopefully a football player). Living in the suburbs, the wives were expected to have children, wear pearls, and serve a drink to their husbands every night when he came home from work. This set of expectations, of course, was a replay of the Angel of the House theme from earlier times.

Why were women forced into playing the aproned housewife in the 1950s after the intoxicating taste of men's work? Betty Friedan (Figure 3.2), author of *The Feminist Mystique* (1963), writes of how the traumas of the Depression and World War II made society weary of change. The American spirit fell into a strange sleep; men as well as women, scared liberals, disillusioned radicals, conservatives bewildered and frustrated by change—the whole nation stopped growing up. All of us went into the warm brightness home, the way it was when we were children and slept peacefully upstairs while our parents read, or played

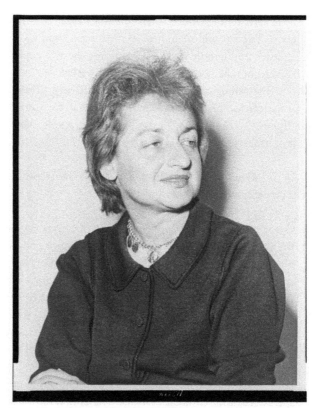

Figure 3.2 *Betty Friedan. (Undated photo courtesy of Library of Congress)*

bridge in the living room, or rocked on the front porch in the summer evening
in our home towns. (Honey, 1984, p. 3)

The Feminist Mystique, which helped spark the second wave, started when Friedan
conducted a survey of her former college classmates. Their responses about the quality of their lives motivated her to write this book. Despite the material comforts of
their homes, these women expressed their frustration about being trapped in the private
sphere.

The problem lay buried, unspoken, for many years in the minds of American
women. It was a strange stirring, a sense of dissatisfaction, a yearning that
women suffered in the middle of the twentieth century in the United States.
Each suburban wife struggled with it alone. As she made the beds, shopped
for groceries, matched slipcover material, ate peanut butter sandwiches with
her children, chauffeured Cub Scouts and Brownies, lay beside her husband at night—she was afraid to ask even of herself the silent question—"Is
this all?"

For over fifteen years there was no word of this yearning in the millions of
words written about women, for women, in all the columns, books, and articles

by experts telling women their role was to seek fulfillment as wives and mothers.... Experts told them how to catch a man and keep him, how to breastfeed children and handle their toilet training, how to cope with sibling rivalry and adolescent rebellion; how to buy a dishwasher ...

The suburban housewife—she was the dream image of the young American women and the envy, it was said, of women all over the world.... "There's nothing wrong really," they kept telling themselves. "There isn't any problem." (Friedan, 1963, p. 1)

In *The Feminist Promise: 1792 to the present,* Stansell (2010) clearly describes the status of women in the 1950s and 1960s.

Overwhelmingly, they worked in jobs that were segmented by sex, although the variety of jobs had increased in the service and clerical sectors since the nineteenth century. Classified ads in newspapers specified male or female; employers bluntly informed women they would not earn as much as men doing similar work. Wages were low—60 percent of men's, on average—and women had little hope for advancement. Schoolteachers seldom became principals; waitresses did not become cooks or restaurant managers; secretaries did not move up to be office heads. Those were men's jobs. The reigning ideology tried to reconcile the contradiction between the female ghetto and the American faith in meritocracy by casting women's underpaid work as an emanation of special feminine choices. Teachers weren't in it for the money, but because they loved children; secretaries took pleasure in waiting on their bosses; waitresses enjoyed the sociability of meeting people and serving them; maids liked tidying up for others....

In the professions, women were subject to the same downward pressures. Physicians and lawyers ended up pediatricians and estate attorneys; Ph.D.s in mathematics taught math to grade-schoolers.... African-American women were more likely to become professionals than whites, but they were clustered in lower-paid, lower-status echelons: nursing, secondary school teaching, and social work. (Stansell, 2010, pp. 184–185)

As Collins (2009) points out in *When Everything Changed: The Amazing Journey of American Women from 1960 to the Present* this was the reality for women before women's lib:

- Women were fined for wearing slacks in the courtroom because dresses symbolized their place in the world.
- In some states, husbands still had legal control of their wives' property and paychecks.
- Divorced women found it difficult if not impossible to get credit or buy a house.
- Women could not get credit without a male to co-sign (a father if there was no husband).

- In some states, women could not serve on juries.
- It was legal for employers to refuse to hire women or have two pay levels for men and women in the same jobs.
- Professional schools (law, medicine) allowed very few women in.
- Some jobs were unthinkable for women, such as news anchors or pilots.

One dean of a medical school stated in 1961, "Hell yes, we have a quota. Yes, it's a small one. We do keep women out, when we can. We don't want them here—and they don't want them elsewhere, either, whether or not they'll admit it" (Collins, 2009, p. 20). As a result, "In 1960 women accounted for 6 percent of American doctors, 3 percent of lawyers, and less than 1 percent of engineers." (Collins, 2009, p. 20). Some college students never once saw a single female professor during their four years. As Box 3.1 indicates, life was quite different for women before Second Wave feminism.

Box 3.1 Five Things Women Couldn't Do in the 1960s

McLaughlin (2014) lists five things that women could not do before second-wave feminism changed the rules. "Can you imagine pregnancy being a fireable offense? How about job security hinging on your weight or the softness of your hands? What if you couldn't open a bank account or establish a line of credit unless you had a husband to cosign for you?" (McLaughlin, 2014).

First, unmarried women could not obtain credit cards and married women had to get their husbands to co-sign for them. The Equal Credit Opportunity Act of 1974 forced banks and financial institutions to treat women as equal to men.

Secondly, women could not serve on juries in some states until 1973. A law article from 1927 describes one reason why women were not allowed to serve: "One picture which is often conjured up is of a mother being dragged off for jury duty while nubby [nursemaid] sings to the crying baby: Nice little baby, don't get in a fury, Mama, it may be, must sit on the jury" (Matthews, 1927, p. 1).

The third thing that women could not do was go on the Pill or buy other forms of contraception. Until the late 1960s, many states banned birth control even for married couples.

Going to most Ivy League schools was another impossibility for women during this era. Not until 1969 did Yale and Princeton admit women, while Harvard waited until 1977.

Lastly, job discrimination was rampant in the 1960s. Since Title VII's equality requirement took years to fully develop, some employers felt it was acceptable to have height and other requirements for stewardesses and other female works. Figure 3.3 is a picture of women applying to be stewardesses—a remarkable example of sexism in the workplace.

Figure 3.3 *Competition for Miss New York City title at an airline hostess school (Undated photo courtesy of Library of Congress)*

Discussion Questions

If you were a social worker in the 1960s, which of the five items would you focus on for your political advocacy project? How would you start a macro-level intervention to achieve your goal?

Do you think that the term "women's liberation" is appropriate for this movement, or is it too strong? Discuss what term you would use otherwise.

Emergence of Women's Lib

The 1960s was a decade of major social changes affecting women, including the introduction of "the Pill" in 1960 and the last-minute inclusion of gender in the 1964 Civil Rights Act (Title VII). Now women could plan their pregnancies and fight job discrimination. Collins (2009) describes how the lawmakers had ridiculed the idea of equal opportunity for working women was seen as such a joke that they called it the "Bunny Law." (Collins, 2009, p. 80). The Civil Rights Act had set up the Equal Employment Opportunity Commission (EEOC) as intended for minorities, but women requested that the Commission take them seriously. Stewardesses, for instance, were not allowed to be married, were fired at 35, and had to endure body measurements to keep their jobs. In another case, Lorena Weeks faced discrimination by Southern Bell based on the excuse that she could not lift 30 pounds. She proved that she could do it by lifting her heavy typewriter, and won not only the legal case but back wages (Collins, 2009).

Two strong advocates against sex discrimination in the workplace, Pauli Murray and Mary O. Eastwood, worked hard against employment discrimination through Title VII. Before this legislation, employers could legally classify jobs for men and women. For instance, men were the telephone repairmen and women were the operators. Men

Figure 3.4 *Advertisement in official program of a chemistry conference, 1963 (Historical artifact, unknown source)*

received higher salaries because they were the breadwinners. Seen as only temporary and uninterested workers, women had to settle for underemployment and lower wages. Some employers claimed that the public would not accept the sight of women in a man's job and vice versa. Other employers stated that women were too emotional to handle certain jobs. The legal weight of Title VII, then, was momentous for women seeking equality. The authors conclude that "We are entering the age of human rights" not just for women but for minorities (Murray & Eastwood, 1994, p. 86).

Besides legal actions such as Title VII, women organized on the grassroots level all over the United States. In 1966, the National Organization for Women (NOW) formed with Betty Friedan as its first president. In the Statement of Purpose, the new organization stated that "NOW is dedicated to the proposition that women, first and foremost, are human beings, who like all other people in our society, must have the chance to develop their fullest human potential" (National Organization for Women, 1966). This statement also includes these points:

- Women should share the "challenges and responsibilities" of all citizens in the public sphere .
- Since women are living for decades past their child-bearing years, they can have identities beyond mothers.
- Men should not have to be the sole breadwinner of the family. "We believe that a true partnership between the sexes demands a different concept of marriage… .").
- Housewives/mothers should receive full recognition for their contributions to society.

Discussion Questions

1. The full text of the NOW Statement of Purpose is available online at: http://now. org/about/history/statement-of-purpose. Discuss which point you most agree with. Is it still relevant today?
2. Now look for a point that you either disagree with or you consider to be outdated. Discuss this point. What would be an acceptable alternative?

Consciousness-raising

For decades, women had been facing discrimination and traumas such as unwanted pregnancies in silence. These issues were kept secret until women started meeting in groups all over the United States to raise their consciousness. "The personal is political" became the strong message of those who rejected "the ideological division of public and private spheres that dismissed women's claims of injustice as merely personal. Power, these feminists realized, operated within and through personal relations, including sexuality and the family" (Freedman, 2002, p. 87).

Although consciousness-raising (CR) was not officially associated with the women's movement, an overlap developed between the personal changes caused by CR sessions and the political goals of NOW and other groups. CR movements grew so fast from the mid-60s that by 1973 an estimated 100,000 women belonged to a CR group (Shreve, 1989). The Redstockings, one famous CR group, issued this Manifesto in 1969:

> We regard our personal experience, and our feelings about that experience, as the basis for an analysis of our common situation. We cannot rely on existing ideologies, as they are all products of male supremacist culture. We question every generalization and accept none that are not confirmed by our experience (Shreve, 1989, p. 11).

The groups met in living rooms and other informal places, and talked about whatever was on each member's mind. One woman discusses how she connected with the group:

> We were having a meeting in a woman's kitchen in Brooklyn. And she was talking about how her husband never took her seriously, about the tricks he had for doing this. I can't remember what all of them were, but one thing she said was how he seemed never to hear what she was saying, how an hour later, or days later, he'd say she hadn't told him the thing she'd said, when she knew she had. It was a way of dismissing her, of subtly suggesting that his mind was so full of important matters that he couldn't be expected to have to listen to the trivia she had to say. I remember that I brought my hands to my face, and I might have said something like, "Oh, my God." I'd been living for months in a state of constant confusion and bewilderment because my husband always did the same thing to me. I'd sometimes thought seriously that I was losing my mind, that he

Figure 3.5 *Women's lib march in New York City, 1970 (Photo courtesy of Library of Congress)*

Women's Lib (Second-Wave Feminism) and the Backlash

was right, that I hadn't actually said the thing to him. But here was this other woman, with the very same experience. And once that opened up, everything opened up. It changed my life. I'm not kidding. (Shreve, 1989, p. 55)

Another woman noted, "When you become a feminist, I don't think you all-of-a-sudden become a totally different person. You regress and you advance. Though my consciousness was raised and it grew, and there were things that I could verbalize that I couldn't before, making emotional and intellectual changes are two different things." (Shreve, 1989, p. 76) One participant described how the CR sessions helped her to fight back when she was told that she was not getting a promotion because she was a woman. She confronted her supervisors and ended up not only with the promotion, but a feeling that she now had powerful insights.

Goals of Second-Wave Feminism

What exactly did the "women's libbers" want? Besides the legal reforms listed in the following paragraph, feminists demanded respect for women. They no longer wanted to be seen as "The Second Sex" (as described by Simone de Beauvoir) that was subordinate because men's realities were the norm. Instead, women wanted their realities to be the center of the discussion. This demand would involve a deep change not just for society but for individuals who were brought up in a male-centered way of thinking.

The legal reforms initiated by the feminists include:

- Equal pay for equal work
- Equal access to jobs and promotions
- Equal access to higher education and scholarships
- Equal spending on women's sports
- Access to birth control
- Access to abortion (this controversy is covered in Chapter 9, Sex and Consequences).
- Rights of victims of domestic violence/intimate partner violence.
- Rights of rape victims.
- Laws prohibiting sexual harassment.
- Legal rights of housewives facing divorce and loss of income.
- Laws prohibiting employment discrimination against married and/or pregnant women (womenshistory.about.com).

Despite the popular conception that feminism led to a high divorce rate, the direct cause of the rise in divorces was the legal changes in the state laws. Before 1969, it was difficult to obtain a divorce because one party had to be at fault (adultery, etc.) The legal profession started a campaign for the "no fault" divorce laws that meant that couples could divorce based on irreconcilable differences instead of a major reason. As states changed their laws, the rates of divorce obviously increased (Kay, 1987). The feminist movement probably contributed to this rise because some women may have felt trapped in their unhappy marriages, but it would be impossible to calculate how many divorces were caused by feminism.

Another popular conception is that feminism looked down on housewives and even treated them as jokes. Although individual women may have said negative things about being a housewife because they had felt forced into that role, the feminists themselves tried to elevate the status of housewife. On the academic level, feminists described the difference between productive labor (which produces a paycheck) and reproductive labor (which does not involve a paycheck, but is still worth millions of dollars). Reproductive labor includes childcare, housework, volunteer work, and caregiving for the sick and elderly. Duffy (2007) claims that reproductive labor has lost its value in modern society. The first part of the article title, Doing the Dirty Work, indicates the low regard for the hard labor. This research on reproductive labor has achieved more recognition for the women whose contributions to society had been invisible for centuries.

> Although housewives did not receive pay, their work had enormous value for industrializing economies. Women's unpaid labor in the home made it possible for families to survive on working men's modest wages.... As mothers, they prepared children for the tasks they would have in the industrial and consumer economies.

> So diverse are housewives' contributions that it is difficult to place a monetary value on their labor. Some economists have attempted to do so by calculating the annual cost of purchasing women's services. In 1993 a family in the United States would have had to pay as much as $50,000 a year to buy all that a housewife contributed. In 1995 the United Nations Development Programme estimated that the worldwide annual worth of women's unpaid or underpaid work was $11 *trillion*. (emphasis added; Freedman, 2002, p. 129)

On the legal level, feminists have fought for the rights of married women in general to ensure that they were not left financially stranded due to divorce or widowhood (Freedman, 2002). Instead of denigrating housewives, feminists have stressed the dignity of their work and demanded full recognition for them. The goal of feminism is to provide women with choices—to have a career, to stay at home, or both.

The First Backlash: The Defeat of the ERA

In 1923, Alice Paul (the suffragist who had endured hunger strikes for her cause) first submitted a constitutional amendment for women's equal rights. The current text reads: "Equality of rights under the law shall not be denied or abridged by the United States or by any state on account of sex" (www.equalrightsamendment.org). Not until the 1970s did this amendment pass Congress and go to the states for ratification. However, the backlash against feminism had gained enough strength to defeat it in 1977.

Phyllis Schlafly (Figure 3.6) led the antifeminist fight because she claimed that the ERA would destroy marriages. (She also warned about same-sex marriages, which have become increasingly common in several states despite the ERA's defeat.) A passage from

Figure 3.6 *Phyllis Schlafly (Undated photo courtesy of Library of Congress)*

her book *Who Killed the American Family?* (2014) exemplifies her middle-American, conservative concerns about the social changes that have occurred since the 1960s.

> *Who Killed the American Family?* explains why and how feminists, judges, lawmakers, college professors and courses, government incentives and disincentives, and Democratic politicians seeking votes oppose the American traditional nuclear family as we knew it and as it was depicted on TV fifty years ago. Each antifamily act may seem minor, but added up, those acts and events are changing America for the worse. It is time to reverse the tide. (Schlafly, 2014, pp. xiii-xiv).

Threats to the American family include: homosexuality, divorce laws, day care, family courts, and the Violence Against Women Act. Following is an excerpt about why she opposes this Act:

> Domestic violence has become whatever the woman wants to allege, with or without evidence. Examples of claims of domestic abuse include name-calling, constant criticizing, insulting, belittling the victim, blaming the victim for everything, ignoring or ridiculing the victim's needs, jealousy and possessiveness, insults, put-downs, gestures, facial expressions, looking in a certain way, body postures, and controlling the money....
>
> No VAWA programs promote intact families or better male-female relationships. The act has no provision for addressing problems within the marriage context. Instead, VAWA promotes divorce and provides women with weapons, such as the restraining order and free legal advice.... (Schlafly, 2014, pp. 65, 68)

Box 3.2 The ERA Is Not Dead Yet!

Politicians such as Representative Carolyn Maloney and Senator Robert Menendez have continued the fight to ratify the ERA. According to a Congressional Research Service report cited on the website www.equalrightsamendment.org, Congresspersons have considered both the "fresh start" approach (starting with a new joint resolution) and the "Three State" approach (since ratification only lacked three states, to try again for just three more states.)

The website also includes a factsheet called "Why we need the Equal Rights Amendment," which includes the point that some women's rights are being reversed by laws and courts. Unlike other countries that provide constitutional rights for women to protect against discrimination, the U.S. Constitution only guarantees women the right to vote.

Discussion Question

Research the arguments for and against the ERA. Do you think that the ERA is still needed in the U.S.? Defend your answer.

The controversy over the ERA, though, continues through the 2010s. Box 3.2 describes the current efforts to ratify this amendment.

Discussion Questions

1. Discuss the significance of reproductive labor as the "invisible work" mentioned in Chapter One. How would you promote awareness of the unpaid but valuable labor provided by parents and other caregivers?
2. Research the Violence Against Women Act (also covered in the Domestic Violence/ Intimate Partner Violence chapter). Which sources would be valid in supporting or opposing Schafly's position?

More Backlash from Antifeminists

Any powerful social movement will inspire a strong reaction. In her book *Backlash: The Undeclared War Against American Women*, Susan Faludi points out that opponents are fighting back so hard because feminism has been so successful. Although the book was published in 1991 and based on the politics of the 1980s, many points are still relevant today.

> The force and furor of the backlash churn beneath the surface, largely invisible to the public eye. On occasion in the last decade, they have burst into view. We have seen New Right politicians condemn women's independence, anti- abortion protesters firebomb women's clinics, fundamentalist preachers damn

feminists as "whores" and "witches." Other signs of the backlash's wrath, by their sheer brutality, can push their way into public consciousness for a time—the sharp increase in rape, for example, or the rise in pornography that depicts extreme violence against women.

More subtle indicators in popular culture may receive momentary, and often bemused, media notice, then quickly slip from social awareness: ... The puzzling news that, as one commentator put it, "So many hit songs have the B-word (bitch) to refer to women that some rap music seems to be veering toward rape music." (Faludi, 1991, p. xxi)

One striking example of this backlash is Mona Charen, a law student who wrote an article entitled "The Feminist Mistake." Ignoring the fact that her admittance to law school was probably due to the feminist reforms, she writes, "In dispensing its spoils, women's liberation has given my generation high incomes, our own cigarette, the option of single parenthood, rape crisis centers, personal lines of credit, free love, and female gynecologists. In return it has effectively robbed us of one thing upon which the happiness of most women rests—men." (cited in Faludi, 1991, p. x).

In contrast to Faludi, Summers opposes second-wave feminists in her book, *Who Stole Feminism? How Women have Betrayed Women* (1994). The First Wave feminists desired legal equality, but now the "gender feminists" (Summers, 1994, p. 17) are self-absorbed individuals always complaining about oppression. For instance, she criticizes the way feminists have exaggerated the rates of violence against women and other social problems. Her opposition to women's studies, seen as a form of indoctrination of young women to start feeling oppressed, includes scorn for the critics of male-dominated curriculum.

Another antifeminist writer is O'Beirne, whose book title *Women Who Make the World Worse: And How Their Radical Feminist Assault Is Ruining Our Families, Military, Schools and Sports* (2006) indicates her opinion. "The radical demand for androgyny and personal autonomy is irreconcilable with the need for different sex roles and mutual self-sacrifice between parents raising their offspring. Influential feminists see two major problems with the family that inhibit women's equality—husbands and fathers" (O'Beirne, 2006, p. 2). She opposes Title IX, which provides equal funding for female athletes in schools, because it takes money away from male sports. Mocking the idea of female soldiers in combat, she calls them "G.I. Janes" (O'Beirne, 2006, p. 113).

Many antifeminists have also blamed feminism for the sexual freedom in modern society, including Wendy Shalit, author of *Return to Modesty: Discovering the Lost Virtue* (2004). It is true that feminists have attacked the double standard (i.e., females had to be chaste but not males) and the second wave occurred during the "Free Love" movement of the 1960s. However, the current raunchy culture of "Girls gone wild" seems unrelated to feminism. Shalit, though, believes the way for women to gain respect was not through feminism but by abstaining from premarital sex or wearing sexy outfits. She criticizes the hook-up culture of casual sex among young people (which the older crowd would call a one-night stand). Traditional cultures such as Judaism gave women the right to "sexual privacy" so that she could refuse sex during her menstrual cycle (Shalit, 2004, p. 56). She extends this idea to single women not being pressured to have sex in the past.

In 2014, a Tumblr site called Women Against Feminism added to the backlash. Women posted pictures of themselves with signs that responded to this prompt: "I don't need feminism because":

- I don't want to politicize my gender.
- I am not a victim.
- I *don't* need something that demonizes men.
- I don't need something that tells me that the action of a slut are okay, and that the evidence of those actions can be thrown away like they were nothing but a clump of tissue.
- And I sure as hell *don't* need anything that makes playing the victim out to be "empowering."
- It has turned from a movement about equality to a hateful sexist corrupt group that disregards people's issues due to "privilege."
- Society does *not* objectify me. Feminists are the ones that tell me that. Do I look oppressed?
- I believe in equality NOT entitlements and supremacy.
- I am NOT a target for violence and there is NO war against me.
- I respect men. I refuse to demonize them and blame them for my problems.

Discussion Question

Pick one theme (e.g., the feminists stress oppression too much) from the preceding section and comment on it. Do you agree or disagree with this theme?

Third-Wave Feminism—and Fourth?

Upon reflecting on the advances made by the second wave, De Hart (1991) writes that even simple goals such as equal pay are problematic because they require a major shake-up. "Given the pervasiveness of sexism, many feminists see no possibility for real equality short of transformation not only of individuals but also of social institutions and cultural values" (De Hart, 1991, p. 511). Instigating real change, then, is exhausting work. "Feminism is not for the fainthearted" (De Hart, 1991, p. 511).

No wonder, then, the term *postfeminist* became such a popular term in the 1980s and later. It seemed that enough had been achieved and people were tired. Journalists and others speculated that enough pro-equality laws and social changes had occurred that the idea that women needed feminism anymore seemed ludicrous. According to Hall and Rodriguez (2003), postfeminists claimed that women no longer found the feminist movement to be relevant to their lives. The disclaimer of "I'm not a feminist, but (I support equal pay, etc.) ..." actually meant that feminism still mattered.

Since the 1990s, Third Wave Feminism has emerged as a counterpart to postfeminism. Rebecca Walker describes the moment when she decided to call women together for the new fight in 1992. She was sitting on a New York subway, watching a mother and young daughter. Two men sat behind Walker and started talking loudly about their sexual conquests in rude terms. Then another man sat next to her before making a sexual remark. He asks Walker her name. "A torrent explodes: 'I ain't your sweetheart, I ain't your bitch, I ain't your baby. How dare you have the nerve to sit up here and talk about women that way, and then try to speak to me.' The woman/mother chimes in to the beat with claps of sisterhood...." (Walker, 2007, p. 400).

Third-wave feminism is more than just an angry response to harassment, of course. Punk rockers such as Kathleen Hanna of Bikini Kill created a version of "girl power" to fight the underrepresentation of women in music and other venues. Following is an excerpt from the Riot Grrrl Manifesto of 1992:

> BECAUSE us girls crave records and books and fanzines that speak to US that WE feel included in and can understand in our own ways....
>
> BECAUSE we recognize fantasies of Instant Macho Gun Revolution as impractical lies meant to keep us simply dreaming instead of becoming our dreams.... (Hanna, 2007, p. 395)

The use of art as social protest is not confined to the United States, since women all over the world have written poetry, performed plays, and painted murals as protests. "A refusal to be 'nice' resonates throughout third-wave creativity" (Freedman, 2002, p. 324). For example, the use of appliqued handiwork on vests and other garments started as a survival strategy for Chilean women prisoners smuggling out messages. Now Peruvian women are creating works of art that are also political messages. One craftsperson said, "The more we work, the more creativity we find in ourselves. We all have a little art in our minds and in our hands; we will have something as a legacy for society. It will stay behind us, in another place, in another time" (Freedman, 2002, p. 325).

Third-wave feminism, then, stresses inclusion of all cultures. Acknowledging the impact of racism is vital for the white middle-class women who had dominated the second wave. One activist advised whites, "Work on racism for your sake, not 'their' sake" (Freedman, 2002, p. 92). In response to challenges like these, the third wave stresses these themes:

- Diversity (as evident in the textbook's middle section).
- Intersectionality—how multiple identities intersect (as discussed in Chapter 12).
- Global issues (Chapters 18–25).

Generational differences also play a role in current feminism. The Third Wave Manifesta of 2000 (Baumgardner & Richards, 2010) delineates thirteen goals. They include reaching out to the younger women so they will become an effective political force. Reproductive health is focus of the next two goals, including the right to fertility treatments and pleasurable sex. The fourth goal is "to bring down the double standard in sex and sexual health, and foster male responsibility and assertiveness in the following areas: achieving freedom from STDs; more fairly dividing the burden of family planning...." (Baumgardner & Richards, 2010, p. 279). Next is the promotion of women's history and the support of queer women (lesbians, etc.).

One key point is to "liberate adolescents from slut-bashing, listless educators, sexual harassment, and bullying at school, as well as violence in all walks of life, and the silence that hangs over adolescents' heads, often keeping them isolated, lonely, and indifferent to the world" (Baumgardner & Richards, 2010, p. 280).

A renewed trend of feminism has emerged since 2010, prompting some writers to claim that this is a fourth wave (e.g., Cochrane, 2013). Valenti, author of *Full Frontal Feminism: A Young Woman's Guide to Why Feminism Matters* (2007), opens her book with this blunt statement:

> The worst thing you can call a girl is a girl. The worst thing you can call a guy is a girl. Now tell me that's not royally f***ed up.... Most young women know that something is off. And even if we know that something is sexist, we're certainly not ready to say we're feminists. It's high time that we get past the "I'm not a feminist but ..." stuff. You know what I'm talking about: "I'm not a feminist or anything, but it is total bullshit that Wal-Mart won't fill my birth control prescription."
>
> Do you think it's fair that a guy will make more money doing the same job as you? Does it piss you off and scare you when you find about your friends getting raped? Do you ever feel like shit about your body? Do you ever feel like something is wrong with you because you don't fit into this bizarre ideal of what girls are supposed to be like?
>
> Well, my friend, I hate to break it to you, but you're a hardcore feminist. I swear....
>
> As different as we all are, there's one thing most young women have in common: We're all brought up to feel like there's something wrong with us. We're too fat. We're dumb. We're too smart. We're not ladylike enough - 'stop cursing, chewing with your mouth open, speaking your mind'. We're too slutty. We're not slutty enough.
>
> F*** that.
>
> You're not too fat. You're not too loud. You're not too smart. You're not unladylike. There is nothing wrong with you. (Valenti, 2007, pp. 5–7)

Valenti has reinvigorated feminism with another book, *The Purity Myth: How America's Obsession with Virginity Is Hurting Young Women* (2010). She condemns the abstinence-only education movement, which revives the ancient idea that the only good woman is a sexually pure one. Valenti writes:

> If you spend any amount of time doing media analysis, it's clear that the most frenzied moral panic surrounding young women's sexuality comes from the mainstream media, which loves to report about how promiscuous girls are, whether they're acting up on spring break, getting caught topless on camera, or catching all kinds of STIs. Unsurprisingly, these types of articles and stories generally fail to mention that women are attending college at the highest rates in history, and that we're the majority of undergraduate and master's students. Well-educated and socially engaged women just don't make for good head-lines, it seems. (Valenti, 2010, pp.45–46)

Discussion Question

Pick one idea from the third- (or fourth-) wave feminists and write a paragraph about it. Why did you agree or disagree with it? What is the idea's significance to your own life?

Key Terms

Rosie the Riveter
Title VII
Consciousness-raising
Betty Friedan
Second-wave feminism
Backlash of antifeminists
Third-wave feminism

4

The Gender Line: Solid Wall or Dotted Line?

Introduction

Some people may think of the gender line as a solid stone wall. Men are men and women are women—there is no in-between. Others, though, may consider it to be a dotted line with plenty of room to cross it. The idea of an ambiguous line could confuse and even upset some people, especially those raised in traditional cultures. How can there be any exceptions to the solid gender line?

Gender beliefs are a women's issue because they relate to biological determinism, the tenet that your body is your destiny. A female body is destined to bear children and display nurturing, passive, and all the other "naturally female" traits. Men are destined to be strong, brave, and assertive because of their physiques. People who believe in biological determinism are more likely to resist women's call for equality, since it is not "natural" for women to cross the gender line.

Another critical purpose of this chapter is to spread knowledge about transgender persons and others who were born outside the male/female gender binary. In December 2014, a seventeen-year-old transgender male-to-female committed suicide by stepping in front of a semitrailer truck on the interstate outside of Cincinnati, Ohio. The suicide note on Leelah (Joshua) Alcorn's blog received worldwide attention. After describing how her parents took her out of public school and kept her isolated for months, she expressed her sense of hopelessness that she could never transition successfully to either adulthood or her true gender. She ends her note:

> The only way I will rest in peace is if one day transgender people aren't treated the way I was, they're treated like humans, with valid feelings and human rights. Gender needs to be taught about in schools, the earlier the better. My death needs to mean something. My death needs to be counted in the number

of transgender people who commit suicide this year. I want someone to look at that number and say "that's f**** up" and fix it. Fix society. Please. (cited on websites such as http://www.dailymail.co.uk/news)

Gender, then, is not a dry academic topic but a matter of life and death for some persons. Because not enough people understand the complexity of gender identity, parents and others may harm a transgender person. Lack of knowledge can lead to hardships and even death for persons who cross the gender line.

Fortunately, public awareness about gender issues is growing and true acceptance is becoming more common. Social workers have a special obligation to not only learn about gender, but also to advocate on behalf of marginalized persons such as this teenager who was in too much despair to see the wonderful life she could have lived.

Biological Basis of Sex/Gender

What makes you a male or female? The first answer may refer to genitalia—of course, I'm a male/female because of what's in my underwear! What could be more obvious? (Note: Gender is often defined as a psychological or social classification of masculine/feminine, as opposed to the male/female classification based on biology. However, biologists may use the terms "sex" and "gender" in a different context.)

A gender difference begins in fetuses with chromosomes. Usually, XX indicates a female and XY indicates a male. But what about XXY (Kinefelter Syndrome), XYY (Jacobs Syndrome), X (Turner Syndrome), and XXX (Triple X Syndrome)? Persons may cross the gender line, then, because of their unique chromosomal structures. In normal development, the indifferent fetal sex phase takes place. Then within eight to ten weeks of development, a fetus develops embryonic gonads: either testis or ovaries. That is when the hormones work on the fetus on three layers: genitals, internal parts (e.g., cervix), and brain. "By birth, then, the baby has five layers of sex. And, as we shall see, these layers do not always agree with one another" (Fausto-Sterling, 2012, p. 5).

After birth, the person goes through even more layers of sexual differentiation (e.g., pubescent growth). Gender and hormones are usually seen as absolutes: women have more estrogen and men have more testosterone. However, a person may have low levels of a hormone that could influence their puberty. Some male teens, for instance, may develop their deep voices and body hair years after their peers. Hormone shots are used by transgender persons as part of their transition. Biological males, for example, develop breasts by taking estrogen (Fausto-Sterling, 2012).

How much do hormones affect sexual differentiation? This debate has been going on for decades. One researcher at the Women's Mood and Hormone Clinic writes of the profound impact of hormones on women's lives (Brizendine, 2006).

What we've found is that the female brain is so deeply affected by hormones that their influences can be said to influence to create a woman's reality. They can shape a woman's values and desires, and tell her, day to day, what's important. Their presence is felt at every stage of life, right from birth. Each hormone state—girlhood, the adolescent years, the dating years, motherhood, and

Figure 4.1 *Gender binary (Photo source: Entofolio)*

menopause—acts as fertilizer for different neurological connections that are responsible for new thoughts, emotions, and interests. Because of the fluctuations that begin as early as three months old and last until after menopause, a woman's neurological reality is not as constant as a man's. His is like a mountain that is worn away imperceptibly over the millennia by glaciers, weather, and the deep tectonic movements of the earth. Hers is more like the weather itself—constantly changing and hard to predict. (Brizendine, 2006, pp. 3–4)

Hormones, then, are critical in a woman's life. Her brief descriptions of some of these hormones include the following:

Estrogen—the queen: powerful, in control, all-consuming; sometimes all business, sometimes an aggressive seductress….
Progesterone—intermittently appears and sometimes is a storm cloud reversing the effects of estrogen; other times is a mellowing agent….
Testosterone—fast, assertive, focused, all-consuming, masculine; forceful seducer; aggressive, nonfeeling; has no time for cuddling;
Oxytocin—fluffy, purring kitty; cuddly, nurturing, earth mother; the good witch Glinda in the *Wizard of Oz*; finds pleasure in helping and serving….
Cortisol—frizzled, frazzled, stressed out; highly sensitive, physically and emotionally. (Brizendine, 2006, pp. xv–xvi)

A male counterpart to this analysis is the popular term "testosterone poisoning," which implies the big, muscular, and dumb male who does destructive things to prove his manhood. Like Brizendine's assertion about women, this stereotype of macho men is essentialist because gender differences are based on nature.

Discussion Questions

1. Do you agree with the concept of hormones being so influential on one's personality and behavior? Are you basing your opinion on personal observations (anecdotes) or research studies?

2. Design a research study to test this hypothesis: Males do stupid things because of testosterone poisoning (hormonal influence). How conclusive would your research be?

3. Design another research study to test this hypothesis: Women are more emotional than men because of their hormones. How would you define "more emotional"?

Nature and Gender

In her book *Evolution's Rainbow: Diversity, Gender, and Sexuality in Nature and People*, Roughgarden (2009) challenges the idea that there are "natural" aspects of gender. For instance, she debates Darwin's concept of sexual selection. Not all males show aggression or other courtship behavior (e.g., a male peacock's feather display) and not all females choose the male with the most desirable traits for its species. Instead, she proposes the concept of "social selection" that allows for several types of variations of sex and gender. (Roughgarden, 2009, p. 6) This view stresses the inclusive nature of animal groups that accept diverse versions of male and female. She also notes that chemists can use a periodic table of elements, but that

> Biological rainbows interfere with any attempt to stuff living beings into neat categories. Biology doesn't have a periodic table for its species. Organisms flow across the bounds of any category we construct. In biology, nature abhors a category. (Roughgarden, 2009, p. 14)

Thus, using names for species and other classifications contradict the wide range of variations in organisms. Essentialists (i.e., those who believe women are "essentially" more nurturing than men because of their ability to bear children, etc.) have tried to use biology to justify their argument that males and females should follow their "natural" roles. To counter this view, she states bluntly that:

> To a biologist, "male" means making small gametes and "female" means making large gametes. Period! By definition, the smaller of the two gametes is called a sperm, and the larger an egg. Beyond gamete size, biologists don't recognize any other universal difference between male and female. (Roughgarden, 2009, p. 23)

Most social scientists distinguish sex (biological attributes) from gender (psychological and social attributes). Biological attributes include: "chromosomes, external genitalia, internal genitalia (e.g., uterus, prostate), gonads, hormonal states, and secondary sex characteristics" (Stoller, 1984, p. 9). Sometimes these attributes overlap, which results in intersexed persons who were once called hermaphrodites. Sexual dimorphism, though, means that a person may be born as intersex—with ambiguous genitalia that is neither male nor female. In one case, a girl was born with an incomplete vagina and no uterus. She did not discover this until she was a teenager and had always identified herself as a female. After corrective surgery, she adjusted to life as a woman and married a man (Stoller, 1984).

When the book was written in the 1980s, professionals did not handle gender issues with the awareness and sensitivity that vulnerable patients needed. For example, a gynecologist told a 14-year-old girl that she had underdeveloped female sex organs and male chromosomes.

> To the patient, despite all accompanying explanations, this meant that she was genetically, and therefore in the most biological sense, no longer a female but a freak, with both male and female qualities. From the day of that pronouncement, she began ruminating on whether she was a female or male.... (Stoller, 1984, p. 25)

These obsessive thoughts triggered an acute distress. After being diagnosed with schizophrenia and sent to a psychiatric unit, she described her struggle:

> As soon as they found out about my condition, I should have been left to die. I am no good to society. I am abnormal. I am different. That is what has always been done since time immemorial. No one can reach me. Not even you. I have to kill myself because society didn't. I am trash of the earth. Not fit to live. (Stoller, 1984, p. 26)

Fortunately, she received competent counseling and was reaffirmed as a female. "What has lingered, but with diminished intensity, are ruminations about whether a particular thought or act is masculine or feminine" (Stoller, 1984, p. 28).

Intersexed persons may or may not identify as transgender (as explained later). Around 0.05 percent of the population are born intersexed, with the doctors usually performing a sex reassignment surgery in the early childhood. According to the Intersex Society of North America, some individuals do not show signs of being intersexed until puberty because some the indications are not based on outer genitalia but inner organs. Advocates for intersexed persons also stress that the "cut first, ask questions later" attitude of doctors may result in the wrong gender being assigned to the child. Since it is easier to construct female genitalia (as the saying goes, "it is easier to dig a hole than build a pole"), most intersexed persons are assigned as females although they may grow up feeling like males (Fausto-Sterling, 2012). Box 4.1 demonstrates how "gender" and "sex" are not easy concepts to define.

Psychological Basis of Gender

Are men and women really from two different planets? Carothers and Reis (2013) would strongly disagree with the assertion that gender differences are that vast. Instead, their analysis of 122 different characteristics such as sexual attitudes, mate selection, and dependence on others produces only a difference in degree rather than a list of categories. "Although gender differences on average are not under dispute, the idea of consistently and inflexibly gender-typed individuals is. That is, there are not two distinct genders"

(Carothers & Reis, 2013, p. 401). The model for male/female differences should be a continuous line of gradations, not two distinct categories.

    Researchers continue to explore the question of gender and the brain. How does one determine whether nature or nurture has created a possible difference in traits such as the level of social interaction? As described in Cahill's summary of brain research (2012), a British team studied newborns in a maternity ward. The researchers themselves did not know the baby's sex. These babies had the choice to look at either a student's face or a mobile that resembled a face. "The girls spent more time looking at the student, whereas the boys spent more time looking at the mechanical object. This difference in social interest was evident on day one of life—implying that we come out of the womb with some cognitive sex differences built in" (Cahill, 2012, no page).

    In *Brain Gender*, Hines (2005) argues that the nature/nurture dichotomy does not exist for this topic because "All of our behavior is controlled by our brain and, in this sense, is biologically based" (Hines, 2005, p. 4). Claiming that research findings about sex differences are more likely to be published than findings about nondifferences, Hines believes that stereotypical thinking has influenced the scientists' work. One researcher who has faced much criticism has been Kimura, who states that gonadal hormones affect cognition and so women lack the ability to excel in science or engineering (Kimura, 2000).

Transgender Persons
....

Brain wiring, then, may be the most important biological component of gender. Transgender persons are those who have the body of one gender but the brain wiring of another. The medical establishment recognizes Gender Identity Disorder (primarily characterized as Gender Dysphoria) as a condition. Scientists state that sexual differentiation, including brain wiring, begins in the womb around the fourth month. Transgender persons may go through hormonal therapy and sex reassignment surgery, or they may choose to live as either androgynous (sexually neutral) or as "genderqueer" (non-conforming to either gender) (www.webmd.com/mental-health/gender-dysphoria).

Children as young as two or three may show signs that they "know" they are the wrong gender. In the 2007 documentary "My Secret Self," a mother tells of finding her toddler son in the bathroom trying to cut off his penis with a nail clipper because it didn't belong on his body. When puberty hits, gender dysphoria can become a crisis as the body starts developing into a mature male or female while the person's mind says otherwise. If the child starts expressing his/her concerns, the family may refuse to listen or even worse, throw him/her out of the house. Homelessness, drug addiction, and other preventable problems often result from the family's rejection of their child.

Sexual orientation is NOT the same as gender identity. The term LGBTIQA (Lesbian/Gay/Bisexual/Transgender/Intersex/Questioning/Asexual) includes the "T" because these groups all deviate from the social norms of sex and gender. Transgender persons may or may not be involved in relationships with persons of the same gender (regardless of whether they have sex reassignment surgery or not).

To counterbalance the negative reactions from society, many advocates have spoken out about their experiences. One of the most eloquent accounts of being transgender, *She's Not There: A Life in Two Genders* by Jennifer Finney Boylan (2003), describes the first time she realized that she was really a female in a male body:

> I was born in 1958, the second day of summer. It was also the birthday of Kris Kristofferson and Meryl Streep, both of whom I later resembled, although not at the same time. One day when I was about three, I was sitting in a pool of sunlight cast onto the wooden floor beneath my mother's ironing board.... I saw her ironing my father's white shirt ..."Someday you'll wear shirts like this," said Mom.
>
> I just listened to her strange words, as if they were a language other than English. I didn't understand what she was getting at. *She* never wore shirts like that. Why would I ever be wearing shirts like my *father's*?
>
> Since then, the awareness that I was in the wrong body, living the wrong life, was never out of my conscious mind—*never*, although my understanding of what it meant to be a boy, or a girl, was something that changed over time.... And at every moment as I lived my life, I countered this awareness with an exasperated companion thought, namely, Don't be an *idiot*. You're *not* a girl. Get over it.
>
> But I never got over it. (Boylan, 2003, pp 19–20)

Boylan went on to fall in love and marry, hoping that becoming a husband would help her to get over it. Then they had two children. Even then, she did not get over it.

> I often woke up and lay there in the dark. Usually this was about a quarter to four. I'm the wrong person, I thought. I'm living the wrong life, in the wrong body.
>
> To which I would respond: You're a maniac. An idiot. You have a life a lot of other people dream about, a life so full of blessings that your heart hurts.
>
> To which I would respond: I know. Still. (Boylan, 2003, p. 102).

Boylan's story is one of love and acceptance. As a college professor, she did not experience any job discrimination. Other transgender persons, though, have faced overwhelming barriers to getting a job, finding suitable health care, and have even suffered violence. The FBI does not track the number of hate crimes committed against transgender persons, but reports indicate that even police officers have attacked this population. According to one study, 90 percent of transgender adults have experienced harassment at work, and 78 percent of transgender youth have been harassed at school (Angell, 2013). Hopefully, society will create a more accepting environment for those who cross the gender line as transgender.

Although the book uses the outdated term *transsexual* instead of *transgender, True Selves: Understanding Transsexualism* (Brown & Rounsley, 1996) offers constructive insights about this issue. This excerpt from "Nature's Cruel Trick" describes the strain of pubescent growth when the body feels all wrong to the person.

Gender dysphoric teens … rarely report feelings of exhilaration (at the bodily changes). Instead of excitement and anticipation, they experience profound disappointment, panic, and confusion. Patients often refer to puberty as a "curse" or "hell for transsexuals."

As children, they may have been able to delude themselves into thinking that a transformation to the opposite sex might still occur. But all hope is lost with the emergence of their secondary sex characteristics. For males, these include deepening of the voice, development of the Adam's apple, growth of body hair, development of a more masculine physique, and maturation of the genitals. For females, they include development of breasts, hips, and a softer, more feminine shape; maturation of the genitals; and the beginning of menstruation. With the arrival of puberty, transsexual teens must face the harsh reality of nature's cruel trick—that their bodies are finally changing but the changes are all the wrong ones.…

Transsexual teens typically feel shame, despair, and anger because they are developing the adult body of the wrong sex. Puberty, to them, feels like "end of the line" because it provides the indisputable evidence that their bodies are never going to match their gender identity.…

(One patient) fully expected that her body would magically straighten out when she "grew up." From an early age her perception had been that "eventually you either got your period or got a penis."

For Malcolm, the unhappiness grew incrementally with the development of each new secondary sex characteristic. "While I was growing up," he said, "I prayed that it wouldn't happen to me. All that hair and the voice and getting tall and everything. And one by one, they all happened. Each one was like a hammer blow to my head.…" (Brown & Rounsley, 1996, pp. 49–61)

Discussion Questions

1. If you were the case manager working with a transgender youth, what three things should you know?

2. How trans-friendly is your school or workplace? Are there any policies against harassment, or a gay–straight alliance?
3. Since an estimated 40 percent of homeless youth identify as LGBT, what policy solution do you suggest? How would you garner support for your cause?

Others Who Cross the Gender Line

Cross-dressers (once called transvestites) are sometimes called drag queens or drag kings. Despite the desire to wear the clothes of the other gender, these persons's sexual orientation could be heterosexual or bisexual. In the 1970s, the TV show MASH had a character called Corporal Klinger (played by Jamie Farr) who dressed as a woman to try to get a psychiatric discharge. This running gag was the first exposure that mainstream Americans had of cross-dressers. Unfortunately, our society still lumps all persons who cross the gender line as a joke like Klinger. One researcher notes that

> Put simply, cross dressing is wearing the garments of another gender, e.g. a man wearing what society deems is women's clothing or a woman wearing what is deemed to be men's clothing. For women in most modern cultures this distinction is somewhat blurred.... (but) heterosexual or homosexual men do not have the (same) freedom (Lewis, 2012, p. 1).

Unlike cross-dressers, the hijras of India are a cultural group with a centuries-old religious background. Biologically male, this third sex dresses and acts like women but identify as neither sex. They worship a mother goddess and perform sacred rites at festivals.

> For the most part, hijras are phenotypic men who wear female clothing and, ideally, renounce sexual desire and practice by undergoing a sacrificial emasculation—that is, an excision of the penis and testicles—dedicated to the goddess Bedhraj Mata. Subsequently they are believed to be endowed with the power to confer fertility on newlyweds or newborn children. They see this as their "traditional" ritual role, although at least half of the current hijra population ... engages in prostitution....
>
> By their own accounts, hijras in most major cities ... have been driven crazy by foreigners or, to translate the more colorful Hindi phrase, have had their "minds eaten by foreign (firangi) people" desperate to capture a story for their audience. In the last decade or so, (there have been several movies and books).... Given this history of near-invisibility, the recent attention focused on hijras has been unsettling for both hijras and non-hijras.... (Reddy, 2005, pp. 2–3)

In India, the third sex allows for a men-to-women shift but not women-to-men. Some Native American tribes, however, honor "Two-Spirits" persons who are either type. "Two-spirit people are part of a historical tradition that was seen in many Aboriginal communities prior to colonization, whereby individuals with diverse gender identities were valued for the unique contributions they made to community life. (They were) asked to fulfill key ceremonial roles" (Meyer-Cook, 2008, p. 246). Modern LGBT activists sometimes use the term "Two Spirits" in recognition of this high level of acceptance.

Legal Status of Transgenders and Others Who Cross the Gender Line

Depending on the country, the new status of a transgender person who has gone through the transition (gender-reassignment surgery) may or may not be legally recognized. In the United States, the states have the right to determine the amount of legal recognition for a transgender person. Marriage certificates, driver's licenses, and other legal papers may or may not be amended to show the new status (Howell, 2014).

Others who cross the gender line also experience legal confusion. In 2010, Norrie May-Welby was recognized by Australia as the world's first nongendered person. Born a male who had become a transwoman twenty years ago, May-Welby stated that neither gender applied to hir (the nongender pronoun). Australia, though, later rescinded this legal ruling (Fausto-Sterling, 2012).

Another international event regarding gender identity occurred in 2009, when the conservative Muslim country of Pakistan officially recognized their hijra population as a third gender. This ruling also prohibits the police from mistreating these persons. In 2014, India followed suit by giving hijras the legal recognition they needed as a third gender (Khaleeli, 2014).

Breasts are often related to gender identity, as discussed in Box 4.2. The norm is for women to have noticeable breasts, but not men.

Discussion Question

In 2011, a Canadian couple announced that their child would be officially genderless until it became obvious. The parents refuse to disclose their child's gender, stating that it is a violation of privacy. In your opinion, is this harmful or beneficial to the baby? Why?

Historical Look at Gender

In history, not every society has followed rigid rules of gender. In ancient Pompeii, for instance, murals depicting erotic scenes reveal a unique view of rape and power. Instead of male dominance and female submission, though, the overriding theme is the "master's gaze" (Severy-Hoven, 2013, p. 35). Male slaves were just as vulnerable as females to being violated. "The way Roman notions of sexuality intersect with slavery reinforces this positioning of the viewer as master. In the same way that a male or female slave's body was treated as penetrable by stick or lash, it was considered open to the master for sexual use as well" (Severy-Hoven, 2013, p. 40). The male/female dichotomy was superseded by the master/slave relationship: social status, rather than gender, determined whether one could be raped at will.

Box 4.2 Breasts and Gender Identity

Brownmiller's classic work, *Femininity* (1984), has several excellent points. The following passages discuss the impact of gender norms, especially regarding how society regards breasts.

What to do with breasts, if one is not actually using them for nursing a baby, has preoccupied the feminine mind for a very long time.

Breasts are the most pronounced and variable aspect of the female anatomy, and although their function is fundamentally reproductive, to nourish the young with milk (placing "Man" among the mammalian species), it is their emblematic prominence and intrinsic vulnerability that makes the chief badge of gender. Breasts command attention, yet they are pliable and soft, offering warmth and succor close to the heart....

Although they are housed on her person, from the moment they begin to show, a female discovers that her breasts are claimed by others. Parents and relatives mark their appearance as a landmark event, schoolmates take notice, girlfriends compare, and boys zero in. No other part of the human body has such semipublic, intensely private status, and no other part of the body has such vaguely defined custodial rights.... breasts belong to everybody, but especially to men. It is they who invent and refine the myths, who discuss breasts publicly, who criticize their failings as they extoll their wonders, and who claim to have more need and intimate knowledge of them than a woman herself....

An uptilted cup shape is idealized in Western art, for high, round breasts are associated with youth. Yet an uplifted sphere is invariably smallish in nature, since a large mass cannot defy the laws of gravity except when securely trussed in a bra or shot up with silicone.... Clothes are never designed for low-slung pendulous breasts, and rarely do we see this shape extolled in the nude.

Who can blame women for being confused about their breasts? And what good does it do to point to our barebreasted sisters in other cultures, for we have seen too many pictures in National Geographic of wizened old females with sagging, shriveled teats or with udderlike breasts that hang forlornly to the waist. No, not sexy. Not pretty and attractive.... Who wants to dwell on the thought that breasts can look like udders, that breasts are udders, dry, full, swollen, dripping with milk, squeezed, sucked on, raw, tender, in pain—and ultimately used up and withered. (Brownmiller, 1984, pp. 40–44)

Discussion Questions

1. Reflect on the importance of breasts in your own life. When were you first socialized to think about them?
2. The social work profession affirms the dignity and value of each person. How does this apply to people who feel objectified for a body part: breasts, muscles, and so forth?

Another striking example appears in nineteenth-century Cuba, in which African-based religions allowed men and women to cross the gender line. In ceremonies, men acted as *orishas* (goddesses) and women acted as hunters. The cross-dressing was forbidden under colonial law, so this behavior challenged the white overlords (Watson, 2014).

Before this modern era, military maidens dressed and fought as men in the military. Some women secretly joined the military out of boredom or to escape their husbands. In some cases, military maids continued to pose as men long after they had left the ranks.

Deborah Sampson (Figure 4.2), for instance, posed as "Robert Shurtliff" in 1782 to join the Revolutionary Army. She later claimed that she was trying to avoid an unwanted marriage and wanted to serve her country. According to her senior officer cited in an article:

> She displayed herself with activity, alertness, chastity, and valour, having been in several skirmishes with the enemy, and receiving two wounds; a small shot remaining in her to this day; she was a remarkably vigilant soldier on her post, and always gained the admiration and applause of her officers; was never found in liquor, and always kept company with the most upright and temperate soldiers.
>
> For several months this galantress (sic) served with credit as a waiter in a General officer's family; a violent illness ... led to the discovery of her sex; she has since been honorably discharged from the army with a reward. (Young, 2004, p. 4)

Although other women posed as men to fight in the American Revolution, Sampson promoted herself for both public attention and a military pension. She later married. Her story, parallel to the Chinese legend of Mulan (discussed in Chapter 22, Women in China), indicates that crossing the gender line can be a valuable experience.

The Social Basis of Gender

Gender identity develops not just through the biological process, but through socialization. What makes a girl a girl, and a boy a boy? The first step is of course determining the gender, which can be done on either a biological or identity-based process. In a 1989 malpractice lawsuit, the widow was deemed not to be a real woman despite the gender reassignment surgery done several years prior. The judge said, "There are some things you cannot will into being. They just are" (cited in Westbrook & Schilt, 2013, p. 33). His biology-based view of gender contradicted the "identity-based determination of gender," which her husband and several others had acknowledged (Westbrook & Shilt, 2013, p. 33).

Doing gender (conforming to rules of one's determined gender) starts early. Girls should like dress-up and glitter, but boys should like toy soldiers. In a 2011 controversy, a J.Crew advertisement showed a five-year-old boy getting his nails painted by his mother. Child psychologists accused the mother of causing damage to her child by crossing the gender line—not only did she paint his toenails, but it was neon pink! (Macedo, 2011).

DEBORAH SAMPSON.

Published by H. Mann. 1797.

Figure 4.2 *Deborah Sampson (Courtesy of Library of Congress)*

Figure 4.3 *Gender as a spectrum (Photo source: Entofolio)*

Meanwhile, places such as the Little Princess Spa state on their website: "Little Princess Spa is dedicated to every True Princess who ever dreamed sneakers were glass slippers and to girls who believe it is better to twirl than walk, sing than talk and that everything goes better with sparkles. For now she wants her own Fairy, a little sprinkling of fairy dust.... " (www.littleprincesspa.com).

Discussion Questions on Doing Gender

1. If an alien from a genderless planet landed on Earth, how would you prove to it that you are male or female? Starting from your first memories of gender, write an essay on how you learned to do gender. You may include:

   - Toys
   - Clothes
   - Shopping habits
   - Eating habits
   - How you walk
   - How you handle conflict

2. Go to a mall (or a mall website) and analyze the gender breakdown of stores. Divide the stores into three categories: female, male, and neutral. For instance, a Hallmark store may be seen as female-specific and a sports store may be male-specific. Count how many stores are in each category. What does this say about consumer society?

3. Go on a website for a multiplex movie theater of at least 14 movies. List the movies in three categories: male-dominant (lead role is male), female-dominant, and gender neutral. For instance, a review of the movies playing in January 2015 include:

Male: *American Sniper, Wedding Ringer, Taken 3, Paddington, Selma, Blackhat, Foxcatcher, Hobbit, Unbroken, Night at the Museum*, and *Big Hero 6*.
Female: *Into the Woods* (Meryl Streep seen as an ugly witch) and *Hunger Games*
Gender neutral: *Woman in Black* (horror movie)
Write a short essay on the list. If you have seen any of those movies on the list, discuss the gender aspects of that movie.

Gender Roles in Latino Culture

Machismo and marianismo, the gender roles in Latino culture, exemplify the strict boundaries that a society can establish. Stevens (1973) proposes the term "marianismo" (based on the Mother Mary) as the female counterpart to machismo. Like a Spanish conquistador, men must act with arrogance and decisiveness. "Life is risky for the Latin American male... forced to act or pretend to act aggressively at all times" (Stevens, 1973, p. 59). In contrast, wives are meant to be more spiritual than men and forgive them their violent behavior and sexual affairs. Hence, "a female cannot hope to attain full spiritual stature until (she has) been tested by male-inflicted suffering. Men's wickedness is therefore the necessary precondition of women's superior status" (Stevens, 1973, p. 62).

Figure 4.4 *Statue of Mary (Photo courtesy of OUP)*

The Gender Line

Other scholars have adapted this model to their research, including Bull (1998). Marianismo influences Latinas' sexual behavior because they are exposed to the Virgin Mary's ideal of chastity. "Women who fit the marianismo profile tend to be women who work for their families in the home, serving husbands and sons and enlisting their daughters' assistance ... (they) teach their daughters to remain virgins until marriage, leaving the sexual education of their sons to male family members" (Bull, 1998, p. 3). As a result, women who follow this traditional role are less likely to work outside the home or assert financial independence.

Marianismo is also linked to the low level of exercise done by Latinas, because they are too busy with family duties to address their own health needs (D'Alonzo & Sharma, 2010). HIV prevention, which stresses the use of condoms, is also affected because Latinas may not be able to insist on protection. In a study of Latinas in prison, one researcher notes that: "It is not surprising, then, that fatalism runs high among these women; they believe that they have no control over their own lives, that nothing they do will affect the inevitable outcome (predetermined by God), and that they may as well let fate take its course" (West, 2001, p. 34).

Discussion Question on Gender Norms

In small groups (preferably mixed-gender groups), write down the rights that men and women should have in this society. Make a list for each gender.
Men have the right to..... Without....
Women have the right to.... Without ...
Examples: Men have the right to have friends who are girls without being called gay. Men have the right to cry without being seen as soft. Women have the right to be angry without being called a bitch. Women have the right to be out late without having a bodyguard.
Share this list with the class, and discuss how gender norms can be challenged.
These lists will include examples of socialization. People experience sanctions (e.g., insults or rejection) for not following the rules. At any age, people must be aware of the expectations not only of their gender, but also of their age, class, and so forth. A boy toddler may cry without being seen as a deviant, but a male teen could be ridiculed or even beat up for that same behavior. Another example is that a female teen may show off her cleavage a little bit, but not older women.

Key Terms

Chromosome
Hormones
Transgender
Intersex
Military maids
Machismo
Marianismo

5

Lesbians and Bisexual Women

Introduction

For the modern person in the twenty-first century, it may be hard to imagine the context of being lesbian when it was forbidden. In the era before World War II, most middle-class lesbians were closeted. It was the working-class lesbians who were more likely to be "out" despite the risks.

> Things were horrible back then and I think that because I fought like a man to survive I somehow made it easier for the kids coming out today. I did all their fighting for them. I'm not a rich person. I don't have a lot of money; I don't even have a little money. I would have nothing to leave anybody in this world, but I have that---that I can leave to the kids who are coming out now, who will come out in the future. That I left them a better place to come out into. And that's all I have to offer, to leave them. But I wouldn't deny it. Even though I was getting my brains beaten up I would never stand up and say, "No, don't hit me. I'm not gay, I'm not gay." I wouldn't do that. I was maybe stupid and proud, but they'd come up and say, "Are you gay?" And I'd say, "Yes, I am." Pow, they'd hit you. For no reason at all. It was silly and it was ridiculous; and I took my beatings and I survived it. (Kennedy & Davis, 2014, p. 1)

During World War II, a senior staff member of the Women's Air Command (WAC) stood before General Eisenhower during World War II. Eisenhower had ordered a list of lesbians in WAC so he could dismiss them all. "I looked at him, looked at the secretary who was there with us, and said, 'If the General pleases, sir, I'll be happy to do that, but the first name on the list will be mine" (Gallo, 2007, p. xxviii). The secretary then said that her name would be second. After being told that lesbians were in every level of WAC and had excellent records, the General rescinded his order.

Although gay-bashing and homophobia still occur, western society is starting to embrace the diversity of sexual orientations. Same-sex marriages, for instance, are no longer a utopian goal for gay activists but a legal reality for many couples. Supreme Court Justice Ruth Bader Ginsburg, for instance, stated in 2015 that "The change in people's attitudes on that issue has been enormous … I think that as more and more people came out and said that 'this is who I am,' the rest of us recognized that they are one of us" (Stohr & Winkler, 2015). Statistics from the Pew Research Center confirm her claim. In 2013, 49 percent of all adults supported the legal right of same-sex couples to marry, whereas 44 percent oppose it. The generational differences are striking: 70 percent of adults born after 1980 support it, whereas only 31 percent of the oldest generation (1928-1945) support it (Pew Research Center report, 2013a). The growing acceptance of same-sex marriage is just one measurement of acceptance of lesbian/gay/bisexual/transgender/questioning/intersex/asexual (LGBTQIA)—shortened to LGBT in this chapter—persons but it does indicate that the world is a much different place for lesbians and bisexual women today.

Life Before Stonewall (1969)

Before gay liberation started with the Stonewall Riots of 1969, countless women felt that they had to hide their identities. Living a secret life was common for lesbians and bisexual women. One lesbian describes her hard work in achieving "sex-role invisibility" (Zevy & Cavallaro, 1987, p. 86) to protect herself:

> I wore feminine camouflage: makeup, seamed stockings, starched crinolines, and endless curlers. I took on feminine habits: I spoke in deliberate tones and flirted with the boys.… I could not act either truly female or truly male. What I had learned very well was how to be invisible.… (Zevy & Cavallaro, 1987, pp. 86–88)

Such invisibility was necessary for survival for those who faced rejection and even persecution. The history of lesbians is a fascinating combination of both hostility and acceptance from societies. The first historical mention of lesbians appeared in the days of ancient Greece (Lesbos Island is the origin of the word lesbian). Historians dispute whether the poet Sappho of Lesbos was actually a lover of women, but her name now symbolizes strong women who are unashamed of their desires (Lardinois, 1991). This following poem is part of her legacy.

> The Moon
> The stars about the lovely moon
> Fade back and vanish very soon,
> When, round and full, her silver face
> Swims into sight, and lights all space (Source: www.poetry-archive.com)

Ancient Roman writers also mentioned lesbians. Although some, such as Juvenal, may have objected to homosexual behavior, they aimed most of their criticisms at men instead of women. Most of Fone's comprehensive work, *Homophobia: A History* (2000), focuses on antimale homosexuality because society felt more threatened by homosexual men. Exemplifying this, the Greek writer Charicles states that it is better for lesbians to have sex than for "the male sex ... (to) become effeminate and play the part of a woman" (Fone, 2000, p. 67). Also, the phallocentric attitude that sex is only "real" if it involves a phallus/penis has partially protected lesbians in history. This attitude is congruent with the modern view that two kissing lesbians are "hot" and really want a man to join in—if there is no man, then it really is not sex.

In western society, the antilesbian sentiments in the Christian Scriptures have influenced today's debate on gay rights. In Romans 1:26, St. Paul states that women had turned to "shameful, unnatural lusts," which may or may not involve lesbianism. Church Fathers and other Christian writers have also condemned lesbians, such as St. Augustine writing that nuns must not do "shameless" things with each other (Fone, 2000, p. 124). The penalty for lesbian sex in the early Church, though, was less than for male homosexual sex.

Medieval authorities would mutilate, torture, and execute lesbians for their "sins." The punishment for a woman in an Italian city in 1574 was that the woman "be fastened naked to a stake in the Street of the Locusts and shall remain there all day and night under a reliable guard, and the following day shall be burned outside the city." (Fone, 2000, p. 200). The church leaders of the Spanish Inquisition committed even worse atrocities against lesbians. In the 1890s, scientists concluded that lesbians were "sexual inverts" who needed serious medical intervention such as surgical removal of the clitoris (Gibson, 1997). Later, psychotherapy became another way to "cure" lesbianism.

Another dark time for all homosexuals was the Nazi persecution, during which men and women were imprisoned and killed because of their sexual orientation. The Nazis had used the pink triangle for the homosexual prisoners, which was comparable to the Jewish Star of David. Not until the 1980s did the international community acknowledge the tragedy, which involved at least 100,000 homosexual victims. Today, the pink triangle is one of the symbols of gay rights (Jensen, 2002).

In some historical periods, though, women could be "out" as lesbians and still be accepted by their societies. Paris in the 1920s, for instance, hosted several famous lesbians such as Gertrude Stein and Colette (Latimer, 2005). One Gertrude Stein quote that still applies today is: "There ain't no answer. There ain't gonna be any answer. There never has been an answer. That's the answer" (cited on www.brainquote.com).

Aldrich's *Gay Lives* (2012) also offers vivid examples of women who were accepted despite breaking gender norms. For instance, the Ladies of Llangollen were two Irish women who lived openly as a couple in the early nineteenth century. For over fifty years, they were celebrities who posed for photographs while wearing men's clothes.

In the United States during the nineteenth century, Boston marriages were a social norm for many women living together. Although they did not openly discuss whether they were physical lovers, displays of affection (both word and action) were completely acceptable. Eva Gore-Booth, who lived openly with her lover around 1900, was a British suffragette and labor organizer who opposed gender norms. "If the world is to see sweetness and independence combined in the same individual, all recognition of their duality must be given up" (Aldrich, 2012, p. 130). Box 5.1 provides another historical perspective on lesbians before the modern gay rights movement.

One woman who stayed with her partner for forty years, Valentine Ackland, wrote:

I love you with a most true, most married love: that I feel as I have done always, since we first lay together, a deep and absolute responsibility for you—which was my greatest joy and happiness. (Aldrich, 2012, p. 134)

Box 5.1 Daughters of Bilitis

One bright spot in the history of lesbians is the formation of the Daughters of Bilitis in 1955. Before this organization started, lesbians usually had to hide in the shadows.

For many lesbians and gays in the late 1940s, the cost of being true to their desires was shame and a constant fear of exposure. It coexisted, however, with the shadowy excitement of developing new and different lives and loves in a handful of major metropolitan areas. There, down dark streets in the warehouse district behind unmarked doors, tucked in alleyways near derelict buildings, or way out near the beach in shacks hardly anyone but the vice squad noticed, gay women and men could experience a secret, sexually charged world hidden from the rest of society.

The discovery and acceptance of one's homosexuality put gay men and women in de facto positions of defiance—of prevailing social norms, of religious teachings, of traditional family values. For many, the possibility of ostracism and punishment meant that they had no choice but to live in two worlds—"normal" and "deviant"—and become adept at negotiating both while maintaining strict segregation between them (Gallo, 2007, p. xxxii).

Besides this social pressure to be heterosexual, anticommunists encouraged a red scare that sometimes targeted homosexuals as possible traitors. In the 1950s, up to five thousand government employees lost their jobs because of their sexual orientation. In this context, the Daughters of Bilitis emerged to fight for justice. These women, inspired by the legacy of both Eleanor Roosevelt and her husband, refused to stay silent in a time when it was dangerous to speak out. Four lesbian couples joined together to form a literary journal, learn more about lesbianism, and educate the public. Perhaps the group's most important goal was to advocate for civil rights by making it legal to be a lesbian. Setting up local chapters and regional conferences, they organized to give a voice for women once invisible. They also broke through racial barriers in a time when the Civil Rights movement was just beginning to flourish (Gallo, 2007). The Daughters of Bilitis disbanded in 1969—right at the time of the modern gay-rights movement.

One couple, Del Martin and Phyllis Lyon, noted that lesbians' issues were less about getting arrested and more about being denied custody of children and other forms of discrimination. They were together for fifty-five years and were the first couple to get married in California in 2008—just two months before Martin died. "Happiness is personal. Some women find it with other women. It's really as simple as that" (Aldrich, 2012, p. 249).

Stonewall

On June 27, 1969, the New York police raided the Stonewall Inn (a gay hangout) as they usually did. But this time was different.

They (the police) expected the usually docile response to what was, after all, a familiar event in New York City's gay bar culture: a few snide remarks, some campy bitchery, but general acceptance of the law. But instead of fading into the Village streets to seek out other haunts, the bar's patrons fought back. The crowd outside the Stonewall grew larger, louder, and increasingly defiant. Bitchy remarks became jeering shouts; hostility grew. A bottle was thrown, a window broken; a paddywagon arrived, blows were exchanged, arrests were made, and suddenly a riot exploded....

For those present it was intoxicating and empowering. For the first time in American memory, gay people had refused to accept the law, which indicted them as second-class citizens, as sick, perverted criminals, as undeserving of its protection as they were of the compassion of the righteous. Instead someone shouted, "Take your hands off me!" (Fone, 2000, p. 407)

Gay males were not the only victims of police harassment. Lesbians such as Karla Jay had also faced persecution before Stonewall:

What scared me most was the prospect of being caught in a bar raid.... A law against masquerading—that is, disguising oneself—was invoked as a pretext for persecuting gay people. When the police raided a lesbian bar, they had to release only those customers over the age of eighteen who were wearing three visible pieces of clothing.... But even customers who evaded arrest might find their lives ruined after a police raid.... Lesbians could be deprived of homes, jobs, an education, or even children without the benefit of a trial, without ever having been arrested—all for being in the wrong place at the wrong time. (Jay, 1999, p. 24)

Lesbians, then, soon joined the fight for civil rights. The Gay Liberation Front quickly formed, using this slogan for their fliers: "Do You Think Homosexuals Are Revolting? You Bet Your Sweet Ass We Are!" (Gay Liberation Front Leaflet cited on www.oocities.org). This quote also expresses the mood of the gay rights movement:

It's amazing to me, that people think gays' and lesbians' not wanting to lose their jobs because of who they are is "special treatment." Not wanting to walk down the street in fear that someone will jump out of a pickup with a baseball bat is "special treatment." Being able to live with the one that you love is "special treatment." No one is talking about quotas or affirmative action. We are talking about the Constitution. That's all. (Dan Mixner quoted on www.oocities.org)

Discussion Question

Why is it critical for a social worker (and everyone else) to know the historical background of LGBT rights? If you were in a marginalized group with a historical trauma, why would you want others to acknowledge its importance?

Lavender Menace

The terms *women's liberation* and *gay liberation* would imply the same goal of fighting oppression, but divisions appeared between the two political groups. Heterosexual women dominated the women's-lib movement as it emerged in the late 1960s. As openly gay women began to get involved, some discomfort resulted because the straight women did not want to be further marginalized. One writer notes:

> The stigma of lesbianism can also be used by the patriarchy to frighten women into subordinate, dependent behaviors.... Any woman who seems strong, athletic, competent, and assertive, or who has intense friendships with other women, can always be called a dyke to intimidate her back into line.... (Pearlman, 1987, 317)

Betty Friedan, one of the feminist leaders, coined the term "lavender menace" because she did not want lesbians to dominate the National Organization of Women. In 1970, lesbian leaders such as Rita Mae Brown were even forced out until they were invited back into the organization a year later.

Brown was one of the first openly gay women to demand that the feminist movement listen to their concerns. Karla Jay, author of *Tales of the Lavender Menace: A Memoir of Liberation* (1999), recalls the meeting of a radical feminist group called the Redstockings. Brown confronted them. "The leaders of Redstockings were disturbed and threatened by Rita's behavior. They turned the conversation back around to men as our oppressors. Still, they looked uncomfortable.... I was thrilled at Rita's daring, but I pitied the leadership" (Jay, 1999, p. 45). She added later:

> What she [one feminist] and many other heterosexist Redstockings overlooked was that lesbians had been raised in families with men, had usually had sexual relationships with men, had worked with men, and had sometimes lived with male roommates. Several lesbians I knew had children from previous marriages. What the straight women couldn't see was that many Redstockings talked about men all the time the way dieters obsess about food. There were times when some of us, including a few of the heterosexuals, felt it would be more productive to focus on ways in which women could interact with one another positively. (Jay, 1999, p. 66)

By the 1990s, Jay reflects that she was no longer angry at the nongay feminists. However, "I got the feeling they would like us to shut up or disappear" (Jay, 1999,

p. 47). Through the decades, the feminist movement has embraced LGBT rights as part of their activist agenda. According to the NOW (National Organization for Women) website:

> NOW is committed to fighting discrimination based on sexual orientation or gender identity in all areas, including employment, housing, public accommodations, health services, child custody and military policies. NOW is committed to educational efforts that combat the adverse effects of homophobia, promote positive images in the media and ultimately ensure civil rights protection for all. NOW asserts the right of lesbians to live their lives with dignity and security, and marriage equality for all. (http://now.org/issues/lgbtq-rights//)

Discussion Question

The National Association of Social Workers (NASW) also strongly supports GLBT rights. In the Diversity section of its website (www.socialworkers.org/diversity), there are documents about SOCE (Sexual Orientation Change Efforts --also called "reparative" and "conversion" therapy). Research the implications of this issue. What is SOCE/reparative therapy? Why is it so controversial, especially for children?

Figure 5.1 *Lesbians in a climate of social acceptance (Photo courtesy of OUP)*

Is "lesbianism" merely a matter of same-sex attraction or defined even more narrowly, simply two women having sex? After discussing the historical development of the word "lesbian," Golden (1987) discusses the assertion that a woman could be a lesbian even if she denies it to herself. Ferguson's definition, though, stresses self-identification:

> A lesbian is a woman who has sexual and erotic-emotional ties primarily with women or who sees herself as centrally involved with a community of self-identified lesbians whose sexual and erotic-emotional ties are primarily with women and who is herself a self-identified lesbian. (Ferguson cited in Golden, 1987, p. 21)

Some theorists claim that there are two types of lesbians: primary (identifying from early childhood) and elective. Those who felt that they had been born lesbian may refer to themselves as "real" lesbians and designate the others as "fake." (Ferguson cited in Golden, 1987, p. 28). This distinction may become even more complicated when some lesbians state that they sometimes want to have sex with men. Bisexuality, as discussed in the following section, indicates the fluid nature of sexual identity.

Sometimes women who have been married to a man for years may fall in love with a woman. This can cause much confusion and distress to somebody who has considered herself to be heterosexual all her life.

> When a married woman suddenly feels attraction to another woman, the experience often turns her world upside down. She is filled with questions and uncertainty. One client described herself as always "surrounded by a fog." Her foundation had been rocked by her discovery. She no longer trusted many of the beliefs she had about herself, her marriage, or her values. (Fleisher, 2011, p. 1)

Sexual pleasure, not deep emotions, can be a motivating factor for same-sex encounters. In a study of 34 married women who were advertising for same-sex encounters online, Walker (2014) found that they refused to consider themselves as lesbian or bisexual. The first part of the article title, " 'I'm not a lesbian, I'm just a freak' " explicates their understanding of why they were seeking female lovers online.

> "Freaky;" "hypersexual," and having a "high sex drive" (were used) to explain their desire to arrange clandestine same-sex sexual encounters. For them, the gender of their partner was not a consideration in their formation of a sexual identity, but instead represented a desire to push boundaries and engage in taboo behavior. (Walker, 2014, p. 923)

These women claimed that they only wanted no-strings-attached sex with no intimacy or interruption of their married lives. Assuming that a random female would be a better lover than a random male, they stated that sexual satisfaction was their primary goal of these encounters.

In sharp contrast are the women who have always felt a strong pull toward other women on many levels. As one lesbian speaker states, "I'm not just sexually attracted to women. I'm emotionally, spiritually, and socially attracted to women. So it's not just about sexual attraction. I'm more attracted to women in lots of ways." (Crawley & Broad, 2004, p. 53) Another writer answers the question this way: "What is a lesbian? Who is a lesbian … In the end, a lesbian must simply be any woman who calls herself one … .For there is no essential or timeless lesbian, but instead lesbians who, by creating our lives day by day, widen the range of possibilities" (Whisman, 1993, p. 60).

Bisexual Women

Like lesbians, bisexual women can experience discrimination and stereotypes. Orlando (2001) discusses how the gay-rights movement has had difficulty defining and even accepting bisexual women. Some lesbians have considered bisexual women as betraying their cause, since they sometimes have male lovers. Mainstream society regards them as "promiscuous or incapable of commitment" because of the hetererosexual/homosexual dichotomy. She adds:

> "Heterosexual privilege" doesn't prevent us from being queerbashed on our way home from the bars or having our children taken away when we come out. We look just like other queers; i.e., we range from blatant to indistinguishable from straights. (Orlando, 2001, p. 147)

The term "biphobia" means fear and/or the negative reactions toward bisexual persons, which is distinct from homophobia. People may believe that bisexuality is only a phase, or just a denial about being homosexual. Also, many are simply unwilling to acknowledge bisexuality as a legitimate sexual orientation (Worthen, 2012).

Lesbians sometimes react negatively to bisexual women, calling them "hasbians" and traitors. "[Bisexuality] makes some lesbians uneasy. In a society where heterosexuality is the norm and lesbianism is still stigmatized, bisexual boundary crossings often lead to hurt feelings, as when a woman is left by her female lover for a man" (Stein, 1993, p. 29).

Discussion Questions

If you had a client who was not sure of which sexual orientation she had, how would you respond? Would you feel more empathy to a woman in love with another woman rather than to a woman just seeking sexual gratification? What are your personal values regarding this issue?

Intersection of Race/Ethnicity

White heterosexist mainstream culture may require that lesbians from diverse backgrounds must develop their identities not just on the level of ethnicity, but also on the level of sexual orientation. Espin (1987) writes of how she developed her identity as a Cuban-American only after arriving in the United States.

Adding to this process of self-discovery was the experience of realizing that one was also lesbian. The first reaction was denial:

> First, total unawareness. Then, after sleeping with a woman, total rejection of her; as if she was an addition. I knew this was "sick." I never went to bed with so many men in my life as I did during that period.... (Espin, 1987, p. 46)

After acknowledging their sexual orientation, some Latinas feel that they have to choose between being a Latina or a lesbian. This conflict causes much distress because both identities are so essential to their personhood (Espin, 1987).

A more recent study (Gallor & Fassinger, 2010) confirms the extra stress for an ethnic minority who is LGBT. In a study comparing white lesbians/gay males with their ethnic minority counterparts, the whites were likely to be "out." The researchers note that

> Previous literature has speculated that ethnic minority gay men and lesbians must function in multiple communities, including their racial/ethnic community and the gay community. Although assimilation into the white-dominated gay and lesbian community can be a difficult task ... the support network of their ethnic group (was found) to be helpful. (Gallor & Fassinger, 2010, p. 311)

However, some ethnic communities can still be homophobic. African-American lesbians, for example, may feel pressure from their churches' teachings against homosexuality (Bates, 2010). In a study of once-married lesbians, the researcher found that being a strong, brave heterosexual woman in the face of racism was the community's ideal. Claiming a lesbian identity, then, may seem like a betrayal to their race. Both racism and homophobia can be internalized for an African-American lesbian. As a result, many of these lesbians married men because being attracted to other women was not an option.

> You got married, went to church, paid your tithes . . . doing the right thing was being married to one man, having children with that one man, and growing old with that one man until one of you all died. And that was it. (Bates, 2010, p. 208)

Older Lesbians

As the aging Baby Boomers transform society's view of the elderly, one component of the older population is gaining recognition: older lesbians. In an interview about her life in 1930s and 1940s, one African American woman expressed surprise at the idea that she would have "come out" in public. "[Do you think I] put a sign on my back? If you think I am, I didn't ... say I was but if you like me well, you know what I am, that's a shame. That's all I can say. Why you gotta tell? If you don't know, shame on you" (Hall & Fine, 2005, p. 181).

These women had to cope for years not only with homophobia but the need to support themselves in a prefeminist era of low pay and low regard for working women. Finances are a major concern for many older lesbians, especially those who were never legally married. Social Security and private pensions heavily favor married couples when they receive their retirement benefits, so same-sex couples often lose thousands of dollars a year because of their "single" status. Older lesbians also have to cope with ageism, since they may feel less valued as they age. However, most have developed considerable strengths—including a supportive community of both straight and lesbian friends (Averett & Jenkins, 2012).

Another concern for aging lesbians is the perceived need to go back into the closet as they receive more social services. Researchers (Jenkins, Walker, Cohen, & Curry, 2010) discuss a case study on Molly, a seventy-eight-year-old who has moved into assisted living. Although she had previously been "out" as a lesbian, now she was retreating from such openness. She described her "keeping her own counsel" as a way to handle the new environment. "I am private and some people just don't accept that, so rather than take a chance, I just don't tell them anything. It is none of their business." (Jenkins, et al., 2010, p. 408).

Sometimes generational differences between lesbians can cause a rift. This case study shows the culture clash between pre-Stonewall and post-Stonewall lesbian identities:

> Ruth was seventy-eight years old. She had come out to herself in 1943 when she worked in a steel factory in Pittsburgh. Three of Ruth's coworkers were also "that way" and the four of them became lifelong friends. Ruth considered herself to be gay and proud of it. However, she could not get over her great-niece, Emily, identifying as "queer." Ruth thought queer was insulting and not at all descriptive of her gay friends. She didn't even like the term lesbian…. (Clunis & Green, 2005, p. 66)

Discussion Question

Fighting social isolation through community building for older lesbians can be a priority for social workers. Are there any lesbian-specific groups for older adults in your area? Can you find an example of one that could be used as a best practice model?

Concerns of Lesbian and Bisexual Women

Butch/Femme Stereotypes

Do lesbians fall into the categories of butch (manly) and femme (feminine)? This has been a controversial question for decades. Before Stonewall, some lesbian communities did emphasize these stereotypes.

> During this period [1930s to 1950s], manipulation of the basic ingredient of patriarchy—the hierarchal distinction between male and female—continued to be an effective way for the working-class lesbian community to give public expression to its affirmation of women's autonomy and women's romantic and sexual interest in women. Butches defied convention by usurping male privilege in appearance and sexuality, and with their fems, outraged society by

creating a romantic and sexual unit within which women were not under male control. (Kennedy & Davis, 2014, p. 6)

However, other lesbians fought this image. In the 1950s, the Daughters of Bilitis tried to persuade butches to behave more conventionally for social acceptance. The founders stated that society would reject women not wearing skirts—in the 1950s, that would not be an overstatement for any woman (Whisman, 1993). The modern stereotype would be a woman wearing a flannel shirt and driving an SUV for a camping trip.

Another consideration about the butch/femme stereotype is that academic researchers take the term seriously. The article title "The Coming-out Process of Young Lesbian and Bisexual Women: Are There Butch/Femme Differences in Sexual Identity Development?" (Rosario, Schrimshaw, Hunter, & Levy-Warren, 2009) typifies the approach. The researchers found that butches were more likely to be exclusively lesbian, whereas femmes were sometimes bisexual. Crawley (2001) notes that working-class lesbians are more likely to identify as butch/femme than their middle-class counterparts, but the butch/femme trend varies through the years.

Discussion Question

Do you agree that the butch concept challenges the patriarchy ideal? Or does it merely reinforce it?

Internalized Homophobia

Another concern for lesbians and bisexual women is internalized homophobia which is the "LGB person's internalization of society's negative attitudes and beliefs about homosexuality and directing these attitudes toward one's self" (Barnes & Meyer, 2012, p. 506). Homophobia also affects men, as discussed in Box 5.2.

Askowitz (2008) describes the painful experience of internalized homophobia as it affected her relationship with her girlfriend. Her reaction is also related to fat-shaming.

> When Kate ate Fritos in bed at night I was sure that instead of growing old together in that romantic way, we'd grow fat together, in that awful, stereotype of a lesbian way. It would only take time before we were sitting up in bed watching college football, eating Ding Dongs and drinking Pabst Blue Ribbon from cans.
>
> I'd learned enough in women's studies classes in college to know that I was experiencing internalized homophobia. It was one thing to become fat, which I worried about enough to avoid, but becoming a fat lesbian was everything I dreaded. When I felt fat, I felt butch. And I didn't want to be one of the butch lesbians—the ones who are often awkward in their bodies.
>
> I knew the butch lesbians took the brunt of oppression because straight people could spot them on the street. I admired them for refusing to conform to society's standards for women and insisting on being themselves. I realized they paved the way for the rest of us. But they are the lesbians people hate. They are the ones who are accused of being men. And even though I didn't look like them, I always feared I was one piece of cake away. (Askowitz, 2008, pp. 60–61)

Box 5.2 Homophobia and Men

Gay and bisexual men, of course, also experience homophobia. The fear of male homosexuality may be only one component of homophobia, as noted by Kimmel (2000):

> This, then, is the great secret of American manhood: We are afraid of other men. Homophobia is a central organizing principle of our cultural definition of manhood. Homophobia is more than the irrational fear of gay men, more than the fear that we might be perceived as gay.... (Kimmel, 2000, p. 133)

Instead, he notes that men's fear of being seen as "sissies" has led them to look away from the oppression of others. Men use violence to prove their masculinity because that is regarded as power in this society. Ironically, this norm has made men feel powerless because only a select few can be confident of their manliness. Feeling trapped by the fear that they are failures, some men become gay-bashers instead of confronting their own feelings.

Discussion Questions

1. Do you believe that homophobia is more harmful to men or women?
2. Has homophobia ever affected you (regardless of your sexual orientation)? Have you ever spoken out against it?

Coming Out

When women come out as lesbians, they may be confused about how to present themselves. This wry commentary expresses this dilemma:

> At the height of my college cruising, I was attending Take Back the Night meetings dressed in Mr. Greenjeans overalls, Birkenstocks, and a bowl haircut that made me look like I'd just been released from a bad foster home. (Walker, cited in Crawley, 2001, p. 180)

Another college woman struggled with whether she was lesbian after her relationships with men failed.

> Suddenly a new thought crept into my consciousness: Maybe I should try to date a girl. But far from feeling that vast sense of relief that many people describe when their "light" goes off, I felt as awkward and confused as I'd been during adolescence. None of the stereotypes of being a lesbian appealed to me—a wardrobe of plaid shirts and motorcycle jackets, the love of granola and all things natural, not to mention a childless future. Still, I decided the only way to find out was to try it. So I decided to take a mature and measured approach: I targeted the "token" lesbian on campus.

I'd seen Becky around campus for years. You couldn't miss her: She had short, cropped hair and wore plaid shirts, pleated pants, and Doc Martens all year round. We were polar opposites—at the time, I favored floral tiered mini-skirts and soft T-shirts—but what we did have in common was the only thing that mattered to me. I was determined to make her show me the way.

When I got back to college after summer break to complete my senior year, I was pleasantly surprised to find Becky sitting in the third row of my science class. I had no idea how to approach her; but as it turned out, I didn't have to give it too much thought, because my feet did the work for me.... I knew what I wanted to say: "Please help me figure out this gay thing!" (Henderson & Ellis, 2011, pp 4–5)

Sometimes girls come out at an earlier age, which requires bravery because so many LGBT youth are kicked out of their homes.

I was young. I was only sixteen so, I'd kinda just like went downstairs one day to my mom was like, you know, I, I think I'm gay and ... she freaked out.... She got a little upset, cried, said it was a phase, girls go through that. (Rossi, 2010, p. 1184)

Whether a lesbian couple is dating or living together, the level of disclosure can affect the relationship. One partner may be more "out" than the other one. In one case, a woman asked her partner not to attend a family function because she looked "too much like a dyke" (Clunis & Green, 2005, p. 1). In another case, this situation caused a problem in the women's relationship.

Leanne was very closeted at work. She was afraid her life would be much more difficult if her coworkers found out she was a lesbian. Carrier, her partner, was as out at work as you could get; she was one of the bartenders at a lesbian bar. When they moved in together, Leanne insisted on getting a two-bedroom apart-ment so people at her work would think they were roommates, not lovers. She also refused to have any explicitly lesbian literature in view at their home. Carrie was upset with this charade but kept it to herself. (Clunis & Green, 2005, p. 144)

Coming out at work may mean losing business to clients, even for professionals. For instance, one lawyer was partially closeted because she was sure that some clients would fire her if they knew about her partner (Clunis & Green, 2005).

Discussion Question
If a lesbian couple were your clients trying to resolve their different degrees of "outness," which resources would you recommend?

Media Portrayals of Lesbians

How the media portrays lesbians may affect their decision to come out or not. In the 1980s, Vito Russo wrote the classic book on film, *The Celluloid Closet: Homosexuality in the Movies* (1987). Although there were occasional mentions of male homosexuality in the movies, the topic was seen as a joke. Lesbianism, in contrast, was mostly invisible in the movies until the 1960s. Then the mainstream media stressed the tragic fate of lesbians: suicide. One lesbian, an older "mannish" woman, kills herself because she is unlovable in *The Killing of Sister George* (1966). Another lesbian movie is *The Children's Hour* (1962), in which a teacher ends her life because of homophobia.

Since the 1980s, many more movies have featured lesbians and bisexual women. Unfortunately, three mainstream movies stressed violence and deviance: *The Hunger* (with lesbian vampires—1983), *Basic Instinct* (with a bisexual serial killer—1992), and *Heavenly Creatures* (about two schoolgirls murdering one girl's mother because of their obsessive love—1994).

The tide shifted in 1997, when the comedian Ellen Degeneres "came out" as a lesbian on national television. This event marked a new direction for lesbians in the media, as indicated by the positive portrayal of lesbian characters on shows such as *Buffy: The Vampire Slayer*. In 2004, Showtime began to present *The L Word*—the first time a major series focused on lesbians and bisexual women.

Discussion Questions

Find a recent media portrayal of a lesbian or bisexual woman. Does it fit the butch/ femme stereotype? How positive or negative is the image?

Figure 5.2 *Pro-gay rights slogan (Photo courtesy of OUP)*

Lesbians and Bisexual Women

Lesbians and DV/IPV

As stated in the chapter on Domestic Violence/Intimate Partner Violence, women can be perpetrators as well as men. Heterosexual relationships are not the only venue for this type of violence.

> Unfortunately, domestic violence and relationship abuse are believed to be equally common among same-sex and heterosexual couples. Estimates of the prevalence of abuse in same-sex relationship range from 20 to 33%, which is about the same as in heterosexual relationships. (Dugan & Hock, 2006, p. 73).

Like domestic violence in heterosexual relationships, the key aspect is "an abuse of power" (Rohrbaugh, 2006, p. 295). Lesbian batterers appear to have similar traits as heterosexual male batterers:

> (They) seem to have an intense fear of abandonment and are therefore threatened by their partner's desire to be independent. They use violence to maintain distance in their relationships and to reject or avoid the partner before the partner can reject them. (Rohrbaugh, 2006, p. 295)

Threats of being "outed" can add to the problem. An abuser may threaten to "out" a victim so she may lose her job or housing. Not all lesbians are "out" to their families or community, so relationship violence can add to their isolation. One lesbian was quoted as saying, "I feel as if the only way to get help is tell my family I'm gay. I'm just not ready to do that" (Dugan & Hock, 2006, p. 71). Even if family and friends knew about the abuse, they may treat it as a joke because it appears as a catfight between two women. Isolation, then, may lead to an inadequate support system. The lesbian community itself may resist the idea of an abuser in their midst, since woman are expected to be more peaceful than men.

Also, the police and agencies may have trouble determining which partner is the abuser and which is the victim. Often an abuser will lie and claim to be the actual victim. Reporting abuse may result in the possible loss of one's child/children in a custody dispute, since the state laws may not recognize the parental rights of same-sex couples (Dugan & Hock, 2006).

Discussion Questions

How is violence by lesbians related to the essentialist argument that women are by nature less aggressive than men?

Box 5.3 describes how lesbians can use humor to cope with social disapproval. Can you think of other examples of how a marginalized person may use humor?

Box 5.3 Humor as a Coping Mechanism

One powerful coping mechanism, of course, is humor. For instance, Kate Clinton's remarks about same-sex marriage provide a wry perspeective:

It has taken me a long time to warm to same sex marriages. One of the cool things about being gay was that you didn't have to get married. Instead of trying to get the right to marry, I thought we should have been going around trying to talk ungay people out of it. If marriage is so natural, why the need for its constant defense, the elaborate ceremonies, the marriage benefit, the tax credits for children? It's as if those old Scared Straight programs have morphed into Paid Straight programs. A piquantly timed *Newsweek* cover on marriage painted a bleak picture of same old sex unions. Perhaps it's a conspiracy. If you want gay people to stop having sex, have them get married. (Clinton, 2005, p. 97)

Another controversial topic is reparative therapy (also known as "pray away the gay" in a religious context), a treatment condemned by the NASW and other professional associations related to mental health. Clinton raises a good point about the organizations out to fix the gays:

When I saw the Exodus International (an organization that "cures" gays by prayer) full-page ad in The New York Times Toward Hope and Healing for Homosexuals, my first thought was that it must not be going well for conservatives if they have to throw away good money to advertise for straight people. All those institutions—marriage, churches, the military, schools—aren't doing their job, I guess. (Clinton, 2005, p. 109)

Motherhood

Lesbians are often mothers, either through an earlier marriage to men or through other ways. The married women coming out as lesbian risk fighting a custody battle. In 70 percent of all custody battles, the fathers win (Chesler, 2011).

On a more positive note, many lesbians are choosing artificial insemination even if they are single. Askowitz (2008) describes her encounter at a fertility clinic where she had to watch a video.

I learned that if you have sex less than once a week you have a 17 percent chance of getting pregnant within six months. Sex once a week almost doubles your chances to 32 percent. Twice a week and you have a 46 percent chance....

When the video was over, I told the nurse I'd discovered my problem.

"What is it?"

"I'm a lesbian."

She seemed too dignified to smile, but made a face that told me she'd seen it all. (Askowitz, 2008, pp. 75–76).

Miller (2010) discusses the wider impact of lesbian couples bearing children.

It's a mixed blessing to have to make an explicit decision about parenthood. While straight people often assume future parenthood in the same way that they might assume the certainty of a spring wedding, the default for gay men and lesbians traditionally has been not to have children. Accidental pregnancies are not a big problem in our community. We generally have to seek out parenthood if we want it to happen. On the plus side, we are almost never harassed by eager grandparents.... As with adoptive parents or infertile couples, our children must be chosen and pursued. There's a certain smugness that often goes with this: we worked for our children, they didn't just happen. (Miller, 2010, p. 11)

She later adds about the desire for gay men and lesbians to be parents, which was rarely an option until recently.

There is a "gayby boom" going on. Estimates of the number of kids being raised by gay, lesbian, bisexual, or transgendered parents vary widely.... an increasing number are the result of some form of assisted reproduction. People in the gay community—especially lesbians, but increasingly also gay men—are assuming that they can have children. This is a sea change. Just twenty or so years earlier, coming out generally meant letting go of expectations of parenthood.... A gay male friend, about ten years older than I, told me once that he became very depressed when he realized that he was gay because he was certain that it meant he would never become a father. And, in fact, he never has.

Historically, the gay community as a whole has compensated for its lack of procreation by more or less ignoring children. Our most distinctive institutions have traditionally been bars. We have been defined by our sexuality and have often played to type.... Only recently has the focus begun to shift to marriage and, for a subset of the community, to kids. (Miller, 2010, pp. 30–31)

As the teen son of lesbian parents, Zach Wahls spoke to the Iowa House Judiciary Committee in support of same-sex marriage. This testimony led to the publication of *My Two Moms: Lessons of Love, Strength, and What Makes a Family* (2011), which is excerpted here:

Yes, even those of you who think my conception was "unnatural" or pity me for my "tragic" upbringing and are convinced that I'm effectively a victim of child abuse. I don't expect my story to convince every one of you that being gay isn't a "choice" or that same-sex marriage should be legal or even that I reached adulthood undamaged by the sexuality of my parents. I promise that I'm not going to ask you to attend a gay wedding and sing show tunes, and I'm not going to try to brainwash you with the "gay agenda." (Wahls & Littlefield, 2011, pp. xi–xii)

He then stresses how his family is ultimately normal, and not remarkable in how they ive their daily routines.

Since the conversation (about same-sex marriages) began, a lot has been said and written about the kids being raised in "gay families." (By the way, I find this label silly. My moms don't live in a gay house, drive gay cars, or have a gay dog—as far as we can tell.) But we, the kids of gay parents, haven't really contributed much because we were busy growing up, and adolescence is hard enough as it is without having to respond to society's incessant questions about your family structure. Further, even though there are an estimated two million children of LGBT parents in the United States, of the folks I know raised by openly gay parents, none of us are more than twenty-five years old. (Wahls, 2011, pp. xii–xiii)

Discussion Questions

Do you think that there is more social acceptance of openly gay men or lesbians being parents? Are there any examples in the media or your own social circle?

Key Terms

Lesbians
Stonewall
Lavender Menace
Bisexual women
Butch/femme
Internalized homophobia

6

Is the Beauty Standard a Feminist Issue?

Introduction/Author's Note

On the TV show *What Not to Wear*, two fashion consultants performed an "intervention" on a hopelessly dressed woman. Along with her friends and coworkers and family, the consultants confronted her with pictures of how she appeared in public. The woman may have been sloppy, frumpy, outlandish, or a combination of fashion errors. She undergoes a transformation, though, and emerges not just with a new wardrobe but a new self-confidence.

I like this show. Watching it has made me ponder the consequences of my poor sense of style through the years. When have my wardrobe choices—or my physical appearance in general—affected not only my social life but my career? For instance, I have had to wear sneakers instead of office shoes because of a disability. Did even my shoes indicate that I was less than professional?

Whatever your political ideology, whatever your opinion on women's rights, you will be judged by others based on your physical appearance. Obviously, men will also face judgment based on their clothes, haircuts, and even facial hair. Beards, for instance, are sometimes prohibited in certain jobs such as the military.

But is the beauty standard for women a feminist issue? One of the first actions of the women's-lib movement was the protest of the Miss America pageant of 1968. No bras were actually burned, but they were placed in the "Freedom Trash Can." (By the way, underwear in the 1960s was very uncomfortable because of the girdles and bras that resembled mechanical contraptions.) What did happen, though, was a lively piece of feminist guerrilla theater that drew international attention. The protesters' Ten Points included this item:

> *The Degrading Mindless-Boob-Girlie Symbol.* The Pageant contestants epitomize the roles we are all forced to play as women.... So are women in our

society forced daily to compete for male approval, enslaved by ludicrous "beauty" standards we ourselves are conditioned to take seriously. (Morgan, 1989, p. 343)

As a bumper sticker slogan says, "Start a revolution. Start loving your body." Trying to look one's best can be pleasurable and empowering. Wearing a nice outfit, for instance, boosts my mood. How does one balance the healthy desire to enhance one's appearance with the destructive impact of the beauty standard? This question affects both genders, since males now face increased pressure to fit the "six-pack abs" ideal.

The Beauty Myth

According to *The Beauty Myth: How Images of Beauty are used against Women* (Wolf, 1991), the feminist movement actually triggered a backlash from the establishment. "The more legal and material hindrances women have broken through, the more strictly and heavily and cruelly images of female beauty have come to weigh upon us" (Wolf, 1991, p. 10). She states that although women have made great advances, they have a "secret 'underlife' poisoning our freedom; infused with notions of beauty, it is a dark vein of self-hatred, physical obsessions, terror of aging, and dread of lost control" (Wolf, 1991, p. 10)

Among the provocative points in her book is the term "beauty pornography," in which women's beauty is linked explicitly to women's sexuality (Wolf, 1991, p. 11). Although this book was written before Victoria's Secret became so popular, this term seems relevant today. In today's society, can a woman be considered beautiful without being considered sexy?

The beauty myth not only regulates physical appearance but also behavior. For instance, some women may feel compelled to buy expensive make-up and fashionable clothes for social acceptance. Their work clothes must be businesslike so they will be taken seriously, but also feminine. Wearing feminine clothes, however, allegedly causes sexual harassment or distracts the male coworkers. Wolf also discusses how the male power structure requires "display behavior" (Wolf, 1991, p. 47) from the female to show that she is playing along:

She may have to will her body to relax and not stiffen at an untoward compliment, or simply have to sit up straighter, letting her body be seen more clearly, or brush the hair from her eyes in a way that she knows flatters her face. Whatever it is she has to do, she knows it without being told, from the expression and body language of the powerful man in whose eyes her future lies.

Researchers reinforce Wolf's reference to the male gaze in the preceding quotation. Calogero (2004) explored the effect of public attention on college women who felt more anxiety about their appearance when men looked at them rather than women.

Increasingly, researchers have investigated diverse samples of women and demonstrated a variety of detrimental effects associated with self-objectification including increased body shame, appearance anxiety, disordered eating, self-surveillance, and diminished mental performance and capacity to achieve peak motivational states. (Calogero, 2004, p. 16)

The male gaze amplifies the beauty myth, as evident in beauty pageants and magazine covers. In the broader context of self-objectification, lesbians have also reported body shame and other related issues (Kozee & Tylka, 2006). Depression is one result of self-objectification (Szymanski & Henning, 2007), as illustrated in Figure 6.1. Media critics such as Jeanne Kilbourne (1998) have pointed out the adverse effects on teen girls when they see so many too-skinny, "perfect" fashion models. In *Deadly Persuasion: Why Women and Girls Must Fight the Addictive Power of Advertising*, she writes:

It is important to understand that these problems go way beyond individual psychological development and pathology. Even girls who are raised in loving homes by supportive parents grow up in a toxic cultural environment, at risk for self-mutilation, eating disorders, and addictions. The culture, both reflected and reinforced by advertising, urges girls to adopt a false self, to bury alive their real selves, to become "feminine," which means to be nice and kind and sweet.... (Kilbourne, 1998, p. 130)

Social pressure may also reinforce the beauty myth, even for children. In *Cinderella Ate My Daughter: Dispatches from the Front Lines of the New Girly-girl Culture*, Orenstein

Figure 6.1 *Self-criticism (Photo courtesy of OUP)*

Is the Beauty Standard a Feminist Issue?

(2011) writes of how she was a feminist mother who wanted to raise her daughter free of gender restrictions. By the age of three, though, the girl wanted to be a Disney princess. It seemed that everybody from waitresses to shop clerks would call her "princess." Even the dentist encouraged this royal fantasy.

> Then, shortly after Daisy's third birthday, our high-priced pediatric dentist … pointed to the exam chair and asked, "Would you like to sit in my special princess throne so I can sparkle your teeth?"
> "Oh, for God's sake," I snapped. "Do you have a princess drill, too?"
> She looked at me as if I were the wicked stepmother.
> But honestly, since when did every little girl become a princess? (Orenstein, 2011, pp. 3–4)

As a result of the girly culture, females as young as six are wearing lip gloss and high heels. In a child's book titled *How to Be a Girly Girl in Just Ten Days* (Papademetriou, 2007) the protoganist looks at a teammate: "Hannah smiled, showing the dimple in her right cheek, and tugged at her perfect blond French braid. I ground my teeth, trying not to look annoyed" (Papademetriou, 2007, p. 10). Unfortunately, the constant comparison to other females' appearances is a behavior that can continue through adulthood.

Fat-Shaming

Comparing one's body to somebody else can include fat-shaming. Also known as weight discrimination or bias, this term needs little explanation. The word *fat* is subjective and depends on culture, age, and gender. A middle-aged woman, for instance, may define the word *fat* differently than a teenager. The shaming part is obvious, though. One woman who gained weight from her medical problems reflected on her new identity. "I am amazed at how inferior I feel now. I feel invisible. People avoid eye contact with me. I am often treated rudely or dismissed" (Brooks, 2014).

According to researchers, fat-shaming includes three elements: disgust, contempt, and anger. Disgust is highly associated with antifat stereotypes such as lazy and sloppy (Vartanian, Thomas & Vanman, 2013). Related to avoiding the object of this reaction, disgust is a strong visceral reaction. Contempt is a feeling of superiority that usually has a moral undertone (e.g., "well, I don't let myself binge like that person probably does every day"). A heavy person may also provoke anger—"how can she *do* that to herself?"

Fat-shaming is related to body shaming (e.g., a male may be perceived as too skinny). Another related concept is food shaming. For example, an anonymous online writer on the Hollaback website (an advocacy tool against street harassment) describes one incident: "I was in South Station in the afternoon with my dad eating a vanilla soft serve and a 50 plus man walked by looking me up and down and said, 'You've got to be kidding'" ("Fighting Back Against 'Food Shaming' Phenomenon," 2014).One instance of fat-shaming occurred in 2006, when a college sorority evicted twenty-two women who were either Asian or perceived as overweight. In *Fat Shame: Stigma and the Fat Body in America*, Farrell (2011) comments:

Within this Delta Zeta controversy, what particularly interests me is the way that "fatness" served as a crucial marker of social status, or rather the lack thereof.... Indeed, the attempt of the Delta Zeta national office to reinstate a hierarchy of "white, thin, and privileged" ... intersect [with gender and the construction of what it means to be a "popular girl." (Farrell, 2011, p. 2)

After discussing how overweight persons faced ridicule since the nineteenth century and how diet fads have shifted through the decades, the author adds:

What began to interest me more than the particular permutations of weight loss methods was the formidable *meaning* attributed to fatness in these dieting tracts. The authors of these weight loss tracts and the advertisements for these weight loss products articulated anxiety, scorn, even outrage toward the fat they promised to eradicate. It is easy for us to assume today that the cultural stigma associated with fatness emerged simply as a result of our recognition of its apparent health dangers. What is clear from the historical documents, however, is that the connotations of fatness and of the fat person—lazy, gluttonous, greedy, immoral, uncontrolled, stupid, ugly, and lacking in will power—preceded and then were intertwined with explicit concerns about health issues. (Farrell, 2011, p. 4)

Weight discrimination can actually lead to more obesity, as noted by Sutin & Terraciano (2013). As one article title states: "If Shaming Reduced Obesity, There Would Be No Fat People" (Tomiyama & Mann, 2013). Older persons may also experience weight discrimination, which harms their physical and emotional health (Sutin, Stephan, Carretta, & Terracciano, 2015). Heavier persons tend to avoid doctors because of possible shaming, which can lead to higher risks for undetected cancers and other conditions (Drury, Aramburu, & Louis, 2002).

In diary postings, women wrote about the daily humiliations they faced: "Teenagers made animal sounds (moo) outside of the store," "Boyfriend's mother denied me access to food; also stated that I was so fat because I was lazy," and "The dentist was worried I might break his chair" (Seacat, Dougal & Roy, 2014). The women also reported job discrimination and being subjected to stares.

It is no surprise, then, that a Glamour survey reports that "women have an average of thirteen negative thoughts about their bodies each day, with 97 percent of women admit(ting) to at least one 'I hate my body' moment a day" (Drelsbach, 2011). This policing of their own bodies is not caused by self-absorption or vanity, but by the harsh reality of fat-shaming. In one research study, a woman reported that her female senior manager had faced criticism for her weight—but not the male CEO, who was much heavier. " 'It's been quite acceptable for him, but it's not acceptable for her.... Since she's been promoted more questions have arisen about her weight. Because she is successful, they think she should be more in control of her diet' " (Germov & Williams, 1999, p. 120).

The preceding anecdote illustrates the wider context of fat-shaming: the lower educational levels, reduced job opportunities, and higher rate of poverty for overweight women (Ernsberger, 2009). For instance, low-income persons live in high-crime areas with little

Figure 6.2 *A person's weight can be a painful number (Photo source: Entofolio)*

options for exercise. Food deserts (the public health term for neighborhoods with corner markets but no full supermarkets) are full of high-carbohydrate food such as pasta. If a person has no easy way to get to a store that sells better quality food, she—or he—must live on cheap but non-nutritious food. However, Ernsberger argues that "Although there is some evidence that poverty is fattening, there is much stronger evidence that fatness is impoverishing" (Ernsberger, 2009, p. 26) because of the powerful effects of discrimination.

Discussion Questions

- On the macro level, how would you address the link between poverty and obesity?
- Does your school and/or workplace have any barriers for overweight persons, such as small chairs? How would you advocate for better accommodations for overweight persons?
- As a social worker, would you treat an overweight client the same as everybody else, or would you have any unconscious bias caused by social conditioning? For instance, some psychiatric medications cause weight gain. Would knowledge of that fact make a difference in how you treated a heavy client on those medications?

Eating Disorders and Compulsive Exercise

Two types of eating disorders, anorexia nervosa (self-starvation) and bulimia (binging and purging) have emerged in the 1970s as major health concerns for females. Another disorder is compulsive exercise, which is often associated with an eating disorder. Using the term "obligatory runners and obligatory dieters," Yates (2013) discusses her research on runners with both conditions. Combining food deprivation with hours of exercise can deprive a body of essential nutrients, leading to serious health problems—and even death.

The history of anorexia nervosa is a fascinating one, as shown by Brumberg (2000). In her book on fasting girls, she starts with the stories of medieval female saints who considered fasting to be the path to sanctity.

> In medieval Europe, particularly in the years between 1200 and 1500, many women refused their food and prolonged fasting was considered a female miracle. The chronicles and hagiographies of this period tell numerous stories of women saints who ate almost nothing or claimed to be incapable of eating normal earthly fare. The best-known of these saints, Catherine of Siena (1347–1380), ate only a handful of herbs each day and occasionally shoved twigs down her throat to bring up any other food that she was forced to eat. (Brumberg, 2000, p. 43)

Centuries later, celebrities such as the Welsh Fasting Girl in the nineteenth century became a tourist attraction. "The presence on the farm changed the nature of the case from a private family agony to a public event that generated intimate graphic descriptions of the starvation process" (Brumberg, 2000, p. 66). The fasting done by Victorian girls were not necessarily the result of religious devotion but compliance to the social ideal of equating weakness and womanhood.

> In Victorian society how and what one ate were important indications of female character for middle-class and upper-class women. The slim body and languishing posture ... epitomized the Victorian ideal of femininity. In the minds of privileged women, fragility and debility were linked to a spirituality that transcended the need for food (Brumberg, 2000, p. 190).

In this setting, eating an orange at the dinner table was regarded as too sensuous an act for a female. Meat and other hearty foods were often taboo, since they symbolized passion and virility. The eating habits were obviously connected to the requirement for ladies (not working-class women) to wear corsets. These tight lacings, connected to a metal structure, compressed the lungs and other vital organs—sometimes leading to death (Steele, 2001). Emmeline in Figure 6.3 exemplifies this fashion trend.

Although anoretic females started receiving medical treatment in the late nineteenth century, not until 1983 was the eating disorder taken seriously. Karen Carpenter, a popular singer, died from complications from years of starving herself. Since then, public awareness has coupled with a sharp rise in the number of females diagnosed with eating disorders (Brumberg, 2000).

Abra Chernik, who required hospitalization for her anorexia, writes of the body hatred created by the diet culture. "I had no weight in the world during my years of anorexia. Curled up inside my thinness, a refugee in a cocoon of hunger, I lost the capacity to care about myself or others. I starved my body and ... I wanted only to vanish." (Chernik, 1995, p. 103).

This desire to vanish is the complete opposite of what feminism wants for women: a voice, a solid body that takes up space without apology. Chernik had resisted the transition from girl to woman, since that meant a rounder body. Why would girls want to avoid maturing into a woman? This may not just be about avoiding adulthood and its responsibilities, but the fears of women: getting pregnant, getting old, getting passed by.

Figure 6.3 *Emmeline (note the tiny waist) (Photo courtesy of Library of Congress)*

A girl still retains her promise of boundless potential, but the realities of womanhood can be restricting. Many females with eating disorders, for instance, are proud when they are too undernourished to be menstruating.

Another girl fighting anorexia nervosa spoke of how her mother was always urging her to lose weight.

I never seemed to measure up to her expectations. I loved sport, but because the exercise made me hungry I gave it up and concentrated on dieting. I knew that, at some level, Mum loved me, but could not understand why she cared more about my size than my happiness. Eventually I decided that if I kept my weight down I would gain her acceptance and feel content, attractive, and loved; instead I was always tired, irritable and hungry. Then I became too scared to eat even if I wanted to. (Treasure & Alexander, 2013, p. 4)

In addition to parental pressure, workplace pressures can trigger an eating disorder. "I moved jobs and became anxious. Concerned that I would appear lazy, I increased my exercise routine and controlled my food intake. My weight fell rapidly as I developed anorexia nervosa" (Treasure & Alexander, 2013, p. 6). An anoretic's hunger for food may be only the tip of the iceberg of her deep needs: sexual, emotional, intellectual, and so forth. As her body shrinks, she may lose her independence and autonomy because the illness has taken away her freedom.

However, this is not to say that eating disorders are merely an individual problem When society assumes a thin woman owes her success to her figure, it is reinforcing a dangerous stereotype.

Discussion Questions

- One point made by Brumberg (2000) is the practice of "secret eating," when a girl eats alone in her room and hides the evidence. Eating in a college cafeteria, for instance, may cause her to show a small appetite. How is appetite related to gender norms? Is secret eating harmless, or could there be consequences?
- Eating disorders and compulsive exercise are common on college campuses. Research what your school does to raise awareness and reach out to students. Do you think the school's efforts are sufficient, or should more be done?

Other Body Image Issues

Weight issues, of course, are only part of the beauty standard. Brumberg, author of *The Body Project: An intimate history of American Girls* (1997), notes that modern young women are also focusing on their skin, hair, "bikini line," and other areas that supposedly need to be fixed. "Why is the body still a girl's nemesis? Shouldn't today's sexually liberated girls feel better about themselves than their corseted sisters of a century ago?" (Brumberg, 1997, p. xxv).

A clear complexion, for instance, indicates a morally clean person. "The expectation of perfect skin has made America's female adolescents extremely vulnerable. Filled with insecurity and anxious about their looks, young adolescents constitute a fertile market for almost any drug or cosmetic that promises perfection" (Brumberg, 1997, p. 91). Another skin-related issue is the new stress on anti-aging creams sold to young women to prevent wrinkles later in life.

Of course, plastic surgery and nonsurgical procedures such as botox are an option for those who want to take their "body projects" a step further. According to the American Society for Aesthetic Plastic Surgery, $13 billion was spent in 2010 on cosmetic procedures. Men are 9 percent of the customers. There has been almost 9.5 million cosmetic procedures done in 2010 with 17 percent being surgeries. (www.surgery.org) Even during a recession, plastic surgery is still a booming industry because of ageism in the job market. The top five surgeries for women are: breast augmentation (increasing bust size), liposuction (removing fat), eyelid surgery, abdominoplasty (stomach reduction), and breast reduction. According to the American Academy of Facial Plastic and Reconstructive Surgery website (www.aafprs.org), women account for 83 percent of the nonsurgical procedures.

Ageism is one reason for these cosmetic procedures. One Canadian feminist, Cynthia Rich, describes her feelings about the multibillion dollar industry to fight wrinkles and other signs of aging. Because of these profits, the industry "actively promoting a fear and loathing around women's aging. Now 30-year-olds are just horrified by their first wrinkle, and it's become a major industry to make younger women see my 72-year-old body as hideous" (Lipscomb, 2013, pp. 417–418).

A new emphasis in the beauty standard is the vaginal rejuvenation surgery, in which female genitalia is modified and even "beautified" to enhance a woman's self-image. One ad for this procedure states, "Feel 21 again." Although some surgeries are medically necessary for women who had traumatic childbirths, other surgeries are cosmetic and related to the anti-aging aspect of the beauty standard. Even teenagers, though, have requested trimming of their labia because their genitalia do not look like the ones in pornography. The American College of Obstetricians and Gynecologists has warned against such cosmetic procedures (Childs, 2007).

Another aspect of the beauty standard is its emphasis on Caucasian/white bodies. Warren (2014) examines the body area dissatisfaction of three groups of college women: white, black, and Latina. The Latinas reported the most dissatisfaction with their eyes and noses, wheres both whites and Latinas were dissatisfied with other body features. A strong sense of ethnic pride lowered the rate of dissatisfaction.

The beauty standard is by no means limited to the United States. De Rivera (2005) describes her experiences in the Philippines, where—"a wide nose is seen as something to hide" (De Rivera, 2005, p. 108). Her mother kept her out of the sun because "Beauty in the Philippines is also associated with light skin" (De Rivera, 2005, p. 108). Drugstores sold skin whiteners, thus profiting from colorism. When she asked her mother why there were no dark-skinned models, her mother said: "Sweetheart, when you are dark, you are not pretty here" (De Rivera, 2005, p. 108).

Pozner (2013) also discusses colorism in her essay entitled "Ghetto Bitches, China Dolls, and Cha-Cha Divas: Race, Beauty, and the Tyranny of Tyra Banks." Indians and other Asians value lighter skin and eyes, especially because the caste system is partially based on skin color. One Indian contestant on a modeling show stated, "I actually want to beat that. Be like, 'Hey, I'm dark, I'm beautiful, and I'm Indian, so I don't have to have light skin or have light-colored eyes to be beautiful" (Pozner, 2013, p. 340).

Beauty Standard for Males

In recent years, the beauty standard for males has become more and more blatant. Researchers (Else-Quest, Higgins, & Morton, 2012) have found that there is little difference between males and females on the self-conscious experiences scale. Both genders have expressed shame and guilt about their bodies. Although several studies have focused on possible gender differences, no single difference can be verified.

Adolescent boys are one population reported to have body shame. Hall (1999) writes of "The bully in the mirror" that is plaguing today's male teens. Alexander, a 16-year-old, had started an exercise regimen to build a muscular body. He had been overweight, so he had been teased mercilessly about it. Even his parents made comments about his weight. Looking in the mirror, "James saw a chubby 13-year-old in his mirror. ("I just want to be skinnier," he said plaintively.) … Willie, a powerfully built 15-year-old with impressive biceps, derived no solace from his solid athletic build. "When I look in the mirror, I wish my ears were bigger and my feet were smaller…." (Hall, 1999). As figure 6.4 indicates, the male beauty standard can be high.

College-age men are also vulnerable to body shame. Like women, men are influenced by the media's portrayals of the perfect body. A dissertation on the possible effect of media exposure on males' internalization of body image concludes that there was a relationship between the two factors (Garrison, 2012).

Two other population groups are at risk of body shame: gay males and weightlifters. In a comment published in the *Journal of the American Medical Association*, researchers claim that gay males are three times more likely to have eating disorders because they are expected to be leaner than heterosexual men (Nguyen & Margo, 2015). This observation

Figure 6.4 *Male beauty standard (Photo source: Entofolio)*

Is the Beauty Standard a Feminist Issue?

about gay men being at higher risk overlaps with a study on weightlifters, who also may suffer from unrealistic expectations. Researchers have found muscle dysmorphia in several men who are obsessed with building their muscles. A high percentage of these men reported themselves as homosexual. These men are more prone to eating disorders, anxiety, steroid use, and other harmful behaviors (Olivardia, Pope, & Hudson, 2014).

Whatever one's gender, this question resonates: why is the beauty standard so important in this society? Nancy Friday, author of *The Power of Beauty* (1996), writes: "I am a woman who needs to be seen. I need it in a basic way, as in to breathe, to eat. Or not to be seen, that is the other increasingly attractive option...." (Friday, 1996, p. 1). From the time of birth, we needed a loving gaze. Adults may later crave "the gaze" not out of vanity but a deep need to be seen.

> You are already thinking that this is not about you, who are not a clotheshorse or a starer into mirrors. Perhaps you have already begun to disdain my vanity. But your life has been as fashioned by mirrors as mine; none of us escapes the influence that our looks have had on our lives. Later we may choose to live without mirrors, but we begin life very much in need of reflection. Did you begin rich or poor, seen as the Christ Child or left, invisible, to make yourself up?
>
> Perhaps you ducked out of the competition over looks so many years ago] that you can't remember. But once you did want to be seen, taken in, and loved. If you don't today, consider that it might be because you tried and lost. Lost to your brother or sister; maybe got lost in the abyss of invisibility, a parent demanding that all eyes be on her or him. Who wants to remember such pain? Perhaps, instead, you won and were hated for it. Envy can be a killer.
>
> The universal power of looks is free-floating, an electrical charge between hungry eyes and the objects of their desire: "Let me feast my eyes on you. Let me take you in." It is an open market, traded on more exhibitionistically today than at any time in my life. Near-naked bodies demand our attention on the streets, undressed fashions fill the restaurants, the television screens in our living rooms: "Look at me!" (and) ... "See me or I won't even know I exist." (Friday, 1996, p. 2)

Discussion Questions

- Do you agree with Friday's assertion that the need for attention is critical to our understanding of the beauty standard?
- What is the most significant point in this chapter? Write a reflection paragraph about it.
- Do you think that because more males are reported to have body shame that there will be a backlash against the beauty standard? Or will this new angle merely strengthen the beauty standard?
- How does this chapter relate to the social work value of the dignity of each person? Do social workers have an ethical obligation to fight body shame and other negative aspects of the beauty standard?

Key Terms

Beauty myth
Male gaze
Fat-shaming
Eating disorders
Beauty standard for males

7

Rape and Sexual Assault

Introduction

"Race you?" Max blew his hair out of his eyes and looked at Basima. His freck-
les were starting to show through. By the end of the summer, he'd be covered.

Basima adjusted her headscarf. "Sure, but you know I always win."

Max took off ahead of her. Cheater. But Basima knew she could beat him.
She'd grown at least two inches last summer.

She caught up with him halfway through the field. "Gotcha!" she yelled
as her fingers grazed his t-shirt. Suddenly, she was tripping, falling. She landed
hard on the ground, hearing a loud snap in her wrist and the spread of pain
searing up her arm. She tasted grass and dirt.

"My wrist," Basima gasped. She turned to look up. Max was standing over
her, staring at her.

Max knelt down in front of her. "You tripped," he said.

"You did it on purpose," she cried. "I think I broke it." Her arm was already
starting to swell. "Help me, Max."

Max was staring at Basima. The look in his eyes made her feel very afraid.

"Max, I need to go home." She was starting to cry.

"No, you don't." Max put his hand on Basima's shoulder. He pushed her,
lightly.

"Don't, Max."

"Shut up." Now he was forcing. Pushing. Pressing. She tried to push him
off but her wrist wouldn't work. And he was so strong. Too strong. (Wilkins,
2011. p. 4)

In her book about date rape for teens, Wilkins (2011) represents a new phase in rape/sexual assault awareness. The awareness movement that started in the 1970s emphasized stranger rape, because at the time it seemed unthinkable that a trusted relative or "friend" could hurt somebody that much. Rape represented an abhorrent crime that only a grotesque, slobbering monster could commit. Like an animal, he would crouch behind the bushes and attack his prey.

Basima's story, though, tells of a normal-looking friend whom she trusted. Not until recently would an incident like this be considered "real" or "legitimate" rape. The good news is that mainstream society has become more open in listening to victims' stories, even if they are decades old. Unfortunately, rape/sexual assault remains so deeply embedded in society that yet another generation has to deal with it.

Author's Note

Growing up in Denver during the 1970s, I felt as if I were living in the epicenter of rape awareness. Police officers would come to safety meetings and urge us to walk a certain way: head up, shoulder back, appearing unafraid to look back at a stranger walking behind you. Look tough instead of fearful, so the attacker will look elsewhere for his target. I do not know whether this advice was valid for rape prevention. However, it did serve me well once during a street harassment incident. I was walking down a busy residential street when I heard a man walking behind me. Since I was a college student unused to wearing a purse, I thought he was planning to grab it so I held it close to me.

Instead, he pinched me on the backside and said something like, "Looking mighty fine today, miss."

I was so startled by the unexpected physical contact that I screamed very loudly. People came rushing over to see what was going on. I turned around to face the man, who turned out to be shorter and smaller than me. Yelling a curse word at him, I felt ready to throw him to the ground. He must have read my mind, because he ran away before I could teach him a lesson.

Like most women of that time, then, we focused our rape prevention efforts on avoiding stranger rape. In high school, I saw the movie *Animal House* (1978) that includes a scene in which a fraternity member has a girl passed out drunk on his bed. A devil on one shoulder tells him to go for it and have sex with her, while the angel on the other shoulder tells him to leave her alone. At the time, that scene was considered to be humorous. The girl obviously deserved anything that would happen to her, since she was the one stupid enough to get drunk in a frat house. He had the right to take advantage of her stupidity. By the 1980s, though, that scene became less funny. Date rape became regarded as not just morally wrong but a criminal action. It is now illegal to have sex with an incapacitated person because she or he is unable to consent to sex.

Today society is recognizing that simply avoiding dark alleys will not be enough to ensure a woman's safety. A few years ago, a student came to my office. Her roommate had invited a male friend to her dorm room and had been raped a few days ago. This student had been the one to find her right after the attack. She said, "I don't ever want to see a person in that state again." Another student of mine, who was the victim's best friend, spent so much time "guarding" her friend after the attack that her grades were affected. This incident made me think about the nature of rape and how many people it affects. A violent attack sends off shockwaves to everybody nearby, and a woman may ask herself, "will it be me next time?"

Rape Culture

Feminists coined the term "rape culture" in the 1970s to describe the social context of rape. "We live in a culture that demands public ownership of the body.... In this sense, rape culture works by restricting a person's control of hir body, limiting hir sense of ownership, and granting others a sense of entitlement to it" (Troost, 2008, p. 171). One example is when people make jokes about rape and other forms of sexual exploitation. Others simply trivialize the idea of rape as a violent crime instead of a misunderstanding between two persons. The phrase "there are no rapists, only bad lovers" is one example of treating rape as a noncrime, just a blunder by a man who does not excel at foreplay.

Blaming the victim for her clothes or behavior is another aspect of rape culture. One antirape blogger, Mike the Mad Biologist, posted this quote:

> Earth to liberated women: When you display legs, thighs or cleavage, some liberated men will see it as a sign that you feel good about yourself and your sexuality. But most men will see it as a sign that you want to get laid (Atrios post quoted in www.mikethemadbiologist.com posted June 16, 2011)

Technology has often amplified rape culture, since some attackers now make recordings for trophies to brag about. For instance, in 2011 the town of Cleveland, Texas was rocked by the allegations that an 11-year-old girl had been gang-raped over a three-month period by eighteen boys and young men (from 14 to 26). The defendants had used cell phone videos to show off at the high school and other places about the attacks. The child had run away from a foster home and was trapped in a house by the attackers. After the arrests, some town members spoke up on the defendants' behalf. At a community meeting, "Supporters didn't claim that the men and boys did not have sex with the young girl; instead they blamed the girl for the way she dressed or claimed she must have lied about her age" (AP report cited in Linkins, 2011). One woman stated that "I'm not taking nobody's side, but if she hadn't put herself in that predicament, this would have never happened" (Linkins, 2011).

Websites such as Facebook have also had to deal with rape culture. One group that was banned had the name "I don't like chicks with tans. It means they've been out of the kitchen." This group posted a picture of a bound and gagged woman with a rifle pointed at her head with this caption: "My girlfriend has a learning disability ... teaching how to make sandwich (sic) can be difficult. Stick with it!"

Street harassment, as discussed in Box 7.1, is one example of rape culture. Another aspect of the rape culture is how women have to learn how to avoid crime. In *Nothing Bad Happens to Good Girls: Fear of Crime in Women's Lives* (Madriz, 1997), the author criticizes the way crimes against women have become entertainment. Usually the

Box 7.1 Street Harassment

What is the difference between a compliment by a man on the street and street harassment? The man who calls out, "Looking really nice today, girl!" may think that he is merely being nice to a pretty female, while she may feel besieged by male attention.

In the documentary *War Zone* (1998), Maggie Hadleigh-Smith walks down the streets of New York City with a video camera. Anytime a man harasses her or a nearby female, she directly confronts him with the camera and asks him why he did that. None of them apologize, since they believe that they had the right to call out comments or be even more intrusive on the females (even young girls) walking by them. She ends the movie with the story of a rape, which is the worst fear of those being harassed on the street.

Another work on street harassment is *Passing By: Gender and Public Harassment* by Brooks Gardner (1995). One interviewee said that she had to change her route to work because she grew tired of "the hassling and the grief from guys. I don't want to be reminded how they, men, have power over me, as a woman" (Brooks Gardner, 1995, p. 10). The author remarks that "Public harassment is a regular and lifelong occurrence for women, not merely the province of young and attractive women …" (Brooks Gardner, 1995, p. 41). Another woman stated that:

> I've been pretty and young, then old and not so pretty. I've had the money to dress well, then not. I've been skinny, then I've been fat. I've been married with children, I've been a gay woman out on the town with my girlfriend. I tell you, after sixty years: It happens everywhere, all the time, sexual terrorism by men in the streets. It shouldn't. (Brooks Gardner, 1995, p. 43)

Unfortunately, street harassment can escalate into violence. In 2014, "One woman in Detroit was shot and killed after refusing to give a stranger her phone number. Another woman in New York got her throat slashed for refusing to go on a date with a stranger" (Culp-Ressler, 2014).

Street harassment, then, has recently received international attention. The United Nations Women's website, for example, promotes Orange Day to stress the need for "safe cities" to increase the safety of females on streets (www.unwomen.org). In India, the term "Eve teasing" is used to minimize street harassment as a harmless diversion for males. However, the recent episodes of violence (rapes and attacks on males trying to help the victims) have created an international outcry against this practice. A news correspondent shares this story: "I was once told by a complete stranger: You can wear a trench coat and be covered from head to toe in the depths of an Indian summer but a man with indecent intentions will still try his best to ruin your day" (Dutt, 2012).

Discussion Question

Research the website www.ihollaback.org and other advocacy sites. Discuss the implications of street harassment.

victims are young and attractive, reinforcing the belief that somehow they deserve their fate. She adds:

> Fear of crime teaches women that some rights are reserved for men, such as the right to use public places, to take a walk at night, or (even a restaurant or movie alone). Although such places are supposed to be open to all, women's access to them is often hampered by the fear of criminal victimization and by the possibility of sexual harassment. (Madriz, 1997, p. 19)

Discussion Question

Find one example of what you consider to be rape culture. How do you think that it is related to oppression? Relate the concept of rape culture to society's objectification of bodies (e.g., the torsos of male models).

A Brief History of Rape and Sexual Assault

In her groundbreaking book, *Against Our Will: Men, Women and Rape* (1975), Brownmiller discusses how rape is not just a personal crisis. According to her research, rape has been a constant presence in human history and should be a public matter. For centuries, women have lived with the threat of rape and had their actions restricted because of this threat. Women had to get married to get protection from rape. In feudal times, the practice of *bride* capture meant that rich women were kidnapped and raped so they would have to marry their captors.

The origin of the word *rape* is to abduct, seize, or plunder. What is regarded as stolen is not the woman's right to her own body, but the sexual property rights of the husband or father. Rape, then, was originally seen as an offense against a man's property instead of a crime against a person. Bourke (2007) reinforces this point with this statement:

> Since rape legislation has often been framed from a male perspective, the victim's unique identity has often been effaced in the legislation, making rape the act of having sex with a woman who does not "belong" to the perpetrator. Thus married men have often been spared prosecution under rape legislation if their actions were directed against their own 'property,' that is, their wife. (Bourke, 2007, p. 9)

Both Brownmiller and Bourke emphasize the historical context of rape. Instead of regarding a rapist as merely a psychopathic deviant, Bourke stresses the social nature of rape.

> The rapist is not a "social virus." He is human.
>
> Deep down, we all recognize the truth. Every one of us is vulnerable, and we all possess the capacity to be vindictive. A significant number of people, however, purposefully set out to exploit the human propensity to suffering. The infliction of cruelty is a choice. Who are these people who opt to deliberately

inflict pain in sexual encounters? They may not be immediately recognizable, but their actions are disconcertingly familiar. Rape is a form of social performance. It is highly ritualized. It varies between countries; it changes over time. There is nothing timeless or random about it. Indeed, meaning has not been stripped bare from deeds of brutality, but has been generously bestowed. For perpetrators of sexual violence, it is never enough to merely inflict suffering; those causing injury insist that even victims give meaning to their anguish.... (Bourke, 2007, p. 6.)

In this context, then, men wrote laws on rape with little attention to the victim's needs. The Bible presents several examples of how the Hebrews did not have a modern understanding of rape. When Lot was facing the Sodomites who wanted to rape his male angel guests, he offered them his virginal daughters instead. No mention is made of him being punished for this action. The Hebrews were typical of other desert tribes in that historical era regarding the status of women. If a woman was raped inside the city gates, the assumption was that she could have cried out for help. Since it was regarded as impossible to truly rape a woman inside the city, she was really a prostitute who deserved to be stoned to death along with the attacker. But if a woman were outside the city gates, she would not be put to death. Instead, she would be forced to marry the rapist if she were unmarried (Deuteronomy 22). According to these laws, the true victims of rape were the husbands or fathers because their property rights were stolen.

In the Middle Ages, property rights also dominated the rape laws as the Catholic Church prohibited bride capture (kidnapping an heiress, raping her, and forcing her to marry the captor) and requiring a woman's consent for marriage. It took centuries for the Church to see rape as a moral offense. Penalties depended on the status of the victim: raping a noblewoman or nuns was seen as much worse than raping a serf (Brownmiller, 1975).

Another aspect of rape laws was the overemphasis on false accusations instead of the victims' rights. Potiphar's wife, for example, falsely accused Joseph of rape. This symbolized the need for men to be protected against false accusations, which influenced rape laws for centuries. The rights of the accused man usually outweighed any rights of the alleged victim. Not until the reforms to the rape laws that started in the 1970s were victims taken more seriously by the legal system. Another reform was redefining "rape" from the forcible penetration of a vagina by a penis to other intrusions (oral and anal). The broader definition of "sexual assault" includes a wide range of offenses, from groping to sadistic torture. Now males and other victims can receive the recognition from the legal system they deserve.

Racial tensions have also affected Americans' perceptions of rape. In the South, for example, whites lynched black men for alleged rapes of "pure white" women. The image of the African-American male as a sexually ravenous beast has been a shameful stereotype for decades. In 1931, nine black teens in Scottsboro, Alabama were wrongfully accused of raping a white woman. This trial galvanized the nation as liberals fought for justice and others feared a racial insurrection inspired by Communists (Carter, 2007). Related to lynchings and false prosecutions was the murder of Emmett Till, a fourteen-year-old black who allegedly approached a white woman in Mississippi (Crowe, 2003).

However, the rapes of black women by white men often went unreported and unpunished. McGuire (2010) posits that the antirape movement in 1940s Alabama, partially created by Rosa Parks, was the real beginning of the civil rights movement.

In later years, historians would paint Rosa Parks as a sweet and reticent old woman, whose tired feet caused her to defy Jim Crow on Montgomery's city buses. Her solitary and spontaneous act, the story goes, sparked the 1955 bus boycott and gave birth to the civil rights movement. But Rosa Parks was a militant race woman, a sharp detective, and an antirape activist long before she became the patron saint of the bus boycott. After meeting with Recy Taylor (a woman who had been raped by six white men), Rosa Parks helped form the Committee for Equal Justice. With support from local people, she helped organize what the *Chicago Defender* called the "strongest campaign for equal justice to be seen in a decade." Eleven years later this group of homegrown leaders would become better known as the Montgomery Improvement Association. The 1955 Montgomery bus boycott, often heralded as the opening scene of the civil rights movement, was in many ways the last act of a decades-long struggle to protect black women, like Taylor, from sexualized violence and rape. (McGuire, 2010, xvii–xviii)

Rape as a Weapon of War

Any history of rape would be incomplete without acknowledging how sexual attacks are used as a weapon of war. In the Hebrew Scriptures, soldiers were expected to rape their captive women. Other Bible passages encouraged the Israelites to kidnap women from another land and force marriage on them, as in Judges 21. Another primitive culture that regarded women as the spoils of war was the ancient Greeks. The *Iliad*, for instance, opens with the story of two warriors fighting over the captive Briseis.

Brownmiller writes of war's impact on male behavior:
War provides men with the perfect psychologic backdrop to give vent to their contempt for women. The very maleness of the military—the brute power of weaponry exclusive to their hands, the spiritual bonding of men at arms, the manly discipline of orders given and orders obeyed, the simply logic of the hierarchical command—confirms for men what they long suspect, that women are peripheral, irrelevant to the world that counts, passive spectators to the action in the center ring. (Brownmiller, 1975, p. 32)

Mass rapes also occur in wartime as a deliberate strategy. The popular misconceptions that "boys will be boys" and that soldiers will act out their frustrations through sex have nothing to do with the reality of war rape. Females of all ages are at risk of attack because the soldiers are sometimes ordered to rape them to humiliate and demoralize the enemy. The symbolic nature of these attacks is not only to prove to the enemy men that they could not even protect their women. In some traditional societies, an unmarried rape victim may never be able to find a husband, whereas a married rape victim may lose her husband. This would decrease the birth rate of the ethnic group under attack, such the Bosnian Muslims in the 1990s. During this civil war, men were also raped by an enemy out to humiliate them. One male victim said, "When you lose an arm or a leg you can see it—but when your soul is hurting it's invisible. I may look like a rock but I'm just a shell of a man. A shell" (Hughes, 2014).

In 2011, Libya was experiencing a civil war and a sharp increase in the number of rapes. At a press conference in a Tripoli hotel, a female law student interrupted the meeting by announcing that she had been gang raped for two days by fifteen soldiers. "She showed reporters bruises and cuts on her legs, scratches on her wrists and face" (NPR, 2011). She was dragged out of the hotel room crying out her outrage. She is now safely in Rumania. "Hundreds of women may have been raped during the eight-month conflict, according to the International Criminal Court, which has collected evidence that pro-Gaddafi forces used rape as a weapon to spread fear among its opponents" (Reuters News Agency, 2014). Sadly, they are only the latest victim of the centuries-old practice of using rape as a weapon of war.

In many societies, rape victims remain silent about their traumas to avoid possible repercussions such as being cast out of a village or even getting murdered by her family to save its "honor." However, sometimes soldiers publicly rape women to ensure that the community knows that she is "tarnished" or "spoiled" (Hagen & Yohani, 2010, p. 16). The victim—and sometimes the entire family—may be ostracized as a result.

Although many victims of war rape may try to hide their trauma, international organizations have begun to take notice of this crisis. For instance, the United Nations Security Council declared in 2008 that "women and girls are particularly targeted by the use of sexual violence, including as a tactic of war to humiliate, dominate, instill fear in, disperse and/or forcibly relocate civilian members of a community or ethnic group" (United Nations Resolution 1820, 2008). Former Secretary of State John Kerry stated, "Thousands of years after rape was written into the lexicon of warfare, we know that it is time to write it out and to banish sexual violence to the dark ages and the history books where it belongs. We can make clear to the world we will not tolerate these horrific tactics" (Penny, 2014).

Rape Myths

The first rape myth is that only adult women get raped. Males are also vulnerable to rape, as indicated in Box 7.2. According to Meloy (2006), these populations are at higher risk of sexual assault: the disabled, immigrants, Native Americans, and college-age women. Those at the most risk, though, are children—two-thirds of all sexual assault cases are under the age of eighteen. Only 7 percent of the attacks are by a stranger, which means that most often a child's trust had been deeply violated by a trusted adult. As Figure 7.1 indicates, the harm can be intense.

> Children who are sexually abused often act out in sexually inappropriate ways, develop severe emotional and behavioral problems, have intense feelings of guilt and shame as a result...and have a strong sense of betrayal by the offender ...

Box 7.2   A Male Victim's Story

As the media, government, and universities grapple with the challenge of sexual assault on campuses, they usually focus on female victims. However, males can also be attacked. In one CDC (Centers for Disease Control and Prevention) study, one in twenty-five male college students answered "yes" when asked if they had been forced to have sex against their will (CDC, 2010).

During his first week at Brown University, Andrew was assaulted in the dormitory bathroom. For months, he pretended to himself that it was just a "hookup" because he did not want to think of himself as a victim. Then, during spring semester, he began to run into his attacker on a regular basis on the other side of campus. He finally reported the attack. After the hearing months later, he was happy to learn that the university had expelled his assailant. Then he found out that this student had been on suspension for two previous sexual assaults.

According to experts, it is common for male rape victims to avoid reporting the crime. Sometimes their physiological response (i.e., erection and orgasm) may betray their state of mind, which may not only confuse the victim but decrease their credibility as victims. Even calling themselves victims or survivors seems problematic, since these terms contradict the social norm of masculinity.

Another social norm that affects male victims is the belief that since men always want sex, a man cannot really be raped. One male victim writes, "a lot of women might not realize they've assaulted someone. It didn't even occur to me that I had been raped until more than a week after it happened" (Anonymous & Mannen, 2015). Gay men especially have had to deal with this stereotype. "The sentiment ... is that because we're being open about our sexuality, when someone assaults us it's not an assault.... Like, 'Oh you were kind of asking for it,' or 'Are you surprised you got assaulted?'" (Kassie, 2014).

Discussion Question

Design an intervention program to reduce the risk of sexual violence against men aimed toward young women who believe that a man should always be ready for sex.

Furthermore, the children are left with a sense of abandonment and the belief that they are powerless to protect themselves and their bodies (Meloy, 2006, p. 4).

The second rape myth has been that the victim is somehow to blame, as discussed in the preceding section. She secretly wanted it to happen or she was just having some "morning after" regrets. Men had the right to sex whenever they wanted, since rape was a natural aspect of their sexuality. In the past, rape prosecutions were difficult if not impossible because the accuser often faced disbelief. She had to show proof of struggle (bruises or injuries) regardless of what really happened. Supposedly, only "loose" women were at risk of sexual assault—and she should not have flirted with him anyway.

When does a victim "deserve" it? A woman walking down a dark street does not cause an attack, since the only cause of rape is the rapist. (Obviously, women should still take common-sense precautions to decrease the risk of crime.) Sometimes a person may

Figure 7.1 *Youth are at high risk for sexual assault (Photo source: Entofolio)*

be reckless and find herself in a risky situation. Does her recklessness imply consent? Rape advocates often stress this point: *bad judgment is not a rape-able offense.*

"Bad judgment," of course, is a subjective term. Unless a woman hides behind triple-locked doors and never leaves the house without a male escort, she could be accused of having bad judgment. This means that any woman leaving her home for school or work or socializing could be at risk for attack. Feminists such as Valenti (2007) use the term *rape schedule* to describe how she had to change her work and social life based on the level of risk. For instance, a woman may not take night classes because of the risk of walking to the car after class.

Yet another rape myth is that men rape primarily out of sexual desire. However, Hazelwood (who worked as a profiler for the Federal Bureau of Investigation [FBI]) presents evidence that most rapists have access to consensual sex with their girlfriends or wives (Michaud & Hazelwood, 1998). Related to this myth is the idea that only unattractive or poor men rape because they cannot attract a mate. Thornhill and Palmer (2000) applied the principles of social evolution to the "natural history" of rape. They propose that sperm competition (males competing to be the one to impregnate a female) and female choice of partners contribute to the "natural history" of rape. If a man is deemed too ugly or poor to attract a mate, rape is more likely. "A sexually coercive male may succeed in the competition for mates by coercing mating even though he loses in male-male competition for females and is not chose as a mate by a female" (Thornhill & Palmer, 2000, p. 54).

If one believes in the social-evolution theory, then she or he may assume that a man is too good-looking or well-off to need to rape and lower one's guard. This could increase the chance of assault. Andrew Luster, the heir to the Max Factor fortune, was both handsome and wealthy. He could likely find a willing partner at a local bar. Notorious for videotaping his multiple assaults on unconscious women, he did not need to rape in order to have sex (www.dailymail.co.uk/news/article-2309942).

A more sophisticated analysis is the 1977 FBI classification system of rapists that researchers still use as a framework (Robertiello & Terry, 2007). The first kind, power reassurance, is sometimes called the "gentleman rapist" because he pretends that he is actually a boyfriend (Robertiello & Terry, 2007, p. 510). In one case, the rapist told his victim to repair the lock on her bathroom window as if he were a concerned friend (Michaud & Hazelwood, 1998). Power assertive rapists are primarily motivated by the urge to prove their masculinity. "The key to understanding him is his macho self-perception. The most important thing in the world for him is for others to see him as a man's man" (Michaud & Hazelwood, 1998, p. 73). A more violent type is the anger retaliation rapist, who is mostly motivated by aggression and the need to punish women. The least common but most dangerous are the anger excitation rapists, sadists who find sexual gratification from hurting and sometimes killing the victim. When asked what aspect of the crime turned him on, one convicted rapist responded, "It was a multitude of things. The rapes were a sexual thing a lot of the time, but it was also mainly the idea of being dominant, having complete control, having the woman at your disposal and mercy to do what you wanted to do" (Michaud & Hazelwood, 1998, p. 119).

The fourth rape myth is that women say no when they really mean yes because they do not want to appear promiscuous. In a study of college-age males, Osman (2003) asked questions about Token Resistance (women saying "no" when they do not mean it) such as: "When a man only has to use a minimal amount of force on a woman to get her to have sex, it probably means she wanted him to force her" (Osman, 2003, p. 685). If a student scored high on items like these, he was more likely to see a date rape scenario as harmless.

Consent, then, is the key aspect about whether an encounter is rape or regular sexual intercourse. Until the 1990s, many assailants felt entitled to force sex on someone without considering themselves rapists. This prompted the no-means-no movement that is intended to empower women. Some critics, though, claim that the no-means-no movement goes too far, especially when verbal coercion is considered to be a weapon (Roiphe, 1994).

The no-means-no movement has shifted into a yes-means-yes version that emphasizes active assent instead of just consent. A law enacted in California in 2014, for instance, states that "Lack of protest or resistance does not mean consent, nor does silence mean consent. Affirmative consent must be ongoing throughout a sexual activity and can be revoked at any time" (Chappell, 2014).

Discussion Question

A study by the Department of Justice (Krebs, et al. 2007) states that one-fifth of college women have been sexually assaulted—mostly by somebody they knew. However, critics such as Sommers (2012) dispute studies that allegedly inflate the number of attacks. "Faulty studies send scarce resources in the wrong directions; more programs on sexism, stereotypes and social structures, for example, are unlikely to help victims of violence" (Sommers, 2012).

Are the government statistics on sexual assault (and violence against women in general) accurate, or are they just a political tool? Using search terms such as *rape statistics inflated*, research this question. Did you see any methodological flaws in the studies? Do you agree with the researchers who claim a high number of attacks, or with their critics who think the number is much lower?

Causes of Rape

No rapist that I've ever heard of ever slipped on a banana peel and "accidentally" raped someone: the decision to rape is a conscious, deliberate act by the rapist (www.mikethemadbiologist.com posted January 3, 2007).

Rape culture is but one possible cause of sexual assaults. This is such a multilayered issue that there is no single cause, since every rapist comes from a different set of circumstances. One aspect of rapists' mentality is their denial of doing harm. In two studies, researchers surveyed males about forcing somebody to have sex without using the word *rape*. The first study used this wording for one of the questions: "Have you ever had sexual intercourse with an adult when they didn't want to because you used or threatened to use physical force ... if they didn't cooperate?" (Lisak & Miller, 2002, pp. 77–78). The average age of the men was 26, with 6 percent self-reporting on sexual assault with the repeat rapists having committed 5.8 attacks. A more recent study (McWhorter, Stander, Merrill, Thomsen, & Milner, 2009) focused on newly recruited male Navy personnel and found a higher rate of self-report—13 percent. The narrative below may shed light on how a rapist may rationalize his actions.

When I was a high school senior, I started dating a girl I really liked named Sharon. Sharon had been giving out lots of hints that she wanted to have sex with me. From the way she talked sometimes, I figured she'd have sex with anybody. She did have a fine body.

I waited for just the right time. Her parents were away, and I gave her a ride home. She invited me into the house, talking about homework, but I knew what it was really all about. I talked a little, then I made my move.

When I kissed her, Sharon started to act like she was afraid or something— I thought she was trying to make herself look good, behaving like a good girl.

She cried and asked me to stop but there was no way I could. When she told me that it was her first time, I realized why she was so scared. By then, though, I couldn't stop. We never spoke again. (Hilgenkamp, Harper, & Boskey, 2010, pp. 79–80)

In Meloy's study of sex offenders (2006), one interviewee framed his assault as not really a crime. "And well, I know I'm not that kinda person (rapist or murderer), you know, deep down you know, just, well you do things ... out of impulse. And when you do things like that you're not thinking, snap judgment, you know...."(Meloy, 2006, p. 83).

Although persons who were abused or neglected as children are at higher risk of becoming sexual offenders, most abuse victims do *not* become offenders (Hilgenkamp,

Harper, & Boskey, 2010). Another risk factor for sexual offenders is low self-esteem, as expressed by this man convicted of having sex with a minor:

> I had real bad self-esteem issues. I mean, my view of myself was real low. I just couldn't seem to do noth'n right. So, when someone showed me some attention … in this case it was an underage person … I was too excited to think right. I made a bad mistake, which I don't know if it would have happened had I been in a better frame of mind. (Meloy, 2006, p. 89)

Rape occurs in all countries, no matter the status of women. Rape occurs when women wear burqas from head to toe or when women wear anything they want. Rape occurs in societies where talking about sex is taboo and where sexual messages are common. Rape occurs because a perpetrator made a conscious choice to hurt another person. No matter the cause of the attack, the behavior that deserves condemnation is the rapist's and not the victim's.

One controversial point is whether the U.S. troops in Vietnam had used rape as a weapon of war (Neill, 2013). Although that point is still debated, few would deny that the sex trade had started expanding in the 1960s in southeast Asia because of the influx of U.S. troops. Four decades after the end of the U.S. involvement in the Vietnam War, women and girls still have to live with the legacy of sexual exploitation.

Figure 7.2 *A woman is more likely to be raped by an acquaintance than a stranger (Photo courtesy of OUP)*

Rape and Sexual Assault

Watching the media's coverage of crime stories, one may assume that almost all rapes are done by strangers. Women are cautioned not to walk home alone at night or take a shortcut down an alley. However, the National Institute of Justice reports that 85 to 90 percent of rapes of college women are committed by acquaintances (www.nij.gov). (Victims' advocates first used the term *date rape* before expanding it to the term *acquaintance rape*.) This fact does not mean that females should take unnecessary chances, such as walking home from the library at midnight when an escort is available. However, it is critical for both women and men to realize that rape prevention is more complicated than avoiding a dark alley.

The book *I Never Called It Rape: The Ms. Report on Recognizing, Fighting, and Surviving Date and Acquaintance Rape* (Warshaw, 1994) describes the pioneering research done in the mid-1980s on the ordeals of women who were attacked but did not report it. In 1982, *Ms. Magazine* (the leading feminist journal) published an article about rape that occurs when the perpetrator is known by the victim. Researchers received funding from the National Institute for Mental Health to conduct a survey of 6,100 college men and women on 32 campuses. According to the report, "One in four female respondents had had an experience that met the legal definition of rape or attempted rape." (Warshaw, 1994, p. 2) The researcher herself had survived an acquaintance rape years earlier, which she told the women she was interviewing. "Each time, my listener visibly relaxed. That piece of information was powerful enough to remove the ever-present fear among acquaintance-rape survivors—the fear of not being believed" (Warshaw, 1994, p. 9).

Fairstein, a former prosecutor in New York City, describes the social reaction to the victims of acquaintance rape that it is not "real rape" because there had been a previous nonviolent encounter. Some experts use the term *confidence rape* in contrast to the stranger rapes, also called blitz rapes.

> In confidence rape, the rapist has gained control over the victim by winning her trust [to] at least some degree before the crime occurs. Studies confirm that these victims are more likely than blitz victims to have consumed alcohol or drugs; that they report feeling more anger (rather than fear for their lives) than blitz victims during the assault; and that they generally wait longer before seeking medical or legal intervention after the occurrence of the assault....
>
> It is my belief that most sexual assaults occur when there is a combination of two critical conditions: opportunity and vulnerability. The rapist needs the opportunity to commit the crime, and he succeeds when a victim is vulnerable at the moment of his opportunity. (Fairstein, 1993, p.132)

For instance, a burglar may break into a house and find a sleeping woman whom he rapes. Few people would blame her for the crime. But if this same woman had invited a long-time male coworker over to her house for dinner and got assaulted, even close friends would question her about whether it was rape.

She was vulnerable precisely because she did know her assailant; she was vulnerable because she trusted him. And we rarely speak with a survivor attacked by a co-worker, date, friend, or relative who doesn't tell us that the reason they were together (and usually together alone) was because she knew him and trusted him. (Fairstein, 1993, p. 133)

How to Fight Sexual Violence

It is beyond the scope of this book to offer safety advice, but the first place to start would be to read de Becker's *The Gift of Fear: Survival Signals That Protect Us from Violence* (1997). This book emboldens the reader because it delineates the difference between anxiety (free-floating and vague) and fear (sharp, intense, and life-saving).

I may have learned many lessons, but my basic premise in these pages is that you too are an expert at predicting violent behavior. Like every creature, you can know when you are in the presence of danger. You have the gift of a brilliant internal guardian that stands ready to warn you of hazards and guide you through risky situations. (De Becker, 1997, p. 7)

Besides self-protection, advocacy is critical to fight this public issue. Obviously, awareness of the problem is the first step. Learning more about this issue and sharing it with your friends and family would be valuable.

If someone you know tells you that she or he has been sexually assaulted, offer them your full support. According to the Rape Awareness and Assistance Program website, these are actions that a friend can take:

Listen. Be there. Communicate without judgment.
If the survivor seeks medical attention or plans to report, offer to be there. Your presence can offer the support they need.
Encourage the survivor to get support....
Be patient. Remember, there is no timetable for recovering from trauma. (www. rainn.org)

Discussion Questions

- Review the safety suggestions for your campus and/or community on their websites. Contact the relevant offices (e.g., campus survivor advocacy services) and ask for a presentation.
- Review websites such as Men can stop rape and the White House campaign It's On Us. Do you think these outreach efforts can reduce the rate of sexual assault? Why or why not?

Box 7.3 When the Victim Has No Legal Recourse

In an article about women crossing the Mexican border into the United States, Perez (2008) discusses how these immigrants face the high risk of rape. According to one expert quoted, "Rape has become so prevalent that many women take birth control pills or shots before setting out to ensure they won't get pregnant. Some consider rape 'the price you pay for crossing the border'" (Watson article cited in Perez, 2008, p. 141). Coyotes, the smugglers who lead the migrant groups through the desert, often commit rapes without little fear of repercussions. "Women are used like meat on a hook (by the smugglers) to attract men to their groups," states another expert (Perez, 2008, p. 141).

Immigration officials, human traffickers, and potential employers are also able to rape these vulnerable women without getting arrested. Falcon (2001), who researched the cases of women who brought charges against the Border Patrol or immigration officials, claims that rape was used as a weapon of war in this militarized setting. Whether the rapist is a U.S. government employee, coyote, or other powerful person, the women must keep silent or fear being deported. As non-citizens, then, these women are especially vulnerable to sexual assault.

When told about the dangerous situations that these women faced, Massachusetts State Representative Ryan Fattman said, "My thought is that if someone is here illegally, they should be afraid to come forward." Disregarding the barriers to citizenship faced by undocumented workers, he added, "If you do it (obtain legal status) the right way, you don't have to be concerned about these things" such as being deported (Diamond, 2011).

However, some government officials are responding with appropriate actions. In 2012, PBS (Public Broadcasting Station) aired a documentary on the 170 allegations of rape by women in detention for immigration offenses. The Department of Homeland Security reacted by creating new rules to protect these women, giving them more legal protection (Planas, 2012). Public pressure, then, can be effective in fighting an injustice.

Discussion Questions

- How is the "silencing of women" concept related to this issue?
- If you were to advocate for these women, how would you address the bigger picture of the U.S. dependence on the labor of millions of undocumented labor?

- The Steppin' Out to Prevent Violence is one example of community organizing. After researching groups like these, write a public service announcement to promote their work.
- Tori Amos, who was raped several years ago, wrote a song "Me and my gun" based on this experience. The lyrics include this statement: "Yes I wore a slinky red thing/Does that mean I should spread/For you, your friends your father, Mr. Ed." After singing this song in concerts, so many rape victims approached her that she created the Rape Awareness and Assistance Program. This organization has helped thousands of victims. Research the website (www.rainn.org) and find three items for advocacy purposes.

Key Terms

....

Street harassment
Rape culture
Rape as a weapon of war
Rape myths
Acquaintance rape
Male victims

8

Domestic Violence/Intimate-Partner
Violence (DV/IPV)

Introduction

When the author was a child, they used to call it wife beating. If the topic was ever discussed, most people thought of it as a joke. For instance, on the *Honeymooners* show the husband would say to his wife with raised fist, "One of these days, Alice, POW! Straight to the moon!" Obviously, this line was not that funny for those living in a violent household.

Then in the early 1970s, the feminists began to publicize this issue and the new term was *wife abuse*. Later on, victims' advocates used the term *domestic abuse* to include girlfriends and other nonwives. *Domestic violence* became the norm, and now the term *intimate-partner violence* is used to include those romantically involved with a batterer. The term *dating violence* usually refers to couples not living together. For purposes of this chapter, the acronym DV/IPV will indicate this social problem.

Of course, DV/IPV is not only about male-on-female violence. Gay male relationships may also include violence and/or abuse. As one male victim said, "I could see the disgusted look on the nurse's face when I mentioned that my partner Bill had given me the black eye. It just wasn't worth talking to her about it, so I left" (Dugan & Hock, 2006, p. 71). Women can be the perpetrators, either toward male or female partners. But since 80 percent of the victims are women (Catalano, 2012) and most perpetrators are male, the pronouns *he* and *she* will indicate this accordingly.

Without the feminist movement, the fight against DV/IPV may never have occurred. Lenore Walker, the researcher who coined the term *Battered Women Syndrome,* wrote in 1977 about how society should no longer allow this to be "cloaked in a conspiracy of silence" (Walker, 1977, no page). Instead, "Women no longer are willing to be treated as men's property—to be disciplined at their will" (Walker, 1977, no page).

Unfortunately, DV/IPV still hurts and kills millions of women all over the world. In the United States, around 1.3 million women are assaulted by their husbands/boyfriends a year (Centers for Disease Control report, cited by—National Center Against Domestic Violence [NCADV] factsheet). Worldwide, twenty countries still consider wife abuse to be legal.

"He's So Romantic!"

An abuser does not walk around town with a sign on his forehead stating, "I'm going to beat up my girlfriend." An abuse victim does not look for a man to kick her around. Instead, two people meet and start dating. According to song lyrics, romantic love in our society includes:

- Extreme dependence on the loved one: for example, the U2 song "All I Want Is You" by U2 (1988) and the Maroon 5 song "The Air That I Breathe" with these lyrics: "It's you that I could never live without/ You're everything" (2010).
- Possessiveness: for example, the classic "You Belong to Me" (1952) and the Demi Lovato song "Until You're Mine" (2008) with these lyrics: "Until you're mine, I have to find/A way to fill this hole inside/I can't survive without you here by my side" (2008).
- Jealousy: for example, the Bryan Adams song "Whoa, jealousy taking control of me/Now ya just gotta know/That I can't let it go" (1981).
- Violent rage with the attitude that if you reject me, you deserve to die: for example, Eminem's song "Kim," in which the man justifies a homicide/suicide: "So long, bitch you did me so wrong/I don't wanna go on/Living in this world without you" (2000).
- Sympathy for those who kill one's lover if he or she is cheating: for example, the traditional ballad of "Frankie and Johnny," in which the girlfriend shoots Frankie because she caught him cheating.

Both men and women may face social pressures to have a romantic partner, especially on Valentine's Day. Figure 8.1 is a typical example of this norm. This attitude of "any boyfriend/girlfriend is better than nothing" increases the likelihood that a person looking for romance may end up with an abuser.

At first, the boyfriend may be extremely attentive and considerate. He brings her flowers, tells her many times that she is beautiful, and even is willing to say "I love you." Then little signs of trouble creep into the relationship, as described in the excerpt below.

At the beginning of your relationship, you may not have even noticed the negative behaviors. You may [have] even felt that some of the behaviors seemed loving and attentive. Your ex-partners was so jealous of your time it seemed extreme, but he convinced you it was because of how much he loved you. Your ex was probably around virtually all the time and told you that he couldn't stand to be without

Figure 8.1 *Romance and love (Photo courtesy of OUP)*

you. He seemed to put you on a pedestal. The relationship developed quickly and when you were not together, he frequently called or e-mailed you. You may have thought at the time that this was the best relationship of your life.

Slowly, however, some of those wonderful things began to change. Perhaps you felt as if your ex-partner wanted to move ahead in the relationship too quickly. He may have pressured you into spending all your time together to the exclusion of other friends and family members. After the times you were apart, he constantly asked where you had been and what you had been doing. And sometimes this questioning may have erupted into outbursts of anger and jealousy.

Next, you may have noticed that your ex was becoming more critical of you. The criticism may have been about whom you went out with, the way you dressed, how you paid the bills, or how you decorated your house. Each time, he followed the criticism by saying he was only telling you these things to "help you." And each time your ex once again professed love for you. (Dugan & Hock, 2006, pp. 4–5)

As mentioned earlier, abusers are usually reluctant to let her spend time with other people, even her own family. He might say, "I love being with you so much that I don't want to miss any time with you." That may be sweet at first, but then it becomes harmful. Nobody should have to ask permission from a boyfriend/girlfriend to socialize with others. For instance, a friend who is constantly cancelling plans for a girl's night out because of her boyfriend may be at risk of being abused.

Another sign is that the abuser is often a "blamer" (Stosny, 2008) who will not take responsibility for his actions. If somebody has been fired from five different jobs in the past year, the problem may not be with the bosses. Later, this blaming can develop into the attitude of "look what you made me do" when he hits her. Related to this blaming is his denigration of his ex-girlfriends. It can be natural to be a little bitter about one's ex, but not extreme hatred and derogatory language. For instance, "You're so smart, sensitive, and loving, not like that bitch I used to go out with" and "Why couldn't I have met you before that self-centered, greedy woman I used to date?" are red flags (Stosny 2008, p. 1). If he seems to have trouble letting go of his anger toward his ex-girlfriends, that may be a warning.

In contrast to the ex-girlfriends, the new girlfriend may feel like she is on a pedestal. This may seem like an odd red flag since most people want to be well liked, but pedestals are hazardous. Inevitably, the girlfriend is going to show an imperfection like irritation. A potential abuser would overreact to this because of his black/white thinking that somebody is either all good or all bad. He may not be able to tolerate a minor disagreement.

An abuser is often more likely to believe in the traditional gender roles. If he sits on the couch and expects his girlfriend to get him a beer because that is her job, that could be a potential problem. Believing in a man's rights could justify abuse later (Berkel, Vandiver, & Bahner, 2004).

Discussion Question

A friend tells you that she is thinking of dating a young man, although she has some doubts. He is insisting that he pick her up at her house although she wants to meet him at the restaurant. She wants to pay for her own dinner, but he is insisting that he will pay because he is the man. Is he being romantic, or are there any red flags?

Verbal Abuse: A Script on Reality Warping

The abuse rarely starts with a violent episode. Instead, it starts gradually with verbal abuse and mental manipulations. Following this paragraph is a script based on *The Secret of Overcoming Verbal Abuse: Getting Off the Emotional Roller Coaster and Regaining Control of Your Life* (Ellis & Powers, 2000), A verbal abuser is one who uses mental tricks to make the victim doubt his/her own reality. Verbal abuse can go on for years before the first act of physical violence, or some relationships contain only verbal abuse but not physical. Discussion questions are included in the script to help readers better understand these mental tricks.

Ellen and Mike are a young couple in their 20s. They dated for two years before marrying. There were no obvious signs of abusive behavior for years, but this pattern has been set in place:

Part 1

Mike: I don't have time to check out the different interest rates at the banks for our accounts. Can you do it this week?

Ellen: Sure, no problem.

Mike: And make sure you get the best rates. You're always in a hurry and might not look too closely.

Ellen: No, I'm not.

Mike: Not what?

Ellen: Always in a hurry. I'm not careless.

Mike: I didn't say that. I never said you were careless.

Ellen: Well, what you said was something like that. You said I was always in a hurry.

Mike: Maybe you need a hearing aid. I never said that.

Ellen: You said I was always in a hurry and might get careless. And I'm not.

Mike: You're making things up. You're crazy.

Ellen: I'm not. You said I was always in a hurry and---

Mike: Will you listen to yourself? Always harping on something you think I said? You've got one overactive imagination, lady.

Ellen: I'm not harping. I'm just saying---

Mike: (mocking): "I'm just saying." Listen to yourself. You sound like an idiot.

Ellen: Look, you asked me to go to the banks to check out the different rates.

Mike (exaggerated patience): Yeah....

Ellen: So I'll do that.

Mike: I'm not so sure now. The way you've been talking nonsense, I don't think you're capable of doing a good job.

Ellen: What? I'm not stupid!

Mike: Are you sure? You can't even figure out what I was saying. I was making one simple request. Only an idiot could screw it up. But you're such an idiot, you would screw it up.

Discussion of Part 1: Look for examples of:
- Denying her reality.
- Making her wonder if she's crazy.
- Mockery.

Part 2

Ellen: Stop calling me an idiot!

Mike: Oh come on, are you going to call your dumb lesbo girlfriends now and complain? All you do is talk and talk to them and you won't even do a simple favor like go the banks---

Ellen: I never said I wouldn't! You said I was too stupid—

Mike: Why are you calling yourself stupid again? Got a problem or something?

Ellen: No, I don't have a problem. You have the problem. You said—

Mike: Stop it already. Look, even if you went to the banks and checked out the rates, you'd probably pick the worst one. There would be a good-looking guy working at the bank and you're so slutty you'd just want to flirt with him and---

Ellen: I'm not---

Mike: Yeah, yeah. "I'm not slutty. I'm not stupid." Why are you always accusing me of calling you names? You're the one calling yourself names. I'm just watching you screw yourself up.

Ellen: You were saying—

Mike: Stop that already! Look, I know what I said. And I didn't say those things. You just make them up because you're such a messed-up person. I don't know why I ever married you. You're pathetic. You're ugly.

Ellen: (crying): That's mean.

Mike: Mean? You think that's mean? You're the mean bitch! I mean, I asked you to do ONE SIMPLE FAVOR and you won't do it!

Ellen: I said I'd do it!

Discussion of Part 2: Look for examples of:

- Constant interruptions.
- Irrational jealousy.
- Constant criticism.
- Efforts to isolate her from others.

Part 3

Mike: Yeah, right. Women can't do business anyway. The only thing they're good for is what's between their legs. And hey, you're not that good at that, either.

Ellen: Why are you doing this?

Mike: I mean, you're not that much to look at. Your hair looks like hell and you're a fat cow.

Ellen: I'm trying to lose weight ...

Mike: Well, you're always pigging out. It's gross just to look at you. And you can't even go to the banks and get some interest rates.

Ellen: I was ready to, but then you—

Mike: There you go again, more excuses.

Ellen: What I was trying to say was ...

Mike: You're just trying to be right. You're trying to control this conversation. Hell, you're trying to control ME. You're always trying to tell me what to say. I can say anything I want. And I think you're absolutely pathetic. You're a lousy wife and that's that.

Ellen: I'm trying ...

Mike: Yeah, yeah, you're trying. Everything you do is wrong. You can't even have a decent conversation with me without starting an argument.

Ellen: But I'm not arguing ...

Mike: You started it, not me. I just asked you to do one simple favor and you start ragging on me. You're such a bitch.

Ellen: Let me go to the banks. Please. I'll try to prove to you that I can do it.

Mike: Never mind. It's not worth it at this point. You know, sometimes you make me so mad … it's like you want me to hit you so you'd stop being so hysterical.

Ellen: Please let me go.…

Mike: I said, forget it. Geez, you're so friggin' stupid you don't even understand plain English? What a loser.

Discussion of Part 3: Look for examples of:

- Projection (accusing her of doing what he is actually doing).
- Extremely negative remarks.
- Rigid gender roles.
- Efforts to make her feel helpless.
- Threat of violence.
- Blaming her for his reaction to her.

Later Stages of Violence

As the verbal abuse worsens, other signs of abuse may occur. He might pin her down for sex and claim that he was only playing. The criticisms may become more frequent and more hurtful, with the unconscious goal of humiliating her so much that she loses her sense of self-assurance. Threats may occur—slamming his fist on the table or throwing a plate against the wall.

The isolation from friends and family usually increases as the abusive relationship progresses. As she gets more and more emotionally enmeshed with her boyfriend, she may start losing friends. One of the author's students told the story of her best friend in high school. The friend had started dating a possessive man and stopped talking to her. The two girls lost touch. Three years later, she found her friend's obituary in the paper—that boyfriend had killed her.

Besides isolation is "The Look," which is one tactic that parents may use on children to control their children in a public place. "Behave or you're going to be in big trouble!" Applied to a relationship between adults, though, "The Look" is troubling.

And then there's The Look. Some abusers have become so skilled at maintaining control over their victims that they can do it without words. If a man has been physically violence once, he is capable of doing it again. His victim realizes this. When he looks at her in a particular way, she knows that she had better shape up. "I called it The Bull," one woman told me. "It was like his nostrils would start flaring and he'd start getting that look in his eyes and he's start pacing. It was just like a bull, you know. Just a bull that's ready to charge." Terrifying, and the more terrifying for being silent.

There is another version of The Look. One woman called her husband's look "The Frozen Tundra," his cold lack of emotion transforming her into a

Figure 8.2 *Intimate partner violence (Photo source: Entofolio)*

nonperson. It was as though he was saying, "You mean no more to me than the table, the refrigerator, or the vacuum cleaner." Objectifying. Dismissive. (Weiss, 2003, p. 41)

The next stage of abuse is an escalated risk of violence. Now the threats are backed up by violence. By then, the victim is so overly attached to the abuser that living without him seems unthinkable. She may mistake her obsession for a healthy love. He may still be charming and loving most of the time, which reinforces her sense that the ugly incidents are only an aberration of his "real" self.

In one woman's words, the husband used an "invisible whip" to control her (Weiss, 2004, p. 33). Advised by a counselor to fight back, she decided to stand up to him.

She slammed pots and pans down on the stove, taking pleasure in the satisfactory clatter. She was a new person! She wasn't going to let Karl push her around ever again! Just let him try!

An hour later, he did. "I was fixing dinner and he started in arguing with me, calling me names. I turned and I just yelled, right in his face, 'If you ever call me dumb f***, or a shithead, or a fat pig, ever again, here's what I'm gonna do to you.'" The next bit is a blank. Her mother has told her what happened, but Judy has never recovered her memory. Head trauma will do that. She gropes for words, summoning her recollections in disjointed fragments. Karl, drawing back his fist. The jolt of pain as his knuckles connected with her jaw. Though she has been told, she doesn't remember that the blow was hard enough to send her flying across the room. She doesn't remember that her head hit a corner of the windowsill, knocking her out cold. She doesn't remember her children screaming, certain that their mother was dead. (Weiss, 2004, p. 38)

How does the violence escalate? Researchers have developed a Danger Assessment for nurses and other health professionals. The first level of violence is "slapping, pushing; no injuries and/or lasting pain" and the highest level of violence is "use of weapon" (Campbell, Webster, & Glass, 2009, p. 655).

Guns are especially dangerous to DV/IPV victims. In 2014, a Congressional hearing on regulating guns for those convicted of domestic violence or stalking stated the following: "Fifty-seven percent of recent mass shootings involved some form of domestic violence; and homicides are the most prevalent cause of death for pregnant or immediately postpartum women in many states" and countless times a gun was used to threaten a victim without being shot (Osell, 2014).

Control: The Key Element of DV/IPV

For whatever reason, the abuser feels the need to control his partner. He controls her social life by isolating her from others. He controls her personal space by crowding into it. He controls her time by requiring her to make him dinner or other tasks.

With the new technology of cellphones and the Internet, control becomes even more dominant in abusive relationships. Relentless texting of insults and threats, besides the demand that she stay in constant touch with him, can overwhelm a person's sense of self. Whenever an abuser becomes a stalker, technology becomes even more dangerous.

Without control, the abuser has little left to encourage the victim to stay with him. At first the control is psychological, then it can become physical (violence or captivity), economic (control of money), and/or sexual. Again, the victim may think that she is still in love with her abuser but he had brainwashed her with mind games.

An interesting parallel to DV/IPV occurred in 1973, when four bank tellers were held hostage for six days by armed robbers in Stockholm, Sweden. After they were rescued, they refused to testify against these men who held them at gunpoint. They sent the men flowers and one of them even got engaged to marry her former captor. Psychologists have called this the Stockholm Syndrome, in which captives "fall in love" with the men who have the power of life or death over them (e.g., Graham et al., 2001). . This syndrome has nothing to do with love, of course, and everything to do with fear. These women could have been killed at any moment. They focused their attention on the men with the guns, who sometimes showed them a little kindness.

These bank tellers are not the only ones to display such behavior. For instance, the release of Jaycee Lee Dugard after eighteen years of captivity renewed the discussion of the Stockholm Syndrome. Abuse victims may also manifest signs of this syndrome as they mistake fearful obsession for romantic love. For those who want to help the victims out of their harmful (and even dangerous) relationships, it can be frustrating because of the victims' loyalty to their abusers. "But he loves me" and "you just don't understand him" are two common statements.

Discussion Question

Since the days of ancient Rome, husbands had the right to "chastise" their wives (Okun, 1986). This historic attitude (physical violence can be used as a corrective action) still exists in some cultural groups today. For instance, one article (Ned and Maria, undated) from the Christian Domestic Discipline website states that:

> The husband (uses) "God mirroring" or "practical godliness" - in other words, a following of God's methods of how He uses authority....
>
> This leads to physical discipline to lovingly keep the wife accountable to her master's God given authority.... (including) physical and painful discipline for sinful habits or other various things.... (www.christiandomesticdiscipline.com)

If you were a social worker with clients from the Christian Domestic Discipline movement, how would you respect their cultural beliefs while supporting a woman's right to live without violence? How does the social work value of self-determination apply to a woman who accepts her husband's God-given right to hit her?

Figure 8.3 *Resentment and anger (Photo courtesy of OUP)*

The Abuser

Is psychopathology the cause of abuse? One research team (Crane, Hawes, Devine, & Easton, 2014) measured the possible relationship between DV/IPV and specific conditions. Bipolar and post-traumatic stress disorder (PTSD) were related to a higher rate of DV/IPV, but not Attention Deficit and Hyperactivity Disorder (ADHD).

In his book *Why Does He DO That? Inside the minds of angry and controlling men*, Bancroft (2002) discusses the mentality of the abuser.

> In one important way, an abusive man works like a magician: His tricks largely rely on getting you to look off in the wrong direction, distracting your attention so that you won't notice where the real action is. He draws you into focusing on the turbulent world of his feelings to keep your eyes turned away from the true cause of his abusiveness, which lies in how he *thinks*. He leads you into a convoluted maze, making your relationship with him a labyrinth of twists and turns. He wants you to puzzle over him, to figure him out, as though he were a wonderful but broken machine for which you need only to find and fix the malfunctioning parts to bring it roaring to its full potential. His desire, though he may not admit it even to himself, is that you wrack your brain in this way so that you won't notice the patterns and logic of his behavior, the consciousness behind the craziness....
>
> Above all, the abusive man wants to avoid having you zero in on his abusiveness itself. So he tries to fill your head up with excuses and distortions and keep you weighed down with self-doubt and self-blame. And, unfortunately, much of the society tends to follow unsuspectingly along behind him, helping him to close your eyes, and his own, to his problem. (Bancroft, 2002, pp. 21–22)

One research study (Whiting, Parker, & Houghtaling, 2014) interviewed thirteen men about their violent relationships. One aspect of their perspective was how much they wanted to control their wives, even to the point of telling her not to cry after being hurt. Another aspect, of course, was anger:

> I felt the rage starting up, the adrenaline, and I just didn't care. I just kept going and going. It was at that moment in time, that I was looking at her. I honestly just wanted to hurt her physically. (Whiting, Parker, & Houghtaling, 2014, p. 281).

Discussion Questions

As social workers, how do we apply the value of "dignity and worth of a person" to this situation? First, how can we teach abusers to see the dignity and worth of their victims? Second, how can social workers affirm the dignity and worth of these abusers while not condoning their actions? Could you ever work with domestic violence offenders? Why or why not?

Anyone can be caught in an abusive relationship—rich, poor, well-educated, poorly educated, Caucasian, African American, Latino—*anyone*. The common characteristic for the victims/survivors is not masochism, since very few people actually want to be abused. Instead, it is the bad luck of dating the wrong person and not knowing the warning signs.

The Stockholm Syndrome partially explains why some victims find it so hard to leave or stay away from the relationship. It can take an average of seven times before the victim makes the final break from the relationship to become a survivor (www.thehotline.org).

Wozniak and Allen (2013) describe two other reasons why a woman may stay with her abuser. The "sense of self" is diminished as she is "feeling small, insecure, lost, afraid, angry, unworthy, and unlovable" (Wozniak & Allen, 2013, p. 26). Another reason is described here:

> Learned helplessness … that occurs when a woman has been so beaten down that she no longer believes that she has any control over her situation and cannot escape it … This process is like brainwashing; it occurs over time and wears away at the woman's self-esteem and sense of self-worth. When all of your energy is spent just trying to survive, you don't have a lot of time to reflect on what is happening around you. (Wozniak & Allen, 2013, p. 28)

Besides learned helplessness is "learned hopelessness" (LaViolette & Barnett, 2014, p. 17) as the victims may despair about the future. Also, a relationship existed before the violence, and memories of that past can be emotionally powerful.

The most commonly asked question regarding abused women remains, Why does she stay? This question is based on the naïve assumption that it's easy to leave. Contrary to frequently held beliefs, most people would not stop liking or loving an intimate partner who hit them. Most of us would say that we don't want to be hit by someone who loves us, but there are conflicting values that occur after the first incident. Most of us make promises and commitments that define who we are as people and in relationship to others. We promise to stick with our partners—to be compassionate, to be forgiving, to keep our families together. Which values weigh more when we are confused with a push, slap, or more from our intimate partners?

In addition, a web of oppression, fear, and confusion occurs over time based on the violent and nonviolent strategies employed by the intimate perpetrator. It is important for helping professionals to understand the intricacies of this web, the individual differences between victims, and the ambiguities of gender that create this entanglement. (LaViolette & Barnett, 2014, p. 15)

One of the first reactions to hearing that somebody is being abused by his or her partner can be anger at the victim—"why does she put up with this?" Financially, she may not be able to leave the situation if she has no outside job. To be successful during a job interview, one must appear self-confident and upbeat—the opposite of how she was brainwashed into becoming.

Figure 8.4 *The rage builds up (Photo source: Entofolio)*

The batterer may have made it impossible for her to go to work by threatening her life if she kept her job. Another possible cause of unemployment is untreated injuries, since only 34 percent of those injured by DV/IPV seek medical treatment (National Coalition Against Domestic Violence, www.ncadv.org/learn/statistics). Other barriers to employment include: facial marks of a beating so she is too embarrassed to be in public, damaged vehicle, and an overload of stress that hurts her work performance. If a batterer calls her place of employment several times a day to check up on her (or even shows up at her workplace), that could also cause her to be fired. Almost eight million days of paid work are lost a year because of DV/IPV (NCADV).

Financial abuse is another barrier to a victim's flight to safety. For instance, one wife had no health insurance and was expected to pay for the hospital bills for two deliveries. An advocate for the National Network to End Domestic Violence stated, "They don't have (money) to fly to a parent's house or rent a hotel room. In a sense, many women are being battered because they can't afford to not be battered" (Jeltsen, 2014).

A support system is another consideration for somebody planning to leave an abusive relationship. Since the batterer usually ensures that she has been cut off from her family and friends, she may not be able to ask for help. She may also be too embarrassed to admit that the man she had chosen was actually hurting her on a daily basis. It often takes more than once before a DV/IPV survivor finally leaves the abuser, so that leads to frustration and even rejection by her family and friends.

In a meta-analysis of DV/IPV literature, Barnett (2001) discusses one major reason for a battered woman to stay in an unsafe relationship: not enough support from the workplace, medical professionals, and other places where she may seek help. "A doctor's silence not only ignores obvious signs of IPV, it tends to reinforce society's general acceptance of IPV" (Barnett, 2001, p. 5).

The biggest consideration about leaving, though, is whether the risk of staying is higher than the risk of leaving. The leading cause of murder of women in the United States is by being in a romantic relationship—almost one-third of female homicide victims are killed by an intimate partner (NCADV).

Another risk to the person who leaves an abusive relationship is stalking, which is one form of Obsessive Relational Intrusion (ORI). Although stalkers may victimize persons they barely know, most victims were in a prior relationship with the stalker. Like DV/IPV, "stalking" is a social construct that is now considered a crime. In 1990, California passed the first antistalking law after several murders took place. Since then, public awareness has made people take this behavior more seriously because of the implicit threat. The behaviors must be repeated to be considered as "stalking." These behaviors may include: information gathering, several unwanted contacts, persistent requests for a date, vandalism, breaking into the victim's car or home, and even violence (Spitzer & Cupach, 2014).

Protection orders and restraining orders are two ways to stop stalkers and other former intimate partners. According to the NCADV, around 20 percent of DV/IPV survivors obtain protection orders and over one-half of these orders are violated. For some violent offenders, a protection order is even a trigger for more violence. In one meta-analysis, researchers found that protection orders can be effective depending on factors such as the timing of the order, involvement of children, and the perpetrator's record of violence (Benitez, McNiel. & Binder, 2010). Survivors trying to escape from their abusers, then, must calculate the risk of re-abuse with the benefits of legal protection. Box 8.1 discusses the complex realities of a survivor who is in a crisis mode.

If a person may not or cannot leave the relationship immediately, safety plans are highly recommended. Examples of safety plans are available on websites such as the National Coalition Against Domestic Violence (www.ncadv.org), the Domestic Violence Organization (www.domesticviolence.org), and police departments. When a person's life is threatened, the person may have trouble thinking clearly. A clearly written list of actions would be valuable to somebody in such a high-stress situation. The list usually includes money, keys, and medicine.

Discussion Question

As discussed earlier, examples of safety plans are available online. Review one of these safety plans, and apply three items on it to this situation: Melanie is 36 and is living in fear of her abusive husband. He controls the money, monitors her phone calls, and will not let her talk to anyone but one neighbor. She goes to a traditional church that opposes the idea of divorce, so she is counseled to obey her husband. How would you help her make plans to leave her home?

Box 8.1 Notes from the Field

Annie Davis, a clinical social worker who works in this field, once survived domestic violence herself as a young woman. She considers herself not only a survivor but a transcender, somebody who is thriving in a rich new life. In her testimony to the Ohio State Senate on a mental health parity bill (which passed in 2008), she describes her experiences with PTSD.

> My journey through healing began over twenty years ago when I was taken into a Ohio Domestic Violence Shelter.... I learned that the mysterious symptoms I have been experiencing were those of PTSD: hives, difficulty talking, hyperventilation, inability to think clearly, loss of visions, and problems with event recall....
>
> I thought I was crazy and did not know that these physical reactions are often symptoms that result from trauma and exposure to violence.... Through the help of a caring shelter staff, I was able to become independent and divorce my abuser....
>
> Despite my new happy life as a mom, wife, student, and volunteer, I have continued to battle other PTSD symptoms. I would wake up at night, screaming and in a cold sweat from the nightmares. Later that morning, I would notice that I had bruised hands from my fingernails driving into the palms. I had been clenching my fists very tightly during these nightmares. With the help of my trauma therapist, I have overcome many of the intense symptoms.
>
> Unfortunately, I had also developed temporomandibular joint dysfunction (TMJ), which resulted from gritting my teeth in anxiety. Over the years, I had difficulty with my jaw because it would click or pop when I talked. The TMJ got so bad that it became painful to open my mouth to talk or eat. Because TMJ was not a covered condition under the insurance policy, we had to pay over $50,000 to cover the bills. We had no choice to take on this financial burden so I could perform the basic functions of life.

Besides being an advocate for DV/IPV survivors, Davis also works directly with this population. When asked by the author to submit comments for this chapter, Davis provided two messages:

Message to the Victim/Survivor
> If abuse happens to you, do not be ashamed. Don't let shame be a barrier to getting the help you need. Don't let this experience diminish you in any way. Statistically, this could have happened to anyone. Make the choice to find healing. Some people will understand your healing journey, and others will not. Keep on trying until someone hears you.

Message to the Social Worker (or anyone who knows a victim/survivor)
> Remember to approach your clients in a spirit of compassion (on an equal footing) instead of pity, which reduces a person. Do not deny their truth. Instead, help them to find the resources they need.

Figure 8.5 *Transcending the trauma (Photo source: Entofolio)*

It is typical for abuse victims to return to their abusers many times before the final departure. This may frustrate you, so consult with your supervisors or peers but do not vent at your client about this decision. Tell them that they can return to get services at any time without feeling ashamed or hearing "I told you so." The national hotline number is 800-799-7233.

It is not easy for a client to leave her abuser. Picture two overlapping circles, with a healthy relationship allowing for extra space for both. In an abusive relationship, the two circles are so enmeshed that the relationship defines her identity. Leaving, then, is like tearing apart her own identity.

If a client tells me that she is returning to her abuser, I usually say, "Okay, that is not uncommon for this to happen" and then bring up safety plans. I always tell my clients, "Violence escalates as the cycle continues. The violence increases in severity." Provide them with the phone number of a local police officer who you know is helpful. At the meeting before her return to the abuser, it is ideal for a police officer or shelter representative to be present. This would make it more likely that she would ask for help instead of being too afraid of being judged.

Finally, always consider your own safety when assisting a domestic violence victim. Do not give her your cell phone number. Be cautious on the social media (obviously, it is unethical to be a Facebook "friend" to any client). Tell her to hide your business card, any pamphlets, and other materials that might trigger violence from an abuser.

Discussion Questions

1. Pick the most relevant point in this section, and write a paragraph reflecting on it.
2. Have you ever known somebody in a destructive (not necessarily abusive) relationship? Or have you ever been hooked in one yourself? Describe how you worked it out.

Female on Male Violence

The research on female on male violence in the DV/IPV context is scanty. One research study (Shorey Brasfield, Febres, & Stuart,2011) measured the levels of anger and impulsivity of 80 female domestic violence offenders, while other researchers focused on the offenders' alcoholism (Chase, O'Farrell, Murphy, Fals-Stewart, & Murphy, 2003). Hall (2012) notes how society treats this type of violence as inconsequential, as seen in the reactions to the reality shows *Jersey Shore* and *Teen Mom*. The women hit their intimate partners with no legal or social consequences. Because of the "feminization of social welfare," males may feel uncomfortable asking for help. They "are unique in that their defining difference (sex) is an experience with which the mainstay of social welfare professionals, including both male and female social workers assigned to domestic violence, lack affinity" (Hall, 2012, p. 21).

In his book *Abused Men: The Hidden Side of Domestic Violence*, Cook (1997) describes the dilemma of a male battered by his wife/girlfriend:

> Men don't hit back, don't tell, often get their genitalia kicked.
> Male victims face ridicule, according to female setting up shelters:
> One of the things that men have to deal with, that women don't have to, is indeed ridicule. I can tell you that from experience, both from working with these men, and from making speaking engagements. When I mention that we are a shelter that provides shelter to battered men, they all laugh, the men and the women. They think it's funny that a man would be battered. They laugh when I tell them that a man can be raped. Of course, I don't think it's funny at all ... I know that there are a lot of battered men out there, but part of the reason they don't seek help is this fear of ridicule....
> I worked with a man who was an ironworker. Now, an ironworker is the epitome of macho. This guy was big, and his wife was tall, but thin, probably no more than a hundred pounds. She kept putting him in the hospital. She kept beating him up with a baseball bat. Every time he came out of the hospital, they (his co-workers) were laughing him off the girders. They had no sympathy or empathy for him. (Cook, 1997, p. 54)

Men's rights activists have claimed that almost half of DV/IPV victims in the United States are male (e.g., www.batteredmen.com), but the Bureau of Justice states that only 20 percent of the victims are male. Since the male victims may be involved in a same-sex relationship, it is impossible to determine how many of the males were assaulted by women. (For women in same-sex relationships, DV/IPV was covered in the Chapter 5, Lesbian and Bisexual Women.)

Discussion Questions

Discuss how you would convert a women's-shelter program into one that includes all genders and sexual orientations. How could you ensure cultural competence in this setting? Would the inclusion of men make some of the female residents uncomfortable? Describe three possible problems that could result.

Violence Against Women Act of 1994

To combat DV/IPV, sexual assault, and other forms of violence against women, Congress passed the VAWA (Violence Against Women Act) in 1994. According to the U.S. Department of Justice, 1.5 million women are victims of DV/IPV a year and one in every four women will experience DV/IPV in her lifetime.

Controversies emerged when opponents stated that the rates of violence were exaggerated. Phyllis Schlafly, the woman who had led the fight against the ERA (Equal Rights Amendment), writes that the laws are written so loosely that they produce "absurdities.... The supply of 1,500 new domestic violence laws enacted by states from 1997 to 2005 is largely the handiwork of targeted lobbying by feminists funded by the multimillion-dollar federal boondoggle called the Violence Against Women Act" (Schlafly, 2009, p. 32).

Another controversy was whether the VAWA was antifamily because it would break up families by funding more women's shelters (RADAR, 2008). Critics such as RADAR (Respecting Accuracy in Domestic Violence Reporting, website: www.mediaRADAR.org) regard this law as another version of male-bashing. However, the Department of Justice is reaching out to men's groups in violence prevention. The Engaging Men and Youth grants, for example, fund projects such as the Bystander Intervention Project in Portland, Maine. (engagingmen.futureswithoutviolence.org/).

Despite the opposition, this law has resulted in better services for anyone in a DV/IPV relationship (Stuart, 2009). Through the Department of Justice, the Office on Violence against Women has funded several community programs to educate the public. Another positive change is the improved training of law enforcement and hospitals so they would treat the victims of violence more appropriately. For instance, the waiting time in the emergency department of a hospital for a sexual assault victim was decreased by several hours.

The Office on Violence Against Women (OVW) currently administers 21 grant programs authorized by the Violence Against Women Act of 1994 and subsequent legislation. These grant programs are designed to continue to develop the nation's capacity to reduce domestic violence, dating violence, sexual assault, and stalking by strengthening services to victims and holding offenders accountable for their action.s (Department of Justice, 2015)

According to the Department of Justice, a sharp decrease in DV/IPV crimes has occurred since the passage of the VAWA. "From 1994 to 2010, the overall rate of intimate partner violence in the United States declined by 64%, from 9.8 victimizations per 1,000 persons age 12 or older to 3.6 per 1,000" (Catalano, 2012). Is this a case of correlation or causation? Regardless of whether or not the VAWA has caused any of the decrease, the news is very encouraging. Not only has public awareness expanded, but widespread indignation over DV/IPV incidents. For instance, in 2014 an NFL football player was caught on camera beating his fiancée in an elevator. Millions of people saw the footage and cried out in outrage. No longer will DV/IPV be acceptable in mainstream society, but regarded as a serious crime.

Discussion Questions

- If a politician wanted to cut funds for the Violence Against Women Act because he sees it as antimarriage, how would you respond? Does this chapter have any key points that could be used to support funding for this Act?
- According to the 2010 National Intimate Partner and Sexual Violence Survey by the Centers for Disease Control, "Nearly half of all women and men in the United States have experienced psychological aggression by an intimate partner in their lifetime." How would you define "psychological aggression" to use in a social work setting? Is it possible to write a definition of "psychological aggression" that could be enacted into law? If you were to advocate a law against it, what should be the penalty for the aggressors?
- One debate about DV/IPV is the mandatory arrest laws. Should a law enforcement officer arrest an alleged abuser at the scene, even if the alleged victim does not want it? Several people debate whether mandatory arrests decrease the incidence of violent incidents. By using the search term "mandatory arrest law" on www.googlesholar.com, find an article for each side of the debate. Summarize their key points. After this research, would you support mandatory arrest laws? Why or why not?
- According to researchers, mothers are three times more likely than nonmothers to be abused by their partners (Buchanan, Power, & Verity, 2013). If you worked in Child Protective Services, what steps would you take to help this mother with her goal?

Apart from wanting to make sure that he's protected forever. I think I put up more of a protection. From that point in time, definitely. Yes, yes from that time I was more determine (sic) to, you know, "I'll not let anything happen to you." (Buchanan, Power, & Verity, 2014, p. 718)

1. Review the Power and Control Wheel graphic on the National Center on Domestic and Sexual Violence website (HYPERLINK http://www.ncdsv.org/images/Power ControlwheelNOSHADING.pdf)
2. How does misogyny apply to this Wheel, especially the silencing of women and diminishing them?

Key Terms

DV/IPV
Red flags
Reality warping
Control (physical, etc.)
Stalking
Stockholm Syndrome
Learned helplessness
Safety plan

9

Sex and Consequences

Sex in History

One remarkable book that discusses this topic is titled, not surprisingly, *Sex in History* (Tannahill, 1980). In prehistoric times, man mated like primates with only a back view of the partner. The primary sexual part of a woman was the buttocks—not until later did the female breasts become the main attraction. The Paleolithic sex symbol was the Venus figurine. Made more than 20,000 years ago, they are usually small and have no face. "All the accent is on the female sexual features of ample breasts and *mons pubis* and on the less exclusively female features of bulging stomach and buttocks" (Tannahill, 1980, p. 35). Anthropologists are still unsure of why the face was not featured on these figurines.

For centuries, people were unaware of the biological facts of life: that intercourse causes pregnancies. Not until the 1930s did a tribe in the Solomon Islands find out that their children were not sent by their ancestral deities but by sexual intercourse. For them, sex was only for pleasure. One Australian tribe believed that a woman became pregnant by "sitting over a fire on which she had roasted a fish given to her by the prospective father" (Tannahill, 1980, p. 42). In another Australian tribe, a woman was told the facts of life. "(She) flatly denied it. 'Him nothing!' she said scornfully" (Tannahill, 1980, p. 42).

Even today, people still have erroneous beliefs about sex. On one health information website, the article "Top 10 Myths About Safe Sex and Sexual Health" includes these two items: a female can get pregnant the first time, and she can get pregnant during her period. Some people also believe that the "morning after" pill can cause abortions, which is impossible (www.health.com/health/gallery/0,,20307293,00.html).

Religion, of course, has affected sexual behavior through the ages. In the Early Church era, theologians did allow for sex to occur in a marriage setting—but only under certain conditions.

> Some rigid theologians recommended abstention on Thursdays, in memory of Christ's arrest; Fridays, in memory of his death; Saturdays, in honor of the Virgin Mary; Sundays, in honor of the Resurrection; and Mondays, in commemoration of the departed. Tuesdays and Wednesdays were largely accounted for by a ban on intercourse during fasts and festivals—the forty days before Easter, Pentecost, and Christmas; the seven, five, or three days before Communion; and so on. (Tannahill, 1980, p. 146)

It appears miraculous, then, that enough Christians were conceived to perpetuate the religion. Obviously, there is only a slight possibility that couples during this era disobeyed these restrictions.

Virginity

Related to such restrictions on marital sex is the stress on the virginity of females. Throughout history and in many cultures, a female's virginity was regarded as more important than her own life. Saint Agnes, for example, is honored for her martyrdom because she would have rather been killed by a would-be rapist than lose her chastity (Salih, 2001).

Virgins are expected to bleed the first time they have intercourse. This bleeding from the broken hymen, though, does not always happen for several possible reasons (www.med-health.net). This is not an obscure medical fact, but a life-threatening misperception that has triggered violence against virgins who do not bleed on their wedding night. In Biblical times, for instance, a new husband could accuse his wife of not being a virgin. If she could not prove her virginity by showing a blood-stained cloth, she should be stoned to death because "She has done an outrageous thing in Israel by being promiscuous while still in her father's house. You must purge the evil from among you" (Deuteronomy 22:21, NIV).

Influenced by the Virgin Mother ideal, the Early Church also emphasized the importance of virginity/chastity. It expanded the concept to include spiritually pure behavior and thoughts. Saint John Chrysostom, for instance, stated that "When a virgin learns to discuss things frankly with a man, to sit by him, to look at him, to laugh in his presence, to disgrace herself in many other ways ... the veil of virginity is destroyed, the flower trampled underfoot" (Kelly, 2000, p. 4).

However, Jewish scholars did take into account the possibility of a chaste bride not bleeding on her wedding night. According to the Jewish Virtual Library, "In *halakhah* a virgin is not necessarily a maiden whose hymen is intact. She can be legally regarded both as a virgin with a ruptured hymen and as a nonvirgin when it is intact. The former applies when she can claim ... that the rupture was caused by an injury" (www.jewishvirtuallibrary.org). In many cultures, virginity was regarded as a gift given to the husband.

Medieval society also emphasized the importance of virginity for females. One scholar (Kelly, 2000) notes that excluding Sir Galahad, all medieval references to virginity refer to females. Because some cultures did not necessarily rely on the traditional tests of virginity (i.e., medical examination and blood-stained sheets), other methods were used. In one thirteenth-century romance poem, the Sultan's women washed their hands in a magic fountain. If the water turned red, it meant that she was unchaste (Kelly, 2000). Virginity in medieval females may also symbolize empowerment, since they were seen as pious and less restricted by male power (Salih, 2001). Centuries later, the Council of Trent supported such attitudes by declaring "that virginity was still a more blessed state than marriage" (Tannahill, 1980, p. 333).

When women did get married, bridal virginity was a source of concern in many cultures. Bridal virginity is not only associated with questions of the legitimacy of the children. For centuries after the Biblical injunction against alleged unchaste women, displaying the blood-stained cloth was a symbol of male triumph. The husband's honor was at stake in the patriarchal setting. He was claiming his wife as his property by taking away her virginity (Mernissi, 1982). Ancient Sumerians and subsequent cultures also developed the institution of the "first night" privilege, in which a king or lord could bed the new bride before the husband. Deflowering the virgin, then, could be a privilege reserved for the upper classes (Tannahill, 1980).

Virginity is also connected to the fear of STIs (sexually transmitted infections). Virgin prostitutes in Victorian England, for example, were seen as "clean" by men who were willing to pay more for them. "Enthusiasts had always claimed that there was a special pleasure in deflowering a virgin, because of the emotional thrill, a blend of aggression, possessiveness, and mild sadism" (Tannahill, 1980, p. 370). As recently as 2013, a news article reports that Taiwanese prostitutes buy blood to insert drops into their vaginas to fake virginity. One prostitute stated that her earnings went up five times since she started this practice (Shagar, Lai, & Raman, 2013).

This focus on the hymen is still relevant in many societies, even in the United States. Doctors are now performing hymen restoration surgeries for women who want to fake virginity on their wedding nights. One New York City doctor says that "several hundred scared young women from many cultures — Latinas, Mideasterners, Chinese, Koreans — have paid her $2,500 each to have their hymens restored. Sure, it's a business, she says, but what's behind the practice makes the doctor angry. 'It's about machismo, 100 percent'" (Sherr, 2014). The article also notes that in some Middle Eastern families, honor killings may result if a new bride is not deemed a virgin. Seen as a disgrace to her family, only her death could restore the honor of those who should have guarded her virginity. Tradition dictates that without an intact hymen, a girl is worthless.

Virginity tests done by government officials are also an indication of the continuing importance of the hymen. In 2011, several women were arrested during the protests in Cairo's Tahrir Square. According to Amnesty International, a man in a white coat conducted virginity tests on them with soldiers watching. "The general justified the abuse by saying these women 'were not like your daughter or mine. These were girls who had camped out in tents with male protesters'" (Coleman, 2011). Authorities, then, were equating social protests with promiscuity—perhaps because these women were in the public sphere and deserved to be punished.

In the United States, the virginity of high school students became a political issue in the 1990s as abstinence sex education replaced the comprehensive version. Thousands of teens took virginity pledges to abstain from sex until marriage. One research study (Bearman & Bruckner, 2001) discloses that these pledges were somewhat successful in delaying the age of the first sexual experience. Those who identified with the church's abstinence-only movement were more likely to keep the pledge. However, the pledge breakers were less likely to use protection for their first sexual experience.

Rosenbaum's longitudinal research study (2009), though, contradicts this earlier finding. He found that 82 percent of the pledges denied that they had even taken the pledge five years earlier. Comparing pledgers to nonpledgers, he found little difference in their rate of self-reported sexual activity and STI's. He did find that the pledgers were less likely to use birth control and condoms.

Discussion Questions

- Did you learn sex education from school, parents, or other sources? How valid was the information? What gaps were not covered?
- The prevalence of Internet porn may affect one's understanding of sexual facts. For instance, female porn stars rarely have pubic hair. What other misconceptions could somebody develop from using porn as sex education?
- The above section only discusses heterosexual sex. Write your own definition of virginity. Would you include or omit mention of same-sex behaviors in your definition?

Figure 9.1 *Vintage birth control ad (Photo source: Cardcow)*

Historically, many women feared childbirth because it was so dangerous. Figure 9.1 proves that pregnancy concerns were nothing new. Preachers warned women that if they were pregnant, they should prepare for death. The special linens used for childbirth were also used as burial shrouds if needed (Collins, 2003). In one Swedish study of nineteenth-century records, almost half of the women who died in their reproductive years died from giving birth. Because of maternal mortality rates, it was riskier to be a female than a male. The motherless children were also at higher risk of dying (Hogburg & Brostrom, 1985).

For women who were pregnant out of wedlock, the consequences were even worse. In colonial times, a pregnant servant would be severely punished even if she had been raped by her master (Collins, 2003). The term *bastard* originally meant an illegitimate child. Bastards lived life as second-class citizens, shamed for their mothers' disgrace. In a judgmental society, bastards often had trouble finding jobs or getting married. Not until the 1950s did the U.S. courts start recognizing the legal personhood of illegitimate persons. No longer deemed "the son of a nobody," illegitimate persons could now have the right to sue for the wrongful death of their parents and in other matters (Mostofi, 2004, p. 453).

It should not be surprising, then that women have been using birth control for centuries. Indigenous peoples have used special herbs to prevent pregnancy, such as the Hopis using a powder made from the jack-in-the-pulpit flower. Ancient Egyptians invented vaginal sponges to absorb the sperm. Another method was *coitus interruptus* (withdrawal method), which is both unreliable and also dependent on the man's motivation to avoid impregnating his mate. Also, the Jewish religion forbade this practice because it violates God's command to bear fruit and multiply (Tannahill, 1980).

When birth control did not work or was not available in the past, unwed or desperately poor mothers have abandoned their newborn babies. Left on the doorsteps of churches or other places where the child might find a good home, these foundlings were common in some societies. In Charles Dickens' novel *Oliver Twist*, the baby was found in a basket with a locket that later identifies him to be of good family. In the meantime, though, he endured cruel treatment. Unwanted babies were also killed (for instance, being left out on a mountain to die), neglected, and exploited for child slavery.

Birth control, then, has been used for centuries as a way to prevent such tragedies. Abstinence was the most obvious form of birth control, but such lack of intimacy could destroy a marriage. Douching with liquids such as Coca-Cola was another questionable method (Tone, 2001). Casanova, famous for his sexual exploits, is also noted for his promotion of condoms. Although he used animal skins in the pre-rubber era, he praised them for "shelter(ing) the fair sex from all fear" (cited in Tone, 2001, p. 87).

Although people have been using different methods of contraception all through history, this practice has not always been legal in the United States. The Comstock Act of 1873 forbade the possession and sale of obscene materials, including contraceptives. This law did not keep Americans from black market manufacture of diaphragms, cervical caps, and other forms of birth control (Tone, 2001).

In 1914, Margaret Sanger (Figure 9.2) defied the Comstock Act to provide birth control information to women. Although she was not the only activist, she became the most

Figure 9.2 *Margaret Sanger (Undated photo courtesy of Library of Congress)*

prominent one. Her 1938 autobiography (Sanger, 2004) reveals how her social views evolved. She tells of a liberal father who lost business because of his nonreligious status. As a child, she connected the idea of small families with better lives. She watched the small families play in their spacious backyards, while the "tiny yards of the (workers) ... were a-sprawl with children.... To me the distinction between happiness and unhappiness in childhood was one of small families and of large families rather than of wealth and poverty" (Sanger, 2004, p. 28).

Having borne three children herself, Sanger expressed a keen appreciation for motherhood. "To see a baby born is one of the greatest experiences that a human being can have.... As often as I have witnessed the miracle, held the perfect creature with its tiny hands and tiny feet, each time I have felt as though I were entering a cathedral with prayer in my heart" (Sanger, 2004, p. 55).

However, she was also aware of the dark side of unlimited childbearing. Her mother's health had suffered greatly from the multiple pregnancies, and Sanger herself probably would have died if she had not used birth control.

Pregnancy was a chronic condition among the women of this class. Suggestions as to what to do for a girl who was "in trouble" or a married woman who was "caught" passed from mouth to mouth---herb teas, turpentine, steaming, rolling downstairs, inserting slippery elm, knitting needles, shoe-hooks. When they had word of a new remedy they hurried to the drugstore, and if the clerk were inclined to be friendly, he might say, "Oh, that won't help you, here's something that may" (giving them the address of an abortionist) ... They asked everybody and tried anything, but nothing did them any good.... On Saturday nights I have seen groups of from fifty to one hundred with their shawls over their heads waiting outside the office of a five-dollar abortionist.

Each time I would return to this district ... I used to hear that Mrs. Cohen "had been carried to a hospital, but had never come back" or that Mrs. Kelly "had sent the children to the neighbor and had put her head into the gas oven" .... I shuddered with horror as I listened to the details and studied the reasons back of them—destitution linked with excessive childbearing. (Sanger, 2004, pp. 88–89)

One haunting story is of a young mother who needed Sanger's help with an infection caused by a self-induced abortion. She begged the doctor for advice on avoiding further pregnancies, but he just told her to make her husband sleep on the roof. Three months later, she died from complications caused by another self-induced abortion (Sanger, 2004).

Sanger's fight for contraception availability led her to endorse eugenics, the movement that promotes selective breeding of "desirable" groups (e.g., white, well-educated, and upper class). In an article titled "The eugenic value of birth control propaganda," Sanger (1921) first describes how making responsible decisions about parenthood can help on both the individual and social levels. However, she then uses terms such as the "submerged masses" and distinguishes between the "fit" and the "unfit" (Sanger, 1921, p. 2). She openly states "Birth Control propaganda is thus the entering wedge for the Eugenics educator" (Sanger, 1921, p. 2) and that "Possibly drastic and Spartan measures may be forced upon society if it continues complacently to encourage the chance and chaotic breeding that has resulted from our stupidly cruel sentimentalism" (Sanger, 1921, p. 3).

Providing a historical context to defend his grandmother, Sanger (2007) shares his opinion about her support of eugenics. She herself was an Irish Catholic, born into a large family with a father who had trouble supporting them. She married a Jewish man, had a criminal record for her labor activism, and suffered from genetic diseases. Most eugenicists, then, would have placed her in the "unfit" category. She was not well-educated and may not have understood the disturbing implications of this movement. Instead, she came from a promother background whose goal is that "every child should be a wanted one" (Sanger, 2001, p. 211).

Having seen much poverty growing up in upstate New York and working as a nurse in the city slums, she advocated for voluntary motherhood so no child would starve. She did support immigration quotas and other racist laws, but so did most Americans at the time. (Despite her father's progressive views, he opposed immigrants because of the perceived threat to white men's jobs.) The question about Sanger's views on eugenics, then, is complex.

Since Sanger, the development of birth control methods has undergone huge changes. Not until 1960, when "the Pill" was introduced to the public, did birth control enter the modern age of science. Other methods are also available, of course, but the most widely used method is still oral contraceptives.

The politics of birth control have also shifted since the 1960s. In 1960, thirty states limited birth control availability and two states actually banned it. The 1965 Griswold case ensured that all married couples would have access to birth control. Since then, unmarried persons also have better access (Stacey, 2015).

The widespread use of birth control in the United States has had a significant impact on both women and men. To live in a world in which every act of sexual intercourse could result in pregnancy is now unthinkable. One author discusses the effect of the birth-control pill on society, especially women:

> Historians and sages are fond of attributing the improved status of women in the Western world to everything from Christianity and democracy to the printing press. But every modern woman knows in her heart that her real liberation began with the Pill. Flawed as it is, and full of hazard, the Pill is more than a chemical contraceptive. It is a symbol of the new technological, psychological and social power of women over her own biology—and ultimately over her own life. (Kolbenschlag, 1988, p. 165)

Opposition to Birth Control

Historically, people have opposed birth control for many different reasons. According to Joyce, author of *Quiverfull: Inside the Christian Patriarchy Movement*, Teddy Roosevelt was concerned about "race suicide" because white women were having fewer babies than women from other ethnicities (Joyce, 2009b, p. 172). His concern was echoed in a more recent article: "When Godly People Stop Having Children, We Are Wasting the Godly Seed" because Muslims are having several more children per family (cited in Joyce, 2009b, p. 183).

Quiverfull, a conservative Christian movement that was mentioned in the Introduction, also expresses concern about the need for more Christians. Comparing children to arrows in a quiver, one writer states:

> Children are our ammunition in the spiritual realm to whip the enemy! Scripture says that one of God's people can chase one thousand enemies, and two can put ten thousand to flight. These special arrows were handcrafted by the warrior himself and were carefully fashioned to achieve the purpose of annihilating the enemy. (cited in Joyce, 2009b, p. 158)

One context for this movement is the requirement that wives submit to their husbands, especially regarding sexual matters. A wife should never refuse sex nor demand physical satisfaction for herself. One writer recommends that "women ... should see sex as their ministry to their husbands, and as such, one that doesn't require their interest, pleasure, or fulfillment" because only his needs matter (cited in Joyce, 2009, p. 79). Instead, a Godly woman should realize that "My body is not my own" (cited in Joyce, 2009, p 115). Even her voice should be carefully modulated to be soft and calming.

Being a wife is more than being just a helper, though. "It means a servant, single or married. If a girl does not know how to be a servant then she is learning how to be a ruler. It's called witchcraft" (cited in Joyce, 2009b, p. 162). Also part of being a good wife is the rejection of birth control. Women who should not get pregnant for health reasons, besides those who did not want to be mothers, should stay single. A wife taking birth control because her body cannot handle a pregnancy should simply avoid sex because "If you're too sick to have babies, you're too sick to have sex" (cited in Joyce, p. 136). Some Quiverfull leaders even hint that a wife who does not bear enough children is risking her salvation.

Another context for this movement is economic, since many of these women are usually lower middle class. They criticize feminism because it does not seem to represent their interests. Many Quiverfull women do not care about equal pay, since they think that their husbands should earn a family wage instead. The author notes that:

> For poorer women, the feminist fight for job equality won them no career path but the right to pink-collar labor, as a housekeeper, a waitress, a clerk. The sexual revolution brought them not self-exploration and fulfillment, but rather loosened the social restraints that bound men to the household as husbands and fathers. (Joyce, 2009b, p. 156)

Of course, the Quiverfull movement is not the only religious entity that rejects birth control. The ultra-orthodox Jews, for example, ban birth control. A doctor who serves this population remarked, "It's pretty depressing to see women get trapped in the circular tasks of housework and childcare like this. They become very de-selfed" (Joyce, 2009b, p. 188).

These anti-birth-control attitudes became a national controversy in 2014, when the debate over alternative forms of birth control erupted over the Supreme Court case of *Burwell v. Hobby Lobby Stores*. The employer opposed the federal mandate to cover two types of contraceptives, the IUD (intrauterine device) and morning-after pills for emergencies, which prevent fertilization of the egg. The Hobby Lobby owners and others who oppose these two types of contraception believe that they can induce abortions, an allegation disputed by the medical community.

The Hobby Lobby case exemplifies the complex realities of birth control when they overlap with anti-abortion concerns. One writer for the website Reproductive Health Reality Check, Amanda Arcotte, writes that the antichoice movement is really about antisex. She cites as an example the opposition to a new Planned Parenthood clinic in a Minneapolis suburb, a clinic that does not provide abortions. Nonetheless, flyers in the neighborhood state that the clinic provides "'dangerous contraception,' 'promotes and encourages sex without limits,' and is 'destroying families.'" Instead, women should be going to a church-based center that stresses that sex is only acceptable if no birth control is used (Marcotte, 2014).

Another writer describes her experience at a rally to celebrate the Hobby Lobby decision. She quotes a speaker as saying, "Providing contraceptives is not health care, it's tyranny." Another speaker said: "The idea that their capacity to become mothers is a disease that needs to be cured is utterly wrong. That they need medical treatments in the form of birth control pills struck me as both a father and as a pro-life activist as outrageous" (Stanley, 2015). Like the second speaker, many men are also concerned about reproductive health. Box 9.1 discusses why men should also care about reproductive health.

Discussion Questions

The Affordable Care Act ("Obamacare") mandates that insurance companies should cover contraceptives for women. Mike Huckabee, a Republican leader, states that:

> If the Democrats want to insult the women of America by making them believe that they are helpless without Uncle Sugar coming in and providing for them a prescription each month for birth control because they cannot control their libido or their reproductive system without the help of government then so be

---

Box 9.1 Why Men Should Care About Reproductive Rights

Solinger, (2013) presents the argument that men should also be concerned about reproductive rights. "The cultural ideas about masculinity that facilitate many men's distance from reproductive and family matters impose burdens on both men and women, including the costs of eliding and neglecting the status of male reproductive health and dignity" (Solinger, 2013, p. 141).

The first point is that the "rise of male reproductive-related health problems" (e.g., environmental) affect not only men but their partners and children. Also, the fertility industry is commodifying males when "sperm banks select donors using eugenically inflected criteria" such as intelligence and appearance traits (Solingr, 2013, p. 142).

On a social justice level, many men support reproductive rights because they agree with the "core claim that a woman has the right to manage her own body, including the right to decide whether or not and when to be a mother, and the right to access the resources she requires to do this with safety and dignity" (Solinger, 2013, p. 142). Last, it occurs to many men that women bear a heavier burden of contraception than them---so these men are "taking responsibility for their own reproductive health and fertility control" (Solinger, 2013, p. 142).

Discussion Questions

- If you were talking to a man who says he does not bother worrying about birth control because that's the woman's problem, what would you say?
- How would you promote more male involvement in the fight for access to reproductive health services?

---

it! Let us take that discussion all across America because women are far more than the Democrats have played them to be (cited in Johnson, 2014).

Do you agree with him that contraceptive coverage should be the financial responsibility of the women (i.e., lifestyle choice) instead seen as a medical necessity? What research would you use to support your argument?

History of Abortion

Consequences of sex, whether a sexually transmitted infection (e.g., HPV as discussed in Box 9.2) or an unplanned pregnancy, can be controversial. According to Mohr's landmark book on the history of abortion (1978), abortion was legal in the United Staates until 1800. Until then, the law defined a pregnancy in two stages: before and after the quickening, which was "the first perception of fetal movement by the pregnant woman herself" (Mohr, 1978, p. 3). This usually occurred in the fourth or fifth month. A person

---

Box 9.2 The HPV Vaccine Controversy

Since 2006, a controversy has raged around the HPV (human papillomavirus) vaccine that can drastically reduce the rate of cervical cancer in women. Public health experts urged the widespread vaccination of girls as young as eleven, which prompted a strong backlash from conservatives who thought it would encourage girls to have more premarital sex (Knox, 2011). Krishnan (2008) clearly explains the issue:

> Proponents of the vaccine argue practicality over morality. Sure, most parents want their children to practice total abstinence until marriage. However, many parents realize that in a society where nearly 50 percent of girls and boys are sexually active before graduating from high school (CDC), total abstinence may not be a practical doctrine. Therefore, they are in agreement to take precautions to protect young women against possible repercussions of their sexual activity. After all, even if a young woman stays a virgin until marriage, the only way to guarantee that she will not contract HPV is if her spouse was also a virgin, no marital infidelity occurs, and the couple never divorces. In addition, most teens who do practice abstinence do not do so because they fear diseases like HPV. Therefore, a vaccine that eliminates the possibility of HPV will not eliminate their reason for abstaining from sex. (Krishnan, 2008, p. 5)

Discussion Questions

Do you see any connection between this controversy and the stress on virginity, especially for females? As a parent of an adolescent girl, what would your reaction be to this controversy?

---

could be prosecuted for harming an unborn child in the postquickening stage, but the penalty was lighter than for a human being. Before the quickening occurred, nobody could be sure that a female was actually pregnant in the days before modern medicine. Doctors and pharmacies, then, assisted women with "obstructed menses" even if the cause was early pregnancy (Mohr, 1978, p. 6). At least thirty-four different medical remedies were sold in the 1860s, besides mail-order products such as "Sir James Clarke's Female Pills" (King, 1992, p. 34).

Besides drugstore remedies that served as abortifacients, women also had these option to end their pregnancies:

- Bloodletting.
- Bathing.
- Violent exercise.
- Reaching too high.
- Jumping.
- Pulling a tooth without anesthetic.
- Getting hit again and again.
- Deliberately falling, like down the stairs (Mohr, 1978, pp. 7–8).

Until the mid-1800s, midwives also assisted with both childbirth and pregnancy prevention, including abortions. These traditional healthcare providers knew about abortifacients such as pennyroyal tea to induce a miscarriage. They hung special flags in their windows that indicated that they helped women who were "in trouble." Midwives rarely faced prosecution for providing abortions, although their actions were an open secret (Collins, 2003).

In the late nineteenth century, abortion became common not only among the lower-income females but the middle-class wives who felt the need to limit their families. Sometimes the abortions were secrets, whereas other times observers noted that it was an acceptable topic between women. One woman even loaned her special device (a wire with a hook) to a pregnant neighbor. (King, 1992).

Historically, then, the laws in the United States have either allowed or prohibited abortions. An upsurge in abortions from 1840 to 1870 alarmed many because it was becoming so mainstream. "Indeed, abortion became one of the first specialties in American medical history" (Mohr, 1978, p. 47). Women who were white, Protestant, middle-class, and married—not the desperate, poor, and unmarried women one would expect—were the majority of those seeking abortions as a form of birth control. Policymakers who wanted more white, Protestant, and middle-class babies enacted laws to restrict access to abortion (Mohr, 1978).

Another cause of anti-abortion laws was the "Physicians' Crusade" that started in the late nineteenth century (Mohr, 1978, p. 147). Physicians began to oppose abortion on both medical and moral grounds, urging the clergy to join in their efforts (King, 1992). As the medical profession started to take over from the midwives, the laws against abortion became stricter. In 1878, a famous abortionist named Madame Restell faced criminal charges and committed suicide. This was a turning point in America's attitude toward abortion, from minor laws to aggressive prosecutions (Mohr, 1978).

By 1900, every state had outlawed abortions except to save the life of the mother. Whatever the legal consequences, though, women continued to have abortions for decades—around a million a year, according to one 1966 estimate.

> That women were willing to risk illegal abortions speaks to the almost impossible calculus between the risk that procedure posed and the burden of an unplanned pregnancy—be it expulsion from college, another mouth to feed when there already wasn't enough to go around, the public shame of premarital sex in the chill dawn of the sexual revolution, or the fear deep in a woman's bones that either her sanity or health would not endure if she had to bear another child. But many, many women took the risk. (Miller, 2014, p. 41)

In 1973, the U.S. Supreme Court ruled that states could no longer prohibit abortion in the *Roe v. Wade* case. This decision has created a firestorm of both verbal attacks and outright violence. Since this decision, millions of women have obtained abortions but few have made it public because of fear of being stigmatized or even threatened.

Discussion Questions

- Advocates for reproductive justice argue that the term *forced motherhood* should be used regarding women's inability to access contraceptive or abortion services. After reading the preceding sections, do you agree or disagree?
- Another term related to limited (or no) access to these services is *reproductive coercion*. One research study states that

> Moreover, mounting evidence that unintended pregnancy occurs more commonly in abusive relationships highlights that victimized women face compromised decision-making regarding contraceptive use and family planning, including condom use. [This includes] Forced sex, fear of violence if she refuses sex, and difficulties negotiating contraception and condom use ... (Miller, et al, 2010, p. 457)

The Controversy of Abortion

In the medical context, there are three types of abortions. Spontaneous abortions (also known as miscarriages) result in 50 percent of all fertilized eggs dying. Usually this occurs before the female even knows that she is pregnant. The number of known miscarriages is around 15 to 20 percent of pregnancies (www.webmd.com).

Besides spontaneous abortions, there are two types of induced abortions: therapeutic and elective. Therapeutic abortions are considered medically necessary for the health of the mother. An ectopian pregnancy, for instance, is when the fetus is growing outside the womb. When a fetus is severely abnormal (e.g., the brain is outside the skull), these types of abortions are also done. Around 90 percent of therapeutic abortions are done before thirteen weeks. After six months, therapeutic abortions are very rare and only done if the mother's life is in danger. Late-term abortions (called partial birth abortions by critics) account for 1 percent of all abortions. They occur almost always because the pregnancy is doomed, such as the fetus having massive tumors (Solinger, 2013).

The second type of induced abortions is elective—the source of most controversy. According to the Centers for Disease Control (CDC), the demographic breakdown of who has an abortions includes: 81 percent are unmarried; 53 percent are white/Caucasian; 50 percent are under 25 years of age, 54 percent have their first abortion; 25 percent have their second one; and 19 percent have three or more. Most of these women later become mothers. The rate of abortions dropped in the 1990s, which has caused speculation that economic pressures are the primary reason for women to end their pregnancies (www.cdc.gov).

According to the Guttmacher Insitute, the reasons for seeking an elective abortion are complex and overlapping: "concern for or responsibility to other individuals" (75 percent); "they cannot afford a child" (75 percent); "having a baby would interfere with work, school or the ability to care for dependents" (75 percent); and "half say they do not want to be a single parent or are having problems with their husband or partner" (Guttmacher Institute Factsheet, available on www.guttmacher.org).

The two surgical methods to induce an abortion are done on an outpatient basis. The vacuum method uses suction to empty the uterus, and the D and C (dilation and curettage) method scrapes the uterus. Many women must have the D and C surgery for nonpregnancy reasons, such as abnormal periods. Both methods are low risk (American College of Obstetrics and Gynecology website: www.acog.org).

A new method, which has faced great opposition in the United States, is the RU-486 pill. This "abortion pill" is widely used in Europe, where there is less controversy about this topic. A woman must see her doctor three times to ensure that the pill works correctly. The medication causes a "medical abortion" (as opposed to a surgical abortion) that resembles a miscarriage (Solinger, 2013).

Another controversy is the "morning after" pill, which is sometimes confused with the RU-486 pill. This method prevents fertilization of the egg, but is not an abortion pill. It must be used within 48 hours of the possible conception for it to be effective. If the condom slips or a couple has unprotected sex, the woman has 48 hours to take heavy doses of hormones to prevent pregnancy. The hormones prevent the uterine lining from supporting the pregnancy. According to the medical experts, it is "not the same as RU-486, which is an abortion pill. It does not cause a miscarriage or abortion. In other words, it does not stop development of a fetus once the fertilized egg implants in the uterus. So it will not work if you are already pregnant when you take it" (www.webmed.com). However, several pharmacists have refused to fill the prescription for these pills on the basis that they still consider it to be abortion (Solinger, 2013).

In describing the abortion debate, the terms themselves are a point of debate. Those who oppose legal abortion call themselves prolife, but that term may offend those who do not consider themselves to be "prodeath." Being called pro-abortion is also problematic, since many advocates who support legal abortion are not necessarily "for" abortion. Those who support keeping abortion legal call themselves prochoice, but that term seems to trivialize the seriousness of the decision.

Those who oppose legal abortion (elective and sometimes therapeutic) argue that the embryo becomes a human being at the point of conception or the first heartbeat. The prochoice advocates consider the answer to be less definite. They often believe that an embryo/fetus does not become a full human being until later in the pregnancy, perhaps when brain activity starts in the fifth month. Because abortion opponents consider the embryo/fetus a full human being from the very beginning, they equate abortion with murder. The other side would state that abortion is a medically necessary procedure for a woman's health and well-being. Obviously, abortion opponents would oppose any public funding for abortion (e.g, Medicaid), whereas the other side would advocate for assistance to low-income women.

The abortion debate also includes the ethics of new fertilization techniques and the fate of unused embryos. When trying to conceive using the latest techniques, patients and doctors often have multiple embryos (fertilized eggs) that cannot be used. Fertility clinics hold thousands of embryos in refrigerators. If these embryos are considered medical waste, then they would be tossed away. If these embryos are considered to be human beings, then who should be impregnated and give birth to them? If these embryos are to be used in stem cell research, is this an ethical use of something that is potentially human? This ethical dilemma has added to the moral complexities of the abortion debate (Solinger, 2013).

Box 9.3 describes one aspect of this issue, the treatment of pregnant women struggling with drug addiction. Another aspect of the debate is over the clinic protests, which are sometimes related to shootings of abortion providers and bombings of women's clinics. Wilson (2013) explores the legal debate between the free speech of the sidewalk protesters and the right to privacy of the clinic's patients.

> As clinic-front anti-abortion protests grew in frequency, magnitude, and intensity, abortion providers and their supporters sought ways to respond. Their search yielded their own direct action strategies, but it also returned abortion-rights proponents to the state, and in particular, to the judiciary. At times, abortion-rights advocates attempted to use state-based means to win dramatic gains against their adversaries. The National Organization for Women (NOW) tried to use federal anti-racketeering (or RICO) laws, which were created to fight organized crime, to criminalize specific anti-abortion tactics and organizations. More commonly, abortion-rights activists sought to obtain court orders and legislation that governed how anti-abortion protests could occur—for example, establishing specific distances that needed to be maintained between activists and clinic doorways. (Wilson, 2013, p. 2)

Figure 9.3 *Abortion debate*

International Debate

Goldberg (2009) discusses the impact of abortion bans on women on a global basis. In Nicaragua, for instance, the ban is so loosely written that doctors are afraid to perform therapeutic abortions to save a woman's life. Several women have died from miscarriages as a result. "Many Managua gynecologists … spoke of the fear and confusion that had descended onto their practices, and said that they, too, might be forced to withhold help from pregnant women with complications like those of Bojorge (a woman who had died)" (Goldberg, 2009, p. 13). Now women who have had miscarriages are treated as potential criminals who had abortions. El Salvador has similar laws and "'forensic vagina inspectors' (who) treat women's bodies as potential homicide scenes" (Goldberg, 2009, p.14).

According to a more recent article, "More than two dozen women are now in prison in El Salvador, convicted of 'aggravated homicide' because of abortions or miscarriages" (Barron, 2013). One 19-year-old woman went to a hospital for a miscarriage, but was charged with homicide because her abusive boyfriend claimed she had induced an abortion. She is now serving ten years.

Human rights organizations, then, have begun to consider therapeutic abortions as a human right. For instance, the UN Human Rights Committee decided in 2005 that a 17-year-old Peruvian girl who was denied a therapeutic abortion had been denied her rights. The fetus had been missing its forebrain and was doomed to die within a few days after birth (Goldberg, 2009).

Box 9.3   When a Pregnant Woman Uses Drugs

In the late 1980s, the media and politicians spoke about a "crack baby" epidemic caused by pregnant women using crack. "Women, particularly minority women of lower socioeconomic status, who used cocaine while pregnant were perceived as immoral and irresponsible" (Coles, 1993, p. 290). So-called experts claimed that crack babies were more likely to be born early, besides being "born addicted and quivering, to experience a host of neurological, digestive, respiratory, and cardiac problems, and to be headed toward a childhood of learning difficulties, hyperactivity, and ultimately, delinquency and jail" (Ortiz & Briggs, 2003, p. 44). This was related to the idea that a child born in poverty in the United States was somehow damaged at birth, as opposed to the "resilient" orphans adopted from Rumania and other desirable locations (Ortiz & Briggs, 2003).

However, research has shown that the "crack babies" problem did not even exist. According to the American College of Obstetrics and Gynecology, there never was such a thing as a "crack baby" syndrome. "It is now understood that poverty, poor nutrition and inadequate health care can account for many of the effects popularly, but falsely attributed to cocaine" (ACOG Toolkit on State Legislation: Pregnant Women & Prescription Drug Abuse, Dependence and Addiction available on website: www.acog.org).

In 2001, the *Journal of the American Medical Association* printed a commentary that asked, "Why then all the hullabaloo about crack babies? Why then the prosecution of 200 women who used cocaine while pregnant? Why was a program established to pay $200 to crack-using women to become sterilized?" (Chavkin, 2001, p. 1626). Unfortunately, society still demonizes pregnant women who abuse drugs despite the medical evidence that treatment—not punishment—works best for both mother and child (ACOG).

Tennessee, for example, passed a law in 2014 that criminalizes drug use by pregnant women. This has resulted in women avoiding prenatal care or leaving the state for medical care. Two women have already faced charges of assault and gone to jail. Although the intention is to push pregnant women into treatment, advocates believe that this approach could backfire and lead to more drug use. "It's no surprise that people under stress, scrutinized by the state, with the threat of their baby being taken away -- that they would experience stress that could lead them to use again" (Ganeva, 2015).

Discussion Questions

- Do you think that the stigmatization of pregnant women who use drugs is related more to race, class, or gender prejudice? Explain your answer.
- Which social work value best applies to this issue?
- How does intersectionality apply to these women?
- If you were a social worker working with a pregnant client who uses drugs, what would be your ethical concerns? How would you address them?

Elective abortions are also an international issue. They are illegal in most of Africa, with the result that 36,000 African women die each year from unsafe abortions.

> Worldwide, complications from unsafe abortions cause 13% of maternal deaths and account for a fifth of the 'total mortality and disability burden due to pregnancy and childbirth,' according to the WHO. Twenty-four million women have been rendered infertile by dangerous procedures, an especially crushing debility in parts of the world where childless women are reviled. Again, the toll is worst in Africa. (Goldberg, 2009, p. 3)

One author makes this provocative point about the desperation of women around the globe who need reproductive services: "In many countries, illegal abortion is a leading cause of death for women in their childbearing years. Could it not be said that denying women the right to safe abortion is itself a form of murder?" (Hartmann, 2013, p. 474).

Discussion Questions

- Should elective abortions be banned in every country? If one considers abortion to be murder, then that would be the logical goal.
- What would be the consequences if the laws are so restrictive that doctors are afraid to provide therapeutic abortions? Or should elective abortions be legal in every country?
- For the past two decades, the United States has not provided financial assistance to international organizations that provide abortions. Should the United States also provide generous financial assistance to the mothers who could not obtain abortions?

Key Terms

Virginity
Birth control
Quiverfull movement
History of abortion
Three types of abortion
RU-486 pill

10

The Politics of Work and Motherhood

Women in the Workplace

Sexual Harassment

As stated in Chapter 2, women have been working outside the home for centuries. Not until the 1970s, though, did women's work receive serious recognition as a policy issue in the United States. Now issues such as sexual harassment and unequal pay are widely debated.

Women leaving the private sphere to compete in the job marketplace were sometimes seen as trespassers onto male territory. The family wage, which assumed that men were supporting their wives and children, was part of the patriarchal structure. In the prefeminist era, "people were supposed to be organized into heterosexual, male-headed nuclear families.... Of course, countless lives never fit this pattern. Still, it provided the normative picture of a proper family" (Fraser, 1994, p. 591). Society expected women to do the invisible work of housekeeping and childcare with little acknowledgement or pay.

In this context, the sexual harassment of working women could be deemed acceptable since they had walked into a man's world. In the romantic comedy *My Dear Secretary* (1948), a playboy hires a secretary and continually harasses her. This movie is only one example of how society regarded lecherous bosses as a joke. If women wanted to keep their jobs, they just had to put up with it.

The 1964 Civil Rights Act, though, provided legal grounds for women (and men) to fight sexual harassment as awareness grew in the 1970s. Title VII states that employers cannot discriminate against persons based on race, sex, etc. (MacKinnon, 1979). The courts established there were two kinds of sexual harassment:

- Quid pro quo, in which a person must provide a sexual favor for a job, promotion, or other benefit. For instance, a professor demanding that a student sleep with him for an "A" would be providing "something for something."
- Hostile work environment, in which a person endures psychological strain by dealing with constant dirty jokes, pornographic images, and other inappropriate behavior. For instance, a work crew may harass a female employee by not allowing her privacy in the locker room. This type of harassment is harder to determine than the quid pro quo type, since cultural standards may vary (Black & Allen, 2001)

One groundbreaking book on this topic, *Sexual Harassment of Working Women: A Case of Sex Discrimination* (MacKinnon, 1979), clearly states the dilemma faced by women before they obtained more legal support.

In addition to being victims of this practice, working women have been subject to the social failure to recognize sexual harassment as an abuse at all. Tacitly, it has been acceptable and taboo; acceptable for men to do, taboo for women to confront, even to themselves. But the systematic silence enforced by employment sanctions is beginning to be broken. The daily impact on women's economic status and work opportunities, not to mention psychic health and self-esteem, is beginning to be explored, documented, and, increasingly, resisted (MacKinnon, 1979, p. 1).

Figure 10.1 *Unwanted touching (Photo courtesy of OUP)*

Sexual harassment became a major issue in the 1990s with the Anita Hill/Clarence Thomas case. In the 1980s, Anita Hill started working for Clarence Thomas in the Department of Education. Both were highly motivated lawyers with bright futures. When he became head of the Equal Employment Opportunity Commission, she followed him to this agency because it was the most beneficial for her career. She left to become a law professor. Then in 1991, President Bush nominated Thomas for the U.S. Supreme Court. During a background check, the Senate staff found out about her allegations of sexual harassment and subpoenaed her to appear at the Senate nomination hearings.

The impact of these hearings is still being felt. One article (Austin, Solic, Swenson, Jeter-Bennett, & Marino, 2014) discusses how the Supreme Court did not rule that sexual harassment was a form of sexual discrimination until 1986, but most of the public was still unaware of the issue.

> After Anita Hill's case "sexual harassment" became a household term. The lengthy and detailed televised interrogation of Anita Hill by an all- white, all-male Senate Judiciary Committee and their unabashed incredulity regarding her testimony galvanized a groundswell of feminist activism (Austin et al., 2014, p. 65).

Indeed, the hearings electrified the nation as millions watched Hill testify about Thomas' alleged inappropriate behavior. Suddenly, sexual harassment was no longer just a minor legal issue. Did he really make all those sexually explicit remarks to her? If so, why did she continue her professional relationship with him?

The image of a lone woman facing a long row of male senators made many realize that men were still in power and they "just didn't get it." Their blundering remarks included accusations that she was delusional, suffered from erotomania (too many romantic fantasies) or was perhaps demon-possessed. The debate still continues on why Senator Hatch held up a copy of *The Exorcist*, but the implication was that Hill was crazy in some way. The defenders of Thomas even flew in psychiatric experts to attack her credibility (Dean, 2007).

> Cool and unflappable, Hill looked the Senators in the eye and handled every question without hesitation.... (she described) what it means to be victimized by sexual harassment — from the fears, embarrassments and humiliations she experienced to the repercussions it had on her work, health and career choices. (time.com)

In his defense, Thomas claimed that this was a "high-tech lynching of uppity blacks" (Dean, 2007, p. 151). The racial angle troubled many, since both Hill and Thomas are African American. Some worried that the stereotype of the oversexed black male was being reinforced by Hill's testimony, whereas others perceived Hill as betraying one of her own.

The Senate approved Thomas's nomination and he now sits on the Supreme Court. Occasional references to the hearings still occur, such as other witnesses supporting

Hill's testimony and Thomas's wife demanding an apology from Hill. Whatever the outcome, the public became keenly aware of sexual harassment and the debate continues: what exactly is sexual harassment? What should society do about?

Some people may assume that "sexual harassment" means that a pretty woman is receiving passes from a male boss. If she insists on wearing that tight skirt, then she should expect it and maybe even wants the attention. However, the key word in the term is not *sexual* but *harassment*. When a child harasses another child on the playground, the attention is not at all flattering. At best, it is obnoxious and at worst, it is a threat.

Instead of the term *sexual harassment*, one variation could be *gender harassment*. For instance, a female who is trying to work on an ambulance crew may be rejected by her coworkers. One aspect of their hostility is sexually explicit language to make her feel that she is "only" a woman and that she deserves to be punished for taking a "man's job."

Harassment can also occur within the same gender with or without homosexual overtones. Men are at higher risk for same-sex sexual harassment than women, especially if the target is seen as a "wimpy male"—which "evokes a clear image of a very powerless target" (Goldberg & Zhang, 2004, p. 824). Another example would be a religious man who feels uncomfortable around his male coworkers saying sexually explicit things. The men may harass him for violating the social norm that all men should be "players" who want to sleep with any female who catches their eye.

Sexual harassment does not just happen in an office, but in all work settings. In the restaurant industry, for example, one survey shows that 60 percent of women have had to deal with it—almost weekly and mostly by customers (Covert, 2014). One bartender "has had customers grope her, slap her butt, and try to get her phone number. She even had one lick her hand. As someone who has been ... supporting herself and her three-year-old daughter, sexual harassment 'is almost expected,' she said ... . 'I'm not even exaggerating when I say it's an everyday thing'" (Covert, 2014, p. 1).

Tragically, female migrant farm workers of sexual harassment are one of the most vulnerable populations in the U.S. In one survey, 80 percent of these workers in California's Central Valley reported some form of harassment (McMillan, 2012).

> There's a presumed level of desperation for anyone seeking work in the fields—the unspoken rule is that anyone with better options would take them—and as frequently happens when the vulnerable depend wholly on the powerful, episodes of sexual quid pro quo and even rape are not unheard of in the fields. In Monterey Valley ... federal lawyers heard workers refer to *el fil de calzon*, the field of panties, a reference to the rapes that occurred there. (McMillan, 2012, p. 60).

Unequal Pay

In 2015, women are still being paid only 78 percent of what men earn. Over forty years, that means $431,000 less for women. According to several sources, the pay gap is a reality for most women. The Payscale website, for example, notes that the pay gap starts

Box 10.1   The Glass Ceiling

Why were only 5.2 percent of the Fortune 500 CEOs women in 2014? (www.fortune.com) Why are only 17 percent of Congresspersons female in 2015? The glass ceiling, a concept of gender inequality that emerged in the 1990s, is one possible cause. One study (Cotter Hermsen, Ovadia, & Vanneman, 2001) describes how an analysis of the Panel Study of Income Dynamics proves the existence of gender disadvantages at the top percentile.

While interviewing male and female professionals about the glass-ceiling concept, Olcott (2006) met one woman who disclosed that she did not like female supervisors because they were "bitches." Men commented that other men might have such frail egos that a strong woman threatens them, while an older white man said that he was now the target of discrimination. On the other hand, one woman noted that women are more likely to be laid off in a downturn.

> One woman commented that organizations are usually controlled by men, men set the rules, and these rules restrict career advancement for women unless they are willing to align their workforce and social behaviors with the male-dominated values of the organization (Olcott, 2006, pp 16–17).

The glass-ceiling concept, then, is complex and not set in stone. One author (Shambaugh, 2008) expresses her opinion in the book title: *It's Not a Glass Ceiling, It's a Sticky Floor: Free Yourself from the Hidden Behaviors That Sabotage Your Career.* Women do not achieve their highest career goals because they do not have enough self-awareness or vision. Instead, hidden behaviors deter them from success. Self-defeating women do too much multitasking, self-criticism, and helping others. Unless women find a good work-life balance, then, they could be stuck forever on a sticky floor.

Discussion Questions

- Based on your personal impressions, do you think that there are systemic barriers to women achieving the highest level of success in the United States?
- Find a research article that supports or disproves the glass-ceiling concept. Discuss the article's most salient point.

immediately after college: $31,900 for women and $40,800 for men. The gap widens after age 39, when women earn only two-thirds of their male counterparts (www.payscale.com). The Institute for Women's Policy Research compares the pay rates based on job description and still found major discrepancies from CEOs to supervisors to store clerks. A regression analysis reveals that "the poverty rate for working women could be cut in half if women were paid the same as comparable men" (www.iwpr.org). The glass ceiling, as discussed in Box 10.1, is related to this topic.

Why do women make less than men after forty years of feminism? The most obvious response would be that women are more likely to take time off from their careers to care for their children. However, researchers (e.g., Institute for Women's Policy Research) claim that they allowed for this possible factor and still found gaping discrepancies no matter the education level or career path.

Gender-based segregation is another possible cause of the wage gap. Despite the antidiscrimination laws, women are still clustered in certain jobs. The construction industry, for example, has had little increase in the number of female workers in the past forty years (Hegewisch & O'Farrell, 2015).

In the United States, "If you pick the twenty top female occupations—meaning the ones that employ the largest absolute numbers of women—you find that, in seven of them, the workplace is over 90 percent female. Make 80 female your cut-off and it is over half the group" (Wolf, 2013, p. 8).

The author once worked in a "pink collar ghetto" at an office that processed insurance claims. I remember standing up and seeing row after row of cubicles, almost all filled by women. This was a low-paying, dead-end job that held little promise of advancement. Two men worked with us, and one of them obtained an administrative job in a different company. Were the women stuck in the cubicles because of their lack of initiative or for other reasons?

- Gender stratification, the class system that places female workers on the bottom. According to this theory, the good jobs are mostly reserved for the men (Seguino, 2013).
- Physically demanding jobs. Some argue that men in physically demanding jobs such as police work deserve better pay. Certain jobs are just too demanding for women, such as a surgeon who must work long hours. Since women are less fit for more demanding work, they deserve less pay. Those who advocate for this position, though, disregard the difficult physical demands of caring for an elderly patient with dementia or other demanding work done by females.
- Nature. Because of testosterone, men are naturally more competitive than women. Men know how to get promoted, ask for higher pay, and dominate the workplace. The obvious question is how a woman acting as an aggressive male would be regarded in the workplace. Would she get the same rewards?
- Man is still the breadwinner. Men's Rights Activist blogs (e.g., https://malemattersusa.wordpress.com/). include several articles that support this claim.
- Business meetings in strip clubs, and other indications that it is still a "man's world." Before feminists challenged the "men's only" clubs, men could meet and make business deals without women having any equal access. If most networking is done outside the office, then women must fight any social exclusion. For instance, the modern counterpart to a "good old boys" network could be sports-related gatherings.
- Women choosing to work in lower-paying jobs, such as teaching. Taking this possibility into account, the American Association of University Women (AAUW) notes that:

After accounting for college major, occupation, industry, sector, hours worked, etc.… a *5 percent difference in the earnings of male and female college graduates one year after graduation was still unexplained.* (Ten years later is) a *12 percent* unexplained difference in earnings. (American Association of University Women, 2015, p. 8)

Calling unequal pay a women's issue is incorrect, since millions of families depend on the mother's income (AAUW). In 2009, President Obama's first act as president was to sign the Lily Ledbetter Fair Pay Act. She had found out twenty years after working at Goodyear that she had been underpaid. Because the law stated that she had to file a complaint within six months of the first paycheck, she lost her lawsuit. "My case set a new and dangerous precedent. According to the Court, if pay discrimination wasn't challenged within six months, a company could pay a woman less than a man for the rest of the woman's career" (Ledbetter, 2007). Fortunately, Congress passed the Lilly Ledbetter Fair Pay Act to tell the Supreme Court it got it wrong in my case. The Act did not help Ledbetter herself, so she had lost hundreds of thousands of dollars through this injustice.

Women of color are even more affected by the wage gap. According to the AAUW, Latinas make 53 percent of white male salaries and African-American females make 64 percent. Besides racism, one possible cause is the lower educational levels of these women (American Association of American Women, 2014).

Discussion Question

According to liberals, the War on Women includes the Republicans' rejection of equal pay legislation. Research the best argument *against* equal pay legislation and write your response.

Figure 10.2 *Office worker (Photo courtesy of OUP)*

Mothers in the Workplace

Box 10.2 describes what it is like when a woman serves in the military, which can be a challenging workplace for women. Motherhood can also be problematic for women in the workplace.

The Motherhood Manifesto: What America's Moms Want—and What to Do about It is a book written in association with the liberal group Moveon (Blades & Rowe-Finkbeiner, 2006). As this quote shows, balancing motherhood and work is a tough job.

Box 10.2   Women in the Military

In her in-depth book about three women who served in Afghanistan, Thorpe (2014) describes an encounter between a soldier and an Afghan woman.

> After two months in Afghanistan, (they) had begun to appreciate keenly the vast difference between their position in American society and the much more precarious station of the women around them in Afghanistan. Michelle thought it pure chance that she had inherited such largesse; she could easily have been born female into this society instead.... Not long after the election had taken place, Desma crossed paths with an Afghan family on the post. The medics at Camp Phoenix had provided care to their son. The father was pushing his son's wheelchair, and in the traditional fashion, his wife was following five paces behind. The woman was holding a black headscarf across the lower half of her face. She looked at Desma, a female soldier wearing desert camouflage and carrying an assault rifle, and stopped walking. To Desma's shock, the woman knelt down before her. "Thank you," she said in English. "Thank you." (Thorpe, 2014, p. 157)

Unfortunately, these women did not receive the full recognition of their military service when they returned home. Some people did not even know where they had served.

> Otherwise, some of the interactions she had with family members proved jarring. She had been gone for a long time, and they could not fathom where.
> "This is my sister—she just got back from Iraq," her sister Tammy told a friend at one point.
> "Actually, I was in Afghanistan," Michelle said.
> "Where in Afghanistan?" asked her sister's friend.
> "I was in Kabul."
> The friend looked blank-faced.
> "It's the capital," Michelle snapped. "Look it up sometime." (Thorpe, 2014,, p. 239)

Unfortunately, the high rate of sexual assault of female soldiers has emerged as a serious problem. In a 2012 report by the Department of Defense, 26,000 sexual assaults were occurred in 2011—a 35 percent rise. Out of that number, only 3,374 attacks were officially reported. The manual *Sexual Assault in the Military: A Guide for Victims and Families* (Scott & Philpott, 2014) was written in response to this crisis. The reasons for not reporting an assault include: a superior officer had been the assailant; fear of possible consequences for reporting; and distrust of the military courts. One reform has been the introduction of restricted reporting, in which the victim receives medical care but can decide when or if an investigation can begin (Scott & Philpott, 2014).

One rape survivor brought her case to a human rights panel. She told the story of how "a coworker 'physically abused and raped her,' and that her command accused her of lying and labeled her a 'troublemaker.' Not only did her command not punish her rapist, she said; it forced her to work with him" (Gliha, 2014, no page).

Several politicians have expressed deep concern about this issue, including Senator Gillibrand. While proposing legislation to remove the reporting process from the chain of command to legal officers, she said, "Not every single commander necessarily wants women in the force, not every single commander believes what a sexual assault is, not every single commander can distinguish between a slap on the ass and a rape. You have lost the trust of the men and women who rely on you" (Scott & Philpott, 2014, p. 7).

Discussion Questions

- How much do you know about the U.S. military operations in Iraq and Afghanistan? If you were going to work with veterans, how would you research this topic before meeting with them?
- Do you think that female veterans would have specific needs different from male veterans?
- Do you agree with Gillibrand's assertion that not every military superior would support the rights of an assault victim? Why or why not?

> I have to wake up, wake my kid up, deal with a morning tantrum, drop him off at daycare, fight traffic, agonize about whether I am a horrible mother for leaving him at daycare, worry if I'm going to be late to work—and that's just the morning before my workday starts at 8 am. (Blades & Rowe-Finkbeiner, 2006, pp. 4–5)

The authors note that 75 percent of mothers work outside the home and 34 percent are the sole breadwinners. The previous chapters discussed the importance of defining "work" properly, since it involves not just a paying job but also unpaid labor such as child care or caring for an elderly parent. Thus, every mother is a "working mother" if she is caring for her child(ren). For purposes of this section, though, the term *working mother* designates only those working outside the home for a paycheck.

Around three-quarters of American mothers work outside the home. However, the financial costs of working mothers include more than day care. The authors state that the "maternal wall" means that becoming a mother can be woman's worst financial decision (Blades & Rowe-Finkbeiner, 2006, p. 7). The book also notes that:

- Women without children earn 10 percent less than their male counterparts, but mothers earn 27 percent less.
- Women's overall wages are dropping.
- Mothers are 44 percent less likely to be hired than nonmothers with the same credentials.
- Mothers are paid $11,000 less than nonmothers.
- It is legal to pay a single mother less in many states.

Other industrialized countries do not have this "mommy wage gap" because they have better family policies. For instance, the United States does not mandate paid family leave because the Family Medical Leave Act is very limited. The argument for paid family leave is that "Mothers need time to have babies. Giving a mother no choice but to come back to work mere days after the birth of a child or face financial ruin is bad social policy. Society needs to share the cost of bringing new life into the world" (Blades & Rowe-Finkbener, 2006, p. 45).

Related issues for working mothers include mandatory overtime, which means that they have much less time for their children or their own needs. Time poverty, the lack of personal time for all workers, is evident in the United States as they are afraid to say "no" to their bosses. Books such as *Take Back Your Time: Fighting Overwork and Time Poverty in America* (De Graaf, 2003) stress the importance of claiming time for oneself to promote health, families, and social relationships.

Figure 10.3 *Motherhood can be rewarding—but expensive (Photo courtesy of OUP)*

Day care is another pressing issue for many working mothers. In an article titled "We're Arresting Poor Mothers for Our Own Failures, Colvert (2014) discusses the dilemma of mothers who need jobs but cannot afford the high cost of day care. One famous case was Shanesha Taylor, who was arrested for leaving her children in the car while she was being interviewed for a job. She was a homeless mother who was trying to escape from her financial crisis. Another mother arrested for neglect was Debra Harrell. She could not find day care for her nine-year-old, so let her play in the park without supervision but with a cell phone for emergencies. "Whose fault is it that these children were put in these situations to begin with? These weren't mothers doing drugs or other dangerous activities and neglecting their children; they were both mothers trying to hold down jobs to provide for their children while stuck swirling in a Catch-22" (Colvert, 2014). When the TANF law was signed, mothers were promised childcare subsidies to help pay for the expense. However, states have drastically cut subsidies (30 to 40 percent) since 2000.

In contrast to the mothers struggling with finding and paying for acceptable day care, other mothers are working at companies that are supportive of their needs. The Working Mother website praises companies such as Credit Suisse, which allows part-time workers to get company health insurance. Other aspects of this company's mother-friendly policy include assistance in finding quality day care and caring for elderly parents (www.workingmother.com).

Companies that offer maternity leave, an affinity group for new mothers, and flex-time are also factors for working mothers. Government policies in the United States

Figure 10.4 *Money worries (Photo courtesy of OUP)*

sometimes fail to address the needs of working mothers (and all working parents) Some private companies, though, are going in a hopeful direction by investing in their workers with children.

Feminization of Poverty

With smaller paychecks and less political power, women have been more vulnerable than men to fall into poverty. Some poor women are married to men who are unable or unwilling to assist with the family, whereas other poor women are unmarried. Both mothers and nonmothers have been at risk of poverty, but obviously mothers carry a bigger burden.

Mimi Abramovitz, author of the classic work *Regulating the Lives of Women: Social Welfare Policy from Colonial Times to the Present* (1988), presents the feminist argument that poor women have been punished for not following social norms.

> Social welfare policy's preoccupation with the nuclear family unit featuring a male breadwinner and an economically dependent female homemaker, reveals the presence of a strong "family ethic"—one that has had a profound influence over the relationship between women and the welfare state. Despite the continued presence of many types of families, social welfare programs have consistently favored the conventional family model that uncritically freezes women and men into rigid gender roles....
>
> Using the family ethic to re-examine the welfare state has uncovered those assumptions about women's proper roles that are buried in social welfare policies and has revealed how compliance with the family ethic became the basis fro distinguishing between deserving and undeserving women.....Why, for example, are widows with young children considered to be among those "deserving" of aid, while other single mothers are treated harshly? (Abramovitz, 1988, pp. 2–3)

By stressing the point that patriarchy and capitalism exploit women, Abramovitz criticizes the welfare system for punishing women. For instance, the reproductive functions of white middle-class women are honored. Women of color who are poor and/or immigrants, though, are valued more for their wage labor instead of their childbearing abilities. The patriarchy tries to reinforce the family ethic by stigmatizing the single mothers and wives whose husbands were not supporting them.

The Social Security system for wage earners, for example, presumes that a worker will work full-time for decades. The system did not consider the effect of sex discrimination and taking time for mothers. Women of color did have more steady employment, but their low wages and working in excluded jobs (maids, teachers, and nurses) meant that they received too little or even nothing from the system. One-earner (male-headed) families are rewarded more than the two-earner families—thus penalizing the working wife.

Unemployment insurance also has inequities that affect poor women. Again, certain women's jobs were excluded from this program. The unemployment offices required that women had to be available for a new job no matter the hours or childcare availability.

Abramovitz's book also includes a critique of welfare, now called TANF (Temporary Assistance to Needy Families.) Although she wrote the book before the 1996 "welfare reform" law, several aspects of the law apply:

- The bill's name is the Personal Responsibility and Work Opportunity Act, which indicates that poor women deserve blame for their plight. Helping women to train for jobs and/or obtain jobs is the new focus. When the economy was booming in 1996, work opportunities were more numerous than in today's recession.
- The bill replaces AFDC (Aid to Families to Dependent Children) with TANF—with the key word of *Temporary*. The federal limit for receiving benefits is 60 months total (five years), but states can impose limits as low as two or three years.
- The bill stresses marriage as a solution to poverty, although most low-income persons marry within the same class. Marriage promotion by state agencies include stricter divorce laws and even marriage incentives.
- Poor women are valued as workers but not as mothers. Even if day care is not available, mothers still have to work outside the home to receive benefits. When the benefits expire, the women are trapped in low-paying jobs with few if any benefits. Restaurants and stores, for instance, have work shifts on nights and weekends when day care centers are closed.

When TANF became law, President Clinton claimed that it "was the end of welfare as we knew it" (www.washingtonpost.com) However, this law did not mean the end of poverty. According to a recent report (Chang & Mason, 2010), the numbers are grim. "In 2009, 4 out of 10 African-American and Latino households headed by single women lived in poverty.... It is estimated that housing and childcare expenses alone account for over three-quarters of the monthly expenditures of single women mothers, leaving very little, if any, money for emergencies or for savings" (Chang & Mason, 2010).

The 2014 Shriver Report on Women in America, which was cosponsored by the Center for American Progress, supports the assertion that women are struggling with poverty. Shriver writes in the introduction, "These are not women trying to 'have it all....' These are women who are already doing it all — working hard, providing, parenting, and caregiving. They're doing it all, yet they and their families can't prosper, and that's weighing the U.S. economy down" (Alter, 2014). For example, almost two-thirds of minimum-wage earners are women who receive no sick days or other benefits.

The economic structure of work is a major factor in the feminization of poverty. Duggan (2012) uses the term the "de-skilling of retail jobs" to describe the trend of companies to break down jobs into smaller units and to hire cheaper workers. The author writes of the corporations who underpay workers as parasitic, since they force them to rely on government benefits such as food stamps for survival.

Discussion Questions

- Research Abramovitz's claim that the structure of Social Security discriminates against women. If this is true, how would you advocate for a policy change?
- Do you think that welfare leavers (those who no longer receive TANF benefits) should still receive some benefits if they are working low-paying jobs? Write an argument for and against.
- Look up the Shriver Report on www.shriverreport.org. Pick three salient points and write a letter to a politician about them.

Older Women in Poverty

Since most older women have spent fewer years than men in the paid workforce, their Social Security benefits are often inadequate. Another factor affecting the amount of Social Security benefits is the lower salaries received by women—especially before feminists challenged job discrimination. Richardson (1999) describes how family obligations (e.g., marriage and caregiving) have affected women's earnings for decades. Since unpaid work does not "count" as paid work in the Social Security system, older women receive fewer benefits.

The Institute for Women's Policy Research reports that as a result of smaller Social Security benefits and private pensions, older women are more likely to be poor than their male counterparts. The retirement system stresses marriage to a male breadwinner as the best way to avoid poverty in old age. Being single, widowed, or divorced, then, carries a higher risk of poverty. "Nearly 20% of unmarried women 65 and older live below the poverty line, compared with 5% of married elderly women. Without Social Security benefits, more than two-thirds of unmarried elderly women would live in poverty" ("Six Key Facts on Women and Social Security" Fact Sheet available on www.iwpr.org).

Stressing women's higher rate of dependence on Social Security, the Older Women's League's website makes these policy suggestions: "1. Creating an improved minimum benefit; 2. Credit for years spent care-giving; 3. Equal benefits for married same-sex couples, and 4. Improving the current COLA (Cost of Living Adjustment)." (www.owl-national.org).

Discussion Questions

- Review the website for the Older Women's League or the Institute for Women's Policy Research. Find a policy suggestion to fight poverty among older women that inspires you, then write a letter to a Congressperson for an advocacy exercise.
- How is the above section related to the invisibility of women's work concept?

Women in Politics

In the era of Hillary Clinton and other women taken seriously as political candidates, it is appropriate to honor the pioneering women who made this possible. Jeannette Rankin, the first female Congressperson who started serving in 1917. She fought hard for women's suffrage and against U.S entry into World War I (http://history.house.gov/People/Listing/R/RANKIN,-Jeannette-%28R000055%29/) "I want to stand by my country, but I cannot vote for war" (Ojibwa, 2011). Like Jane Addams, she was a peace activist who faced harsh criticism for her principled stance.

Another politician who deserves special mention is Bella Abzug, who served as both activist and politician for fifty years. The title of an oral history, *Bella: How One Tough Broad from the Bronx Fought Jim Crow and Joe McCarthy, Pissed Off Jimmy Carter, Battled for the Rights of Women and Workers, Rallied Against War and for the planet, and Shook Up Politics along the Way* (Braun Levine & Thom, 2007) indicates the feisty character that she was. She wanted to go to Harvard Law School, but was rejected because she was a woman and attended Columbia instead. As a female lawyer in the 1940s, she was a rarity who shocked others with her forthrightness.

> When I went to court, especially when I was pregnant in 1948 and 1949 and again in 1951 and 1953, lawyers would make remarks about "menstruating lawyers." Judges would not know where to look. Even my own clients were afraid I might lose their case. (Braun Levine & Thom, 2007, p. 55)

After working for years as a civil rights lawyer, she entered Congress in 1970. Besides trying to end U.S. involvement in Vietnam, she was the first Congressperson to propose a gay rights bill in 1975. Later, she became involved in international issues and established the Women's Environmental Development Organization.

In discussing her peace activism in the 1960s, Abzug noted:

> Well before anyone thought up the gender gap, we used my slogan, "The woman's vote is a peace vote." Women were trained to speak softly … and carry a lipstick. Now we demanded a bigger stick. We want to be everywhere, at every table, not just the kitchen table. Because women were outside, because they had nothing to do with making policy and did not get trained to solve problems violently, I always thought they could make a big difference in peace. Not every woman is for peace. Golda Meir took us to war, and Indira Gandhi and Margaret Thatcher. But these women did not come out of the women's culture and women's agenda. They happened to be women who came out of male power structures. (Braun Levine & Thom, 2007, p. 71)

Gender politics, then, still affect women who run for office today. An analysis of Clinton's 2008 run for the White House (Lawrence & Rose, 2010) provides insights about public perceptions of women leaders—as evident even in the polling questions.

> Overall, the public opinion data reveal a striking and significant dilemma: People in the United States report favorably that they would vote for a woman, *if she were qualified* for the job. What do these responses mean? The very fact that pollsters have phrased the question in this way for decades reveals a presumption that most women are not qualified. Clearly, more is at stake in the mind of the pollster and the voter than the basic constitutional requirements of the job. (Lawrence & Rose, 2010, p. 33)

Clinton faced two double binds (i.e., "damned if you do and damned if you don't") in her race. First was the Femininity versus Toughness dilemma (Lawrence & Rose, 2010, p. 37). The authors note that "despite her demonstrable toughness.... many detractors mocked Clinton when she occasionally showed emotion on the campaign trail" (Lawrence & Rose, 2010, p. 37). However, others "were just as likely to brand her a 'castrator' or 'ball-buster,' revealing the deeply ingrained sense that any woman who holds power emasculates men" (Lawrence & Rose, 2010, p. 38). Clinton had to act assertively to be a viable candidate, but that meant violating the gender norm for females being quiet and modest.

The second double bind was the split between equality feminism (which stresses that women are the same as men) and difference feminism.

> In an electoral context, gender strategies based in difference feminism claim that unique feminine attributes bring added value to the candidate's capacity to govern. Difference strategies seek to turn gender from a liability into an asset in winning office by claiming and deploying positively framed sex stereotypes, such as women's allegedly greater honesty and compassion. These claims often operate in tandem with claims of outsider status, such as some suffrage arguments that claimed women could clean up government, just as they cleaned up their homes and communities.... Alternatively, however, a female candidate who embraces equality feminism and asserts her equitable qualifications for the job potentially sacrifices her very womanhood by establishing her ability to fill a masculinized role. (Lawrence & Rose, 2010, pp. 39–40)

Besides presidential politics, Congress is another venue for women leaders. Congresswoman C. B. Maloney, author of *Rumors of Our Progress Have Been Greatly Exaggerated: Why Women's Lives Aren't Getting Any Easier—and How We Can Make Real Progress for Ourselves and Our Daughters* (Maloney, 2008), stresses policy issues for women. Some highlights include: the Paycheck Fairness Act, equality for fathers in the workplace, equal business opportunities for women (only 3 percent of Small Business Administration loans go to women), protection of Social Security benefits for older women, and ending sex tourism. She also writes of how encouraged she is by the younger generation of women who will continue the battle.

Political dialogues about women should also include the topic of racism. Patricia Hill Collins (2005) challenges the idea that there is such a thing as "new racism."

> What's new about the new racism? First, new patterns of corporate organization have made for an increasingly global economy. In particular, the concentration of capital in a few corporations has enabled them to shape many aspects of the global economy. One outcome is that, on a global scale, wealth and poverty continue to be racialized, with people of African descent disproportionately poor. Second, local, regional, and national governmental bodies no longer yield the degree of power that they once did in shaping racial policies. The new racism is transnational. One can now have racial inequality that does not appear to be regulated by the state to the same degree. For example,

the legal support given racial segregation in the United States has been abandoned yet African Americans remain disproportionately at the bottom of the social hierarchy. Third, the new racism relies more heavily on the manipulation of ideas within mass media. These new techniques present hegemonic ideologies that claim that racism is over. They work to obscure the racism that does exist, and they undercut antiracist protest. Globalization, transnationalism, and the growth of hegemonic ideologies within mass media provide the context for a new racism that has catalyzed changes within African, Black American, and African-Diasporic societies. From one society to the next, Black youth are at risk, and in many places, they have become identified as problems to their nations, to their local environments, to Black communities, to themselves. (Collins, 2005, p. 54)

The full picture of racism intersecting with sexism, then, is global and complex. Classism is also critical to include in political dialogues about women. In her critique of neoliberal feminists, Jaffe (2014) writes that focusing on individual salaries neglects the bigger picture. "Neoliberal feminism is a feminism that ignores class as a determining issue in women's lives" (Jaffe, 2014,). For instance, the equal-pay-for-equal-work movement is beneficial to the middle and upper classes. Women trapped in low-paying jobs, though, would benefit little from the proposed policy change.

Politically active women, then, should ally themselves with those working in low-status jobs such as housekeeping. As one labor organizer notes, "the fight for fair pay might seem an individual struggle for high-end workers ... but for (the others), the best way to improve your job isn't to get promoted through the ranks, but to organize with your fellow workers" (Jaffe, 2014). The cause is not about a single paycheck, but the millions of working poor who deserve fair pay.

Not all women involved in politics, of course, are liberal and/or feminist. Sarah Palin and Liz Cheney are famous conservative women. One rising star is Nikki Haley, governor of South Carolina, who strongly supports tax cuts and immigration reform. As a Sikh Indian who converted to Christianity, she sometimes encounters racist remarks. She proudly claims her heritage: "The fact that I happen to be an Indian female, of course that brings a new dynamic. But what I hope it does is cause a conversation in this state where we no longer live by layers, but we live by philosophies" (cited on www.biography.com/people/nikki-haley-20939217). For anyone who wants to be a political advocate, Box 10.2 provides valuable advice.

Discussion Questions

- This section included both moderate reformers (e.g., Mahoney) and advocates for radical change (e.g., Collins). Would you define yourself as moderate, radical, or apathetic?
- Find three sources on Clinton and three on Haley that are unbiased. For instance, the Huffington Post website is left-wing and the Red State blog is right-wing. How difficult was it to find nonpartisan information on these two women?

Box 10.3 How to Advocate

Senator Kirsten Gillibrand (New York) has been an inspirational leader for many. In her book *Off the Sidelines: Raise Your Voice, Change the World* (2014), she offers this advice on advocacy.

Please believe me: Your story matters. Keep telling it until it falls on the right ears. Once, a veteran who lost a limb in Vietnam told me, "When I strap on my leg, I strap on my patriotism. Why isn't the VA supporting me?" Those two sentences moved my office to work until we got him $60,000 in benefits and back pay. This story also opened my eyes to the backlog of veterans' claims caused by the chronic underfunding of the Veterans Administration.

I also hear stories from mayors, church leaders, activists, philanthropists, and community leaders about all kinds of suffering we must address. "Our food bank sees more families and more children than ever before, but less food is coming in, because of the tough economy. Could you help?" Or, "My church runs an after-school program for at-risk youth, and we're running out of funding. Can you get us federal money to stay open?" When people raise their voices, they give leaders opportunities to truly help and serve (Gillibrand, 2014, p. 60).

Discussion Question

- Self-advocacy can be the first step to learning how to advocate. Discuss an example of self-advocacy that you have done.
- Based on Gillibrand's advice, write a letter or prepare a script to share a story for advocacy purposes.

Social Workers in Politics

Representative Ronald Dellums spoke these words during his first term in Congress: "I am not going to back away from being called a radical. If being an advocate of peace, justice, and humanity toward all human beings is radical, then I'm glad to be called a radical" (website history.house.gov/People/detail/12109). He epitomizes the social worker as activist. An African American who was born during the Depression, he had a keen awareness of how poverty and racism were connected. He worked as a psychiatric social worker in northern California during the early 1960s before becoming a community organizer. During his twenty-eight years in Congress, he was unafraid to hold hearings on war crimes committed by U.S. soldiers in Vietnam and to fight apartheid in South Africa.

Another social worker who turned to political action is Barbara Mikulski, a Democratic senator from Maryland. She started her career helping at-risk children and seniors. Like Dellums, she turned to community work when she fought a highway that would have destroyed a neighborhood. Her political focus is on social services such as maintaining the Older Americans Act. On her website she states: "I will always stand up and fight to end discrimination of any kind, anywhere in the United States of America. We must say no to hate crimes, racial profiling, racial redlining and racial sidelining. And we must say yes to equal work for equal pay and equal access to opportunity and protection under the law." (www.mikulski.senate.gov/)

Key Terms

Feminization of poverty
TANF
Glass ceiling
Sexual harassment
Unequal pay
Gender-based segregation
Gender stratification
Women in the military
Mothers in the workplace
Daycare
Bella Abzug
Hillary Clinton
Nikki Haley

11

From Teens to Crones: A Lifespan Perspective of Women

Introductory Note: This chapter is a unique interpretation of the human-behavior-in-the-social-environment emphasis in social work education. It discusses women in four stages: adolescence, higher education, nurturing, and old age. This lifespan-view chapter has a different structure than the rest of the book because it does not focus on any specific issue or group. Instead, the chapter illuminates topics that are common for most women.

Adolescence

Introduction

How should a young woman break up with her boyfriend using a text? *Elle Magazine* offers these suggestions:

- "We have to break up. I slept with your brother."
- "We're done, but if you let me keep your vintage The Kinks T-shirt, we can totally have sex one more time."
- "We have to break up, I turned a witch down for a loan and she turned me into a parakeet." (Breslaw, 2015)

Texting, of course, can be hazardous if a message is sent to the wrong person. One woman admits that "I wanted to give my boyfriend a sneak peek of this new lingerie I'd bought, so I snapped a pretty racy picture with it on—and sent the photo to my mom.... To say I wanted to d ie was an understatement!" (Kramer, 2015).

Contrast this behavior with the ones recommended by writers in the nineteenth century. In the Victorian era, society taught girls to keep pure not just regarding sexual behavior but all behaviors. In *Good Girls Make Good Wives: Guidance for Girls in Victorian Fiction*, Rowbotham (1989) examines the moral lessons that girls read in novels.

First, a girl must be nurturing. Being maternal and caring prepared her for being the perfect mother later in life. Although many females at the time became invalids for no known reasons (was it the tight corsets?), novelists called this behavior unfeminine. In one novel, a "poor-spirited" girl is told by her robust sister, "I do think you would be much better if you would make up your mind to try, and would resolve to go through a little discomfort and fatigue for the sake of strengthening your muscles, and getting out of your invalid ways" (Rowbotham, 1989, p. 36).

Another important goal is to become an Angel of the House: self-sacrificing, sweet-tempered, and committed to family duty. "If girls only understood what angels they might be to men," they would realize how great it was to stay at home (Rowbotham, 1989, p. 52). Besides keeping house, these angels had the burden of being the religious influence in the home. One writer advised, "Say to yourself, dear girls—'With God's help I will be a good angel to this man, who has to meet trials and temptations from which I am exempt. So far as in me lies I will make him respect all women and help, not hinder him in his work'" (Rowbotham, 1989, p. 89).

Education was important for these young women, but not too much education. It was improper to excel or outshine anybody else, as it was enough to be a good conversationalist. Too much introspection led to "selfish apathy" (Rowbotham, 1989, p. 30).

Marriage was central in these stories, but romantic love mattered less than the man's respectful behavior and good morals. Girls who flirted were called heartless and deceitful and often ended up as spinsters.

Discussion Questions
- Using magazines such as *Cosmopolitan* and *Seventeen*, review the advice for girls and young women that is both explicit (e.g., articles on how to get a man) and implicit (e.g., hidden messages in ads).
- Write a set of rules based on your analysis of these magazines. Is there any mention of moral character, education, or the other issues from Victorian novels? What are the new rules for girls and young women today?

The Protective Umbrella

One Victorian idea that was beneficial to young girls was the "protective umbrella" of mentors and other supports to to guide the girls (Brumberg, 1997, p. 197). As discussed in Chapter 6, modern females often regard their bodies as projects to work on.

The beauty standard can start affecting girls at an early age, encouraging even children to diet. In her analysis of diaries of girls in both the nineteenth century and 1980s, Brumberg (1997) discovers the different foci in their lives. For instance, mirrors were rare in the 1800s. Society stressed spiritual matters over physical appearance. Although girls wanted to look pretty with a new ribbon, they were not driven to think about their appearance very much.

Like the Angel of the House ideal, these girls wanted to perform good works. One 1892 diary entry reads: "Resolved, not to talk about myself or feelings. To think before speaking. To work seriously. To be self restrained in conversation and actions. Not to let my thoughts wander. To be dignified. Interest myself more in others" (Brumberg, 1997, p. xxi). In contrast, a girl in 1982 wrote these resolutions: "I will try to make myself better in any way I possibly can with the help of my budget and baby-sitting money. I will lose weight, get new lenses, already got new haircut, good makeup, new clothes and accessories" (Brumberg, 1997, p. xxi). Her physical appearance, then, left no room to consider personal growth.

Brumberg recommends reintroducing the Victorian "protective umbrella" of mentors to help modern girls navigate today's society (Brumberg, 1997, p. 197). They are starting their menstrual cycles years before their emotional maturation. An eleven-year-old girl, for example, may develop breasts but still be a child. Older women can guide them on dealing with society's reaction to their bodies.

One research study would support the need for some type of protection for these girls. According to Hlavka (2014), young women normalize sexual violence so much that they do not report it. The interviews reveal the wide range of behaviors tolerated by the girls who believe that it is acceptable to be treated like that. One 13-year-old girl believed that since it also happened to other girls, it seemed normal. " 'They grab you, touch your butt and try to … touch you in the front … I never think it's a big thing because they do it to everyone' " (Hlavka, 2014, p. 340). A 14-year-old shares how a man would sit on the bus next to her and slide his hand under her buttocks. When she shoved him away, he threatened to rape her. " 'And then, I know he's just joking, but that can be a little weird to hear…. I know he's joking, (but) why would he say that?' " (Hlavaka, 2014, p. 341).

Discussion Questions

- Imagine that you could look in the mirror only once a week or so. How different would your life be? Would you be happier or sadder if you could not make sure that your hair was combed right or your outfit looked fine? How much time do you spend in front a mirror on an average day?
- Do you agree with Brumberg's assertion that young girls need a protective umbrella? Why or why not?
- Did anybody mentor you during your adolescence? What did you learn from that experience?
- Design an intervention program for the girls quoted in Hlavka's article about thinking that sexual violence is not a "big thing."

Bullying

One form of bullying is slut bashing. In the book *Slut: Growing Up Female with a Bad Reputation,* Tanenbaum (2000) discusses the impact of this insult on her own life and on the lives of other girls. "In Kentucky in 1998, two high school students were denied membership in the National Honor Society because they were pregnant—even though boys who engaged in premarital sex faced no such exclusion." (Tannenbaum, 2000, p. 4). Besides the schools and other official institutions that have denigrated females for being sexually active (regardless of whether or not they actually were), harassment based on the words slut, tramp, ho, and so forth is common in both high schools and colleges.

Tanenbaum writes that when she did her research by soliciting letters from girls who had experienced slut bashing, she did not realize how many of them were harassed for reasons other than sexual activity. Many times virgins are picked on because of their body type (e.g., a large bust) or for not fitting into the crowd because of race/ethnicity. Sadly, many raped girls are later called sluts.

> "She asked for it;" The raped girl—I never expected to find so many "sluts" who had been raped or attempted-raped. In fact, when I first thought about why certain girls might be singled out as "sluts," the issue of sexual coercion did not occur to me, nor did I ask a single interviewee if she had been assaulted or raped. And yet over and over again my interviewees volunteered that they had been raped.... The "slut" reputation protects rapists because it makes the victims believe that they are partly to blame. Julie, for instance, did not press charges against her rapists. "I knew no one would believe me ..." She did confide in a few of the girls at school, but as expected, they thought she was making the rape up. "They felt, 'Oh, she's just saying it because she has a bad reputation'" (Tanenbaum, 2000, p. 9).

One key point is that many girls are slut bashing other girls. Many times, the girls had initiated the harassment or were crueler than the boys. One girl who had been called "slut" and even physically attacked by male students reacted by thinking that "she had no right to be sexual. Janice began to hunch her shoulders and wear a coat whenever possible" (Tanenbaum, 2000, p. 11). To this day, she has never felt comfortable with her own body.

Although bullying such as slut bashing has been going on for decades, technology has resulted in the new social problem of cyberbullying. Englander (2013), director of the Massachusetts Aggression Reduction Center, stresses that regular bullying and cyberbullying are connected. However, even the best policies cannot stop this behavior. Youths need to change their behavior on an individual level.

Public awareness, of course, has been one strategy for reducing the amount of cyberbullying among young people. One website, www.makeadifferenceforkids.org, shares stories of suicide victims who could not stand the harassment anymore. The father of Rachel Nesbitt, for example did not fully understand the impact of the threatening emails that she was receiving. He writes, "We found out she was being cyber stalked. I was like the old-school dad and told her not to worry. In my day, we were eye to eye and this stuff didn't last. She said, 'You don't understand, it's different.' She was right."

Figure 11.1 *Adolescent girl (Photo courtesy of OUP)*

At her funeral, he said that she had "a fear so deep and so real she felt her only way was to end her life."

Relational violence is another form of bullying. When girls use exclusion, insults, and other methods to dismiss an "out" girl, the results can be devastating. In *Queen Bees and Wannabes: Helping Your Daughter Survive Cliques, Gossip, Boyfriends, and the New Realities of Girl World* (2009), Wiseman discusses the group dynamics of preteen and adolescent girls. The mother of an excluded daughter frets that she did not want to see her child put up with such humiliation. Another mother says asks, "What do you do when your daughter is the Queen Bee? My daughter talks so badly about other people that she's starting to lose all her friends. I'm having a hard time liking her myself" (Wiseman, 2009, p. 1).

Power plays can occur either in person or via texting. When insults are used as a weapon, the target may answer back. Responses may be: "You can't take a joke. You're so uptight"; "You're so emotional and oversensitive. Are you PMSing?"; and "I'm sarcastic---you know that's the way I am" (Wiseman, 2009, p 234). Even 10-year-olds are developing cliques and using technology to tear down a classmate or destroy a friendship.

Discussion Questions

- Have you ever been the victim of slut bashing or other forms of bullying? How did you respond?

From Teens to Crones

- If you were the counselor for a girl who is being slut bashed at her high school, what would be an appropriate intervention?
- If you were the school counselor where cyberbullying was taking place, what actions would you take?
- Bullying, of course, does not only occur among young people—it is a wider social problem. What macrolevel intervention would be effective in reducing this culture of diminishing others?

Dating Violence

According to the CDC, one in ten teens had been attacked by a boyfriend/girlfriend within the last twelve months—and one in ten also reported sexual coercion (www. cdc.gov/Features/DatingViolence/index.html). The psychologist Dr. Jill Murray, author of *But I Love Him: Protecting Your Teen Daughter from Controlling, Abusive Dating Relationships* (2000) also asserts that teen dating violence is a serious problem. She writes that peer approval is so important for young women that they have trouble seeing that no boyfriend is better than dating a jerk. Less experienced than an older woman, they are less likely to see the warning signs. They are usually unaware of the resources available for abuse victims, especially since they may not consider their boyfriends' behaviors to be abusive.

Recommending that parents regard their daughters not as victims but as active participants, she also stresses that parents cannot control their daughters' decisions on whom to date. Instead, parents should teach them that "love is a behavior" because "It is not possible for love and fear to coexist. It is not possible for love and immense sadness to coexist. When a partner displays loving behavior, his mate feels joyous, carefree, energized" (Murray, 2000, p. 17).

The story of Heather illustrates how a teen girl could get involved with an abuser. He started criticizing her clothes: "He told me I looked ridiculous in my clothes. He said I looked like a mall rat and should distinguish myself from all the pathetic girls at school if I wanted to hang out with him" (Murray, 2000, p. 19). He even picked out new clothes for her, besides hair dye to make her look more "goth." She started listening to new music based on his guidance. When she started talking about how they were thinking of dying together by taking an overdose of ecstasy, the parents had to intervene by sending her out of state. Later she realized that although her boyfriend had never hit her, he had been an abuser.

Another abusive situation that did not involve physical violence appears in the following story.

He didn't hit me. But I always thought he would, if I made him mad. The stuff he did was mind-twisting. Sometimes I thought it would be better if he hit me. I'd think, "If he gave me a black eye, I'd know what was wrong." But I was so confused. He'd search my purse and go through my things, finding things so he could accuse me of seeing someone or doing something wrong. If I brought up a subject to talk about or if I disagreed with him when we were with friends, he'd ridicule me publicly. I walked on eggshells. I never talked about anything important with him and other people.

He constantly told me I looked ugly, heavy, like an old lady. He made me cut my hair short, though I loved it long. He watched what I ate, and put me on a workout program. No matter how much or how well I did he criticized me for doing badly. I was always too fat or too weak. For example, when I did forty-seven pushups, and couldn't get to fifty, he'd make me start over, and tell me I was too weak.

Then, every time, after he got mad, he'd turn around and get me gifts and say, "I love you." I'd say, "He wouldn't hurt me; he loves me. I must be crazy." (Levy, 1997, p. 7)

Fortunately, these types of traumas do not have to cause permanent damage. As discussed in Box 11.1, adolescents have shown resilience and strength as a healthy response to traumas.

Discussion Question

- What adolescent traits would make a teen more vulnerable to dating violence than an adult would be?
- Look up the Dating Matters Initiative on the www.cdc.gov website. Would you consider this to be an effective intervention? Why or why not?

Box 11.1 Resiliency in Adolescents

Although adolescent girls face many difficulties, they also have possible strengths to build on. Zimmerman (2013) defines Resiliency Theory as: "focus(ing) attention on positive contextual, social, and individual variables that interfere with or disrupt developmental trajectories from risk to problem behaviors, mental distress, and poor health outcomes" (Zimmerman, 2013, p. 381). Adolescents may experience risk factors such as poverty and peer pressure, but they also have promotive (sometimes called protective) factors such as families and mentors. Fostering a sense of self-efficacy means that a person feels that her efforts do pay off. Cultural identity and self-esteem are also promotive factors.

Kim and Esquivel (2011) apply Resiliency Theory to spirituality for adolescents. Buddhism and other spiritual traditions could encourage young people to find meaning in their lives. By connecting to the community—especially with elders, young people can find healthy strategies for coping with setbacks.

Discussion Questions

1. Design an intervention program to promote resiliency in at-risk adolescent females, such as those arrested for minor offenses.
2. Do you think that applying the Resiliency Theory to helping adolescent should be gender-specific or for mixed genders? Explain your reasoning.

Women and Higher Education

A Brief History

Now that over half of college graduates are women, it is hard to remember a time when a female attending college was not only rare but condemned. In *College Girls: Bluestockings, Sex Kittens, and Coeds, Then and Now,* Peril (2006) writes about the initial resistance of higher education for females. Too much studying could destroy a woman's ability to reproduce, since energy would be drained away to the brain. The word *bluestocking* denoted an overly intellectual woman who read too many books and was not mother material—in other words, a woman too smart for her own good.

For centuries in the United States, most colleges did not admit women. The highest education a girl could attain to was in a lady's academy, which sometimes included vigorous curriculum. One prototype of a woman's college was Troy Female Seminary in 1821, which included strict monitoring of the students. Waking up at 6:30 every morning for a regimen of study and exercise, the girls received demerits for even having wrinkles on their beds. Most of the graduates became teachers, a common experience for females in academia.

Newspapers mocked the idea of higher education for females, suggesting such degrees as: "Mistress of Petticoat Literature," "Mistress of Pudding Making," an honorary degree of "Mother of a Well Regulated Family" (Peril, 2006, p. 27). These corresponded with the common concept that girls went to college only for an MRS degree, since marriage had to be the only possible goal of these students.

Figure 11.2 *Class of 1905, Western College for Women (Photo courtesy of Library of Congress)*

Besides female-only colleges such as Vassar, some colleges began to offer coeducational options. The Black colleges that emerged in the mid-1800s were open to women because the new educational system could not afford separate schools for women. The author also notes that

> ... while white women were still largely bound by ideals of True Womanhood that made homebound domesticity a woman's highest achievement, the black community recognized that marriage and work were not incompatible, and that its married women often needed to earn a living. Higher education not only increased a black woman's income-earning potential, it helped her "uplift" the race, a widespread concern at the time. (Peril, 2006,, p. 41)

White colleges, though, resisted the idea of coeducation because of the dangers it posed to the females. At the University of Wisconsin in the 1860s, for instance, identical

Figure 11.3 *Ideal female student (Undated photo courtesy of Library of Congress)*

classes were offered to men and women in separate classrooms. Stanford University began to have so many female students that the founder's widow decided to limit their number to 500 a year to make sure that it did not become a woman's college. Mrs. Stanford did comment favorably, though, on how "the refining influences of girls is wonderful" (Peril, 2006, p. 46).

Rules, of course, have always been an unavoidable part of college life. The term "in loco parentis" means that colleges were acting in place of the parents, so the students were still regarded as too young to behave themselves. Strict curfews and housemothers tried to keep the girls from getting into trouble. Even weekend visits to out of town places were under scrutiny. Sometimes the girls self-reported on themselves, such as the 44 students who confessed to smoking in their dormitory rooms in 1930 and faced a ban on dating for six months.

Midnight feasts, often composed of boxes of goodies from home, were a common feature among college girls. Another popular form of socializing was the sorority system, in which girls had to pay initiation fees and look pretty enough to belong to these exclusive groups. Sororities still have rules for members, as indicated by one email from Alpha Chi Omega at University of Southern California in 2015: members must wear Spanx (body shapers), groom their eyebrows, and touch up their hair. The make-up requirements are as follows:

> You need to have foundation, concealer, something pinky neutral for lips (stain, gloss, etc.), BLOT POWDER/OIL BLOTTERS, eyeliner (BLACK or BROWN only), mascara.... If you are not wearing the required makeup, I will stop you and apply it myself. I don't care if you're late for class. (email text accessed through www.wtsp.com/story/news/2015/01/16).

Discussion Questions
- In your opinion, are female college students taken as seriously as male students? Explain how you arrived at this opinion.
- Would knowing the history of women in college (and the stories of most women who were not allowed to attend college) motivate adolescent girls to appreciate their future educational opportunities? Why or why not?

Safety Threats on College Campuses

College can be an exciting phase in a woman's life. Unfortunately, safety threats for young women do not end if they attend college. In both the mainstream media and academic literature, much attention has been focused on sexual assaults on college campuses. Sexual harassment is also a safety threat to both genders in this setting. Both safety threats, of course, occur in the wider societal context of sexism and other forms of oppression.

In the early days of awareness of sexual harassment on campuses, one study breaks down this problem on campuses into two categories: gender harassment (e.g., offensive remarks) and unwanted sexual attention (Shepela & Levesque, 1998). In a recent survey, Hill and Silva (2010) disclose that 89 percent of students reported harassment on their campus and 21 percent said it happened often. The researchers defined sexual harassment to include homophobic names, flashing, and mooning. Both men and women were being harassed, with women reporting more physical types of harassment. Most of the behaviors were done by other students. One male reported getting pornographic images sent to his email account, and a female reported: "People who lived in the same hall as me in the dorms started spreading rumors about my sex life, which were not even close to true. They also spread condoms around my room" (Hill & Silva, 2010, p. 155). This harassment made the victims feel "upset and embarrassed;" "threatened" and "afraid of being raped"; and "self-conscious, pissed off, and concerned, in that order" (Hill & Silva, 2010, p. 159). It also affected the victims' concentration on their work and even made some reluctant to go to class.

One interesting angle is found in the article title "The sexual harassment of uppity women" (Berdahl, 2007). In one study, she tests whether the "desirable" (i.e., feminine woman who arouses sexual interest) is more likely to be harassed than the "deviant" (i.e., masculine woman who defies gender roles). After surveying 175 persons in management courses, she concludes that the masculine women were more likely to be harassed. She rules out the "whiner hypothesis" that these women are more likely to be more sensitive to harassment than the feminine women in another study (Berdahl, 2007, p. 430).

Sexual harassment, then, can be related to gender roles. It can also intersect with racism, as discussed in a meta-analysis of research on racial climate and sexual harassment on campuses, by Lundy-Wagner and Winkle-Wagner (2013). The authors note that although many researchers regard sexual harassment as normal and even to be expected, they still deem racist incidents as unacceptable. Sexual harassment cases are often handled on an individual case and racist incidents on an institutional level, which means that the interventions against racism are more successful.

The other safety threat, sexual assault, has been a controversial topic because of the light (or nonexistent) punishments of the alleged perpetrators. The website of the American Association of University Women (AAUW) includes a toolkit for ending sexual assault (www.aauw.org).

The introductory paragraph reads, "Our campuses are in crisis. The chance of a woman being sexually assaulted during college is about the same as her chance of catching the flu during an average year — except she can't just take Nyquil and rest in bed for a few days. Sexual assault has lasting effects on students." Suggestions include: using social media, fighting back against victim-blaming, and ensuring that one's school complies with the VAWA law called Campus Save Act.

The toolkit also recommends holding a bystander intervention program to encourage persons to step in when they see a possible situation. This is related to using theater to fight sexual assault on campus, which one qualitative study concludes is effective. One male student said later that he would feel more confident in stepping in to prevent a possible assault: I think a lot of the time you know your friends, but if it's someone not so familiar being able to I think it would feel a lot more comfortable to me … you've seen it [in the play] and that actual physical action of stepping in might really help at a party (Christensen, 2014, p. 1465).

Box 11.2 Too Scared to Learn

In her study of the impact of violence on female students in adult literacy and job training, Horsman (2000) stresses the long-term effects. Many adult women are so traumatized that they have trouble concentrating on their work. The victims of childhood trauma, for instance, may experience flashbacks because they are back in the classroom setting again. Those who are in an abusive relationship may face extra beatings because they are attending these classes.

The author, though, rejects the deficit model and urges educators to focus on the students' strengths. She notes that many literacy workers who were themselves victimized found recovery through books. The benefits of reading, then, are not just practical but transcendent.

Discussion Question

What interventions would you suggest for adult learners who experienced (or are still experiencing) violence?

Female college students are not the only ones dealing with safety threats. Box 11.2 describes how adult learners in literacy and job training classes face barriers to their education.

Discussion Questions

1. Write a code of ethics for high school or college students regarding sexual harassment. For instance, "I will not use derogatory language."
2. Is there a sexual harassment policy at your school? Have you heard about or experienced this problem yourself?
3. Review the quote from the student who says that he would be more likely to step in to stop a possible sexual assault at a college party if he did not know the perpetrator. How would you address an intervention strategy for this situation?

Women in STEM

One controversy regarding women in education is the relatively low numbers of women in certain professions, especially STEM (science/technology/engineering/mathematics). The United States is facing a shortage of STEM professionals; the AAUW (American Association of University Women) estimates a gap of 1.7 million professionals in the next ten years. However, only 12 percent of engineers are women. The percentage of females in the computer and mathematics field actually dropped from 35 percent to 26 percent since 1990 (Hill, 2015).

Why are there so few women in STEM when their talents are so needed? Many women choose a STEM major and work in the field, but leave out of frustration. According to Janet Bandows Koster, executive director of the Association for Women in Science, the reason why women leave the STEM fields is because "It's death by a thousand cuts. Every day you're faced with some comment, some snide remark, some inability to get a name on a research paper. And with an accumulation of those experiences, women tend to walk with their feet" (Cooper-White, 2014a, no page).

The business world, even *Fortune Magazine,* has started to take notice about this sexist culture. In one article, a woman who was leaving the field is quoted as saying, "Literally 28 of the 30 people in our company were white, straight men under 35. I was the only woman. I was one of only two gay people. I was the only person of color other than one guy from Japan. My coworkers called me Halle Berry" (Snyder, 2014).

Sexist assumptions begin affecting females in the classroom. One student posted on Whisper, "My chem teacher said I was good enough in his subject that I could have been a boy. When I told him I was interested in a career in it he laughed at me and said, "Girls don't make good scientists, too emotional." Educational researchers have found that high school science teachers will consider males to be naturally gifted, whereas females are hard workers. Teachers spent almost 40 percent more time interacting with the male students (Shumow & Schmidt, 2014).

As a result, it can be lonely being a female STEM student. Cooper-White (2014b) writes that in graduate school, "I work with primarily male engineers and my classrooms are almost all male. Last week during lecture, I looked up in a class of fifty and realized there were only two other women in the room" (Cooper-White, 2014b).

Sadly, the barriers to women in the STEM field include the diminishment of their work. In *The Madame Curie Complex: The Hidden History of Women in Science,* Des Jardins (2010) relates the stories of women who did not receive the credit or appreciation for their work. The Madame Curie Complex, she notes, is based on the focus of that one female scientist while ignoring all the others. One example is Lillian Gilbraith, who worked with her husband Frank for years on industrial efficiency research. After his death, though, she had trouble making a living for herself and her brood. The scientific establishment did not take her seriously as a researcher without her husband. She developed a reputation for knowing what female customers wanted, which she transformed into a lucrative career. In 1932, she was hired for a project on which no males could claim expertise: the design and marketing of sanitary products.

> Men with business degrees were stymied about how to amass consumer data on a product that, until years before, women had privately made themselves. Kimberly Clark had tried to market Kotex pads, the first commercial feminine hygiene product, but no marketing team had mastered the art of selling them women, who were too embarrassed to offer product feedback. Because Lillian and her research team were female, she got candid responses from consumers. They wanted greater comfort, protection, and inconspicuousness in a product they could discreetly obtain and throw away. Back in Montclair she created her own research lab, flushing, submerging, and pulling apart products already on the market and observing women's reactions to the size and shape of the boxes they came in. Lillian seized on the rare fact that a corporate bottom line relied on a thorough study of women's bodies; her report to Johnson & Johnson included exhaustive data on women's cycles and their attitudes about menstruation (Des Jardin, 2010, p. 79).

Figure 11.4 *Students performing atmospheric pressure experiments (Undated photo courtesy of Library of Congress)*

Discussion Questions
- After reading this section, make a recommendation to increase the rate of female graduates with STEM degrees.
- If you were a female STEM professional facing overt sexism, how would you fight it when you would have so few female colleagues?

Feminism and Higher Education

Since the 1970s, feminists have confronted the male-dominated system of higher education. Men determined the research questions, ran the research projects, and controlled the research funding. Also, women were barely visible in the curricula. Feminist theory, then, challenges traditional pedagogy by stressing the importance of lived experience and critiquing the idea of "impartial" research conducted by those unaware of their own biases (Culley, 1984).

In the 1980s, academic feminists still tried to bridge the gap between "hard" intellectualism and "soft" feelings. Applying Simone de Beauvoir to their situation, they noted, "The feminist in the classroom is indeed in a position of permanent imbalance and endless debate.... As mothers, we are expected to nurture; as professionals, we are required to compete" (Culley Diamond, Edwards, Lennox, & Portuges 1984, p. 13).

The struggle of feminists for full recognition in academia continued in the 1990s (Davies, Lubelska, & Quinn, 1994). Noting that patriarchy was maintaining its hold on higher education, the authors questioned whether feminists should let themselves be marginalized (i.e., speak out despite the risk of being called radical) or joining the "malestream" (Davies, Lubelska, & Quinn, 1994, p. 8). Women hesitated to support each other, fearful of becoming further marginalized if they were not seen as individuals. Disrespect in the classroom was another problem, as described by one professor: "Male students are difficult to deal with, they have the power of their maleness. Although it may not be in my mind it's in theirs and it makes it difficult to be assertive. Boys are skilled at manipulating women, they've done it all their lives" (Bagilhole, 1994, p. 19).

Recent articles also reveal continuing problems for women in academia—especially for women of color. Because mainstream curricula rarely mention black women, academia can be an isolated place for them. Besides their racial/class/gender identities, the women must also integrate an academic identity into their lives. One scholar expresses it this way: "Essentially, I was taught that as a black female in America, I have no existence, and that which is, is not worthy of being taught.... Though I am unsure of my next challenge, I am confident that I will succeed—even though my skin is brown and I do not wear a tie" (Clark, 2006, p. 21–22).

Another woman experienced culture shock in the United States because she was educated in Japanese schools, where she internalized a different perspective on knowledge (Murata, 2006). She defines herself as a "connected knower" because in her culture "knowledge is more valued when it is expressed through people's own experiences, and I am a large part of what I know. I am also a woman, and my life experiences ... directed me toward the connected orientation for knowing with emphasis on empathy and feelings" (Murata, 2006, p. 27).

A medical student in Britain also expresses frustration. Not only is she a woman, but she is of Greek descent and has to listen to barbed comments about Greeks. She continues to fight for respect in this setting. "In battles, I was addressed as 'girl' by some surgeons, described as 'controlling' by men when I was calm and rational; I was told that as a social scientist I should understand that most things were a matter of perception and I should not get upset ..." (Tsouroufli, 2012, p. 474).

Discussion Question

What direction do you think that feminism should take in higher education for this decade?

Women as Nurturers

Can Women Have It All?

Traditionalists usually believe that women are nurturing by nature, which has both stimulated and stymied the recognition of motherhood and other unpaid labor. Chapter 9 discussed how mothers in the workplace experience discrimination and low pay because employers may not support their dual roles as mothers and workers. If a society determines that a woman's role as nurturer is more important than her career goals, then the question emerges: can women "have it all?"

In *Wonder Women: Sex, Power, and the Quest for Perfection*, Spar (2013) writes of how she had considered feminism to be irrelevant in her life. With both a successful career and two children, she thought she could have it all without any problems. However, she began to realize that undercurrents of sexism were affecting women in this society.

> (Women) were acknowledging that even if they "had it all," they still had lives that were fundamentally different from and more difficult than men's. They were still, almost always, in the minority. They were still dodging comments and innuendos that took them aback. They were juggling playdates and dental appointments and flute recitals, all of which were somehow absent from the to-do lists of their male partners. And they were still worrying about how they looked.
>
> These were the issues that feminism sought to slay. By fighting to give women equal access to higher education and workplace opportunities, the feminist movement tried to push women over the barricades that separated them from power and privilege....
>
> Indeed, the transformation was so profound that many girls of my generation—girls who were born and raised in the immediate aftermath of the tumultuous 1960s—simply presumed that it was over and won. We thought, often without thinking, that we could just glide into the new era of equality, with babies, board seats, and husbands in tow. We were wrong. (Spar, 2013, p. 7)

In contrast to Spar's perspective, Wolf (2013) argues that most women in the United States value their families over their careers. Except for the minority of women who made it into the elite world of CEOs, women in general are still in traditional roles. No sisterhood unites the highly educated and well-paid women with the women in the pink-collar ghetto. "But adult female employment today isn't a common shared experience in the way that tending home and family used to be. On the contrary, it sorts and separates" (Wolf, 2013, p. 6).

Discussion Question

Do you agree with Spar's assertion that the modern working woman still needs feminism, or do you think that Wolf's point that women are prioritizing family over career? Are you basing your opinion on personal experience or any research?

Caregiving

Besides being mothers, many women face the challenges of caregiving. Both motherhood and caregiving consist of acts of love, but are also emotionally and physically demanding. A "young old" (60–74) daughter may be a caregiver for a parent, or a wife may be caring for her husband during a health crisis. Although women have received the most attention as parental caregivers (e.g., Smith, 2007), a new recognition of male caregivers has emerged. According to the Pew Center, 45 percent of parental caregivers are now men (Greene, 2012).

Figure 11.5 *Mother and daughter (Photo courtesy of OUP)*

As the baby boomers (i.e., the 79 million persons born between 1946–1964) advance toward their senior years, many have become caregivers to their parents and other family members. The "young old" (65–74) are taking care of their "old old" (75 and older) parents. These adult children have their own health problems and financial stressors, so caregivers have many unmet needs. For example, one finding from the National Study of Caregiving is that caregivers for people with dementia face special stresses. "In 2012, over 15 million unpaid caregivers … provided care for people with dementia at an estimated $216 billion" (Moon & Dilworth-Anderson, 2015, p. 300). These caregivers report a higher rate of hypertension and/or arthritis than the other caregivers. The additional stress of caring for a parent with dementia fell especially on women, who had other family responsibilities and their own jobs. "The demands of these multiple roles might cause (the caregivers) … to experience worse general health as compared with other counterparts" (Moon & Dilworth-Anderson, 2015, p. 305).

Parenthood and caregiving, then, have created the dilemma of the sandwich generation. This term applies to the middle-aged parents who are also caring for their parents either despite the costs—including financial burdens. The Pew Research Center reports that almost half of adults aged 40 or older have elderly parents, with 21 percent providing financial support. Emotional and practical support, of course, are also essential elements of caregiving provided by the sandwich generation (Pew Research Center, 2013b).

Elderly parents are not the only ones who require caregiving. Deinstitutionalization for persons with severe mental illness or developmental disabilities has resulted in a caregiving burden for their parents, many who are aging. Research shows that mothers of schizophrenic adults experience more caregiving burden and less social support than the mothers of developmentally disabled adults. The challenge is to prepare the consumers for the transition when the elderly parents are no longer able to care for them (Lefley & Hatfield, 1999).

Caring for one's spouse is another challenge for many older persons. In one Brazilian study (Neri et al., 2012), the researchers conclude that elderly caregivers had difficulties with the physical demands of the tasks. These caregivers were more likely to be stressed and depressed when there was not enough outside support. Another study discusses the gap between the complex demands of caring for a heart-failure patient and the inadequate training for the caregivers (Holden, Schubert, & Michelson, 2015).

Discussion Questions

- What kind of interventions do you suggest to help caregivers stay healthy despite the heavy demands put on them?
- Do you think that the *sandwich generation* term also applies to men? Why or why not?
- The author asserts that male caregivers are receiving more attention from researchers and the media. Verify this assertion. Do you think that this section should have devoted more attention to female caregivers specifically? How does male caregiving fit into the gender norm of women being more nurturing?

Women and Self-Sacrifice—When Is It Too Much?

Can a person give too much of herself to a client or loved ones? For some persons, self-sacrifice can become a negative trait. The book title *Pathological Altruism* (Oakley, Knafo, Madhavan, & Wilson, 2012), a volume of articles by psychologists and other researchers, can be perplexing at first. How can a socially desirable trait such as altruism be considered harmful to self or others?

> *Pathological altruism* might be thought of as any behavior or personal tendency in which either the stated aim or the implied motivation is to promote the welfare of another or others. But instead of the overall beneficial outcomes, the "altruism" has irrational and substantial negative consequences to the other or even to the self (Oakley, Knafo, & McGrath, 2012, p. 3).

Examples of pathological altruism include an animal hoarder (i.e., a pet owner who has so many animals that they are extremely neglected) and an enabler (e.g., the spouse of a drug addict who sacrifices her health and happiness). One extreme example would be a suicide bomber sacrificing himself for a cause. However, simply being a nice person who cannot say no to others can lead to difficulties. This condition is related to survivor's guilt (e.g., "Why am I doing so well when others are suffering?"). Compassion fatigue,

Figure 11.6 *Mother Mary, ideal of self-sacrifice (Photo courtesy of Library of Congress)*

otherwise known as "burnout" in the social work profession, is another related concept (Oakley, Knafo, & McGrath, 2012).

Since women dominate the social work and nursing fields, a gender-based discussion of self-sacrifice would be appropriate. In *Slaying the Mermaid: Women and the Culture of Sacrifice*, Golden (1998) relates the original story of *The Little Mermaid* by Hans Christian Andersen.

> In order to acquire human legs so she can go on land and make the prince fall in love with her, the mermaid obtains from a sea witch a magic potion. Drinking it, the witch warns her, will make her feel "as if a sword were going through your body." And once she does have legs, "every time your foot touches the ground it will feel as though you were walking on knives so sharp that your blood must flow." Andersen dwells on the pain and bleeding of the mermaid's

feet as she dances for the prince and climbs mountains with him: "But she suffered it gladly," he assures us.

The mermaid's sacrifice, however, is more than an expression of her devotion to the prince; it is also a quest for transcendence (Golden, 1998, pp. 16–17).

This archetype of a self-sacrificing woman may resonate with those who have been socialized to ignore their own needs to help others. The author shares the story of her experience as a volunteer at a homeless shelter founded by Catholic sisters. Another volunteer persuaded the sisters to become vegetarian and then later to live in the shelter instead of in their nice homes. This man even told one of the sisters to give up her social work classes because that would make her apart from the low-income clients.

Discussion Questions: Case Study

This anecdote illustrates the effects of too much self-sacrifice.

Because our culture places so much value on sacrifice and suffering, people who feel aggrieved ... are likely to cling to their victimhood as a badge of merit and become enraptured with their own suffering. Anger and resentment do generate a surge of energy that provides an illusion of power and strength, but ultimately these emotions are counterproductive.

Amy, a community activist, habitually did much of the "grunt work" that nobody else in her community group would take on. Sitting before her computer one day, putting together a summary of the group's bylaws, she grew resentful, even though she had volunteered for the task. With the resentment came a surge of adrenaline, and it occurred to Amy that what looked like sacrifice or selfless service on her part might actually be a form of addiction to that adrenaline rush. To experience the rush, she needed something to provoke her resentment, which was why she took on these tedious tasks. As a consequence, her activism was tainted and her energy wasted.... (Golden, 1998, pp. 20–21).

- If you were Amy, what actions would you take to remedy the situation? What types of self-care do you already practice (e.g., meditating or watching comedies)?
- If you were Amy's coworker, how would you handle this situation if you became concerned about her distress?
- Social work supervisors must be alert to possible cases of burnout and overwork. What would be a good strategy for ensuring the health of your staff?
- As Amy's client, how would you react to her if she were acting resentful? Even if she did not say anything about her mood, how would you be able to detect it?

Older Women

Introduction

In her book *The Measure of My Days: One Woman's Enduring, Vivid Celebration of Life and Aging*, Florida Scott-Maxwell (1968) shares her thought about her old age:

We who are old know that age is more than a disability. It is an intense and varied experience, almost beyond our capacity at times, but something to be carried high. If it is a long defeat it is also a victory, meaningful for the initiates of time, if not for those who come less far. (Scott-Maxwell, 1968, p. 5)

She ponders the losses in her life, including the hobbies no longer enjoyed. Her writing, though, stimulates her to laugh at her past self with all the self-righteousness. Later, she discusses the impact of aging on her worldview:

Age puzzles me. I thought it was a quiet time. My seventies were interesting and fairly serene, but my eighties are passionate. I grow more intense as I age. To my own surprise, I burst out with hot conviction. Only a few years ago, I enjoyed my tranquility; now I am so disturbed by the outer world and by human quality in general that I want to put things right, as though I still owed a debt to life. I must calm down. I am far too frail to indulge in moral fervor (Scott-Maxwell, 1968, p. 13–14).

Writers such as Scott-Maxwell remind us to regard older women beyond the stereotypes of a warm-hearted nana or the bitter recluse. Old age can be just as complicated and energizing as any other life stage. Anybody who advocates for the rights of this

Figure 11.7 *Joy (Photo courtesy of OUP)*

population should be aware of social attitudes, since these assumptions do affect policy. Does society deem older women as unworthy of its attention? Or is society finally appreciating these women's multiple gifts?

Ageism

Coined in 1969, the term *ageism* refers to negative attitudes toward aging people but could also mean prejudice against younger persons. A sexist/ageist society may regard older women as losing their prime asset—their sexual attractiveness (Palmore, 2001).

In Simon de Beauvoir's discussion of old age in *The Coming of Age* (1996, first published in 1972), she delves into the classical literature that declared that old people were non-productive and lacked strength. She contradicts both assertions, especially regarding the other types of strength besides physical. Then she quotes the fifteenth-century poet Villon who mourns the death of beauty in an older woman. "Drooping, mossy ears, dead, pale, colourless face, puckered chin and leather lips—this is the last end of human beauty" (de Beauvoir, 1996, p. 147).

Another traditional form of ageism addressed by de Beauvoir is the expectation that old people should be serene.

> Why should an old person be better than the adult or child he was? It is quite hard enough to remain a human being when everything—health, memory, possessions, standing, and authority—have been taken from you. The old person's struggle to do so has pitiable or ludicrous sides to it, and his fads, his meanness, and his deceitful ways may irritate one or make one smile; but in reality is a very moving struggle. It is the refusal to sink below the human level, a refusal to become the insect, the inert object to which the adult world wishes to reduce the aged. There is something heroic in desiring to preserve a minimum of dignity in the midst of such total deprivation....
>
> On the intellectual plane, old age may also bring liberation; it sets one from false notions. The clarity of mind that comes with it is accompanied by a bitter disillusionment.... all at once a man discovers that he is no longer going anywhere, that his path leads him only to the grave. He has climbed to a peak, and from a peak there can be a fall. "Life is a long preparation for something that never happens," said Yeats.... Freedom and clarity of mind are not of much use if no goal beckons us anymore: but they are of great value if one is still full of projects. The greatest good fortune, even greater than health, for the old person is to have his world still inhabited by projects: then, busy and useful he escapes from both boredom and decay....(De Beauvoir, 1996, p. 491)

Ageism, then, affects women because they live in a youth culture. Invisibility is one extreme form of marginalization because somebody is not even recognized as a full person. One woman discussed how some older women liked to hide under a cloak of invisibility. "But I don't like that because I think it's not just about invisibility in terms of a sex object, I think you can be invisible about everything and I don't want to be invisible. I do want to have power and I do want to act and I do want to matter"(Halliwell & Dittmar, 2003, p. 681).

Besides invisibility, ageism presents a double-bind dilemma for aging women. "The oppressed old woman is required to be cheerful. But if you're smiling all the time, you acquiesce to being invisible and docile, participating in your own 'erasure.' If you're not cheerful, then you are accused of being bitter, mean, crabby, complaining! A real Catch-22" (Healey, 1986, p. 61).

Looking at the bigger picture, Copper (1986) notes that ageism is a political issue because it robs women of power by pitting them against each other. "The ageism that old women experience is firmly embedded in sexism—an extension of the male power to define, control values, erase, disempower, and divide. Woman-to-woman ageism is an aspect of the horizontal conflict that usurps the energies of the colonized—part of the female competition for the crumbs of social power" (Copper, 1986, p. 47). Until women fight ageism as a united front, they will fail to achieve full equality.

One way to fight ageism is to fight the stereotypes. The media is a powerful force that molds social attitudes, so it must stop ignoring or minimizing older women. One writer notes, "We need fiction that counteracts ageism. We want stories that present older women as individuals, not as stereotypes. We would like to avoid stale, popular notions and read about spirited, capable, resilient aging females" (Horn, 1986, p. 64).

Discussion Questions

- Find one example of ageism and discuss its impact not just on an older person, but also on those afraid to grow old. What would be a positive response?
- Pick the most striking point from de Beauvoir's essay and write a paragraph in response.
- Betty White achieved popularity as an older actress in the recent past. Look up a "Golden Girls" episode on the YouTube website and write a short response paper after watching it. Do you think this show was anti-ageist? Can you think of more examples in the media that portray older women in a positive light?
- Healey's point about the Catch-22 dilemma for older women (conforming to the role versus acting like oneself) may also apply to other stereotyped groups. Can you think of another group that faces the same dilemma?

Physical Appearance

Both men and women can be ageist and disrespectful to older persons, as indicated in this quote by an older woman who was a jobseeker.

> I was so depressed by the hostility of the young women who took over the magazine, by those other young women not even looking at me when I went in for interviews. I felt like a non-person. As if they didn't want to wait on me at the pantyhose counter at Bloomingdale's because I had some disease repelling them that they didn't want to catch from me: my age. (Friedan, 1993, pp. 229–230)

The concern about looking older, then, is not simply a matter of vanity but related to age-related discrimination. Charla Krupp, author of *How Not to Look Old*, stated in an interview, "My whole focus is about the workplace. It's not about getting a man, or holding on to your relationship. Of course, it spills over. But my focus is for the Boomer woman who is finding herself looking older than everybody else at work, and realizing that she's very vulnerable" (Sachs, 2008). This book became popular during the 2008 recession, during which millions of older Americans were unemployed and sometimes unemployable because of discrimination.

One cause of this appearance-based discrimination is the grandmother stereotype. Although regarded warmly, grandmother types are often seen as incompetent. The first part of one article title "Doddering but dear," expresses this assumption (Cuddy & Fiske, 2004). The researchers note, "The grandmother most closely mirrors the global elderly stereotype as nurturing but ineffectual, resulting in feelings of pity. She is high on communal qualities, but absent from her description are competence-related traits, such as independence, intelligence, and confidence" (Cuddy & Fiske, 2004, p. 13). Because of this kind of stereotype, potential employers are more likely to rate younger applicants higher even if the qualifications are identical.

Should older women dye their grey hair to look younger in response to this pressure? Facing both sexism and ageism in the workplace, some women feel that they have no choice. Others, though, reject this concession to any employers who prefer younger, prettier staff. One woman stated, "I'm stubborn that way. It's costing me I know but I don't believe in catering to that. I don't believe the color of your hair should be an influence on how people treat you (McMullin & Berger, 2006, p. 218).

A British study (Ward & Howe, 2011) confirms that grey hair triggers discrimination for older women. The article title, " 'If I Look Old, I Will Be Treated Old': Hair and Later-life Image Dilemmas," articulates the symbolic importance of aging bodies as the focus of those who marginalize these women.

"And then there was my face. Oh God, my face. The lines, the wrinkles, the sags and bags. Every few months it got worse. Makeup only accentuated it, and unlike my body, I could not cover it up. Your face simply cannot be hidden" (Domitrovich, 1986, p. 131). The beauty industry, of course, is quite aware of these sentiments of many aging women. An article on the Professional Beauty Association website offers this marketing advice to its beauticians and stylists: "women in their 40's and older are, for the first time, likely facing some signs of aging that they have never faced before: fine lines, crow's feet, age spots, grey hair and the dreaded expression lines between their brows and around their mouth and nose" (Beyer, n.d.).

Viewing wrinkles as repulsive instead of attractive is ironic, since they represent a long life instead of illness. In *What Are Old People For? How Elders Will Save the World* (Thomas, 2004), the author/doctor states bluntly: "The surest method of wrinkle prevention is death at a young age" (Thomas, 2004, p. 6). He adds that "The cosmetics and medical industries are happy to fuel an arms race that perpetuates our fear of wrinkles. They view (and want you to view) those little lines at the corners of your eyes as advance scouts from the evil empire of age" (Thomas, 2004, p. 7). Instead, we should regard older persons as an irreplaceable treasure. "An African proverb says: "The death of (an) old person is like the loss of a library" (Thomas, 2004, p. 59).

Discussion Questions

- Thomas also writes, "The genius of human aging transforms an inevitable physical decline into something new, a reinvention of the self, a portal that leads to a new freedom from the burdens of adulthood" (Thomas, p. 61). Write a paragraph reflecting on this insight.
- Does ageism also affect men? Can men show grey hair or baldness without any negative repercussions? How would you research these two questions? Would anecdotal evidence be useful for exploring this issue?

Meaning of Menopause

For many women, menopause occurs in their fifth decade and symbolizes their entry into old age. Women's bodies stop producing estrogen and the menstrual cycles begin to end. According to the American College of Physicians (acponline.org), some women may experience severe symptoms during the "change of life," whereas others may barely notice the event. Hot flashes, mood swings, depression, and low sex drive are the major symptoms of menopause. If the symptoms are bothersome enough, women have the option of hormone replacement therapy. Controversies rage on whether menopause is a medical condition or a natural event, and whether hormone replacement is harmful or beneficial.

Beyond the medical facts is the deeper meaning of menopause for women's roles. In *Goddesses in Older Women: Archetypes in Women over Fifty,* Bolen (2001) reflects on the three phases of a woman's life: maiden, mother, and crone. The word "crone" used to connote an ugly old hag, but she reclaims it to be a proud symbol of maturity. "It is possible for this third trimester to be a time of personal wholeness and integration; when what you do is an expression of who you deeply are" (Bolen, 2001, p. x). The author continues:

> There have been and still are cultures with women elders or wisewomen in which menopause is acknowledged as marking the transition into a new and honored status. This happens when women and nature are seen as positive reflections of each other. As in many Native American tribal traditions, menarche (the onset of menstruation) and menopause mark major traditions in the awesome cycle—the *blood mysteries*—in which women, the moon, and the divine feminine are related.
>
> Whether it is a crescent sliver or gloriously full, we know we are only observing a facet of the same spherical moon. (Bolen, 2001, p. xi)

In *The Fountain of Age* (1993), Betty Friedan writes of how society—especially the medical establishment had once viewed menopause as an illness.

> At that time, if menopause was talked about at all—and like other aspects of female biology, this shameful sexual sickness was better not discussed—the

end of a woman's childbearing function was seen as ultimate trauma, the end of her sexual function, her life as a woman. She was told to expect painful, even agonizing, physiological symptoms and depressions that might send her to bed for weeks, even years, sometimes requiring hospitalization....

But in the 1960s, women, myself included, were moving beyond that definition of ourselves solely in terms of our biological sexual role.... When women grow beyond the limits of their biological role and find new purposes for their lives, could that larger human dimension change the very biology of the aging process? (Friedan, 1993, pp. 14–15)

In another excerpt, Friedan quotes a woman who had spent years raising her children and was now in graduate school. Her positive view of menopause is evident in this quote: " 'I've been remembering how we are all so forgiving of pregnancy (e.g., a little foot kicking her liver) because of the anticipated birth of a child.... Can we be as forgiving of menopause, giving birth to ourselves?' " (Friedan, 1993, p. 143).

For mothers, menopause often occurs when the grown children are moving out and leaving behind an "empty nest." Many women return to school, start new careers, or simply enjoy their new life phase. As one woman wrote:

I was so unhappy about how old I was, but people at the school knew my age, and they wanted me! When I got my degree, I remember saying, "I'm sixty-one, I've got a new career and the rest of my life ahead of me," and feeling so *excited*! (Friedan, p. 161)

Friedan also points out the late-late creativity of great artists such as Yeats. "By his seventies, his language revealed the height of its powers. He now stood for something beyond himself: the Irish people" (Friedan, 1993, p. 122).

Grandma Móses (Anna Mary Robertson), who did not start her painting career until she was 78, also exemplifies the expanded opportunities of old age. She grew up in a rural setting, which she lovingly depicted in her folk art. Another late-life artist is Louise Bourgeois, who is quoted as saying that growing older made her a better artist: "you become better in every way, morally, intellectually.... You become better, which is really the Chinese philosophy—the wisdom of the elders" (Galenson, 2009, p. 107).

Discussion Questions
Look up the art of Grandma Moses and Louise Bourgeois. After picking your favorite works, write a reflection paragraph on why they affect you.

Working Past Retirement Age

Women Still at Work: Professionals Over Sixty and on the Job (Fideler, 2012) explicates the reasons some women work past their retirement age. Finances, of course, are a crucial factor because the 2008 recession lowered the retirement savings of millions of Americans. Another reason is feeling "professionally naked" after decades of being connected to a career (Fideler, 2012, p. 2). For some people, retirement symbolizes a decline

Figure 11.8 *Professional woman (Photo courtesy of OUP)*

in their lives for which they are not yet ready. The struggles of feminism are also a factor, as stated in Margaret Gaston's letter: "Maybe we are holding on because it was so damn hard to get here" (Fideler, 2012, p. 18). She also states, "The retirement question has changed for our generation because employment has become our life's work. It is a deep pleasure, honor, and privilege to carry out our responsibilities in the everyday world" (Fideler, 2012, p. 22).

Another woman, Davi-Ellen Chavner, grew up in the prefeminist era when she was expected to go to college, get married, and bear children. But she found that tennis dates and shopping did not fill her life. Noting that, if she had been born ten years later, she would have gone to medical school, she was thrilled when feminism emerged as a movement.

> With consciousness-raising groups proliferating everywhere in the sixties and seventies, Davi embraced women's lib. She also started teaching biology part time at an alternative school for unwed mothers. She quickly discovered that her students did not know the first thing about reproduction and birth control. At the same time, she discovered that she positively loved teaching. (Fideler, 2012, p. 23)

Box 11.3 Feminist Gerontology

For years, feminism focused on younger women's goals while gerontologists did not consider gender as an issue. However, both feminists and gerontologists share the same goal of energizing oppressed persons to claim their full identities (Garner, 1999). The relationship between the youth culture and patriarchy becomes clear in how they value—or devalue—persons. Feminists must work with direct service practitioners to ensure that older persons are treated with respect. For example, an old woman in a retirement home whispered to the writer, "I'm tired of being petted like a dog" by a staff nurse who "spoke to them as if they were children. Rather than sit beside them, she always stood over them" (Garner, 1999, p. 8).

Discussion Question

What is one practical way to integrate feminist principles into social work practice with the elderly?

Based on this experience, she wrote books on medical terminology that sold millions. She cannot imagine retiring because she wants to work as long as her health is holds up. "As long as you have the passion and can help others, don't let age stop you. The number does not mean anything!" (Fideler, 2012, p. 25). Box 11.3 discusses the synthesis of feminism and gerontology.

Successful Aging

Researchers have come up with new terms for aging well: successful aging, healthy aging, and resilience in old age. They all connote the same goal of aging with as much fulfillment as possible. In his study on the benefits of digital games for older adults, Kaufman (2013) defines aging well as "maintaining older adults' vitality, independence and quality of life" (Kaufman, 2013, p. 1943).

One Finnish study (Nosraty Jylhä, Raittila, & Lumme-Sandt, 2015) interviewed forty-five persons who were 90 and 91 years old about successful aging. When asked to define a "good old age," one woman responded: "I've been able to take care of things and my work and everything, so in that sense nothing has been that important. And being myself. Living how I want to live and not caring too much about other people's lives. I mean, let them live as they want to live (Nosraty et al., 2015, p. 54).

Staying busy in activities such as volunteer work has also contributed to successful aging. In one qualitative study, participants described the need to have a purpose in life instead of simply waiting to die. One woman who uses a scooter describes her work at a dog club and other groups. She sometimes "wonders, [am I] doing too much. And yet I'm happy. And by being happy and in the right state of mind, my illness and disability have taken a back seat" (Wiles et al., 2012, p. 420). Even her scooter symbolizes her positive attitude. Although it slows her down, it allows her to visit more with people along the way.

Volunteering for the community appears to cross cultural boundaries. In a study of Canadian Inuits, the younger people were asked to describe how they regarded their elders. One overriding theme was the contributions of elders to the group, whether it is wise advice or active helping. One person noted, "Elders doing good are always keeping busy with their life. I always see them in the community doing completely different things and then an hour, two hours later I see them somewhere else doing something else. I wonder where they get their energy from" (Collings, 2001, p. 135). Some elders even continued hunting for the community.

Besides staying active, reflection is a key component of successful aging. One example is Brody (2010), a gerontologist who found old age to be a surprise. Writing as an 86-year-old, she muses that "I do not remember becoming old. All of a sudden, I was there. Others perceive me as old. Cars stop to let me cross. People offer to help carry my packages. My grandchildren 'check up' on me when my children are out of town and hold my arm when we cross a street" (Brody, 2010, p. 5).

Another quote by an octogenarian stresses a positive outlook on her age despite her initial shock at becoming so old. "But eighty? Holy smoke! This is DEAD! Or supposed to be. This is the end, or supposed to be. This is not rich, it is dying. This is not time to make new friends, it is time to settle in warm and cozy by the fires of remembrance…." (Mattlage, 1986, p. 79).

Making peace with the past is another result of reflection as an older person. A study of Japanese-American older adults, for instance, discusses how they held little bitterness about the internment camps of World War II. Their culture had stressed endurance and patience over anger. The Japanese concept of persevering without complaints still influenced their worldviews, thus resulting in successful aging (Iwamasa & Iwasaki, 2011).

Aging persons must not only make peace with the past, but also with the present situation. One study (Wild, Wiles, & Allen, 2013) shares the insights of older persons also facing disability. They acknowledge that they are living in a new reality that requires resilience—but that they considered themselves to be successfully aging.

In the end, only the person herself can define what successful aging means to her. One woman summarizes it perfectly: "I'm artistic in many ways. It gives you a lot of roads to go. I like to do many things and I can express myself in many ways. Sewing, painting, gardening, listening to music, singing. You can see that my roads are many…. Aging is like an open window" (Fisher & Specht, 1999, p. 458).

Discussion Questions

- The Red Hat Society (www.redhatsociety.com) is an organization of women fifty and over who want to wear red hats and have fun in group activities. Based on the poem "Warning" by Jenny Joseph, "When I am an old woman I shall wear purple/With a red hat which doesn't go, and doesn't suit me" (full poem available on www.poemhunter.com), this society encourages women to enjoy their senior years. Go to the RedHat Society's website and write a paragraph about how this society is an example of the strengths perspective.

- Write a short essay describing an older woman in your life (e.g., grandmother or teacher) who has changed your life. What would be the best way to honor her for her contributions to society?

Key Terms

Protective umbrella
Slutbashing
Cyberbullying
Queen Bee
Dating violence
Sexual harassment on campuses
STEM
Caregiving
Ageism
Menopause

2

Diversity

12

Diversity and Intersectionality:
An Introductory Note

Intersectionality

As discussed in the introductory chapter, *intersectionality* refers to the "mutually consti-
tutive relations among social identities ... [identity is defined here as] social categories in
which an individual claims membership as well as the personal meaning associated with
those categories" (Shields, 2009, p. 302). Intersectionality amplifies the different ways
a person can be in an outside group: gender, race, disability, etc. For example, women
of color are likely to be underpaid on two levels. As a result, "The long-term wage gap
hurts families of color tremendously.... On average, an African American woman working full time loses the equivalent of 118 weeks of food each year due to the wage gap.
A Latina loses 154 weeks' worth of food" (Kerby, 2013).

Because lesbian women of color are more likely to be underpaid on three levels,
they experience more financial hardships and housing instability than straight women
of color. "Black lesbians are hyper-marginalized within their race, gender, and sexual
orientation. The rates of poverty and unemployment for Black lesbians means that our
society must think more critically about policy and legislation that would improve the
quality of life across *all* marginalized groups" (Bateau, 2014,).

Pay inequity is but one example of the "matrix of domination" established by intersectionality (Collins, 2008, p. 228). This matrix is related to the first two dimensions of
oppression that affect black women, as described in the following:

> African-American women's oppression has encompassed three interdepen-
> dent dimensions. First, the exploitation of Black women's labor essential to
> U.S. capitalism—the "iron pots and kettles" symbolizing Black women's

long-standing ghettoization in service occupations—represents the economic dimension of oppression....

Second, the political dimension of oppression (including the right to vote, hold public office, and receive fair treatment from the criminal justice system).... (Collins, 2014, p. 4)

The third dimension of oppression is ideological, which uses negative portrayals of black women as a tool. Collins continues her analysis with this statement:

Finally, controlling images applied to Black women that originated during the slave era attest to the ideological dimension of U.S. Black women's oppression.... In this context, certain assumed qualities are applied to Black women are used to justify oppression. From the mammies, jezebels, and breeder women of slavery to the smiling Aunt Jemimas on pancake mix boxes, ubiquitous Black prostitutes, and ever-present welfare mothers.... (Collins, 2014, pp. 4–5)

This ideological dimension is by no means an abstract idea with no actual impact on women. On the website of the University of Michigan's Sexual Assault and Prevention Center is the article "Sexual Assault and Women of Color," which states that race amplifies the problem. The myths that African American women are promiscuous and that Asian American women always want sex contribute to the minimization or denial of the attacks.

Assumptions about race make women of color vulnerable to sexual assault in a number of ways. Sexual violence committed against women of color is often seen as insignificant and/or acceptable and is justified by stereotypes of women of color that serve to portray these women as "unrapeable" (Article available on sapac.umich.edu).

In another discussion of intersectionality, Collins (2008) explains how this concept is not a theory to be proven or disproven. Instead, intersectionality is an "interpretative framework" of "multiple axes" that intersect with one another (Collins, 2008, p. 208). She points out that not all oppressions are equivalent. For instance, a white lesbian may experience more oppression as a lesbian than as a woman.

Discussion Questions

A Pakistani girl growing up in Britain writes of her experiences as a disabled child. She felt like an outsider in both the white-dominated clinics and her own neighborhood full of able-bodied persons.

It took me a long time to understand why people who did not know me ... called me "spastic," "bandy legs" or "Ironside" and why people with disabilities called me "paki" or "nigger." Eventually I learned that where I went I would probably stand out as being different from the majority. (Begum, 1994, p. 50)

1. In your opinion, are her three identities (female, Pakistani, and disabled) equally important in her life, or just one? Explain your answer.

2. What assumptions could be made about her regarding her intelligence and other traits? In what ways could people prejudge her?

Classism is another part of the intersectionality framework, as delineated by the author bell hooks (2000). Noting that the second-wave movement started with a focus on dissatisfied middle-class housewives, she stresses that more than one-third of women were working outside the home in the early 1960s. Her life experience in the working class, then, differed considerably from the middle-class world. Because they only focus on gender, "Privileged feminists have largely been unable to speak to, with, and for diverse groups of women because they either do not understand fully the interrelated-ness of sex, race, and class oppression or refuse to take this interrelatedness seriously" (hooks, 2000, p. 15).

Claiming that "Being oppressed means the *absence of choices*" (hooks, 2000, p. 5), hooks expresses frustration with those who believe that black women needed white feminists to tell them about sexism.

> There are white women who had never considered resisting male dominance until the feminist movement created an awareness that they could and should. Growing up in a Southern, black, father-dominated, working-class household, I experienced (as did my mother, my sisters, and my brother) varying degrees of patriarchal tyranny, and it made me angry—it made us all angry. Anger led me to question the politics of male dominance and enabled me to resist sexist socialization. Frequently, white feminists act as if black women did not know sexist oppression existed until they voiced feminist sentiment. They believe they are providing black women with "the" analysis and "the" program for liberation. (hooks, 2000, p. 11)

Intersectionality, then, is a powerful tool for feminist analysis. Religion adds another layer of possible oppression by the dominant groups. One African-American woman who wears a headscarf in honor of her Muslim faith muses on whether she should take it off so she could pass as "normal." "However, my otherness is layered, thereby relegating me to a life at the intersection of many "isms"; even without a headscarf, I am still a dark brown black woman, and underneath that, I am still a woman, and an overweight woman at that" (Medina, 2011, p. 139).

The opposite extreme is coming out as a nonbeliever in a heavily religious setting. In her memoir *Infidel* (a word which literally means person of no faith), Ayaan Hirsi narrates the story of her escape from an arranged marriage. Her Somali culture demanded obedience from her. Instead, she fled to the Netherlands and gained refugee status. As an African living in a European country full of blonde, pale-skinned persons, she stuck out. She could not connect to the African groups living there because she started rejecting traditional views. It took her years to realize that she was an atheist, which made her even more the "Other."

> When Marco gave it [The Atheist Manifesto] to me, I felt as if he were handing me his holy book, as if I had pressed the Quran on him, and it put me off. But

Figure 12.1 *Muslim woman (Photo source: Entofolio)*

now I wanted to read it. I wanted to think this thing through. My questions were taboo. According to my upbringing, if I was not a follower of God, I must be a follower of Satan. But I couldn't be spouting answers for Holland's problems when I still had questions about my own religious faith.…

I read the book, marveling at the clarity and naughtiness of its author. But I really didn't have to. Just looking at it, just wanting to read it—that already meant I doubted, and I knew that. Before I'd read four pages I already knew my answer. I had left God behind years ago. I was an atheist.

I had no one to talk to about this. One night in that Greek hotel I looked in the mirror and said out loud, "I don't believe in God." I said it slowly enunciating it carefully, in Somali. And I felt relief.

It felt right. There was no pain, but a real clarity. The long process of seeing the flaws in my belief structure and carefully tiptoeing around the frayed edges as parts of it were torn out, piece by piece—that was all over. The angels, watching from my shoulder, the mental tension about having sex without marriage, and drinking alcohol, and not observing any religious obligations—they were gone. The ever-present prospect of hellfire lifted, and my horizons seemed broader. God, Satan, angels: these were all figments of human imagination. From now on I could step firmly on the ground that was under my feet and navigate based on my own reason and self-respect. My moral compass was within myself, not in the pages of a sacred book. (Ali, 2007, pp. 280–281)

Besides religious differences, political oppression based on classism and racism is part of intersectionality. One remarkable story is of Benedita da Silva, an Afro-Brazilian woman who rose from the shantytowns to become a major political figure. She grew up in such poverty that she often went to bed hungry. Her parents could not afford a birth certificate until later, so the wrong date is on it. Only eight of thirteen children survived in her family. She only had one outfit to wear to school, so the children made fun of her. Her homemade underwear once fell down around her ankles, which made things even worse.

At the age of seven, da Silva started work as a candy seller and shoe shiner to help her family survive.

> I learned early on the prejudices against girls. The market venders didn't want to hire us because they said we weren't as strong as boys and it would take us twice as long to carry the boxes to and from the market. I insisted on proving that I could work as hard as the boys did. That's when they started calling me macho woman—a reputation I have to this day. (Benjamin & Mendonca, 1997, p. 8)

After fighting to bring water and electricity to her town as an adult, this "macho woman" helped to found the Workers Party and ran for office. As a politician, though, she still faced sexism.

> These gender stereotypes make it difficult for women to be assertive. Men are more accustomed to being in control and they don't want to take orders from women. I see this in my own professional life. Sometimes I have difficulty with men I work with. They belittle my political position and call me mulher mandona—a bossy woman. I've even overheard men calling me negrinha metia a besta—an arrogant nigger. That's because I don't like to follow orders. I can't stand someone telling me how to act or what to do. (Benjamin & Mendonca, 1997, p. 104)

Sexism becomes entangled with racism when Brazilian black women are regarded as sexier and "easier" than lighter-skinned women. This stereotype leads to a higher risk of prostitution, exploitation, and violence—a striking parallel to the mention of sexual assault and women of color excerpted earlier.

Da Silva has also fought against the mass sterilization of indigenous women in remote areas where birth control is not available. In one northeastern province, 80 percent of the women had been sterilized. It may be difficult to restore justice in cases like these, but she notes that the feminist movement has become stronger in both Brazil and the world,

> Today, the women's movement is much broader and there is greater understanding and solidarity across classes. Now there are women's groups all over Brazil focusing on all kinds of issues—women's health, reproductive rights, domestic violence, affirmative action. These issues not only cross class lines, but international boundaries. (Benjamin & Mendonca, 1997, p. 116)

Da Silva and the other women in this chapter, then, exemplify the concept of inter-sectionality. Although they must prevail over more oppressions than others, they also have more sources of strength through their multiple identities. The following chapters provide glimpses in the lives of diverse women, lives that are filled with abundance and light.

Discussion Questions

- Do you have any personal connection to any of the stories in this chapter so far?
- If you were an activist, which woman would you prefer as an ally? Discuss the qualities that you admire about her.
- The word *nigger* appears in both the British and Brazilian stories. What do you think is the significance of this observation?

Incarceration of Women

In the United States., one of the clearest examples of intersectionality is the mass incarceration of women. According to the advocacy group The Sentencing Project, the rate of incarcerated women has escalated almost ten times since 1980—from 13,258 to 113,605 in 2012. "The number of women in prison, a third of whom are incarcerated for drug offenses, is increasing at nearly double the rate for men. These women often have significant histories of physical and sexual abuse, high rates of HIV infection, and substance abuse" (www. sentencingproject.org). Women of color are more likely to live in jail or prison, according to these striking numbers: all women have a 1 in 56 chance of being incarcerated; white women, 1 in 111, black women, 1 in 18, and Latinas 1 in 45. With the racial disparity being even worse for males, the mass incarceration in the United States has had a profound impact on the disproportionately affected.

As a result of this high rate of incarceration, family ties—especially the mother/child relationships—are damaged. Rathbone (2005) describes her research setting at MCI-Framingham in Massachusetts:

> The housing units were crowded, dark, and noisy, and the aimless vacuum of the daily life there often made you want to curl into yourself on your thin little bunk up close to the ceiling and cry. But it was nothing, *nothing*, like Denise thought it would be. There were the locks, of course—including, most impressively, the one to her own cell—to which she would never hold a key. And there were the guards and the continually blaring intercoms, which controlled the smallest minutiae of her everyday life. There were full, bend-over-and-cough strip searches both before and after a visit, and random urine checks, and cell searches, called raids, which left her prison-approved personal items (mostly letters and drawings from her son, Patrick) scattered all over the floor. She'd heard there were punishment cells too. Dismal, solitary cages with nothing but a concrete bed and a seatless toilet, to which women sometimes disappeared for months.
>
> Despite all this, Framingham seemed more like a high school than a prison. Some of the guards were rougher than teachers would ever be, of course. Dressed

in quasi-military uniforms and calf-length black leather boots, a few also flaunted their power, making irrational demands simply because they could. For the most part, though, Denise found it easy to keep out of the way. No, it was the inmates, not the guards, who reminded her of her days at Wecausett High—as did the unfamiliar experience of being with so many women.... the overwhelming majority were mothers, as well, their walls decorated not, as she'd imagine, with images of muscle-bound men but with photos of their kids and sheets of construction paper scrawled over with crayon—valentines and birthday and Christmas cards saved year after year. (Rathbone, 2005, pp. 4–5)

Another aspect of prison life for women is loneliness. According to Owen (2005), women prisoners are less likely to be socialized as criminals or gang members. As a result, they have fewer social ties in prison. Another difference is that although most women's prisons allow for bathroom stalls, most of the time women have no privacy.

Figure 12.2 *Women in prison (Photo courtesy of OUP)*

Women in prison rarely escape the male gaze.… While privacy is already eroded by crowded conditions, shared housing units, and the need for surveillance, the presence of male staff further undermines one's ability to attend to personal hygiene and grooming without the scrutiny of men. (Owen, 2005, p. 272)

Why are so many women in prison? As mentioned earlier, the war on drugs has been one major cause of the rise "with its emphasis on street-level sweeps of those engaged in the drug trade and harsh mandatory sentencing.… despite their roles as relatively minor players in the drug trade, women—disproportionate numbers of them African American and Latina—have been 'caught in the net'" ("Women and the Drug War" article on drugwarfacts.com). Mandatory sentencing policies, intended to capture the drug lords, have caused women with minimal involvement in the drug trade to be harshly punished.

Prostitution may also lead to the higher rate of incarceration, although most sex workers may need treatment for childhood trauma instead of a jail term (Belknap, 2014). Another risk factor is being a previous victim of violence (e.g., getting beat up by a gang or a husband). Belknap also discusses the criminological theories that explain why women break the law, especially the women's-liberation theory. Because women have become more equal, they are more likely to become criminals. However, she asserts that the rate of women committing violent crimes has not significantly increased since the 1970s. The rate of women committing property crime, though, has risen. This may be the result of the feminization of poverty or simply more opportunities to embezzle or steal.

Another feminist interpretation (Chesney-Lind & Pasko, 2013) stresses how laws criminalize girls' survival. Delinquent girls who got in trouble for running away, for instance, often were victims of their families.

Young women, a large number of whom are on the run from sexual abuse and parental neglect, are forced by the very statutes designed to protect them into the lives of escaped convicts. Unable to enroll in school or take a job to support themselves because they fear detection, young female runaways are forced into the streets. Here, they engage in panhandling, petty theft, and occasional prostitution to survive. Young women in conflict with their parents (often for legitimate reasons) may actually be forced by present laws into petty criminal activity, prostitution, and drug use. (Chesney-Lind & Pasko, 2001, p. 28)

Other issues also affect women in prison, including sexual assault and inadequate services. Substance abuse treatment, for instance, is urgently needed for many of these women (Women's Prison Association website: www.wpaonline.org). One troubled teenager who started using meth after being raped wrote of one experience after being arrested: "I was seventeen years old, I was terrified, I had no clue what was going to happen to me, and I had absolutely no one fighting for me. I was taken to county jail. In county the cops were horrible to me" (Waldman & Levi, 2011).

Figure 12.3 *Woman in trouble with the law (Photo courtesy of OUP)*

The concerns of incarcerated mothers are also critical, since their children are the most vulnerable victims of the "get tough on crime" mentality. According to the Women and Prison website (womenandprison.org), at least 65 percent of incarcerated women have a child under 18. Fifty-three percent of the 1.5 million people held in U.S. prisons by 2007 were the parents of one or more minor children. This percentage translates into more than 1.7 million minor children with an incarcerated parent.

African-American children are seven times more likely, and Latino children two-and-a-half times more likely, to have a parent in prison than white children. The estimated risk of parental imprisonment for white children by the age of 14 is 1 in 25, whereas for black children it is 1 in 4 by the same age.

Previous research has shown a close yet complex connection between parental incarceration and adverse outcomes for children, including:

- An increased likelihood of engaging in antisocial or delinquent behavior, including drug use
- An increased likelihood of school failure.
- An increased likelihood of unemployment.
- An increased likelihood of developing mental health problems (Women and Prison website, www.womenandprison.org).

Besides the impact on the children, the community may also have depended on the woman prisoner. She may have been a caregiver to an elderly parent or helping to support a disabled relative. Incarceration affects not only the immediate family, but also the wider community.

Once an invisible population, women prisoners are receiving more attention by the media in shows such as *Orange is the New Black*. Stigmatization of this population still occurs, but public awareness is shifting. For example, a blog by a woman who visited a facility in Marysville, Ohio, to sing in a choir performance states: "As the program starts, I look at these women, our audience. I am struck by their *ordinariness*. They look like the women I see downtown, in the grocery, in my neighborhood. Many are chomping gum — the prison is a nonsmoking facility. They could be my daughters and my grandmothers" (The Women in the Mirror: A First-Hand Account of MUSE's Visit to an Area Women's Prison, citybeat.com).

Discussion Questions

- Describe how intersectionality relates to incarcerated women.
- Micro level: As a social worker at a woman's homeless shelter, you meet Kate. She has recently been released from prison and is estranged from her family. To maintain her sobriety, she has been cautioned to avoid her old friends who might encourage her to get high again. What are three immediate goals that you would suggest for her action plan? What are three long-term goals for Kate? (Maslow's Hierarchy of Needs may apply here.)
- Mezzo level: You work at an agency located in a neighborhood that is economically depressed. When you start seeing more and more female ex-felons on your caseload, you realize that some people at the agency (both client and staff) express resentment at how many resources "those women" are getting. How do you generate more social acceptance for the stigmatized women at your agency?
- Macro level: The Incarceration of Women section contains many examples of problematic policies, such as the war on drugs. Pick one of the macro issues and discuss how you would advocate for a policy change.

Key Terms

Intersectionality
Matrix of domination
Classism
Religion
Political oppression
War on drugs

13

Latinas in the United States

Who Is a Latina?

Latinas, who may also be called Hispanic American or Chicana, have cultural heritages that range from the islands in the Caribbean to South America. (In this section, the term *Latina* and *Hispanic* will be used interchangeably.) Geographical diversity, along with variations of economic class and acculturation level, ensures that this group could never be a homegeneous entity. For instance, the United States took away half of Mexico's land in the 1848 Treaty of Guadelupe Hidalgo. Many of the residents in the Southwest, then, have ancestors going back for centuries living in the same area. Other Latinas may be recent immigrants or their families had settled in the United States in the 1900s wave.

According to the 2010 Census (www.census.gov), "More than half of the growth in the total population of the United States between 2000 and 2010 was due to the increase in the Hispanic population" (Overview of Race and Hispanic Origin: 2010, available on www.census.gov, p. 3). Hispanics now compose 16 percent of the U.S. population. The 2010 Census asked the question about Hispanic origin this way: "Is this person of Hispanic, Latino, or Spanish origin?" If so, the options were: Mexican, Mexican American, Chicano; Puerto Rican; Cuban; and other, such as Argentinian or Colombian. The U.S. Census Bureau stresses that this question had nothing to do with race. To precisely define *Latino/a*, then, can be an elusive task. On a personal level, Cepeda (2013) writes of her search for identity as a Latina through DNA testing. Disagreeing with the official definition of *Hispanic* as based on country of origin, she found out that her ancestral origins came from several different races.

On the macro level, Martinez speaks out against the "deadly dualism" of black/white racial relations that cannot tolerate shades of brown. (In this passage, the author uses the term *La Raza* for Latino/a.)

Figure 13.1 *Mexican woman standing in front of a bureau, San Antonio, Texas (Undated photo courtesy of Library of Congress)*

As a people, La Raza combines three sets of roots—indigenous, European, and African—all in widely varying degrees. In short we represent a profoundly un-American concept: mestizaje … the mixing of peoples and emergence of new peoples. (Martinez, 1994, p. 58)

No matter the country of origin or other differences, though, Latino/as have a "shared history of conquest and colonization" (Aquino, Machado, & Rodriguez, 2002, p. 3). This shared history is related to the concept of intersectionality:

- Class (i.e., economic worth).
- Language (not only Spanish/English but indigenous languages as well).
- Skin color (since lighter skin is sometimes valued more).
- Level of education.
- Country of origin (e.g., Puerto Ricans are U.S. citizens).
- Gender.
- Immigration status—"You are not a person unless you have a green card, right?" (Mederos, 2001, p. 237).

Challenges Faced by Latinas

Like most indigenous groups, Latinas face prejudice, discrimination, and other indignities. Supreme Court Justice Sonia Sotomayor, for example, was born in the same year as the 1954 Supreme Court decision *Hernandez v. Texas*, the landmark case on discrimination against Hispanics. (Box 13.1 discusses her life as a Supreme Court justice.) She grew up in New York City as the civil rights movements of different groups emerged, including the Puerto Ricans. As a child, she was visiting a friend's house when they watched a Puerto Rican pride parade on TV. The father said:

> "Aren't those disgusting people?,"

Sotomayor stood up and turned to her friend's father. "Those people? They're my people. I'm Puerto Rican," she said as she walked out (Biskupic, 2014, p. 14).

A more recent example is from the memoir by Cepeda (2013), who was attending a tennis academy with mostly upper-class whites. She writes in her memoir about have a crush on a young man there.

> "Can you watch my sister when she goes to the bathroom in the women's locker room?" Simon asks me.
>
> "Yes, of course," I respond.
>
> He smiles warmly. "You know, you look like a younger version of my baby sister's nanny," he continues. "Are you from Central America?"
>
> "No," I respond, deflated.

Box 13.1 Do Nail Polish and Jewelry Really Matter?

Even after appointed to the U.S. Supreme Court, Sotomayor said that she felt different from mainstream culture and that she did not really belong. According to one of her biographers:

> Sotomayor's looks, particularly her bright nail polish and flashy jewelry, were scrutinized by the news media…. Latoya Peterson [stated,] "Assimilation requires a very high price and her refusal to do so is an amazing stand for individual truth. There is nothing inferior about wearing colored nail polish, or wearing an off-the-rack suit to work, or rocking hoop earrings. Just as many of us are asked to remove our ethnic and regional markers in exchange for success (straightening hair, tightening diction, and avoiding items that call attention to the wearer) Sotomayor's subtle—but persistent—refusal to fall in line implies much more than a love of candy apple red polish." (Biskupic, 2014, p. 174)

Discussion Questions

1. Do you agree that Sotomayor's fashion details were an appropriate topic for commentators? Do you think that the comments were based more on gender or ethnicity?
2. Do you agree with Peterson's statement about assimilation requiring a high price? Give an example of assimilation that you would consider harmless, and one that you think would be destructive.

"Anyway, you're sort of hot in an exotic way. Maybe one day you'll work for me and we can fool around." He laughs.

"You mean maybe you'll work for *me*."

"Come on, let's be realistic. You could be my cleaning lady." (Cepeda, 2013, p. 82)

In another incident, she was playing on the tennis team and had a painful encounter with her teammates:

When we hit the road, I learn a whole new lesson about team camaraderie and humor. On an off day, one of the girls relaxing by the pool calls a few of us over to share a joke her mom just told her on the phone.

"My mom is so funny," she says to us. "Okay, check this out—"

"Yeah, okay. I'm game," I say.

"So we just bought a new dishwasher." She pauses. "His name is Juan."

She starts laughing. The other girls chuckle, except Number One and me.

"You don't think that's funny?" she asks, still laughing.

"Um, what exactly did that joke mean?"

"Dude, she's Hispanic," says Number One. "That was kind of a stupid joke."

"How was I supposed to know what she was?" says the jester. "And I was talking about Mexicans—she doesn't look like one of them."

"You mom taught you that?" I ask. "Does she keep Juan shackled all day to your dishwasher and then to a tree at night?" I laugh. "What's wrong, mass [master]?"

The jester bolts up and retreats to our room without a word. A couple of the other girls follow. (Cepeda, 2013, p 119)

In a research study at a midwestern high school, young Latinas expressed their own experiences with discrimination. "Here, Americans think that we all travel on donkeys, and that we are all called Maria. My name is not Maria" (Williams, Alvarez, & Andrade Hauck, 2002, p. 51). Because they had to do so many chores at home, they could not get jobs to pay for more "American" clothes. At school, the ESL (English as a Second Language) classes had low expectations of the students so they did not expect to have any college or career goals.

No matter the class, then, Latinas sometimes still have to deal with prejudiced attitudes and discriminatory behavior. Biculturalism (the adaptation to two different cultures) can lessen the amount of prejudice/discrimination but cause other problems. For example, one Latina writes of how she was told that she was not white but that she could not be Puerto Rican because she was not pregnant or on drugs. "This denial rendered me silent, frozen on the border between my Latina and my *gringa*, wondering which face to look to or turn from in order to find myself" (Molinary, 2005, p 189).

Biculturalism may lead to a person feeling in between two places. One Mexican American (Fernandez, 2005) writes of people in her white high school who made her feel that she was less than them. During her visits to Mexico, though, she felt that she did not belong there either. Mexicans regarded her as a *gringa* who looked down on

Figure 13.2 *Mexicans at the U.S. immigration station, El Paso, Texas (Undated photo courtesy of Library of Congress)*

them, so she worked hard on her language skills to be able to pass as Mexican. "I wanted to be such a *good* Chicana, to recapture my Mexican roots so thoroughly that even the Mexicans would think I was one of them. I wanted their approval" (Fernandez, 2005, p. 135).

Language appears as a salient aspect of biculturalism in another Latina's experience, who links the loss of one's native tongue with "Historical trauma, or soul wound, (which) is a result of colonization. It is a wound we experience in our spirits, our minds, and our bodies" (Chavez Leyva, 2003, p. 4). When mentioning in class that some Hispanic parents did not teach their children Spanish, some of her students who could not speak Spanish were "ashamed and angry" (Chavez Leyva, 2003, p. 5) because they were not "real" Mexicans. The author told them about going to school before the 1960s, when students had to pray in English or be punished by the teachers. Anyone who spoke Spanish in school could even be paddled.

The parents who were trying to protect their children by not teaching them Spanish, then, were not bicultural but attempting acculturation. In contrast to biculturalism, acculturation stresses adaptation to the dominant culture. Acculturation may be inevitable in many cases, especially for the younger generation. However, one research study of Latina sexual minority women (i.e., lesbians and bisexual women) indicates that acculturation was actually a risk factor for substance abuse (Matthews et al., 2014).

One Latina expresses her intricate relationship with the English language:

When I was younger I thought of myself as an English speaker with the ability to speak Spanish. My view of who I was changed when my mother and I went to one of those amusement areas where you play a game and end up winning a little plastic toy. Not being very coordinated, I avoided the games where you would try to toss rings around a wooden block.

As I randomly threw the rings, I was surprised when my last ring toss ended perfectly over the block. I knew instantly that I had won the largest stuffed animal. In my joy I shouted, "Gane! Gane!" (I won! I won!) I don't know what surprised me more—that I won or that I announced my joy in Spanish.

At that moment it became clear to me that culture was very complex. I knew that I spoke English 98 percent of the time, but when the moment came to express deep emotions, I did so in Spanish. (Delgado, 2010, p. 26)

Whether a Latino/a is bicultural or acculturated, economic injustice is often a prominent feature of their lives. According to the 2010 census, Cuban Americans have a 16.2 percent rate (slightly higher than the 14.3 percent national average), whereas Dominicans have the highest rate at 26.3 percent (www.census.gov). Hispanics were the only ethnic group to see a drop in their poverty rate, but it is still 23.2 percent—almost nine points higher than the national average. According to the National Women's Law Center, "Hispanic women working full time year-round were paid only 55 cents for every dollar paid to white, non-Hispanic men" ("Women's Poverty Rate Stabilizes, But Remains Historically High," September 12, 2012 press release available on nwlc.org). Immigrant women are particularly vulnerable to economic exploitation, especially if they are undocumented (Sullivan & Lee, 2008).

Machismo and Marianismo

As discussed in the Gender chapter, Latino culture sometimes emphasizes the sharply delineated gender roles of machismo (male) and marianismo (female). Machismo is related to patriarchy, since the strong male should be lord and master over his family. However, Latinos are also expected to honor their mothers to a high degree. Marie Arana, author of *American Chica: Two Worlds, One Childhood* (2001), describes how her mother interacted with her husband's mother. "The difference between my mother and my grandmother ... was not one between woman and woman. It was the difference between an Anglo's daughter and the mother of a Latin male.... The mother of a Latin male is the mother of a Latin male no matter what her class or education." (Arana, 2001, p. 65) Arana goes on to explain how Latin men often flirt with women on the street not to show off their masculinity but because:

Latin men worship women. They are trained to. Mothers admit sons to secrets, pamper them, teach them to cherish babies, prize beauty, pray to the Madonna, wear perfume. A love of the feminine is a mother's legacy to her son. Boys learn to use it. Fathers understand its importance. A Latino is admired for revering his mother. He is sent from mother to wife, strutting, preening, adored. He is allowed vanities few men on this earth enjoy. But a bargain is struck in the process: A man is bound fast by women, tied back to family, held tight by obligation. It is the core of the Latin soul. (Arana, 2001, p. 66)

Palacio (2013) discusses how the term *caballerismo* is a positive alternative to the negative aspects of machismo, since it implies chivalry. A gentleman should not only be protective of his family, but also kind and considerate.

The gender expectations of marianismo may overlap more with caballerismo than with machismo, since they both stress honoring tradition and self-sacrificing for their families. Unfortunately, too much self-sacrifice can hurt the health of Latinas. D'Alonzo (2012) writes of how marianismo beliefs affect the level of physical activity of immigrant Latinas. In the study, one woman stated that "The woman is the center of the family," whereas another one said that "If I go spend an hour at the gym (I would love to go), I feel I am robbing time from my children" (D'Alonzo, 2012, p. 129). Although focusing on their families made them feel special, they admitted that they were neglecting their own health concerns.

One major health concern is HIV prevention, which two research studies (Cianelli, Ferrer & McElmurry, 2008; Wood & Price, 1997) relate to machismo/marianismo and

Figure 13.3 *Latina saying "no" to IPV (Photo source: Entofolio)*

sexual attitudes. A submissive woman is less likely to insist on condom usage, even if she knows that her male partner is unfaithful to her. The machismo ideal emphasizes manliness through having many sexual partners and the marianismo ideal encourages women to find spiritual superiority through their suffering.

Latinas and DV/IPV

HIV risk is also associated with DV/IPV (domestic violence/intimate partner violence), which Cianelli et al. (2013) found in their study of fifty older Latinas in Miami, Florida. In another study (Raj, Silverman, & Amaro, 2004), the researchers recommended that HIV prevention programs should target male abusers because they are more likely to engage in risky behaviors.

"A lot of times women think that because we are living with a man who pays our rent, who gives us a gift, we have to tolerate everything" (Moreno, 2007, p. 344). This statement from a Latina escaping from IPV is from the article entitled "The Relationship Between Culture, Gender, Structural Factors, Abuse, Trauma, and HIV/AIDS for Latinas" (Moreno, 2007). As indicated by the article title, complex factors affect this social problem. One structural factor is economic dependence, especially for newly arrived immigrants. Being HIV-positive increases the risk of abuse from men who believe that the woman has no other option but to stay.

Cultural norms such as machismo are also related to IPV, as indicated by this quote from a survivor: "And you know ... you think that's normal ... in Mexico it is normal to have fights ... that they [partners] can drink ... is like there is still machismo in marriage ... I thought it [domestic violence] was part of marriage" (Reina, Maldonado, & Lohman, 2013a). Social isolation and feelings of shame also affected these Latinas' decisions when they reached out for help.

Immigration status also affects women who are undocumented and at risk of being deported (Reina, Maldonado & Lohman, 2013b). Often the batterers are permanent residents or citizens who threaten their wives with deportation. (Box 13.2 discusses the immigration issue in more detail.) Understandably, immigrant women who have tried to stay invisible from the authorities would be reluctant to reach out for help or call the police. Informal social networks have helped many of these women to survive their ordeals (Silva-Martínez & Murty, 2011).

In another study, Marrs Fuchsel (2012) writes of the mixed record that the Catholic Church and other churches had regarding IPV. For example, one priest helped a woman to end her marriage through annulment (instead of divorce). One woman, though, reached out to her priest when her life was threatened and was told to make an appointment. At a Protestant Bible study, one woman was advised "to avoid talking to her husband when he was angry and not to anger him generally because he would hit her" and that God would not want her to leave her marriage (Marrs Fuchsel, 2012, p. 77).

The good news about Latinas and IPV, though, is that the rate has dropped sharply 78 percent from 1994 to 2010 (National Center on Domestic and Sexual Violence, www.ncdsv.org/). The Violence Against Women Act may be partially responsible for this dramatic decline, as are intervention programs. One pilot program for immigrant

Box 13.2 Immigration Issues

Immigration concerns have created an uncomfortable and sometimes even hostile atmosphere for many Latinos. In her book about four Mexican girls growing up in Denver, Thorpe (2009) describes the growing rift between the girls with papers and those without.

> The four girls explained that they had met in eighth grade, back when they were awkward adolescents at an urban middle school in Denver.... By the time the four girls started their freshman year at Roosevelt High, they had become inseparable. They slept over at one another's houses, went to parties together, took the same courses. All four spoke English fluently by this point, even though they spoke Spanish at home; among themselves, they switched back and forth. They were oblivious to the differences in their legal status since it did not affect them in any tangible way during the early years of their friendship.
>
> Back in those days, Clara had been illegal, too. Clara could not recall precisely when she learned that two of her friends also lacked documents—she just remembered that in middle school they were all "on the same level." When she was seven, Clara had crawled under the wire fence that separated the town of Nogales, Sonora, from the town of Nogales, Arizona, with her mother and three siblings. She had no concept of what it meant to be an illegal immigrant at the time; the main thing on her mind was that now she would get to live with her father....
>
> The slow accumulation of ordinary things that they could not do became painful for the two illegal girls to endure, especially given that their two legal friends were able to accomplish basic tasks without difficulties. But nothing was more painful than the subject of college, which had also come up during their junior year. "The teachers say: 'Everybody can go to college! Everybody can do it, no matter what!'" Yadira recounted. "And it's hard, because I can't just raise my hand and say, 'Well, miss, I don't have my papers....'" (Thorpe, 2009, pp. 23–25)

Discussion Question

Related to this dilemma is the DREAM (Development, Relief, and Education for Minors) Act, a proposed law that would allow illegal immigrants who had grown up in the United States to become eligible for citizenship through going to college or joining the military. In 2012, President Obama issued an executive order for DACA (Deferred Action for Childhood Arrivals.) Research the latest developments related to the immigration concerns of children who arrived in the United States without proper documentation. Does the NASW have a position on immigration?

Mexican women, held at a community health center for eleven weeks, used Spanish-language and other culturally specific materials. One woman commented, "Every class, I feel better and prettier because they (group members) give me more tools to keep going. I receive a lot of support, love, and friendship from my group members" (Marrs Fuchsel & Hysjulien, 2013, p. 10).

Strengths

Latinas show their strengths in many venues, such as families and communities. Even when many Latinas are unable or unwilling to attend college, they can still challenge the gender roles as a fellow wage earner in the family. Working-class Latinas, then, can emerge as feminists without higher education (Harklau, 2013).

Most articles about successful Latinas, though, do focus on higher education as the avenue toward fulfilling their goals. Cejda (2010) emphasizes how cultural capital that a student develops through her family and faculty is vital to academic success. Even when students are living in the shadows as undocumented immigrants, many strive for success because they feel so much support from their families (Enriquez, 2011).

Although language can be a barrier to any level of education, one student urged, "Don't be afraid of speaking out even if you think you don't know enough English! Try to avoid speaking Spanish at school but don't forget your roots" (McWhirter, Luginbuhl & Brown, 2014, p. 11). The student recommendations also included ending discrimination and allowing undocumented students full access to the education they deserve.

In her qualitative study of Latina high school principals, Palacio (2013) conducted interviews with women who overcame the marianismo influence in their lives to achieve professional recognition. Below are selected quotes from these women:

> My dad has always pulled my sister and I aside and said, "you know what, you girls can do way better than boys." He always told us we were "better at doing things, and we were stronger than men." So there was a lot of support... . (Palacio, 2013, p. 106)

> Mom graduated from high school in the United States. My dad did not formally go to high school... Both parents attended all of our school events. My dad modeled good work ethics. He was a mechanic. He went to night school to get his community college credentials to teach automotive technologies. Watching dad attend night classes and work to make sure we had what we needed, made us value education... From an early age, my parents really instilled in me the non-negotiable of going to college. At an early age, I knew from the get go, I was not going to be allowed to stay home after graduating from high school. I was going to have to go to college. I was going to have to move somewhere to attend college and...get A's, A's and B's. (Palacio, 2013, pp. 110-111)

> My parents are [immigrants] from another country.... They are children from immigrants... I am first generation in the United States. I was born here, but I also lived in another country. I attended school [off shore and] in the United States urban community. My ex-husband is from a country [other than from my family's or mine]. I spent quite a lot of time in his country for several years... I am able to understand American culture. I can understand Latin culture. I can understand immigrant culture. I can understand minority culture. You know, I can be anywhere. Help anyone. (Palacio, 2013, p. 129)

Discussion Questions

- In this section on Latinas, find one example of both male privilege and intersectionality.
- If you were a counselor in a women's shelter, how would you make sure you were culturally competent with Latinas?
- If you were a school counselor, how would you increase the impact of family support as described in the Strengths subsection?
- After reading this section, which political cause would you most advocate for? What would be the next step for your advocacy?

Key Terms

Latina/Hispanic defined
Biculturalism
Immigration issues
Machismo/Marianismo

14

African-American Women

Introduction

Despite the great advances made toward racial equality, racism still haunts today's society. The height of the civil rights movement of the 1960s led to the norm that overt racism was unacceptable. This scene at a white boarding school, written by Cary (1991), describes the post-civil rights attitude that whites thought was acceptable in the 1970s:

> I did not, however, tell the girls what I was thinking. We did not talk about how differently we saw the world. Indeed my black and their white heritage was not a starting point for our relationship, but rather was the outer boundary. I could not cross it, because there sprang up a hard wall of denial impervious to my inexperienced and insecure assault. "Well, as far as I'm concerned," one girl after another would say, "it doesn't matter to me if somebody's white or black or green or purple. I mean people are just people."
>
> The motion, having been made, would invariably be seconded.
>
> "Really. I mean, it's the person that counts."
>
> Having castigated whites' widespread inability to see individuals for the skin in which they were wrapped, I could hardly argue with "it's the person that counts." I didn't know why they always chose green and purple to dramatize their indifference, but my ethnicity seemed diminished when the talk turned to Muppets. It was like they were taking something away from me.
>
> "I'm not purple." What else could you say?
>
> "The truth is," somebody said, "I ... this is *so* silly ... I'm really embarrassed, but, it's like, there *are* some things, you, God, you just feel ashamed to admit that you think about this stuff, but I always kind of wondered if, like, black guys and white guys were, like, different ..." (Cary, 1991, p. 84)

The author reflects on the age-old racist stereotype of the hypersexualized black male after the girls leave her room. "It always came down to this, I thought, the old song of the South. I wanted something meaningful (after King's assassination and other events).... It couldn't be just that I was to become like them or hang onto what I'd been. It couldn't be that lonely and pointless" (Cary, 1991, p. 84).

What is it like to grow up as an African American female? If the United States is now a post-racist and post-sexist society, then there should be no unique challenges for these women. However, this chapter will reveal perspectives different from the popular perception that there is no more need for activism against racism and sexism.

Challenges

Racism and Sexism

Before the civil rights movement took hold in the 1960s and 1970s, most products and advertising were "white." The author bell hooks writes of a doll she wants, which is "brown, brown like light milk chocolate." (hooks, 1997, p. 23) She wants to have this doll instead of the white dolls. "Deep within myself I had begun to worry that all this loving care we gave to the pink and white flesh-colored dolls meant that somewhere left high on the shelves were boxes of unwanted, unloved brown dolls covered in dust" (hooks, 1997, p. 24). This poignant story shows the impact of racism on children—that because of their skin color, they may feel unwanted and unloved. And for girls, this feeling of exclusion can be amplified by sexism.

Even as a child, bell hooks also caught on to the historical impact of slavery on women. Visiting the "white folks" (hooks, 1997, p. 32) in the neighborhood, she and her brother want some popcorn. She is told that if she kisses the white man, she will get the popcorn.

> She gives the kiss, gives him (her brother) the popcorn for already she is ashamed. She knows better, knows that kisses are for friends and other loved ones. She fears the history in this exchange. White men taking black girls, black women, the word they do not understand but hear the grown-ups use: white man raping black women. After eating the popcorn he assures her that he will tell as soon as they are home, that she will be punished. Rushing home, running through the dark, she hopes the punishment will wipe away the feeling of shame. (hooks, 1997, p. 33)

Michele Wallace, author of *Black Macho and the Myth of the Superwoman* (1980), also speaks of the reality of being a Black woman. She grew up in Harlem, thinking that she must succeed in school or end up as an Aunt Jemina—the stereotype of a servant who happily serves a white family. The Black movement for political power was seen as a man's movement, while the feminist movement was for white women. Society accused Black women of being too powerful, too matriarchal, and even emasculating of their Black brothers. "The American black woman is haunted by the mythology that surrounds the American black man. It is a mythology based on the real persecution of

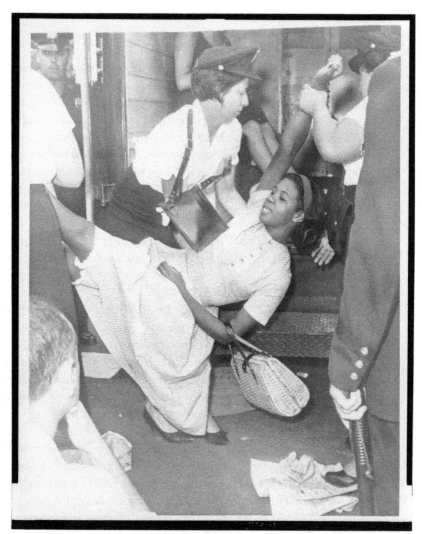

Figure 14.1 *African American woman being carried to police patrol wagon during demonstration in Brooklyn, NY (Undated photo courtesy of Library of Congress)*

black men: castrated black men hanging by their necks from trees; black men shining shoes; black men behind bars...." (Wallace, 1980, p. 303). These painful images, of course, obscure the fact that black women have also suffered deeply from slavery and racism. Their own history has been ignored. "History has been written without us. The imperative is clear: Either we will make history or remain the victims of it" (Wallce, 1980, p. 309).

Angela Davis (1981), another black activist, also writes of how slavery has affected today's relationships between African Americans. She stresses that black women worked just as hard in the fields as the men, and were not just pampered house slaves. Unfortunately, domestic service was often the only occupation available to black women after emancipation. This continuation of serving whites and was often still called their "nigger" (i.e., slave). Many times, the white employers subjected these women to sexual abuse and labor exploitation. Their wages were usually lower than those of white or immigrant house servants. Even after blacks moved to the north, the women were often stuck in domestic work again. Not until World War II did these women manage to get jobs that no longer treated them as ex-slaves.

Like Wallace and Davis, Cynthia Stephens experienced the tensions between black men and women during the civil rights era. As a student organizer at the University of Michigan in 1970, she helped to lead BAM (Black Action Movement). Unfortunately, the male coleaders saw her as a "pushy broad" and tried to minimize her initiative (Cole, 1994, p. 312). Although several women were faithfully working on the picket line for days, the men later stated that only Stephens was involved in the protests. In the 1990s, the next generation of activists at the same school also confronted sexism. One activist was told that "'outspoken' women … were labeled lesbians in an attempt to silence them and discredit their work" (Cole, 1994, p. 317). The women decided not to be homophobic by denying it, but to keep on speaking up.

Lorde (2007) is a black lesbian who also had to deal with sexism and homophobia. She describes the frustration she had with black males who did not respect women as their equals.

> All too often the message comes loud and clear to Black women from Black men: "I am the only prize worth having and there are not too many of me, and remember, I can always go elsewhere. So if you want me, you'd better stay in your place which is away from one another, or I will call you 'lesbian' and wipe you out." Black women are programmed to define ourselves within this male attention and to compete with each other for it rather than to recognize and move upon our common interests. (Lorde, 2007, p. 48)

Political activists, of course, are not the only ones to show sexist tendencies. Religious leaders in the black community often urge women to submit to their husbands because it is God's will. For example, Munroe (2001) writes that "God designed the woman to fulfill her purpose of being a compatible helper for the man" (Munroe, 2001, p. 95). Men should be the visionaries, leaders, teachers, and protectors. Because women were created to help men fulfill their destiny, they should obey God's plan instead of defying it.

Discussion Question

If you were involved in a political movement and your peers did not respect you, would you keep on working with them? What would be the alternatives?

Poverty

Racism, sexism, and poverty are all interlocking problems that are difficult to separate from each other. (Box 14.1 describes one form of racism, micro-aggressions.) African Americans experience more poverty than whites for several reasons, including the overincarceration of both men and women. Not only does prison "socialize men to be more violent," it reduces the chances of employment and staying in relationships (Hattery & Smith, 2014, p. 128).

Box 14.1 Micro-aggressions

In her book *It's the Little Things: Everyday Interactions That Anger, Annoy, and Divide the Races,* Williams (2000) uses the term "micro-aggressions" to describe how people can alienate each other unintentionally. Dr. Alvin Pouissant, who calls micro-aggressions "the death of a thousand cuts," is quoted in the book explaining this term.

> The things you experience every day that then add up and take their toll. Everything from being in a place and feeling invisible or ignored or questioned about your credentials or your feelings about race matters. They may seem minor, but people don't know how much this society makes blacks constantly think about being black. (Williams, 2000, p. 10)

Social workers and anybody else who want to be culturally competent should consider the possibility that they may be giving nonverbal cues or saying inappropriate things that are harmful. Williams expands on this concept.

> Too much still remains unsaid, and too much assumed, imagined, or inferred. Blacks as well as whites are guilty of making false assumptions about the other group's motives. Resentments over seemingly small slights are felt by both. I know of blacks who refuse to relinquish an inch to whites on narrow city sidewalks, because it smacks of the bygone days of Jim Crow; of black men who feel it is the height of condescension for white men to refer to them by their first names. I remember parties that were dead on arrival the minute the words "So, what do blacks think about…" were uttered, and job offers that were rejected on the spot because a white interviewer used the word *articulate* to compliment a well-spoken black applicant. I've seen whites on a crowded subway stand through several stops rather than approach a black youth sitting alone in a seat for two. I've seen whites called racists for acts that had little or nothing to do with race. And I've seen confusion on the faces of white Americans when blacks call each other 'niggers' but dare these whites to even think about it. (Williams, 2000, p. 4)

Going beyond micro-aggressions, Smith (1998) confronts white feminists with the behavior shown to their black counterparts. She believes that whites should do more to fight the entrenched racist systems.

> I am sure that many women here are telling themselves they aren't racist because they are capable of being civil to Black women, having been raised by their parents to be anything but. It's not about merely being polite: "I'm not racist because I do not snarl and snap at Black people." It's much more subtle than that. It's not white women's fault that they have been raised, for the most part, not knowing how to talk to Black women, not knowing how to look us in the eye and laugh *with* us. Racism and racist behavior are our white patriarchal legacy. What is your fault is making no serious effort to change old patterns of contempt—to look at how you still believe yourselves

to be superior to Third World women and how you communicate these attitudes in blatant and subtle ways. (Smith, 1998, p. 97)

Discussion Questions

1. Have you ever experienced a micro-aggression? How did you react?
2. Have you ever inadvertently said or done something that could be seen as derogatory to somebody else? How did you handle it?

Another cause—and result—of poverty is the higher rate of teen mothers, which is three times higher than whites although the rate of sexual activity is only 10 percent higher (Hattery & Smith, 2012). As educational options are limited and the chances for marriage are lower for young black females, motherhood represents a sign of adulthood. Domestic violence is also related to poverty both as a cause and result. Lower-income black women are not only at higher risk of abuse, they are at a higher risk of economic hardships caused by the abuse. Lastly, class differences between the middle class and lower class may occur when successful blacks disassociate themselves from "the abandoned" who did not fight their way out of poverty like they did (Slattery & Smith, 2012, p. 110).

Poverty, of course, has been a recurrent problem for decades. Growing up African American in the 1960s, Rosemary Bray (1998) describes how the welfare system and the Catholic Church impacted her and her family in Chicago.

Certain things shape you, change you forever. Years later, long after you think you've escaped, some ordinary experience flings you backward into memory, transports you to a frozen moment, and you freeze. Being poor is like that. Living surrounded by fear and rage is like that. I grew up hating the cold, dreading the approach of night. Thirty years later, a too-cold room at night can trigger a flash of terror, or a wash of ineffable sadness. Voices raised in anger can still make me shrink (Bray, 1998, p. 3).

Her mother had to survive beatings from her husband, humiliating treatment at the welfare office, and the daily rigors of poverty. "My mother's endurance was a mystery to me. I understood why she said she could not leave us. I was grateful that she refused to disappear. But what I never understood was how she was able to do what she did for as long as she did it.... There was only the relentless quest for survival" (Bray, 1998, p. 10).

Despite the popular belief that living on welfare is pleasant, Bray describes the way it was for her family:

One of the truths that seem to elude most welfare reformers is the pervasive sense of fear and tension that accompanies that monthly check. I learned to decipher that look of tension in my mother's eyes.... Not one of these bitter people (welfare critics) understands how hard it is simply to live with the money any state provides. There is no money to plan ahead, to shop cheaply, to prepare for an emergency. There is no ability to set aside a bit for the future; the present occupies all the attention of anyone on welfare (Bray, 1998, p. 13).

Although African Americans are more likely than whites to be poor, whites are the majority of TANF (Temporary Assistance to Needy Families) recipients. The media's images of the Welfare Queen imply that she is an African American, which strengthens the false belief that welfare recipients are mostly African Americans or Latinos. However, all three groups (whites, Latinos, and African Americans) have a rate around 30 percent for receiving TANF benefits (Department of Human Services 2010 report, cited on www.democraticunderground.com). This misconception is related to the racist assumption that blacks are freeloaders. In one survey, whites were less likely to support Hurricane Katrina victims if the picture showed blacks instead of whites (Harris-Perry, 2011, p. 152).

Poverty, then, is linked to economic injustices caused by discrimination, as Collins (2014) notes:

> Despite differences of age, sexual orientation, social class, region, and religion, U.S. Black women encounter societal practices that restrict us to inferior housing, neighborhoods, schools, jobs, and public treatment and hide this differential consideration behind an array of common beliefs about Black women's intelligence, work habits, and sexuality. (p. 25)

For example, Collins quotes from an essay by a sixth-grade girl living in a high-crime neighborhood and then comments about the child's reality.

> "My world is full of people getting rape (sic). People shooting on another. Kids and grownups fighting over girlsfriends (sic). And people without jobs who can't afford to get an education so they can get a job ... winos on the streets raping and killing little girls." Her words poignantly express a growing Black feminist sensibility that she may be victimized by racism, misogyny, and poverty. They reveal her awareness that she is vulnerable to rape as a form of sexual violence. Despite her feelings about her neighborhood, Sandra not only walked the streets daily but managed safely to deliver three siblings to school. In doing so she participated in a Black woman's legacy of struggle. Sandra prevailed, but at a cost. Unlike Sandra, others simply quit. (Collins, 2014, pp. 26–27)

Stereotypes

Girls like Sandra must grow up in a setting full of stereotypes about her as a black female. Even the most successful black women must grapple with these stereotypes, including First Lady Michelle Obama (Figure 14.2). Her public role meant different things for different people, of course. Kaplan (2008) writes how some started associating

Figure 14.2 *First Lady Michelle Obama official portrait (Photo courtesy of Library of Congress)*

Michelle Obama with the ghetto as soon as she stopped playing the one-dimensional role of supportive wife.

> It's worth noting how Michelle was admired as long as she filled the prescription of a successful black woman on paper … But (later she was seen as) another kind of black woman altogether: angry, obstinate, mouthy…. (Kaplan, 2008).

Angry Black Woman (Sassy Mammy) Stereotype

Journalists and other critics have called Obama the Angry Black Woman. This stereotype began in the 1800s, when popular media portrayed the Sassy Mammy as controlling their families and talking back to their white superiors.

Stressing the "misrecognition of African American women" (Harris-Perry, 2011, p. 21), one writer notes that the Mammy stereotype was applied to Representative Stephanie Tubb Jones. A journalist had called her "Hanky Head" in 2008 for supporting Clinton—a white candidate—over Obama (Harris-Perry, 2011, p. 70). Another Congressperson, Representative Maxine Waters, worked hard in Congress for 20 years but all her efforts were dismissed in a column by Cal Thomas: "Angry black women … They're usually angry about something" (Harris-Perry, p. 87).

Are black women really that angry? In the article "Debunking the Myth of the 'Angry Black Woman': An Exploration of Anger in Young African American Women,"

Walley-Jean (2009), reports that these women are less likely to show anger and more likely to repress any outbursts. However, the stereotype persists. One modern version of the Angry Black Woman relates to their alleged resistance to black men dating/marrying white women (Childs, 2005). One woman states, "Black men are in fashion; call it the resurgence of the black male. It's like interracial dating is a fashion statement, a token especially when it is an African American athlete" (Childs, 2005, p. 553). As a result of so many black men rejecting black women for white girlfriends, many black women feel even more victimized by the European standard of beauty that does not honor them.

Discussion Questions

- Using a search engine, type in the term "Michelle Obama angry face" to verify the author's assertion that some people apply the Angry Black Woman stereotype to the First Lady. Try to find similar pictures of former First Ladies, such as Laura Bush. What do you conclude from this exercise?
- Find three examples of Angry Black Woman in movies or TV shows. For instance, would you consider Madea to fit that stereotype?
- The Jim Crow Museum website (www.ferris.edu/jimcrow) is a rich source of data about racial stereotypes. Pick a stereotype and find modern versions of it.

Strong Black Woman Stereotype

A variation of the "Mammy" is the Strong Black Woman stereotype, as described in Sheri Parks' *Fierce Angels: The Strong Black Woman in American Life and Culture* (2010).

> The Mammy myth was central to the nostalgia for a grand Old South, which Southern whites used to return to the delusions that made slavery palatable to them in the first place. The myth fulfilled their need to redefine themselves as a once great and powerful people, loved and cared for by wonderful black women. It reassured poorer whites that they had shared in the glorious past of the Old South, although they had really been hurt by the competition with slave labor. The myth also positioned the black woman as the protector from the more "savage" black man. The docile, happy male slave, according to the myth, became dangerous and angry when freed. Many believed that blacks were physically stronger than whites and that black men could not be assimilated. At the same time, many whites thought that black women were already assimilated. (Parks, 2010, p. 67).

This perceived division between the "savage" black man and the assimilated (and safer) black women has affected media coverage and even policymakers. The disproportionately high rate of incarceration of African-American males, for instance, has received international attention for its possible human-rights abuses. Unemployment and underemployment (low-paying, dead-end jobs) have also affected African-American males more than their female counterparts.

On the political level, policymakers have attacked these women who had to support their families and others. On the political level, policymakers have attacked these women who had to support their families and others. In 1965, the Moynihan Report stated that too many black households were headed by females, instead of males. Criticisms of "welfare mothers" and other racially loaded terms have continued this tradition of blaming the women for chasing their men away. Parks describes the social expectations of African-American women to be strong:

> I was raised to be strong and nurturing. As far back as I can see, so were all the women of my family. We never asked why. The survival of our family and of our race seemed enough. In black life, women are the fierce girlies, mamas, and grandmamas who hold together black families and neighborhoods through sheer determination. Folks consider them to be the "backbone" of their families and culture, with "back" being an important operative word. Black females in this country are born in the army of Fierce Angels, and they have no choice in the matter. (Parks, 2010, p. xiv)

As a result of these pressures, the extreme stress has affected their health to the point of a higher mortality rate for this population. "The diseases that kill black women—diabetes,

Figure 14.3 *Nursing student (Undated photo courtesy of Library of Congress)*

heart conditions, obesity, hypertension—are all connected to and worsened by stress" (p. xix). However, Parks stresses that these Fierce Angels ultimately "remind us that strong love, intelligently and energetically applied, can evoke great change" (p. 206)

The author bell hooks agrees about the negative repercussions of too-high expectations for black women.

> Racist stereotypes of the strong, superhuman black woman are operative myths in the minds of many white women, allowing them to ignore the extent to which black women are victimized in this society, and the role white women may play in the maintenance and perpetuation of that victimization.... By projecting onto black women a mythical power and strength, white women both promote both a false image of themselves as powerless, passive victims and deflect attention away from their aggressiveness, their power.... These unacknowledged aspects of the social status of many white women prevent them from transcending racism.... (hooks, 1997, p. 15)

Discussion Question

Find an example of the Strong Black Woman stereotype. Do you agree with Parks and hooks about the possible harm of this stereotype?

Jezebel Stereotype

Another long-term stereotype of African-American women is the Jezebel stereotype, the one with unrestrained sexuality. During the centuries of slavery in the United States, this stereotype was used to justify the sexual abuse of the slave women. They were not quite human, so it was acceptable to brutalize them. In the era of slavery, black women were displayed on the auction blocks with their bodies fully exposed. Collins (2000) calls this an early form of pornography. Another writer states that "Black women's sexuality is often described in metaphors of speechlessness, space, or vision; as a 'void' or empty space that is simultaneously ever-visible (exposed) and invisible, where black women's bodies are already colonized" (Collins, 2000, p. 123).

Collins also connects this stereotype to the black rapist, both with "abnormal or pathologized heterosexuality. Long-standing ideas concerning the excessive sexual appetite of people of African descent conjured up in White imaginations generate gender-specific controlling images of the Black male rapist and the Black female jezebel ..." (Collins, 2000, p. 129).

Even the civil rights movement has not removed the impact of this stereotype. The glamorization of the ghetto ethos, including the word *pimp* to mean to improve something ("Pimp your ride"), has given new life to the hypersexualized black female image. Music videos also promote a hypersexualized view of black women, inspiring the term "video ho." The Urban Dictionary defines this term as " 1) A women in a video who is wearing the most revealing clothes always trying to be near the rapper or singer in a video trying to get the most camera shots; 2) A women who wears revealing clothes" (www.urbandictionary.com).

Discussion Questions

• In the recent past, pornographic images of black females included the submissive posture of women on their knees performing fellatio and being locked up in chains. Connect these images with Collins' observations about slavery.

- Do you agree with some observers that black women are sometimes portrayed as partly animal? Can you think of any recent examples in advertising or music videos, or is this theme no longer used in popular culture?
- How do these stereotypes differ from the women from other ethnic groups?

Strengths

Writers such as Maya Angelou have shown strength in their lives and written stories about the women who inspired them. In her autobiographical work *I Know Why the Caged Bird Sings*, Angelou (1970) writes of her childhood in rural Arkansas in the 1930s. Segregation was a bitter fact of life. Maya occasionally came into contact with few whites, only the "powhitetrash" (Angelou, 1970, p. 28), who were disrespectful toward the blacks. Even white children were rude to the adults in her family store, calling them by their first name.

When Maya was 10, some white girls came to the store to harass her grandmother. The woman stood still and hummed a hymn to herself while the children mocked her. One girl even exposed herself as a sign of extreme disrespect. The grandmother had to accept this humiliation, and even say goodbye to the girls by calling them "Miz." Maya confronted her after the girls had left.

> I burst. A firecracker July-the-Fourth burst. How could Momma call them Miz? The mean nasty things. Why couldn't she have come inside the sweet, cool store when we saw them breasting the hill? What did she prove? And then if they were dirty, mean and impudent, why did Momma have to call them Miz?
>
> She stood another whole song through and then opened the screen door to look down on me crying in rage. She looked until I looked up. Her face was a brown moon that shone on me. She was beautiful. Something had happened out there, which I couldn't completely understand, but I could see that she was happy. Then she bent down and touched me as mothers of the church "lay hands on the sick and afflicted" and I quieted.
>
> "Go wash your face, Sister." And she went behind the candy counter and hummed, "Glory, glory, hallelujah, when I lay my burden down."
>
> I threw the well water on my face and used the weekday handkerchief to blow my nose. Whatever the contest had been out front, I knew Momma had won.
>
> I took the rake back to the front yard. The smudged footprints were easy to erase. I worked for a long time on my new design and laid the rake behind the wash pot. When I came back to the Store, I took Momma's hand and we both walked outside to look at the pattern.
>
> It was a large heart with lots of hearts growing smaller inside, and piercing from the outside rime to the smallest heart was an arrow. Momma said, "Sister, that's right pretty." Then she turned back to the Store and resumed, "Glory, glory, hallelujah, when I lay my burden down." (Angelou, 1970, pp. 32–33)

Another memoir of an African-American woman is Dickerson's *An American Story* (2000). Growing up in north St. Louis, she joined the Air Force and the middle class in 1980. She looked down at her former home as a depressed city with depressed people.

In the Air Force, then, Dickerson found her home. By working diligently, she believed that she had no need to worry about race or gender. However, the prevalence of rape on the military bases made her rethink her position on gender issues. She knew many women who had been date raped or beaten by their boyfriends. Dickerson also dealt with internalized racism. In the military, she came across blacks who spoke ungrammatically or seemed unmotivated.

Then she was raped by a fellow serviceman. She had woken up in the middle of the night with him on top of her. This trauma affected her deeply. "Passing men, I felt as if I had a bull's-eye drawn in blood red on my pelvis. I had a vivid new image of myself, of all women, as walking targets" (Dickerson, 2000, p. 121). Struggling with the aftermath, she did not receive enough support from the military.

Another event that caused her to reexamine her identity was how the Reagan recession affected her relatives. She noticed that many of her relatives had been laid off. Poverty, then, was a more complex matter than that of poor motivation. Later, she had a dream about being in a nightclub back home in St. Louis.

> What I felt was wistfulness because I wasn't part of it. Even so, it was a soothing dream, one that filled me with hope and humility. I envied my oblivious brethren their places at the table and I wished I could move so unselfconsciously among them. For the first time, I also knew that anyone in that room who was wasting his time judging me and critiquing my every move wasn't worth worrying about. I even considered the possibility that nobody was paying me the least attention. How self-absorbed to carry on as if no one but me had mastered mainstream English or ever cracked the covers of serious literature. The weight of the community off my shoulders, I woke up smiling. It hit me like a thunderbolt. I was alone. Truly alone.
>
> I didn't like it.
>
> I wanted to be black.
>
> I admitted to myself how ashamed I'd been of us and I simply let it go. I just walked away from it.
>
> It was much easier than I would have imagined it would be. Once I stopped kidding myself about my true feelings, I just stepped out of that shell of self-hatred and felt a hundred pounds lighter. Once I did, my overwhelming emotion was---foolishness. I felt silly. How could I hate black people? That's like hating my elbows. If black people were no good, then I was no good. My mother, my sisters, strangers on the street. That couldn't be. I had a lot more thinking to do, but the more I lived, the more all my old assumptions were crumbling. (Dickerson, 2000, p.146)

Rediscovering her identity as a black woman, then, became the sources of Dickerson's strength. The internalized racism had evolved into an intense love for herself and her fellow blacks.

Motherhood, of course, can be one source of strength for women. However, Box 14.2 describes the dilemma of African American mothers trying to protect their sons in a society that calls them thugs.

Box 14.2 Raising Black Sons in the Ferguson Era

In 2014, a policeman shot to death a young African-America male in Ferguson, Missouri. This tragedy resulted not only in several protests across the country, but a frank discussion about racial profiling (coverage is available on several news websites, such as www.abcnews.com). The earlier shooting death of Trayvon Martin by a neighborhood vigilante in 2012, besides several other acts of violence against black males that went unpunished, reinforced the idea that it is dangerous to be an African American on the streets.

Comedian Chris Rock (1997) shares his thoughts about being the target of so much suspicion.

> Sometimes I hate life that I was born a suspect. All black men are born suspects. When I came out of my mother, right away, if anything happened within a three-block radius, I was a suspect. As a matter of fact, the day I was born, somebody's car got stolen from the hospital parking lot. They made me stand in a lineup. That was pretty tough, considering I wasn't even a day old and couldn't crawl, much less walk. Good thing I had a couple black nurses to help hold me up. I got lucky. They were in the lineup, too (Rock, 1997, p. 9).

Unfortunately, Rock's satire is not too far from the truth. A mother of a toddler discusses the early labeling of her son, even when he is still wearing diapers. Below is her description of one such incident.

> An acquaintance…spotted us and came over to say hello. She looked at my son, marveling over how much he had grown since she last saw him a few months ago.
> 'Yes,' I smiled, "He's a big boy!"
> She replied, "Such a cute little thug."
> My son is 2 years old (Garlinghouse, 2015).

Why are blacks targeted as though they are not even human? One article, "Not Yet Human: Implicit Knowledge, Historical Dehumanization, and Contemporary Consequences" (Goff, Eberhardt, Williams, & Jackson, 2007) describes the results of six separate research studies with the same conclusion: many college students connect blacks with apes and would endorse violence against them, including capital punishment. These students were too young to have been raised in the pre-civil rights milieu that often depicted apelike blacks. However, even in 2015, celebrities such as the Univision host Rodner Figueroa compared Michelle Obama to a character on *Planet of the Apes* (Hutchinson, 2015). Implicit bias, then, may be one cause of the threat against black males.

This racial profiling concerns many mothers who want to protect their sons from being harassed for wearing a hoodie or walking with their hands in their pockets. Taraji P. Henson, an actress and mother of a college-age son, decided to transfer her son from a California campus to the historically black college Howard University. She hopes that this setting will decrease the number of times her son will be stopped by policemen (Williams, 2015). Obviously, this

Figure 14.4 *Mother and son (Photo courtesy of OUP)*

is not a feasible solution for parents without enough income to move their sons away from white-dominated areas.

Another black mother, Kelly Rowland, expresses her concerns about teaching her son about his self-worth while being stigmatized. "He needs to get it from home so that when he goes into the world he has a great sense of self-respect and identity and he knows who he is and he has respect for others as well" (Gebereyes, 2015) Many parents, of course, want to instill the right values in their children—but black parents face the additional burden of raising their sons in a society that would label them as thugs.

Discussion Questions

1. If you were/are the mother of a child of a stigmatized population, what would be your strategies in addressing that stigma?
2. What macrolevel interventions do you suggest to fight racial profiling and other aspects of implicit bias?

Strength, then, can come from many sources. Some writers emphasize that besides claiming one's identity, black women must also be warriors. Lorde's words contain a message intended to embolden her sisters:

I am not only a casualty, I am also a warrior. What are the words you do not yet have? What do you need to say? What are the tyrannies you swallow day by day and attempt to make your own, until you sicken and die from them, still in silence? Perhaps for some of you here today, I am the face of one of your fears. Because I am woman, because I am Black, because I am lesbian, because I am myself—a Black woman warrior doing my work—come to ask you, are you doing yours? (Lorde, 2007, pp. 41–42).

Key Terms

Civil rights movement
Micro-aggressions
Sassy Mammy/Angry Black Woman
Strong Black Woman
Jezebel
Internalized racism
Ferguson Era

15

Asian-American Women

Introduction

Like other groups that are not the dominant culture in the United States, Asian Americans are by no means a monolithic group. Layers of complexity include class, level of education, country of origin, rural or urban background, and the number of generations who have lived in the United States. Some Asian Americans came as little children and have no memory of their homeland, whereas others have family roots for decades (Nomura, 2003). This can lead to acculturation differences between the young and old. Helie Lee (1996), a Korean American writer, shares her feelings about the culture clash with her elders. As she became more Americanized, her grandmother and mother feel that they are losing her.

> Grandmother was the one who devised a plan for us to flee Korea. And it was Mother's idea to raise us like the other American kids in the San Fernando Valley. She filled my head with dreams, telling me I could become anything I wanted. I believed her so much I thought I could be white. My light-eyed friends were my role models, people I emulated. I copied their dress, manners, and Valley girl speech in order to lose myself and fit in.... To me, my parents and grandmother were from Mars—out of sight and out of touch—too Korean for my good.
>
> "Your makeup too heavy. Try soft color. Dark lipstick make your face look sick." Mother's voice steers my mind back to the moment.
>
> "You sick? Stick out tongue." Grandmother sticks out hers to demonstrate.
>
> "Grandmother, not here," I whine, embarrassed.
>
> "Grandmother right. You not eat enough," Mother remarks as she brushes the bangs out of my face, ruining a perfectly styled hairdo.

"It's too late," I protest. "I am who I am. I'm not like you."

"What?! You think you better than your mother? You shame because we Korean?"

"No, I didn't say that." I'm totally flustered. I regress back to a little whimpering girl whenever I'm with these two women who intimidate me so much.

"You Korean, you always be Korean. Our people so good."

"Then why did you bring us to America if you didn't want us to be American?" (Lee, 1996, pp. 12–13)

After explaining to her that they had to flee the war, her mother adds:

I know you tired me tell you eat more, do nice hairstyle, change lipstick color, wear nice dress, but I do because when others see your Oriental face I want them to say, "Ah, the Korean lady, they so proud people." (Lee, 1996, p. 13)

Koreans, of course, are not the only Asian group that expresses cultural pride. As Asian American women encounter common challenges and demonstrate their strengths, a vibrant spirit emerges from their stories.

Challenges

History

As with everyone else, history still affects the lives of Asian-American women. In the nineteenth century, the United States used the labor of the Chinese men to build the transcontinental railroad. These laborers endured brutal and life-threatening work conditions. However, the government did not reward them with citizenship but instead repressed them. In 1882, the Chinese Exclusion Act barred all Chinese from citizenship (Foo, 2002). More importantly, the Act and its successors banned legal migration from China until 1943.

Fear of the Yellow Peril (i.e., hordes of Asians taking over) had led to this prohibition of Chinese immigration. Another reason was that the government assumed that all Chinese were prostitutes. Mazumdar (2003) discusses the barriers faced by the women, including overt racism and legal exclusion that occurred before the 1882 Chinese Exclusion Act. Using the Asian women's exotic sexuality as an excuse to use them as objects, men patronized Chinese prostitutes in the Old West. Lawmakers, assuming that all Chinese female immigrants were prostitutes, passed a law in 1870 to allow immigration officers to exclude women of questionable character. Because of such restrictive immigration laws, thousands of Asian women were left behind in their countries while their husbands worked for decades in the United States. One Indian man did not reunite with his wife for forty years.

Another scholar notes, "The only Chinese women whose existence American society acknowledged were the prostitutes who lived miserable and usually short lives. Senate hearings on Chinese immigration in 1876 resounded with harangues about prostitutes and slave girls corrupting the morals of young white boys. 'The Chinese race is debauched....'" (Yu, 1989, p. 35). Instead of being able to reunite with their wives or sending home for a bride, then, most Chinese men had to remain unmarried.

Other Asian groups also had to deal with restrictive immigration laws, including the Japanese and Koreans. One result of these laws was the practice of picture brides, in which men arranged to marry complete strangers based on the pictures. This practice is reminiscent of today's Internet advertisement for husbands in the United States and Europe by Asian women. Escaping from their home countries meant a huge gamble, but it sometimes paid off. One 78-year-old Korean grandmother stated, "Ah, marriage! Then I could get to America! That land of freedom with streets paved of gold!... Since I became ten, I've been forbidden to step outside our gates, just like all the rest of the girls of my day.... Becoming a picture bride, whatever that was, would be my answer and release" (Mazumdar, 1989, p. 7).

Many Asian immigrant women ended up working in the farm fields, which was hard work that rarely paid as well as for men. One Korean picture bride recalled that she would go to the sugar cane fields at 4 A.M. and work until dark. She was glad that she was too short to see past the cane plants, since she did not have to see how much work lay ahead. (Mazumdar, 1989).

Another striking example of Yellow Peril concerns affecting U.S. policy occurred in World War II, when the Japanese Americans were herded into internment camps. The bombing of Pearl Harbor in 1941, of course, affected not only Japanese Americans but all Asian Americans who faced open hostility and racism (Mazumdar).

Noda (1989) writes of her reaction to her parents' past internment.

"Why did you go into those camps," I raged at my parents, frightened by my own inner silence and timidity. "Why didn't you do anything to resist? Why didn't you name it the injustice it was?" Couldn't my parents even think? Couldn't they? Why were we so passive? (Noda, 1989, p. 246)

She realized later, though, that the Japanese Americans were already facing restrictions such as five-mile travel limits and early curfews. The banks had frozen their accounts and the neighbors stole from them without fear of any legal consequences. When the soldiers with machine guns did come to round up these American citizens, then, the new prisoners went quietly to the internment camps.

Since then, anti-Asian prejudice has continued. In the 1950s, the Korean War resulted in a wave of refugees (including Lee, the author cited in the Introduction of this chapter). Kim (1989) expresses her feelings about leaving her homeland: "Throughout my life, it has seemed to me that being Korean meant living with *han* every day. *Han*, the anguished feeling of being far from what you wanted, a longing that never went away, but ate and slept with you every day of your life, has no exact equivalent in English" (Kim, 1989, p. 81).

Like the Korean War, the Vietnam War resulted in an influx of refugees into the United States. One writer who worked with refugee children notes that "Then I notice that some of the children who have walked through fire in Southeast Asia have emerged not destroyed, but tempered with strength, hope, and resilience. For these children, obstacles simply mean finding another way" (Kam, 1989, p. 97). Another refugee, who had to bury her own sister during wartime, had trouble adjusting to her new life. "Huu

Tien was already beginning to hate English…. It would be very hard to fit in here. No, the time of joy was not yet. Nonetheless she was no longer in a city at war, or on a sickening boat with pirates around, nor in a camp" (Lee & Oberst, 1989, p. 112).

The Vietnam War also inspired many Asian Americans to protest the war as racist and unjust. Rejecting the term "oriental," these activists adopted the term "Asian American" instead. The term "oriental" was not overtly racist, but its connotations of exotic stereotypes seemed outdated (Foo, 2002).

The history of Asian Americans in the United States, then, is one of challenges partially caused by anti-Asian sentiments. The Immigration and Naturalization Act of 1965 mandated that more non-Europeans could migrate to the United States, thus diversifying the population with more Asian immigrants. In the 1980s, fear of economic competition from Japan led to a resurgence of anti-Japanese feelings. The current fear of China's economic boom has led to a version of the Yellow Peril. Fortunately, Asian Americans have shown great resilience through the 150 years in the United States. One historian encourages Americans to learn their history. As one elderly Japanese laborer is quoted as saying, " 'Our stories should be listened to by young people. It's for their sake. And we had a hard time, you know' " (Takaki, 1998, p. 12).

Stereotypes

As noted in the previous section, stereotypes affected U.S. policy. Not only were Asian American women characterized as exotic temptresses, but they were also regarded as Dragon Ladies. Based on a Chinese empress, this stereotype stresses the "cruel, perverse, and inhuman ways" of these perfidious creatures (Shah, 1997, p. xiii).

Figure 15.1 *Chinese American woman (Photo courtesy of OUP)*

In her analysis of the Dragon Lady and other negative stereotypes of Asian American women, Bow (2011) states that society has distrusted women through history. "Accusations of disloyalty clearly serve to regulate female sexuality" (Bow, 2011, p. 8). Asian-American women are seen as even more treacherous because they were the "Other." One example is Tokyo Rose, a legendary radio personality during World War II in the Pacific theater. She allegedly used her seductive voice to persuade American G.I.s that their girls back home were cheating on them. Bow also asserts that the denigration of Yoko Ono, the wife of John Lennon, was related to anti-Asian prejudice because she was accused of breaking up the Beatles.

The article title "Nancy Reagan: China Doll or Dragon Lady?" (Benze, 1990) proves that the power of stereotypes extend beyond Asian-American women. Media portrayals of Asian Americans continue to present three memes: Dragon Lady, Lotus Blossom, and the male as a sexless nerd. The Dragon Lady has too much power, whereas the Lotus Blossom and the male loser have too little power (Ono & Pham, 2009). The title of the feminist anthology, *Dragon Ladies: Asian American Feminists Breathe Fire* (Shah, ed., 1997) is one appropriate comeback to the persistent stereotypes.

Discussion Questions

- Find three examples of a Lotus Blossom (exotic Asian girl) on the Internet or in the popular media. (Hint: use search terms such as "Asian Girls" and "Asian women"). How long did it take you? Find three examples of Asian woman who are *not* stereotypical Lotus Blossoms or Dragon Ladies. How long did that take you?
- Ono and Pham (2009) consider some roles played by Lucy Liu to reinforce the Dragon lady stereotype. Use search terms such as "Lucy Liu Kill Bill fight scene" and "Lucy Liu Charley's Angels massage" on the YouTube website (www.youtube.com) to look up some movie scenes. Do you agree with the authors, or do you think that her characters satirize the Dragon Lady image?
- Do you think that the Lotus Blossom and Dragon Lady stereotypes are related to essentialism? Defend your answer.
- One response by Asian American women is to boost their image as successful career women. Lu (1997) criticizes this approach, though, by stating, "proving that some Asian women can succeed on the terms of the dominant culture fails to question the injustices that remain in place" (Lu, 1997, p. 19). Do you agree or disagree with this comment? Why or why not?

Model Minority Myth

One current stereotype of Asian Americans is the Model Minority, in which they are seen as highly successful compared to other minorities. As an Indian woman, Roshanrawan (2009) writes of how belonging in the model minority prevented her from claiming a minority status altogether. She still experienced racism, but had nobody to whom she could relate. As an honorary white who could sometimes "pass," she felt that she did not really belong to any social group. One Korean American college student, for example, joined Latino groups on campus because she could be herself with them. The author encourages the use of the term "Woman of Color" because the "identity may

Figure 15.2 *Chinese immigrant children in Manhattan (Undated photo courtesy of Library of Congress)*

be especially appealing for the politicized woman who is racialized as inferior and who lacks resistant sociality" (Roshanrawan, 2009, p. 11).

Another writer (Pegues, 1997) describes her experiences as a "Model Minority" person in leftist groups. The white leftists ignored her Asian identity because they considered her to be an honorary white. She felt invisible to these non-Asian leftists, who thought that Asian Americans had no social justice issues like other minorities. The group members regarded her this way:

> (I received) more compliments about my appearance than my viewpoints. One leftist friend referred to me as "his little Mao." Asian American women are considered a safe bet for leftist groups; we boost their proportions of people of color, yet are expected to be cute, well-behaved, hard-working, and obedient. (Pegues, 1997, p. 9)

Besides the question of self-identity, the Model Minority myth is harmful because of the assumption that all Asian Americans are prospering. Li (2013) uses the term "bamboo ceiling" instead of "glass ceiling" to describe the invisible barriers to success, such as discrimination and exclusion. Many Asian American women work in low-paying, dead-end jobs that lead to health problems (Foo, 2002). In *The Myth of the Model Minority: Asian Americans Facing Racism*, Chou and Feagin (2014) emphasize the high level of racism faced by Asian Americans in general.

"Lumping different Asian ethnic groups into a single Asian-American category hides the variation of economic success and academic achievement across ethnic groups" (Kwon & Au, 2010, p. 224). Southeast Asians, for example, have lower rates of college attendance and higher rates of poverty. Socioeconomic class and language proficiency, not ethnicity, are the key factors in academic success. The author also points out that the higher household income is the result of more working adults living in the same household, not necessarily higher salaries.

Research reported by Kim and Zhao (2014) supports this assertion about the Model Minority. Measuring the labor-market performance of college-educated female workers, the researchers conclude that Asian-American women are more likely than whites to be unemployed and less likely to be promoted to management.

Discussion Questions

1. If you were entering a room in a campus library looking for a quiet place to study, would you sit near Asian Americans or whites? Describe your first reaction to this question. Were you prejudging the two groups?
2. Discuss two disadvantages of being called a Model Minority. Which minority would you consider to be the most opposite of an idealized one?
3. Asian Americans are less likely to seek health care—especially mental health treatment—because of the cultural expectations of appearing strong and stoic (Augsberger, Hahm, & Dougher, 2015). What would be an effective outreach to overcome the resistance to asking for help, especially because of the Model Minority ideal?

Parental Expectations: Challenge or Strength?

Parental expectations of a highly successful child can be either a challenge or strength. The stereotypical overachieving Asian is related to the new stereotype of the Tiger Mother, a term that resulted from Amy Chua's account of her parenting style in *Battle Hymn of the Tiger Mother* (2011). Her tough discipline in forcing her young daughters to practice their music and study for hours has resulted in controversy.

Some might think that the American sports parent is an analog to the Chinese mother. This is so wrong. Unlike your typical Western overscheduling soccer mom, the Chinese mother believes that (1) schoolwork always comes first; (2) an A-minus is a bad grade; (3) your children must be two years ahead of their classmates in math; (4) you must never compliment your children in public; (5) if your child ever disagrees with a teacher or coach, you must always take the side of the teacher or coach; (6) the only activities your children should be permitted to do are those in which they can eventually win a medal; and (7) that medal must be gold. (Chua, 2011, p. 5)

Chua proudly describes her own childhood as a second-generation immigrant. Her father worked long hours and was very strict, but she was happy. Once when she won a history prize as a child, her parents went to the award ceremony. "Somebody else had won the Kiwanis prize for best all-around student. Afterward, my father said to me: 'Never, never disgrace me like that again'" (Chua, 2011, pp. 16–17).

Concerned that her daughters would grow up too comfortably in their middle class setting, Chua urged them to do physical labor and listen to classical music. She continued to feel determined to not slack off herself, as indicated by the passage below.

> As the eldest daughter of Chinese immigrants, I don't have time to improvise or make up my own rules. I have a family name to uphold, aging parents to make proud. I like clear goals, and clear ways of measuring success. (Chua, 2011, p. 26)

When she told others about how strict she was with her daughters regarding school-work and other requirements, culture clashes with her non-Chinese acquaintances resulted. For instance, she did not understand why the other guests at a dinner party got upset when she mentioned that she had called her daughter "garbage." As a child, she herself had been called that by her parents. "It worked really well. I felt terrible and deeply ashamed of what I had done. But it didn't damage my self-esteem or anything like that. I knew exactly how highly he thought of me. I didn't actually think I was worthless or feel like a piece of garbage" (Chua, 2011, p. 50).

Parental expectations, then, can inspire Asian Americans to try to please their parents. In a qualitative study of young Korean Americans, one woman stated about her father, "I almost felt like I was living his life for him and my mom's as well (Hahm & Kim, 2010, p. 34). Another woman described her burden to please her family: "If I did something wrong it would reflect bad on my parents.... I wouldn't want to like shame my family or make my parents look bad" (Hahn & Kim, 2010, p. 34).

According to another study led by the same researcher (Hahm, Gonyea, Chiao, & Koritsanszky, 2014), parental expectations are a factor in the high rate of suicide among Asian-American women. In the article "Fractured identity: A framework for understanding young Asian American Women's self-harm and suicidal behaviors," the women felt that they could not comply to the "dutiful daughter" or "perfect Asian woman" ideal (Hahm Gonyea, Chia, & Koritsanszky, 2014, p. 63). The researchers add that the results could be harmful.

> They feel suffocated by the idealized Asian woman image and wished to escape these norms and instead follow their own desires, a path that often leads in involvement in risky healthy behaviors, including unsafe sexual behaviors and/or drug use. (Hahm, Gonyea, Chia, & Koritsanszky, 2014, p. 63)

Discussion Questions

- If you were a social worker with a client who came from a similar culture and treated her child like Chua, what would be the appropriate response?

- Asian Americans must be bicultural and comply with two sets of norms—white mainstream and their Asian culture. If you were a social worker leading a support group for this population, what resources or actions would you recommend?
- One study of young Asian-American women engaging in high-risk sexual behavior (i.e., not using condoms) is related to gender power control. Do you think that strict parenting makes an Asian girl more or less likely to engage in safer sex practices by insisting on condom usage?

Strengths

Louie's book on labor activists, *Sweatshop Warriors: Immigrant Women Workers Take on the Global Factory* (2001) provides a clear example of the strengths of Asian American women. Despite the alleged protections provided by labor laws, the workers in the garment industry experienced low wages (e.g., less than $2 an hour) and long hours (e.g., over 100 hours a week). Some of these women had emigrated from Hong Kong, where the working conditions were much better. Louie claims that half of these shops violate U.S. labor codes. As a result, several health problems plagued these workers. One woman said, "'I got X-rays taken and it shows that the (back) bone is kind of bent. If I sit or work too long, my back just can't take it anymore. That's why I need to rest a little'" (Louie, 2001, pp. 19–20). Repetitive stress injuries hampered the hands' functions, and poor circulation for sitting too long caused even more problems. In a garment shop in New York City for the DKNY brand, one worker reported that:

> It felt like being in prison....We had to keep our heads down all the time once we started working. No looking up. No talking to anyone. Can you imagine? A big room with rows and rows of machines and all of us looking down. (Louie, 2001, p. 44)

Fortunately, many of these women rose up in protest. "They transformed themselves from women exploited by the subcontractors and elites to women who clearly understood the 'big picture'" (Louie, 2001, p. 13). This big picture consists of a large web of international exploitation of workers. Labor organizers helped them to build workers' centers for mutual support.

Joining together to force employers to give them their back pay, these women refused to back down. One organizer commented on them:

> Quite a few of the women are very strong. They get a lot of pressure from the bosses, from their families to back down. It's not easy for women workers to fight for justice. They have to deal with survival, how to take care of their kids, and what to do with their husbands. Through our activities we try to stay in touch. We stress that problems just can't be solved alone by oneself. (Louie, 2001, pp. 39–40)

Besides collective action, another cultural strength is filial piety. In a study of Asian-American caregivers, researchers found many women finding joy and gratification in their assistance to their aging parents. One woman stated, "My parents have been very giving, generous people.... It is our turn to do something. It means one way to show them I love them, care for them. Besides, Oriental people are not expressive. They don't go to tell you 'I love you' all the time. So you do for them" (Jones, Zhang, & Meleis, 2003, p. 848).

Discussion Questions

- After reading both the Challenges and Strengths sections, write a paragraph that emphasizes what every social worker should know about this population.
- Find one challenge that is shared by another group discussed in this textbook. Are the challenges identical? How could the Asian-American women and the other group unite to fight the same challenge?

Case Study: South Asian Women Immigrants

Despite the growing number of immigrants from India and its neighbors, the number of research studies on South Asian women immigrants is scanty. Their journey to the United States and other western nations is called the Diaspora, a reference to the historic dispersion of Jews throughout the world. South Asians are sometimes mistaken for persons of Arab descent. Since the 9/11 terrorist attacks of 2001, this similarity has been a disadvantage for them. An immigration advocate in New York City writes of the aftermath in 2011:

> Ten years later, the South Asian community and other immigrant communities are still grappling with anti-immigrant backlash and xenophobia. This has contributed to the stalling of workable solutions to immigration reform in Congress and to a widespread movement in the states to restrict immigrants' ability to integrate. (Sayu Bhojwani, 2011, p. 374)

Religion has played a significant role in helping South Asian immigrants to adapt to their new countries. For example, Mir (2013) describes the activism of South Asian Shia Muslim in the New York/New Jersey area. The religious centers host events that keep the community cohesive, and a soup kitchen is open to anyone. Young South Asians are organizing by reaching out to non-Shia groups to build relationships in the larger community. The author concludes that "The South Asian Shias in the USA have a formal history of less than half a century, but have managed to produce an impressive network of institutions that carry the community forward" (Mir, 2013, p. 335).

Another example of religion uplifting South Asian immigrants is a Canadian study on social capital, which involves befriending established immigrants for assistance and advice (George & Chaze, 2009),. For these women, the temple is the center of the social network and helps them to stay grounded. One woman expressed her connection to the temple this way:

Figure 15.3 *Indian mother and son (Photo courtesy of OUP)*

> Okay I could still go to the temple..... just going to the temple really gave me
> peace of mind......I'm doing something which still associates me from India.
> I know like we totally changed over here ... but still there is something which
> I could rely on in making me like 100% Canadian as Indian. (Georg & Chaze,
> 2009, p. 275)

Like other cultures, though, the Indian culture can also have destructive elements.
In an article titled " 'There Is Such a Thing as Too Many Daughters, but Not Too Many
Sons': A Qualitative Study of Son Preference and Fetal Sex Selection Among Indian
Immigrants in the United States" (Puri, Adams, Ivey, & Nachtigall, 2011), women disclose the family pressure to have prenatal tests to determine the gender and to have a
sex-selective abortion if it is a girl. One woman told of her sister-in-law urging her to get
a test, and her mother-in-law threatened to remove her from the family if she did not
comply. Another woman told of how she got pressured after giving birth to two daughters. Her mother-in-law refused to hold the second granddaughter and "yelled at me that
I should have had this test to know if I had a boy or girl. This is why I am getting the test
now for my third child" (Puri, 2011, p. 1172).

A husband's family, then, can be the source of conflict and even violence. In a study
on family violence in Indian immigrant families, Dasgupta (2007) explicates the phenomenon of mother-in-law abuse. The mother-in-law colludes with the son to discipline

his wife, even resorting to violence. The traditional role of mothers-in-law is to punish their sons' wives as they themselves had been punished earlier. Other in-laws can be also abusive to the wife. Many times, the wife's birth family is either back in India or will not accept her decision to leave her husband. Another form of family violence is the abandonment of the wife, who must face stigma and poverty from this rejection. Daughters also can be subject to family violence if they appear too Americanized or date a man not approved by the family.

The wider context of family violence in South Asian immigrant communities has many culturally specific traits (Venkataramini-Kothari, 2007). In one case, a husband partially starved his wife because he wanted to keep her slim like the American models. Not only is divorce a source of shame for women, though, but being unmarried is also stigmatized. This culture stresses family loyalty over individual needs, so divorce seems like a betrayal of an entire family. Educated and/or working wives may experience domestic violence. The stress of being a model minority adds to the dilemma of not wanting to disgrace their community.

Canadian activists have responded vigorously to the prevalence of domestic violence in their South Asian communities (Kang, 2006). Like the wife who does not want to shame her community, however, these women

> … thus face the dilemma of bringing changes in women's status while upholding their own cultural esteem. Due to fear of exposure and resultant discursive perception and treatment by the majority community, women's action groups often conceal the evils of Indian culture as this may undermine their cultural identity. (Kang, 2006, p. 158)

Fighting both racism and domestic violence, then is difficult when the Canadian media stresses the violent nature of Indian men. Another complication is the extreme hardships of an Indian woman who is divorced. A white woman may feel comfortable identifying herself as divorced, but Indian women would probably be left stranded both financially and socially (Kang, 2006).

In another article about fighting domestic violence in the South Asian communities, Bhattacharjee, (1997) stresses how the Western model of individualism does not work for this population. Instead, "collective action would greatly alleviate the burden on individual women. For example, when a woman decides to leave her batterer, the burden of her guilt and responsibility could be lightened by a collective show of solidary from other women" (Bhattacharjee, 1997, p. 34). For example, she recommends that protective orders may not be effective against abusive husbands. In one group, several women with baseball bats promised to stay in the woman's house so she could feel safe. The author connects these actions with cases in India, where villagers sometimes gather together to confront an abuser.

Discussion Questions

- Discuss an intervention to enhance the strengths of a South Asian immigrant community, especially for the women and girls.

- Much of the research on this population focuses on domestic violence. What other aspects of South Asian women do you want to know more about? How would you design a research study to explore that topic?
- In your opinion, what would be the most difficult aspect of being the case manager for an Indian woman who is being battered by her husband and/or in-laws. How would you plan an appropriate intervention?

Perspective of a Japanese-American Woman

In *Polite Lies: On Being a Woman Caught Between Cultures* (1997), Mori describes how the house she shared with her Caucasian husband symbolized the cultural rift between them. She felt social pressure to make the house a home not only because she was the woman, but because of her Japanese heritage. "Everyone who asked Chuck and me about home decorating addressed me more than Chuck" (Mori, 1997, p. 88). She describes her angry reaction to such assumptions.

> Every time someone asked me if I ironed Chuck's shirts, if I planned to work part-time or stay home once we had children, I wanted to cry or slam the door and walk out. I never got used to being reminded that I was "just a woman" and that a woman's place was in the house. I couldn't help seeing the house as something that was used to put a woman "in her place"—a form of punishment. (Mori, 1997, p. 90)

In Japan, women were meant to stay at home. "The most common Japanese word for a wife is ka-nai, literally 'house inside'" (Mori, 1997, p. 90). However, Japanese wives ran the household and controlled the money. "It is a woman, not a man, who gives a sense of security to a house in Japan ... [however], A person can be in charge of her house and still be trapped by it" (Mori, 1997, p. 91).

Her aunt, for instance, rarely went out although her husband worked such long hours that she was alone most of the time. She did not install central heating in her house not because of the cost but because her comfort did not seem important to her. When her husband was home, she did all the work but never asserted herself as a person. "An ideal Japanese woman effaces—rather than expresses—herself. She is valued for her ability to pretend that her hard work is nothing, that she is scarcely there. The home she creates is a pure, empty space. Its beauty is elegant but cold" (Mori, 1997, p. 94).

The cold kitchen, then, symbolizes for Mori the empty hours spent by the lonely Japanese women who deserved more from life. Her cousin, a traditional housewife, spent hours every week creating beautiful flower arrangements that nobody ever saw. "Sitting in front of the tower of flowers my cousin had made, I thought of all the women driven to be alone at night, craving solitude and yet lonely for a different life; night after night, they practiced flower arrangement or embroidery—disciplines of beauty against so much sadness" (Mori, 1997, p. 96).

Vowing to make her life different from her mother's unhappy one, Mori divorces her husband and lives in a studio apartment in the city. "Doing the right thing doesn't mean that we have no regrets. Still, I love the temporary home I have made in an almost public place in the midst of traffic. It's a good place to be" (Mori, 1997, p. 106).

Discussion Question

What was the most striking aspect of Mori's story? Write a paragraph about your reaction.

Key Terms

Chinese Exclusion Act
Yellow Peril
Lotus Blossom
Dragon Lady
Model Minority
Parental expectations

16

Native-American Women

Introduction

As there are over 500 legally recognized tribes, it is impossible to generalize about Native American women. These tribes exemplify the "diversity within diversity" principle because of the wide range of variations. According to the U.S. Census Bureau, the 2010 Census counted 2.9 million persons identified as American Indian/Alaska Native (AI/AN) alone and 2.3 million more identified as AI/AN combined with other races. (Note: Due to the precedent set by this Census classification, this chapter will use the terms *Native American, Indian*, and *indigenous* interchangeably.) This 5.2 million total comprises 1.7 percent of the U.S. population, but represents a 39 percent increase since the 2000 Census. Most AI/AN live in locations other than the reservation (67 percent AI/AN alone and 78 percent AI/AN combined). (http://www.census.gov/prod/cen2010/briefs/c2010br-10.pdf).

Today's popular images of Native Americans are of sweat lodges, gambling casinos, and sexy half-animal types such as the werewolf Jacob in the *Twilight* series. The reality of the lives of Native Americans, of course, is far more complex and deserves serious study. Perdue's description of Native American women (2001) is an excellent starting point.

> Throughout Native North America, women acted as sifters (sorting out corn for bread), giving life and sustaining life. Native peoples honored mothers, not through empty sentimentality, but by recognizing the social, economic, and political importance of their reproductive role. Many Native peoples

Figure 16.1 *Native American woman (Photo courtesy of OUP)*

attributed the earth's creation and peopling to women, not men. Mothers nurtured small children and exercised enormous influence over their adult offspring. In some societies, such as the Iroquois, motherhood conveyed political power to women through clan mothers who chose chiefs and had the authority to depose them.

The status of women also rested on their economic role. Native women, whether they lived in the hunting and gathering societies of the Great Basin or the agricultural societies of the Southeast, provided much of the food for their communities. . . .

Women controlled their own labor and the goods they produced. Feminist anthropologists have referred to "arenas of power" and "complementary" roles in describing the relationship between Native women and men: each gender had its own responsibilities, and Native societies recognized that the contributions of each were essential to survival. Similarly, each gender had access to spiritual power, although perhaps in different forms. Women, for example, had songs and rituals that made the corn grow, while men's ceremonies brought success in hunting and war. Gender, therefore, distinguished in profound ways the kind of life—from work to prayer—that a person would live (Perdue, 2001, p. 4).

Challenges

Historical Traumas

Native Americans live with many historic traumas, such as the attempted genocide of some tribes in the nineteenth century. One historian claims that the Native American genocide was worse than the Nazi's mass murders of the Jews, since "many American Indian peoples became extinct" (Thornton, 1987, p. xvi). Conservative estimates of the Indian population before the Europeans' arrival are around five to seven million. By 1900, though, the Indian population had declined to 250,000—its lowest point (Thornton, 1987). Government officials were quite explicit about their genocidal intent, including the Governor of California speaking before the Assembly in 1852:

> That a war of extermination will continue to be waged between the two races until the Indian race becomes extinct, must be expected; while we cannot anticipate this result with but painful regret, the inevitable destiny of the race is beyond the power and wisdom of man to avert (Trafzer & Lorimer, 2014, p. 64).

In this context, the Indian woman was either glorified as a princess or despised as a "squaw." Either way, sexual exploitation was one major factor in the war against the Indians. The first European settlers bragged about how they beat and raped native women until they acted like courtesans. If a native man did not mine enough gold for the day, the Spanish supervisors would come to his hut to rape his wife (Miranda, 2011).

California was especially a horrific place for Indian women. Men in Spanish missions routinely raped women who "necessarily became accustomed to these things, but their disgust and abhorrence never left them till many years after" (cited in Miranda, 2011, p. 98). When the women gave birth, they sometimes killed and buried the babies in secret because of the trauma. Slavery was also endemic as the children left behind in massacres were "protected" by their white masters. Not until 1867—two years after the Civil War ended slavery in the South—did California agree to abide to the antislavery laws of Congress to achieve statehood.

These traditions of sexual violence perpetuated against Native women continue to this day. Smith's article, "Not an Indian Tradition: The Sexual Colonization of Native Peoples" (2003), discusses how rape has two layers of meaning for Indian women. The attack "is not just an attack on her identity as a woman, but on her identity as a Native.... This explains why, in my experience as a rape crisis counselor, every Native survivor I ever counseled said to me at one point, 'I wish I was no longer Indian'" (Smith, 2003, p. 71).

Violence Against Native Women

"Historically, violence against Native women was rare because such behavior was inconsistent with the role of women within the worldview of Indian nations" (Agtuca & Sahnevah, 2014, p. 31) Before the Europeans came, the tribal languages did not even have a word for domestic violence. Some tribes would punish batterers with whipping, exile, or even execution.

Figure 16.2 *Native American woman from Plains region (Undated photo courtesy of Library of Congress)*

Poverty is associated with domestic violence, especially related to the high unemployment rate (Gurr, 2015). Whether fueled by poverty or other causes, domestic violence is now a dominant issue for Native women. In a 2000 report, the Department of Justice reports that 64 percent of women reported being "raped, physically assaulted, and/or stalked since age 18" by an intimate partner (Tjaden & Thoennes, 2000, p. iv). Children exposed to domestic violence are at special risk. "This exposure not only contradicts traditional understandings that children are to be protected and viewed as sacred, but it leaves hundreds of children traumatized and struggling to cope over the course of their lifetime" (www.justice.gov/ovw/tribal-communities).

Social isolation is one risk factor for Native women, especially in Alaska. The founder of a women's shelter in Alaska describes the dilemma of finding a safe place to hide in the following excerpt:

Since my journey began working and helping women in rural, remote Alaskan villages, I have seen and listened to countless stories filled with so much pain and have heard the crying voices of our Native women, our sisters, our aunties, grandmothers, and children, often with nowhere to go for safety. In reality, there is no safe place to go in the villages, except to local churches (if doors are left open), inside willows, in steam baths, and/or fish smokehouses (caches). There are no readily available resources and many women and children have no reliable police protection. We cannot simply get into a car and drive away---we run, many times with five children with us as we hide under our homes in the dark, cold winter months. Sometimes, if we're lucky, we might see a porch door open and we run inside the house, not knowing whom the house belongs to or whether someone is home … this we do to keep ourselves alive (Agtuca & Sahnevah, 2014, p. 19).

The legal question of tribal sovereignty versus the authority of the U.S. government has hampered efforts to fight violence against women. In 1885, the Major Crimes Act enabled the U.S. government to exercise joint jurisdiction on the tribal lands, but prosecutions of rape and domestic violence were rare. A loophole for perpetrators emerged from the 1978 Supreme Court ruling on tribes having no legal jurisdiction over non-Indians—they could get away with raping Native women on reservations (Agtuca & Sahnevah, 2014). According to the Department of Justice website, "American Indians are 2.5 times more likely to experience sexual assault crimes compared to all other races, and one in three Indian women reports having been raped during her lifetime" (www.justice.gov/ovw/tribal-communities). Not until the 2013 revisions of the Violence Against Women Act (VAWA) was this loophole addressed.

Reproductive justice is related to the issue of violence against Native American women (Gurr, 2015). They have a higher risk of illness and death from health hazards such as unclean water and limited access to medical services, Native American women have a higher risk of illness and death. For instance, cervical cancer cases are often diagnosed at a stage too late to treat. Forced sterilizations have been part of their history, a troubling legacy of a "racist patriarchal state" (Gurr, 2015, p. 27). The writer claims that the inadequate health care for Native women is a continuation of the past treatment of them as disposable people.

> The violent oppressions enacted on Native communities in the ongoing project of "disappearing" Native peoples—from land, from history, from contemporary stories about the nation—are enacted in part through the bodies of Native women, including Native women's sexuality and reproduction, as indigenous communities continue to be targeted in particular ways under a heteropatriarchal, white supremacist settler colonial regime. (Gurr, 2015, p. 30)

Intellectual Apartheid

In her introduction to an anthology of Indian women's writings, Allen (1989) uses the term *intellectual apartheid* to describe how Indian writers have faced exclusion from mainstream literature (Allen, 1989, p. 3).

> The literature and arts of non-Western peoples have thus remained obscure to people educated in Western intellectual modes. Moreover, non-Western literature and art appear quaint, primitive, confused, and unworthy of serious critical attention…. Aesthetic colonization affects everyone. (Allen, 1989, p. 3).

She also links intellectual apartheid to political apartheid, since this ignorance of Indian culture leads to harmful policy decisions. Native women are especially invisible to mainstream society. Intellectual apartheid is also related to the historic trauma of the Indian boarding schools, in which the children were not allowed to speak their tribal languages or show any cultural traits.

Indian boarding schools, which tried to "civilize" Native children from the 1880s to the 1950s, were another form of intellectual apartheid. Sometimes authorities kidnapped these children, while other times parents gave permission to give their children an educational opportunity. Johnson (1989), a Canadian activist, describes her experience at an Indian boarding school:

> The first grief of my life was when we reached the mission. They took my buckskin dress off, saying I was now a little Christian girl and must dress like all the white people at the mission.... My next serious grief was ... that they forbade me to use any Cree words whatever.... (Johnson, 1989, p. 71)

Kenney, who was sent to a mission school by her alcoholic parents, endured separation from her siblings. "We had to speak English, so most of us forgot our language. We couldn't even ask about traditions or stories—nobody did. We didn't have names, we were called by numbers—like I was Miss 14.... our souls and spirits were all in the same mold. We were little frozen people" (Kenney, 1995, p. 36).

The 1950s saw the end of the Indian boarding school era, and subsequently the adoption of Native children into white families continued until the 1970s (Agtuca & Sahneyah, 2014). In 1978, Congress tried to remedy the harm done to Native Americans by passing the Indian Child Welfare Act. This law stresses the need to keep Indian children with their families and/or tribes instead of being sent away to non-Indian families. (www.nicwa.org) Although Indian boarding schools no longer exist, Allen (1989) claims that the mainstream educational system of today still represses Indian culture.

Discussion Questions
- If you plan to work in child welfare, what else should you know about the Indian boarding schools and the Indian Child Welfare Act?
- In your opinion, is the "squaw" image a social construction? Why or why not?

Stereotypes of Native Women

One element of intellectual apartheid is the media image of the squaw—the silent, submissive wife. In the movies, "We did not see her making medicine to heal a sick child, or praying. We did not see her addressing a tribal council or planning military strategy" (Katz, 1995, p. 6). Because Europeans associated manual labor with servitude, they assumed that Indian women were oppressed by men, instead of partnering with them. These misconceptions continue among non-Natives. When asked to present on Indian woman, a guest speaker noted that "'when I didn't show up in buckskin and moccasins, the audience was disappointed; I felt like they didn't really hear what I had to say'" (Katz, 1995, p. 7).

Another common stereotype is the Indian Princess, which is also a product of intellectual apartheid. In Chrystos' poem "I Am Not Your Princess," the poet expresses her anger toward those who see only a stereotype that epitomizes a nature-based spirituality.

I won't chant for you
I admit no spirituality to you
I will not sweat with you or ease your guilt with fine turtle tales (Chrystos, 1988, p. 66).

Since then, the Disney movie *Pocahontas* was released to a new generation of children. The Indian Princess is beautiful, uplifting, and the "Other." Does this movie reinforce the historic image seen in advertisements and literature, or present a new portrayal of Native American women?

Discussion Questions

- Before starting the analysis described next, write a paragraph about your view of Native American women. How much do you know? Which images have influenced you?

Figure 16.3 *Native American woman and child (Photo courtesy of OUP)*

- Review the Indian Princess pictures on the Authentic History website's article, Native Americans and American Popular Culture. (www.authentichistory.com/diversity/native). How many of these images are familiar or new? Does viewing this collection increase your awareness of stereotypes in general?
- Conduct a content analysis of the *Pocahontas* movie (or at least the song "Colors of the Wind" as available on www.youtube.com). Count the number of times a certain phrase, symbol, color, or other aspects of the Indian Princess appears. For instance, she moves like a deer in the forest—a symbol that she is closer to nature than the rational European male. Look for themes, such as her relationship with animals. Do you think that this movie increases a child's knowledge of Native American culture, or does it denigrate the culture?
- If you had a new client who was a Native American woman, what would be the appropriate steps to ensure a high level of cultural competence in your encounters with her? Did the preceding exercises increase your sensitivity to possible stereotyping? If not, what would be a good approach to recognizing and negating the power of a stereotype?

Wounded Knee 1973

The conflict between the U.S. government (and its Indian allies) and the Indian resistance movements did not end in the nineteenth century. Although the 1890 Wounded Knee massacre is a milestone in the history of Indian resistance, a new wave of defiance emerged through the AIM (American Indian Movement). In 1973, the activists decided to occupy the site of this tragedy on the Pine Ridge Reservation. They were opposed to the tribal chairman and his alleged obeisance to the U.S. government. This event developed into a two-month siege that ended with fatalities on both sides, the AIM and the FBI (Federal Bureau of Investigation). The violence ensued sporadically for two more years—leaving additional and deep scars on the Native American population.

In 2012, a local college hosted a conference on the Wounded Knee protests. "Thirty nine years later, the anger stemming from the occupation and its turbulent aftermath had not cooled. Some observers believe that the Pine Ridge Reservation, one of the poorest places in the United States, still suffers from the trauma inflicted by the warring sides in the 1970s" (Magnuson, 2013).

Below is an excerpt from Mary Crow Dog's memoir, *Lakota Woman* (1990), about her experiences at Pine Ridge Reservation.

I am Mary Brave Bird. After I had my baby during the siege of Wounded Knee they gave me a special name—Ohitika Win, Brave Woman, and fastened an eagle plume in my hair, singing brave-heart songs for me. I am a woman of the Red Nation, a Sioux woman. That is not easy.

I had my first baby during a firefight, with the bullets crashing through one wall and coming out through the other. When my newborn son was only a day old and the marshals really opened up upon us, I wrapped him up in a blanket and ran for it. We had to hit the dirt a couple of time, I shielding the baby with my body, praying, "It's all right if I die, but please let him live."

When I came out of Wounded Knee I was not even healed up, but they put me in jail at Pine Ridge and took my baby away. I could not nurse. My breasts swelled up and grew hard as rocks, hurting badly. In 1975 the feds put the muzzles of their M-16s against my head, threatening to blow me away. It's hard being an Indian woman....

At age fifteen I was raped. If you plan to be born, make sure you are born white and male.... It is not the big, dramatic things so much that get us down, but just being Indian, trying to hang on to our way of life, language, and values while being surrounded by an alien, more powerful culture. It is being an *iyeska*, a half-blood, being looked down upon by whites and full-bloods alike. It is being a backwoods girl living in a city, having to rip off stores in order to survive. Most of all it is being a woman (Crow Dog & Erdoes, 1990, pp. 3–5).

Discussion Questions
- To achieve cultural competence, a social worker must know the basics of the group's history. What do you know about the Wounded Knee massacre of 1890? If you do not know much about it, why do you think it was not taught in your history classes?
- How much did you know about the Wounded Knee incident of 1973? After researching this topic, highlight three points that every culturally competent person should know.
- If you were a social worker on Pine Ridge Reservation in 1973, how would you have reacted during this violent clash?
- In what year were Native Americans allowed to vote? Why is this also a significant fact?

Strengths

One famous Cheyenne saying is, "A nation is not conquered until the hearts of its women are on the ground. Then it is done, no matter how brave its warriors, nor how strong its weapons (Daly, 1994, p. 240). As feminism reemerged in the 1970s in the United States, some Native women claimed that economic survival—not any gendered oppression—was their primary focus. Many saw themselves as "the keepers of the culture" (Daly, 1994, p. 236) through the decades of repression. This theme is common in diverse groups of women who do not know which primary identity to claim. Daly also points out the tensions caused by acculturation—how "Indian" should they be?

In the hundreds of tribes in North America, the role of women in these tribes varied greatly. The Navajos, for instance, expected husbands to move into their wives' families and work for them. Women were allowed to divorce her husband this way: "In earlier times, it was easy. She just picked up all his stuff and put it outside the door of the hogan, and that was it. He couldn't contest it. He had to go" (Whitehorse, 1995, p. 57).

Archeologists and historians claim that the Iroquois tribes were also an egalitarian society (e.g., Bursey, 2004). Another indication of how some indigenous groups honored the strength of women follows:

> The arrival of horses to the Plains in the 1700s brought major changes to the lives of the Lakota and others. One innovation was an increasing emphasis on male activities and maleness. Even so, many ceremonies and societies continued to honor women.
>
> These included a women's society known as Praiseworthy Women. Before performing a ceremony, members wrapped strips of otterskin around their foreheads and wore eagle feathers in their hair. While a group of men sang for them, the women danced in a circle.
>
> Another group, the Tanners, honored women as teepee makers. When a woman needed to make a teepee cover, she sent a messenger to throw tent-making tools through the doorways of each of the other teepee-makers in the encampment. On the appointed day, the women feasted together and sewed skins provided by their hostess into a new teepee cover.
>
> One of the most sacred and powerful societies of all was the Women's Medicine Cult. Only women who had had certain kinds of dreams of buffalo and other large animals could belong. These dreams gave them the power to forecast success in war during the coming year. It also made them responsible for blessing and protecting young men who were going to war.
>
> The women made the young men war shields and imbued the shields with sacred powers. To each young man the women also gave a small medicine bag with feathers, bird skins, or some other sacred objects attached (Hazen-Hammond, 1999, p. 102).

Tribes also revered older women not only for their wisdom, but also for their nurturing. One inspiring story is of the Wise Old Woman who "lives deep inside a spring. She knows that people are starving, and she wants to help" (Hazen-Hammond, 1999, p. 36). She tricks two medicine men into jumping into the spring.

> At the bottom of the spring, the wise old woman gives each man a bowl of food to take back to the people. It seems like such a small amount of food, but when people begin to eat, the bowls keep filling themselves from within. No matter how much people eat, the bowls never empty. The people are saved. (Hazen-Hammond, 1999, p. 36)

Many oral traditions have also honored the female image of a fertile earth. The Pawnees, for instance, sing this prayer during the Mother Corn ritual:

> Mother Corn, who led our spirits over the path we are now to travel, leads us again as we walk in our bodies, over the land ... She led our fathers and she leads us now because she was born of Mother Earth and knows all places and all people, and because she has on her the sign of having been up to Tirawahut, where power was given her over all creatures. (Fitzgerald & Fitzgerald, 2005, p. 36).

Figure 16.4 *Native American elder (Photo courtesy of OUP)*

Another tribute to Mother Corn in Pawnee culture indicates the awe that this tribe felt toward the gifts of women:

> As I lay sleeping, as I lay dreaming, out of the distance came one advancing one whom I ne'er had seen before, but when her voice addressed me, straight-way I knew her—Lo! 'Twas our Mother, she whom we know. I rose from sleeping, my dream remembering. Her words I pondered, words of our Mother. Then I asked of each one I met, Tell me, how far may Her shrine be? When I found it sweet smoke I offered unto our Mother. (Fitzgerald & Fitzgerald, 2005, p. 26)

Like the prayers cited earlier, this song excerpt for girls' puberty rites from the Chicicahua Apache tribe acknowledges the power of women.

> I come to White Painted Woman,
> By means of long life I come to her.
> I come to her by means of her blessing,
> I come to her by means of her good fortune,
> I come to her by means of all her different fruits.
> By means of the long life she bestows, I come to her,
> By means of this holy truth she goes about.

Native-American Women   **283**

I am about to sing this song of yours,
The song of long life.
Sun, I stand here on the earth with your song,
Moon, I have come in with your song.

White Painted Woman's power emerges,
Her power for sleep.
White Painted Woman carries this girl;
She carries her through long life.
She carries her to good fortune,
She carries her to old age,
She bears her to peaceful sleep. (Fitzgerald & Fitzgerald, 2005, p. 39)

A modern version of a revered grandmother is Rita Pitka Blumenstein, a 76-year-old who lives in the Alaskan tundra. Here is her story:

Today Rita, a Yup'ik Indian, lives on the Alaskan tundra but she was born on a fishing boat on Nelson Island in the Bering Sea. Her father, half Russian and half Aleut, died a month before she was born, but he left instructions for her to attend a Montessori school in Seattle, and a bond to pay her tuition.

Rita grew up to enjoy a 43-year marriage with a Jewish man; their daughter calls herself a "Jewskimo." Not surprisingly, Rita's ceremony is a creative, eclectic mix of cultural influences.

She has placed 13 stones around the Sacred Fire Circle to represent the 13 planets and the 13 grandmothers. She prays for healing water, earth, fire, and air. Chanting in the Yup'ik language, she tosses cedar into the fire from the four directions.

She invites the Thirteen Grandmothers plus all the grandmothers in the audience to form a circle around the Sacred Fire, and then invites the children to stand in front of them. She greets each youngster, and invites the children to bless themselves by touching their hearts, then their heads. After the children scatter cedar in the fire, Rita asks everyone to howl like an Alaskan wolf, creating a deafening cacophony....

Rita passes the crowd a large ball that is painted to look like the planet. It travels overhead from hand to hand. Each trip, the ball circles closer to the Sacred Fire until it is transferred from grandmother to grandmother, and finally, from child to child....

I ask whether Rita considers herself a doctor, healer, shaman, or medicine woman. "My name is Rita," she smiles. "I am special. There is no better than—and no less than—me. That's who I am." (Gianturco, 2012, p. 178)

Ceremonies like that of the Sacred Fire, then, provide strength to both the individual and community. The Corn Dance, for instance, celebrates the harvest time. Planting also inspires a reverent attitude, as expressed by one writer: "When I plant my garden,

I give an offering to Mother Earth, and pray for a good crop.... You have to be in a calm state of mind. It's almost a meditation" (Track, 1995, p. 26).

Discussion Questions

- If you were working with a group of Native women on a community project, which strengths mentioned in this section could be helpful?
- This chapter includes several examples of misogyny. Find one and write a paragraph on how Native women could reclaim their heritage to overcome it.

Key Terms

Intellectual apartheid
Indian boarding schools
Indian princess
Tribal sovereignty
Wounded Knee 1973

17

Women with Disabilities

Introduction: Author's Note

What does *disabled* really mean? This question is intensely personal for me, since I have been coping with disabilities for years. The doctors diagnosed me with juvenile rheumatoid arthritis when I was only eight. I misheard the term as "author-itis" and thought that meant that I was going to grow up to be a writer one day. For decades, though, I did my best to ignore the pain. People laughed at me for being a klutz, since I wiped out all of the time. (Later, I found out that both knees had cartilage and bone chips that often made me trip.) Otherwise, this was an invisible disability because I did not limp at the time. I never considered this condition to be a disability, only as "bad knees" that slowed me down.

My first visible disability, then, came from a bizarre cancer episode in which half of my left thumb had to be amputated. Later, I had to have a skin graft on the stump because of some possible melanoma spreading there. At the age of 35, I stared at my mutilated hand and was repelled by it. Having read that trying to hide a deformity only makes it more obvious, I resolved never to cover up my left hand. This still goes against my instincts, especially if I am talking to an attractive man.

"I am now disabled," I said to myself. The thumb provides around half of a hand's function; as I now tell my friends, be nice to your thumbs. Every day, I have to adjust my hand functions for simple tasks such as washing dishes. My right hand and shoulder developed such severe tendinitis from overuse that both sides were disabled for months.

"I am disabled," I say to employers who must provide me with special keyboards to comply with the ADA (Americans with Disabilities Act) requirements. One reason why I left the business world to enter academia was because I could no longer use a computer for eight hours a day. I needed to make a living somehow.

Then the arthritis hit me with a vengeance in my forties. This time the disabilities were extremely visible as I struggled with canes, walkers, crutches, and walking boots. Being a full-time professor meant being on one's feet for hours. Even when I started teaching from a chair, I had to get up numerous times to run the classes. Luckily, I taught on a small campus so the walking was minimal—but it was enough to wipe me out from the pain.

What, then, is a disability? The visible symbols of handicap placards and walking aids are indicators but do not really define the term. One writer expresses it well:

> How, I wondered, should I handle my flawed body? What attitude do I take? What language do I use? The answers did not come easily. All my life I had been taught to ignore my skin condition, to pretend—against manifest evidence—that the problem didn't exist. (Kaler, 2011, p. 228)

I certainly went through years of denial, trying to "pass" as nondisabled as many others have tried. "Sometimes the notion of calling myself disabled makes me want to disappear ..." (Dorris, 2011, p. 346). As I delay travel plans until I recover from my latest surgery, I think of the famous expression "biology is destiny." In this case, how much of my life has been determined by my body's limitations?

> Bodies are not absolute. As an artist, as a disabled person, as one who believes in the possibility of social as well as personal change, I resist any attempts to make our bodies determinative, to keep disabled people in their places, to force our bodily facts to be destiny. (Ferris, 2011, p. 90)

Another aspect of being disabled is developing a new identity, regardless of whether or not it is desired. Society gives me two choices: pitiful sufferer or heroic survivor. Neither choice fits me. Asking for pity would only increase my own self-pity, which is abundant enough. And I reject the term *cancer survivor* although it is meant to empower people like me. I did not fight any harsh battles, I only went to the doctors and submitted to the surgeries and managed not to die. To me this was common sense, not courage.

Playing the role of comedian was one way I gained social approval. In the doctors' waiting room waiting for the latest biopsy result (i.e., news of whether I was going to live or die), I would compose comedy routines in my head. They were not really funny jokes. However, people praised me for my attitude for making light of my situation. A writer dealing with quadriplegia notes:

> As with other social roles, a person can succeed or fail at sickness. A key rule for being a successful sick person is: Don't complain! The person who smiles and jokes while in obvious physical misery is honored by all (Murphy, 1990, p. 20).

This diversity chapter, then, is not intended to evoke pity or admiration for women living with disabilities. The title of Rousso's book, *Don't Call Me Inspirational: A Disabled Feminist Talks Back* (2013), expresses the frustration of many who just want to be seen as they are. Like me, Rousso was able to "pass" for years because the cerebral palsy (CP) symptoms were minor at first. She resisted her new identity as the symptoms worsened and became more obvious.

> Despite my disability activism, somewhere in my head I still saw myself as nondisabled. Also, I continued to feel uneasy when I encountered some people with CP. They, too, served as mirrors, challenging that image of myself as "normal."
>
> Such grappling continued for years—decades, in fact—and I'm not entirely comfortable with my disabled body even today. But other experiences, besides disability activism, helped me progress in the process of truly embracing myself as a woman with CP. First, I fell in love. Or, more to the point, a few men whom I wanted fell in love with me....
>
> Some of my women friends also helped me develop a more positive body image. For example, when I complained about my clumsy, unfeminine walk to one of my closest friends, who had a disability herself, she said, "I love to see your 'crooked' walk, because when I see it, it means you are coming to visit." (Rousso, 2013, p. 8)

Challenges for Women with Disabilities

Ableism

One challenge for anybody with a disability is ableism, which can be defined as "society's pervasive negative attitude about disability" (Hehir, 2007, p. 8). Why do some people respond differently to a disabled person than to a nondisabled person? One possible explanation is simply fear.

> Ableism has been noted to cause fear, in part because of ignorance concerning whether a particular disability is contagious. Additionally, fear is often projected on disabled people by nondisabled people as seem to be triggered by the representation of disability to process their mortality and the frailty of their bodies. (Stevens, 2011, p. 3)

Micro-aggressions, a term first used regarding race-based indignities but now expanded to other out-groups (Sue et al., 2007), may be a common occurrence for women with disabilities. One example of a micro-aggression is the treatment of somebody in a wheelchair as a nonentity, as described by this writer.

> A store clerk will listen to my question, and then turn to face my attendant, replying, "The elevator is at the back ..." Some strangers must see my attendants as keepers, as wardens wholly responsible for me, serving alternately as nurse, as guardian, as conduit to the world of the normal. (Hershey, 2011, .p 131)

Women with noticeable disabilities, then, can feel invisible to others. Even feminists have neglected to include this population in their call for equality. Saxton (2012) noted that in the past, feminists marginalized disabled women because they could not "meet traditional feminist stereotypes—if we cannot be powerful, autonomous, highly intelligent, financially or physically independent, in the typical ways." She ended with a quote from Bonnie Klein, "These notions hurt and limit all women, but they especially have kept women with disabilities disconnected from the feminist community. But, 'feminism is strongest when it includes its weakest'" (Saxton, 2012).

Besides invisibility, some persons with disability may feel objectified by the medical profession. Saxton, who was born with a disability had to endure many surgeries as a child. During one doctors' round, she was on her bed with a crowd of men staring down at her. One doctor tried to pull away her underwear to show her hip. "Pleading-eyed, I begged him to let me keep this token of privacy. Miraculously, he let go" (Saxton, 1987, p. 54). As an adult, she has this message for those who provide care to disabled children: "People do the best they can to help in meaningful ways, I know. I just wish all disabled children would say to their helpers: 'Before you do anything else, just listen to me'" (Saxton, 1987, p. 55).

Social reactions like the doctors' disregard for the child's dignity can be debilitating, as noted by one author: "Like many people with a disability, I am always slightly amazed to realize I have suffered more from other people's perceptions of my condition than I have from my own real 'disabilities'" (Black, 2011, pp. 208–209). One reaction is to impose stereotypes on persons who are too unique to be categorized. For example, one woman at a grocery store was seen as too independent to need help. "People apparently think they know what crips look like. I startle them. I am clearly not helpless, not pathetic or sickly" (Stewart, 1987, p. 135). As a result, she did not get the help she needed to load up the car. Keith (1994) concurs with the dilemma of being seen as completely helpless and completely independent: "It is important to try to counteract the popular view of ourselves as sick, tragic figures, but if we do this by denying the realities of our lives, which are sometimes painful and sad, we are just swopping the "tragic but brave" model … (that) we must always be fighters … .(Keith, 1994, p. 7). As figure 17.1 indicates, disability does not mean disempowerment.

On the other hand, some persons react with extreme pessimism when they see a severely disabled person. Kafer (2013) describes her experience in the rehabilitation center after being injured in a fire:

> I have never consulted a seer or psychic; I have never asked a fortune-teller for her crystal ball. No one has searched my tea leaves for answers or my stars for omens, and my palms remain unread. But people have been telling my future for years. Of fortune cookies and tarot cards they have no need: my wheelchair, burn scars, and gnarled hands apparently tell them all they need to know. My future is written on my body.
>
> In 1995, six months after the fire, my doctor … thought graduate school would remain out of reach; it was simply not in my future.… My friends were likely to abandon me, alcoholism and drug addiction loomed on my horizon, and I needed to prepare myself for the futures of pain and isolation brought on by my disability. Fellow rehab patients, most of whom were elderly people recovering from strokes or broken hips, saw equally bleak horizons before me.

Figure 17.1 *Triumph over ableism (Photo source: Entofolio)*

One stopped me in the hall to recommend suicide, explaining that life in a wheelchair was not worth living.…

A common response is for people to assume that they know my needs better than I do, going so far as to question my judgment when I refuse their offers of help. They can apparently see into my immediate future, forecasting an inability to perform specific tasks and predicting the accidents and additional injuries that will result. (Kafer, 2013, pp. 1–2)

Body image concerns also affect women with disabilities, as described in Box 17.1 In a society that stresses an unrealistic beauty standard, women who are "different" may experience self-hatred.

Box 17.1 Case Study About the Body Image of a Teen Girl

One writer had to wear a big boxy hearing aid as a child, so she struggled with her body image. Below is a quote from her essay:

> As a vain child trapped in a monster's body, I was frantic for a way to survive the next few years. Glimpsing my reflection in mirrors became such agony that I acquired a habit of brushing my teeth and hair with my eyes closed (Galloway, 1987, p. 6).

1. If you were her parents, how would you help her to adjust?
2. How should a friend react to such a statement? What would you say?
3. Research the term *body image* on an Internet search engine. What would be some good ideas for a counselor to consider with this girl?

Discussion Questions

The term *micro-aggression* can apply to anybody who has felt marginalized or put down by somebody based on class, race, gender, etc.

1. Have you ever experienced a micro-aggression? Did you acknowledge it or just let it pass? What did it make you feel?
2. Have you ever dismissed a person's intelligence or committed another type of microaggression? What triggered this action? Did your socialization affect your behavior?

Invisible Disabilities

Considering stories such as Kafer's about being told that it would be better to commit suicide than to live in a wheelchair, it is no wonder that some persons try to hide their physical disabilities for as long as possible. As a child with cerebral palsy, Gritz (2011) writes of how she managed to "pass" as normal while her symptoms were still mild. She did have to wear a special shoe at night, though. "Though I understood that what I had was cerebral palsy, I thought of that shoe as my disability. More precisely, I thought of it as my secret inner ugliness. After all, it was kept hidden and mentioned only in private as my mother helped me put on at night" (Gritz, 2011, p. 191).

In contrast, a woman who lost her leg has made her peace by not trying to walk without a limp. At first she tried to "pass" despite wearing a prosthetic leg, then gave it up. "My gimpy gait is mine, and it is very 'normal' to me.... Above all, why should women amputees even care about what others think about their gait? Just being able to walk or to get where we want to go … is the point, isn't it?" (Walton, 2011, p. 6).

Box 17.2 discusses the concepts of stigma and "passing as normal. "Passing" does have its disadvantages, however. Siebers (2004) writes of how he needed accommodations at the airport but he was disregarded. Not until he had to use crutches for another condition did people consider him to be a legitimately disabled person. "For one thing, it was the first time I found myself on crutches since I had come out as disabled. The crutches projected to the public world what I felt to be a profound symbol of my inner life as well as my present status as a person with a disability" (Siebers, 2004, p.1). People can be especially judgmental about possible fakers, especially those who use the handicapped spaces. Mollow (2012) shares this story in a co-written essay:

> The second time I was confronted about parking in a handicapped spot was right after I moved to Berkeley.... This woman had all these pride stickers on her car: disabled, Jewish, queer. And she was yelling at me. "Nobody," she said, looking me up and down, "nobody who looks as good as you can be disabled!" I was twenty-nine years old, wearing a sundress and high-heeled sandals. "You need to educate yourself about invisible disability!" I said. "You need to edu-cate *your*self!" she shot back. I walked away, shaking and feeling sick to my stomach. I really did need that parking spot; I was in too much pain to walk through even the whole grocery store. But what I hate most about my memory of that moment was that a little part of me sort of liked it: in a way, I liked the

Box 17.2 The theories Behind Stigma and "Passing"

Erving Goffman, author of *Stigma: Notes on the Management of a Spoiled Identity* (1968), defines stigma as "an undesired differentness from what we have anticipated" (Goffman, 1968, p. 5). He writes of three possible stigmas: "abominations of the body—the various physical deformities." The second one is "blemishes of the individual character such as weak will, domineering or unnatural passions, treacherous and rigid beliefs, and dishonesty...." Lastly is the tribal stigma of belonging to a discredited group (Goffman, 1968).

He also notes the difference between discredited and discreditable persons. A discredited person has a visible sign that leads to social rejection, whether a skin color or obvious disability. Discreditable persons, however, have hidden traits that could lead to negative reactions if discovered. This theoretical insight directly relates to LGBT persons and their decisions to come out (Corrigan et al., 2009). A "lipstick lesbian," for example, could "pass" as straight if she wants to manage her identity (Medina, 2011, p. 138).

Apply this theory to these examples:

- An African-American student who has a learning disability. In your opinion, which stigma would be more harmful?
- An overweight woman with a severe mental illness. Do you consider her to have three stigmatized conditions, or only two? Defend your answer.
- An openly gay male has severe headaches that affect his ability to work full time. In your opinion, should he disclose his condition to anybody or should he keep it hidden? How does the theory of stigma apply to his case?

idea of looking too good to be disabled, had even been working on looking that way. (Mollow & McRuer, 2012, p. 19)

Other invisible impairments are dyslexia, ADHD (Attention Deficit/Hyperactivity Disorder), and other learning disabilities. In a qualitative study about college students with learning disabilities, researchers found that professors and classmates judged them as not having a real disability. Seen as either stupid or lazy, the students also had to face some who were skeptical about their condition. One student said, "Because [my learning disability is] hidden, it's not physical, some people think, 'Well, he's just trying to get by. It's a game' ... that [I'm] faking" (McDonald, Keys, & Balcazar, 2007, p. 152). However, they were motivated to overcome these prejudices. As another student said, "Only you are the architect of your life. Only you can shape it. Only you can say what you can or cannot do ... messages around you can lie to you" (McDonald, Keys, & Balcazar, 2007, p. 156).

One fascinating insight about invisible disabilities is their connection to Queer (LGBT) studies (e.g., Sherry, 2004). Samuels (2003) discusses the coming-out process "in each context as a person whose bodily appearance does not immediately signal one's own sense of identity" (Samuels, 2003, p. 233). Both disabled and LGBT persons have encountered oppression and rejection, besides the temptation to "pass" as normal.

Box 17.3 Case Study About TBI (Traumatic Brain Injury)

A woman was brutally attacked by assailants who left her for dead. Both her physical injuries and TBI require months of rehabilitation. Her brain injury has left her especially isolated from others, especially since she has trouble connecting with people. For instance, she finds it hard to read facial expressions and to respond appropriately to others' feelings. Emotionally, her functions have been affected by post-traumatic stress that is aggravated by her losses. She has lost some memories, besides her old identity.

> My parents told me that once back home, living with them, I would need to learn how to live life anew. Like a limp marionette I went along with the program…. But problems prevailed…. I felt isolated and mutilated (Mukherjee, Reis, & Heller, 2013, p. 9).

- If you were a family member, how would you reach out to her?
- Because her personality change is caused by an invisible disability, it may be hard not to take things personally. How could her family and friends learn to cope with these changes?

Traumatic Brain Injury is another invisible disability, as discussed in Box 17.3. Social workers and other professionals should become aware of how deeply this injury can affect a perons's life.

Other Challenges

Besides social reactions, many women with disabilities must also cope with poverty. Researchers (Parish, Rose, & Andrews, 2009) assert that this population is among the poorest in the United States because of the high rates of food insecurity, housing instability, and insufficient medical care. Because these women's needs are so complex, the Federal Poverty Level is not an adequate measure of their material hardships.

As mentioned earlier, the medical establishment sometimes fails to respond appropriately to this population. Pinto (2013), for example, states that the rehabilitation system was based on the needs of war veterans and other men. Ignoring the specific needs of women could be related to the controversy of chronic fatigue syndrome, which is usually suffered by women and often dismissed as not a real condition. On a micro level, a doctors' lack of respect can be upsetting to a female patient: "Even beyond medical settings disabled women are caught between the intense "visibility" of their different bodies and the "invisibility" of their selves, desires, and needs as women and human beings" (Pinto, 2013, p. 446).

Employment discrimination is also related to poverty, leading to economic losses. In a study of adults with MS (Multiple Sclerosis), one research team found that 20 percent of those surveyed had experienced discrimination in the workplace (Roessler, Neath, McMahon, & Rumrill, 2007). Another study stresses the link between gender and disability, which leads to lower wages for women with disabilities (O'Hara, 2004).

Unfortunately, domestic violence/intimate partner violence (DV/IPV) is another challenge faced by some women with disabilities. According to one conference paper,

"A woman with a disability may experience lower self-esteem when she is not seen as a woman but only as a person with a disability, or even worse—only as her disability ..." (International Network of Women with Disabilities, 2011, p. 8). Banks (2013) claims that doctors often ignore the signs of DV/IPV and just prescribe pain medications for their injuries. Also, researchers know very little about disabled women who are forced into prostitution by their male partners.

The article title " 'I Thought I Was Less Worthy': Low Sexual and Body Esteem and Increased Vulnerability to Intimate Partner Abuse in Women with Physical Disabilities" (Hassouneh-Phllips & McNeff, 2005) clearly expresses the extra dimension of being a disabled woman in an abusive relationship. Feeling an intense need for a partner and for not being stranded, she may think that nobody else would love her. Many women with disabilities, then, are more vulnerable to batterers than a nondisabled person.

Another dimension to DV/IPV and other forms of abuse is the restricted access to the outside world. An article entitled, " 'Bring my scooter so I can leave you': A study of disabled women handling abuse by personal assistance providers" (Saxton et al., 2001) exemplifies the extra control an abuser may have in this situation. "You see, there [are] two levels of isolation going on if you are disabled and abused, a double level and layer so you are more isolated in all sorts of ways" (Thiara, Hague, Bashall, & Harwin, 2012, p. 40). Because of the isolation from family or friends who may help her, a woman's dependence on the abuser may grow. This dependence sometimes outweighs her concerns about her right to be treated with love and respect. She may resist seeing him arrested because she cannot be left alone. Women's shelters and other services may be inaccessible for her. "Isolation, vulnerability and neglect" occur in a cycle as both her physical condition and the abuse worsens (Thiara, 2012, p. 33).

Abusers may refuse to help her get to the bathroom, or keep sanitary supplies out of reach. Taking batteries out of wheelchairs and holding the wheelchair so she cannot move are also abusive behaviors. Although nondisabled abuse victims may be humiliated by their abusers, the humiliation can be worse for disabled women when they may need help with toileting or bathing. One woman states,

> Severely disabled women are often quite abused, anyway, throughout their lives. And it's not obvious abuse, it's not violence particularly, it's kind of some-times quite manipulative and that ... because you have to receive care, you're quite passive and people can abuse that very easily. It's a very easy thing, to abuse. So I don't think it's that unusual, either. (Thiara, Hague, Bashall, & Harwin, 2012, p. 35)

Sex and Reproduction: Challenge or Strength?

Although DV/IPV is definitely a challenge for this population, the topic of sex and reproduction may be either a challenge or strength. Like most people, women with dis-abilities desire physical intimacy. Some also want to bear children. These desires deserve recognition as strengths, especially by social workers who value the self-determination of a client. Unfortunately, social attitudes can challenge these women's rights to make decisions about their own bodies.

Should women with physical disabilities even consider having sex like a "normal" person? Walton (2001), who lost a leg to cancer, writes about how people react to her sexual attitudes:

> It is rather comical and equally disturbing how folks—both men and women— view me as a disabled woman, particularly when it comes to sexuality. They have so many misconceptions. Straight women, for example, want to know how I catch a man.... I like sex! I am very sexual! (Walton, 2001, p. 126).

Sometimes people try to discourage women with disabilities from dating, since they think that nobody would want them as partners (Banks, 2013). This could lead to internalized ableism that inhibits a woman from even trying to date. One writer, for instance, was afraid to express her feelings to a male friend to whom she was attracted. "But is it possible any more to be honest in talking affairs of the heart—or body, more's the point—when there's a fundamental, insuperable barrier between us? The twisted, scarred and sagging deformity that I perceive to be me...." (Fulton, 1994, p. 89).

Odette (2013) describes how the beauty ideal affects women with disabilities. Few role models exist, since women with disabilities are rarely seen at all in the media. "Society believes that lack of physical attractiveness, as defined by the dominant culture, hampers our ability to be intimate" (Odette, 2013, p. 415). Another barrier is finding accurate information about sexual health, especially for intellectually disabled women (Christian, Stinson, & Dotson, 2001). This is probably related to one researcher's claim that society assumes the disabled to be asexual (Kangaude, 2014).

Women with disabilities have also faced barriers to becoming mothers, especially in the past. In some countries, forced sterilizations and other contraceptive methods are common (Frohmader & Ortoleva, 2012). One American woman, who bore a child despite some opposition, writes,

> Even in the absence of outright bans on reproduction, the attitude that disabled people should not have children is common. Disabled women and men are still sometimes subject to forced and coerced sterilizations—including hysterectomies performed without medical justification but to prevent the "bother" of menstruation. (Finger, 2000, p. 245)

Pregnancy and childbirth can be higher risk for women with physical disabilities (Signore, Spong, Krotoski, Shinowara, & Blackwell, 2011). However, one paper presented at the ICPD (International Conference on Population and Development) 2012 Conference states unequivocally that:

> Sexual and reproductive rights are fundamental human rights.... They include the right to autonomy and self-determination—the right of everyone to make free and informed decisions and have full control over their body, sexuality, health, relationships, and if, when and with whom to partner, marry and have children.... (Frohmader & Ortoleva, 2012)

Discussion Questions

- Consider the quote by Fulton about feeling too deformed to express her attraction to a man. If you were in her place, would you act like her? Or would you be like Walton, who openly expresses her sexual feelings?
- If you were the friend of Fulton, what would be your advice? Is she realistic about her fear of rejection, or should she take the risk? Does it depend on the disability?
- In 2015, a fashion model who is intellectually disabled made a famous appearance. More than one disabled character appears in *Glee*, Can you think of other examples of public acceptance of persons with disabilities? Have the media or personal experiences influenced your views on the disabled?
- Read over the statement at the ICPD Conference about Sex and Reproductive Rights (http://papers.ssrn.com/sol3/papers.cfm?abstract_id=2444170). How would you advocate for these rights in the U.S. and other countries?

Strengths of Women with Disabilities

> Yet I love how I am and the life I lead. I like what I see when I look in the mirror. I value so much the contact I have with other disabled people—and with non-disabled allies—in our struggle against prejudice and discrimination. (Morris, 1994, pp. 170–171)

Happiness is not restricted to the able-bodied community. Going beyond just coping, women with disabilities can transcend to a full life. One strength is the acceptance of one's new identity: "But to wish that I could walk again would be wanting to turn myself into something so completely different that I wouldn't know who I was any more. Like wishing I was a man or wishing I was Japanese" (Keith, 1994b, p. 72).

Of course, acceptance is much harder if chronic pain is related to the condition. "The most frustrating thing about unwelcome and chronic pain is its mandate to revise your life…. (but) when I consider the contrast between the time of hopelessness and my growing abilities to proceed with life despite the condition, I make those compromises gratefully" (Hardesty, 1987, p. 23).

Besides pain, women with disabilities may have to work with others to succeed in the workplace. One writer, a deaf woman, uses matter-of-fact language and is explicit about her needs to those talking to her: "I smile as I begin my daily patter. 'Could you speak more slowly please, and move your lips, as I am deaf. This will help me to understand what you are saying.' This smile is not conjured up to sell my deafness. I am a naturally cheerful person…." (Kenyon, 1994, p. 136). Another woman, who dealt with a learning disability before there was much public knowledge, educated herself about this topic. "Basically, however, information about my learning disability was very useful. Weaknesses, I realized, could be worked on systematically" (Brown, 1987, p. 38). For instance, she found out that her right arm was weaker than the left one, so she adjusted accordingly. She also asked her employers for extra training time.

"All that is left now is to change the attitudes of society. To let them see that we understand our own needs. With our guidance they could get things right…. "

(Rushworth, 1994, p. 40). In the 1970s, disability activists occupied a federal building and protested for equal access to public spaces. Not until 1990, though, did the Americans with Disabilities Act (ADA) pass—called "the last inclusion" by many (Weise, 2011, p. 139). One woman notes that her very existence defies the stereotypes of a depressed and pathetic patient:

> I have a physical disability which is considered severe, as it restricts my bodily movement so completely. Using resources and supports … I live independently, work as a free-lance writer, advocate for my rights, and give and receive love and friendship. All of these are acts of rebellion (Hershey, 2013, p. 10).

Another activist, Susan Sygall, began her work in the 1970s after she was injured in a car accident. "Of course we should think beyond our atrophied legs! Of course we should feel good about ourselves and like who we are! Let's tell our story the way we want: 'We are loud, proud, and passionate!'" (Gianturco, 2007, p. 217). She co-founded Mobility International USA, which conducts leadership trainings for disabled persons in 90 countries. Aware that women with disabilities are at higher risk for sexual assault, she also stresses self-defense classes. Noting that her identity is like a series of concentric circles, she adds,

> First, I am a woman; the second ring is people with disabilities; the third ring is women with disabilities and fourth is Jewish people. I am equally proud of all those.
>
> In the Jewish tradition, there is a tikkun olam, "to make the world better." I am lucky to have a way to do my part. I never wanted a "job." I wanted something I could be passionate about every day. (Gianturco, 2007, p. 218)

Discussion Questions

- A young woman has agoraphobia (fear of going out in public), but is determined to attend college. Find resources in your local community so she can fulfill her dream.
- A visually impaired (but not legally blind) woman works for a supervisor who has made "reasonable accommodations" (ADA requirement) for her disability. However, he does not understand why traveling around the country could be a problem for her. Research the ADA requirements and write a paragraph explaining why or why not the supervisor is compliant with the law.
- As a social worker, you have a client with MS. One common symptom is fatigue, which many MS patients may deny until they end up collapsing. Your client says, "My life often seems a series of small failures to do as I ought" (Mairs, 1987, p. 120). Discuss how you would address this issue with her.
- Box 17.4 describes the experiences of one woman facing a new disability. Discuss your reaction to this essay.

Box 17.4 One Woman's Perspective

(Author's note: Jill Anderson, my research assistant, wrote this essay about her experiences.)

At nineteen, most people do not think about their health, since their physical abilities are a given. On an unusually snowy October morning, I woke up unable to walk without assistance. My world collapsed around me. Never before had I considered the possibility of disability. Never before had I encountered the world of hospitals, MRIs, blood draws, consults, and so much waiting around. I would have never considered losing my job because of my physical limits. I even had to drop out of college during this health crisis.

I tried to deal with this change as bravely and calmly as possible. Needing a cane, I selected a beautiful wooden one that had the reddish-brown color of cherry wood. The traditional Japanese designs were hand-carved. I thought that if I found a cane that made me happy, I would feel better about using it. But the cane did not help me when it came to people's reactions to me.

Hardest of all was my social transition from "normal" to "disabled." I had been a perfectly average young person, blending well into the background with my peers. Suddenly, I became "the girl with the cane"—a *disabled person*. I have always noticed many people can never use this phrase without a whisper and a frozen smile, as if to prove that they are absolutely comfortable with me or others with disabilities. These reactions made me feel even worse than my frightening health crisis—I was still the same person I had been the day before I could not walk. Overnight, though, I had turned into an object on display for public examination and comment.

Walking down the street, I saw many people who would whisper or point at me. One incident happened months after I began using a cane. I was buying groceries at a convenience store. A new cashier was working that evening. As I browsed the cereal aisle, I heard a shout:

"Oh, my God! What happened?"

I whirled around, looking for whatever crisis must be occurring. Then I locked eyes with the cashier, whose mouth was agape. He seemed bewildered by my mobility aid. Then he began to engage in what had become a painfully familiar and humiliating ritual for me: asking intensely personal questions about my medical history. As a visibly disabled young woman, I am now subject to the public feeling that entitles others to ask details of my life that would be unthinkable to ask an able-bodied person. My right to privacy is unimportant to them.

When I went back to school, it amazed me that so many people felt that they had the right to touch me. To put their hands on my back to guide me. To poke my arms or legs. To take the cane from my hands to laugh about it, assuming that I must be using it as some bizarre fashion accessory. Continually, people would ask about my health, my medical history, and why I was using the cane.

"What's wrong with you?"

"What happened?"

"Why are you using that?"

If I met someone while seated, we would have a normal, friendly conversation. But then I would arise from my seat. The look on their faces immediately transformed from congenial to tight-lipped half-smiles. People would occasionally say, "Oh..." then trail off, as if they had suddenly realized my new identity. I was no longer a possible friend, but a *disabled person*, and there was no way a regular person could be friends with a *disabled person*.

Currently, I am able to walk without assistance but may suffer a relapse in the future. What frustrates me most is the decision on using my cane for walking and balance. If I opt to honor my body by acknowledging its needs, I am also opting to allow the public the perceived right to dishonor my body and autonomy. To some people, disability transforms me from a human being to something lesser.

Although my health problems have disrupted my life, they have also increased my sensitivity to others. My respect for persons who do not fit a norm has deepened. I expect others to look beyond my cane, and expect myself to look beyond the other indications of difference in others.

Key Terms

Ableism
Stigma
Passing
Invisible disabilities
Social attitudes
Reproduction concerns

3

Women in the International Context

18

Global Feminism

West Is Best?: Debate on Universal Rights

The key question regarding global feminism is: should universal rights apply to *every* woman in *every* culture? In contrast to the concept of universal rights is cultural relativism, which stresses the possible ethnocentrism of the West-is-best view. Brems (1997) argues that the dichotomy between universal rights and cultural relativism need not lead to conflict. "There seems to be enough common ground to allow for building a bridge between the two strands of thought. Instead of wasting part of their creative potential in opposing each other, feminists and cultural relativists could join forces and combine their insights into a constructive critique" (Brems, 1997, p. 136).

The compelling question, then, is whether feminism can be truly universal—or only an ideology for the white, middle-class mainstream based in Europe and the United States. Feminists must confront several international issues while acknowledging their own cultural biases. Can there really be a global feminism?

One eloquent defense of the universal rights of women appeared in this essay by Women Living Under Muslim Laws, a trans-feminist group. After discussing the realities of honor killings and punishment by stoning, the authors conclude that "Introducing and defending any reactionary and suppressive measure against people, especially under the name of respecting different cultures must be condemned because it is against humanity at large. One cannot have thousands of sets of standards for women's human rights" (Moghadam, p. 154).

The story of Nujood Ali (2010) is a striking example of the culture clash between modern feminism and traditional values. "I Am Nujood, Age 10 and Divorced" is the striking title of her memoir about child marriage in Yemen. "I'm a simple village girl who has always obeyed the orders of my father and brothers. Since forever, I have learned to say yes to everything. Today I have decided to say no" (Ali & Minoui, 2010, p. 18).

Forced by her father to marry a man three times her age, young Nujood Ali had to leave her parents and beloved sisters. She lived with her husband and his family in an isolated village in rural Yemen. There she suffered daily from physical and emotional abuse by her mother-in-law and nightly at the rough hands of her spouse. Flouting his oath to wait to have sexual relations with Nujood until she was no longer a child, he took her virginity on their wedding night. She was only 10 years old.

Unable to endure the pain and distress any longer, Nujood fled—not for home, but to the courthouse of the capital, paying for a taxi ride with a few precious coins of bread money. When a renowned Yemeni lawyer heard about the young victim, she took on Nujood's case and fought the archaic system in a country where almost half the girls are married while still under the legal age. Since their unprecedented victory in April 2008, Nujood's courageous defiance of both Yemeni customs and her own family has attracted a storm of international attention. Her story even incited change in Yemen and other Middle Eastern countries, where underage marriage laws are being increasingly enforced and other child brides have been granted divorces. (Ali & Minoui, 2010 p. 7)

Unfortunately, Nujood's story as a child bride is all too common. Other nations also continue this tradition because the girl's virginity is assured. According to the International Center for Research on Women (ICRW), "One third of girls in the developing world are married before the age of 18 and 1 in 9 are married before the age of 15.... Girls younger than 15 are five times more likely to die in childbirth than women in their 20s" (www.crw.org/child-marriage-facts-and-figures). Besides the risks of pregnancy, HIV/AIDS and domestic violence also threaten the lives of these girls. As a counterargument against universal rights, though, Box 18.1 makes a case for cultural relativism.

Discussion Questions

- Write an argument supporting the right of traditional cultures to practice child marriage without penalty.
- Discuss why you would consider this girl's case to be a violation of universal rights. Start with: "every child has the right to …" with specific provisions.

International Human Rights Treaties

Although tradition allows for child brides, the United Nations explicitly states that this practice violates both the United Nations Charter and the Universal Declaration of Human Rights. This declaration, a milestone in history, was adopted in 1948 by the United Nations. Its preamble reads:

Whereas recognition of the inherent dignity and of the equal and inalienable rights of all members of the human family is the foundation of freedom, justice and peace in the world,

Box 18.1 The Case for Cultural Relativism

In her article "Transnational Feminism and 'Local' Realities: The Imperiled Muslim Woman and the Production of (In)justice," Siddiqi (2011) presents a case study in Bangladesh. In 1994, a woman was abandoned by her husband and had a relationship with a married man. After she became pregnant, the village tribunal was called to resolve the issue. Requiring the man to marry her as his second wife would mean giving a legitimate status to the child and providing limited economic security for her. However, tradition demanded that on the day of the wedding she would have to be caned 101 times as punishment for *zina* (adultery).

This case received much publicity in the country, with feminist groups converging on the village on the woman's behalf. One activist, though, shared her concerns about this intervention with the author. "Unlike the other feminists, (she) took the fatwa order for caning (her) to be a token gesture of punishment, not a genuinely coercive sanction. It was…a way to ritually cleanse the village of (her) sin and for the community to solve its problems on its own terms" (Siddiqi, 2011, p. 85). The author notes that the caning probably would have been more symbolic than painful.

As a result of the intervention, the man had to give a piece of land to the pregnant woman. The village ostracized her and she could find no one willing to work the land. As a result of being stigmatized, she left the village to join an ashram (religious community). The baby's fate is unknown, but some accounts speculate that it died from neglect.

Discussion Questions

1. Feminists usually oppose polygyny (multiple wives) because of the possible harm to women. In this case, would you support the man taking on this woman as a second wife?
2. Do you think that a public ceremony that shames the alleged wrongdoer and cleanses the village can result in healing for the person? Are there any parallels in Western society?

Whereas disregard and contempt for human rights have resulted in barbarous acts which have outraged the conscience of mankind, and the advent of a world in which human beings shall enjoy freedom of speech and belief and freedom from fear and want has been proclaimed as the highest aspiration of the common people,

Whereas it is essential, if man is not to be compelled to have recourse, as a last resort, to rebellion against tyranny and oppression, that human rights should be protected by the rule of law,

Whereas it is essential to promote the development of friendly relations between nations,

Whereas the peoples of the United Nations have in the Charter reaffirmed their faith in fundamental human rights, in the dignity and worth of the human person and in the equal rights of men and women and have determined to promote social progress and better standards of life in larger freedom,

Whereas Member States have pledged themselves to achieve, in co-operation with the United Nations, the promotion of universal respect for and observance of human rights and fundamental freedoms,

Whereas a common understanding of these rights and freedoms is of the greatest importance for the full realization of this pledge.... (www.un.org)

The first treaty regarding women's rights was the Convention on the Political Rights of Women of 1952. Countries that signed this treaty promised to give women the right to not only vote but to also run for office. "Recognizing that everyone has the right to take part in the government of his country directly or indirectly through freely chosen representatives, and has the right to equal access to public service in his country, and desiring to equalize the status of men and women in the enjoyment and exercise of political rights ..." (www.un.org). Although compliance to these treaties is voluntary, the power of these documents is that they force nations to confront the inequalities that affect women's lives every day.

In 1956, a treaty allowed for the alimony and child support to be collected across country borders. The next treaty, the Nationality of Married Women, stated that "everyone has the right to a nationality" that cannot be taken away by marriage or divorce (www.un.org).

The Convention on Consent to Marriage, Minimum Age for Marriage and Registration of Marriages was signed in 1964. "Men and women of full age, without any limitation due to race, nationality, or religion, have the right to marry and to found a family. They are entitled to equal rights as to marriage, during marriage and at its dissolution." The Convention also states that "Marriage shall be entered into only with the free and full consent of the intending spouses"—which directly applies to child brides (www.un.org). Also, marriages must be registered so the spouses will have legal rights.

Discussion Questions

- What if a culture believes that it is sinful for women to be leaders or be active outside the home? Should this treaty be imposed on all countries?
- If a country allows only men to vote, should the United States label this country as a democracy or insist that it is violating human rights?
- What would be the implication if a woman got married and was stripped of her nationality? What could happen to her?
- If parents want to arrange a marriage for their children, how should the Convention on Consent to Marriage apply? Should all arranged marriages be abolished?

CEDAW

The most important treaty for women's rights, CEDAW (Convention on the Elimination of all Forms of Discrimination Against Women), was written in 1979. Following is a short excerpt from the introduction:

Recalling that discrimination against women violates the principles of equality of rights and respect for human dignity, is an obstacle to the participation of women, on equal terms with men, in the political, social, economic and cultural life of their countries, hampers the growth of the prosperity of society and the family and makes more difficult the full development of the potentialities of women in the service of their countries and of humanity.... (www.un.org / womenwatch/daw/cedaw/text/econvention.htm#intro)

Provisions regarding human trafficking, reproductive freedom (which does not specify abortion rights, but has been interpreted that way), and equal access to jobs and education are also included. Nations have used it to pass laws to promote literacy and fight domestic violence.

The United States is the only developed nation that has not ratified it, and only six other nations (including Somalia and Iran) have refused to ratify it. Conservative groups such as Concerned Women for America (CWA) have argued against ratification because of concerns about abortion, prostitution, and family rights. The CWA website claims that "Radical Western feminists are using poor women's disadvantages to push a Marxist agenda" (www.cwfa.org/cedaw-harms-families).

However, the fight for U.S. ratification of CEDAW continues. In 2015, Senator Barbara Boxer and other senators held a hearing on how CEDAW could be used to fight violence against women around the world. Boxer expressed embarrassment that the United States had not yet ratified this treaty. "(One) Nigerian attorney who is engaged in efforts to return the kidnapped girls and defends women sentenced under Sharia law for abuses such as death by stoning, testified that U.S. ratification 'would be a huge partnership with our own work and make our work much easier....'" (cedaw2010.org).

Discussion Question

Research CEDAW on several websites, then write the strongest (and weakest) argument for ratification by the United States.

Global Violence Against Women

War

In the article title "Women's bodies were the ultimate battleground of war-torn 2014," Shah (2014) expresses the discouragement felt by many supporters of women's rights. In Nigeria, hundreds of schoolgirls were kidnapped by warlords and not yet returned. The author compares the tide of war violence to a "tsunami to drown out the precious advances that women have made in those countries" (Shah, 2014, no page). With the political and economic instabilities comes a resurgence of male domination. "Patriarchy gives men a sense of security in insecure times" (Shah, 2014). Egypt, for example, went through a revolution that resulted in a backlash against women's rights.

In war-torn countries all over the world, the military sometimes kidnaps and enslaves both boys and girls. Ishmael Beah, the author of *A Long Way Gone: Memoirs of a Boy*

Soldier (2007), describes a horrifying, vicious life with several atrocities. Fortunately, the staff of UNICEF (United Nations Children's Fund) rescued him and others to reconnect them to a peaceful life. Now he works as a human-rights activist.

Besides experiencing firsthand the violence of war, girl soldiers must also contend with sexual slavery. In northern Uganda, the Lord's Resistance Army kidnapped schoolgirls from a seminary and forced them into a harsh world. Grace Akallo, at the age of fifteen, was one of these girls.

> The place had the smell of death. Before I went far into the camp, I knew there was great trouble, but I had given up. I had no hope of escape, and home was many miles away. I was in a strange land with the most heartless people ever known.
>
> We had to assemble before the leader of the rebel movement, Joseph Kony, on the parade ground. "Aboke girls should forget about going back to Uganda," Kony said. "They should be trained to fight."
>
> A week later, the commanders gave us AK-47 assault rifles and taught us how to dismantle, clean and assemble them. "Hunger will teach you how to shoot," they said.
>
> Kony distributed us among his commanders. I was given to a man older than my father. His eyes were so hard that my sweat made a pool.
>
> "Remove your clothes," he ordered. I was too scared to move. How could this man do this to me? I wanted to shout, "Who can help me? God, help me." He seized me and forced me to bed. I felt like a thorn was in my skin as my innocence was destroyed.
>
> They were right. Hunger taught me how to fight. We raided villages, looking for food and water. Our commanders, our so-called husbands, provided nothing. We were forced to eat lizards, rats, wild fruits, leaves, roots and soil. We walked about three miles from the camp to look for water. We had to dig in the sand with our fingers.... The path to the water places was strewn with corpses. (McDonnell & Akallo, 2007, pp. 109–110)

Discussion Questions

- Using Maslow's hierarchy of needs, describe how you would address the needs of a girl soldier who had just been rescued. How would you prioritize her needs? How would you help her to reconnect with life after war?
- In the foreword to McDonnell & Akallo's 2007 book about Ugandan girls, Dan Haseltine cites an activist from International Justice Mission who recommends that "the way to communicate the awful realities of girls in brothels is to give people 30 percent despair and 70 percent hope" (McDonnell & Akallo, 2007, p. 13). Do you agree that advocacy requires a mixture of bad news and good news? Write a positive, strengths-based perspective of how a girl soldier could recover from her trauma.

Nationalism

Related to war, of course, is nationalism. As traditional societies evolve into modern nation-states, feminists must confront a new form of patriarchy. Women have participated in revolutionary and anticolonial movements, from France in 1789 to El Salvador in the 1980s. However, nationalism can become another form of oppression for women. "Wars may 'bring women out of their kitchens,' but the end of the war may just as easily pressure women to return to them if the process has not been accompanied by major transformations in men's and women's consciousness" (Chinchilla, 1997, p. 215).

For former colonies, the nationalist movement symbolized the rejection of the modern West—including women's rights. Male nationalists defended the right of Indians to rule themselves even to the point of rejecting reforms such as banning suttee, the burning of widows on their husbands' pyres. One Indian scholar "argues that women's association with the home came to represent the very essence of Indian nationalism—as the spiritual, private world of Indian tradition and customs untainted by colonialism" (West, 1997, p. xvii).

Besides anticolonial movements, war and occupation can result in more oppression of women. When civil war erupted in Yugoslavia in the 1990s, for example, mass rapes were used as a way to express nationalism. Bosnian women, for instance, often faced imprisonment for months after a rape to ensure that they would give birth to the enemies' babies (Benderly, 1997). The women's bodies became another battlefield for the ethnic cleansing, the attempt to wipe out an ethnic group. The feminist groups that had existed before the civil war, which were once spread all over the now-dismantled Yugoslavia, now split up by nationalities. Some feminists spoke out for the rape victims and the larger purpose of these crimes, but others claimed that this advocacy was merely propaganda.

> When the war started, nationalist hatred increased dramatically and the Serbian government began to produce propaganda and the notion of the Enemy. All of a sudden Slovenians became an enemy, then Croats, then Muslims.... Deep conflicts emerged in families, in workplaces, and women began to separate on that basis. (Benderly, 1997, p. 68)

Becoming refugees can also cause severe distress for women. Since the statehood of Israel in 1948, Palestinians, have faced monumental difficulties in maintaining their culture. Living in exile in Lebanon and other nations, Palestinian men may enforce their patriarchal rule as one way to assert their masculinity. Palestinian society had once supported women's rights, "but after 1948 this changed: in the camps the Palestinian became ultrastrict, even fanatic about the 'honour' of his women. Perhaps this was because he had lost everything that gave his life meaning and 'honour' was the only possession remaining to him" (Gluck, 1997, p. 106).

Other Forms of Violence

In December 2011, over 300 men in Accra, Ghana, participated in a march to protest violence against women. This was a hopeful sign that the efforts by UNIFEM (United Nations Development Fund for Women) to raise awareness of this critical issue are taking root. "It was the second time that such a march was organized. This year, it gathered men from various backgrounds and professions, from police officers to taxi drivers.... A male doctor [said], 'What affects women and children affects men too'" (www.saynotoviolence.org)

One type of violence that persists is honor killings, which occur all over the world and is not confined to the Muslim culture. Families murder a female family member if she has been raped or suspected of having sex outside of marriage. In Brazil, a husband killing his allegedly cheating wife is seen as an honor killing. Even rape victims have been murdered by their own families for their alleged disgrace. Related to honor killings are dowry burnings in India, in which thousands of Indian wives are killed because the husband's family considers her dowry to be too small (Mayell, 2002).

A controversial practice in several countries is female genital mutilation (FGM—also called female genital cutting and female circumcision). FGM deserves special attention because of its extreme impact on women's health. This surgery is designed to reduce a woman's sexual desire and ensure her virginity. According to the World Health Organization,

> FGM includes procedures that intentionally alter the female genital organs for non-medical reasons. The procedure has no health benefits for girls and women. Procedures can cause severe bleeding and problems urinating, and later cysts, infections, infertility as well as complications in childbirth and increased risk of newborn deaths. (Factsheet available on www.who.int)

FGM, practiced on an estimated 125 million girls, often involves primitive instruments instead of sharp scalpels. Thorns, knives, and razor blades are used without any measures for safety or pain control. Girls may bleed to death or die from infections, or later on die in childbirth. On their wedding nights, brides scream from being "disvirgined" by knives because they have to be cut open for intercourse. If a knife is not used, it can take weeks or even months for full penetration by the man (Lightfoot-Klein, 1989).

Mothers and other women usually conduct FGM on the girls (starting at age six or so) to make sure that they would get husbands. Like the Chinese mothers who had bound their daughters' feet to attract good husbands, these women sincerely believe that they are helping the girls. However, the practice is tremendously painful with lifelong consequences.

Type I FGM is the mildest, since it only removes the clitoral hood and perhaps the clitoris. In contrast, Type II is more extensive and more widely practiced. The entire clitoris is removed, besides part or all of the labia minora (small vaginal lips). Type III is the most severe, since it not only removes most if not all of the external genitalia but also sews the opening of the vagina almost completely shut. Since the hole is only the width of a matchstick, passing of menstrual blood can become a lifelong ordeal(World Health Organization [WHO], 2014 Factsheet available on www.who.int/mediacentre/factsheets/fs241/en/).

Even urination can cause great distress, since FGM may permanently damage the uretha (www.path.org/files/FGM-The-Facts.htm).

Considering by many international organizations as a violation of human rights, this cultural practice is practiced in both Muslim and non-Muslim countries. Wrongly believed to be a religious tradition, FGM is actually opposed by Muslim leaders and others who are concerned about the girls who suffer and even die from it.

Girls as young as six are held down by a group of women to be cut. One Somali woman told the author about the experience: "I will never forget the pain." Villagers often celebrate this event as a coming-of-age ceremony. After the cutting, the girls' legs are often tied together and the girls are kept in a separate hut for forty days. Many girls die during this time since no medical resources are available. Convinced that female genitalia must be cut or it looks deformed, many girls grew up to support the practice and force their daughters to undergo it (WHO).

The United Nations has worked with WHO to eliminate FGM, including the adoption of a resolution in 2012. The Centers for Disease Control and Prevention has also participated in the International Zero Tolerance to FGM Days. However, FGM is no longer found only in the 29 countries where it is the tradition. In the United States, estimates of over 200,000 cases may have occurred among immigrant families (Trohlic, 2015).

Waris Dirie is one of the most famous advocates for protecting women against FGM. As a victim herself, she knows firsthand the excruciating pain and emotional trauma that results from this procedure. She gave up her career as an international model to work as the United Nations Special Ambassador for the Elimination of Female Genital Mutilation, besides establishing foundations for the empowerment of women. Her efforts have spread to Europe, since many immigrant families secretly perform FGM on their young daughters (Dirie & Milborn, 2005). Dirie shares her thoughts about her fame as an activist against FGM:

> For me the worst thing is that, wherever I go, everyone knows what happened to me. I am not seen first and foremost as a woman, because they think of me as the "woman who's been circumcised." When I was writing my first book I bared my soul, announcing in public, "Look what happened to me. They took my genitals and cut them, mutilating me in the cruelest way." Since then, whenever I meet someone all they really want to ask me is what I look like down there and if I can have sex and how. They don't have to say anything; I can feel it in the way they look at me. Perhaps it is worse when they don't mention it at all but just stare at me.…
>
> A year ago was a fair on in Austria and my books were on display at one of the stalls. Donations for my Somali projects were being collected. When I arrived, the first thing I saw was a huge yellow poster with a photo of a circumcision operation taking place. I was even more shocked to read the text on the poster, which said in big letters Come and meet circumcision victim Waris Dirie. What gives them the right to treat me like that? Just imagine a woman asking for donations to a fund for abused children and posters saying Come and meet the victim of childhood abuse, Stella Stereotype. Would you even dream of asking her right at the start of every interview what it was like when she was abused as a seven-year-old by her uncle? Of course not. It is vital to respect people's privacy.
>
> As victims of FGM we are not shown such sensitivity. (Dirie, 2005, pp. 23–24)

Besides dealing with this type of thoughtlessness, FGM survivors in the West must also live with the deprivation of most sexual pleasure. However, one French doctor has pioneered a way to restore a women's genitals and nerve sensitivity. "It can certainly improve women's pleasure and lessen their pain," the doctor said in a statement in 2012 after studying the results of 3,000 such surgeries. "It also allows mutilated women to recover their identity." (Goldberg, 2015). One woman who had the procedure done wrote, "I was immediately overcome by a feeling of completeness. It was an unfamiliar feeling" (Goldberg, 2015).

Another hopeful sign is a new public awareness campaign for men. The advocacy group Safe Hands for Mothers produced a video on FGM and showed it to young men, who broke down and cried. The comments included: "This is just barbaric" and "I felt powerless. I felt like I couldn't do anything to help" (Couch, 2015). After the movie, the men vowed to fight against FGM.

Discussion Questions

- Ali, a Somali woman, shares her thoughts about FGM. "In itself, it does not prevent a woman from developing an independent mind. But the scar may be a constant reminder of the punishments in store for the rebellious" (Ali, 2010, p. 20). If you were a social worker with a client who was traumatized by FGM, what kind of emotional responses would you expect?
- American women sometimes have cosmetic surgery on their genitalia, besides undergoing breast enhancements. Would you consider these surgeries to be comparable to FGM? Why or why not?
- Research to find a defense of FGM that relates to cultural relativism. Does the defender's argument persuade you?
- Widows' rights is another global issue for feminists. Look up the website of Widows Rights International (www.widowsrights.org) and connect three aspects of this issue to misogyny. If you were an international activist, what actions would you take on behalf of widows?

Gender Imbalance

Considering the amount of misogyny in many countries, it is not surprising that parents do not value their daughters. Hvistendahl, author of *Unnatural Selection: Choosing Boys over Girls, and the Consequences of a World Full of Men* (2011), has researched an unsettling trend in several countries. Globally, this is happening not just in Asia but Eastern Europe and other continents.

> For as long as they have counted births, demographers have noted that on average 105 boys are born for every 100 girls. This is our natural sex ration at birth.... [The fact that] more boys are born is itself a form of balance, neatly making up for the fact that males are more likely to die young.... Boys outnumber girls at birth because men outnumber women in early deaths. (Hvistendahl, 2011, p. xiii)

Today, however, demographers are noticing that many countries are developing a higher and higher ratio of males to females. China is notorious for the large number of unwanted female babies, but India is following this trend. Using ultrasound machines to determine the fetus's sex, Indian women often felt pressure from their families to abort a female fetus.

Not only are there fewer females, but the declining birth rate in the world means that there will be a shortage of mothers in the near future. Some experts predict that even if the sex ratio were to be corrected today, it would take until 2050 to make the balance 105:100 again.

Although one may expect that a shortage of females would benefit the women, the opposite is actually true because women would be treated as commodities instead of independent persons. For instance, countries such as Taiwan that lack women are now importing brides from poorer countries such as Vietnam; "the trade in women is now an entrenched industry negotiated by established agencies" (Hvistendahl, 2011, p. 163) Despite the fact that women may be able to negotiate a high price, that is not the same as ensuring that they will be treated kindly by their husbands. In fact, a groom "may fixate on the amount of capital he amassed in order to attract her and watch her like a hawk out of fear she will leave him" (Hvistendahl, 2011, p. 169).

Prostitution and forced marriages are becoming more common because of the sex ratio imbalance. Some women are even being kidnapped and serve as a wife to several men.

Males will also suffer from the shortage of women, since marriage is considered a sign of adulthood in many cultures. These men are called "bare branches" because they will never produce children. "Bachelors remain perpetual adolescents who cannot play a full role in society.... an unmarried youth can have no face" (Hvistendahl, 2011, p. 209). Unable to produce legitimate children or be taken seriously as a man, some bachelors may commit violence as a way to compensate. "Another way to get some sense of the impact millions of surplus men will have on societal stability is to look at the toll bachelorhood takes on a man's quality of life.... A failure to marry, then, may negatively impact a man's physical health" (Hvistendahl, 2011, p.223). The knowledge that he may never be in a long-term relationship may make him depressed.

China is already facing a severe shortage: "By 2013, one in ten Chinese men will lack a female counterpart. By the late 2020s, a projected one in five men will be surplus" (Hvistendahl, 2011, p. 165). As a result, some provinces have begun a Care for Girls program that encourages parents to keep their daughters.

Ironically, parents in the United States prefer girls to boys. Although sex-selective abortions are rare, the fertility experts have tried to help couples conceive a child of their chosen gender. The issue of sex selection, then, presents several ethical dilemmas.

Discussion Questions

- Should parents have the right to choose the sex of their child?
- Should the government interfere with the parents' desire to find out the sex of the fetus?
- What should be the international response to this imbalance sex ratio?

Despite the setbacks suffered by women worldwide, many hopeful trends are developing. Ecofeminism is one such trend that started decades ago and still has the power to inspire millions of women. Shortly before she died in 1998, the feminist pioneer Bella Abzug stated.

> Women do not want to be mainstreamed into a polluted stream. We want to clean the stream and transform it into a fresh and flowing body. One that moves in a direction—a world at peace, that respects human rights for all, renders economic justice and provides a sound and healthy environment. (Moghadam, 2005, p. 105)

Abzug was one of the founders of WEDO (Women's Environment and Development Organization) in the 1990s. An Indian woman influenced by Abzug added her own words:

> In my heart I believe that women will change the nature of power rather than power change the nature of women.
>
> For we are the Old Ones, the New Breed, the Natives, who came first but lasted, indigenous to an utterly different dimension. We are the girl-child in Zambia, the grandmother in Burma, the woman in El Salvador and Afghanistan, Finland and Fiji. We are the whale-song and rainforest, the deep wave rising huge to shatter glass power on the shore....
>
> We are the women who will transform the world. (Moghadam, 2005, p. 114)

Seeing a connection between the oppression of women and the exploitation of nature, the ecofeminists have supported the causes of conservation and equal rights. In patriarchal thought, nature is seen as something to conquer and women are seen as somebody to dominate. Ecofeminists try to connect the international women's community with the imperative to save the environment from further destruction.

Green Fuse, one activist group, states, "Ecofeminists do not seek equality with men as such, but aim for a liberation of women *as* women. Central to this liberation is a recognition of the value of the activities traditionally associated with women; childbirth, nurturing and the whole domestic arena" (thegreenfuse.org). Emphasizing the nurturing aspects of women, the movement can be called essentialist in its association of females with nature.

Ecofeminism also applies to animal rights. One writer states, "The feminist care tradition focuses on affective connections, including compassion and empathy, and shows how these connections have a cognitive or rational component.... Ecofeminist theory provides ethical guidance to challenge inequities arising along racial, gendered, and species boundaries" (Adams & Gruen, 2014, pp. 3, 5). Vegetarians and other animal rights activists have a long history with feminism. In the past, both animals and women have been deemed as mute objects subject to the dictates of male owners. Animal ethics, then, is a growing concern among ecofeminists.

Unfortunately, it can be dangerous to be an ecofeminist in some countries. In Latin America, twelve environmental leaders have been murdered in the past three years. Indonesian women are murdered for speaking out against companies that are destroying the land. "The perpetrators include corporations the activists are opposing, state agencies that see them as a nuisance, paid thugs and even members of their own community, which are often male-dominated.... 'The media criminalises us too. They try to take away our credibility, say we're bitches and corrupt....'" (Win, 2014).

However, these women are still fighting deforestation and other abuses of the land. The Indonesian activist Mama Aleta, winner of the 2013 Goldman Environmental Prize, is a tribal woman who will not back down. Corporations have been mining for marble in her region, causing landslides and pollution. Even though Aleta has been assaulted, she continues as a movement leader. "The forest is the life of my people, the trees are like the pores in our skin, the water is like the blood that flows through us ... the forest is the mother of my tribe" (Perera, 2014).

Discussion Questions

- Discuss the most striking aspect of oppression in this chapter.
- In your opinion, what was the most salient feature in this chapter? Write a paragraph about it.
- Which social work value best applies to global feminism? Why?
- Research an ecofeminist group and share the information with the class.

Key Terms

West is best
Universal rights
CEDAW
FGM
Honor killings
Gender imbalance
Ecofeminism

19

Women in Developing Nations in the Age of Globalization

Introduction: The New India

The term *developing nation* (once called the third world) evokes images of dusty villages and barefoot peasants. However, countries such as India are developing into major economic powers. Skyscrapers, not huts, are emerging as a dominating motif. Since the 1990s, India received an influx of international capital after investors realized the high number of English-speaking, well-educated workers who could perform "outsourced" work such as customer service. The status of women sometimes improved, but traditional patriarchal attitudes can still prevail even in the most modern of settings.

Siddhartha Deb, author of the 2011 book *The Beautiful and the Damned: A Portrait of the New India* (2011), writes of his meetings with Indian women in the modern workforce. He met women who had left their poor villages to "the globalized metropolises of the mainland. Their journey was longer and harder than mine had ever been, and although there were tens of thousands of them in Delhi alone, they were in some sense utterly isolated, always visible in the malls and restaurants but always opaque to their wealthy customers...."(Deb, 2011, pp. 207–208).

Esther, one of the women he interviewed, was the daughter of a government official and a teacher. She majored in biochemistry in college and earned a master's degree in botany, but was unable to go to medical school. Instead, she took a training course in tourism. She moved to Delhi, where she was a travel agent who faced daily harassment on the bus to work. Then she found a better-paying job in the F & B (Food and Beverage) business at the Taj Mahal Hotel. It was hard work, serving the rich customers who sometimes assumed that she was a prostitute.

Figure 19.1 *A modern Indian woman (Photo courtesy of OUP)*

When she met the author at a café, "she stood out among the carefully made-up women meeting their dates or friends. Even though she was the same age as these other women, mostly in their twenties, she looked older, more worn down" (Deb, 2011, p. 217) Unfamiliar with the menu, she had trouble ordering a soda. She knew how to be a server, but not a customer.

Working long hours, she gets home at 3:30 A.M. and has to work later that morning. "Esther's long working hours left her little time for reflection. Yet whenever we met, she liked to talk about who she had become, and was still becoming, in the course of her long journey from Imphal to Delhi. In this vast city, she found herself among a wide range of strangers...." (Deb, 2011, p. 221). She considers herself a strong fighter who is not afraid to stand up to others.

If Esther had left her village, she had done so as much out of a strong sense of independence as out of a need for employment. "I'm a graduate," she had told me the first time we met, clenching her fist to emphasize the point. "Why should I depend on my husband for money?" (Deb, 2011, p. 231). But Esther's independence in Delhi had turned out to be a strange thing, with others depending on her. "Most of my friends in Imphal didn't finish graduation.... I did my degree and came here to work. But still, in spite of the money I make, I have to think twice before I do anything.... I don't have money to buy new clothes or even a pair of chappals [sandals]" (Deb, 2011, p. 231).

Despite the gleaming skyscrapers, India's cities are still places of poverty and discrimination. For instance, Esther and her roommates have to pay extra for their apartment because they were from the northeast and not part of the upper-caste elite. Besides the ethnic discrimination, these women from the northeast also face sexual discrimination. Street harassment and rape are constant threats. The police sometimes look on, or tell the women to wear different clothes.

The local men, suddenly forced to work alongside women as equals, sometimes reacted violently. Some men came from "neighbourhoods where the local women went around wearing veils while the men eyed the outsiders, lusting after them and yet resenting them, considering themselves to be from more superior cultures while also feeling that they were less equipped to take advantage of the service economy of globalized cities like Delhi" (Deb, 2011, pp. 229–230).

Esther's roommate Mary works in a call center. Once considered to be ideal jobs, call-center work became less promising as the 2008 Recession affected the global economy. Mary's job was to call Americans who were behind on their car-loan payments and about to have their cars repossessed. "It was a sudden, reversed camera shot of the American recession, viewed from a flat in a slum-like neighbourhood in north Delhi. It was unpleasant work, Mary said, but she did it to earn a living" (Deb, 2011, p. 225).

These women, then, tell stories of risk-taking, independence, drudgery, and discrimination. This brief glimpse of India represents the successes and challenges of a

Figure 19.2 *Call center in India (Photo courtesy of OUP)*

developing nation in the context of globalization. Not all developing nations, of course, are experiencing a similar growth boom. The history of women in development shows the current relevance of initiatives such microcredit.

Women in Development: A Brief History

> There is a familiar self-help aphorism, "If you give a man a fish, he will eat for a day, but if you teach him to fish, he will eat for a lifetime." A veteran develop-ment expert once quipped to me: If you teach a man to fish, he will eat for a lifetime, but if you give a woman title to the fish pond, she will clean it up, preserve it for the next generation, stock it with new fish, and create a fish farm to employ the village. (Coleman, 2013, p. 8)

For too many years, those who invested in development efforts ignored the possible contributions of women. Charlton (1984) writes of how development efforts began in the 1950s, when colonies (mostly in Africa and Asia) became independent nations. For decades, the World Bank and other development funders apparently had little idea that women even existed in these nations. Instead, male-dominated projects such as factories and bridges were the focus of development. Political concerns also affected decisions on development, since the Cold War (competition between the United States and the now-defunct USSR) dominated the discussion on foreign aid. Forgotten were the social aspects of development such as nutrition, education, and health care.

In the 1980s, then, feminists and other advocates spoke out on behalf of women in nations such as India and Angola. The cultural context of each nation includes its colonial past. In French colonies, for instance, girls received education only for religious reasons. The former colonial government may have tried to improve women's lives (e.g., the British laws against suttee—the burning of widows) or actually worsened them (e.g., the stress on cash crops instead of subsistence crops needed to feed the families.) (Charlton, 1984).

Another factor is corporate influence. Since many multinational corporations (MNC) are worth billions more than many smaller nations, the power of these MNCs can reach even the smallest village. For instance, the decision to breastfeed should be an individual choice but MNCs promoted infant food formula in the 1970s. Health professionals and sales agents visited villages and gave away free samples. By the time the mothers ran out of the free samples, their breasts were no longer producing milk. An international outcry ended this marketing practice in 1981 because it had resulted in mothers diluting the for-mula due to cost, infants dying from malnutrition and diseases caused by impure water, and families affected by the high cost of the formula (Sethi, 1994).

As the corporate powers took over from the colonial powers as the dominant eco-nomic force, neoliberalism (free-market ideology) stressed the financial instead of nonfinancial contributions to the household. Because child care and other family respon-sibilities are rarely paid for, the cash economy no longer honors the work of women. Men gained more dominance as they went in the public sector to do "real work." The follow-ing story illustrates this attitude that work is not work without a paycheck involved.

A peasant and his wife present themselves to the local government administrator. They want to get national identity cards. The bureaucrat asks and records the information....

—You're a farmer, right?

—Yes.

—And what does your wife do?

The man and woman answer at the same time:

—Nothing.

The bureaucrat writes on the paper:

—Occupation: housewife.

This story ... takes place every day here, in the rural area, but also in the town. This peasant woman, however, goes to the field every day alone or with her husband, she takes care of the family and their land allotment; she makes and sells products in the market. (Charlton, 1984, p. 40)

The invisibility of women's work is one possible cause of the unequal treatment of females in the family. The belief that females are parasites has resulted in the neglect of female children as they are fed less, besides receiving less medical care and education. If girls receive vocational training (e.g., health aide), they could add to the family income and receive more respect.

A big, bearded Afghan named Sedanshah once told us that his wife and son were sick. He wanted both to survive, he said, but his priorities were clear: A son is an indispensable treasure, while a wife is replaceable. He had purchased medication for the boy alone. "She's always sick," he gruffly said of his wife, "so it's not worth buying medicine for her." (Kristof & WuDunn, 2009, p. xvi)

Such unequal treatment leads to an increased risk of malnutrition for women. In many nations, women are less likely to get adequate nutrition than men, even if they are pregnant or lactating. For instance, some cultures prohibit females from having meat, certain vegetables, and even milk. Men usually eat first, leaving the scraps to the women (Charlton, 1984). People rarely die from malnutrition but from its resulting weakness, so official records often underreport this problem. For obvious reasons, malnourished persons are less to speak out in protest. Although females are traditionally deprived of food (even pregnant and nursing mothers), females are more likely than males to be food producers in a developing nation. According to the International Fund for Agricultural Development (IFAD), women in Africa had produced 80 percent of the continent's food in 2009 (www.allAfrica.com)

Another contribution that women are making to their home economies is sending paychecks from overseas employment. Since the 1990s, women have become the primary labor migrants for jobs mostly located in Europe or the United States. Working as nannies, maids, and prostitutes, they face both exploitation and pressure to send most of their earnings home. Josephine, a nanny in Greece, had to leave behind her three children in Sri Lanka. Her checks sent home are supporting not just her children but also her parents but at a high costs. One daughter has attempted suicide three times, and the son has to live in an orphanage with little family contact. "This is the female underside of globalization.... These migrant workers often leave their own children in the care of grandmothers, sisters, and sisters-in-law. Sometimes a young daughter is drawn out of school to care for her younger siblings" (Ehrenreich & Hochschild, 2002, p. 3).

Women are not the only labor migrants; millions of men have migrated within their countries for jobs (Momsen, 1991). As developing nations began to industrialize, men left the village to the city (or mines) and the families stayed behind. Wives had to cope with the responsibilities of child care and village commitments while awaiting paychecks and/or visits from the men. Sometimes the men had girlfriends or even second families in their work location.

> For instance, the women of Lesotho are gold widows; left behind to make of life what they can while the men work in the gold mines of South Africa. The border between the two countries forms a sex-specific barrier as, since the 1960s, only men have been allowed to enter South Africa to work. Lesotho society is, therefore, one in which women do most of the work of agriculture and social reproduction. Yet women are generally better educated than men and have developed considerable autonomy. This leads to a deep sense of frustration among women because they are denied access to the modern industrial world. All that most of them can now do is to remain on South Africa's periphery, reproducing its labour force, doing unpaid domestic work, cultivating infertile soil, seeking low-paid local employment, providing a market for South Africa's goods and becoming increasingly dependent on the unreliable supply of remittances from male wage earners.... About two-thirds of rural households are headed by women but only half of these have migrant husbands and receive remittances; the rest are widows, reflecting the high rate of fatal accidents in South African mines. (Momsen, 1991, p. 23)

Female-headed households result not only from male labor migration, but also from the husbands' death or desertion. Twenty years ago, for instance, about one-third of the households in the Caribbean were headed by women (Momsen, 1991) The women's right to own property becomes a survival issue, besides the right to participate in the cash economy by earning a paycheck or starting a small business.

Regardless of whether or not the households are female-headed, women usually do the bulk of household chores in developing countries. Momsen (1991) describes how gathering firewood and water can take hours every day. On average, women do 80–100 percent of these household chores in Sri Lanka:

> Food preparation
> Winnowing and parboiling rice
> Preserving food for the hungry season
> Storing grain at harvest time
> Production of fruits, etc. for home consumption
> Fetching water
> Collecting firewood

Upkeep of house and yard
Bringing up children
Bathing children
Attending to the sick in the family. (Momsen, 1991, p. 38)

Related to this topic are time budgets, the analytical tools to determine how each family member contributes to the household. "Women on small farms in the Third World often have a triple burden of work" that includes the chores just listed, besides "unpaid labour on the family farm and to earn money by working on another farm or by selling surplus produc." (Momsen, 1991, pp. 56–57).

Mrs. T, a woman tobacco farmer in Trinidad (West Indies), starts her working day at 3 am "to clean the house, prepare and serve the family breakfast and get the children ready for school. At 7 am she leaves the house to work in the tobacco or vegetable fields until noon. Between noon and 1 pm she eats lunch and rests. From 1 to 3 pm she sells in the markets and from 3 to 6 pm she prepares produce for sale the next day. (Momsen, 1991, p. 61)

Case Study: Eritrea

Eritrea, a small nation on the Horn of Africa, has experienced colonialism, war, and poverty. Mostly Christian and Muslim, Eritreans have stressed traditional values over modern change. This nation experienced civil war for thirty years, until it won its independence from Ethiopia in 1991. Women fought alongside men in the EPLF (Eritrean People's Liberation Front).

The woman fighter with her characteristic unisex dress and unkempt hairstyle, moreover, personified an image of progress, a rupture with the past, and liberation from oppressive traditions. Within EPLF, national liberation and advancement for women were seen as going hand in hand. (Bernal, 2001, p. 133)

However, the Front was less feminist than Marxist. Political ideology, not women's issues, was the only focus of the Front. For example, women's illiteracy rate was 95 percent in the 1970s (Bernal, 2001). Women's participation in thirty years of war, then, affected gender roles to a great extent. In another study (Hale, 2001), women told the researcher how they did everything that men did. The researcher "began to understand that women's bodies (if not men's) became desexualized—neutralized for the purposes of war. In a way, one could make some of the same statements about men's bodies when women first began to enter the field. Men were forbidden to have sex with women...." (Hale, 2001, p. 163)

When the war ended, most men wanted to return to domestic life and reinstate traditional roles. Women fighters were seen as undesirable wives because of their unwomanly pasts. Also, many were past their peak childbearing years. Some of these women felt disregarded and discarded after the war (Bernal, 2001). Hale's study supports this assertion, noting that many of the interviewees complained about the social pressures to become submissive wives after being warriors. Some organized into women's groups to fight child marriage and other abuses of females.

The long years of war, of course, stripped Eritrea of the resources needed for a developing economy. After the wars, another economic challenge emerged—international financial policies that required the government to reduce its social spending (Hale, 2001). Gebremedhin (2002) explicates the factors affecting development in Eritrea, including gender roles that limit women's lives. Whether Muslim or Christian, most Eritreans value traditions such as FGM and arranged marriages.

However, the government has expressly supported women's equality since the Proclamation of 1991. Another bright spot has been the female entrepreneurs, who sell goods and provide services such as haircuts. In the cities, women are branching into business ventures despite any social disapproval.

Safe drinking water has been another priority in this drought-ridden land. As the population grows, the water supply diminishes. The Donkey Project is an initiative by concerned Europeans to send donkeys to these women, which would reduce the burden of obtaining water. "With the help of donkeys donated from the project many poor and single mothers can earn a daily income and sustain their standard of living; to have the opportunity to send their daughters to school; and to become role models for their children by showing care and love for them" (Gebremedhin, 2002, p. 107).

Education for females is slowly taking root in Eritrea, which offers hope for the nation's future. In one study (Muller, 2006), the researcher relates the story of a girl who was married at the age of ten. Two years later, she bore her first child. After she bore her second one, her husband supported her decision to delay having more babies and to return to school. He drove her on his motorbike every morning to school. "Ashar is an unusual woman in more than one way; about her interest in education she says: 'Education for me

---

Box 19.1 Neoliberal Policies and the Environment

In her article on the ecological crisis in Tanzania, Turshen (1999) explicates the complex causes—including neoliberal policies that degrade the environment. Neoliberalism prioritizes the free market over human (and environmental) concerns. As a result, desertification is spreading in this region of the world.

Is overpopulation the major source of desertification? The author disputes this assertion by the World Bank, claiming that the colonial policies of cutting down so many forests started the problem. Noting that the neoliberal policy of SAPs (Structured Adjustment Programs) overrides social needs such as health care and education, the author calls for accountability from the international financial policymakers.

Discussion Question

Pick a country affected by desertification and research the causes of this problem. How much desertification was caused by overpopulation and how much by other causes?

is not only to have a better job, I also want to know things, know how the world works'" (Muller, 2006, p. 367). The possibility of college is now being discussed.

Discussion Question

Using the strengths perspective, discuss the skills and other resources of Eritrean women.

Family Planning and Birth Control

One major controversy regarding family planning center is whether a women should have access to any form of birth control, including abortion. Since international family planning may include abortion as one of their services, American politicians often refuse to fund them. For instance, the Mexico City Policy, also known as the Global Gag Rule, has periodically interrupted funding for all birth control provided by NGOs (non-government organizations) if abortion were provided. In *The Means of Reproduction: Sex, Power, and the Future of the World,* Goldberg (2009) states, "Botched abortions kill 36,000 African women each year, representing more than half of the global total of between 65,000 and 70,000 annual deaths." (p. 3) The scarcity of contraceptives is also related to the U.S. policy on limiting funding. As a result, the number of unwanted births in countries such as Kenya has nearly doubled. Warning against the dangers of too much cultural relativism, Goldberg reminds readers that some issues are universal.

> But another (danger) is assuming that women in other cultures are so different from us that situations we would find intolerable—bearing child after child into grinding poverty; being utterly at the mercy of fathers, husbands, and brothers; having one's clitoris sliced off with a razor—do not also cause them great pain. The search for human commonality among vastly diverse people is tricky and elusive, but it is callous to surrender to relativism when so many women are clearly suffering (Goldberg, 2009, p. 9).

> Kristof and WuDunn (2009) reinforce Goldberg's point when they write of the "God gulf" (Kristof & WuDunn, 2009, p. 132). Women in the developing world desperately need medical services. Because of the Mexico City Policy, clinics all over the world have closed down and laid off hundreds of doctors and nurses who had once saved lives every day.

> Rose Wanjera, a twenty-six-year-old woman in Kenya, showed up at a maternity clinic one afternoon. She had a small child in tow, and her stomach bulged with another on the way. Rose was sick and penniless and had received no prenatal care. She was an unusual visitor to a slum clinic because she had attended college and spoke English. She sat in a corner of the squalid, dimly lit clinic, patiently waiting for the doctor, and told us how wild dogs had mauled her husband to death a few weeks earlier.
> A nurse eventually called her, and she lay on a cot. The doctor examined her, listened to her abdomen, and then announced that she had an infection

that threatened her life and that of her unborn baby. He enrolled her in a safe motherhood program, so that she would get prenatal care and help with the delivery.

[Because this clinic was associated with a consortium that had provided abortions in China, funds were cut off for all clinics in many countries.] One might have understood cutting funds to the China program, but slashing funds for the consortium in Africa was abhorrent.... [Rose] became one of untold victims of American abortion politics that effectively eliminated her only source of health care. "These were clinics focusing on the poorest, the marginalized, in the slums...." (Kristof & WuDunn, 2009, pp. 131–132)

Other controversies include the forced sterilization not just for women but also for men. Some communities were not taking birth control seriously. In Pakistan in the 1970s, for instance, the USAID (Agency on International Development) officials found out that children were using condoms as holiday balloons. India, which had also tried mass promotions of birth control, decided to use more aggressive measures. "Millions of men were bribed, threatened, or physically forced into vasectomy camps" as the police woke the village up in the middle of the night to herd the men into clinics (Goldberg, 2009, p. 83).

Despite politicians' opposition to funding contraceptives, a woman unable to control her fertility will face diminished educational and career prospects. Not only is it a personal issue, but also a development issue. Family planning also saves lives, since multiple pregnancies can become dangerous in an environment without adequate health care and/or nutrition.

Discussion Questions

- Do you agree with Goldberg's point that allowing local communities to prohibit the use of birth control is taking cultural relativism too far? Why or why not?
- In many cultures, the primary achievement of women is motherhood. Would it be ethnocentric to present other possible goals for women?
- Would you consider the U.S. policy on limiting funding for family planning as one aspect of the war on women? Or is the term *war on women* only applicable to U.S. politics?

Microcredit

How do you empower women when they have no money? One Egyptian woman states, "As long as women earn money, the rest of development will come about on its own.... Empowerment is a luxury the poor cannot fathom when they are fighting to survive" (Drolet, 2010, p. 637). Microcredit projects are one possible solution for the very poor to rise out of poverty.

Traditional development efforts have involved major projects costing millions of dollars. (For example, Box 19.2 describes one overlooked barrier to women's success—the lack of sanitation during menstruation.) In contrast, a new form of development

Box 19.2 Menstrual Hygiene as a Development Issue

In developing countries where females cannot afford sanitary products, they stay home from work or school to avoid being embarrassed (Kristof & WuDunn, 2009). Many schools do not provide clean waters or toilets to girls who need access to them during their periods. According to UNICEF, an estimated one in ten African girls do not go to school at that time. This hurts their academic performance and increases the risk of dropping out. Sometimes girls had sex with older men just to pay for sanitary supplies.

Women also suffer from the lack of clean facilities or sanitary supplies. In countries such as Bangladesh, women lose an average of six workdays a month due to vaginal infections. This is not only bad for their incomes, but the nation's economy (Klasing, 2014). Menstrual management, then, is both a human rights and an economic issue for developing nations.

Discussion Question

Design an intervention program to help girls and women obtain supplies and facilities to meet their needs.

---

has focused on low-income women who want to set up small businesses. Also called microfinance, microcredit is a cooperative venture in which women receive small loans (e.g., a few hundred dollars) that they pay back for other entrepreneurs. The director of Grameen Bank (the first venture) received the Nobel Peace Prize in 2006 for the profound impact of their microcredit program in Bangladesh (Selinger, 2008).

Grameen Bank's microcredit program "promotes credit as a human right; It is aimed towards the poor, particularly poor women; It is based on 'trust,' not on legal procedures and system; It is offered to create self-employment; (and) It gives high priority to building social capital" (Karim, 2008, p. 9). The system uses shame as a way to motivate borrowers to pay back the loans as promised. In the Bangladeshi and other communities, family honor is important to uphold. Defaulting on a loan, then, may seem unthinkable (Karim, 2008).

Drolet (2010) writes of how microcredit affects the feeling of empowerment among women in Cairo, Egypt. After interviewing sixty-nine participants, she found that the women wanted to fulfill both their practical needs (food, TV, etc.) and the desire to earn cash for themselves. They wanted respect from their men for their household work. Not seeing themselves as primary providers for the households even if they often were, they saw themselves as merely helping their husbands be the breadwinner. Gender roles, then, still dominated the women's lives.

Earning money, then, does not necessarily create an equal status for women in traditional countries. Desiring to avoid fights with their husbands, the women "develop covert acts of resistance to ensure their ongoing participation. One of the specific examples given in an interview was when women kept their financial resources secret from their husbands and family members" (Drolet, 2010, p. 640). Although some women readily handed over their earnings to their husbands, others openly resisted this subordinate role. Some women also wore the veil to gain social acceptance of their business activities. Stressing the need to invest in their children's futures, the women were building their community through their hard work.

Unfortunately, recent news reports indicate that microcredit is not an unqualified success. In an article titled "The Dark Side of Micro-credit," Rozario (2007) writes of how dowry demands to brides' parents have escalated. "While micro-credit has benefited large sections of the rural population in many ways, it has also worked against women's solidarity and contributed heavily to the inflation of dowry. Grooms' families are aware that money is available to brides' families more easily now through Grameen Bank, (etc.) ..." (Rozario, 2007).

Discussion Question

Design a microcredit program that could work in your local community. What possible problems could result? How would you increase the chances for success?

Education
....

The power of educating women is undeniable. The militant group ISIS, for example, has threatened to execute any male teachers who educate girls (no author, 2014). In his article "What's So Scary about Smart Girls?," Kristof (2014) writes about the mass kidnapping of Nigerian schoolgirls. "Why are fanatics so terrified of girls' education? Because there's no force more powerful to transform a society. The greatest threat to extremism isn't drones firing missiles, but girls reading books" (Kristof, 2014). Educated girls represent modernism to many traditionalists.

Numerous studies indicate that women have fewer children if they are educated— even if it is only elementary school. Educated females earn more money, have healthier children, and add to a country's economic growth. UNICEF (United Nations Children's Fund) reports that investing in women's education could boost Africa's agricultural production by 25 percent (www.unicef.org).

One barrier to female education is the cultural belief that it is a worthless investment. Sometimes a community builds a school, but there are no teachers to do the work. Iodine deficiency is one surmountable problem, since the simple act of iodizing the salt would reduce fetal brain damage. Surprisingly, another barrier is the need to deworm the students because worms cause anemia in menstruating girls (Kristof & WuDunn, 2009).

One study in Ethiopia (Mulugeta, 2004) discusses how household chores and the long distances to school can be barriers for girls to continue their education. However, sometimes female teachers in the village served as role models and mentors for the girls. Siblings and other family members can be supportive of the girls' efforts. One girl told the researcher, "Our parents were invited to the school day at the end of the academic year.... My parents were happy to see that I was one of those students [who got rewarded]. I think that was one of the reasons why they kept me at school despite relatives' pressure to marry me off" (Mulugeta, 2004, p. 78).

Figure 19.3 *Hope for education (Photo source: Entofolio)*

According to the UNICEF website, other barriers to female education include early marriage and lack of resources. Some schools do not have books or desks, so students sit on mats and read from photocopied texts. Teacher turnover is high in many countries. However, many communities are showing their determination to educate their young—including the girls. The goal is to establish child-friendly schools, as described here:

> A child-friendly school is a school where life is enjoyable. It is a school where the basic needs are met, including shade trees, latrines, water points, classrooms with enough benches and tables, well-trained teachers. It is a learning environment where the community is involved in everything we do (www.unicef.org)

One program that stresses education as a force for development is Camfed, which has provided services in five African countries since 1993. Over one million girls have received an education through its efforts. By concentrating on the girl as an individual, the organization provides mentoring and funding for her education. The community selects the girls for this opportunity. According to a quote on their website, "Teachers, parents, students and local officials are actively working together to help vulnerable local children. Camfed doesn't work 'with the community.' It is the community itself" (www. camfed.org). After they finish their schooling, the girls go through training to set up businesses and be community leaders.

Discussion Questions

Write a paragraph for each item below that describes the macrolevel program that could empower these women. Be as specific as possible. What NGOs (nongovernmental organizations) could be allies in your efforts?

- A community health worker in India. She gives medical advice to women, administers polio shots to children, and fights with the local authorities to remove the garbage and set up safe drinking water.
- A mother of three children in Ghana. Her husband spends most of the time in the city working, so she rarely sees him. Sometimes he sends money, sometimes he doesn't. To supplement her income, she decides to sell her embroidery and weaving crafts in a nearby village. She will need money for a cart, craft supplies, and a booth.
- A group of women who want to reforest the hillsides. Land erosion has resulted in mudslides and flooding, so they need grant money to pay for the trees. They are also dealing with a scarcity of wood.
- A recently widowed woman who is fighting to inherit the land left by her husband. His family opposes the inheritance, so she faces a hard battle.

Key Terms

Multinational corporation
Neoliberalism
Labor migration
Time budgets
Eritrean women
Microcredit
Family planning

20

Women in Muslim Countries

Introduction

> Muslim Women—we just can't seem to catch a break. We're oppressed, submissive, and forced into arranged marriages by big-bearded men.
> Oh—and let's not forget—we're also hiding explosives under our clothes.
> The truth is—like most women—we're independent and opinionated. And the only things hiding under our clothes are hearts yearning for love.
> Everyone seems to have an opinion about Muslim women, even those—*especially* those—who have never met one (Mattu & Maznavi, 2012, p. 1)

Another Muslim woman writes, "Not only does the Qur'an make it clear that man and woman stand absolutely equal in the sight of God, but also that they are 'members' and 'protectors' of each other" (Hassan, 1991, p. 262). This second statement about the Quran (the Holy Book, sometimes spelled as Koran) also exemplifies Muslim feminism:

> Mercifully, the more research I did into the Qur'an, unfettered by centuries of historical androcentric reading and Arabo-Islamic cultural predilections, the more affirmed I was that in Islam a female person was intended to be primordially, cosmologically, eschatologically, spiritually, and morally a full human being, equal to all who accepted Allah as Lord, Muhammad as prophet, and Islam as *din* [religion, way of life]. (Wadud, 1999, p. ix)

These quotes may surprise those who think of Muslim women as faceless creatures who are heavily veiled and allowed outdoors only if escorted by a male. Saudi Arabia is especially infamous for its treatment of its female citizens. Under Sharia law, Saudi

Figure 20.1 *Mosque (Photo courtesy of OUP)*

women cannot vote, cannot drive, and cannot leave the country without their husband's permission (e.g., "Saudi women drivers freed from jail" article dated February 13, 2015 on the BBC website: www.bbc.com/news/world-middle-east-31449972). But are all Muslim women in this situation?

According to the Pew Research Center, 1.6 billion Muslims compose 23 percent of the world's population. Over 62 percent live in the Asian Pacific area. Indonesia—not the Middle East—has the highest number of Muslims in the world (www.pewresearchcenter. org). Because Islam is a decentralized religion within a wide range of cultures, it is impossible to describe Muslim women as a single entity. The wide range of the different schools of Islam is but one variation. In immigrant communities, the number of generations a family has been in the new country and the strength of their ties back home can vary widely (Aitchison, Hopkins, & Kwan, 2007). This chapter focuses on the diversity within diversity of Muslim women, especially in the conflict between traditionalists and feminists.

Brief Description of Islam

In 600 CE (Common Era—used to be called AD), several nomadic tribes populated the Arabian Peninsula. They worshipped many gods until the Prophet Mohammed introduced monotheism (belief in one god) and unity to the tribes (Donner, 1999). Mohammed received his first revelation in 610 CE, which the Quran records as: "Read! In the Name of your Lord, Who has created (all that exists), has created man from something that clings. Read! And your Lord is the Most Generous, Who has taught (the writing) by the pen, has taught man that which he knew not. Surah 96: 1-5 (cited by www.alim.org/library/biography/stories/content).

The five pillars of faith are:

- Fasting (during the month of Ramadan, believers fast during the day).
- Charity (the Red Crescent Society is the Muslim counterpart of the Red Cross).
- Faith in Allah, the one God.
- Praying five times a day.
- Pilgrimage to Mecca and other holy sites if the believer is able. (Cornell, 1999)

As the direct word of the Prophet, the Quran is seen by believers as the Holy Book that should never be disputed. The Hadith ["Tradition," or sayings of the Prophet] has more room for interpretation. Islamic feminists often focus on the Holy Book, since the traditions of the Hadith can be more patriarchal. Writers such as Turner (2006) posit that many repressive measures against women are based on culture, not tradition.

> The fact that most of the laws by which Muslims have endeavored to regulate their lives are in fact human concoctions may come as a bracing surprise to most readers, and a shock to many, particularly if they are Muslims with traditionalist views. However, that "Islamic law" is mostly "human law" is not particularly earth-shattering. What is shocking is the fact that it masqueraded as a sacred code for so long, its spurious provenance allowing it to avoid criticism and to act as a virtually impregnable barrier to legal, social and political reform. (Turner, 2006, p 206)

Traditionalists, of course, would strongly disagree. They often support Sharia law, the religious authority that may supersede secular law in some Muslim countries. Sharia courts in Afghanistan, for example, have ordered the amputation of the hands of thieves. This has led to some anti-Muslim feeling in the West. For instance, even the title of Brighton's polemic against Muslim domination is a warning: *Sharia-ism Is Here: The Battle to Control Women and Everyone Else* (2014). Stressing that mainstream Islam is separated from this extremism, she calls Sharia law "totalitarian, supremacist, global, (and) theocratic" (Brighton, 2014, p 14). Many Muslim countries such as Turkey, though, are secular and do not practice Sharia law.

Another essential fact about Islam is that this religion divided into two major groups, the Sunnis and Shiites, soon after Mohammed died (Donner, 1999). Shia, then, came from the Succession Crisis. This religious split has influenced the politics of the Middle East, especially when the two groups live in the same country such as Iraq. Around 85 percent of the world's Muslims are Sunni (www.bbc.com).

Mohammed and Women

When reviewing Mohammed's attitudes to women, one must remember how brutally the desert tribes had treated women before Islam emerged. In this context, the fact that Mohammed granted formal rights to women (including property rights) is remarkable.

He also abolished slavery, female infanticide, and forced marriages between the widow and her brother-in-law. According to the Hadith, "All people are equal, as equal as the teeth of a comb. There is no claim of merit of an Arab over a non-Arab, or of white over a black person, or of a male over a female. Only God-fearing people merit a preference with God" (cited on www.angelfire.com). He stressed that Muslims should treat their women well and to be kind to them.

> Islam's prophet loved women. He married his first wife when he was twenty-five years old. Illiterate, orphaned and poor, he hardly expected to receive a proposal from his boss, Khadija, a rich Meccan businesswoman at least ten years his senior who hired him as a manager for her international trading company. While it wasn't typical for women to propose to men in Meccan culture, Khadija was among those with the clout to do so. She gave him money, status and four daughters—his only children to survive infancy....
>
> It was to Khadija that Muhammad crawled, trembling, the first time he heard the voice of the angel Gabriel pronouncing the word of God. Despairing for his sanity, Muhammad found himself repeating the first words of the Koran—which means simply "recitation." Then he made his way to his wife on his hands and knees and flung himself across her lap. "Cover me! Cover me!" he cried, begging her to shield him from the angel. Khadija reassured him that he was sane, encouraged him to trust his vision and became the first convert to the new religion, whose name, Islam, means "the submission...."
>
> For twenty-four years Khadija was Muhammad's only wife. It wasn't until she died, nine years after that first vision, that Muhammad began receiving revelations from God on the status of women. So Khadija, the first Muslim woman, was never required to veil or seclude herself, and never lived to hear the word of God proclaim that "Men are in charge of women, because God has made the one of them to excel the other, and because they spend of their property [to support them]." Such a revelation would have come strangely from Muhammad's lips had Khadija still been alive and paying his bills. (Brooks, 1995, p. 3–4)

Based on the preceding excerpt, it is understandable why Islamic feminists refer to Khadija as a symbol of female empowerment. Not only was she the first follower of Islam, but she supported him while he went through his revelations. During Khadija's lifetime, women were politically active and allowed to work with men.

After his first wife's death, though, Mohammed married multiple wives. Sometimes the wives were not subordinate to him, even quarreling with him and among themselves. These quarrels led to political schemes, which resulted in the wives being confined to the backroom when there were visitors. Purdah (confinement), then, arose not from religious doctrine but political infighting (Brooks, 1995).

Mohammed's widow Aisha became a respected authority on what he had done or said in certain situations. Even male leaders consulted her on questions of religion and the proper way of life since she had been his closest wife. Over 2000 traditions (part of religious text) were attributed to her. Fatima, Mohammed's daughter, was also close to Mohammed and is a vital link to the Shiite succession of religious leaders (Ahmed,

1992). When reviewing the Prophet's attitude toward women, one scholar notes that he raised them to leadership roles and praised one female warrior who had fought beside him (Al-Khalaf, 2005).

Discussion Questions

- After reading this section, do you consider Mohammed a prowoman leader? Why or why not?
- The stories of Khadija, Aisha, and Fatima symbolize what empowered women can do in a male-dominated culture. Which aspect of these stories could be relevant today?

Traditional Views of Women in Islam

After the Prophet died, the early days of Islam were a time of shifting roles for women. At first they were allowed to worship alongside men in public prayer, but mosques began to separate the sexes because of possible distractions (Walther, 1995). (Other religions also require segregated worship.) In some Muslim countries, women are not even allowed to attend burials because "It is believed that their presence is disruptive; they might become hysterical, perhaps even hurl themselves into the grave to be with the corpse (Ali, 2010, p. 9)

> With the social degradation of women that accompanied the economic and political decline of the Islamic countries, they were increasingly deprived the right to pray in a mosque. A woman of any self-respect was not even expected to leave the house once she was married, unless she was obliged to. (Walther, 1995, p. 52)

Seclusion from the public sphere is still approved by traditionalists, who emphasize that Islam liberates women by saving them from harmful "men's jobs." Instead, motherhood is a woman's ultimate good (Yuan, 2005). One scholar stresses that women cannot be leaders because they are naturally inferior. Women must depend on men not only for economic survival, but because they are weaker both in body and mind. They cannot perform religious rites during menstruation, which makes them less pure than men. Because of these deficiencies, "Men are overseers of women" (Karolia, 2005, p 26). These overseers need more rights than women because of their obligations. He advises, "women should not complain of men having an additional right over them. If they do, they would be questioning the wisdom of Allah" (Karolia, 2005, p. 28).

Al Qaradawy (2005) would agree with such views. He regards women working outside the home as less feminine, besides being inadequate wives and mothers. "Islam considers the home as the great kingdom of the woman. She is its mistress, its head and axis. She is the man's wife, his partner, the solace of his loneliness ..." (Al Qaradawy, 2005, p. 41).

However, does the split between public and private spheres apply in this context? In one research study, traditional Muslim women spoke of how the homes were connected to each other with a constant flow of visitors. The private/public sphere concept in Western society, then, may not apply to this arrangement. Instead, a "home-centred, family-oriented religion" actually honors women because they are in charge of their domain (Bunting, 2005, p. 56).

Historically, not every traditional Muslim would agree with the subordination of women. Although men like Umar the second caliph wrote in the seventh century, "Take refuge in God from the Evils caused by women, and beware even of the most pious of them!" (Walther, 1995, p. 40), others were more respectful to women. One famous mystic, Ibn-al-Arabi wrote in the twelfth century that: "Whoever knows the worth of women and the mystery reposing in them will no refrain from loving them; indeed, love for them is part of the perfection of a man who knows God, for it is a legacy of the Prophet and a Divine love" (Walther, 1995, p. 40). Ibn-al-Arabi also criticized the treatment of Muslim women:

> In these states, however, the ability of women is not known, because they are merely used for procreation. They are therefore placed at the service of their husbands and relegated to the business of procreation, child-rearing and breast-feeding. But this denies them their (other) activities. Because women in these states are considered unfit for any of the human virtues, they often tend to resemble plants. One of the reasons for the poverty of these states is that they are burden to the men (Walther, 1995, p. 40).

Some Muslim thinkers, then, promoted the well-being of women, whereas others blamed women for the world's problems. Women sometimes emerged as powerful forces in Islamic history, though. The Islamic mystical tradition includes Nafisa of Egypt who is revered as a saint. When people complained to her about the injustice of the Egyptian governor, she stood in his path and handed him a note that accused him of tyranny and called on him to be more just (Walther, 1995).

Feminist Perspectives in Islam

One critic of the traditionalists, Kamguian (2005), opines that the Quran does stress inequality between the sexes. Although there are four gender-neutral verses in the Quran, hundreds of verses are anti-equality. For instance, "Men are managers of the affairs of women because Allah has preferred men over women and women were expended of their rights" (Al-Baqara 2:228; Kamguian, p. 16). The image of ungrateful women filling up hell is another example of misogyny. Wives must submit to sex at any time: "A wife should never refuse herself to her husband even if it is on the saddle of a camel" (Kamguian, p. 17). Although women are allowed to divorce their husbands, cruelty is not viewed as a legitimate reason.

However, some Islamic feminists would disagree with the assertion that the Quran is anti-equality. The previously cited Wuhad states, "It is clear to me that the Qur'an aimed to erase all notions of women as subhuman" (Wahud, 2005, p. 9). The Creation story, for example, stresses the dualism of male and female to imply that both are important. Islam also improved women's status through the right to own property (which occurred centuries before the West allowed that right).

One Indonesian feminist, Maria Ulfah Ansor, explained the importance of women gaining access to religious texts. "I think the most important thing of all is to implement the teachings of Islam in our everyday lives, and because life is dynamic, there is always room for reinterpretation of texts" (Rinaldo, 2014, p. 834). Pious women can use their critical thinking skills to create an Islamic feminism.

Besides the right to interpret religious texts, some Muslims are promoting women's mosques and women prayer leaders. Nomani (2005) cites the Prophet, who allowed a woman to lead prayer in her house with a male slave. In building a mosque, she notes that "We challenged one of the deepest denials of women's full expression: her ability to lead prayer" (Nomani, 2005, p. 148).

In any culture, feminism involves work in the community. One woman who worked at a women's shelter describes a Muslim client who wrongly believed that it was her husband's right to hit her. The advocate found local Muslims to help her. When an *imam* (religious leader) read the police report, he did not hesitate in writing the divorce papers. The writer concludes with the reminder that the Quran had banned female infanticide, which usually involved being buried alive. "We have allowed the bodies of women to become the sacrificial victims again. And we have allowed the female body of Islam to be buried alive in the sand, over and over again" (Kahf, 2005, p. 135)

Marriage and Divorce

One aspect of Islam is its emphasis on marriage, especially with specific roles for husband and wife. The religion requires the male in the family (husband, father, etc.) to be responsible for the family's economic survival. "This is an honor Islam gave to women," one woman explains. Women can work outside the home for other reasons such as to help others, but the primary burden is on the male. "Islam regards the duty of raising the children in the best manner as the noblest occupation a woman can do" (Namou, 2010, p.31).

Many Muslims believe that because of the man's economic and spiritual responsibilities, he should head the household. Another reason was expressed by one Muslim husband: "If you have a ship with two Captains it will sink, in the same way in the family you will not survive if you have two heads" (Siraj, 2010, p. 203).

Polygyny (multiple wives) is sometimes part of a Muslim society. (The term "polygamy" is also used, which means multiple partners.) As an orphan, Mohammed "often regarded himself as the advocate of the weak and underprivileged. Consequently, at a time when marriage represented the only way for a woman to be provided for, the Quran recommends marriage to widows and female orphans" (Walther, 1995, pp. 57–58). In this context, polygyny was a necessity for stranded women. Mohammed himself had many wives, often for the political advantages of tribal alliances. However, he set the limit of four wives per man. The requirement is that the husband must treat each wife equally. Modern scholars interpret this to mean that since it is impossible to treat more than one wife equally, men should limit themselves to one wife (Walther, 1995).

Ayaan Hirsi Ali, who had been raised Muslim in Somalia and has rejected the religion, discusses the impact of polygyny on her own family.

> We who are born into Islam don't talk much about the pain, the tensions and ambiguities of polygamy. (Polygamy, of course, predates Islam, but the Prophet Muhammed elevated it and sanctioned it into law, just as he did child marriage.) It is in fact very difficult for all the wives and children of one man to live happily, in union. Polygamy creates a context of uncertainty, distrust, envy, and jealousy. There are plots. How much is the other wife getting? Who is the favored child? Who will he marry next, and how can we manipulate him most efficiently? Rival wives and their children plot and are said to cast spells on each other....
>
> My mother's story was similar (to my grandmother's). Even though she was my father's second wife, from the day she learned that my father had married a third woman and had another child, Sahra, my mother became erratic, sometimes exploding with grief and pain and violence. She had fainting episodes and skin diseases, symptoms caused by suppressed jealousy. From being a strong, accomplished woman she became a wreck, and we, her children, bore the brunt of her misery. (Ali, 2010, pp. 24–25)

Besides polygyny, child marriage was common in traditional Islam because it ensured the girl's intact virginity. Families arranged the marriages, sometimes with the help of matchmakers. The recommended prayer for the bridegroom was:

> Oh God, I beg Thee for the goodness of her and for her good inclinations which Thou hast created and I take refuge in Thee from the wickedness in her and from the wicked inclinations which Thou hast created. (Walther, 1995, p. 83)

A lesser known aspect of marriage in Muslim society is the marriage contract. These contracts do not have to be written. The parties to the contract are usually the bridegroom and the bride's guardian (father, etc.) The bride should not be married without her consent, but silence is assumed to be agreement. When the girl is a minor, her guardian can also force her into marriage, but she has the right to annul this as soon as she is of age. Some Islamic schools do permit an adult women to be forced by her guardian to contract marriage (Walther, 1995).

Marriage contracts can even specify sexual rights, including the rights of wives to have "respectful and pleasurable sexual experience(s)" and to "make independent decisions about their bodies, including the right to refuse sexual advances" (no author, 2005, p. 155).

Regarding the economic rights of Muslim women in India, the marriage agreement must include some financial security for the woman. "No Muslim marriage is valid without *mahr* (dowry to women). The main object of *mahr* is to offer protection to the wife against the arbitrary powers of the husband in exercising the right of divorce" besides payments to the divorced wife (Hussain, 2013, p. 29). Social practices, of course, may ignore this requirement so it is essential that women know their rights under Islamic law.

If a couple failed to produce children, the blame was usually laid on the wife. In these cases, the husband would be more likely to obtain another wife. Custody rights were

Figure 20.2 *Woman wearing hadith (Photo courtesy of OUP)*

based on the belief that the father had planted a baby in the mother, who only acted as a field for the seed. Fathers, then, had dominant legal status in custody issues. However, mothers were honored for their role as acknowledged in this saying: "Paradise is at the mothers' feet" (Walther, 1995, p. 87).

Veiling

One of the most controversial aspects of Muslim women is the *hijab*, the various forms of veiling. In her book *What Is Veiling?*, Amer (2014) defines the term *hijab* really means "to screen, to separate, to hide from sight, to make invisible" (Amer, 2014, p 12). She stresses that "Islam did not invent veiling, nor is veiling a practice specific to Muslims. Rather, veiling is a tradition that has existed for thousands of years, both in and far beyond the Middle East ..." (Amer, 2014, p. 1). During the time of Islam's development in the Middle East, it was common for Jewish and Christian women to also cover their heads. The covering symbolized an honorable woman who was protected by her family. It also indicated that this was a free woman who was not a slave available for sex. For many Muslim women, *hijab* is still a protective barrier against unwanted attentions.

The Quran does not have any specific clothing guidelines, nor does the Hadith. "For progressive Muslims, *hijab* in Islam is much less about clothing, much less about an injunction to wear specific attire, than it is about adopting a modest demeanor, remaining humble, and avoiding pride and conceit" (Amer, 2014, p 43). The different types of *hijab* include these variations: head scarf, veil that may or may not cover the eyes, and garments that cover the entire body (e.g., the *burqa* in Afghanistan and Pakistan).

Each type of *hijab* is the result of a complex interplay between factors such as religious interpretation, customs, fashion, race, ethnicity, geographic location, and the po system in place at a given time. Within each society, within each subgroup within that society, the term hijab refers to a different set of clothing (Amer, 2014, p. 13).

Wearing the hijab is sometimes optional and sometimes required. When it is optional, several different factors affect the woman's decision on hijab. One American woman, who grew up wearing hijab, decided to stop wearing it after studying her religion. "As I read the Qur'an and secondary texts on Islam and meditated on hijab, I realized that my spirituality had nothing to do with whether or not I wore hijab. My access to Islam was not located in my outer appearance" (Abdul-Ghafur, 2005, p. 14).

However, many others choose to wear hijab. "Hijab, as a conscious choice, gives me great feelings of serenity, security, and elation that being bullied into doing it could never deliver" (Muhammad, 2005, p. 45). One writer says that headscarves "create a tent of tranquility. The serene spirit sent from God is called by a feminine name '*sakinah*' in the Quran ..." (Kahf, 2005). Another writer explains in a poem, "For this scarf is/ Simply, a blessing" (Abdul-Khabeer, 2005, p. 101).

Does a woman wearing the *hijab* (headscarf) in the West represent oppression or autonomy? After interviewing second-generation college students, Williams and Vashi (2007) concluded that the hijab represented their faith. "Wearing hijab, an outward, public display of piety and religious identity, can finesse the constraints that conservative gender roles might impose upon them" (Williams & Vashi, 2007, p. 282). They belonged to Muslim student associations that offered self-defense classes and encouraged them to apply to medical school.

In contrast to those who choose to wear hijab, Ayann Hirsi Ali (the ex-Muslim quoted in the previous section), strongly opposes the veil being forced on women in Somalia and other countries.

> The Muslim veil, the different sorts of masks and beaks and burkas, are all gradations of mental slavery. You must ask permission to leave the house, and when you do go out you must always hide yourself behind thick drapery. Ashamed of your body, suppressing your desires—what small space in your life can you call your own?
>
> The veil deliberately marks women as private and restricted property, nonpersons. The veil sets women apart from men and apart from the world; it restrains them, confines them, grooms them for docility. A mind can be cramped just as a body may be, and a Muslim veil blinkers your vision and your destiny. It is the mark of a kind of apartheid, not the domination of a race but of a sex (Ali, 2010, p. 16).

Discussion Question

In 2004, the French government prohibited Muslims and other persons from showing religious symbols in state schools, government jobs, and public spaces. This meant that Muslim women could not wear any sort of hijab. A French politician said, "We've been very perturbed about the veil. To see those very young girls veiled.... Perhaps the veil once said something religious, but now it's a sign of oppression. It isn't God, it's men who want it" (Amer, 2014, p 94). Human Rights Watch has strongly protested against this ban, stating that "Some in France have used the headscarf issue as a pretext for voicing anti-immigrant and anti-Muslim sentiments" (Human Rights Watch, 2004).

Write one paragraph defending the ban, and one paragraph opposing it. Do you agree with the ban? Why or why not?

Islamic Fundamentalism and Women

Veiling is often associated with Islamic fundamentalists. In many religions, a tension may develop between moderates and fundamentalists (also called extremists.) Fundamentalists believe in certain basic beliefs (fundamentals) that are non-negotiable. Anybody who disagrees with them is wrong—there are no gray areas. The rise of Islamic fundamentalism has concerned not only the West, but many moderate Muslims. Some Westerners consider the Sharia court one example of fundamentalist thinking (Corbin, 2013).

Under Islamic fundamentalism, women become the symbol of their men's commitment to Islam. If she is regarded as impure, then she brings shame upon the family. One woman noted that "My two girlfriends and I grew up believing that we were priceless vases that could easily shatter, thus shattering our family's reputation ... .we believed that we were victims to our femaleness" (Ali, 2005, p. 25).

The practice of honor killings (as further discussed in chapter 18) is one extreme example of this attitude. A teenage girl who wears lipstick or has a boyfriend could be seen as bringing disgrace to the family. The only way to save the family's honor is by murdering her. Another practice related to the honor placed on a girl's virginity is Female Genital Mutilation (FGM), also covered in chapter 18.

Besides honor killings and FGM, the impact of fundamentalism on women has been profound. The women in Afghanistan have been especially hard hit by this trend, as discussed in the Case Study that follows. Through the 1990s, the ultrareligious Taliban took over the country and forced women to stay in their homes unless they had a male escort. This made life difficult for the widows and daughters without brothers or fathers. The *burqa*, an extreme form of *hijab*, was required for all women. The beehive mesh in front of the face meant that the women were semiblind when walking down the street, which resulted in many deaths.

You paint the windows of your house black so you cannot be seen from the outside. You are forbidden from walking on your balcony or in your backyard. It has been years since the sun shone on your face. And all public references to you have disappeared. (Lynch, n.d.).

Case Study: Afghanistan

For anyone who associates Afghan women only with *burqas* and oppression, it might be surprising that the veil had actually been banned by the King in 1959. The government tried to modernize the country in the 1960s and 1970s. In Kabul and other cities, women walked around freely without veils or male escorts to protect their honor (Chavis, 2003). Many women went to college and became doctors and other professionals. The cataclysmic invasion by the Soviets in 1978 led to war and the mobilization of Afghan men fighting for their homeland. The following decade was a period of women working outside the home to support their families. In 1989, the Soviets left the country and the Mujahadeen (Afghan rebels) gradually took over the country. One Afghan girl witnessed the violence firsthand.

> During these years the Mujahadeen fired rockets in and around Kabul.... It became a daily routine at school that whenever we heard the sound of a big explosion we would leave our desks and follow the teacher to the corridor, which was considered a safe haven.
>
> But in the summer of 1989, one of these rockets changed my life. The first missile of the day landed in our school corridor, creating a huge explosion. It was so close by that the bang of the rocket rang in my ears. I can still recall the sound today. Children and teachers were running around in confusion and screaming. I looked down and could see blood and panicked but quickly realized it wasn't coming from my body. It was from another girl. One of my classmates was lying unconscious, her clothes soaked in blood.
>
> That explosion has never left my mind. After seeing a fellow school girl die, I went into shock and became deeply depressed (Kargar, 2012).

The story of Afghan women, then, is one of promised liberation cut short by war and the subsequent regime of militant Muslims who tried to push females back into subjugation. Under the Taliban (religious leaders who took over the country), women have been living severely restricted lives. In 1996, for example, the Taliban forbade women from working outside the home although many were widows. "From their inception, the Taliban have passed edicts legislating the exclusion of women from public life and dividing the country into public and private spheres, both of which are subject to Islamic law" (Telesetsky, 1998, p. 296). However, many Afghan heroines have fought for their rights even in the face of death threats.

One example is Fawzi Koofi, the first female Parliament speaker. Growing up in a northern province of Afghanistan in the 1970s, she learned very early that boys were valued more than girls. Her father, a local leader, had seven wives and twenty-three children. On the day she was born, Koofi was left outside the hut to die because her mother was too distraught and ill to take care of her. Fortunately, she was brought in later and her mother took pity on the baby's sunburned face. Later, she grew up hearing the expression "less than a girl" (Koofi, 2012, p. 26) as the most derogatory insult used in her culture. Koofi grew up to be an activist who risked death threats and gunfire to work for women's rights.

One inspiration for Koofi was Meena Keshwar Kamar (better known simply as Meena), who founded the RAWA (Revolutionary Association of the Women of Afghanistan) in Kabul in 1977. When she was still in high school, she heard about the acid attacks on female college students by fundamentalists. Inspired by one teacher who noted that the attackers violated Islam, she went to rallies and spoke out in classes. She then dropped out of college to found RAWA the year before the Soviet invasion. Rejecting foreign ideologies, she stated that "I want to liberate Afghan women for Afghan women, in the Afghan way. I am a democrat. I have my own mind" (Chavis, 2003, p. 61).

Literacy campaigns were the first RAWA initiative, then the first women-focused magazine in the country. Meetings were one way to fight the repressive Soviet-backed regime.

> Always, the age-old women's culture of Afghanistan that oppressed them also sustained them. Though the separation of the sexes stifled women who wanted to move into work and learning, it also meant that women traditionally spent long hours together. A group of men meeting together might look suspicious, but women gathering to talk was as normal as naan (bread). RAWA turned every common women's custom into a tool of liberation. Every woman walked out at dawn or dusk to the hamom, the communal baths, carrying a change of clean clothes with her. The bath bundles of a few women concealed books and leaflets. (Chavis, 2003, pp. 65–66).

Meena was only able to fight for Afghan women (and the country's liberation) until 1987, when government-backed agents assassinated her. One famous quote still resonates for those who honor her bravery:

> Afghan women are like sleeping lions. When we are aroused, we react with the same courage and charisma as lions. There are only two paths to choose from: Side with the criminal regime, or oppose them, and be ready to fight like lionesses. We might have to risk our lives, and even lose them. (Chavis, 2003, p. 94)

Zoya, whose mother had worked for RAWA before the fundamentalists murdered both parents, has carried on Meena's legacy. Growing up in the 1980s in occupied Afghanistan, she did not attend school because of bomb threats by the Mujahadeen.

> Grandmother insisted that I study at home as much as possible. She was so adamant about this that she quarreled often with a neighbor who sometimes called on us. "I'm not saying that she should grow up to become a housewife," the neighbor would say, "but this girl should know something about cooking and keeping a clean house. Otherwise how can she live with a husband?"
>
> "Wrong," Grandmother would retort. "She should do the work that boys do. There's no future in cooking and cleaning. Education and knowledge, that's what she needs. Zoya, get out of the kitchen and go read a book."
>
> I never did learn how to cook. (Zoya, Follain, & Cristofari, 2002, pp. 40-41)

Zoya grew up to be an international spokesperson for women's rights, risking her life many times to travel to Kabul. RAWA continues to earn praise. The organization opposed the 2001 invasion by allied troops (led by the United States) because it made things worse for Afghan women. One activist by the name of Hamasa recently stated, "Women have to snatch our rights, fight to get them. No one is ever going to liberate us or give us equality but us" (www.rawa.org).

Abu-Lughod (2013) agrees with RAWA that the U.S.-led invasion did more harm than good for Afghan women. Her book, *Do Muslim Women Need Saving?*, criticizes the western view that there is even such an entity as a "Muslim woman." So much diversity exists that it is impossible to make correct generalizations about this population. Distorted views result, such as the tragic figure of a veiled woman who needs the West to rescue her. The author posits that the cause of problems for most Muslim women is not necessarily religion, but poverty and war.

> How many who felt good about saving Afghan women from the Taliban are also asking for a radical redistribution of wealth or sacrificing their own consumption radically so that Afghan, African, or other women can have some chance of freeing themselves from the structural violence of global inequality and from the ravages of war? How many are asking to give these women a better chance to have the everyday rights of enough to eat, homes for their families in which they can live and thrive, and ways to make decent livings so their children can grow? These things would give them the strength and security to work out, within their communities and with whatever alliances they want, how to live a good life. Such processes might very well lead to changing the way those communities are organized, but not necessarily in directions we can imagine. It is unlikely that such changes would not include being good Muslims, and debating, as people have for centuries, how to define a good Muslim, or person. (Abu-Lughod, 2013, pp. 42–43)

Discussion Questions

- How does the concept of public/private spheres apply in the Taliban rules for Afghan women?
- Oppression can crush both men and women. What rules for men do the Taliban enforce? Research how the Taliban treats male rule breakers. In this case, are men and women separate groups with separate causes or should they unite to fight extremism?

Case Study: Egypt

Feminism had an early start in Egypt, when nineteenth-century nationalists linked their cause with liberating women. Although it was beneficial that male feminists started speaking out for the rights of all Muslims, women themselves needed their own voice. Baron's analysis of women-centered publications from 1892 and 1920 discusses the wide range of topics. In a call for contributors for her new journal, one editor stressed, "Do not imagine that a woman who writes in a journal is compromising her modesty or violating her purity and good behavior" (Baron, 1994, p. 1). As a result of these literary journals, a "woman's awakening" occurred. Class differences did matter, since the upper middle class was more open to women's rights than the lower classes. However, many female writers stressed that all women faced the same realities as wives and mothers so they should be united.

These women did not necessarily agree with Western feminists, especially regarding paid jobs. One leader, Fatima Rashid, expressed some concerns.

> Fatima considered a woman who earned wages outside the home to be like a man, disturbing the sexual order. She wrote about a "third sex"—not men and not women—that was developing in Europe in large numbers. As some Egyptian women attempted to follow the path of Western women, Fatima wondered what freedom there was in "coming and going, working with man shoulder-to-shoulder." Women's mixing with men in their work would only lead to "disgrace and difficulty" for them and "misery and misfortune" for the family. Fatima realized that some women in Europe had to work because their families would not provide for them. But in Egypt the family or state had to take care of women, and if Muslim women had to work, it meant that both the family and the state had neglected their duty. (Baron, 1994, p. 147)

A third sex, then, would ignore their primary mission in life—motherhood—and risk losing their womanhood. Other writers approved of women in professions such as medicine and education, but not the labor-intensive jobs (Baron, 1994). Islamic tradition stressed the economic dependence of women because that was the historical context. In the early days of Egyptian feminism, independence was not necessarily a desired outcome for women.

The anthropologist Lila Abu-Lughod, who was quoted about Afghanistan, had spent years in Egypt. She stayed with Amal, a village woman who needed major surgery. Her family was unable to pay for private care, so she had to go to a public clinic. "With structural adjustment, the Egyptian government has been forced to reduce funding of public health care so that patients now have to pay for the medicines and the anesthetic" (Abu-Lughod, 2013, p.74). Structural adjustments are the funding cutbacks required by international financiers such as the World Bank, which has created hardship in the developing world.

Although Amal worked hard, so did her devoted husband. Although he had joked about getting a second wife who would be a rich European, the author interpreted it in this way: "What lay behind his comment was sheer exhaustion and frustration about how unfair it was that others in this unequal world had it easier" (Abu-Lughod, 2013, p.76). Women are not trapped in the home. Instead, they help their neighbors or celebrate their good news as part of their social role. Amal's primary concern is economic survival, not religious restrictions. "So why is Amal not appropriate as a representative of 'the Muslim woman' of IslamLand? She suffers. She has troubles. She has to make compromises. She is poor and hardworking" (Abu-Lughod, 2013, p.79). This point is related to Box 20.1, a discussion on the "Othering" of Muslim women.

Discussion Questions

- Do you agree with Abu-Lughod's view that an Egyptian woman such as Amal is more oppressed by poverty than by sexism?
- Consider the possibility that the public/private sphere concept is a Western construct that does not fit a tradition society if women are honored in their homes. Write one paragraph supporting this assertion and one paragraph opposing it.

Box 20.1 The "Othering" of Muslim Women

McAuliffe (2007) writes of the "anonymous veiled women" representing Iran and needing rescue from the West (McAuliffe, 2007, p. 34). This symbol of Muslim women as the "Other" has affected many Westerners' perspectives on Islam. In her interviews with young European women, Scharff (2011) found that they did not see the need for feminism in their own lives. The "oppressed Muslim woman" stereotype, though, did inspire them to express their desire to fight patriarchal control. One interviewee stated, "I have never come across anything that made me upset about anything the way that a woman is treated…Muslim women for instance are treated, and I think that's very wrong" (Scharff, 2011, p. 129).

What is the impact of seeing Muslim women as the "Other" on the international scale? In writing about a Brazilian soap opera, Simpson (2009) discusses how it "depicted Muslim characters in Morocco as un-modern, but also valorized certain aspects of easternness, such as through

Figure 20.3 *Stereotype of Muslim woman (Photo source: Entofolio)*

brilliant images of feminine beauty, art forms, and certain customs" (Simpson, 2009, p. 306). The Orient appears as an exotic but backward place, quite the opposite of the modern West. The researcher, who watched the show with a family in the Muslim country of Kyrgyzstan, reflects on the irony of seeing the belly-dancing images with Central Asian women whose lives were nothing like that television show.

Ali, a Jordanian scholar, posits that the West's view of Muslim women justified their colonial expansion because Islam was seen as so backward. He states that males do dominate the world, not just Muslim countries. However, he argues that imposing Western culture on the "vastness of the Islamic world" is not the answer because "what if the majority of these women do not want to be emancipated in the western sense of the word?" (Ali, 2003, p. 86).

Supporting this point about perceived Western superiority, Nashat (1995) writes that the "European use of women's status to denounce Islam…aroused the wrath and fear of traditional sectors, led by the clergy" (Nashat, 1995, p. 8). One group, the apologists, "present an idealistic picture of women in Islamic society," whereas the critics stress the women as only victims of a male-dominated religion (Nashat, 1995, p. 9).

The "Othering" of Muslim women, then, can lead to polarization between Muslims and the West, a polarization that breaks down communication and even leads to violence. An accurate picture of Muslim women is one of complexity, contradictions, and courage in the face of many prejudices.

Discussion Questions

- Find an example (picture, movie character, etc.) of how the popular media portrays a stereotypical Muslim woman in *hijab*.
- Find an example of a Muslim woman in the media who contradicts the stereotype.
- In the Disney movie *Aladdin*, Jasmine is portrayed as an exotic Arab woman. (If you have not seen this movie, clips should be available online.) Do you think that Jasmine is the "Other?"
- How do these three images affect your view of Muslim women? Would this view have any impact on your social work practice with Muslim clients?

Empowerment of Muslim Women

For some women, religion can be a catalyst for both social and personal transformation. One study on "piety in politics" focuses on Sri Lankan women preachers who have come together and developed their skills (Haniffa, 2008). One activist states, "I think that every woman in the Muslim community has a talent which is hidden. We ourselves aren't aware that we have that talent. And once we come here … we somehow find out" (Haniffa, 2008, p. 355). Because of the training center, women can be community activists and still be considered pious and modest.

Another example of empowerment is the young woman who was awarded the Nobel Peace Prize, Malala Youvsafzi. One critical factor in her empowerment is her family.

Born in Pakistan, she was blessed with a father who fully appreciated her. As a teacher, he stressed that everybody—both boys and girls—needed an education for the nation's future.

> When I was born, people in our village commiserated with my mother and nobody congratulated my father. I arrived at dawn as the last star blinked out. We Pashtuns see this as an auspicious sign. My father didn't have any money for the hospital or for a midwife, so a neighbor helped at my birth. My parents' first child was stillborn, but I popped out kicking and screaming. I was a girl in a land where rifles are fired in celebration of a son, while daughters are hidden away behind a curtain, their role in life simply to prepare food and give birth to children.
>
> For most Pashtuns it's a gloomy day when a daughter is born.... My father, Ziauddin, is different from most Pashtun men.... He says he looked into my eyes after I was born and fell in love. He told people, "I know there is something different about this child." He even asked friends to throw dried fruits, sweets, and coins into my cradle, something we usually only do for boys. (Yousafzi & Lamb, 2013, pp. 13–14)

Malala was named after a woman warrior who had fought the British forces. Her parents' marriage was not one of male oppression but of mutual respect.

> Though she cannot read or write, my father shares everything with her, telling her about his day, the good and the bad. She teases him a lot and gives him advice about who she thinks is a genuine friend and who is not, and my father says she is always right. Most Pashtun men never do this, as sharing problems with women is seen as weak. "He even asks his wife!" they say as an insult. I see my parents happy and laughing a lot (Yousafzi & Lamb, 2013, p. 22)

At the age of 11, she began a blog about the Taliban (religious extremists). She advocated for both education and women in her hometown until she was 15. On her school bus, she was approached by a Taliban gunman who shot her three times. She almost died, and had to be airlifted to England for life-saving surgery. Now she is living in England because of death threats from the Taliban. Despite this ordeal, she remains confident and determined. "My father always said, 'Malala will be free as a bird'" (Yousafzi & Lamb, 2013, p. 26).

To stand up for women's rights in Pakistan and other conservative countries, then, can be a dangerous enterprise. Benazir Bhutto, the first woman elected to head a Muslim nation, was prime minister twice. Those who saw wives as the husbands' property were shocked that she was allowed to be in politics. As the daughter of a president, she acknowledged the advantages of upper-class women. "For me, the empowerment of women lies less in laws and more in economic independence. And it lies also in men. Our fathers who encourage us. Our male colleagues who stand by us" (Bhutto, 2005, p. 37). Tragically, Bhutto was assassinated in a political rally in 2007. Box 20.2 describes the journey of another Pakistani activist, Humaira Awais Shahid.

Box 20.2 One Pakistani Woman's Story

Humaira Awais Shahid, journalist and member of the Provincial Assembly of Punjab, exemplifies the prowoman advocate who works within her religious culture. Her book, *Devotion and Defiance: My Journey in Love, Faith, and Politics* (Shahid & Horan, 2014), is a proud statement of her activism in a conservative country. She converted a newspaper helpline into a tool for social change.

> The more time I spent listening to the stories of the aggrieved, the more I realized how little I really knew about Pakistan beyond my tidy, privileged corner of it. What I had understood at an intellectual level I came to know at a visceral one: that swaths of Pakistani culture sanctioned the inhumane treatment of its women and girls—and, in many cases, boys. While this was a cultural practice based in clan and tribal culture, Islam was often evoked by perpetrators in their own defense. As I would come to understand, the misperception of Islam as a religion that permits and even calls for certain abuses is not only widespread in the Western world; among the populations of Pakistan's tribal regions, where adherence to tribal tradition prevails, practices such as honor killings and revenge rapes are so common, they are customs. If Pakistan's law enforcement agencies are ineffectual in urban areas where literacy rates and income levels are higher, in tribal regions, law enforcement isn't even recognized. Tribal councils set laws and determine punishments, and the question of what is or isn't prescribed in the Qur'an is moot in a population that cannot read it. In the tribal regions, the illiteracy rate is 71 percent for men and 97 percent for women. Islam is not to blame for the crimes against women and children that are carried out in its name; ignorance is. (Shahid & Horan, 2014, p. 71)

To prove her argument that ignorance and not Islam is the problem, Shahid uses the example of predatory lending as one cause of oppression.

> A young woman had sold one of her kidneys. I was aware of organ-selling in Pakistan, but the particular details of the woman's story were entirely new and shocking to me: She had sold the organ to get out of debt with a predatory moneylender, who was pressuring her for more money still. (Shahid & Horan, 2014, pp. 71–72)

As a result of her investigation, Shahid uncovered an international network of brutal moneylenders, illiterate borrowers who could not read the terms of the agreement, hospitals that harvested the organs, and "transplant tourists" from all over the world (Shahid & Horan, 2014, p. 73). Stories such as these affected her greatly, and she had trouble dealing with all the pain she encountered.

Discussion Questions

- Besides being vulnerable to economic exploitation, what are the other implications of being illiterate?
- Predatory lending also occurs in the United States, especially through the payday-lending stores. What kinds of predatory lending exist in your community? Design an action plan to fight this practice (e.g., a proposed law on interest rates).
- Based on this story, would you call Shahid a feminist? Why or why not?
- After reflecting on Shahid's work, describe which social work value best applies.
- Like Shahid, social workers can experience stress and pain that they cannot shut off when they go home at night. What methods of self-care do you plan to use as a social worker (or activist) when the problems seem so huge?

Muslim Women in the West

"My background as an American Muslim of Arab descent is an asset, and once balanced, it is the most powerful part of my identity" (Omar, 2005, p. 66). Regardless of whether or not Muslim American women wear the hijab, they often encounter other discrimination they faced from both non-Muslims and other Muslims. One woman described being fired from her job after her conversion to Islam: "It was really tough for me because I couldn't understand. My work didn't change, and I as a person hadn't changed" (White & Hernandez, 2013, p. 73–74). In contrast, one African-American woman was rebuffed when greeting persons of Arab descent even though she was wearing hijab. Marriage is another issue, since they are not allowed to marry non-Muslim men because husbands are head of the household.

In a culture with strict gender roles, it is not surprising that Muslim lesbians should be conflicted between their sexual orientation and religious teachings. The first part of one article title, "I Don't Want to Taint the Name of Islam" expresses the inner struggle of lesbians who find it hard to find strength in their faith (Siraj, 2012). Another lesbian writes, "Being gay and Muslim? That's like sinning automatically, for no reason, all the time!" (Saed, 2005, p. 90).

Ali, the former Muslim who advocates for more Western influence in the world, recommends these three goals for Muslim women in the West: "The first is to ensure that Muslim girls are free to complete their education; the second is to help them gain ownership of their own bodies and therefore their sexuality; and the third is to make sure that Muslim women have the opportunity not only to enter the workforce but to stay in it" (Ali, 2010, p. xix).

Discussion Question

In an article about Muslim and non-Muslim battered women and the police, researchers (Ammar Couture-Carron, Alvi, & San Antonio, 2013) describe why Muslim women are less likely to call the police in a domestic violence situation. Immigration concerns, especially the fear of deportation, are one reason. Also, "they feared reprisal from the abuser or family members, the abuse was not a police matter, or that police could not do anything about the problem anyway" (Ammar et al., 2014, p. 1464).

Based on these concerns, design an intervention program with these objectives:

- Outreach to battered Muslim women so they will feel safe to call the police.
- Public awareness to the Muslim community about domestic violence.
- Coalition with Muslim religious leaders (imams) to assist with prevention and interventions when family violence is occurring.

Key Terms

Quran
Sharia Law
Hadith
Polygyny/Polygamy
Marriage contract
Hijab/Burqa
Taliban

21

Women in Latin America

THE wide diversity of cultural and ethnic groups in Central and South America makes it impossible to generalize about this population. This chapter, then, merely presents highlights that include a historical overview and the contexts of politics and economics.

Historical Overview

As the Spaniards and other Europeans invaded Latin America in the sixteenth century, brutal governments and economic exploitation were the norm. Unfortunately, Latin America has been struggling against these two types of injustice since then. In El Salvador in the 1970s and 1980s, for example, an oppressive regime slaughtered thousands of its citizens. A Salvadoran human rights activist, Maria Teresa Tula, writes of her reaction to the Archbishop Romero's murder by the government death squads in 1980: "They took his life because he was telling the truth. Telling the truth was his death sentence" (Tula, 1994, p. 87). Economic exploitation is also an ongoing issue. In *Open Veins of Latin America: Five Centuries of the Pillage of a Continent*, Galeano (1997) writes, "For those who see history as a competition, Latin America's backwardness and poverty are merely the result of its failure. We lost; others won" [because the Indians had so many resources such as gold] (Galeano, 1997, p. 2).

In this context, the status of women cannot be separated from the political and economic realities. European colonial rulers may have imported the *machismo* version of patriarchy that suppressed women, but there were always exceptions to the stereotype of the meek and obedient Latina (Skidmore, Smith, & Green, 2010). For instance, family dynamics sometimes allowed women to dominate their homes. Husbands were often absent in lower class households, so the wives had to take over the households to survive.

In the upper classes, widowhood gave many women the chance to rule as matriarchs in charge of their children's properties.

The Europeans also introduced the concept of public and private spheres as modern capitalism took hold (Meade, 2010). Around 1790, the capitalists started to encourage women to work in their factories to produce cigars and textiles. Stressing the work ethic (which obviously ignored the fact that most women had plenty of work to do at home), these new employers encouraged even middle-class women to work in the public sphere.

Politics also propelled women into the public sphere before the twentieth century. As early as the 1850s, for example, Chilean women printed newspapers about legal issues—even demanding the right to vote (Meade, 2010). Anticolonial revolutions inspired women to not only support their men but also to be active fighters themselves. The Bolivian March of the Women of Socorro of 1781, for instance, inspired Simon Bolivar to praise them years later for their daring. During the Comero Revolt, a woman "stepped forward to rip the hated tax decree from the wall on which it was posted" (Skidmore, Smith, & Green, 2010, p. 38).

One colorful figure in Ecuadoran history is Manuela Saenz, who was Bolivar's lover and inspiration (1797–1859). As a young girl in a genteel household, she was sent to the convent but still managed to meet a man after Mass one Sunday. After Mass one day, she took off with him and never wore a veil again. Her family forgave her and arranged a marriage for her to an English doctor. Once she met the new President Bolivar, though, she broke convention again by leaving her husband for him. Not only did she fight on the battlefields, but one night she confronted several would-be assassins in Bolivar's bedroom and saved his life. Once when some of Bolivar's soldiers were planning a mutiny, she showed up on a horse with a gun in her hand. She managed to persuade them to stay loyal (promising them extra money did not hurt). Saenz kept fighting for the cause even after Bolivar himself gave up. After being arrested and sent into exile, she opened up a small tobacco shop in Peru and delighted in telling her stories (Adams, 2010).

Besides fighting colonial powers, many Latin Americans also had to confront repressive governments. The Mexican Revolution against the Diaz regime, which started in 1910, involved women not only as fighters but as military leaders. Despite the fact that a few women were leaders, though, most female participants still acted submissively by walking behind the men's horses and carrying their rifles. A witness wrote that "A thick and heartbreaking book could be written upon the *soldadera*—the heroic woman who accompanies the army, carrying in addition to her baby, any other mortal possession, such as a kettle.... These women are the only visible commissariat for the soldiers ..." (Navarro & Sanchez Korrol, 1999, p. 95).

One heroic figure of the Mexican Revolution, Juana Belen Gutierrez Mendoza, had to survive jail terms for her newspaper's support of the rebels. Since she was in her sixties, she answered the question about possible retirement by stating, "I have that right, but I don't have a corner. In all the world's corners lives a pain; in all the world's corners is coiled a treachery with open jaws, ready to swallow; and I don't have the indifference necessary to ignore it, nor the cowardice to flee it, nor the gentility to accommodate it" (Adams, 2010, p. 131).

Political Context

In many Latin American countries, then, women have had to confront oppression as both citizens and women. El Salvador, for example, experienced a civil war in the 1980s as rebels fought against a government that committed countless human rights abuses. Maria Teresa Tula, who was quoted earlier, describes in her book *Hear My Testimony* (1994) the story of how she grew up with a father who barely recognized her and a mother who lived with an abusive man. Her older brother beat her up on a regular basis. At 15, she got pregnant. Her boyfriend deserted her, so she had to clean houses right until the day she gave birth. She had to walk forty minutes to the hospital, since there were no buses and they had no money for a cab.

She sold tamales on the street for a living. When she was 16, she fought back against her violent brother.

> The anger I felt was so intense that I wouldn't have wanted to express it, even if I had time to think about it. At that moment I did not even recognize him as my brother. I couldn't feel who I was either. I felt like my body was a shadow. After that fight, my whole being changed. Everything about my life felt different. I knew that the way I was being treated was unjust. (Tula, 1994, p. 24)

Later, she worked with others to protest against the repressive government in 1979. They demanded from the government an explanation of what had happened to several thousand missing persons. Then the activists found the body dumps—mass graves all over El Salvador. The violence escalated so much that Archbishop Oscar Romero was assassinated in his church in 1980. "He was a very humble man. He was extremely sincere. He truly believed that there was no difference between the poorest peasant child and the richest city child. We were all equal in his eyes" (Tula, 1994, p. 87).

After the police murdered Maria's husband, she herself went through torture and prison. She managed to move her family to the United States, where she continued to speak out against the killings in El Salvador. "Personally, I don't think about my own future very much. My future is in my children.... I hope they will use what happened to our family as a way to educate other people. I hope that they will be 'maestros de la realidad,' teachers of reality." (Tula, 1994, p. 177)

Another touching story is the one of Maria Izabel, a Mayan woman who had endured repression in Guatemala and was exiled in Mexico for years. She grew up in the highlands, where the military attacked her people in the 1980s. Her family spent ten years with the Communities of People of Resistance. The Mayans endured helicopter bombings, crop burnings, rapes, and torture. "We were various young people, cousins and neighbors. We saw so much injustice so we said that this could not continue, that we had to do something. They had killed several of our relatives, and they had killed our first cousins. And this gave us more rage ..." (Lykes, 1994, p. 99) At 16, she started her life as an activist on behalf of her Mayan people.

Besides visiting other countries to describe the atrocities, she also started a small business selling crafts in Mexico. Her group also wrote about Mayan history. "It was then, I believe, that we also began to talk about women's rights.... These were experiences that helped me to argue that as women we also have our own rights." (Lykes, 1993, p. 101)

After her exile in Mexico for eleven years, she returned to Guatemala to help rebuild her country. She began wearing the traditional clothes again and tried to get rid of her Mexican accent. Many men in the village had been killed (her aunt lost six of her eight sons), so the women were still grieving their losses. She states that her exile helped her to grow as a person, which could be jeopardized if she got married in this traditional society. "Since birth I have had this sense that I have something to give. Doing what I do, I feel good. To think of myself as a housewife with children, without being able to go out.... If I had really not had the opportunity to leave Guatemala, I think that my life might have taken a very different turn" (Lykes, 1993, p. 108).

Discussion Questions on Tula and Izabel

- Do you agree with Maria Izabel, who saw a connection between her oppression as a Mayan and her oppression as a female?
- If you had experienced governmental violence as these women did, how would your life be different today?
- Using the strengths perspective, describe these women. What kind of social work program would you develop to reinforce these strengths?

Women Activists in Chile

Evita Peron's movement (Box 21.1) and others in Latin America prove that not all women movements were left wing. Baldez (2002) studies two eras in recent Chilean history that provoked protests: Salvador Allende's socialist government (1970–1973) and General August Pinochet's subsequent dictatorship that lasted until 1990. During the brief presidency of Allende, conservative women organized the March of the Empty Pots movement in 1970 to symbolize the food shortages. Historians dispute whether only middle- and upper-class women participated in these marches. The women did not call this this movement "feminist" but "feminine power" to indicate how women could rise above party politics. These activists did not fight for political power themselves, instead urging their men to action (Baldez, 2002, p. 87). During these silent marches, women wore black to indicate mourning and sometimes had to face tear-gas attacks.

In support of Pinochet's coup in 1973, the Chilean Navy issued pamphlets that read, "The mother is sacred. The nation is sacred. Both are in grave danger. Extremism doesn't even respect women. The best guarantee Chile has are its armed forces" (Baldez, 2002, p 114). With support of the United States and other outside agents, Pinochet's military dictatorship committed many acts of horrific violence. Thousands of citizens went "missing" (secretly arrested and usually tortured and/or killed) as his forces suppressed any possible opposition. Even women wearing pants instead of skirts were beaten by soldiers for not looking feminine enough.

This time the Empty Pots emerged as an image by leftists and other citizens who opposed Pinochet. Few citizens dared to march openly as the anti-Allende protesters

Box 21.1 Eva Peron: Feminist or Fascist?

The story of Maria Eva Duarte Peron (1919–1952) (Figure 21.1), the wife of the Argentinian dictator Juan Peron, has fascinated people for decades. As an illegitimate daughter of an unacknowledged second wife, Evita faced class prejudice and dusty poverty. At 15, she moved to Buenos Aires to find work as an actress and model. She later became Juan Peron's mistress and then his wife. How this young woman became one of the most powerful figures in Latin American history is a story of a charismatic woman who lit up Argentina.

Because Juan Peron presented himself as the hero of the "Shirtless One" (laborers and other populists), Eva Peron appeared as a saintly benefactress who handed out charity with open hands. She also fought for clean water, child care, and decent housing (Adams, 2010). She called herself the "mother of my people" (Skidmore, Smith, & Green, 2010, p. 383). Argentinians came up with many names for her, including "Lady of Hope" and the "Mother of Innocents" (Fraser & Navarro, 1980, p. 111). Some even compared her to the Mother Mary.

But was she a feminist? She did support a woman's right to vote and run for public office. However, she rarely spoke of women-specific issues and made rude remarks about feminists. Perhaps the most lasting consequence of her legacy to Argentinian women is the Peronist Women's Party, which grew to over half a million members. This party resulted in thousands of women being politically involved in politics for decades (Fraser & Navarro, 1980).

Another key question was her possible link to fascism. Juan Peron's connections with Nazis and other fascists are well documented, with Eva Peron implicated in a secret deal to let Nazis hide in Argentina in exchange for wealth stolen from Jews (Gardner, 2011). As president, Juan Peron controlled the press and political parties. One reason he stayed in power was because his wife was so popular. Whether loved or despised, Eva Peron symbolizes how one woman can impact history despite the barriers of class and gender.

Figure 21.1 *Eva Peron (Photo source: Entofolio)*

had. Since political meetings were prohibited and every neighbor a possible spy, people had few ways to protest. "Banging on empty pots and pans offered several strategic advantages as a means of protest" because the noise was so loud (Baldez, 2002, p. 148). However, the police did shoot into several homes to stop this wordless protest.

Another method of protest during Pinochet's regime was the weaving of tapestries with "messages combining the personal and the political, [as] women depicted their lost children, or better times, or even scenes of human rights violations and antiregime protests" (Skidmore, Smith, & Green, 2010, p. 301). Not only did these tapestries allow them to express the women's grief, but they were sold by a trading network set up by the Catholic Church. "But their most important function was to provide an avenue for protest in a society in which 'de-politicization' was enforced by gun and bayonet" (Skidmore, Smith & Green, 2010, p. 301).

One survivor of Pinochet's prisons, Michelle Bachelet, emerged from her experience to become a doctor and later the President of Chile in 2007. Meade (2010) writes that a conservative Catholic nation elected "a socialist, atheist, unmarried mother of three children from different fathers, a former political prisoner who was tortured" (Meade, 2010, p. 317) Bachelet managed to win the election despite lacking the family ties normally associated with a woman's political success. As an advocate for women's health, she introduced sex education and free contraceptives (but abortion is still illegal in Chile.)

In a fascinating article about Bachelet, Thomas (2011) analyzes how Bachelet refused to act like an honorary male to win votes. Instead, she stressed the strength of her "Liderazgo Femenino" (feminine leadership) that the country needed instead of the traditional male (Thomas, 2011, p. 63). One political opponent stressed the theme that "She does not have the weight," implying that only men could handle the presidency (Thomas, 2011, p. 70). Both opponents stressed how their roles of father would make them powerful leaders, while one used the tie symbol of maleness. Bachelet responded by stating:

> Your wife, your girlfriend, your daughter and your mother can do it—they demonstrate it every day of their lives. Strength knows no gender, and neither does honesty, conviction or ability. I bring a different kind of leadership, with the perspective of someone who looks at things from a different angle. Let us change our mentality; when all is said and done, a woman president is simply a head of government who doesn't wear a tie (Thomas, 2011, p. 76).

The Roman Catholic Church's Role

As a dominant force in Latin America for centuries, the Roman Catholic Church has a mixed record regarding the welfare of women. Perhaps the most striking aspect of the Church's treatment of women is its doctrine against birth control and abortion, which is covered in chapter 9. Historically, the Church has also reinforced the colonial ideal of the submissive woman who stays at home. When indigenous or African people rebelled against the Church (and colonial rule) by practicing their own religions, they faced harsh punishments. Most of the "heretics" arrested and punished were women.

"African women emerged from the colonial era as priestesses of powerful religions that still flourish today in both the Caribbean and Brazil" (Navarro & Sanchez Korrol, 1999, p. 37).

However, convents were one avenue for women in Latin America to obtain not only a higher education but some relative independence. Medieval women in Europe had also used convents as a way to escape the worst aspects of patriarchy. When there were not enough convents in Brazil because of the government's concerns about a wife shortage, many women risked their lives to sail to Portugal to join an order. The benefits of escaping an unwanted marriage (often arranged by parents) outweighed the difficulties of convent life. The convent system, though, was far from egalitarian. Not only did a female have to come from the right social class to be accepted, but indigenous females were rejected for almost 200 years. Only European women of the right class, then, could enter these exclusive institutions (Navarro & Sanchez Korrol, 1999).

Figure 21.2 *Catholic Church in Latin America (Photo source: Entofolio)*

Liberation theology, which emerged in 1968 from the Medellin Conference of Latin American bishops, has also strengthened the role of women. This conference "denounced capitalism and communism as equal affronts to human dignity and placed the blame for hunger and misery on the rich and powerful" (Skidmore, Smith, & Green, 2010, p. 105). Although liberation theology started with bishops, it was the lower-level priests and nuns who supported it the most, since they lived in the impoverished areas. Grassroots organization, peaceful protests, and Bible studies inspired many devout Catholics to become political activists even under repressive regimes (Skidmore, Smith, & Green, 2010). Because of liberation theology, women linked the damages caused by patriarchal practices with the damages caused by excessive capitalism and repressive governments. "Latin American feminists, including theologians, do not wish to import North American or European feminism. They are careful to place the women's agenda within an overall liberation context rather than have it compete with economic and political liberation" (Berryman, 1987, p. 173).

One inspiration for the liberation-theology movement is the figure of Our Lady of Guadalupe. In the sixteenth century, a Mexican peasant had a vision of Mother Mary that still resonates today. One theologian, Natalia Imperatori-Lee, states, "Because Guadalupe is in solidarity with those who suffer, she points the way for the rest of the Church: where the poor are the Church should be too" (McBrien, 2008, pp. 343–344).

Another aspect of Our Lady of Guadalupe is the partial empowerment of Latinas during the festivities. Matovina (2005) writes:

> Guadalupe celebrations have often enabled women to exercise greater leadership and authority than they have been able to in other areas of public life, illustrating what Ana Maria Diaz Stevens calls the "matriarchal core" of Latin American Catholicism. Women's autonomous authority in religious devotion at San Fernando has enable them to oppose presumptions of male privilege, forge bonds of sisterhood for mutual support, and contest, reinterpret, and reimagine Guadalupe's meaning for their lives in the home and in community activism, politics, and civic affairs. (Mantovina, 2005, p. 18)

Economic Contexts

Maquilas

As the Latin American economies shifted from mercantile (i.e., colonial) to globalist (i.e., neoliberal and free trade), the stark difference between the developed and developing nations appeared on the U.S.-Mexico border in the 1990s. Maquila factories, which were often old warehouses converted into makeshift workplaces, became the new face of industrialization south of the United States border.

> On the way to the El Paso airport, I found a place to pull over on US Route 85, which runs alongside the border. Setting up the camera at the side of the road, I could shoot right through two rows of chain-link fence and into Anapra. Just thirty yards inside Mexico, you could see cardboard shacks, crumbling

cinderblocks and open sewers. As I looked across the border at the people who make Levi's for us, I realized that the skyscrapers of El Paso were almost immediately behind me. First-world and third-world, separated only by a chainlink fence (Abrahamson, 2007, p. 1)

Maquila factories dominated the border after 1993, when governments of Mexico, Canada, and the United States signed the NAFTA (North American Free Trade Agreement). This new policy reinforced the existing structure of outsourced (and low-paid) labor that U.S. companies were using in Mexico. Capitalism is famous for its boom and bust cycles, however. Two years later, the World Trade Organization (WTO) Agreement made it possible for more U.S. factories to move to China. Factories also started to leave Mexico because of the 2004 CAFTA (Central American Free Trade Agreement). This means that the factories are moving southward into Guatemala and other areas south of the U.S.-Mexico border for even cheaper wages.

The context of these maquilas, then, is globalization. The core nations (e.g., the United States and western Europe) use the peripheral nations such as Mexico for economic profit. This is parallel to the female role in many societies, since their labor is used but their position is rarely central. The advantages of outsourcing (also called offshore assembly) are not just low labor costs but also tax advantages and fewer environmental restrictions. In this coproduction mode, the labor in the developing nations is less skilled but much cheaper (Tiano, 1994).

The cultural context related to Mexican women stressed that the family was the cornerstone of society, and that mothers held it together. Married women should stay pure by remaining in the private sphere. But there were push/pull factors that motivated women to start factory jobs. The most obvious push factor was that the families needed the money. Either the husband was unemployed or was not making enough money. Single women also faced family pressures to start a factory job. The pull factors (the attractive aspects) were the personal autonomy symbolized by the paychecks. The news that new jobs were available was exciting, besides the fact that the maquilas were hiring women who were not employable before.

According to the women surveyed in Tiano's study, 93 percent of them cited inflation and the bad economy for the reason they were working there. However, 64 percent stated that they would still work there even if the money were not needed. They considered the job as part of their family role (a daughter or mother helping to support the family) and a way to develop personal growth. One positive result of the maquilas was the stress on education, since the factories offered free classes.

One common view of the maquila worker was that she was exploited by being forced to work in bad conditions and accept low pay. Another view, though, was that the women had stable jobs. They were gaining self-respect and were even able to challenge male authority at home. Society stereotyped maquila workers as temporary staff who did not really need the money. Following the Mexican tradition of Marianismo (female passivity based on the Mother Mary's self-sacrifice model), employers expected these women to be docile and easy to handle.

However, some of these women were anything but docile. Maquila workers have gone on strike and conducted other protests. The resistance factors include the call for autonomy, gender equality, and solidarity of both workers and women. They have not been reluctant to criticize the workplace. Globalization obviously had a profound impact on both workers and society, as also described in Box 21.2.

Another important study of *maquila* workers is Fernande-Kelly's research as an actual factory worker (Fernandez-Kelly, 1997). Getting hired in a Juarez factory, she found out that finding a job was best done through an informal network of friends and relatives, who could recommend factories to the jobseekers and potential employees to their supervisors. The manager's paternalistic interest resulted in each worker feeling obliged to produce more products without more pay. As one worker said, "He gave me the job in the first place! Besides, it makes me feel good to know that I can return the favor, at least in part." (Fernandez-Kelly, 1997, p. 205)

The term *unskilled labor* did not apply to the garment-making procedure that Fernandez-Kelly had to perform. Sewing patch pockets onto jeans required "perfect coordination of hands, eyes and legs.... Too much pressure (on the machine) inevitably broke the thread or produced seams longer than the edge of the pocket. The slightest deviation

---

Box 21.2 Author's Reflections on Globalization

As a writer, I am aware that using terms such as *globalization* and *neoliberal* can make the readers' eyes glaze over. The average U.S. consumer may benefit from the low prices of clothes and other products but not actually be exposed to the human cost of free trade policies. In 1995, I had a brief experience in Juarez, Mexico as faculty for a group of students on a poverty immersion trip. We stayed in the homes of host families living on a vast garbage dump (the size of several football fields). My eyes and nose stung from the smell of chemical waste that had been improperly—but legally—disposed of from the factories. After this trip, I became sick with bronchitis for weeks because of the toxic fumes that these Mexicans had to live with every day.

As this chapter mentioned, corporations started shifting the factories to even less expensive locales by the mid-1990s. My visit had occurred right when many maquilas were shutting down but before the drug war exploded into insane violence. One U.S. politician noted, "About 300 Maquiladoras have left Mexico to go to China where labor is found even cheaper. So they came in here, took up the human resource, used that, manufactured their goods, took their profits, and left" (U.S. Representative Hilda Solis quoted in Abrahamson, 2007). The poverty in Mexico grew even worse as unemployment rose—and now Juarez is too unsafe for most travelers. When I think of the lovely people I met in Juarez, I hope that the drug war has not affected them too much.

Another aspect of globalization that struck me was that the "free market" can fail when millions of people have so little capital (in this case, money for spending or investing). This became evident in the futility of vendors trying to sell their wares. Men would stroll the streets with wagons filled with merchandise such as brooms. As the vendors called out in the neighborhoods looking for customers, nobody came. Nobody had any money even for the smallest of items. As I heard the vendors' calls echoing down the streets, I had to ask: How can globalization work when so many people have no money to spend at all?

---

produced lopsided designs …" (Fernandez-Kelly, 1997, p. 206) She was expected to sew up to 396 pockets an hour, or over 3,000 a day. Not surprisingly, chronic back pain was a problem for these workers.

The researcher befriended one coworker, who took her aside to say that she wanted to help her buy better clothes and a haircut. Her new friend helped her to cope with the difficult demands of the job, including the supervisors walking around the workplace and yelling, "Faster! Faster! Come on, girls, let's hear the sound of those machines!" (Fernandez-Kelly, 1997, p. 210)

Many of the women expressed a desire to find a man, even though they denigrated them as worthless. The young women went out dancing even after long hours of factory work. Once when a group was on a bus, a man came on board and was subjected to teasing and even catcalls. As one woman said later, "Factory work is harder than most people know. As long as you don't harm anybody, what's wrong with having a little fun?" (Fernandez-Kelly, 1997, p. 214)

Tomato Industry

The impact of globalization can be seen in the grocery store, especially in the produce section. As agribusinesses expand their operations to several countries, a simple tomato can symbolize the complex relationships between free trade, environmental concerns, and ethnic/racial discrimination. Brandt (2008) describes how agroexports impact people's lives in Mexico as big business took over agriculture.

Before the multinationals moved into countries like Mexico, the *campesinos* (peasant farmers) had an organic relationship with their land. As one *campesino* stated:

> There is a link between the earth and the [hu]man, between the plant and [hu] man that goes further than simply the idea of cultivating a plant, no? One feels the growth of the plant, it's a relation that grows, it's like a child. It's like talking in silence, getting to know what the plant needs. You feel it very deeply. (Brandt, 2008, p. 212)

Women usually had two work shifts: home and family plot. Then the economy shifted as it became harder and harder to live off the corn and beans they grew. Two family members were once needed to sustain a family with their wages, then the entire family (usually five) had to work for agribusiness. Now women had a third shift as they had to work for low wages while still maintaining home and family plot.

Gender discrimination (e.g., usually women were used as sorters because of their smaller hands) and racial/ethnic discrimination (e.g., indigenous workers were usually given the least desirable jobs) add to the sense of hierarchy. Workers from the city, for instance, received better treatment than the rural workers.

Because child care (and often schools) are usually not available, "Some women carry their children on their backs while they're working" (Brandt, 2008, p. 242). With handkerchiefs over their mouths to protect them from pesticides, these workers often face a quota of forty buckets a day.

Figure 21.3 *Agricultural workers in Latin America (Photo source: Entofolio)*

Working Overseas

Although the immigration issue remains unresolved in the United States, millions of Latino/as continue to migrate north to find jobs. Many Latinas work as maids or nannies in households. The forced intimacy between worker and employer in a house can create conflicts in which the employer usually wins. Hondagneu-Sotelo (2004) discusses the consequences of living so closely to the employer/family:

> Many Latina immigrant employees and their U.S. employers fall easily into a familial rhetoric, referring to the worker as "just like one of the family." Indeed, this attitude has a long history in paid domestic work, and, as many analysts have noted, it helps to blur the boundaries between paid work and unpaid favors, which in turn leads to exploitation. (Hondagneu-Sotelo, 2004, p. 67)

Forced labor, one form of human trafficking, is sometimes associated with this form of employment. In one Texan case, a housewife drove over the border to Vera Cruz, Mexico to hire a housekeeper. She negotiated with the parents of a twelve-year-old girl, promising to educate her and give her a hopeful future. After smuggling her into the United States, this pleasant-looking woman held the girl captive for four years.

> On arrival, Maria was dragged into hell. Sandra Bearden used violence and terror to squeeze work and obedience out of the child. From early morning to midafternoon, Maria cooked, cleaned, scrubbed, and polished. If Maria

dozed off from exhaustion, or when Sandra decided that she wasn't working fast enough, Sandra would blast pepper spray into Maria's eyes…. When Maria wasn't working, Sandra would chain her to a pole in the backyard without food or water. An eight-foot concrete fence kept her hidden from neighbors. After chaining her, Sandra would sometimes force Maria to eat dog feces. (Bales & Soodalter, 2010, p. 4)

It is critical, then, to remember that immigrants are particularly vulnerable to forced labor. As indicated by the book title of *The Slave Next Door: Human Trafficking and Slavery in the U.S. Today* (Bales & Soodalter, 2010), such abuses can occur in any city or state. Maria was one of the lucky ones, because she was rescued. Her traumatic story is a reminder that social workers and other professionals must be alert to possible cases of forced labor.

Discussion: First Case Study on Women in Belize

In McClaurin's book *Women of Belize: Gender and Change in Central America* (1996), the author gives voice to the women in this impoverished nation. Below are some excerpts and discussion questions:

[When asked if she had any message for other women, Rose responded]: We women have to be strong. Women have to be not only emotionally strong but physically. We have to be strong for our family and for ourselves. The father is important. The woman is the one in the family who have all the obligations. We have to be fighters. We have to be strong. This is a battle we have to face with a smile even though it is hard. We have to face it in a positive way. I'm very proud of myself that I am stepping forward not backwards. It's not the end of the world. (McClaurin, 1996, p. 55)

Discussion Questions:

- What kind of program would you set up for women like Rose to achieve her goals?
- If you were Rose's counselor, what would you say to her if she got discouraged?

[After her husband got very sick and had to go to the U.S. for treatment, Zola faced a financial crisis]: I said to myself, if he dies tomorrow I haven't anywhere to go. Where will I go? I got to my brothers but it's only for two days with the kids. So I went to this chairman of this village that I know and I said hey, I'm a Belizean and I need a piece of land. He says, "Humph, it's a hard thing your husband have." I said listen, "I am a Belizean, I have five kids and I born in this village here that I am asking this piece of land from. I has a right to get a piece of land here." (McClaurin, 1996, p. 95)

Discussion Questions:

- If you were a women's group leader and heard about Zola's demand for land, how would you mobilize the group to support her?
- If you were a counselor for a woman in Zola's situation, how would you encourage her to find inner strength like Zola did?

Discussion: Second Case Study on Women in Belize

In her field study of domestic violence in a Mayan community in Belize, McClusky (2001) tells the story of Francesca, who was forced to marry at the age of thirteen.

> "But it's not long before the man likes to lash me too much. Maybe he start to lash me after two months. Then, all the time he lash me."
>
> "But why?"
>
> "I don't know, gal. Maybe he likes to drink too much." Francesca stands and tosses the orange into the bush. It lands far away, next to a cacao tree. Then she sits on the bench again and stretches out her legs. "When he drinks he gets jealous. But I don't go anywhere, I stay at home, I wash the clothes, I cook the corn, I sweep my house. Only sometimes, I like to go visit my mother. But he thinks I go all kinds of places."
>
> "So he lash you?"
>
> "Yes, he lash me. Every day, he like to lash me. I say to myself, why do I have to live like this? I have done nothing wrong. I only do my work.... So, I decide to lef him."
>
> "You left your husband?"
>
> "Yes, I tell him I will not stay with him because he likes to lash me too much." She nods with finality. "When I tell him I'm going to lef him he gets vexed, gal." She laughs. "Aiy, he grabs my hair."
>
> I suck air through my teeth. "Aiy!"
>
> "Yes, gal." She mimes his actions while narrating the story.... "I go back to my poor mother."
>
> "How old were you then."
>
> "I don't know, gal. Maybe sixteen, that's all." She repeats it, perhaps to make it more certain. "Maybe, I was sixteen when I went back to my poor mother."
>
> We are silent for a few moments. I can't think of anything to ask her. Maybe she can't think of what to say next. (McClusky, 2001, pp. 54–55)

Discussion Questions

- If you were starting a women's center in Francesca's village, which issue would you focus on first: child marriage, forced marriage, domestic violence, or poverty?
- If you were a counselor for a woman like Francesca who had left her husband at 16, what do you think could further empower her?

- Describe how the concept of Marianismo may impact a Latina's decision decision to stay with an abusive husband.
- Find examples of the following terms and describe their significance: *patriarchy, oppression,* and *intersectionality*.
- The 2010 movie *Made in Dagenham* describes how some factory workers in England went on strike in 1968 for equal pay, which parallels the maquila situation. These women's protests resulted in the Equal Pay Act of 1970. One point made in the movie was that the lack of equal pay does not just affect women, but also their families. The child of an underpaid worker receives fewer food and clothes. In your opinion, is this a strong argument for equal pay? Why or why not?
- Also in this movie, an executive says that they could not afford to give women equal pay. What would you say to this argument?
- After reading the following chapter on China, compare the factory workers' lives (i.e., Factory Girls excerpt) to the maquila workers. What similarities do you see?

Key Terms

Maquilas
El Salvador's civil war
Mayans in Guatemala
Eva Peron
Chilean activists
Roman Catholic Church
Liberation theology
Globalization
Tomato industry

22

Women in China

Introduction

With a population of over one billion and an economy experiencing unprecedented growth, China presents several complexities. It is both the world's oldest living civilization and an emerging global force in the twenty-first century. Once a nation committed to communism (stressing state ownership instead of private property), China has become a hypercapitalist society. Traditions that have lasted for centuries continue alongside innovative technology in a dictatorship that is no longer Marxist (i.e., collectivist). Osnos (2014) reflects on this enigma:

> The (Chinese Communist) Party no longer promises equality or an end to toil. It promises only prosperity, pride, and strength. And for a while, that was enough. But over time the people have come to want more, and perhaps nothing more ardently than information. New technology has stirred a fugitive political culture; things once secret are now known; people once alone are now connected. And the more the Party has tried to prevent its people from receiving unfiltered ideas, the more they have stepped forward to demand them....
>
> In the early years of the twenty-first century, China encompasses two universes: the world's newest superpower and the world's largest authoritarian state. Some days, I spent the morning with a new tycoon and the evening with a dissident under house arrest....
>
> Forty years ago the Chinese people had virtually no access to fortune, truth, or faith—three things denied them by politics and poverty. They had no chance to build a business or indulge their desires, no power to challenge propaganda and censorship, no way to find moral inspirations outside the Party. Within a

generation, they had gained access to all three—and they want more. (Osnos, 2014, pp. 2–3).

Chinese women especially want more for their lives. Their road to liberation sometimes ran parallel to the Communist Party's drive to modernize, but sometimes verged into new directions. Theirs is the story of fighting seclusion and invisibility to achieve recognition as contributors to society beyond bearing sons. Although women have not yet achieved full equality in China, the progress in the past sixty years has been striking.

Women in Traditional China

As a radio talk show personality in China, Xinran (2002) collected letters from women telling the truth about their lives. She places their struggles in this historical context:

> From the matriarchal societies in the far distant past, the position of Chinese women has always been at the lowest level. They were classed as objects, as a part of the property, shared out along with food, tools and weapons. Later on, they were permitted to enter the men's world, but they could only exist at their feet— entirely reliant on the goodness or wickedness of a man. If you study Chinese architecture, you can see that many long years passed before a small minority of women could move from the side chambers of the family courtyard (where tools were kept and the servants slept) to chambers beside the main rooms (where the master of the house and his sons lived).
>
> Chinese history is very long, but it has been a very short time since women have had the opportunity to become themselves and since men have started to get to know them.
>
> In the 1930s, when Western women were already demanding sexual equality, Chinese women were only just starting to challenge male-dominated society, no longer willing for their feet to be bound, or to have their marriages arranged for them by the older generation. However, they did not know what women's responsibilities and rights were; they did not know how to win for themselves a world of their own. (Xinran, 2002, p. 54)

This excerpt indicates the stunning changes that Chinese women went through during the twentieth century, since tradition dominated most households until the Revolution in 1949. Chinese history started in the early ancient period, followed by several centuries of dynastic emperors from 221 BCE to 1911. During this time, the influence of Confucius (551–479 BCE) through his *Analects* pervaded Chinese culture. He stressed a "harmonious society" above all (Wasserstrom, 2013, p. 15). The concept of yin and yang meant that yin (weak, yielding) should allow yang (strong, positive) to dominate (Hong, 1997). Harmony would be impossible without a hierarchy: emperor over subjects; father over son; husband over wife; and elder brother over the younger ones. Only friendships could be equal relationships. Emperors ruled because they had received the Mandate of Heaven, a divine appointment that his rulers should not question. In the same way, women should never challenge their male's authority or turbulence would result. A woman must obey her father, then her husband, then her eldest son.

Confucius emphasized not only ritualism for correct behavior, but also filial duty. A good son must care for his parents. In this context, the mother-son bond is more important than a husband-wife bond (especially if he should have more than one sex partner). Mothers-in-law usually had great power over their sons' wives. One Confucian writer instructs: "Let a woman not act contrary to the wishes and the opinions of parents-in-law about right and wrong, let her not dispute with them what is straight and what is crooked" (Ban Zhao, c. 80 CE).

In a harmonious society, then, females should be obedient within the family hierarchy. Because chastity was another key aspect of ideal women, a cloistered woman symbolized the honor of her family. Around the age of 12, a girl would join the seclusion of the women's quarters to embroider, play the zither, and other allowed activities. A good woman was somebody who stayed in the private sphere to stay pure from the outside world. One writer noted:

> When a family wanted to know more about a girl who had been suggested for a daughter-in-law and asked what kind of girl she was, the neighbors would answer, "We do not know. We have never seen her." And that was praise (Ning Lao T'ai-t'ai, ca. 1900, cited in Mann, 2011, p. 1).

Women who did appear in the public sphere were considered low class, such as shopkeepers and laborers. Even girls who went to school or temples were suspected of impurity. In one painting of a house in a flood, a "chaste and obedient wife" refuses to go with an escort because he did not have written permission from her husband. She drowns in order to keep her virtue (Mann, 2011, p. 14). Rape victims, then, were often blamed for their plight:

> If a man plots to have illicit sex in broad daylight, it is usually when he happens to encounter a woman in some lonely village or remote empty place.... [if a girl is under sixteen, then it is considered rape].... But women who walk alone without any company are rarely chaste (Magistrate's Handbook, early nineteenth century, cited in Mann, p. 1).

In this context, unwed mothers faced severe treatment from the community regardless of whether or not the pregnancy had been caused by rape. Kingston (1976), for example, writes of her nameless aunt who was staying with her family when a mob attacked the house with vegetables and other missiles. Her mother told her that "The old woman in the next field swept a broom through the air and loosed the spirits-of-the-brooms over our heads. 'Pig.' 'Ghost.' 'Pig,' they sobbed and scolded while they ruined our house" (Kingston, 1976, p. 5). Later that night, the woman delivered her baby in a pigsty. "The next morning when I went for the water, I found her and the baby plugging up the family well" (Kingston, 1976, p. 5). The author reflects that "Mothers who love their children take them along. It was probably a girl; there is some hope of forgiveness for boys" (Kingston, 1976, p. 15).

Besides chastity and seclusion, women had to learn the virtue of self-effacement. "Humility means yielding and acting respectful, putting others first and oneself last, never mentioning one's own good deeds or denying one's own faults ..." (Ban Zhao, cited in Ebrey, 2010, p. 81). Sometimes a daughter had no name except for "Number Two Girl" (Chang, 1991) or "Old Number Two" for a grandmother (Shen, 2007). It is not surprising that many families committed female infanticide to avoid feeding a child who would belong to her future husband's family. In this context, parents often did not consider a daughter to be their own. Sometimes a daughter's only value to her birth family was the amount of money stated in a contract as she became a wife, concubine, maid, or prostitute (Ebrey, 1991).

If marriage was a girl's destiny, arranged marriages were so strictly enforced that a daughter may be imprisoned for refusing to marry a chosen mate. Even as an infant, a daughter did not really belong to her birth family but to her future husband's family. Parents arranged betrothals for infants and children, which could result in a girl as young as eight being sent to her new family. Her status was "child raised to be a daughter-in-law" (Hershatter, 2011, p. 5). She would later be married at an altar at her husband's home to symbolize that she would produce sons to continue the family's ancestor worship (Sommer, 2000). Staying loyal to her husband protected the family from any illegitimate children. Also, she should devote herself to her husband's well-being: "Your husband is like heaven to you" (Mann, 2011, p. 14). After his death, the widow should stay chaste to honor him—even if this caused severe poverty for the women and their children.

However, the word *marriage* is a problematic one because of its variations in traditional China. Although some men may have been monogamous, having many sex partners was a mark of prestige for the man because it proved his wealth. Not only was there a First Wife (the highest rank), there were Second Wives with legal status when allowed by the government. Concubines (comparable to mistresses in western culture) had no legal standing. The lowest ranks were prostitutes and servants (Ebrey, 1991). Such arrangements could create many complications, especially for the families of rulers. Hans Feizi, a Legalist writer (Legalism was a philosophy like Confucianism), warned rulers about scheming women in a piece written around 230 BCE:

> A woman is not tied by flesh and blood. When a ruler loves her, they are close; when he does not love her, they are distant. It is like the saying, "The child whose mother is loved is cherished." The opposite holds true: The child whose mother is hated is cast aside. A man of fifty has not lost his interest in women, but a woman begins to lose her looks before thirty. When a woman whose looks are deteriorating serves a man who still loves sex, she will be despised and her son is not likely to be made heir. This is the reason queens, concubines, and consorts plot the death of a ruler. When the mother of the ruler is the queen, all orders are carried out and all prohibitions are effective. (Hans Feizi cited in Ebrey, 1993, p. 34)

Indeed, the traditional Chinese regarded women's involvement in politics with alarm. "Disorder does not come down from heaven; It is produced by women" (Ebrey, 2010, p. 34).

Life was different for lower-class women, though, because of lighter social restrictions. Not trapped in seclusion, they could interact with men without being condemned. Marriage was less common and concerns about illegitimate children were not as important among the poor. For prostitutes and maids forced to have sex with their masters, nineteenth-century reformers wrote laws in an effort to protect them (Sommer, 2000).

For the lower-class women, sexual servitude often went along with a lack of education. The respected Confucian scholar, Ban Zhao (quoted earlier), supported the dignity of women through education: "Yet only to teach men and not to teach women—is that not ignoring the essential relation between them?" (Ban Zhao, c. 80 CE). One example of this attitude is apparent in the education of elite women in thirteenth-century China, since they were valued by their families (Barlow, 2004). Female writers and scholars publicly shared their work because literacy was a source of pride. Poetry was another form of expression for these cloistered women.

Besides education, marriage sometimes gave elite women a chance for advancement through hypergamy (marrying up the social ladder). In some cases, women gained property rights through marriage (Ebrey, 1991; Barlow, 2004). Without marriage, a woman could not gain legal recognition as an adult.

Linking marriage with adulthood created one disadvantaged group, unmarried men who could not afford a wife. According to Mann (2011), almost every woman had a mate, but 20 percent of men were unmarried because of the skewed sex ratio caused by both female infanticide and rich men having multiple wives and concubines. Single men, called "bare sticks" who would sire no legitimate children, were often outcasts who joined criminal gangs (Mann, 2011, p. 5).

Discussion Questions

- Select one aspect of the preceding section and apply it to the concept of patriarchy. Compare traditional Chinese culture to another traditional culture described in this textbook.
- How would you apply the concept of essentialism to the traditional Chinese view of males and females? In your opinion, is it harmful or beneficial in this case?
- Review the preceding section and select one aspect that may apply to social work practice with clients of Chinese origin. Why should a culturally competent social worker know this aspect?

Foot Binding

Traditional Chinese culture includes stories of strong women such as Mulan (Box 22.1). Class differences, of course, also impacted a Chinese woman's life. One striking difference between upper- and lower-class women was the size of their feet.

During the dynastic period, women in the upper classes had high standards of beauty to achieve. One male novelist, Li Ruzhen, wrote a chapter in *Flowers in the Mirror* around 1810 entitled "Country of the Women." He imagined a country in which women

Box 22.1 The Legacy of Mulan

Those familiar with the story of Mulan, the girl who dressed up as a man to fight as a soldier in her father's place, would appreciate how her story inspired Chinese women for centuries. One writer with the pen name of "A Hunan Woman" noted the importance of Mulan in a 1903 pamphlet:

In the long thousands years (of history), except for the fortunate Mulan who became prominent, has there been no one else with unique ideas? It is all because women have been restrained by customs and controlled by the family. Even those with remarkable talents and aspirations have been unable to cross the boundaries to demonstrate their talent and express their aspirations. (Wang, 1999, p. 41)

Another writer, Maxine Hong Kingston, reminisced about how she responded to her mother's "talking-story" about this heroine.

Instantly I remembered that as a child I had followed my mother about the house, the two of us singing about how Fa Mu Lan fought gloriously and returned alive from war to settle in the village. I had forgotten this chant that was once mine, given me by my mother, who may not have known its power to remind. She said I would grow up to be a wife and a slave, but she taught me the song of the warrior woman, Fu Mu Lan. I would have to grow up a warrior woman. (Kingston, 1976, p. 20)

were the rulers and the men were the subjugated ones. The hero had to undergo a beauty treatment:

In due course, his feet lost much of their original shape. Blood and flesh were squeezed into a pulp and then little remained of his feet but dry bones and skin, shrunk, indeed, to a dainty size. Responding to daily anointing, his hair became shiny and smooth, and his body, after repeated ablutions of perfumed water, began to look very attractive indeed. His eyebrows were plucked to resemble a new moon. With blood-red lipstick, and powder adorning his face, and jade and pearl adorning his coiffure and ears, Merchant Lin assumed, at last, a not unappealing appearance. (Spence, 1990, p 146)

This "Golden Lotus" practice started around 1,000 years ago when women with tiny feet who swayed as they walked were seen as lovely. By crippling a female, this guaranteed that she would need to be protected by a rich husband who could afford a nonworking wife. Women with unbound feet appeared ugly and low class. So if a mother wanted her daughter to marry well, she started the foot binding process around the age of five. The process included breaking the foot and binding it up so it would become deformed.

Foot binding was probably not intended as misogynistic torture. Mothers who bound their daughters' feet thought they were creating a better future for them. The husbands who married these girls were seen as protectors, not oppressors. In her revisionist history of foot binding, Ko (2005) writes that this practice persisted for centuries despite many governmental attempts to stop it. Not only did mothers want it for their daughters so they did not have to work in the fields, but women themselves hid from government inspectors to keep their small feet. Only slaves had big feet. Sometimes girls fought back, as did this child:

> At the age of three my grand aunt proclaimed her independence by categorically refusing to have her feet bound, resolutely tearing off the bandages as fast as they were applied. She was born in Shanghai (city by the sea) in 1886 during the Qing dynasty when China was ruled by the child Kuang Hsu, who lived far away up north in the Forbidden City. The pampered baby of the family, eight years younger than my grandfather, Ye Ye, Grand Aunt finally triumphed by rejecting all food and drink until her feet were, in her words, "rescued and set free." (Yen Mah, 1997, p. 5)

Since the nineteenth century, both foreigners and Chinese reformers tried to eliminate foot binding. Chinese liberals were so mortified by this sign of backwardness that they tried to humiliate women with bound feet. Political leaders such as Mao Zedong banned the practice after he became leader, so there are only a few elderly women left in China who still have the smaller feet. One Chinese woman recalls:

> As a child, I can remember my grandmother being in constant pain. When we came home from shopping, the first thing she would do was soak her feet in a bowl of hot water, sighing in relief as she did so. Then she would set about cutting off pieces of dead skin. The pain came not only from the broken bones, but also from her toenails, which grew into the balls of her feet (Chang, 1991, p. 25).

In writing about the dreams of Chinese girls becoming warrior queens instead of "wives or slaves," Kingston speculates, "Perhaps women were once so dangerous that they had to have their feet bound" (Kingston, 1976, p. 19). Hong (1997) relates this practice to the physical liberation of women necessary for China to develop as a nation. Walking with sturdy feet instead of hobbling on misshapen stumps, Chinese women could start on the road to equality.

Discussion Questions

- Describe one modern Western parallel to foot binding, such as breast enhancement surgery. In what ways are the practices similar and different?
- Consider a practice to comply with modern fashion that you or your social circle may do to enhance your appearance, such as tattoos. How would a person from another century regard this practice? Research the history of this practice to see if there is any prior cultural meanings. What is the current cultural meaning of the practice?

May Fourth Era (1911–1925)

A few cracks in the stone wall of male domination did appear in the early 1900s, when thousands of young Chinese women went to Japan to study. Their families allowed them to unbind their feet and many modern men made pledges to marry those with "large feet" (Spence, 1990, p. 240). Exposed to western culture and role models such as Joan of Arc, some women became even more revolutionary. Qiu Jin, for instance, dressed like a man and tried to start an uprising in 1907. Although her story ended tragically with her execution, she represented to many young Chinese a new kind of woman.

In 1911, the last dynasty fell to Nationalists who tried to transform China after centuries of deep-seated traditions. In reaction to this momentous change, rebellious intellectuals generated the New Cultural Movement of the May Fourth Era for a decade. Embracing western ideals such as democracy, these reformers considered women's emancipation from their subjugation to be a primary goal (Chow, Zhang, & Wang, 2004). Nationalists who wanted a China free from foreign powers stressed that modernization required needed strong men *and* women.

One example of a successful woman in this era was Yen Mah's Grand Aunt, the one who had rescued herself from foot binding.

> In 1924 Grand Aunt founded her own bank, the Shanghai Women's Bank. It is impossible to overestimate the scale of her achievement. In a feudal society where the very idea of a woman being capable of simple everyday decisions, let alone important business negotiations, was scoffed at, Grand Aunt's courage was extraordinary. (Yen Mah, 1997, p. 9)

Xianqi liangmu, the "doctrine of good wives and wise mothers" (Chiang, 2007, p. 70) was another aspect of this feminism. In a study of *The Ladies' Journal* from 1915 to 1925, the researcher noted that this stage of feminism still had traditional features.

One young woman reinvented tradition by writing about the Chinese character for "woman" that includes a broom. This student notes that this symbol could represent more than just a clean house:

> Women have lived in darkness for two thousand years. Dependency has become their nature; jealousy, partiality, and superstition have become their natural habits, which are hard to break. They are all like dust in the heart. Only learning can correct the mistakes. Learning is like a broom that will sweep away all the dust in the heart. (Wang, 1999, p 72)

Era of Mao Zedong

As noted earlier, China experienced political turmoil after the Nationalists became the new rulers. This time of transition occurred from 1911 through the 1930s, in which the Nationalist Party tried to consolidate its power over the warlords.

During this time, Mao Zedong and his cohort developed the Communist Party. He spoke out on behalf of oppressed women, especially by speaking out against arranged marriages. As early as 1919, he noted that China would need all citizens—not just males—for the revolution and rebuilding of China. Arranged marriages were one way that prevented women's power from being realized. After a young woman committed suicide on the way to her wedding, Mao wrote, "It happened because of the shameful system of arranged marriages, because of the darkness of the social system, the negation of the individual will, and the absence of the freedom to choose one's own mate" (Spence, 1990, p. 304). Later in 1927, Mao showed even more awareness of women's inequality when he wrote that they had to live under more levels of authority than men. He did note that peasants were more egalitarian simply because of economic need because both genders had to work in the fields.

The 1930s ushered in a new era of political chaos when Japan invaded different parts of China to add to the political chaos. Mao and the Chinese Communists fought against the Japanese as well as the Nationalists. After World War II, Mao Zedong created the People's Republic of China in 1949. The Chinese Communist Party (CCP) has been ruling since then. Mao was a strict communist who tried to completely change Chinese society overnight. Some of his reforms were beneficial (such as improving the status of women) and some were catastrophic (such as the Great Leap Forward and the Cultural Revolution).

Almost overnight, the status of women changed under Maoist rule. He often quoted the ancient proverb that "Women hold up half the sky." Before Mao, prostitutes were blinded because that increased their appeal. Now the government prohibited polygamy, which exploited the extra wives, or concubines. The Marriage Act of 1950 prohibited arranged marriages and allowed millions of women to get divorced after years of being trapped in an unwanted marriage. Rights to land inheritance and voting were also granted. Women could now go to school and get jobs. Although they are still not fully represented in the government, women still have some access to power (Ebrey, 2010).

However, the Chinese had to make some heart-breaking sacrifices as the CCP wrenched the nation into the twentieth century. Citizens had to put aside their personal loyalties for the sake of the community's needs. One writer describes the new social norms in the 1950s when her mother barely ever saw her children:

> My mother did not have as much physical contact with us as she would have liked. This was because she fell under another set of rules: those of the Communists' puritanical life-style. In the early 1950s, a Communist was supposed to give herself so completely to the revolution and the people that any demonstration of affection for her children was frowned on as a sign of divided loyalties. Every single hour apart from eating or sleeping belonged to the revolution, and was supposed to be spent working. Anything that was regarded as not to do with the revolution, like carrying your children in your arms, had to be dispatched with as speedily as possible.
>
> At first, my mother found this hard to get used to. "Putting family first" was a criticism constantly level at her by her Party colleagues. Eventually, she became drilled into the habit of working nonstop. By the time she came home

in the evening, we had long since gone to sleep. She would sit by our bedsides watching our faces as we slept and listening to our peaceful breathing. It was the happiest moment in her day. (Chang, 1991, pp. 209–210)

Another dark aspect of the Maoist era was the Great Leap Forward (1958–1961), which was a failed attempt to modernize China almost overnight. Trying to create an industrialized nation from a primarily agricultural one, Mao used a collectivization principle to eliminate private farms. The Communists also used brutal force. Considered an economic catastrophe, the Great Leap Forward resulted in an unnecessary food shortage. Historians estimate that up to 32 million people died either from violence or starvation (Dikotter, 2010).

One woman who survived starvation shared her story:

All the trees in the village had been cut down. Any nearby were all stripped of bark. I peeled off the bark of a locust tree and cooked it as if it were rice soup. It tasted like wood and was sticky.

At the time the villagers looked quite fat and even healthy because they were swollen but when they were queuing up at the canteen to eat, they would suddenly collapse and could not get up. Some could only walk using a stick.…

More than half of the villagers died, mostly between New Year (1960) and April or May. In one of our neighbours' houses, three boys and a girl starved. In one brother's family two children died. Another family of sixteen died. Many families disappeared completely with no survivors at all. The production team chief's daughter-in-law and his grandson starved to death. He then boiled and ate the corpse of the child but he also died. When the village teacher was on the verge of death, he said to his wife, "Why should we keep our child? If we eat him then I can survive and later we can produce another child." His wife refused to do this and her husband died (Wright, 2011, p. 156).

When giving their oral histories, some rural women referred to this time of dining halls instead of family meals. The government had tried to collectivize every aspect of their lives, including communal birthing clinics. However, women still had their domestic chores to do despite the long hours of labor because these chores were invisible labor (Hershatter, 2011). Another researcher noted that the Great Leap Forward did advance women's rights for rural women encouraged to be leaders (Manning, 2007).

As a totalitarian leader, Mao created yet another wrenching era for China called the Cultural Revolution from 1966–1976. Wright's description of this time as "China goes mad" (Wright, 2011, p. 164) is apt because of the widespread chaos. Using the youth as his new vanguard, Mao created the Red Guard to attack anybody seen as counter-revolutionary. Political oppression dominated the nation as anything deemed as "western" (anything not Chinese—music, books, etc.) was prohibited. Mass rallies and Mao's picture overwhelmed any possible dissension. "On the dawn of August 18, 1966, Mao propelled his new personality cult to a frenzy when he spoke to one million of them at a rally in Beijing's Tiananmen Square" (Wright, 2011, p. 166).

Students refused to attend school, electing instead to roam the country to enforce Mao's teachings. The Red Guards only accepted those with the proper "family class origin," so many were ostracized (Zhang, 2001, p. 3). One woman, recalling how a doctor refused to visit her injured brother because their family was blacklisted, also told this story of when the Red Guard set fire to her home and arrested her father.

> In the light of the fire, a girl wearing a red armband walked over to me carrying a big pair of scissors. She caught hold of my plaits and said, 'This is a petit-bourgeois hairstyle.'
>
> Before I had realised what she was talking about, she had cut my plaits off, and thrown them into the fire. I stood wide-eyed, watching dumbly as my plaits and their pretty bows turned to ashes (Xinran, 2002, p. 175).

The government forced millions of students and city dwellers into the countryside to work on farms, although the newcomers had no idea of how to farm. One researcher writes of those who were "going up to the mountain and down to the village" (Zhang, 2001, p. 4). Women as well as men had to live on scanty rations and work up to fourteen hours a day with the villagers.

Although the government had been encouraging women to work in factories since the 1950s, the pressure became intense during the Cultural Revolution. Iron Girl Brigades worked in heavy industry doing "man's work." One woman, reflecting that she

Figure 22.1 *Modern woman at ancient monument (Photo courtesy of OUP)*

had become the family breadwinner, stated that: "If I were in the old society, and didn't know how to do needlework, I would have been beaten to death, or at least, I would have been driven out" (Yihong, 2006, p. 627). However, many families did insist that women had to do the domestic chores as part of being a heroic worker.

Discussion Questions

- Why is it important for every American to know the basics of Chinese history, especially about Mao Zedong?
- Why would the Cultural Revolution be a historical trauma for a Chinese person who had lived through it?

Modern Era

Mao's death in 1976 ended the Cultural Revolution, ushering in a new era that included capitalism instead of communism. The new leader, Deng Xiaping, instituted economic reforms that opened China to the world. Now private businesses have replaced the centrally planned economy, and there is a rich/poor gap and unemployment. Despite China's shift from collectivism, however, the government is anything but democratic. Protesters are regularly imprisoned or otherwise mistreated. The most famous example of government repression occurred in 1989 at Tiananmen Square, when thousands of peaceful protesters were killed or imprisoned.

In this context, the road to women's equality in China has not been always smooth. Despite the Communist Party's public commitment to women's equality, on the political level they were often relegated to lower positions. Women also were less likely to hold any higher positions in education in the 1980s (Spence, 1990).

Old attitudes toward women can persist, especially in rural areas. In the 1980s, a girl who grew up on a rice farm had to face her mother's rejection.

> I could never make my mother smile. She told the villagers that not only was I ugly, but my personality was bad too. "She's just not lovable," she told her younger brother, whom I called Small Uncle....
>
> After school, instead of going out to catch cicadas, frogs, and eels with the other kids, I would study hard all evening until my father yelled at me to stop. "You're going to use up all the kerosene," he would say. I didn't mind working hard or being scolded, because school was the sweetest thing in the world....
>
> One hot day early in the summer, when I was ten, my mother threw a roll of thin plastic strings next to my feet, handed me a straw hat, and said, "Even if you read all the books on earth and you can rise into the sky, it doesn't matter. A girl is a girl, and the matchmaker will only care how fast you can plant rice shoots when she looks for a husband for you." (Shen, 2007, p. 3)

Overcoming traditional biases against women is an arduous task. The All-China Women's Federation, created by the government in 1949, has been both a blessing and a curse for Chinese women. The Federation is the "mouthpiece for Party propaganda and has been associated with both positive and negative government policies, such as the promotion of more liberal marriage laws versus the draconian measures used to enforce the one-child campaign." The Federation is also part of a male hierarchy (Perry, 2001, p. 93). However, any NGO (nongovernmental organization) related to women's rights has to work with the Federation.

In China, women's NGOs are often grassroots that start from the bottom up. The Federation must mediate between the strict government, which stresses rigid planning over spontaneous actions, and the NGOs (Jaschok, Milwertz, & Hsiung, 2001). As Chinese women set up services for single mothers and others in need, they must cooperate with the Federation. Several projects have emerged, such as agencies for abused women. Unlike the western model of offering shelter for a woman leaving her abuser, Chinese agencies must recognize the reality of offering the "just leave him" advice. Leaving the abuser is often impossible due to lack of housing and finances for many women. Instead of a shelter, then, the agencies offer hotlines and advice centers.

As mentioned earlier, one major controversy regarding the Federation was the one-child policy. The background of this policy starts in the 1950s, when the government began to realize the threat of overpopulation. Much of the Chinese land is not suitable for agriculture, so there are limited resources. According to the website World Population Statistics, the 2013 estimate for China is 1.39 billion Chinese people (www.worldpopulationstatistics.com//?s=china). The CCP, first concerned about having enough food and other essentials for China, had to first deal with the traditional preference for large families. Many Chinese did not see the need to worry about overpopulation because their culture has lasted for 5,000 years. Also, the massive death tolls of World War II and the Great Leap Forward alleviated overpopulation concerns until the 1970s. Mao himself had strong faith that the more people the better for his dreams for China (Ebrey, 2010).

Not until Mao's death in 1976, then, did the Chinese government prioritize the issue of encouraging couples to limit their families. Pro-birth-control propaganda began to appear in the villages and cities as the CCP urged people to consider the social impact of a pregnancy. Having a baby was no longer a private decision but a public issue because of food and housing shortages (Mosher, 1983).

As the Chinese government considered solutions to the overpopulation problem, one proposal was to discourage marriage. However, both the culture and the Party were so promarriage that this was not a feasible idea (Spence, 1990). Deng then implemented the one-child policy in 1979 that stated that city dwellers had a strict limit of one child no matter the sex. In the country, a couple with a daughter could try again for a son. Ethnic minorities are allowed two or more children (Wright, 2011).

The one-child policy has resulted in horrific stories of forced abortions and sterilizations. Social pressure on the pregnant woman, besides economic coercion by employers, also made women choose abortions (Guilbert, 1998). It is impossible to verify how many women were victimized by the strict enforcement of the policy. Although these stories have tapered off, a recent account by Osnos (2014) describes how he met fifteen women detained by the village council for violating the population policy. Above a shop was a fenced-in area where a woman stepped up to speak to him.

> I asked why she was there. "We cannot leave. We have no freedom," she said. She was calm. She said that local family-planning officials had locked her there, above the fertilizer store, because her daughter-in-law would not agree to a forced sterilization or pay the fees for having too many children, the equivalent of about a year's income. (Osnos, 2014, p. 29)

The one-child policy has also affected the female population because there is still a strong prejudice against daughters. Several thousand female babies are abandoned to orphanages while couples try to have sons. As noted in chapter 15, these girls are being adopted by Americans and other Westerners. However, Fong (2008) stresses that many urban parents are empowering their daughters because they do not have any sons to favor.

Another result has been the alleged spoiling of a family's only child, resulting in "little emperors" (Fong, 2004, p. 28). In interviewing the first generation of only children, the researcher elicited these responses:

> "Yes, singletons are spoiled," said Tian Xin, a lively, friendly girl. "Singletons' parents don't eat anything, and they let their children eat everything, so children grow fatter and fatter!"
>
> "That's right!" said Luo Jun, a boy known for his sense of humor. "For instance, this classmate here is a singleton," he said, pointing Shen Na, a slightly plump girl sitting nearby. "So her parents let her eat too much, and that's why she's so fat!" He ducked as she tried to hit him with a textbook, to the delighted laughter of their classmates.
>
> "I don't think singletons are spoiled!" said Sun Pei, an outspoken girl. "We face pressure to get into good colleges so we can get good jobs to support our parents when they're old. We'll have to make a lot of money to support our parents all by ourselves! So our parents are always nagging us to study harder. How can we be spoiled when we're always being scolded for not studying hard enough?" (Fong, 2004, p. 1)

The girl's concern about her parents is a valid one, since there has been a decrease of care for the elderly. According to medical researchers, "The rapid decrease in the birth rate, combined with stable or improving life expectancy, has led to an increasing proportion of elderly people and an increase in the ratio between elderly parents and adult children" (Hesketh, Lu, & Xing, 2005). Around 70 percent of the elderly do not have pensions, so the family is their major source of income. The future financial burden on the singletons, then, may consist of parents, grandparents, and maybe even great-grandparents—with no siblings to help care for the older generations. Another factor affecting Chinese society is the rise of industrialization and increase of women working in factories, as described in Box 22.2.

Box 22.2 Factory Girls

Rural life is still harsh for women, so many try to move to the cities for jobs in the new factories. Chang's *Factory Girls: From Village to City in a Changing China* challenges the stereotype of a meek girl being hopelessly exploited by her employer. These young women are bold, adventurous, and willing to jump from job to job without hesitation.

> The girls talked constantly of leaving. Workers were required to stay six months, and even then permission to quit was not always granted. The factory held the first two months of every worker's pay; leaving without approval meant losing that money and starting all over somewhere else (Chang, 2008, p. 4).

Despite this barrier, many Chinese workers were willing to start new jobs. Min, one girl who was interviewed by the author, was able to get all her earnings from her employer and go to the new factory. "She should have been scared. But all she knew was that she was free." (Chang, 2008, p. 9). Meeting two teens in a city park, the author describes the joy they felt. "They were sixteen years old, on the loose in one of China's most chaotic boomtowns, raising themselves with no adults in sight. They were prey to all sorts of cons, making life decisions on the barest bits of information. They missed their mothers. But they were also having the time of their lives" (Chang, 2008, p. 23).

Chang also writes of young women daring themselves to do better and better in this chaotic city: "To die poor is a sin." Some workers take English lessons or other self-improvement classes to increase their marketability.

> The stories of migrant women shared certain features. The arrival in the city was blurry and confused and often involved being tricked in some way. Young women often said they had gone out alone (to the city), though in fact they usually traveled with others; they just felt alone. They quickly forgot the names of factories, but certain dates were branded in their minds, like the day they left home or quit a bad factory forever. What a factory actually made was never important; what mattered was the hardship or opportunity that came with working there. The turning point in a migrant's fortunes always came when she challenged her boss. At the moment she risked everything, she emerged from the crowd and forced the world to see her as an individual.
>
> It was easy to lose yourself in the factory, where there were hundreds of girls with identical backgrounds: born in the village, badly educated, and poor. You had to believe that you mattered even though you were one among millions. (Chang, 2008, p. 55)

More Challenges

Hesketh, Lu, & Xing (2005) also note the sex ratio has become a serious problem because of gender imbalance. In many cities and villages, a scarcity of brides for the young men has resulted from so many cases of sex-based abortions and female infanticide. (The topic of gender imbalance was covered further in chapter 19.) Although the one-child policy did prevent a demographic crisis, overpopulation remains a concern for the long-term plans of China and "the implications of both ignoring it and remedying it present vexing ethical questions" (Wright, 2011, p. 184).

Because of the bride shortage, Chinese women have faced increasing pressure to get married even if they are not interested. In *Leftover Women: The Resurgence of Gender Inequality in China*, Fincher (2014) writes about how women over the age of 27 (or even 25, in some cases) are seen as "leftovers" like spoiled food in a refrigerator. Both the government and media are promoting this message, which is reinforced by families. Young urban women resist marriage because of the patriarchal structure that still exists, including the dominance of the mother-in-law. These women would prefer independence and their own paychecks. As one interviewee said, "The institution of marriage basically benefits men, and when women get hurt this institution doesn't protect our rights. The most rational choice is to stay single" (Fincher, 2014, p. 11).

The Women's Federation, which has a mixed record of supporting equality for women, posted this admonition to women:

> Pretty girls don't need a lot of education to marry into a rich and powerful family, but girls with an average or ugly appearance will find it difficult. These kinds of girls hope to further their education in order to increase their competitiveness. The tragedy is, they don't realize that as women age, they are worth less and less, so by the time they get their M.A. or Ph.D., they are already old, like yellowed pearls. (Fincher, 2014, p. 3)

A newspaper article also tried to nudge women to stop being so selective when picking out a husband. "While holding out for a man, if you say he must be rich and brilliant, romantic and hard-working ... this is just being willful. Does this kind of perfect man exist? Maybe he does exist, but why on earth would he want to marry you?" (Fincher, 2014, p 19).

Many women succumb to these messages that they need to get married to be validated by society. Few of them are able to accumulate wealth because the real estate boom, the major investment opportunity in China, is centered on male property ownership. Feeling like a "leftover" with little chance to become rich on her own, a woman often accepts a proposal even if she has doubts about her future husband.

Another feature of women in modern China is that although their condition has much improved in the past few decades, women are not fully equal yet. Kristoff and Wudunn (1994) express the development of new social mores under the new capitalism. Whatever happened to Mao's belief in equality?

> As I talked to more women and got better acquainted with their status, it became clear that the problems ran far deeper. The obstacle was not just the strength of traditional beliefs but the invisible hand of the market itself. The market economy raised living standards for women along with men, but it also led to the return of the male-dominated Chinese society—coupled with the sexist features of Western society. Advertisers quickly discovered that the best way to market their products was by airing commercials showing lovely young women,

preferably wearing as little as possible.... and bosses began to hire pretty young women as ornaments or playthings.

"These days if you're a woman, you're as good as a commodity...."

Women face greater economic opportunity than they did under Mao but also more discrimination; they can find work more easily, but many of the jobs are on assembly lines in the noisiest, dirtiest industries; they may drive buses and taxis, but they usually take only one-third of spots in universities....

Worst of all, the rising market economy now embraces women themselves as tradable commodities [due to human trafficking]. (Kristof & Wudunn, 1994, pp. 215–216).

This story of women in China, then, starts with daughters without names and ends with both career women and commodified females. Women may not have achieved full equality in China, but the drastic social changes enacted by Mao and his successors have ensured a place in the public sphere for women.

Discussion Questions

- If you were working to reduce domestic violence in China, would you work with or against the Women's Federation? Explain your answer.
- If you were a policymaker in China, how would you handle the bride shortage without forcing marriage onto unwilling Chinese and foreign women?
- Does the "Leftover Women" concept have any parallel in U.S. society? In your social group, what is the age at which a woman should give up looking for a husband?

Key Terms

Chinese Communist Party
Mandate of Heaven
First Wife/Second Wife
Hypergamy
Foot binding
Great Leap Forward
Cultural Revolution
All-China Women's Federation
One-child campaign
"Leftover women"

23

Prostitution and the Sex Trade

The World's Oldest Profession or World's Oldest Oppression?

In the 1990 movie *Pretty Woman*, Julia Roberts plays a streetwalker who looks great. She ends up with a good-looking prince in a business suit. This movie would be just another romantic comedy except for its portrayal of prostitution as just a harmless way to make a living before you meet your true love. For girls like Maria, they can spark dreams of a glamorous life.

Although she was raised in a loving and stable home, Maria had a turbulent adolescence. Raped at 12 by a neighborhood boy, she had trouble coping with this trauma. The movie *Pretty Woman* inspired her to run away at 13 to achieve her dream. Later in Atlantic City, a pimp ("Daddy") recruited her to be one of his "bitches." He knew how young she was and named her "Baby Girl." (Sher, 2013, p. 23). Like many prostitutes, Maria felt a strong attachment to her Daddy.

> Too young to recognize they are being manipulated and too old to see themselves as helpless children, they come to endure, if not accept, their own exploitation because rightly or wrongly, they do not see a better alternative. And all they see in popular culture—from music to movies—is a glorification of the pimping world. (Sher, 2013, p. 24)

Thrilled at the idea of working on the casino floors of Vegas, she finally got her wish. She soon learned that as a light-skinned Latina, she could not charge the higher rates of white girls but could charge more than the African Americans.

"When you get to Vegas, you've made it."

Maria could hardly believe her luck. She had been selling her body since she was fourteen on some of the toughest "tracks" in the country—the ghetto corner in Hunts Point in the Bronx, the dark alleys of Philadelphia, the cheap hotels of Boston.

"Do you know how many times I got raped?" she says. "Do you know how many guns I got put to my temples? How many times I've had knives to my throat? How many times I got beaten---with hangers, brooms, whips, and belts?"

Now here she was, just seventeen years old, once an aspiring choir-girl from a small town just outside of Atlantic City, New Jersey, riding in a white Mercedes-Benz past the dazzling lights on the Las Vegas Strip. She had a pile of money by her side and a snazzy car to drive, and it could not get much better than that.

True, she told herself, the car wasn't hers. The money wasn't hers, either. Like everything else she had, including her body, it all belonged to her pimp. But that didn't matter to the young girl, not then. Nothing was going to diminish the glitter and glamour of this moment. At long last, she had graduated from being a "track ho," working the streets, to a "carpet ho," walking the casino floors.

There was just one refrain running through the teenager's head: *I feel so cool.* (Sher, 2013, p. 1)

Prostitution customers (johns) and other defenders of the practice would emphasize that girls like Maria are making the choice to work in the sex trade. Hard data on prostitutes (also known as sex workers) is difficult to find, since the problems of researching this

Figure 23.1 *Free choice or coercion? (Photo source: Entofolio)*

population are obvious. Obviously, there must be some adults in the United States who engage in the sex trade as a job. The major controversy, then, is whether it is primarily about adults consenting to a business arrangement or a form of oppression not just for adults but for children.

Prostitution on the Macrolevel

Although men, women, and children have been prostituted for centuries, new awareness of sex trafficking (a form of human trafficking) has troubled many. Others see prostitution as a victimless crime with this dichotomy: men are the buyers, women are the sellers. However, Davidson (2005) states that this framework is troubling because it assumes that women have equal power in the transaction. The historical—and current—reality is that adult males are in an advantageous position. Females and male children are noncitizens who cannot enter a business contract with adult male citizens.

Jeffreys, author of *The Industrial Vagina: The Political Economy of the Global Sex Trade* (2008), discusses the implications of this power imbalance. Asserting that prostitution has become both "industrialized and globalized" in the free market (Jeffreys, 2008, p. 3), he notes that countries such as Indonesia are highly dependent on sex tourism for its economy. Hotels, airlines, restaurants, and taxi services all rely on the johns for business. One striking example of the extent of prostitution is that in 2005, there were 80,000 Filipinas who had work visas to Japan and 90 percent of these women were *required* to work in the sex trade.

Defenders of the sex trade note that it is an age-old tradition. They also frame it as reproductive labor (i.e., caring for others) and emotional labor. This perspective stresses how men have their "needs" and woman are helping society by providing an outlet for the men. However, Jeffreys labels prostitution as a "harmful cultural practice" as defined by the United Nations protocol (Jeffreys, 2008, p. 10). Like slavery, prostitution is inherently destructive to the person who is regarded as a commodity.

The Caribbean countries serve as an example of how the sex trade is connected to slavery. Kempado (1999) describes the historical context of Caribbean prostitution, which the Europeans institutionalized five centuries ago through slavery. Society almost required European men to have a black mistress. "Assertions of this form of racialized, colonial masculine power rested in part on the ideological constructions of black slave women in the Caribbean as sexually promiscuous and immoral ..." (Kempado, 1999, p. 5). Women of mixed blood—mulattos—were especially desirable and "emerged thus during slavery as the symbol of the prostitute—the sexually available, socially despised, yet economically profitable body" (Kempado, 1999, p. 6).

Although it appears impossible to separate the legacy of slavery from the business of sex tourism, Kempado adds that Caribbean women also used sex to gain freedom from their masters. For example, Haitian women helped the slave revolts by entering the camps of the European soldiers to trade sex for weapons. Today, then, some Caribbean women may be using sex not just for economic advantage but as a tool for empowerment.

Without demand for paid sex, of course, sex tourism would cease to exist. Mullings (1999) discusses how the demand side of prostitution is related to the "Othering" of the Caribbean woman as their "so-called traits simultaneously serve to confirm their status as inferior human beings and their suitability as commodities for consumption" (Mullings, 1999, p. 72). One alternative to sex tourism would be community tourism, in which local groups would manage local sites. Since so many sex workers have worked as unofficial tour guides for their customers, they could transfer their skills to this enterprise.

Another aspect of sex tourism is that not all customers are male. Single female tourists fly to Jamaica and other locations to buy the services of "beach boys." (Phillips, 1999, p. 183). These women consider these younger men to be healthier and something different to try. Like the occasional male tourist, these women tourists may marry their sex partners. However, these marriages often fail because these men have defined their masculinity by having many girlfriends and the wives feel betrayed by the infidelities.

Discussion Questions

- When reading the story about Maria, do you view her as a victim of prostitution or as an adult making a free choice? How is this related to Davidson's point about contracts?
- Discuss the "Othering" of Caribbean women. How is this related to essentialism? In colonial times, how do you think that European women were regarded?
- If an American woman married a beach boy and brought him back to her home, what role could he play in a marriage like this? Discuss the inequalities involved: economic, citizenship status, and social status.

The Culture of Prostitution in Asia

Related to the macroview of prostitution is the consideration of cultural traditions in Asia. In *The Dancing Girls of Lahore: Selling Love and Saving Dreams in Pakistan's Ancient Pleasure District*, Brown (2005) explores the historical aspects of prostitution in a neighborhood in Lahore.

The two older daughters, 12 and 14, do not seem pretty enough to be successful prostitutes. But nobody would marry them because they are the daughters of a prostitute. In this culture, a courtesan wants to give birth to a girl when she is 15 so that by the time she is 30, her daughter can take her place. Daughters are their pension plans. A courtesan working in her 30s is seen as a failure.

The daughters are barely literate. Their only world is the small apartment, hanging around the entrance to the alleyway, and occasional trips in a rickshaw to buy food.

Girls in Heera grow up in a completely different environment than ordinary Pakistani girls. Female beauty and sexuality are openly celebrated. From the time they are babies, girls witness a stream of men coming to the doors of their mothers and aunts and know that these men will visit them too in a few years. Not all live easily with this, but most do. There is no alternative. In Heera, it is not considered wrong or bad. Indeed, those who perform the task well, expensively and with dignity are lauded and envied (Brown, 2005, p. 19).

Brown also emphasizes the historic significance of this prostitution culture, which emerged centuries ago.

> Places like Heera Mandi are not new, and dancing and sex have been linked on the Indian subcontinent for millennia. For centuries, women like Maha have lived by selling their beauty, youth, and skills. Maha is from the Kanjar, one of the region's prostitute groups.
>
> What we see today in Lahore are the remnants of Islamic and Hindu social practices that produced the tawaif—the courtesan (Brown, 2005, p. 26).

Like the dancing girls of Lahore, geisha girls in Japan are famous for their artistic performances. Noting that geisha girls were better off than many wives with demanding mothers-in-law, Foreman (2005) stresses that these independent women were rarely sex slaves. "In Japan, the avoidance of family responsibility and monogamy to focus on careers in the performing arts renders geishas as 'bad' within a society that measures female 'goodness' on humility and loyalty" (Foreman, 2005, p. 33). Geisha girls, then, are not synonymous with prostitutes.

However, traditional prostitution does still thrive in Japan. Constantine (1993) describes a red light district in Osaka. This scene becomes even more haunting when he later mentions how the HIV/AIDS epidemic has affected the sex trade—girls often wear their blood test results pinned to their kimonos.

> These days most of the action takes place after midnight. Walking around the blocks with their 150 brothels, the unsuspecting pedestrian might think he is in a quaint late-night noodle shop district, with row upon row of tiny weatherworn restaurants conveniently huddled one next to the other. As he looks in, past the colorful and short *noren* curtains hanging over the top half of the door, he will see an elderly lady in a kimono kneeling silently on a cushion next to a girl he might mistake for a fashion-conscious granddaughter. The pedestrian's suspicions, however, might be aroused as he peeks into the next store and sees yet another traditional matriarch with another young companion, and then further down another and another. As he walks back up the block in confusion, he notices that men are disappearing off the street to be led up staircases by the old women. (Constantine, 1993, pp. 21–22)

Another location for the sex trade is along the Mekong River in Vietnam where prostitution is not simply a matter of women being forced into servitude. Molland (2012), a former advisor for a United Nations antitrafficking project, describes the family ties and friendly connections between bar owners, prostitutes, and other parties. He claims that the international efforts to fight trafficking do not necessarily fit the situation when a woman recruits a friend into prostitution as a favor. The intersection of race, class, and gender are also critical to consider, as discussed in Box 23.1.

Discussion Question

How do you reconcile the principles of global feminism (basic human rights) with the concept of cultural competence regarding this issue?

Box 23.1 Intersection of Race, Class, and Gender

The sex trade exemplifies the Intersection Theory because so many prostitutes are women of color and from a disadvantaged class. The preceding section's discussion of prostitution as a legacy of colonialism also relates to North American women. In Canada, feminists have spoken out about the disproportionate number of prostitutes who are indigenous. "Race, class, and sex intersect in the worst ways to subjugate Native women — and in the act of prostitution it's *the* most racist, *the* most sexist... And the man holds all of the economic power in that," stated one advocate (Murphy, 2014). The colonial legacy of treating indigenous women as not fully human amplifies the perception that they can be discarded. If girls are growing up in poverty and enduring abuse, they are more likely to believe that their "bodies aren't actually [theirs] but that they are to please men" (Murphy, 2014).

In the United States, women of color are more likely to become involved in sex trafficking than Caucasian women. According to the Department of Justice website (www.bjs.gov/content/pub/press/cshti0810pr.cfm), "Confirmed sex trafficking victims were more likely to be white (26 percent) or black (40 percent)" although whites comprise 75 percent and blacks comprise 13.4 percent of the of the U.S. population (2010 census; census.gov). Also troubling is the reported increase of Latino residential brothels that feature female immigrants who entered the United States for either a boyfriend (who turned out to be a pimp) or for job opportunities. The Polaris Project, an advocacy organization against human trafficking, states that brothels run by Latinos and other ethnic groups are spreading through the United States (www.polarisproject.org).

Despite these disproportionate numbers, an article in *Ebony Magazine* discusses the media's focus on only white victims of sex trafficking.

> Black females are 40% of confirmed sex trafficking victims in the U.S. but under-represented in news coverage on missing children and over-represented among women and girls arrested for prostitution. Perhaps as a function of the deafening silence on their presence "in the market," African American girls remain vulnerable to [sex trafficking] (Morris, 2014).

This media silence about black victims may be related to the Jezebel stereotype that legitimized sexual violence against black women for centuries. MISSEY is one organization that is intervening on behalf of the women of color being trapped into prostitution. The following extract is one client's story from the MISSEY website:

> The Oakland Police Department got a tip from a pediatrician's office about a 13 year old with severe bruises. By the time she was rescued—at age 13—and MISSSEY got involved, nine different pimps had exploited "Jacqueline" in thirteen cities. Luckily, "Jacqueline" had a family and recovered through therapy at MISSEY (Client story available on missey.org)

Discussion Questions

- Using the term *little black ho* on a search engine, research the portrayal of black prostitutes on the Internet. Write a paragraph about your reaction.
- In your opinion, is there any connection to the "video ho" meme with the high rate of black trafficking victims? Can you think of other examples of hypersexual women of color who will do anything for money?
- Do you agree that women of color have been under-represented in the media's coverage of human trafficking stories? Research ten stories on the mainstream media websites about human trafficking and share your results with the class.

Johns and Other Defenders of Prostitution

All through history, people have defended prostitution with several arguments. Some women, for example, regard prostitution as not necessarily a form of male oppression but a choice that some women make freely. Writers such as Camille Paglia state that prostitution could even be seen as a form of empowerment because women control the situation. "The prostitute is not, as feminists claim, the victim of men but rather their conqueror, an outlaw who controls the sexual channel between nature and culture" (Paglia, n.d.). Books such as *Jane Sexes It Up: True Confessions of Feminist Desire* (Johnson, 2002) typify the prosex feminist view about pornography and other aspects of the sex trade.

Men, though, usually dominate the defense of prostitution. Ringdal, a Dutch writer, opines about the need for prostitution in his historical work (2004). Most men will be fathers to their children in a family setting but not for offspring related to paid sex. "In most societies, a man who takes responsibility for his children is considered more moral than one who does not. Understood in this way, the family is a positive servitude, while prostitution is a negative freedom" (Ringdal, 2004, p. 2). Viewed in this way, prostitution is both natural and desirable for society. He presents an essentialist argument in defense of the sex trade: "Simply by nature, men are promiscuous to a far greater degree than women" (Ringdal, 2004, p. 6).

In a self-published book, *The Art of Whoring: Adventures in Prostitution*, Saunders (2011) would agree with Ringdal about the "man has his needs" argument. He attacks the critics of his practice:

> And please don't even get started on nonsense statements like, "Whores are victims of an oppressive patriarchal society. Maybe some *are* indeed victims of abuse and sure, some *are* dope fiends, but a lot of them are just horny young women who like to f***, and figure they might as well make a mint from their little honey-pots while there's an audience willing to pay.
>
> You can also skip the following piece of horseshit: "What if it was your daughter, would it be OK then?"
>
> Guess what?
>
> I avoided having any little youngins' for any number of reasons....

And here's another thought: You want your daughter to avoid being a prostitute?

Don't raise a little whore and you won't have to worry about it (Saunders, 2011, p. 1).

In his groundbreaking study of johns, Malarek (2009) describes his encounters with men like Saunders. He criticizes the viewpoint that "boys will be boys" in this statement: "From the moment of man's first erection, the male sex drive takes on an aura of almost mythical proportions, infused by centuries of lore and widely accepted views about men's entitlement to sex" (Malarek, 2009, p. 15). Although some johns may claim to "love" the girls they are using, a deep-seated misogyny is an undercurrent in their lives. For instance, Malarek shares a story about a man he met in a Costa Rican bar:

"Well, let me give you a little advice to keep you from making a fool of yourself. These girls all smile and make you think you're a king, acting all lovey-dovey … going gaga for you. They may seem sincere, but half of what they tell you is a lie and the other half is a line. Don't fool yourself into thinking any one of them really thinks you're something special. These girls are nothing but a bunch of whores.…"

"Look at them. Look at that one over there." He motioned with a beer bottle, pointing to a young woman in jeans and a yellow tank top. "I was here six months ago when she first hit the bar. She was sweet. I saw her with this guy … had to be three hundred and fifty pounds of whale blubber. He brings her a bag of goodies … make-up, perfume, chocolates, a stuffed teddy bear. Like he's going to somehow make her think he's a nice guy and maybe get better service. Look at her now. She's jaded. She has what I call fish eyes."

"Fish eyes?"

"That hardened, dead look. It's what happens to most of these whores after they've been humped by so many fat, sloppy, ugly guys."

"So there's no respecting these girls?" "I don't respect whores.

I don't get sucked into the whine about them having to feed their families. I pay to f*** them. That's why I come down here" (Malarek, 2009, pp. 147–148).

Websites of sex resorts, besides the blogs of sex tourists, offer researchers a valuable source of information about the johns (Ukockis, 2015). These men conform to mainstream society in their belief that if men do not have convenient sex, they are losers. The movie title *The Forty-Year-aOld Virgin* underscores the ridicule of men who do not get laid. Often the johns frequent websites of pick-up artists (i.e., how to get a girl into bed in five minutes) and men's rights activists. Other mainstream values are their support of the beauty ideal and fat-shaming. In fact, the opinion that American women are too ugly and fat for them dominates their blog postings. Complaints about the bossiness of western women contrast with praise of the lovely *chicas* who serve their every need at a resort.

Another window into the mindset of johns is the book *Porn Nation: Conquering America's #1 Addiction* (Leahy, 2008). Written by a recovering sex addict, this book could apply to many customers of the sex trade although the author was not a john. He calls pornography the "Great Escape" because it made him forget his problems (Leahy, 2008, p. 37). However, this led to his inability to connect to women in a truly meaningful way. On his wedding day, he was distracted by checking out the girls at the reception. That night, he rolled over and went to sleep—he was uninterested in having sex with his wife even on their wedding night. "The continual fantasizing led to the atrophy of my sexual desire for her, which was crazy because we were still newlyweds. But she was only one woman, and there is one thing that one woman can never provide ... the endless variety that porn provides" (Leahy, 2008, p. 51).

His addiction even caused him to lose jobs because he could not concentrate on his work. He graduated to voyeurism (i.e., being a peeping tom) before he finally started therapy. As he continued to objectify women, he became attracted to the images that showed violence and/or bondage (hard-core porn). This excerpt relates to many sex trade customers who may start with standard "adult entertainment" but escalate to hard-core porn or a deeper involvement in the sex trade, such as becoming a john.

> Once I figured out that I could get a higher high and zone out even more by using hard-core porn as my drug of choice, I started spending more time exploring darker genres of images. The more disturbing the image, the more I found I had to separate my relational emotions and values from what I was looking at and view the women as objects instead of people. That was the only way I could reconcile what I was doing with these images in my mind. Even though they were only images, I still found I had to separate or dissociate my emotions from how I was "using" these people for my gratification. Otherwise, I couldn't cope with my own repulsive thoughts about myself and what I was actually fantasizing about doing. The more I went there, the more I started hating myself for who I was as a person.
>
> What I didn't realize at the time was that this would somehow transfer over to the way I treated real people in relationships in the real world, especially women. My objectification and sexualization of the women I had relationships with in my life—including Patty [his wife]. In time, I started caring less about others....
>
> Real women like Patty were no match for what I was getting from porn. Porn didn't ask questions, never complained, and had no needs for me to meet. It was always there, waiting on me hand and foot, ready to meet my sexual needs on demand.... (Leahy, 2008, pp. 60–61).

Discussion Questions

- If a married couple came in for counseling about the husband's porn addiction, what resources would you use?
- If you were the wife of a porn addict, how would this affect your self-image and sexual desire?
- Do you think that the johns described in the this section could learn to see the humanity of the sex workers? How?

When Sex Work Is Voluntary

Despite all the media attention on sex trafficking, not all sex workers are forced to enter or stay in the profession. COYOTE (Call Off Your Old Tired Ethics) is one advocacy group that promotes not only the decriminalization of prostitution, but government oversight of labor conditions. The group recognizes that some sex workers are coerced, but those who are not should receive the same respect as any other worker. Sex workers have the right to work without violence or getting arrested, and also the right to health care without being treated as a public hazard (www.coyotela.org). International organizations such as the Dutch-based International Committee on the Rights of Prostitutes in Europe also encourage sex workers to unionize (www.walnet.org).

Besides these advocacy groups, numerous websites offer young women the chance to find "dates" who will pay for luxuries. Sugar Daddy websites (e.g., www.sugardaddyforme.com) urge females to "experience luxury" while showing a picture of a woman being given an expensive necklace. This movement is parallel to the plot of *Fifty Shades of Grey* (James, 2011), in which a recent college graduate falls in love with a billionaire who showers her with gifts for sexual favors.

Related to this movement has been the rise of "raunch power," which is described by Levy (2005) as girls acting out sexually in public. The book starts with the story of college women trying to get onto the "Girls Gone Wild" bus because they want to show off their sexual power. One barely-dressed girl comments, "The body is such a beautiful thing. If a woman's got a pretty body and she likes her body, let her show it off! It exudes confidence when people wear little clothes" (Levy, 2005, p. 9). Some women link this display of flesh with feminism because "Women have come so far … we no longer needed to worry about objectification or misogyny. Instead, it was time for us to join the frat party of pop culture, where men had been enjoying themselves all along" (Levy, 2005, p. 4).

In fact, Levy notes, these women just wanted acceptance from men as one of them. "Going to strip clubs or talking about porn stars was a way of showing themselves and the men around them that they weren't 'prissy little women' or 'girly-girls.' Besides, they told me, it was all in fun…." (Levy, 2005, p. 4).

Discussion Questions

- If you had a friend who was planning to "date" a man from a Sugar Daddy website, how would you react? Connect your reaction to a point in this chapter.
- What is your reaction to raunch culture, in which girls flash their breasts in public settings? Do you agree with those who believe that "objectification of female bodies" is an outdated concept?

Sex Trafficking

Although some persons may consent to be sex workers, experts stress that most of the sex trade is involved in human trafficking—also known as modern day slavery (Hepburn & Simon, 2013). Human trafficking is nothing new, but it has grown to a frightening extent because of the global marketplace and the Internet. It has never been easier than today to sell and buy humans. The three types of trafficking are human, arms, and drugs. When a quantity of drugs is sold, it is a one-time sale. But when a human is for sale, the trafficker can make money for years on the same "product."

The term *human trafficking* refers to two types—forced labor and sex trafficking. In 2005, an estimated $44.3 billion was made from exploiting over twelve million persons (Hepburn & Simon, 2013). Around half of the victims are children. The word *trafficking* does not necessarily mean that a victim will be transported over international or even state lines. It simply means a criminal enterprise, so a trafficked person could be close to home. Trafficking can be both international and domestic (within the same country). Research studies provide different ratios for how much human trafficking is involved in the sex trade, from 17 to 43 percent (Hepburn & Simon, 2013).

Movies such as *Taken* (2008) have raised awareness of the darker side of globalization—the international trade in humans for sex work or forced labor. However, most trafficked persons in the United States are not foreign born (Sher, 2013).

The United Nations defines sex trafficking as involving "a sex act for profit induced by force, fraud, or coercion or in which the person induced to perform the sex act is under 18 years of age" (Savino & Turvey, 2011, p. 58). The force part usually involves kidnapping, whereas the fraud involves cons such as fake job ads or modeling agencies. Coercion could be threats to either the victim or her family, or involuntary servitude (i.e., being forced to work against one's will). Debt bondage occurs when a family sells a child to pay off a family debt (e.g., to save the family farm) and peonage occurs when somebody is obligated by a contract that can never be paid off (e.g., airfare to the United States becomes a debt impossible to discharge.) Over 90 percent of sex trafficking victims are female (Hepburn & Simon, 2013).

Organized criminal networks from all over the world are involved in sex trafficking. But on a smaller scale are the families, acquaintances, newspaper ads for modeling, and fake employment agencies. Sometimes recruiters are a trusted village member who comes to a village to talk about restaurant jobs in the city. The families trust this person to watch over their girls in the city. Other times, simple kidnapping is used to obtain victims. Sex trafficking involves not only prostitution, but also pornography, strip clubs, and other forms of the sex industry. A potential customer, then, must remember that there is a chance that he is paying a trafficker who is brutalizing the sex worker (Fedina, Trease, & Williamson, 2008).

A former codirector of CATW (Coalition Against Trafficking in Women) argues that prostitution is neither a job or a choice (Raymond, 2013). Instead, modern trafficking is similar to the Atlantic slave trade because both were seen as inevitable and good for the economy. As mentioned earlier, sex tourism has been profitable in many countries such as the Dominican Republic. A quick Internet search yields results such as the Red Diamond website, which lists these prices: $500 for four hours and $700 for eight hours. (Author's note: Although the website insists that the girls are 18 or older, many pictures show teens who look only 14 or 15.)

> With Red Diamond girls, you know who you will be with, and what you will be doing with them. No drama, no clock watchers, and no disappointments....

Take a smart person's vacation with guaranteed adult fun and sexy girls; each of them makes for the perfect adult companion (www.reddiamonds.com).

If johns prefer to stay in the States, they can easily find an escort service on a website (as of 2015, *Craigslist* had banned these ads so *Backpage* had become the dominant site). Some escort services such as the former Emperor's Club portray themselves as high-class and intended to "make life more peaceful, balanced, beautiful and meaningful" (Emperor's Club former website, cited on Huffington Post website www.huffingtonpost.com) Eliot Spitzer, the former governor of New York, patronized this expensive club before getting caught. He allegedly paid the 22-year-old escort $1,000 an hour, but it is unclear how much money she actually kept for herself. She spoke of child abuse, drug addiction, and homelessness in her life—realities that are far from the glamour of this advertisement.

Despite these glitzy websites, the reality of human trafficking is grim. Although children are prime victims, adults can also be victims of human trafficking. According to the Institute on Migration, the average age of a Dominican female trafficked into Europe is the mid-twenties (IOM, 2011). Some women went willingly at first, whereas others were forced by their husbands/boyfriends. Girls are lured into marriages under false pretenses, then end up being prostituted or sold by their husbands. (Coalition Against Trafficking in Women website: www.catwinternational.org).

One article on the CATW website, "I'm an inspirational example and that makes me proud," tells the story of Marcela Loiaza, an author and advocate. A Japanese gang had kidnapped and forced this Colombian woman into prostitution. Unable to speak Japanese, she was isolated from any help. Even when she was recuperating in a hospital after a severe beating, she was heavily guarded by the gang. She managed to escape when a customer gave her a wig and coat so she could escape to the Colombian embassy. Once she came home, her mother would not speak to her because of the shame. The courts ignored her case, so she received no justice.

> I was raped and beaten up to the point where I ended up completely disfigured and broken. I was forced to sleep with 20 men a day, 7 days a week…. I still do not understand how some men, despite seeing me exhausted, sick and sobbing non-stop, would not care (Balbi, 2014).

Domestic Minor Sex Trafficking—DMST

As noted earlier, the Internet has changed the sex trade significantly. Many escort services with motel room encounters have reduced the presence of streetwalkers. Although there may be fewer sex workers walking the streets, the dynamics of prostitution remain the same. One major dynamic is the victimization of children under 18. As evident in Maria's story in the Introduction, the sex trade is about victimization and not just an inevitable aspect of society.

The average age of a girl entering prostitution is 12 to 14, with half of the prostitutes being under age 18. (For boys and transgender youth, the age is even younger—11.) A john, then, has the fifty-fifty chance of raping a child. Most prostitutes report being victims of sexual abuse as children, so the sexual act can be a replay of this trauma. Johns may reassure themselves that they are paying good money for the services. However, most of the money goes to the pimps, brothel owners, and other exploiters in the sex trade. According to the Department of Justice, 75 percent of the youth working on the street have a pimp. He makes up to $200,000 a year from *each* victim—unfortunately, pimping is quite profitable (Savino & Turvey, 2011).

Child sex trafficking occurs in every community in the United States. With 90 percent of runaways being involved in the sex trade, children from troubled families are at high risk. As society begins to recognize the causes of somebody becoming a prostitute, law enforcement and others who come into contact with streetwalkers and other sex workers are now treating them as victims instead of offenders. The offender is the pimp, who is considered a trafficker even if no force was used against the child. "When a minor, with few visible choices, sells sex at the hands of an exploitative adult, it is generally a means of survival" (Fedina, Trease, & Williamson, 2008, p. 4)

Previous history of sexual abuse is also a risk factor, with one Oakland study noting that 61 percent of the youth had been raped as children. Pimps look for "broken girls" who need a Daddy. They groom their victims by treating her with kindness and presents, then often use drugs to create even more dependence on them. One pimp would lock disobedient girls in a dark closet for days. "When girls were released from the box, (he) would tell them that their Daddy still loved them" (Savino & Turvey, 2011, p. 65).

Although recruitment methods may include a female friend persuading her friend to work at a strip club or apply for "modeling" work, most prostitutes become enmeshed with Romeo pimps. These men portray themselves as loving boyfriends. One day a pimp may ask her to go on a "date" with one of his friends, then the truth emerges about her status.

> (One) case is instructive because it typifies a method of operating common to sex traffickers: befriend a young girl (perhaps a runaway), kidnap her to large metro area, rent a hotel room, put up some online ads, take the calls, make the appointments, and collect the money (Savino & Turvey, 2011, p.70).

Researchers have detected a common pattern for how these Romeo pimps entrap their victims. The first stage is ensnaring, in which he acts as a "boyfriend/protector." Next he makes her dependent on him by isolating her from family and friends. He gradually takes control of her life, throwing her off balance by being kind one minute then turning cruel. The last stage is "total dominance" when he imprisons her in a room (De Chesnay, 2013, p. 6).

A trafficked person may feel a "trauma bond," similar to an abused wife experiencing the Stockholm Syndrome (Savino & Turvey, 2011, p. 65). This enmeshment makes her reluctant to reject her boyfriend although he may have several other "bitches" and mistreats her. She may also stay with her pimp because she is afraid of returning to her family or a mainstream life. Emotional dependence, as well as drug addiction, add to the difficulties of separating a sex worker from her pimp. Another parallel to domestic violence is the reality of threats—too often, pimps murder "bitches" who try to escape from them (Savino & Turvey, 2011).

Organizations such as the Polaris Project provide services to trafficking victims. Usually medical personnel are the first to see a victim, who may be diagnosed with pregnancy, malnutrition, physical trauma, sexually transmitted infections (STIs), and drug abuse (De Chesnay, 2013). Then case managers find emergency housing such as hotels, besides basic needs such as clothes and toothpaste. English as a Second Language (ESL) classes are essential for foreign-born victims. Later, rent assistance and job coaching will help prevent a sex worker from returning to the life (Busch Fong, Heffron, Faulkner, & Mahapatra, 2007).

Discussion Questions

- Write an in-depth comparison between trafficking victims who "love" their pimps and domestic violence victims. What are the similarities and differences?
- Discuss the impact of rape on trafficking victims. They may have been raped as children, raped by the pimp as an initiation into the trade, raped by the pimp as punishment, and/or raped by the customers. (Savino & Turvey, 2011). Find a concept from the Rape and Sexual Assault chapter (chapter 7) to apply to this situation.
- Case study: A 14-year-old African-American girl was treated nicely by her older boyfriend, then he started asking her to go on "dates." He later turned abusive if she did not make enough money. "He called it the 25/25 rule: $25 a trick at a rate of $25 men a night" (De Chesnay, 2013, p. 13). If you were a case manager at a youth shelter, what intervention would you consider using to help her?
- Case study: A 15-year-old girl had been sold by her father when she was 12 to pay off his gambling debts. She limped into the Emergency Room, severely injured by a gang rape. The intake person laughed about this and asked how a whore could possibly be raped. The girl left the hospital without getting any medical attention (De Chesnay, 2013, p. 14). If you were her case manager, how would you notify the hospital about this incident? Would you do anything else to advocate for this girl?
- Case study: At 14, a Cambodian girl is rescued by a police raid at a massage parlor. She had been married at the age of six, then her husband sold her to a brothel when she was nine. A Chinese gang had shipped her and many others in a crate to the United States. Now she feels too ashamed to return to her family because she is convinced that they would reject her. However, she wants to continue working so that she can make money to send home to them. (De Chesnay, 2013) If you were her case manager, how would you respond in a culturally competent manner? Do you think it would be appropriate to force her to accept services when she just wants to go back to work?
- Look up the Polaris Project website and other human trafficking advocacy sites. Which organizations would be the most helpful for the three case studies above?

How to Fight Human Trafficking

Groups such as the Polaris Project, the International Labor Organization, and the U.S. government (both the Justice Department and Health and Human Services) have worked hard to promote public awareness of this problem. Local groups have formed coalitions, such as the Rescue and Restore Coalition in Columbus, Ohio.

Besides raising awareness, advocates can work on the issues of legal protections for the victims and reducing demand for the sex trade. In 2000, the TVPA (Trafficking Victims Protection Act) was passed on the federal level to treat trafficking as a serious crime. Continued funding for TVPA is an ongoing concern, since the Recession has hurt many government programs. On the state level, several states either have no laws or inadequate laws regarding human trafficking. State laws are necessary for the smaller cases, since the TVPA can only focus on the bigger crime networks.

On the international level, some countries are fighting sex tourism. Thailand, for example, is a developing nation that relies heavily on the profits of sex tourism. However, since the 1990s, it has attempted to halt human trafficking by a policy that includes treating the prostitutes as victims instead of criminals. Prevention goals include vocational training for women and a theater group that travels to villages with the anti-trafficking message. The government has also stepped up law enforcement against the traffickers (Banerjee, 2006).

Reducing demand for the sex trade is essential to end this form of trafficking. The United States is a major market, with billions of dollars spent per year. If social attitudes could change and the sex buyers are stigmatized instead of being seen as a "real man," then there will be hope for the millions of trafficking victims. Sex should be a glorious and beautiful gift, not a commodity for sale that results in the pain of too many.

Discussion Questions

- After reading the section When Sex Work Is Voluntary, do you agree with the point that women who show off their bodies are empowered because they have sexual power? Why or why not?
- If you were to talk to a man who is bragging about his "adult vacation" in the Dominican Republic, what would you like him to know?
- If you were running a john school (mandatory classes for men arrested for solicitation), which points from this chapter would you cover? Why?
- This chapter shows an obvious bias against the sex trade because it can victimize children and women. What could be a good argument against this bias?
- If you had to go to a business meeting at a strip club, what would your reaction be? Would it be different if you were the other gender? Explain why.

Key Terms

Sex tourism
Johns
DMST
Sex trafficking
Romeo pimp
Raunch culture

24

Women and HIV/AIDS

Introduction: Author's Note

Of all the health issues to focus on, why am I devoting an entire chapter to HIV/AIDS (Human Immunodeficiency Virus/Acquired Immune Deficiency Syndrome)? It is not because HIV/AIDS was my dissertation topic, although it certainly made this chapter easier to write. It is because HIV/AIDS is the leading killer of women aged 15–44 in the world. This stunning fact has affected the debate on women's position in society, especially since almost 50 percent of HIV-positive persons are female. UNAIDS (2012) states that almost 60 million persons have been infected since the epidemic was first reported in the early 1980s—and 30 million have died.

But as one HIV-positive woman stated, "Statistics are human beings with the tears wiped off" (Lather & Smithers, 1996, p. xxvi). HIV/AIDS is a critical issue, but it is also fairly recent. I want the younger readers to picture a world before HIV/AIDS became known. When I was in high school in the late 1970s, the worst sexually transmitted infection (STI) that we could get was called a venereal disease. A quick penicillin shot in the buttocks would solve the problem in a few seconds. (I had not heard about herpes and other more troublesome conditions). If anybody had said that a person could get sick and even die from having sex, it would have seemed preposterous.

What also seemed preposterous was the idea that an infectious disease could actually affect a country, much less the world. "Modern science had congratulated itself on the eradication of infectious disease as a threat to humankind" (Shilts, 1987, p. 20). When odd outbreaks such as Toxic Shock Syndrome and Legionnaire's Disease appeared, the CDC (Centers for Disease Control and Prevention) would quickly take care of it. I had so much faith in public health and advanced medicine that when I first heard about this "gay plague," I assumed that it would be over in a few weeks. The news story seemed so unimportant.

As a child, I had heard about the Black Death that had swept across Europe and killed millions. Villages became ghost towns and fields were left unfarmed because so many had died. If anybody had told me that a virus would arrive in the late twentieth century, wipe out millions worldwide, and leave farm fields untended—I never would have believed it. I am still amazed that over thirty years after its first appearance, the HIV virus is still a pandemic (i.e., widespread epidemic).

For years, though, HIV/AIDS mattered little to me. I did little besides objecting to those inhumane persons who claimed that AIDS was God's punishment against gays, besides feeling outraged by Reagan's inaction when thousands started dying. It happened by accident that my second field placement was at an HIV/AIDS resource office at the Ohio Department of Health. I quickly learned about the macro aspects of this disease and met several consumers (clients who used the services) and activists. When I decided to interview caregivers for my research, the social reactions were interesting. Many people assumed that I was lesbian, as if I had to belong to the LGBT community to care about a disease that affects everybody.

My research topic itself caused confusion because many believed that there was no more need for caregiving after the arrival of HAART (Highly Active Anti-Retroviral Treatment) in 1996. Everybody was supposed to be getting better. Before HAART, an HIV diagnosis was practically a death sentence because there was no effective treatment. When talking about how many friends' funerals he had attended, one man whom I had

Figure 24.1 *Condoms are only happy if they are used (Photo source: Entofolio)*

interviewed said: "After the first forty, I stopped going." Then the new medications finally began to save thousands of lives and provide hope for persons who were HIV-positive. The assumption was that after 1996, no HIV-positive person needed caregiving anymore. However, my agency contacts indicated that people were still getting sick and dying from HIV/AIDS. Poverty and race were the major factors, not sexual orientation. The medications can only go so far to save lives if there are obstacles to proper care. To state it bluntly, people who are poor and/or African American or Latino were more likely to die from HIV/AIDS than others.

HIV/AIDS, then, is not just about sexual activity or using needles to get high. This infectious disease is like a tornado that has shredded the vulnerable buildings and left the town stripped bare. Rebuilding the community with a foundation of social justice—gender equality and economic fairness—will provide as much hope as the HIV medications did in 1996.

HIV/AIDS: Basic Facts

Technically, HIV/AIDS is not a disease but a syndrome. It breaks down the immune system so that a person can die from an opportunistic illness such as pneumonia. Scientists have concluded that HIV is zoonotic (of animal origins). Like the Bird Flu and the Swine Flu, this virus was able to jump from the animal population to the human population. Cats can get feline leukemia (FIV—Feline Immunodeficiency Virus) and apes can get SIV (Simian Immunodeficiency Virus.) Based on blood samples stored in central Africa, researchers state that the retrovirus first appeared in the human population in the 1908. Most experts believe that persons eating bush meat (apes) may have caused this jump. In *Spillover: Animal Infections and the Next Human Pandemic*, Quammen (2012) speculates that "A man kills a chimpanzee and dresses it out, hacks it up, in the course of which he suffers blood-to-blood contact through a cut on his hand" (Quammen, 2012, p. 428).

For decades, then, HIV probably appeared intermittently in African villages but was never recognized as a separate medical problem. Patients were instead diagnosed with an illness such as pneumonia or cancer. Not until 1981 did this virus emerge as the cause of the pandemic we know today. International travel had spread the disease to other parts of the world, including the United States and Europe. Since the first known victims in the United States were gay males, HIV/AIDS was first labeled GRID—Gay Related Immune Disorder (Stine, 2004).

Don Francis, one of the CDC researchers who fought the pandemic from the beginning, linked the syndrome to feline leukemia in 1981.

> Cancer and immune suppression, Francis said. Both feline leukemia and this new gay disease were marked by a trail of opportunistic infections that seemed to take advantage of an immune system weakened by a primary infection.... Clearly, some similar virus was doing the same thing to these homosexual men, and they were getting cancer too. Secondly, feline leukemia has a long incubation period; this new disease must have long latency too, which is the only way it was killing people in three cities on both coasts before anybody knew it existed....

Francis (knew that) viruses were crafty little creatures constantly trying to outsmart humans in their bid for survival (Shilts, 1987, p. 73).

Of course, from the very beginning of the pandemic the victims were not just gay men. It took researchers a while to realize that several other groups could also be infected—even babies who had received blood transfusions.

The young parents were frantic. Their other child had been normal, but what was the matter with their baby boy? They knew, of course, that his first months had been difficult, after the series of transfusions to alter his Rh factor. But now he was seven months old and he still kept getting sick. He suffered from candidiasis and an ear infection that did not respond to antibiotics. The child's immunologists could tell the baby was suffering from some kind of immune dysfunction, but the pattern didn't fit the profile of babies born with congenital immune impairment (Shilts, 1987, p. 95).

The tragic consequence of the misperception of AIDS being a "gay cancer" was that gay-bashing flared up. Fear of the new illness, which had appeared so suddenly and stricken so many healthy people, added to the homophobia. "The poor homosexuals—they have declared war upon nature, and now nature is exacting an awful retribution" (Shilts, 1987, p. 311). President Reagan's budget cuts in the early 1980s also delayed the urgent response needed from both the political and scientific establishments. Shilts, author of *And the Band Played On: Politics, People, and the AIDS Epidemic*, himself died of AIDS in 1994. He writes,

There was no excuse, in this country and in this time, for the spread of a deadly new epidemic. For this was a time in which the United States boasted the world's most sophisticated medicine and the world's most extensive public health system, geared to eliminate such pestilence from our national life.... But from 1980, when the first isolated gay men began falling ill from strange and exotic ailments, nearly five years passed before all these institutions ... mobilized the way they should in a time of threat (Shilts, 1987, p. xxii).

Another factor that delayed the response was the sheer complexity of HIV, which is actually a retrovirus. This type of virus will "REVERSE the usual flow of genetic information within the host cell in order to reproduce themselves" (Stine, 2004, p. 56–57). As a result, the retrovirus hijacks the immune system to make it the body's own worst enemy. The transcription process of making RNA copies is complicated, so the HIV drugs must be multifaceted in their approach. The medications include: nucleoside/nucleotide reverse transcriptase inhibitors (NRTIs), NNRTIs Non-nucleoside reverse transcriptase inhibitors (NNRTIs), protease inhibitors (PIs), entry inhibitors, and integrase inhibitors. The medications and doctors' visits are usually expensive.

The HIV virus reproduces very quickly in a host body. It essentially turns the immune system's CD-4 cells into an HIV-making factory. As a result, a person's immune system collapses and she or he becomes vulnerable to infections. A person with a low CD-4 count (below 200) could literally die from being exposed to the common cold. Without HAART treatment, then, HIV could develop into AIDS (Stine, 2004).

History of HIV/AIDS and Women

When the "gay plague" first appeared in the United States, many people wrongly assumed that only gay men were at risk. This belief has lasted for many years. For instance, Fumento's *The Myth of Heterosexual AIDS: How a Tragedy Has Been Distorted by the Media and Partisan Politics* was published as late as 1990. If only gay men could get the disease, then women were not at risk from this disase.

As stated earlier, the fear of a new deadly disease added to the stigma of male homosexuality in the 1980s. (Lesbians were at much lower risk than their heterosexual counterparts, an irony that has escaped the notice of antigay activists.) Not until the 1990s did the U.S. government and other entities begin to properly fund the effort to fight this epidemic.

The government and doctors especially ignored women in the early days of AIDS. In *The Invisible Epidemic: The Story of Women and AIDS* (1992), Corea describes how doctors and politicians ignored the emergence of the health threat to women in the 1980s. When the CDC first began a surveillance of possible cases, it did not include female-specific aspects of AIDS until 1993 (www.cdc.gov/mmwr). A higher rate of gynecological cancers, for instance, indicated HIV infection. At first, the only women seen as at-risk were prostitutes and drug users. In one scene, a doctor talked to a female patient who had gotten infected by her husband. She had three young children who were going to lose her soon. After going home to read medical articles about AIDS, the doctor reflected that:

> None of the physicians or scientists talked about the women with AIDS as being sick themselves. They all saw women simply as vectors of disease to men and fetuses, as organisms, like insects, that transmit a pathogen.... Those innocent babies getting it from those irresponsible moms. Those bad women in prostitution giving it not only to innocent men—the johns—but to "good" women, the johns' wives. As if the guy in the middle had nothing to do with it. And the reason that it mattered that the "good" women were getting AIDS, according to the physician-experts, was not that they would suffer from the disease but that they would give it to the innocent man's innocent babies (Corea, 1992, pp. 29–30).

Corea claims that the male-dominated medical profession had consistently treated women as the "other." When HIV/AIDS emerged, then, the marginalization of female patients grew even worse.

> The AIDS virus thrives on precisely what permeates the U.S. medical system: the notion of "otherness." This is also called "sexism," "racism," and "homophobia"—words too puny and mild-mannered to convey the savagery they represent....

Otherness: We don't need to care for the worthless "others" afflicted with AIDS. They have only themselves to blame. Nor need we take decisive, effective action to prevent the further spread of AIDS among them. Certainly we don't have to worry about catching AIDS ourselves if it is something "others" get (Corea, pp. 4–5).

Kitzinger (1994) would agree with Corea's point about marginalization. She notes that either a woman is a white, middle-class, heterosexual innocent victim or "the prostitute, the nymphomaniac, the evil mother and the 'African woman'" (Kitzinger, 1994, p. 95). Only when the public perceived HIV/AIDS as affecting the suburban wife did the issue become relevant. Movies that portrayed loving mothers of dying gay sons added to the motif that this disease only mattered if the right sort of person was involved—not the "Other."

As public awareness grew, HIV-positive women were no longer invisible. The story of Elizabeth Glaser, an actor's wife who became infected from a blood transfusion and died in 1994, decreased the stigma of HIV-positive women. Unfortunately, the public still perceived HIV-positive women in two categories: the "innocent" victims (e.g., somebody who got an unsafe blood transfusion) and those who were to blame (e.g., sexually active women who were called promiscuous).

One Latina, who died of AIDS in 1991, wrote about how when she first attended support groups, there were only gay white men. Then she "discovered other women with the virus. There were black women, white women, Latinas, rich women, and poor women.... They were mothers and sisters and lovers and daughters and grandmothers...." (de la Cruz, 1995, p. 44).

Women with HIV/AIDS, however, had to hide in the shadows for their own survival. Stigma has been an obstacle to full disclosure. One nurse describes her dilemma:

> I lead a double life ... as if I were a split personality. People are always telling me, "Oh, you're a nurse, an intelligent girl, you should have known better." But it's not intelligence, it's an emotional problem. I had low self-esteem, having been physically abused by my father, and had used drugs a few times. I gave them up ten years ago and went to nursing school, but I can never escape my past. It seems unfair to have worked so hard to get clean and then find out I have the virus. I'm mad at myself. I've seen a lot of friends die from it. So many young people get sick and die after they have straightened out their lives and gotten back on the right track. They're being punished all their lives for a mistake they made. My drug addiction is a weight I can never get rid of. I got my life together, but I'm still stuck with this thing, and it keeps coming back in my face, following me around. It's always going to be there, held against me....
>
> My coworkers' attitudes outrage me. Well-educated nurses and doctors say, "I'd never take care of a person with AIDS because everything isn't known about it, and I wouldn't risk my life. I have to think of my children. People with the virus deserve it. Look at the kind of life they're living."

Sitting around, one secretary said, "When I go to church I'm afraid to drink from the cup because somebody with AIDS might have drank from it." Then another woman I work with said, "Oh, you don't have to worry about that. Those type of people don't go to church" (Klitzman, 1997, pp. 46–47).

Gender Aspects

Because HIV/AIDS is primarily transmitted through sexual activity, many troubling questions have emerged. Why are women so high risk? Should we regard female prostitutes as disease carriers or as victims themselves? Can a developing nation create a strong economy without addressing this major threat to stability, especially since there are now 14 million orphaned children in sub-Saharan Africa?

Prostitution

Females are more likely to be prostitutes/sex workers than males. As discussed in the chapter on prostitution and human trafficking (chapter 23), most of the persons involved in the sex trade are forced by either poverty or coercion by pimps, brothel owners, and so forth. In countries such as India, trucking routes become a major avenue of transmitting the virus because truckers and migrant workers are more likely to be customers.

Lack of Economic Power

In many developing nations, women do not have the resources to be independent of men. They must either marry or become a "girlfriend" to help pay the bills. In these relationships, women find it hard to insist on condom usage. They are frightened of either being beaten up or deserted. According to UNAIDS and other organizations, one of the best ways to reduce the rate of infection would be to empower women through education and other ways to gain independence. Otherwise, abstinence messages (e.g., delay sex) are of little use.

Violence Against Women

As the World Health Organization reports on the connection between HIV/AIDS and violence against women who cannot protect themselves from the virus:

> Violence against women (physical, sexual and emotional), which is experienced by 10 to 60% of women (ages 15–49 years) worldwide, increases their vulnerability to HIV. Forced sex can contribute to HIV transmission due to tears and lacerations resulting from the use of force. Women who fear or experience violence lack the power to ask their partners to use condoms or refuse unprotected sex. Fear of violence can prevent women from learning and/or sharing their HIV status and accessing treatment. (www.who.int/gender)

Domestic violence and rape, then, are highly dangerous to women if they are involved with HIV-positive men. Because of a myth that having sex with a virgin can cure AIDS, countries such as South Africa are experiencing an alarming increase in rapes of girls and even babies. A South African researcher came up with an interesting solution: Rape-ex, a female condom that has barbs in it. A woman can insert it before she leaves the house. Only a doctor could remove the condom from the rapist's penis. This product was even distributed at the World Cup games in 2010 in Cape Town (Freeman, 2010).

HIV/AIDS and Women of Color in the United States

As a teenager, Marvelyn Brown knew little about HIV/AIDS. In her memoir *The Naked Truth: Young, Beautiful, and (HIV) Positive* (2008), Brown recalls that "there was a chapter about STIs and HIV in our health books. HIV was limited to a page, and half of that page was taken up by the picture of a skinny, gay, white man. In other words, not me, not me, not me" (Brown, 2008, p. 21). At 19, she began to experience flulike symptoms.

> The nurse at the clinic said that it must be some short-term virus or bug that was going around the city's youth and gave me some antibiotics, but in my heart I knew she was wrong. I knew there was something more serious going on....
>
> [Later at work] Suddenly everything around me started to fade into one tiny circle of bright light, and then I was gone. Later I would learn that I had fainted on the stairs, tumbling down a few steps before landing—a pile of skin and bones where I had once been muscular and alert (Brown, 2008, p. 77).

After the hospital tested her and told her that she was HIV-positive, she called her mother to tell her. "'Do not tell anyone anything, Marvelyn. If people want to know what is wrong with you, tell them you got cancer or something.... Anything but HIV'" (Brown, 2008, p. 87). However, she had to call her ex-boyfriends to tell them about her status before anybody else

> At just that moment, anger welled up inside of me. How did I not know that this virus was sexually transmitted? I felt I had been robbed, by my community, my school, and my church. The mantras I'd heard over and over again growing up— "Don't do.drugs." "Don't get pregnant." "Don't smoke."—suddenly seemed so worthless. I had seen family members struggle through drug addiction and lung cancer, so that was all very real to me.... But never had someone mentioned the possibility of me, Marvelyn Brown, contracting HIV from unprotected sex. I had seen it as something only Africans or gay men got (Brown, 2008, p. 89).

Approximately one million persons are HIV-positive in the United States. One of the most striking features of the epidemic in the United State is the disproportionate infection rate.

Although African Americans comprise only 13.6 percent of the U.S. population, they represent 59 percent of the HIV-positive persons in the United States Latinas are also at higher risk—4.2 times higher rate of infections than for white women (Centers for Disease Control, www.cdc.gov/hiv/statistics/overview/ataglance.html).

Why is the rate so high for women of color? First, black and Latino men are disproportionately represented in the prison system. During their incarceration, they may have participated in same-sex relationships that put them at risk of infection. When they return from prison, they may end up infecting their wives or girlfriends. Another possible reason is the "down low" culture of men who refuse to call themselves gay or bisexual. Instead, they have wives or girlfriends and secretly engage in sex with men. This controversial book by J. L. King, *On the Down Low: A Journey into the Lives of "Straight" Black Men Who Sleep with Men (King, 2004)*, describes how he had lived a life of denial even though he had male friends dying of HIV/AIDS. Poverty is another risk factor, since it is related to unsafe sexual practices and lack of health care. Box 24.1 discusses how the HIV/AIDS epidemic is related to the social work profession.

HIV prevention for African American women can be a challenge, especially because it requires frank discussion of sex. In this novel excerpt, the sister of an HIV-positive woman decides to teach prevention in her church.

> I knew there was going to be trouble when Joyce came home with four packages of juicy jumbo hot dogs and six boxes of latex condoms, but I don't think any of us had any idea how *much* trouble until Gerry walked into the fellowship hall and saw Aretha unrolling a very slippery lubricated condom over a jumbo juicy that, to facilitate matters, had been mounted straight up on a chopstick like a hard-on from hell.
>
> The evening started off calmly enough, considering that most of these girls had not only never *used* a condom, they had never seen one, except in drugstore displays with smiling white couples on the front and the mysterious thing itself well concealed within. The words safe sex were not a part of their erotic vocabularies any more than birth control entered into their family planning options....
>
> She just asked them what they thought was the number one killer of young black folks all over America. They guessed homicide, drug overdose, cancer, and car accidents, in that order. When Joyce said AIDS, they thought she was kidding.
>
> "You just trying to scare us into reading this stuff, right?"....
>
> "You need to be scared," Joyce said calmly, "if you want to stay alive."
>
> That sort of got their attention and they started asking questions.....
>
> They wanted to know where it came from, how you could get it, could your kids get it, did you always die from it, and how could you tell who had it and who didn't.
>
> "You can't tell," Joyce said. "That's why we have to use condoms every single time." (Cleage, 1997, pp. 90–91)

Box 24.1 Social Workers and the Epidemic

In *Ashamed to Die: Silence, Denial, and the AIDS Epidemic in the South*, Skerritt (2011) discusses how a South Carolinian town deals with the epidemic. The rate of HIV/AIDS in the South is higher than the national average, with 40 percent of the cases, although this area has only 36 percent of the U.S. population.

> The region's health care systems became increasingly overburdened as HIV/AIDS devastated vulnerable populations, especially poor black men and women…. [it is] rife with pervasive poverty, lack[s] adequate health services, [has] poor infrastructure, high unemployment and underemployment, and too many people who can't afford health insurance. (Skerritt, 2011, p. 9)

For instance, local doctors often do not have the expertise to analyze test results or determine the proper medication therapy. In the 1980s when the epidemic first started, one doctor even ordered a woman out of her office and told her never to come back. Case managers usually have a high caseload and a high number of miles to drive each day in the rural area.

Social workers who deal with welfare mothers expect to attend a court hearing occasionally. But social workers who counsel people with AIDS attend funerals. And for Linda, attending African American funerals was a surprising cultural excursion. "I went to more funerals in that first year in that job than I did in my whole life," she said later.

White and black southern folks bury their dead differently, she soon learned. She remembers her first African American AIDS funeral. She was totally unaware that such events were like an open-mike afternoon mixed in with a camp meeting. They went on for hours. Linda didn't anticipate all the weeping, clapping, and singing. She was struck by the sight of of the women who wore white nurse-like uniforms and white gloves and ran around fanning people who fell out in the aisles (Skerritt, 2011, p. 165).

Discussion Questions

- On the macrolevel, make one policy suggestion regarding the high rate of HIV in the South and its link to systemic poverty. What would be one change you would make to fight the epidemic?
- HIV medications can cost up to $2000 a month, which is too expensive for a low-income client. Write an advocacy letter on behalf of public funding for HIV medications to help persons retain their health (Aguirre, 2012).
- As a social worker, you will probably encounter dying and grief in your career. Discuss the boundaries you plan to set to ensure that you will care for your clients, but not be overwhelmed by the clients' pain. In what circumstances would you attend a client's funeral? In the context of a small Southern town, when would it be appropriate to be involved in a community's grieving—and when would it appropriate to pull back?

Three-quarters of the HIV-positive women in the world are Africans. Several factors contribute to the high rate of HIV in several African countries, including the migration of men looking for work in cities. Although extramarital sex is prevalent among African men, they are often reluctant to admit it even when they test positive for HIV. Governments are sometimes slow to respond to this health emergency.

Besides this climate of silence and denial about HIV, churches hinder prevention efforts by opposing the use of condoms. Both Christians and Muslims may believe in witchcraft, which encourages a supernatural view of the disease as an inevitable event. Belief in witchcraft also promotes the stigma of HIV by blaming somebody (usually a woman) for causing it (Gordon, 2006).

However, countries such as Zimbabwe have been successful in lowering the HIV rate by promoting the delay in sexual activity and the use of condoms (Gordon, 2006). Botswana is another example of a country that went from disaster to hope. This southern African country was once the "hot zone" for HIV/AIDS as it epitomized the frightening implications of this disease. "In the year 2000, the World Health Organization estimated that 85 percent of 15-year-olds in Botswana would eventually die of AIDS" because the rate was already 25 percent for adults (Dow & Essex, 2010, p. ix). The impact would not be just on HIV-positive persons, but on all of society.

> It has been said that many more are affected by AIDS than just those who are infected with HIV: orphans have lost parents, parents have lost children, spouses have lost partners, schools have lost teachers, farms have lost farmers. So behind every HIV infection is some form of personal tragedy for others—not just for the deceased, the sick person, or the stigmatized person who is infected....
>
> HIV is a stealth type of killer. It sneaks in through events of human bonding: conjugation and childbirth. Events that should be sacred and wonderful, not the seeds of death. The virus usually stays hidden in the body for a few years, gradually rising to strangle the immune system—the ultimate death sentence (Dow & Essex, 2010, p. ix).

As the population became decimated by AIDS, people had to reserve Saturdays for funerals. One older woman, noting that there were many more funerals than weddings these days, noted that "Nature has gone crazy.... There had always been a balance between death and birth, but not anymore. 'We are burying babies with their parents! How can there be a future?'" (Dow & Essex, 2010, p. 5).

Fortunately, the national government took bold actions to fight the epidemic. Working with international agencies, the president vowed to make HIV medications available to the entire nation. Now 95 percent of the Botswana citizens who need the HIV medication have access to it. The mother-to-child transmission rate has dropped from 40 percent to 4 percent. One farmer, who said he would have been dead if not for the drugs, told the reporter how he had recently built his own house. "I was surprised seeing myself going on top of the roof of the house and making some bricks for the house" (Beaubien, 2012).

Cultural Norms

In many countries, the sexual norms stress that men should have as many sexual partners (or even wives, in some cases) as possible. A "real" man does not limit himself to monogamy. In contrast, women are supposed to be monogamous or risk being stigmatized. Marriage, then, is the highest-risk activity for women in most developing nations.

Women are also not supposed to know about their bodies or seek services that would help them, such as a family planning clinic. If she were seen obtaining a condom, for instance, she would be called a slut. Researchers have developed female condoms so women could protect themselves, but they are not widely used. Microbicides (gel that a woman could apply to kill the viruses in the sperm) are not yet fully developed (Dow & Essex, 2010).

Another norm in some African and Asian countries is the cruel treatment of widows. For instance, the practice of widow cleansing forces her to have sex with a man appointed by the village or a relative from her husband's family. This practice is meant to "cleanse" the dead husband from the widows, but also is increasing the HIV rate because many widow cleansers are HIV-positive.

However, the wide-scale impact of HIV/AIDS in many developing countries has challenged centuries-old cultural norms. For instance, it was once traditional that only women cared for the terminally ill. Now one program in Zimbabwe has recruited men to provide hospice care in the villages. One male participant stated, "To me it is encouraging to see men becoming less idle and less chauvinistic. Their decision to participate in community-based caregiving is a great shift ..." (UNAIDS, UNFPA, & UNIFEM, 2004, p. 44).

Another cultural norm being questioned is the devaluing of women in the workplace and family. Because of their second-class role, many women do not have access to employment or business capital. Economic empowerment, then, is essential in this struggle to control the pandemic. One aspect of female powerlessness is the widespread practice of *dharas*, or sugar daddies who pay young girls for sex. In Zimbabwe, it is estimated that one-third of these sugar daddies are HIV-positive but rarely use condoms. Called a "financial prophylactic (protection)," one program not only teaches girls health education but provides businesswomen as mentors to avoid needing a sugar daddy (UNAIDS et al., 2004, p. 25).

Rape is another cultural norm that must be addressed. The Zimbabwean program called Girl Child Network (GCN), empowers girls to fight the rape epidemic. In a country in which men believe that having sex with a virgin will cure them of AIDS, young girls are at high risk. GCN provides self-defense courses and assistance to rape victims. One 15-year-old girl shares how GCN made her more assertive after being a shy child.

But now I have to stand on my own and talk in assemblies. I am confident in what I do and say, and proud of our work. There was a so-called White

House where girls were abused. The first time we reported it, the police didn't react. So we marched as a club to the police station and said we would not go away unless the officers accompanied us to the White House. They did. The girls had been impregnated. The boys smoked cannabis. Everything was scruffy. The police closed the house and put the boys in jail for five years. We said if they were allowed out on bail, we would come back. (Gianturco, 2007, p. 15)

Besides rape, marriage also poses risks of infection for women. In India, for example, "marriage is actually women's primary risk factor" because wives do not feel comfortable refusing sex or insisting on condoms (UNAIDS et al., 2004, p. 16). Since most couples want to have families, they are reluctant to use condoms. Prevention activists, then, focus on frank discussion of sexuality not just in the clinic, but also between couples.

Fighting Back

In the face of a pandemic, spreading knowledge about a disease can be a challenge if there is a low literacy rate. In *Singing for Life: HIV/AIDS and Music in Uganda*, Barz (2006) studies how songs have become one method of public health awareness. Following are some samples of lyrics that are sung from village to village:

This song describes the concern of parents whose children have predeceased them because of HIV/AIDS. Nobody would be burying the parents or tending their graves.

> We are all in danger, Ugandans
> Let us pull up our socks—those who are still alive
> Let us fight the disease that wants to destroy us (Barz, 2006, p. 9).

Another song shares knowledge about the services available:

> I caught the virus at home and then I had a problem
> I caught the virus at home and thought I was dying....
> (But) IDAAC looks after many AIDS victims (Barz, 2006, p. 24).

One song is about women now empowered to stand up to their husbands:

> We ladies, we used to sit behind the hours
> The real truth is that we used to cry from behind there....
> We now drink water in cups (Barz, 2006, p. 42).

Drama is another way to spread the message. One drama group, TASO, sings: "We now without parents, we should all come together, Now and all times, for those in need, It is a challenge; we should all come together...." (Barz, 2006, p. 53).

Discussion Questions

- According to *A Woman's Guide to Living with HIV Infection* (Clark, Maupin, & Hammer, 2004), the side effects of HIV medications may include: diarrhea, nausea, nightmares, headaches, rash, neuropathy (nerve pain), and liver/kidney damage. If you were a case manager with a client who was having trouble with some side effects, what kind of actions would you suggest to her for coping? If she were unwilling to continue her medication regime because of the side effects, how would the social work value of self-determination influence your discussion with her? Is there an ethical argument for forcing an HIV-positive person to take their medications?

- When facing a health crisis such as HIV, a common question is "why me?" This question is especially hard for women who may be blamed for their past drug use or sexual behavior. One HIV-positive woman states, "I don't think I deserve this…. I believe it's something that just happens" (Klitzman, 1997, p. 111). Other persons report feeling punished by God. Discuss how you would help an HIV-positive client adjust to her diagnosis as related to her worldview and spirituality. What would be a healthy response?

- Relate the concept of male privilege to condom use.

- Research the advocacy efforts by groups such as the Center for Women and HIV Advocacy (http://hivlawproject.org) and the United Nations Women Organization (www.unwomen.org). Design a poster to advertise one aspect of their work.

Key Terms
....

HIV/AIDS

Retrovirus

Gay cancer/gay plague

Condoms

Cultural norms

Gender aspects

25

Conclusion: A Proud Future

It takes emotional labor to read this textbook, since it is filled with stories of oppression and sadness. When writing these chapters, I would sometimes get depressed because topics such as domestic violence can be so dark. For centuries, women have faced challenges that appear impossible to overcome. The fact that gang rapes and child marriages still occur all over the world can be discouraging. Also disheartening are the messages from mainstream media that belittle women as if the women's-lib movement had never taken place. Beauty contests in the twenty-first century? Really?

However, the stories of strength—women's strength in initiating the struggle for justice, men's strength in supporting their cause, and grassroots-groups' strength when they confront systemic wrongs—are the counterbalance to any pessimistic thoughts. The fight for equality and respect is a fight for women, men, and those who cross the gender line because everybody benefits. Like racism, sexism damages both the oppressed and oppressor. Before the Civil Rights movement, millions of talented persons were excluded from better education and jobs. Racism is harmful to the United States as long as barriers prevent the best and the brightest to rise to the top. Sexism, too, is harmful because no society can truly flourish without all citizens being able to fulfill their dreams. Although feminism primarily benefits women, their issues actually apply to all humans. Child care, for instance, is not a "woman's issue" because everyone should want healthy and stimulating environments for children. The poster from the National Network to End Domestic Violence (Figure 25.1) reinforces the book's point that all persons are involved in these issues—not just women.

Domestic violence and
sexual assault are never
the victim's fault. It's time
we all speak out to stop
the violence.

No more excuses.
No more silence.
No more violence.

NNEDV
NATIONAL NETWORK
TO END DOMESTIC
VIOLENCE

© 2013 Joyful Heart Foundation. All rights reserved. All content and trademarks used with permission.

NO MORE
TOGETHER WE CAN END DOMESTIC VIOLENCE & SEXUAL ASSAULT
www.nomore.org
Nick Lachey

Figure 25.1 *Advocacy poster (Printed with permission from NNEDV)*

In a speech to the United Nations announcing the HeForShe program in 2014, Emma Watson addressed the men with this statement: "Gender equality is your issue too." Fathers are less valued than mothers, young men would rather kill themselves than ask for help, and many men suffer from the "distorted sense of what constitutes male success. Men don't have the benefits of equality either." Until men are free from gender stereotypes, women will be forced to comply with the norms of submission. "Both men and women should feel free to be sensitive. Both men and women should feel free to be strong" (full text of speech available on www.un.women.org).

Patriarchy and Misogyny

This book's Introduction presented several themes for this textbook, including patriarchy and misogyny. In her book *He's a Stud, She's a Slut and 49 Other Double Standards Every Woman Should Know*, Valenti (2008) uses her critical thinking skills to fight these types of male dominance. Examples include:

- "He's the boss, she's a bitch." (p. 86)
- "He's successful, she's a showoff" about women expected to be self-effacing. (p. 78)
- "He's superdad, she's shittymom" regarding the too-high standards for mothers. (p. 82)
- "He's manly, she's sasquatch" regarding body hair. (p. 74)
- "He's getting an education, she's getting in his way." (p. 102)
- "He's independent, she's pathetic" regarding being single. (p. 106)
- "He's fun, she's frivolous" regarding the hobbies of watching sports and shopping. (p. 146)
- "He's pussy whipped, she's a 'good girlfriend' " regarding relationship dynamics. (p. 182).
- "He's a porn watcher, she's the show" regarding man-centered pornography. (p. 154)

Valenti and other social critics, then, are gadflies who attack inequalities. The term "gadfly" comes from the famous Socratic quote about how the gods had sent this philosopher to the city to wake it up. Comparing the city to a large and lazy horse, Socrates called himself a gadfly that would sting it with upsetting questions. Gadflies are meant to arouse, persuade, and reproach those who would resist progressive changes. Society may regard gadflies as annoyances, but they are sometimes necessary to fight patriarchy and misogyny.

Objectification

Objectifying other people can be fun, such as being a member of the fashion police when celebrities are on the red carpet. At the Oscars and other award ceremonies, a common sight is the full-body pictures of women in gowns. In this venue, fat-shaming and other forms of ridicule are acceptable. After a British awards show in 2014, several commentators criticized the appearance of comedian Sarah Millican. She responded this way: "I'm sorry. I thought I had been invited to such an illustrious event because I am good at my job. Putting clothes on is such a small part of my day. They may as well have been criticising me for brushing my teeth differently to them" (Gervais, 2014).

Millican and other women are objecting to objectification, which psychologists state diminish the perceived value of women. Focusing on a woman's appearance can lower a person's opinion of her—she is seen as less intelligent, less capable, and less pleasant. Unfortunately, women themselves objectify other women; by spending so much time analyzing their appearance they forget to see the person. Men, too, can be objectified

(Gervais, 2014). When fighting the objectification of any person, self-awareness is the first step. An activist cannot hope to change this norm if she conforms to it herself.

On a larger scale, objectification also involves the media images of females as either hypersexualized or passive victims of violence. The advertising industry, for example, displays breast-centric pictures that are almost caricatures of themselves. For the 2015 Superbowl, the burger chain Carl's, Jr. spent millions to show an ad of an almost-naked woman walking through a farmer's market. "While social media lights up with claims of sexism, industry insiders say the fast food chain is giving its male customers what they want" (Corneau, 2015). Fifty years ago, activists had few communication tools besides a mimeograph machine that printed pamphlets. An ad like this could have passed unnoticed without public awareness. Now that the social media is available, activists can amplify their fight against this type of objectification.

Oppression

As the first female black president who had been elected, Ellen Johnson Sirleaf of Liberia has had to fight oppression on both the personal and professional levels. At seventeen, she married a young man who abused her and even pointed a gun at her head. The subsequent divorce did not stop her from working in the government. In 1985, though, she became a political prisoner under a repressive regime and had to flee the country. Liberia later underwent a civil war that tore her country apart. Although she was living a comfortable life in the Unite States, she felt compelled to return to run for president in 2005. Some detractors accused her of being from an elite class. In her autobiography *This Child Will Be Great: Memoir of a Remarkable Life by Africa's First Woman President.* (2009), she rejects the label of elitist.

> I told them I knew what it was to be part of a family denied opportunity. My mother and father had been blessed to have broken through the barriers, but when life circumstances struck our family hard, those barriers had risen again. Our gift, our strength, lay in our having always been mindful that such barriers still existed and that others were struggling mightily against them, because our grandmothers were always part of our lives. Neither one of my grandmothers could read or write any language—as more than three quarters of our people still cannot today—but they worked hard, they loved their country, they loved their families, and they believed in education. They inspired me then, and their memory motivates me now to serve my people, to sacrifice for the world and honestly serve humanity. I cannot and will not betray their trust (Sirleaf, 2009, p. 22).

Her grandmothers' legacy gave her the strength to become an outspoken proponent of not only women but of those suffering from political corruption and economic deprivation. In her 2011 acceptance speech of the Nobel Peace Prize, she stated, "Yet there is occasion for optimism and hope. There are good signs of progress and change. Around the world slowly, international law and an awareness of human rights are illuminating dark corners, in schools, in courts, in the marketplace.... and the light is coming in" (Sirleaf, 2011).

Male Privilege

As discussed in the Global Feminism chapter (chapter 18), one of the worst forms of male privilege is child marriage. In some traditional cultures, men prefer to marry young girls because they are more likely to be virgins and easier to control. An encouraging development has emerged in Nepal, where poverty compelled many families to force their daughters into marriage because there would be one less mouth to feed. One 14-year-old girl joined nine others in her village to fight child marriage with the help of NGOs such as UNICEF. According to one organizer, " 'These girls are local heroes; they have really proven themselves [in their] persistent educational campaigns, and by inspiring their parents to join their cause' " (Newar, 2015). Instead of alienating their parents and other elders, the girls persuaded them to join the movement. At least eighty-four schools in the area have worked with these girls to create "child marriage-free zones" (Newar, 2015).

Amazingly, this movement has spread all over Nepal—there are 20,000 of these clubs run by girls. The next step, of course, is to ensure that these girls have a brighter future through more education and economic opportunities. The government is working on initiatives to help the girls develop financial skills so they can help their families. Getting married as adults instead of as children is a significant triumph for these girls in Nepal, which now reports a 20 percent decrease in the ancient tradition of child marriage (Newar, 2015).

This activist strategy of working with the elders also appears in Carter's book *A Call to Action: Women, Religion, Violence, and Power* (2014). Fighting male privilege with men as allies instead of excluding them from the battle may be one path to success. For instance, persuading enough men to marry women with uncut genitals may encourage mothers not to inflict genital cutting upon their daughters. Carter tells the story of a village chief who attended a human rights conference. When he returned to the village, he found out that a 14-year-old girl had been raped by a soldier. He tied the soldier to a chair until the police came, and told the villagers to avoid shaming the girl.

> After years of concerted effort by The Carter Center to alleviate the mistreatment of women and girls, one of the most important lessons we have learned is that outside organizations like ours, even when working with women who are fighting their own abuse, cannot bring about an end to child marriage, genital cutting, or exclusion of women from equal treatment without the support of the entire community, including traditional chiefs and other male leaders. Molly Melching, the head of Tostan, said that when men were asked to join their discussion groups the women began calling their goal "human rights" instead of "women's rights." Including men had a positive effect, because Tostan began making real progress in ending genital cutting and child marriage only when the men gave their quiet approval or began speaking out in favor of the reforms.

Figure 25.2 *Suffragette Trixie Friganza, New York (Undated photo courtesy of Library of Congress)*

One of the most effective inducements for local chiefs and other men to oppose child marriage, for instance, is to show them how families can become more prosperous if the girls can go to school and be gainfully employed [rather] than sold at an early age to become a servant in their husband's home (Carter, 2014, pp. 194–195).

Author's Final Note to Reader

Activism is always hard work, but it is much harder to live with the despairing thought that nothing ever changes. I wrote this book not to demoralize anyone, but to embolden those who want to fight an injustice. First, do not let the list of injustices overwhelm you. It is valuable to see the big picture of how these social problems may interconnect, but only pick one problem.

Then develop your expertise on that problem. Don't look stupid. The Internet and other media have plenty of uninformed morons publicizing their opinions—the world does NOT need another one. It takes hours of research and critical thinking (e.g., avoiding questionable websites) to not look stupid. When writing this book, I consulted countless sources and asked several people for the primary purpose of not looking stupid. Hopefully, you will also invest the time to do your homework. That is the only way to make people to take you seriously.

The next step is a life-affirming and enjoyable one: find others who share your mission. Join the group(s) that have already started working on the problem. You will probably meet some wonderful people and have some fun. During this process, groups may inundate you with several other issues that may seem just as important. Remember to focus your attention on the problem or you will lose your efficacy. If your activist work jumps from topic to topic, you will lose your way. Also, you will risk getting drowned in a sea of sorrow.

Lastly, preserve a sense of joy as you develop your activism. You may even feel liberated as you start (or continue) this journey toward social justice. Doing any sort of volunteer work is good for one's health, besides increasing the hope that things can change for the better. Yes, there will be setbacks and idiots and aggravations. But social activism is a way to enhance the beauty of this world. Take a deep breath (or take a nap), then think about your first goals. As Gandhi once said, "First they ignore you, then they ridicule you, then they fight you, and then you win."

References

Abdul-Ghafur, S. (2005). Saleemah's story (pp. 7–16) In *Living Islam out loud: American Muslim women speak*. Boston, MA: Beacon Press.

Abdul-Khabeer, S. (2005). Connotations of the Crown. In *Living Islam out loud: American Muslim women speak* (pp. 99–102.) Boston, MA: Beacon Press.

Abrahamson, P. (2007). Free trade and social citizenship: Prospects and possibilities of the Central American Free Trade Agreement (CAFTA-DR). Retreived from *Global Social Policy* online journal gsp.sagepub.com

Abramovitz, M. (1988). *Regulating the lives of women: Social welfare policy from colonial times to the present*. Boston, MA: South End Press.

Abu-Lughod, L. (2013). *Do Muslim women need saving?* Cambridge, MA: Harvard University Press.

Adams, C. J. & Gruen, L. (2014). Introduction. In C. J. Adams & L. Gruen, L. (Eds.), *Ecofeminism: Feminist intersections with other animals & the earth* (pp. 1–6). New York, New York, NY: Bloomsbury.

Adams, J. R. (2010). *Liberators, patriots, and leaders of Latin America: 32 biographies,* (2nd ed.). Jefferson, NC: McFarland.

Agtuca, J. & Sahneyah, D. (2014). *Safety for Native women: VAWA and American Indian tribes*. Lame Deer, MT: National Indigenous Women's Resource Center.

Aguirre, J. C. (2012). Cost of treatment still a challenge for HIV patients in U.S. Retrieved from *National Public Radio* website: www.npr.org.

Ahmed, L. (1992). *Women and gender in Islam*. New Haven, CT: Yale University Press.

Aitchison, C., Hopkins, P., & Kwan, M., (2007). Introduction. In C. Aitchison, P. Hopkins, & M. Kwan (Eds.), *Geographies of Muslim identities: Diaspora, gender and belonging* (pp. 1–10). Hampshire, UK: Ashgate Publishing.

Al-Khalaf, M. (2005). Islamic tradition proves that women have the right to be leaders. In Yuan, M.S (Ed.), *Women in Islam* (pp. 29–33). Detroit, MI: Thomson Gale.

Al Qaradawy, Y. (2005). Islamic women must obey restrictions on work. In Yuan, M.S, (Ed.), *Women in Islam* (pp. 41–48). Detroit, MI: Thomson Gale.

Aldrich, R. (2012). *Gay lives*. New York, NY: Thames & Hudson.

Ali, A. H. (2007). *Infidel.* New York, NY: Atria.

Ali, A. H. (2010). *Nomad: From Islam to America.* New York, NY: Free Press

Ali, N. & Minoui, D. (2010). *I am Nujood, age 10 and divorced.* New York, NY: Three Rivers Press.

Ali, S (2005). How I met God. In *Living Islam out loud: American Muslim women speak.* (pp. 19–35). Boston, MA: Beacon Press

Ali, W. (2003). Muslim women: Between cliché and reality. *Diogenes, 50*(3), 77–87.

Allen, P. G. (1989). Introduction. In *Spider Woman's granddaughters: Traditional tales and contemporary writing by Native American women.* (pp. 1–25). New York, NY: Fawcett Books.

Alter, C. (2014). 11 surprising facts about women and poverty from the Shriver Report. Retrieved from *Time Magazine* website: time.com.

Amer, S. (2014). *What is veiling?* Chapel Hill, NC: University of NC Press.

American Association of University Women (AAUW). (2014). How does race affect the gender wage gap? Retrieved from http://www.aauw.org/2014/04/03/race-and-the-gender-wage-gap/

American Association of University Women (AAUW). (2015). The simple truth about the gender wage gap. Retrieved from http://www.aauw.org/research/the-simple-truth-about-the-gender-pay-gap/

American College of Obstetrics and Gynecology (no date). ACOG Toolkit on State Legislation: Pregnant Women & Prescription Drug Abuse, Dependence and Addiction Retrieved from: www.acog.org

Ammar, N., Couture-Carron, A., Alvi, S., & San Antonio, J. (2013). Experiences of muslim and non-muslim battered immigrant women with the police in the United States a closer understanding of commonalities and differences. *Violence Against Women, 19*(12), 1449–1471.

Anderson, B. S. & Zinsser, J. P. (1988). *A history of their own: Women in Europe from prehistory to the present.* New York, NY: Harper & Row.

An Islamic Bill of Rights for women in the bedroom. (2005). In *Living Islam out loud: American Muslim women speak* (pp. 155–156). Boston, MA: Beacon Press

Anonymous & Mannen, A. (2015). 5 bizarre realities of being a man who was raped by a woman. Retrieved from *Cracked Magazine* website: http://www.cracked.com/article_21884

Angell, M. (2013). Basic freedoms: Why Chelsea Manning's transition matters. Retrieved from *Brown Political Review* website: www.brownpoliticalreview.org

Angelou, M. (1970). *I know why the caged bird sings.* New York, NY: Bantam Books.

Aquino, M. P., Machado, D. L., & Rodriguez, J. (2002). Introduction. In M. P. Aquino, D. L. Machado, & J. Rodriguez, J. (Eds.), *A reader in Latina feminist theology: Religion and justice.* Austin, TX: University of Texas Press.

Arana, M. (2001). *American chica: Two worlds, one childhood.* New York, NY: Delta Books.

Askowitz, A. (2008). *My miserable, lonely, lesbian pregnancy.* San Francisco, CA: Cleis Press.

Augsberger, A., Hahm, H. C., & Dougher, M. (2015). *Suffering alone: Understanding barriers to healthcare utilization amongst Asian-American women.* Presentation at SSWR Conference, abstract retrieved from sswr.confex.com/sswr/2015/webprogram/Paper22858.html

Austin, S., Solic, P., Swenson, H., Jeter-Bennett, G., & Marino, K. M.. (2014). Anita Hill roundtable. *Frontiers: A Journal of Women's Studies, 35*(3), 65–74.

Averett, P. & Jenkins, C. (2012). Review on the literature of older lesbians: Implications for education, practice, and research. *Journal of Applied Gerontology, 31*(4), 537–561.

Badowska, E. (1998). The anorexic body of liberal feminism: Mary Wollstonecraft's A Vindication of the Rights of Women. *Tulsa Studies in Women's Literature, 17*(2), 283–303.

Bagilhole, B. (1994). Being different is a very difficult row to hoe: Survival strategies of women academics. In S. Davies, C. Lubelska, & J. Quinn (Eds.), *Changing the subject: Women in higher education* (pp. 15–28). London: Taylor & Francis.

Baker, J. H. (2005). *Sisters: The lives of America suffragists.* New York, NY: Hill and Wang.

Balbi, M. (2014). Marcela Loaiza: "I'm an inspirational example and that makes me proud." Retrieved from Coalition Against Trafficking in Women website: www.catwinternational.org

Baldez, L. (2002). *Why women protest: Women's movements in Chile.* New York, NY: Cambridge University Press.

Bales, K. & Soodalter, R. *The slave next door: Human trafficking and slavery in America today.* Oakland, CA: University of California Press, 2010.

Ban Zhao, "Lessons for a woman," *Chinese Cultural Studies*. Retrieved from http://academic/ brookly.cuny.edu/core9

Bancroft, L. (2002). *Why does he DO that? Inside the minds of angry and controlling men.* New York: NY: Berkley Books.

Banerjee, U. D. (2006). Migration and trafficking of women and girls: A brief review of some effective models in India and Thailand. In K. Beeks & D. Amir (Eds.), *Trafficking and the global sex industry* (pp. 189–200). Lanham, MD: Lexington Books.

Banks, M. E. (2013). Preface. In M. E. Banks & E. Kaschak (Eds.), *Women with visible and invisible disabilities: Multiple intersections, multiple issues, multiple therapies* (pp. xxi–xxxix). New York, NY: Routledge.

Barlow, T. E. (2004). *The question of women in Chinese feminism.* Durham, NC: Duke University Press.

Barnes, D. M. & Meyer, I. H. (2012). Religious affiliation, internalized homophobia, and mental health in lesbians, gay men, and bisexuals. *American Journal of Orthopsychiatry, 82*(4), 505–515.

Barnett, O. W. (2001). Why battered women do not leave, Part 2: External inhibiting factors—Social support and internal inhibiting factors. *Trauma, Violence & Abuse, 2*(1), 3–35.

Baron, B. (1994). *The women's awakening in Egypt: Culture, society, and the press.* New Haven, CT: Yale University Press.

Barron, A. (2013). Pro-zygote policies ut U.S. on path to Nicaragua. Retrieved from Women's ENews website: womensenews.org

Barz, G. (2006). *Singing for life: HIV/AIDS and music in Uganda.* New York, NY: Routledge.

Bateau, A. M. (2014). Equal pay day for (some) African-American women. Retrieved from *Reproductive Health* website: www.rhrealitycheck.org

Bates, D. D. (2010). Once-married African-American lesbians and bisexual women: Identity development and the coming-out process. *Journal of Homosexuality, 57*, 197–225.

Baumgardner, J. & Richards, A. (2010). *Manifesta: Young women, feminism, and the future* (10th anniv. ed.). New York, NY: Farrar, Straus and Giroux.

Beah, I. (2007). *A long way gone: Memoirs of a boy soldier.* New York, NY: Sarah Crichton Books.

Bearman, P. S. & Brückner, H. (2001). Promising the future: Virginity pledges and first intercourse. *American Journal of Sociology, 106*(4), 859–912.

Beaubien, J. (2012). Botswana's 'stunning achievement' against AIDS. *National Public Radio.* Retrieved from www.npr.org/2012/07/09/156375781/

Begum, N. (1994). Snow White. In L. Keith (Ed.), *Mustn't grumble: Writing by disabled women* (pp. 46–51). London, UK: The Women's Press.

Belknap, J. (2014). *The invisible woman: Gender, crime, and justice* (Cengage Learning.

Benderly, J. (1997). Rape, feminism, and nationalism in the war in Yugoslavia. In L. A. West (Ed.), *Feminist nationalism* (pp. 59–74). New York, NY: Routledge.

Benitez, C. T., McNiel, D. E., & Binder, R. L. (2010). Do protection orders protect? *Journal of the Academy of Psychiatry Law, 38*(3), 376–385.

Benjamin, M. & Mendonca, M. (1997). *Benedita da Silva: An Afro-Brazilian woman's story of politics and love.* Monroe, OR: Food First Books.

Benze, J. G., Jr. (1990). Nancy Reagan: China doll or dragon lady?. *Presidential Studies Quarterly,* 777–790.

Berdahl, J. L. (2007). The sexual harassment of uppity women. *Journal of Applied Psychology, 92*(2), 425–437.

Berkel, L. A, Vandiver, B. J., & Bahner, A. D. (2004). Gender role attitudes, religion, and spirituality as predictors of domestic violence attitudes in white college students. *Journal of College Student Development, 45*(2), 119–133.

Bernal, V. (2001). From warriors to wives: Contradictions of liberation and development in Eritrea. *Northeast African Studies, 8*(3), 129–154.

Berryman, P. (1987). *Liberation theology: Essential facts about the revolutionary movement in Latin America—and beyond.* New York, NY: Pantheon Books.

Beyer, A. M. (n. d.). So much more than numbers: The magic of marketing to your target demographic. Retrieved from Professional Beauty Association website: www.probeauty.org

Bhattacharjee, A. (1997). A slippery path: Organizing resistance to violence against women. In S. Shah (Ed.), *Dragon ladies: Asian American feminists breathe fire* (pp. 29–45). Boston, MA: South End Press,.

Bhutto, B. (2005). Islamic women in South Asia must fight for economic independence. In M. S. Yuan (Ed.), *Women in Islam* (pp. 34–40). Detroit, MI: Thomson Gale,.

Biskupic, J. (2014). *Breaking in: The rise of Sonia Sotomayor and the politics of justice.* New York, NY: Sarah Crichton Books.

Black, A. E. & Allen, J. L. (2001). Tracing the legacy of Anita Hill: The Thomas-Hill hearings and media coverage of sexual harassment. *Gender Issues, 19*(1), 33–52.

Black, S. (2011). Waiting to be dangerous: Disability and confessionalism. In J. Bartlett, S. Black, & M. Northen (Eds.), *Beauty is a verb: The new poetry of disability* (pp. 205–210). El Paso, TX: Cinco Puntas Press,.

Blackwelder, J. K. (1977). Quiet suffering: Atlanta women in the 1930s. *The Georgia Historical Quarterly, 61*(2), 112–124.

Blades, J. & Rowe-Finkbeiner, K. (2006). *The Motherhood Manifesto: What America's moms want-and want to do about it.* New York, NY: Nation Books.

Bolen, J. S. (2001). *Goddesses in older women: Archetypes in women over fifty.* New York, NY: HarperCollins.

Borgmann, C. E. (2011). What the Mississippi Personhood Amendment tells us about "life." *Mississippi Law Journal, 81,* 115–121.

Bourke, J. (2007). *Rape: Sex, violence, and history.* Berkeley, CA: Counterpoint Press.

Bow, L. (2011). *Betrayal and other acts of subversion: Feminism, sexual politics, Asian American women's literature.* Princeton, NJ: Princeton University Press.

Boylan, J. F. (2003). *She's not there: A life in two genders.* New York, NY: Broadway Books.

Brandt, D. (2008). *Tangled routes: Women, work and globalization on the tomato trail,* (2nd ed.). Lanham, MD: Rowman & Littlefield.

Braun Levine, S. & Thom, M. (2007). *Bella: How one tough broad from the Bronx fought Jim Crow and Joe McCarthy, pissed off Jimmy Carter, battled for the rights of women and workers, rallied against war and for the planet, and shook up politics along the way.* New York, NY: Farrar, Straus and Giroux.

Bray, R. L. (1998). *Unafraid of the dark.* New York, NY: Anchor Books.

Brems, E. (1997). Enemies or allies? Feminism and cultural relativism as dissident voices in human rights discourse. *Human Rights Quarterly, 19*(1), 136–164.

Breslaw, A. (2015). 10 perfect breakup texts for every kind of guy in your life. *Elle Magazine.* Retrieved from www.elle.com.

Brighton, J. (2014). *Sharia-ism is here: The battle to control women and everyone else.* Sharia-ism Education Center.

Brizendine, L. (2006). *The female brain.* New York, NY: Broadway Books.

Brody, E. M. (2010). On being very, very old: An insider's perspective. *The Gerontologist, 50*(1), 2–10.

Brooks, G. (1995). *Nine parts of desire: The hidden world of Islamic women.* New York, NY: Anchor Books.

Brooks, K. (2014). On being fat. Retrieved from www.huffingtonpost.com.

Brown, D. (1987). Learning to work. In M. Saxton & F. Howe (Eds.), *With wings: An anthology of literature by and about women with disabilities* (pp. 34–40). New York, NY: Feminist Press,.

Brown, L. (2005). *The dancing girls of Lahore: Selling love and saving dreams in Pakistan's ancient pleasure district.* New York, NY: Fourth Estate.

Brown, M. (2008). *The naked truth: Young, beautiful, and (HIV) positive.* New York, NY: Amistad.

Brown, M. L. & Rounsley, C. A. (1996). *True selves: Understanding transsexualism.* San Francisco, CA: Jossey-Bass.

Brownmiller, S. (1975). *Against our will: Men, women and rape.* New York, NY: Bantam Books.

Brownmiller, S. (1984). *Femininity.* New York, NY: Linden Press, Simon & Schuster.

Brumberg, J. J. (1997). *The body project: An intimate history of American girls.* New York, NY: Vintage Books.

Brumberg, J. J. (2000). *Fasting girls: The history of anorexia nervosa.* New York, NY: Vintage Books.

Buchanan, F., Power, C., & Verity, F. (2013). Domestic violence and the place of fear in mother/Baby relationships "What Was I Afraid Of? Of Making It Worse". *Journal of interpersonal violence*, *28*(9), 1817–1838.

Bull, S. S. (1998). Work and sexual behavior among Latin American women. *Journal of Gender, Culture & Health*, *3*(1), 1–27.

Bunting, M. (2005). The traditional Islamic view of sexuality benefits women. In M. S. Yuan (Ed.), *Women in Islam* (pp. 49–59). Detroit, MI: Thomson Gale.

Bursey, J. A. (2004). Women and cabin sites: Understanding the Iroquoian economic system. *North American Archeologist*, *25*(2), 161–187.

Busch N. B., Fong, R., Heffron, L. C., Faulkner, M., & Mahapatra, N. (2007). An evaluation of the Central Texas Coalition Against Human Trafficking. Report issued by the School for Social Work Research, University of Texas at Austin.

Cahill, L. (2012). His brain, her brain. *Scientific American*. Retrieved from www.scientificamerican. com

Calogero, R. M. (2004). A test of objectification theory: The effect of the male gaze on appearance concerns in college women. *Psychology of Women Quarterly*, *28*, 16–21.

Campbell, J. C., Webster, D. W., & Glass, N. (2009). The danger assessment validation of a lethality risk assessment instrument for intimate partner femicide. *Journal of Interpersonal Violence*, *24*(4), 653–674.

Carothers, B. J. & Reis, H. T. (2013). Men and women are from earth: Examining the latent structure of gender. *Journal of Personality and Social Psychology*, *104*(2), 385–407.

Carter, D. T. (2007). *Scottsboro: A tragedy of the American South*. Baton Rouge: Louisiana State University Press.

Carter, J. (2014). *A call to action: Women, religion, violence, and power*. New York, NY: Simon & Schuster.

Cary, L. (1991). *Black ice*. New York, NY: Vintage Books.

Catalano, S. (2012). Intimate partner violence in the United States [Electronic Version]. Retrieved from http://bjs.ojp.usdoj.gov/index.cfm?typbdetail&iid1000

CDC (Centers for Disease Control and Prevention). (2010). The National Intimate Partner and Sexual Violence Survey summary. Retrieved from www.cdc.gov/violenceprevention.

Cejda, B. D. (2010). In their own words: Latina success in higher education. *Journal of women in educational leadership*, *8*(3), 179–193.

Chase, K. A., O'Farrell, T. J., Murphy, C. M., Fals-Stewart, W., & Murphy, M. (2003). Factors associated with partner violence among female alcoholic patients and their male partner. *Journal of Studies on Alcohol*, *64*(1), 137–149.

Case, K. A. (2007). Raising male privilege awareness and reducing sexism: An evaluation of diversity courses. *Psychology of Women Quarterly*, *31*(4), 426–435.

Cepeda, R. (2013). *Bird of paradise: How I became Latina*. New York, NY: Atria Books.

Chang, J. (1991). *Wild swans: Three daughters of China*. New York, NY: Simon & Schuster.

Chang, L. T. (2008). *Factory girls: From village to city in a changing China*. New York, NY: Spiegel & Grau.

Chang, M. & Mason, N. (2010). At rope's end: Single women mothers, wealth and assets in the U.S. Report retrieved from Women of Color Policy Network website, www.wagner.nyu.edu

Chappell, B. (2014). California enacts "Yes Means Yes" law, defining sexual consent. Retrieved from www.npr.org.

Charlton, S. E. M. (1984). *Women in third world development*. Boulder, CO: Westview Press.

Chavez Leyva, Y. (2003). "There is great good in returning:" A testimonio from the Borderlands. *Frontiers: A Journal of Women's Studies*, *24*(2), 1–9.

Chavis, M. E. (2003). *Meena: Heroine of Afghanistan*. New York, NY: St. Martin's Press.

Chavkin, W. (2001). Cocaine and pregnancy—Time to look at the evidence. *JAMA*, *185*(13), 1626–1627.

Chernik, A. F. (1995). The body politic. In Findlen, B. (Ed.), *Listen up: Voices from the next feminist generation* (pp. 103–111). New York, NY: Seal Press.

Chesler, P. (2011). *Mothers on trial: The battle for children and custody* (2nd ed.) Chicago, IL: Lawrence Hill Books.

Chesney-Lind, M. & Pasko, L. (2013). *The female offender: Girls, women, and crime,* (3rd ed.). Thousand Oaks, CA: Sage Publications.

Chiang, Y. (2007). Womanhood, motherhood and biology: The early phases of The Ladies' Journal 1915-25. In D. Ko & W. Zhen (Eds.), *Translating feminisms in China.* Malden (pp. 70–103). MA: Blackwell Publishing,.

Childs, D. (2007). Intimate Operations: OB-GYN Organization Issues Warning. Retrieved from *ABC News* website, www.abcnews.go.

Childs, E. C. (2005). Looking behind the stereotypes of the "Angry Black Woman" An exploration of Black women's responses to interracial relationships. *Gender & Society, 19*(4), 544–561.

Chinchilla, N. S. (1997). Nationalism, feminism, and revolution in Central America. In L. A. West (Ed.), *Feminist nationalism* (pp. 201–219). New York, NY: Routledge,.

Chou, R. S. & Feagin, J. R. (2014). *The myth of the model minority: Asian Americans facing racism* (2nd ed.). Boulder, CO: Paradigm Publishing.

Chow, E. N., Zhang, N., & Wang, J. (2004). Promising and contested fields. Women's studies and sociology of women/gender in contemporary china. *Gender & Society, 18,*(2), 161–183.

Christensen, M. C. (2014). Engaging theater for social change to address sexual violence on college campuses: A qualitative investigation. *British Journal of Social Work, 44*(6), 1454–1471.

Christian, L., Stinson, J., & Dotson, L. A. (2001). Staff values regarding the sexual expression of women with developmental disabilities. *Sexuality and Disability, 19*(4), 283–291.

Chrystos. (1988). *Not vanishing.* Vancouver, Canada: Press Gang.

Chua, A. (2011). *Battle hymn of the tiger mother.* New York, NY: Penguin Press.

Cianelli, R., Ferrer, L. & McElmurry, B. J. (2008). HIV prevention and low-income Chilean women: machismo, marianismo and HIV misconceptions. *Culture, Health & Sexuality: An International Journal for Research, Intervention and Care, 10*(3), 297–306.

Cianelli, R., Villegas, N., Lawson, S., Ferrer, L., Kaelber, L., Peragallo, N., & Yaya, A. (2013). Unique factors that place Older Hispanic Women at risk for HIV: Intimate partner violence, machismo, and marianismo. *Journal of the Association of Nurses in AIDS Care, 24*(4), 341–354.

Clark, M. P. (2006). My skin is brown and I do not wear a tie. In T. R. Berry& N. Mizelle (Eds.), *From oppression to grace: Women of color and their dilemmas in the academy* (pp. 13–23). Sterling, VA: Stylus Publishing,.

Clark, R. A., Maupin, R. T., & Hammer, J. H. (2004). *A woman's guide to living with HIV infection.* Baltimore, MD: Johns Hopkins University Press.

Cleage, P. (1997). *What looks like crazy on an ordinary day.* New York, NY: Avon Books.

Clinton, K. (2005). *What the L?* New York, NY: Carroll and Graf.

Clunis, D. M. & Green, G. D. (2005). *Lesbian couples: A guide to creating healthy relationships.* Berkeley, CA: Seal Press.

Cochrane, K. (2013). *All the rebel women: The rise of the Fourth Wave of feminism.* Guardian Shorts available on Kindle.

Cole, E. R. (1994). A struggle that continues: Black women, community and resistance. In C. E. Franz & A. J. Stewart (Eds.), *Women creating lives: Identities, resilience, and resistance* (pp. 309–323). Boulder, CO: Westview Press.

Coleman, I. (2011). 'Virginity tests' and the abuse of Egypt's women. *CNN.* Retrieved from www.cnn.com.2011.

Coleman, I. (2013). *Paradise beneath her feet: How women are transforming the Middle East.* New York, NY: Random House.

Coles, C. D. (1993). Saying "Goodbye" to the "Crack Baby." *Neurotoxicology and Teratology, 15,* 290–292.

Collier-Thomas, B. (2010). *Jesus, jobs, and justice: African American women and religion.* New York, NY: Alfred A. Knopf.

Collings, P. (2001). "If you got everything, it's good enough": Perspectives on successful aging in a Canadian Inuit community. *Journal of Cross-Cultural Gerontology, 16,* 127–155.

Collins, G. (2003). *America's women: 400 years of dolls, drudges, helpmates, and heroines*. New York, NY: Harper Collins

Collins, G. (2009). *When everything changed: The amazing journey of American women from 1960 to the present*. New York, NY: Back Bay Books.

Collins, P. H. (2005). *Black sexual politics: African Americans, gender, and the new racism*. New York, NY: Routledge.

Collins, P. H. (2008). *Fighting words: Black women and the search for justice*. Minneapolis, MN: University of Minnesota Press.

Collins, P. H. (2014). *Black feminist thought: Knowledge, consciousness, and the politics of empowerment*, (2nd ed.) New York, NY: Routledge.

Collis, L. (1964). *Memoirs of a medieval woman: The life and times of Margery Kempe*. New York, NY: Harper Collins.

Colvert, B. (2014). We're arresting poor women for our own failures. Retrieved from the *Nation* website: www.nation.com

Constantine, P. (1993). *Japan's sex trade: A journey through Japan's erotic subcultures*. Tokyo, Japan: Charles E. Tuttle.

Cook, P. W. (1997). *Abused men: The hidden side of domestic violence*. Westport, CT: Praeger.

Cooper-White, M. (2014a). Read the nasty comments women in science deal with daily. Retrieved from *Huffington Post* website: www.huffingtonpost.com.

Cooper-White, M. (2014b). These stories will help you understand why it can be hard to be a woman in science.. Retrieved from *Huffington Post* website: www.huffingtonpost.com.

Copper, B. (1986). Voices on becoming an old woman. In J. Alexander, D. Berrow, L. Domitrovich, M. Donnelly, & C. McLean (Eds.), *Women and aging: An anthology by women* (pp. 47–57). Corvallis, OR: Calyx Books.

Corbin, J. (2013). Inside Britain's Sharia courts. Retrieved from *The Telegraph* website: www.telegraph.co.uk.

Corea, G. (1992). *The invisible epidemic: The story of women and AIDS*. New York, NY: HarperCollins.

Corneau, A. (2015). Carl's Jr. strikes again? Watch their (nearly) naked super bowl ad. Article available on *US Magazine* website: www.usmagazine.com/entertainment/news.

Cornell, V. J. (1999). Fruit of the tree of knowledge. In J. Esposito (Ed.), *The Oxford history of Islam* (pp. 65–106). Oxford, UK: Oxford University Press,.

Corrigan, P. W., Larson, J. E., Hautamaki, J., Matthews, A., Kuwabara, S., Rafacz, J., ... & O'Shaughnessy, J. (2009). What lessons do coming out as gay men or lesbians have for people stigmatized by mental illness?. *Community mental health journal, 45*(5), 366–374.

Cotter, D. A. Hermsen, J. M., Ovadia, S., & Vanneman, R. (2001). The glass ceiling effect. *Social Forces, 80*(2), 655–681.

Couch, R. (2015). Men break down watching footage of female genital mutilation, vow to speak out against practice. Retrieved from *Huffington Post;* www.huffingtonpost.com.

Covert, B. (2014). In the restaurant industry, "If you're not being harassed, then you're not doing the right thing." Retrieved from *Think Progress* website: www.thinkprogress.com.

Crane, C. A., Hawes, S. W., Devine, S., & Easton, C. J. (2014). Axis I Psychopathology and the perpetration of Intimate Partner Violence. *Journal of Clinical Psychology, 70*(3), 238–247.

Crawley, S. L. (2001). Are butch and fem working-class and antifeminist? *Gender & Society, 15*(2), 175–196.

Crawley, S. L. & Broad, K. L. (2004). "Be your (real lesbian) self" mobilizing sexual formula stories through personal (and political) storytelling. *Journal of Contemporary Ethnography, 33*(1), 39–71.

Crow Dog, M. & Erdoes, R. (1990). *Lakota woman*. New York: NY: HarperCollns.

Crowe, C. (2003). *Getting away with murder: The true story of the Emmett Till case*. New York, NY: Dial Books.

Cuddy, A. J. C. & Fiske, S. T. (2004). Doddering but dear: Process, content, and function in stereotyping of older persons. In T. D. Nelson (Ed.), *Ageism: stereotyping and prejudice against older persons* (pp. 3–26). Cambridge, MA: MIT Press.

Culley, M. (1984). Introduction. In M. Culley & C. Portuges (Eds.), *Gendered subjects: The dynamics of feminist teaching* (pp. 1–8). New York, NY: Routledge.

Culley, M., Diamond, A., Edwards, C., Lennox, S., & Portuges, C. (1984). The politics of nurturance. In M. Culley & C. Portuges (Eds.), *Gendered subjects: The dynamics of feminist teaching* (pp. 11–20). New York, NY: Routledge.

Culp-Ressler, T. (2014). This week, two incidents of street harassment escalated into violent attacks against women. Retrieved from *Think Progress* website: www.thinkprogress.org.

D'Alonzo, K. T. (2012). The influence of marianismo beliefs on physical activity of immigrant Latinas. *Journal of Transcultural Nursing, 23*(2), 124–133.

D'Alonzo, K. T. & Sharma, M. (2010). The influence of marianismo beliefs on physical activity of mid-life immigrant Latinas: a Photovoice study. *Qualitative Research in Sport and Exercise, 2*(2), 229–249.

D'Antonio, P. (1999). Revisiting and rethinking the rewriting of nursing history. *Bulletin of the History of Medicine, 73*(2), 268–290.

Daly, F. Y. (1994). Perspectives of Native American women on race and gender. In E. Tobach. & B. Rosoff (Eds.), *Challenging racism & sexism: Alternatives to genetic explanations* (pp. 231–255). New York, NY: Feminist Press.

Dasgupta, S. D. (2007). Introduction. In S. D. Dasgupta (Ed.), *Body evidence: Intimate violence against south asian women in America* (pp. 1–9). New Brunswick, NJ: Rutgers University Press.

Davies, S., Lubelska, C., & Quinn, J., (1994). Introduction. In S. Davies, C. Lubelska, & J. Quinn (Eds.), *Changing the subject: Women in higher education* (pp. 3–12). London, UK: Taylor & Francis.

Davidson, J. O. (2005). *Children in the global sex trade.* Malden, MA: Polity Press.

Davis, A. Y. (1981). *Women, race & class.* New York, NY: Vintage Books.

De Becker, G. (1997). *The gift of fear: Survival signals that protect us from violence.* Boston, MA: Little, Brown.

De Beauvoir, S. (1996). *The coming of age.* New York, NY: W.W. Norton.

De Chesnay, M. (2013). *Sex trafficking: A clinical guide for nurses.* New York, NY: Springer Publishing.

De Graaf, J. (Ed.) (2003). *Take back your time: Fighting overwork and time poverty in America.* San Francisco, CA: Berrett-Koelher.

De Hart, J. S. (1991). The new feminism and the dynamics of social change. In L. K. Kerber & J. S. De Hart (Eds.), *Women's America: Refocusing the past* (3rd ed., pp. 493–521). New York, NY: Oxford University Press,

De la Cruz, I. (1995). Sex, drugs, rock-n-roll, and AIDS. In m. Howe & M. Klein (Eds.), *In the company of the my solitude: American writings from the AIDS pandemic.* New York, NY: Persea Books.

De Pizan, C. (2007). Cited in E. Freedman, Ed., *The essential feminist reader.* New York, NY: The Modern Library, pp. 3–9.

De Rivera, J. (2005). A lesson in posture. In A. J. Fountas (Ed.), *Waking up American: Coming of age biculturally* (pp. 107–117). Emeryville, CA: Seal Press.

Dean, J. (2007). *Broken government: How Republican rule destroyed the legislative, executive, and judicial branches.* New York, NY: Viking Press.

Deb, S. (2011). *The beautiful and the damned: A portrait of the new India.* New York, NY: Faber & Faber.

Decoste, R. (2013). Gloria Steinem is wrong: Blame Miley, not the game. Retrieved from www.huffingtonpost.ca/rachel-decoste/gloria-steinem-miley-cyrus_b_4101786.html

Department of Justice (2015). Retrieved from website for office: www.justice.gov/ovw

Des Jardins, J. (2010). *The Madame Curie complex: The hidden history of women in science.* New York, NY: Feminist Press.

Delgado, J. L. (2010). *The Latina guide to health: Consejos and caring answers.* New York, NY: Newmarket Press.

Diamond, M. (2011). Massachusetts Republican: Undocumented immigrant rape victims 'should be afraid to come forward.' Article available on *Think Progress* website: www.thinkprogress.com.

Dickerson, D. J. (2000). *An American story.* New York, NY: Anchor Books.

Dikotter, F. (2010). *Mao's great famine: The history of China's most devastating catastrophe 1958–1962.* New York, NY: Walker Publishing.

Dirie, W. & Milborn, C. (2005). *Desert children.* London, UK: Virago Press.

Domitrovich, A. (1986). Thoughts on aging. In J. Alexander, D. Berrow, L. Domitrovich, M. Donnelly, & C. McLean (Eds.), *Women and aging: An anthology by women* (pp. 131–133). Corvallis, OR: Calyx Books.

Donner, F. (1999). Muhammed and the Caliphate. In J. Esposito (Ed.), *The Oxford history of Islam* (pp. 1–64). Oxford, UK: Oxford University Press.

Dorris, K. (2011). Benign bone tumor city. In J. Bartlett, S. Black, & M. Northen (Eds.*), Beauty is a verb: The new poetry of disability* (pp. 346–347). El Paso, TX: Cinco Puntas.

Dow, U. & Essex, M. (2010). *Saturday is for funerals*. Cambridge, MA: Harvard University Press.

Drelsbach, S. (2011). Hate your body? Most do, at least once a day. *Glamour Magazine*. Retrieved from Today Show website: www.todayshow.com.

Drolet, J. (2010). Feminist perspectives in development: Implications for women and microcredit. *Affilia, 25*(3), 212–223.

Drury, A., Aramburu, C., & Louis, M. (2002). Exploring the association between body weight, stigma of obesity, and health care avoidance. *Journal of the American Academy of Nurse Practitioners, 14*(12), 554–561.

Duffy, M. (2007). Doing the dirty work: Gender, race, and reproductive labor in historical perspective. *Gender & Society, 21*(3), 313–336.

Dugan, M. K. & Hock, R. R. (2006). *It's my life now: Starting over after an abusive relationship or domestic violence* (2nd ed.). New York, NY: Routledge/Taylor & Francis.

Duggan, L. S. (2012). Retail on the "Dole": Parasitic employers and women workers. In C. Morrow. & T. A. Fredrick (Eds.), *Getting in is not enough: Women and the global workplace* (pp. 40–60). Baltimore, MD: Johns Hopkins University Press.

Durschmied, E. (2005). *Whores of the devil: Witch-hunts and witch-trials*. Phoenix Mill, UK: Sutton.

Dutt, N. (2012). Eve teasing in India: Assault or harassment by another name. Retrieved from *BBC News* website: www.bbc.com.

Ebrey, P. B. (1991). Introduction. In R. S. Watson & P. B. Ebrey (Eds.), *Marriage and inequality in Chinese society* (pp. 1–24). Berkeley, CA: University of California Press.

Ebrey, P. B. (1993). *The inner quarters: Marriage and the lives of Chinese women in the Sung period*. Berkeley, CA: University of California Press.

Ebrey, P. B. (2010). *The Cambridge illustrated history of China* (2nd ed.). London, UK: Cambridge University Press.

Ehrenreich, B. & English, D. (1978). *For her own good: 150 years of the experts' advice to women*. NY: Anchor Books.

Ehrenreich, B. & English, D. (1993). *Complaints and disorders: The sexual politics of sickness*. New York, NY: Feminist Press.

Ehrenreich, B. & Hochschild, A. R. (2002). Introduction. In *Global woman: Nannies, maids, and sex workers in the new economy* (pp. 1–14). New York, NY: Metropolitan/Owl.

Ellis, A. & Powers, M. G. (2000). *The secret of overcoming verbal abuse: Getting off the emotional roller coaster and regaining control of your life*. Hollywood, CA: Melvin Powers/Wilshire Book Co.

Else-Quest, N. M., Higgins, A., & Morton, L. (2012). Gender differences in self-conscious emotional experience: A meta-analysis. *Psychological Bulletin, 138*(5), 947.

Englander, E. K. (2013). *Bullying and cyberbullying: What every educator needs to know*. Cambridge, MA: Harvard Educational Press.

Enriquez, I. E. (2011). "Because we feel the pressure and we also feel the support": Examining the educational success of undocumented immigrant Latina/o students. *Harvard Educational Review, 81*(3), 476–500.

Ernsberger, P. (2009). Does social class explain the connection between weight and health? In E. Rothblum. & S. Solovay (Eds.), *The fat studies reader* (pp. 25–36). New York, NY: New York University Press,

Espin, O. M. (1987). Issues of identity in the psychology of Latina Lesbians. In Boston Lesbian psychologies collective (Eds.), *Lesbian psychologies: Explorations and challenges* (pp. 35–55). Urbana, IL: University of Illinois Press.

Ezer, T. (2012). Innovating justice for widows in Kenya. Retrieved from www.opensocietyfoundations.org/voices/innovating-justice-widows-kenya

Fairstein, L. A. (1993). *Sexual violence: Our war against rape*. New York, NY: Berkley Books.

Falcon, S. (2001). Rape as a weapon of war: Advancing human rights for women at the US-Mexico border. *Social Justice, 31*–50.

Faludi, S. (1991). *Backlash: The undeclared war against American women*. New York, NY: Crown Publishers.

Farrell, A. E. (2011). *Fat shame: Stigma and the fat body in America*. New York, NY: New York University Press.

Fausto-Sterling, A. (2012). *Sex/gender: Biology in a social world*. New York, NY: Taylor & Francis.

Fedina, L, Trease, J., & Williamson, C. (2008). *Human trafficking in Ohio: A resource guide for social service providers*. Toledo, OH: Second Chance

Fernandez, M. E. (2005). Fooling Mexicans. In A. J. Fountas (Ed.), *Waking up American: Coming of age biculturally* (pp. 131–139). Emeryville, CA: Seal Press.

Fernandez-Kelly, M. P. (1997). Maquiladors: The view from the inside. In N. Visvanathan, L. Duggan, L. Nisonoff, & N. Wiegersma (Eds.), *The women, gender and development reader* (pp. 203–215). London, UK: New Africa Books,.

Ferris, J. (2011). Keeping the knives sharp. In J. Bartlett, S. Black,. & M. Northen (Eds.), *Beauty is a verb: The new poetry of disability* (pp. 89–93). El Paso, TX: Cinco Puntas,

Fideler, E. S. (2012). *Women still at work: Professionals over sixty and on the job*. Lanham, MD: Rowman & Litchfield.

Fields, M. G. (1989). Black women enter the teaching profession. In S. Ware (Ed.), *Modern American women: A documentary history* (pp. 50–54). Belmont, CA: Wadsworth Publishing Co.

"Fighting Back Against 'Food Shaming' Phenomenon." (2014). Article available on miami.cbslocal.com website.

Fincher, L. H. (2014). *Leftover women: The resurgence of gender inequality in China*. New York, NY: Zed Books Limited.

Finger, A. (2000). Forbidden fruit. In E. Disch, E. (Ed.), *Reconstructing gender: A multicultural anthology* (2nd ed., pp. 244–247). Mountain View, CA: Mayfield

Fisher, B. J. & Specht, B. K. (1999). Successful aging and creativity in later life. *Journal of Aging Studies, 13*(4), 457–472.

Fitzgerald, J. & Fitzgerald, M. O. (Eds. (2005). *The spirit of Indian women*. Bloomington, IN: World Wisdom.

Fleisher, J. (2011). *Living two lives: Married to a man & in love with a woman*. Philadelphia, PA: Lavender Visions.

Fone, B. (2000). *Homophobia: A history*. New York, NY: Henry Holt and Company.

Fong, V. L. (2004). *Only hope: Coming of age under China's One-Child Policy*. Stanford, CA: Stanford University Press.

Fng, V. L. (2008). China's one-child policy and the empowerment of urban daughters. *American Anthropologist, 104*(4), 1098–1109.

Foo, L. J. (2002). *Asian American women: Issues, concerns, and responsive human and civil rights advocacy*. Lincoln, NE: iUniverse, Inc.

Ford, L. G. (1991). *Iron jawed angels: The suffrage militancy of the National Woman's Party 1912–1920*. Lanham, MD: University Press of America.

Foreman, K. (2005). Bad girls confined: Okuni, geisha, and the negotiation of female performance space. In L. Miller & J. Bardsley (Eds.), *Bad girls of Japan* (pp. 33–47). New York, NY: Palgrave MacMillan.

Frank, M., Ziebarth, M., & Field, C. (1984). Rosie the riveter. *Society, 21*(3), 75–78.

Fraser, A. (1984). *A weaker vessel: Women's lot in seventeenth century England*. New York, NY: Knopf.

Fraser, A. (1989). *The warrior Queens: From Britain's Boadicea to Elizabeth I*. New York, NY: Alfred A. Knopf.

Fraser, N. (1994). After the family wage: Gender equity and the welfare state. *Political Theory, 22*(4), 591–618.

Fraser, N. & Navarro, M. (1980). *Evita: The real life of Eva Peron*. New York, NY: W.W. Norton.

Freedman, E. B. (2002). *No turning back: The history of feminism and the future of women*. New York, NY: Ballantine Books.

Freeman, D. W. (2010). Anti-rape condoms: Will jagged teeth deter World Cup sex assaults? Article available on *CBS News* website: www.cbsnews.com

Friday, N. (1996). *The power of beauty*. New York, NY: HarperCollins.

Friedan, B. (1963). *The feminine mystique*. New York, NY: W.W. Norton.

Friedman, B. (1993). *The fountain of age*. New York, NY: Simon & Schuster.

Frohmader, C. & Ortoleva, S. (2012). *The sexual and reproductive rights of women and girls with disabilities*. Paper presented at ICPD International Conference on Population and Development Beyond 2014, July 2012. Retrieved from SSRN: ssrn.com/abstract=2444170

Fulton, J. (1994). Journey. In L. Keith (Ed.), *Mustn't grumble: Writing by disabled women* (pp. 84–89). London, UK: The Women's Press.

Galeano, Eduardo (1997/1973). *Open veins of Latin America: Five centuries of the pillage of a continent*. New York, NY: Monthly Review Press.

Galenson, D. W. (2009). *Conceptual revolutions in twentieth-century art*. New York, NY: Cambridge University Press.

Gallo, M. M. (2007). *Different daughters: A history of the Daughters of Bilitis and the rise of the lesbian rights movement*. Emeryville, CA: Seal Press.

Gallor, S. M. & Fassinger, R. E. (2010). Social support, ethnic identity, and sexual identity of lesbians and gay men. *Journal of Gay & Lesbian Social Services, 22*(3).

Galloway, T. (1987). I'm listening as hard as I can. In M. Saxton & F. Howe (Eds.), *With wings: An anthology of literature by and about women with disabilities* (pp. 5–9). New York: NY: Feminist Press.

Ganeva, T. (2015). Woman thrown in jail for having an addiction while pregnant. *Alternet* online magazine. Retrieved from www.alternet.org/woman-thrown-jail-having-addiction-while-pregnant

Gardner, D. (2011). First lady Eva Peron 'allowed Nazis to hide out in Argentina in exchange for treasures looted from rich Jewish families.' MailOnline, Sept. 2, 2011. Retrieved from www.dailymail.co.uk

Garlinghouse, R. (2015). To the lady who called my toddler a thug. Retrieved from *Huffington Post* website: www.huffingtonpost.com

Garner, J. D. (1999). Feminism and feminist gerontology. In J. D. Garner (Ed.), *Fundamentals of feminist gerontology* (pp. 3–12). New York, NY: Haworth Press,.

Garrison, M. C. (2012). Size matters: Television Media Effects on Male Body Image. Dissertation retrieved from http://rave.ohiolink.edu/etdc/view?acc_num=xavier1395151552.

Gebereyes, R. (2015). Kelly Rowland had a 'mild anxiety attack' when she realized the pressures of raising a black son. Retrieved from *Huffington Post* website: www.huffingtonpost.com.

Gebremedhin, T. G. (2002). *Women, tradition and development: A case study of Eritrea*. Lawrenceville, NJ: ,Red Sea Press.

George, U. & Chaze, F. (2009). "Tell me what I need to know": South Asian women, social capital and settlement. *International Migration and Integration, 10*, 265–282.

Germov, J. & Williams, L. (1999). Dieting women: Self-surveillance and the body panopticon. In J. Sobal. & D. Maurer (Eds.), *Weighty issues: Fatness and thinness as social problems* (pp. 117–132). Hawthorne, NY: Aline de Gruyter,

Gervais, S. J. (2014). Daring to fight sexual objectification. Retrieved from *Psychology Today* website: www.psychologytoday.com

Gianturco, P. (2007). *Women who light the dark*. Brooklyn, NY: Powerhouse Books.

Gianturco, P. (2012). *Grandmother power: A global phenomenon*. Brooklyn, NY: Powerhouse Books.

Gibson, M. (1997). Clitoral corruption: Body metaphors and American doctors' construction of female homosexuality, 1870–1900. In V. A. Rosario (Ed.), *Science and homosexualities* (pp. 108–132). New York, NY: Routledge.

Gillibrand, K. (2014). *Off the sidelines: Raise your voice, change the world*. New York, NY: Ballantine.

Gliha, L. J. (2014). Exclusive: Victims of military sexual assault appeal to human rights panel. Retrieved from *Aljazzera* website: aljazzera.com

Gluck, S. B. (1997). Shifting sands: The feminist-nationalist connection in the Palestinian movement. In L. A. West (Ed.), *Feminist nationalism* (pp. 101–129). New York, NY: Routledge.

Goff, P. A., Eberhardt, J. L., Williams, M. J., & Jackson, M. C. (2008). Not yet human: Implicit knowledge, historical dehumanization, and contemporary consequences. *Journal of Personality and Social Psychology, 94*(2), 292–306.

Goffman, E. (1968). *Stigma: Notes on the management of a spoiled identity.* Englewood Cliffs, NJ: Prentice-Hall, Inc.

Goldberg, C. & Zhang, L. (2004). Simple and joint effects of gender and self-esteem on responses to same-sex sexual harassment. *Sex Roles, 50* (11/12), 823–833.

Goldberg, E. (2015). Little-known surgery restores sexual pleasure to female genital mutilation victims. Retrieved from *Huffington Post* website: www.huffingtonpost.com

Goldberg, M. (2009). *The means of reproduction: Sex, power and the future of the world.* New York, NY: Penguin Press.

Golden, C. (1987). Diversity and variability in women's sexual identities. In Boston Lesbian Psychologies Collective (Eds.), *Lesbian psychologies: Explorations and challenges* (pp. 19–34). Urbana, IL: University of Illinois Press.

Golden, S. (1998). *Slaying the mermaid: Women and the culture of sacrifice.* New York, NY: Three Rivers Press.

Goldin, C., Katz, L., & Kuziemko, I., (2006). The homecoming of American college women: The reversal of the college gender gap. NBER Working Paper No. 12139 Retrieved from http://www.nber.org/papers/w12139

Gordon, A. A. (2006). Population, urbanization, and AIDS. In A. A. Gordon. & D. L. Gordon (Eds.), *Understanding contemporary Africa.* Boulder, CO: Lynne Rienner.

Graham, D. L. R., Rawlings, E. I., Ihms, K., Latimer, D., Foliano, J., Thompson, A., Suttman, K., Farrington, M., & Hacker, R. (2001). A scale for identifying "Stockholm Syndrome" reactions in young dating women: Factor structure, reliability, and validity. In K. D. O'Leary & R. D. Maiuru (Eds.), *Psychological abuse in violent domestic relations* (pp. 77–100). New York, NY: Springer Publishing.

Greene, K. (2012). Men at Work—As Caregivers. Retrieved from *Wall Street Journal* website: www.wsj.com

Gritz, O. (2011). A conscious decision. In J. Bartlett, S. Black, & M. Northen, M. (Eds.), *Beauty is a verb: The new poetry of disability* (pp. 191–192). El Paso, TX: Cinco Puntas Press.

Guilbert, J. (1998). Strapped down: Chinese women and the logic of American feminism. *Bad Subjects, 38.* Retrieved from http://eserver.org/bs/38/guilbert.html

Gurr, B. (2015). *Reproductive justice: The politics of health care for Native American women.* New Brunswick, NJ: Rutgers University Press.

Guy, M. E. & Newman, M. A. (2004). Women's jobs, men's jobs: Sex segregation and emotional labor. *Public Administration Review,* 289–298.

Hagen, K. & Yohani, S. (2010). The nature and psychosocial consequences of war rape for individuals and communities. *International Journal of Psychological Studies, 2*(2), 14.

Hahm, H. C. & Kim, A. (2010). In the path of establishing ethnic identity: Stories of young Korean-American women. *Journal of Korean American Education, 27,* 31–37.

Hahm, H. C., Gonyea, J. G., Chiao, C., & Koritsanszky, L. A. (2014). Fractured identity: A framework for understanding young Asian American women's self-harm and suicidal behaviors. *Race and Social Problems, 6*(1), 56–68.

Hale, S. (2001). The state of the women's movement in Eritrea. *Northeast African Studies, 8*(3), 155–177.

Hall, E. J. & Rodriguez, M. S. (2003). The myth of postfeminism. *Gender & Society, 17*(6), 878–902.

Hall, R. E. (2012). The feminization of social welfare: Implications of cultural tradition vis-à-vis male victims of domestic violence. *Journal of Sociology and Social Welfare, 39*(3), 7–27.

Hall, R. L. & Fine, M. (2005). The stories we tell: The lives and friendship of two older Black lesbians. *Psychology of Women Quarterly, 29*(2), 177–187.

Hall, S. S. (1999). The troubled life of boys; The bully in the mirror. Retrieved from *New York Times* website: www.newyorktimes.com

Halliwell, E. & Dittmar, H. (2003). A qualitative investigation of women's and men's body image concerns and their attitudes toward aging. *Sex Roles, 49,* 11.

Hancock, A. M. (2004). *The politics of disgust: The public identity of the Welfare Queen*. New York: New York University Press.

Haniffa, F. (2008). Piety as politics amongst Muslim women in contemporary Sri Lanka. *Modern Asian Studies, 42*(2,3), 347–375.

Hanna, K. (2007). Riot Girrrl Manifesto. In E. Freedman, E. (Ed.), *The essential feminist reader* (pp. 394–396). New York, NY: Modern Library.

Hapke, L. (1995). *Daughters of the Great Depression: Women, work, and fiction in the American 1930s*. Athens, GA: University of Georgia Press.

Hapke, L. (2004). *Sweatshop: The history of an American idea*. New Brunswick, NJ: Rutgers University Press.

Hardesty, C. (1987). Pain. In M. Saxton. & F. Howe (Eds.), *With wings: An anthology of literature by and about women with disabilities* (pp. 19–23). New York, NY: Feminist Press.

Harklau, L. (2013). Why Izzie didn't go to college: Choosing work over college as Latina feminism. *Teachers College Record, 115*.

Harris-Perry, M. V. (2011). *Sister citizen: Shame, stereotypes, and black women in America*. New Haven, CT: Yale University Press.

Hartmann, B. (2013). Sterilization and abortion. In M. Hobbs & C. Rice, (Eds.), *Gender and women's studies in Canada: Critical terrain* (pp. 473–486). Toronto, Canada: Women's Press.

Hassan, R. (1991). Muslim women and post-patriarchal Islam. In P. M. Cooey, W. R. Eakin, & J. B. McDaniel (Eds.), *After patriarchy: Feminist transformations of the world religions* (pp. 39–64). Maryknoll, NY: Orbis Books.

Hassouneh-Phillips, D. & McNeff, E. (2005). "I thought I was less worthy": Low sexual and body esteem and increased vulnerability to intimate partner abuse in women with physical disabilities. *Sexuality and Disability, 23*(4), 227–240.

Hattery, A. J. & Smith, E. (2014). Families of incarcerated African American men: The impact on mothers and children. *Journal of Pan African Studies, 7*(6), 128.

Hazen-Hammond, S. (1999). *Spider woman's web: Traditional Native American tales about women's power*. New York, NY: Perigree.

Healey, S. (1986). Growing to be an old woman: Aging and ageism. In J. Alexander, D. Berrow, L. Domitrovich, & C. McLean (Eds.), *Women and aging: An anthology by women* (pp. 58–62). Corvallis, OR: Calyx Books.

Hegewisch, A. & O'Farrell, B. (2015). Women in the construction trades: Earnings, workplace discrimination, and the promise of green jobs Retrieved from www.iwpr.org/publications/pubs/women-in-the-construction-trades-earnings-workplace-discrimination-and-the-promise-of-green-jobs

Hehir, Thomas. (2007). Confronting ableism. *Educational Leadership, 64*(5), 8–14.

Henderson, K. & Ellis, S. K. (2011). *Times two: Two women in love and the happy family they made*. New York, NY: Free Press.

Hepburn, S. & Simon, R. J. (2013). *Human trafficking around the world: Hidden in plain sight*. New York, NY: Columbia University Press.

Hershatter, G. (2011). *The gender of memory: Rural women and China's collective past*. Berkeley, CA: University of California Press.

Hershey, L. (2011). Getting comfortable. In Bartlett, J., Black, S., & Northen, M., eds., *Beauty is a verb: The new poetry of disability* (pp. 129–132). El Paso, TX: Cinco Puntas Press.

Hershey, L. (2013). Coming out in voices. In M. Willmuth & L. Holcomb (Eds.), *Women with disabilities: Found voices* (pp. 9–18). New York, NY: Routledge.

Hesketh, T., Lu, L., & Xing, Z. W. (2005). The effect of China's one-child family policy after 25 years. *The New England Journal of Medicine, 353*(11), 1171–1176.

Hilgenkamp, K., Harper, J., & Boskey, E. (2010). *The truth about rape* (2nd ed.). New York, NY: Facts on File.

Hill, C. (2015). Solving the equation: The variables for women's success in engineering and computing. American Association of University Women Report retrieved from http://www.aauw.org/research/solving-the-equation/

Hill, C. & Silva, E. (2010). Drawing the line: Sexual harassment on campus. In J. H. Skolnick & E. Currie (Eds.), *Crisis in American Institutions* (14th ed., pp. 150–164). Boston, MA: Allyn & Bacon,.

Hines, M. (2005). *Brain gender*. New York, NY: Oxford University Press.

Hlavka, H. R. (2014). Normalizing sexual violence: Young women account for harassment and abuse. *Gender & Society, 28*(3), 337–358.

Hogburg, U. & Brostrom, G. (1985). The demography of maternal mortality—seven Swedish parishes in the 19th century. *International Journal of Gynecology and Obstetrics, 23,* 489–497.

Holden, R. J., Schubert, C., & Mickelson, R. S. (2015). The patient work system: An analysis of self-care performance barriers among elderly heart failure patients and their informal caregivers. *Applied Ergomonics, 47,* 133–160.

Hondagneu-Sotelo, P. (2004). Blowups and other unhappy endings. In B. Ehrenreich & A. Russell Hochschil (Eds.), *Global woman: Nannies, maids, and sex workers in the new economy.* New York, NY: Metropolitan/Owl Books.

Honey, M. (1984). *Creating Rosie the Riveter: Class, gender, and propaganda during World War II.* Amherst, MA: University of Massachusetts Press.

Hong, F. (1997). *Footbinding, feminism and freedom: The liberation of women's bodies in modern China.* New York, NY: Frank Cass.

hooks, b. (1997). *Bone black: Memories of girlhood.* New York, NY: Henry Holt and Co.

Hooks, B. (2000). *Feminist theory: From margin to center.* Cambridge, MA: South End Press.

Horn, B. (1986). Beyond hags and old maids: Women writers imaging aging women. In J. Alexander, D. Berrow, L. Domitrovich, M. Donnelly, & C. McLean (Eds.), *Women and aging: An anthology by women* (pp. 63–67). Corvallis, OR: Calyx Books.

Horsman, J. (2000). *Too scared to learn: Women, violence, and education.* Mahwah, NJ: Erbaum.

Howell, A. W. (2014). *Transgender persons and the law.* Chicago, I: American Bar Association Press.

Hughes, S. (2014). Bosnia's wartime rape survivors losing hope of justice. Retrieved from www.bbc.com

Human Rights Watch (2004). France: Headscarf ban violates religious freedom. Retrieved from www.hrw.org

Hussain, S. (2013). Unfolding the reality of Islamic rights of women: Mahr and maintenance rights in India. *Pakistan Journal of Women's Studies: Alam-e-Niswan, 20*(2), 29–50.

Hutchinson, E. A. (2015). Nothing new in the ape crack about Michelle Obama. Retrieved from *Huffington Post* website: www.huffingtonpost.com

Hvistendahl, M. (2011). *Unnatural selection: Choosing boys over girls, and the consequences of a world full of men.* New York, NY: Public Affairs.

International Network of Women with Disabilities (2011). Violence against women with disabilities. Paper for Center for Women Policy Studies. Retrieved from www.centerwomenpolicy.org

IOM (2011). International Organization for Migration. (2011). Case Data on Human Trafficking. Retrieved from www.humantrafficking.org

Isis "Threatens to Execute Male Teachers who teach Female Students." (2014). Retrieved from *International Business Times* website: www.ibtimes.co.uk

Iwamasa, G. Y. & Iwasaki, M. (2011). A new multidimensional model of successful aging: Perceptions of Japanese American older adults. *Journal of Cross-Cultural Gerontology, 26,* 261–278.

Jaffe, S. (2014). Neoliberal feminists don't want women to organize. Retrieved from *Truth Out* website: www.truthout.com

James, M. L. (2011). *Fifty shades of grey.* New York, NY: Vintage Books.

Jaschok, M., Milwertz, C., & Hsiung, P. (2001). Introduction. In P. Hsiung, M. Jaschok, & C. Milwertz, eds., *Chinese women organizing: Cadres, feminists, Muslims, queers* (pp. 3–24). Oxford, UK: Berg.

Jay, K. (1999). *Tales of the Lavender Menace: A memoir of liberation.* New York, NY: Basic Books.

Jeffreys, S. (2008). *The industrial vagina: The political economy of the global sex trade.* New York, NY: Routledge.

Jeltsen, M. (2014). Financial abuse takes heavy toll on domestic violence survivors. Retrieved from *Huffington Post* website: www.huffingtonpost.com.

Jenkins, D., Walker, C., Cohen, H., & Curry, L. (2010). A lesbian older adult managing identity disclosure: A case study. *Journal of gerontological social work*, *53*(5), 402–420.

Jensen, E. N. (2002). The pink triangle and political consciousness: Gays, lesbians, and the memory of Nazi persecution. *Journal of the History of Sexuality*, *11*(1/2), 319–349.

Johnson, E. P. (1989). As it was in the beginning. In P. G. Allen (Ed.), *Spider Woman's grand-daughters: Traditional tales and contemporary writing by Native American women* (pp. 69–78). New York, NY: Fawcett Books.

Johnson, K. (2014). Huckabee: Women who can't control their libidos dependent on 'Uncle Sugar.' Retrieved from *Liberals Unite* website: samuel.warde.com

Johnson, M. L. (Ed.). (2002). *Jane sexes it up: True confessions of feminist desire*. New York, NY: Four Walls, Eight Windows.

Jones, P. S., Zhang, X. E., & Meleis, A. I. (2003). Transforming vulnerability. *Western Journal of Nursing Research*, *25*(7), 835–853.

Joyce, K. (2009a). "Inside the Duggar Family's Conservative Ideology," *Newsweek*. Retrieved from www. newsweek.com

Joyce, K. (2009b). *Quiverfull: Inside the Christian Patriarchy Movement*. Boston, MA: Beacon Press.

Kafer, A. (2013). *Feminist, queer, crip*. Bloomington, IN: Indiana University Press.

Kaler, A. (2011). River creature. In J. Bartlett, S. Black, & M. Northen, M. (Eds.), *Beauty is a verb: The new poetry of disability* (pp. 228–231). El Paso, TX: Cinco Puntas Press.

Kahf, M. (2005). The Muslim in the mirror. In S. Abdul-Ghafur (Ed.), *Living Islam out loud: American Muslim women speak* (pp. 130–138). Boston, MA: Beacon Press.

Kam, K. (1989). The hopeland. In Asian Women's United of California (Ed.), *Making waves: An anthology of writings by and about Asian American women* (pp. 92–97). Boston, MA: Beacon Press,

Kamguian, A. (2005). The Koran teaches that women do not have the same rights as men. In M. S. Yuan (Ed.), *Women in Islam* (pp. 14–23). Detroit, MI: Thomson Gale.

Kang, N. (2006). Women activists in Indian Diaspora: Making interventions and challenging impediments. *South Asia Research*, *26*(2), 145–164.

Kangaude, G. (2014). Disability, the stigma of asexuality and sexual health: A sexual rights perspective. *The Review of Disability Studies: An International Journal*, *5*(4).

Kaplan, C. (2002). Wild nights: Pleasure/sexuality/feminism. In M. Evans (Ed.), *Feminism and the enlightenment* (pp. 351–370). New York, NY: Routledge.

Kaplan, E. A. (2008). Who's afraid of Michelle Obama? *Salon*. Retrieved from www.salon.com/mwt/ feature/2008/06/24/michelle_obama/index.html.

Kargar, Z. (2012). *Dear Zari: The secret lives of Afghan women*. Napierville, IL: Sourcebooks.

Karim, L. (2008). Demystifying micro-credit: The Grameen Bank, NGOs, and neoliberalism in Bangladesh. *Cultural Dynamics*, *20*(1), 5–29.

Karolia, M. M. (2005). The Koran teaches that women cannot be leaders. In M. S. Yuan (Ed.), *Women in Islam* (pp. 24–28). Detroit, MI: Thomson Gale.

Kassie, M. (2014). Male victims of campus sexual assault speak out. *Huffington Post*, 1/27/15. Retrieved from www.huffingtonpost.com

Katz, J. (1995). Introduction. In J. Katz (Ed.), *Messengers of the wing: Native American women tell their life stories* (pp. 1–20). New York, NY: Ballantine Books.

Katz, S. T. (1994). *The Holocaust in historical context: The Holocaust and mass death before the modern age* (Volume 1). New York, NY: Oxford University Press.

Kaufman, D. (2013, October). Aging lwell: Can digital games help older adults? *World Conference on E-Learning in Corporatee, Government, Healthcare, and Higher Education*, *2013*(1), 1943–1949.

Kay, H. H. (1987). Equality and difference: A perspective on no-fault divorce and its aftermath. *University of Cincinnati Law Review*, *56*(1), 1.

Keith, L. (1994a). Introduction. In L. Keith (Ed.), *Mustn't grumble: Writing by disabled women* (pp. 1–9). London, UK: The Women's Press.

Keith, L. (1994b). This week I've been rushed off my wheels. In L. Keith (Ed.), *Mustn't grumble: Writing by disabled women* (pp. 61–72). London, UK: The Women's Press.

Kelly, K. C. (2000). *Performing virginity and testing chastity in the Middle Ages*. New York, NY: Routledge.

Kempado, K. (1999). Continuities and change: Five centuries of prostitution in the Caribbean. In K. Kempado (Ed.), *Sun, sex, and gold: Tourism and sex work in the Caribbean* (pp. 3–36). Lanham, MD: Rowan & Littlefield.

Kennedy, E. L. & Davis, M. D. (2014). *Boots of leather, slippers of gold: The history of a lesbian community, 20th anniversary ed.* New York, NY: Routledge.

Kenney, F. (1995). Men and women lived with the seasons. In J. Katz (Ed.), *Messengers of the wing: Native American women tell their life stories* (pp. 33–45). New York, NY: Ballantine Books.

Kenyon, D. (1994). Reaction-interaction. In L. Keith (Ed.), *Mustn't grumble: Writing by disabled women* (pp. 136–139). London, UK: The Women's Press.

Kerber, L. K. & De Hart, J. S. (1991). Introduction. In L. K. Kerber & J. S. De Hart (Eds.), *Women's America; Refocusing the past* (3rd ed., pp. 3–25). New York, NY: Oxford University Press.

Kerby, S. (2013). How pay inequity hurts women of color. *Center for American Progress Report.* Retrieved from www.americanprogress.org

Khaleeli, H. (2014). Hijra: India's third gender claims its place in law. Retrieved from *The Guardian* website: www.theguardian.com

Kilbourne, J. (1998). *Deadly persuasion: Why women and girls must fight the addictive power of advertising.* New York, NY: Free Press.

Kim, C. H. & Zhao, Y. (2014). Are Asian American women advantaged? Labor market performance of college educated female workers. *Social Forces (2014).* doi: 10.1093/sf/sou076

Kim, E. H. (1989). War story. In Asian Women's United of California (Ed.), *Making waves: An anthology of writings by and about Asian American women* (pp. 80–92). Boston, MA: Beacon Press.

Kim, S. & Esquivel, G. B. (2011). Adolescent spirituality and resilience: Theory, research, and educational practice. *Psychology in the Schools, 48*(7), 755–766.

Kimmel, M. (2000). Masculinity as homophobia. In E. Disch (Ed.), *Reconstructing gender: A multicultural anthology* (2nd ed., pp. 132–139). Mountain View, CA: Mayfield.

Kimura, D. (2000). *Sex and cognition.* CO: Bradford Books.

King, C. R. (1992). Abortion in nineteenth century America: A conflict between women and their physicians. *Women's Health Issues, 2*(1), 32–39.

King, Helen (1993). Once upon a text: Hysteria from hippocrates. In S. Gilman; H. King; R. Porter, G. S. Rousseau, E. Showalter. *Hysteria beyond Freud* (pp. 3–90). Berkeley, CA: University of California Press.

King, J. L. (2004). *On the down low: A journey into the lives of "straight" black men.* New York, NY: Broadway Books.

Kingston, M. H. (1976). *The woman warrior: Memoirs of a girlhood among ghosts.* New York, NY: Vintage International.

Kitzinger, J. (1994). Visible and invisible women in AIDS discourses. In L. Doyal, J. Naidoo, & T. Wilton (Eds.), *AIDS: Setting a feminist agenda* (pp. 95–110). London, UK: Taylor & Francis.

Klasing, A. (2014). Menstrual hygiene day links periods and human rights. Retrieved from *WeNews* website: www.womensenews.org

Klitzman, R. (1997). *Being positive: The lives of men and women with HIV.* Chicago, IL: Ivan R. Dee.

Knapp, B. L. (2000). *Voltaire revisited.* New York, NY: Twayne.

Knox, R. (2011). HPV Vaccine: The science behind the controversy. Retrieved from *National Public Radio* website: www.npr.org

Ko, D. (2005). *Cinderella's sisters: A revisionist history of footbinding.* Berkeley, CA: University of California Press.

Kolbenschlag, M. (1988). *Kiss Sleeping Beauty goodbye: Breaking the spell of feminine myths and models.* New York, NY: HarperCollins.

Koofi, F. (2012). *The favored daughter: One woman's fight to lead Afghanistan into the future.* New York, NY: Palgrave MacMillan.

Kozee, H. B. & Tylka, T. L. (2006). A test of objectification theory with lesbian women. *Psychology of Women Quarterly, 30*(4), 348–357.

Kramer, J. (2015). "I once sent a naked pic to my parents" and other hilarious dating stories. *Glamour Magazine.* Retrieved from: www.glamour.com

Krishnan, S. S. (2008). *The HPV vaccine controversy: Sex, cancer, God, and politics: A guide for parents, women, men, and teenagers.* Westport, CT: Praeger.

Kristof, N. D. (2014). What's so scary about smart girls? Retrieved from *New York Times* website: www.nytimes.com

Kristof, N. D. & WuDunn, S. (1994). *China Wakes: The Struggle for the Soul of a Rising Power.* New York, NY: Times Books.

Kristof, N. D. & WuDunn, S. (2009). *Half the sky: Turning oppression into opportunity for women worldwide.* New York, NY: Alfred A. Knopf.

Kwon, H. & Au, W. (2010). Model minority myth. In E. W. Chen & G. J. Yoo (Eds.), *Encyclopedia of Asian American issues toda,* (Vol.1). Santa Barbara, CA: ABC-CLIO.

Landes, J. B. (1988). *Women and the public sphere in the age of the French Revolution.* Ithaca, New York, NY: Cornell University Press.

Lardinois, A. (1991). Lesbian Sappho and Sappho of Lesbos. In J. N. Bremmer (Ed.), *From Sappho to De Sade: Moments in the history of sexuality* (pp. 15–35). New York, NY: Routledge.

Lather, P. & Smithers, C. (1996). *Troubling the angels: Women living with HIV/AIDS.* Boulder, CO: Westview.

Latimer, T. T. (2005). *Women together/women apart: Portraits of Lesbian Paris.* Piscataway, NJ: Rutgers University Press.

LaViolette, A. D. & Barnett, O. W. (2014). *Why battered women stay: It could happen to anyone* (3rd ed.). Los Angeles: Sage Publishing.

Lawrence, R. G. & Rose, M. (2010). *Hillary Clinton's race for the White House: Gender politics & the media on the campaign trail.* Boulder, CO: Lynne Rienner.

Leahy, M. (2008). *Porn nation: Conquering America's #1 addiction.* Chicago: Northfield.

Ledbetter, L. (2007). Lily Ledbetter: In her own words. Transcript retrieved from http://action.nwlc. org/site/PageServer?pagename=FairPay_LillyLedbetter

Lee, E. & Oberst, G. (1989). My mother's purple dress. In Asian Women's United of California (Ed.), *Making waves: An anthology of writings by and about Asian American women* (pp. 99–114). Boston, MA: Beacon Press.

Lee, H. (1996). *Still life with rice: A young American woman discovers the life and legacy of her Korean grandmother.* New York, NY: Touchstone Books.

Lefley, H. P. & Hatfield, A. B. (1999). Helping parental caregivers and mental health consumers cope with parental aging and loss. *Psychiatric Services, 50*(3), 369–375.

Legge, N. J., DiSanza, J. R., Gribas, J., & Shiffler, A. (2012). "He sounded like a vile, disgusting pervert …" An analysis of persuasive attacks on Rush Limbaugh during the Sandra Fluke controversy. *Journal of Radio & Audio Media, 19*(2), 173–205.

Levy, A. (2005). *Female chauvinist pigs: Women and the rise of raunch culture.* New York, NY: Free Press.

Levy, B. (1997). *In love and in danger: A teen's guide to breaking free of abusive relationships.* New York, NY: Seal Press.

Lewis, A. (2012). On being a gender maverick: An exploration of male cross dressing. *Counseling Australia, 11*(1), 1–12.

Lewis, J. J. (no date). Blackstone commentaries. Retrieved from http://womenshistory.about.com/cs/lives19th/a/blackstone_law.htm

Li, P. (2013). Recent developments hitting the ceiling: An examination of barriers to success for Asian American women. *Berkeley Journal of Gender, Law & Justice, 29*(1). Available at SSRN: http://ssrn.com/abstract=2318802

Lightfoot-Klein, H. (1989). *Prisoners of ritual: An odyssey into female genital circumcision in Africa.* New York, NY: Harrington Park Press.

Linkins, J. (2011). Residents of town where awful gang-rape occurred are also awful, apparently. Retrieved from *Huffington Post* website: www.huffingtonpost.com

Lipscomb, V. B. (2013). "We need a theoretical base": Cynthia Rich, women's studies, and ageism: An interview. In M. Hobbs & C. Rice (Eds.), *Gender and women's studies in Canada: Critical terrain* (pp. 417–423). Toronto: Women's Press.

Lisak, D. & Miller, P. M. (2002). Repeat rape and multiple offending among undetected rapists. *Violence and Victims, 17*(1), 73–84.

Lorde, A. (2007). *Sister outsider: Essays and speeches*. (Crossing Press Feminist Series). New York, NY: Random House Tenspeed Press.

Louie, M. C. Y. (2001). *Sweatshop warriors: Immigrant women workers take on the global factory*. Boston, MA: South End Press.

Lu, L. (1997). Critical visions: The representations and resistance of Asian women. In S. Shah (Ed.), *Dragon ladies: Asian American feminists breathe fire* (pp. 17–28). Boston, MA: South End Press.

Lundy-Wagner, V. & Winkle-Wagner, R. (2013). A harassing climate? Sexual harassment and campus racial climate research. *Journal of Diversity in Higher Education, 6*(1), 51–68.

Lykes, M. B.. (1994). Speaking against the silence: One Maya woman's exile and return. In C. E. Franz & A. J. Stewart (Eds.), *Women creating lives: Identities, resilience, and resistance* (pp. 97–114). Boulder, CO: Westview.

Lynch, D. (n.d.). Afghan women reach out via web. Retrieved from *ABC News* website: http://abc-news.go.com

Macedo, D. (2011). J. Crew ad showing boy with pink nail polish sparks debate on gender identity. Retrieved from *Fox News* website: www.foxnews.com

MacKinnon, C. (1979). *Sexual harassment of working women: A case of sex discrimination*. New Haven, CT: Yale University Press.

Madriz, E. (1997). *Nothing bad happens to good girls: Fear of crime in women's lives*. Berkeley, CA: University of California Press.

Magnuson, S. (2013). *Wounded Knee 1973: Still bleeding*. Chicago, IL: Now and Then Reader.

Mairs, N. (1987). On being a cripple. In M. Saxton & F. Howe (Eds.), *With wings: An anthology of literature by and about women with disabilities* (pp. 118–127). New York, NY: Feminist Press.

Malarek, V. (2009). *The johns: Sex for sale and the men who buy it*. New York, NY: Arcade Publishing.

Maloney, C. B. (2008). *Rumors of our progress have been greatly exaggerated: Why women's lives aren't getting any easier—and how we can make real progress for ourselves and our daughters*. New York, NY: Rodale.

Mann, S. L. (2011). *Gender and sexuality in modern Chinese history*. Cambridge, UK: Cambridge University Press.

Manning, K. E. (2007). Making a great leap forward? The politics of women's liberation in Maoist China. In D. Ko & W. Zheng (Eds.), *Translating feminisms in China* (pp. 138–163). Malden, MA: Blackwell Publishing.

Marcotte, A. (2014a). Anti-choice groups increasingly reveal their anti-contraception agenda. *Reproductive Health Reality Check* article. Retrieved from www.rhrealitycheck.org

Marcotte, A. (2014b), Republican Congressional Nominee: A Woman Can Run for Office With Husband's Permission, *Slate Magazine* Retrieved from www.slate.com,)

Marrs Fuchsel, C. L. (2012). The Catholic Church as a support for immigrant Mexican women living with domestic violence. *Social Work & Christianity, 39*(1), 66–87.

Marrs Fuchsel, C. L. & Hysjulien, B. (2013). Exploring a domestic violence intervention curriculum for immigrant Mexican women in a group setting: A pilot study. *Social Work with Groups, 36*(4), 304–320.

Martens, A. M. (2009). *Working* women *or* women *workers?* The *Women's Trade Union* league and the transformation of the American constitutional order. *Studies in American Political Development, 23*(2), 143–170.

Martinez, E. (1994). Seeing more than Black & White: Latinos, racism, and the cultural divides. *Z Magazine, 7*, 56–60.

Matovina, T. (2005). *Guadalupe and her faithful: Latino Catholics in San Antonio, from colonial origins to the present*. Baltimore, MD: Johns Hopkins Press.

Matthews, A., Li, C. C., Aranda, F., Torres, L., Vargas, M., & Conrad, M. (2014). The influence of acculturation on substance use behaviors among latina sexual minority women: The mediating role of discrimination. *Substance Use & Misuse, 49*(14), 1888–1898.

Matthews, B. S. (1927). The woman juror. *Women Lawyers' Journal, 15*(2), 1–4.

Mattlage, L. (1986). Getting there. In J. Alexander D. Berrow, L. Domitrovich, M. Donnelly, & C. McLean (Eds.), *Women and aging: An anthology by women* (pp. 79–81). Corvallis, OR: Calyx Books.

Mattu, A. & Maznavi, N. (2012). *Love inshallah: The secret love lives of Muslim women.* Berkeley, CA: Soft Skull Press.

Mayell, H. (2002). Thousands of women killed for family "honor." *National Geographic News* article. Retrieved from news.nationalgeographic.com.

Mazumdar, S. (1989). General introduction: A woman-centered perspective on Asian American history. In Asian Women's United of California (Ed.), *Making waves: An anthology of writings by and about Asian American women* (pp. 1–22). Boston, MA: Beacon Press.

Mazumdar, S. (2003). What happened to the women? Chinese and Indian male migration to the United States in global perspective. In S. Hune . & G. M. Nomura (Eds.), *Asian/Pacific Islander American women: A historical anthology* (pp. 58–76). New York, NY: New York University Press.

McAuliffe, C. (2007). Visible minorities: Constructing and deconstructing the 'Muslim Iranian' diaspora. In C. Aitchison, P. Hopkins & M. Kwan, M. (Eds.), *Geographies of Muslim identities: Diaspora, gender and belonging* (pp. 29–56). Hampshire, UK: Ashgate Publishing.

McBrien, R. P. (2008). *The Church: The evolution of Catholicism.* New York, NY: HarperOne.

McClaurin, I. (1996). *Women of Belize: Gender and change in Central America.* New Brunswick, NJ: Rutgers University Press.

McClusky, L. J. (2001). *"Here, our culture is hard:" Stories of domestic violence from a Mayan community in Belize.* Austin, TX: University of Texas Press.

McDonald, K. E., Keys, C. B., & Balcazar, F. E. (2007). Disability, race/ethnicity and gender: themes of cultural oppression, acts of individual resistance. *American Journal of Community Psychology, 39*(1/2), 145–161.

McDonnell, F. J. H. & Akallo, G. (2007). *Girl soldier: A story of hope for Northern Uganda's children.* Grand Rapids, MI: Chosen.

McGuire, D. L. (2010). *At the dark end of the street: Black women, rape, and resistance—A new history of the civil rights movement from Rosa Parks to the rise of black power.* New York, NY: Vintage Books.

McLaughlin, K. (2014). 5 things women couldn't do in the 1960s. Retrieved from www.cnn.com

McMillan, T. (2012). *The American way of eating: Undercover at Walmart, Applebees, farm fields and the dinner table.* New York, NY: Scribner.

McMullin, J. A. & Berger, E. D. (2006). Gendered ageism/age sexism. In T. M. Calasanti & K. F. Slevin (Eds.), *Age matters: Re-aligning feminist thinking* (pp. 201–223). New York, NY: Routledge.

McWhirter, E. H., Luginbuhl, P. J., & Brown, K. (2014). Apoyenos! Latina/o recommendations for high school supports. *Journal of Career Development, 41*(1), 3–23.

McWhorter, S. K., Stander, V. A., Merrill, L. L., Thomsen, C. J., & Milner, J. S. (2009). Reports of rape reperpetration by newly enlisted male Navy personnel. *Violence and victims, 24*(2), 204–218.

Meade, T. A. (2010). *A history of modern Latin America: 1800 to the present.* West Sussex, UK: Wiley.

Mederos, F. (2001). National Symposium on La Violencia Domestica: An emerging dialogue among Latinos. In G. Kirk & M. Okazawa-Rey (Eds.), *Women's lives: Multicultural perspectives.* (pp. 232–242). Mountain View, CA: Mayfield.

Medina, J. X. (2011). Body politicking and the phenomenon of 'passing.' *Feminism & Psychology, 21*(1), 138–143.

Meloy, M. L. (2006). *Sex offenses and the men who commit them: An assessment of sex offenders on probation.* Lebanon, NH: University of New England Press.

Mernissi, F. (1982). Virginity and patriarchy. In *Women's Studies International Forum, 5*(2), 183–191.

Meyer-Cook, F. (2008). Two-spirit people: Traditional pluralism and human rights. In S. Brotman & J. J. Levy (Eds.), *Intersections: Cultures, sexualites et genres.* (pp. 245–279). Quebec, Canada: University of Quebec Press.

Michaud, S. G. & Hazelwood, R. (1998). *The evil that men do: FBI profiler Roy Hazelwood's journey in the minds of sexual predators.* New York, NY: St. Martin's.

Miller, A. K. (2010). *She looks just like you: A memoir of (nonbiological lesbian) motherhood.* Boston, MA: Beacon Press.

Miller, E., Jordan, B., Levenson, R., & Silverman, J. G. (2010). Reproductive coercion: Connecting the dots between partner violence and unintended pregnancy. *Contraception, 81,* 457–459.

Miller, P. (2014). *Good Catholics: The battle over abortion in the Catholic Church*. Berkeley, CA: University of California Press.

Mir, R. A. (2013). Religion as a coping mechanism for global labor: Lessons from the South Asian Shia Muslim diaspora in the US. *Equality, Diversity and Inclusion, 32*(3), 325–337.

Miranda, D. A. (2011). "Saying the padre had grabbed her": Rape is the weapon, story is the cure. *Intertexts, 14*(2), 93–112.

Mirkinson, J. (2014). George Will says being a rape victim is a 'coveted status' in college. Retrieved from www.huffingtonpost.com

Mitchell, M. (1985). The effects of unemployment on the social condition of women and children in the 1930s. *History Workshop Journal, 19*(1), 105–127.

Moghadam, V. M. (2005). *Globalizing women: Transnational feminist networks*. Baltimore, MD: The John Hopkins University Press.

Mohr, J. C. (1978). *Abortion in America: The origins and evolution of national policy*. New York, NY: Oxford University Press.

Molinary, R. (2005). The latina in me. In A. J. Fountas (Ed.), *Waking up American: Coming of age biculturally*. Emeryville, CA: Seal Press, pp. 185–196.

Molland, S. (2012). *The perfect business? Anti-trafficking and the sex trade along the Mekong*. Honolulu, HI: University of Hawaii Press.

Mollow, A. & McRuer, R. (2012). Introduction. In R. McRuer & A. Mollow (Eds.), *Sex and disability*. Durham, NC: Duke University Press.

Momsen, J. H. (1991). *Women and development in the third world*. New York, NY: Routledge.

(Moved to correct spelling Matovina)Moon, H. & Dilworth-Anderson, P. (2015). Baby boomers and dementia caregiving: Findings from the National Study of Caregiving. *Age and Ageing, 44*, 300–306.

Moreno, C. L. (2007). The relationship between culture, gender, structural factors, abuse, trauma, and HIV/AIDS for Latinas. *Qualitative Health Research, 17*(3), 340–352.

Morgan, M. (1989). Feminist guerilla theater, 1968. In S. Ware (Ed.), *Modern American women: A documentary history*. Belmont, CA: Wadsworth Publishing.

Mori., K. (1997). *Polite lies: On being a woman caught between cultures*. New York, NY: Fawcett Books.

Morris, J. (1994). The fall. In L. Keith (Ed.), *Mustn't grumble: Writing by disabled women*. (pp. 167–171). London, UK: The Women's Press.

Morris, M. W. (2014). Black girls for sale. Retrieved from *Ebony Magazine* website: www.ebony.com

Mosher, S. W. (1983). *Broken earth: The rural Chinese*. New York, NY: Free Press.

Mostofi, L. (2004). Legitimizing the bastard: The Supreme Court's treatment of the illegitimate child. *Journal of Contemporary Legal Issues, 14*, 453.

Muhammad, P. R. (2005). To be young, gifted, black, American, Muslim, and woman. In S. Abdul-Ghafur (Ed.), *Living Islam out loud: American Muslim women speak* (pp. 36–50). Boston, MA: Beacon Press.

Mukherjee, D., Reis, J. P., & Heller, W. (2013). Women living with traumatic brain injury: Social isolation, emotional functioning and implications for psychotherapy. In M. E. Banks . & E. Kaschak (Eds.), *Women with visible and invisible disabilities: Multiple intersections, multiple issues, multiple therapies* (pp. 3–26). New York, NY: Routledge.

Muller, T. R. (2006). Education for social change: Girls' secondary schooling in Eritrea. *Development and Change, 37*(2), 353–373.

Mullings, B. (1999). Globalization, tourism, and the international sex trade. In K. Kempado (Ed.), *Sun, sex, and gold: Tourism and sex work in the Caribbean* (pp. 55–80). Lanham, MD: Rowan & Littlefield.

Mulugeta, E. (2004). Swimming against the tide: Educational problems and coping strategies of rural female students in Ethiopia. *Eastern Africa Social Science Research Review, 20*(2), 71–97.

Munroe, M. (2001). *Understanding the purpose and power of men*. New Kensington, PA: Whitaker House.

Munyoro, F. (2015). Zimbabwe: Call to protect spouses (sic) property rights. Retrieved from http://allafrica.com/stories/201509280462.html

Murphy, R. F. (1990). *The body silent: The different world of the disabled*. New York, NY: W.W. Norton1.

Murata, A. (2006). Bridging identities. In T. R. Berry & N. Mizelle (Eds.), *From oppression to grace: Women of color and their dilemmas in the academy* (pp. 24–33). Sterling, VA: Stylus Publishing.

Murphy, M. (2014). In prostitution, 'race, class, and sex intersect in the worst of ways to subjugate Native women.' Retrieved from *Feminist Current* website: feministcurrent.com

Murray, P. & Eastwood, M. O. (1994). Jane Crow and the law: Sex discrimination and Title VII. In M. Schneir (Ed.), *Feminism in our time: The essential writings, World War II to the present* (pp. 76–86). New York, NY: Vintage Books.

Murray, J. (2000). *But I love him: Protecting your teen daughter from controlling, abusive dating relationships*. New York, NY: HarperCollins.

Namou, W. (2010). Muslim women empowered by their religion. *Multicultural Review, 19*(2), 30–33.

Nashat, G. (1995). Introduction. In W. Walther (Ed.), *Women in Islam: From medieval to modern times* (pp. 3–12). Princeton, NJ: Markus Wiener.

National Coalition Against Domestic Violence (n.d.). Domestic Violence Facts. Retrieved from www.ncadv.org

National Organization for Women (1966). Statement of Purpose. Retrieved from http://now.org/about/history/statement-of-purpose/

National Women's Law Center (2012). Women's poverty rate stabilizes, but remains historically high. September 12, 2012 press release. Retrieved from nwlc.org

Navarro, M. & Sanchez Korrol, V. (1999). *Women in Latin America and the Caribbean: Restoring women to history*. Bloomington, IN: Indiana University Press.

Neill, K. G. (2013). Duty, honor, rape: Sexual assault against women during war. *Journal of International Women's Studies, 2*(1), 43–51.

Nelson, S. C. (2014). 'Virginity tests' forced on female police recruits in Indonesia. Retrieved from http://www.huffingtonpost.co.uk/2014/11/18/virginity-tests-forced-female-police-recruits-indonesia_n_6176872.html

Neri, A. L., Yassuda, M. S., Fortes-Burgos, A. C. G., Mantovani, E. P., Arbex, F. S., de Souza Torres, S. V., Perracini, M. R., & Guariento, M. E. (2012). Relationships between gender, age, family conditions, physical and mental health, and social isolation of elderly caregivers. *International Psychogeriatrics, 24*(3), 472–483.

Newar, N. (2015). By girls, for girls – Nepal's teenagers say no to child marriage. Retrieved from *Inter Press Service* website: www.ipsnews.net

Nguyen, G. T. & Margo, K. L. (2015). Male body image and weight-related disorders. *Journal of the American Medical Association, 313*(8), 856–856.

Noda, K. E. (1989). Growing up Asian in America. In Asian Women's United of California (Ed.), *Making waves: An anthology of writings by and about Asian American women* (pp. 243–251). Boston, MA: Beacon Press.

Nomani, A. Q (2005). Being the leader I want to see in the world. *In Living Islam out loud: American Muslim women speak* (pp. 139–152). Boston, MA: Beacon Press.

Nomura, G. M. (2003). Introduction. In S. Hune & G. M. Nomura (Eds.), *Asian/Pacific Islander American women: A historical anthology* (pp. 16–24). New York, NY: New York University Press.

Nosraty, L., Jylhä, M., Raittila, T., & Lumme-Sandt, K. (2015). Perceptions by the oldest old of successful aging, Vitality 90+ Study. *Journal of Aging Studies, 32*, 50–58.

NPR News Service (2011). Libyan woman accuses Gadhafi soldiers of rape. Retrieved from www.npr.com

Oakley, B., Knafo, A., Madhavan, G., & Wilson, D. S. (Eds.) (2012). *Pathological altruism*. New York, NY: Oxford University Press.

O'Beirne, K. (2006). *Women who make the world worse: And how their radical feminist assault is ruining our families, military, schools and sports*. New York, NY: Sentinel.

Odette, F. (2013). Body beautiful/body perfect: Where do women with disabilities fit in? In M. Hobbs & C. Rice (Eds.), *Gender and Women's Studies in Canada: Critical terrain* (pp. 414–416). Toronto: Women's Press.

O'Hara, B. (2004). Twice penalized employment discrimination against women with disabilities. *Journal of Disability Policy Studies, 15*(1), 27–34.

Ojibwa (2011). Jeannette Rankin. Retrieved from www.dailykos.com /story/2011/03/10/954533/ -Jeannette-Rankin

Okun, L. (1986). *Woman abuse: Facts replacing myths.* Albany, NY: State University of New York Press.

Olcott, D. Jr. (2006). Women, leadership, and technology: A brave new world. In D. Olcott, Jr. & D. Hardy (Eds.), *Dancing on the glass ceiling.* Madison, WI: Atwood Publishing.

Olivardia, R., Pope, H. G. Jr, & Hudson, J. I. (2014). Muscle dysmorphia in male weightlifters: a case-control study. *The American Journal of Psychiatry, 157*(8), 1291–1296.

Omar, M. (2005). My own worst enemy. In *Living Islam out loud: American Muslim women speak* (pp. 55–66). Boston, MA: Beacon Press.

Ono, K. A. & Pham, V. N. (2009). *Asian Americans and the media.* Cambridge, UK: Polity.

Orenstein, P. (2011). *Cinderella ate my daughter: Dispatches from the front lines of the new girly-girl culture.* New York, NY: HarperCollins.

Orlando, L. (2001). Loving whom we choose. In G. Kirk & M. Okazawa-Rey (Eds.), *Women's lives: Multicultural perspectives* (2nd ed.) Mountain View, CA: Mayfield.

Ortiz, A. T. & Briggs, L. (2003). The culture of poverty, crack babies, and welfare cheats: The making of the "healthy white baby crisis." *Social Text, 21*(3), 39–57.

Osell, T. (2014). Senators push for better gun regulations to protect survivors of intimate partner violence. *RH Reality Check.* Retrieved from at www.rhreality.org

Osman, S. L. (2003). Predicting men's rape perceptions based on the belief that "no" really means "yes." *Journal of Applied Social Psychology, 33*(4), 683–692.

Osnos, E. (2014). *Age of ambition: Chasing fortune, truth, or faith in the new China.* New York, NY: Farrar, Straus and Giroux.

Owen, B. (2005). Afterword: The case of the women. In J. Irwin, *The warehouse prison: Disposal of the new dangerous class.* Los Angeles, CA: Roxbury Publishing.

Paglia, C. (n.d.) Quote cited in *Columbia World of Quotations.* Retrieved from Dictionary.com website: http://quotes.dictionary.com

Palacio, C. A. (2013). The career development of Latina women achieving the position of public high school principal. *Theses and Dissertations.* Paper 368. Retrieved from http://dc.uwm.edu/ etd/368

Palmore, E. B. (2001). Sexism and ageism. In J. M. Coyle (Ed.), *Handbook on women and aging* (pp. 3–13). Westport, CT: Praeger.

Papademetriou, L. (2007). *How to be a girly girl in just ten days.* New York, NY: Scholastic..

Parish, S. L., Rose, R. A., & Andrews, M. E. (2009). Income poverty and material hardship among US women with disabilities. *Social Service Review, 83*(1), 33–52.

Parks, S. (2010). *Fierce angels: The strong black woman in American life and culture.* New York, NY: Ballantine Books.

Paul, A. (1976). Suffrage militant Alice Paul goes to jail. In S. Ware (Ed.), Modern American women: A documentary history (1989) (pp. 150–156). Belmont, CA: Wadsworth Publishing,.

Pearlman, S. F. (1987). The saga of continuing clash in lesbian community, or will and army of ex-lovers fail? In Boston Lesbian Psychologies Collective, (Eds.) *Lesbian psychologies: Explorations and challenges.* (pp. 313–326). Urbana, IL: University of Illinois Press.

Pegues, J. (1997). Strategies from the field: Organizing the Asian American feminist movement. In S. Shah (Ed.), *Dragon ladies: Asian American feminists breathe fire* (pp. 3–16). Boston, MA: South End Press.

Penny, T. (2014). Kerry says world can agree to stop rape in war. Retrieved from www.bloomberg. com.

People for the American Way (no date). How the war on women became mainstream: Turning back the clock in Tea Party America. Retrived from www.pfaw.org/media-center/publications/ war-women

Perdue, T. (2001). Introduction. In T. Perdue (Ed.), *Sifters: Native American women's lives* (pp. 1–13). New York, NY: Oxford University Press.

Perera, A. (2014). Women warriors take environmental protection into their own hands. Retrieved from *Inter Press Service* website: www.ipsnews.net

Perez, M. Z. (2008). When sexual autonomy isn't enough: Sexual violence against immigrant women in the United States. In J. Friedman & J. Valenti (Eds.), *Yes means yes!: Visions of female sexual power & a world without rape* (pp. 141–150). Berkeley, CA: Seal Press.

Peril, L. (2006). *College girls: Bluestockings, sex kittens, and coeds, then and now.* New York, NY: W.W. Norton.

Perry, S. (2001). Between a rock and a hard place: Women's organizations in China. In S. Perry & C. Schenk (Eds.), *Eye to eye: Women practising development across cultures* (pp. 89–101). New York, NY: Palgrave Press.

Pew Research Center (2013a). Growing support for gay marriage: Changed minds and changing demographics. Retrieved from on www.people-press.org/2013/03/20

Pew Research Center (2013b). The sandwich generation: Rising financial burdens for middle-aged Americans. Retrieved from on www.pewsocialtrends.org

Phillips, J. L. (1999). Tourist-oriented prostitution in Barbados: The case of the Beach Boy and the white female tourist. In K. Kempado (Ed.), *Sun, sex, and gold: Tourism and sex work in the Caribbean* (pp. 183–200). Lanham, MD: Rowan & Littlefield.

Pinto, P. C. (2013). Women, disability, and the right to health. In M. Hobbs & C. Rice, (Eds.), *Gender and women's studies in Canada: Critical terrain* (pp. 444–455). Toronto, Canada: Women's Press.

Planas, R. (2012). Rape, sexual abuse of immigrant detainees addressed with new DHS rules. Retrieved from *Huffington Post* website: www.huffingtonpost.com

Pozner, J. L. (2013). Ghetto bitches, china dolls, and cha-cha divas: Race, beauty, and the tyranny of Tyra Banks. In M. Hobbs & C. Rice (Eds.), *Gender and women's studies in Canada: Critical terrai.* (pp. 339–348). Toronto, Canada: Women's Press.

Puri, S., Adams, V., Ivey, S., & Nachtigall, R. D. (2011). "There is such a thing as too many daughters, but not too many sons": A qualitative study of son preference and fetal sex selection among Indian immigrants in the United States. *Social Science & Medicine, 72*(7), 1169–1176.

Quammen, D. (2012). *Spillover: Animal infections and the next human pandemic.* New York, NY: W.W. Norton.

RADAR (Respecting Accuracy in Domestic Violence Reporting) (2008). VAWA: Threat to families, children, men, and women. Retrieved from on website: www.mediaRADAR.org

Rainey, L. S. (2010). Secretarial fiction: Gender and genre in four novels, 1897–1898. *English Literature in Transition, 1880–1920 53*(3), 308–330.

Raj, A., Silverman, J. G., & Amaro, H. (2004). Abused women report greater male partner risk and gender-based risk for HIV: Findings from a community-based study with Hispanic women. *AIDS Care, 16*(4), 519–529.

Rathbone, C. (2005). *A world apart: Women, prison, and life behind bars.* New York, NY: Random House.

Raymond, J. G. (2013). *Not a choice, not a job: Exposing the myths about prostitution and the global sex trade.* Dulles, VA: Potomac Books.

Reddy, G. (2005). *With respect to sex: Negotiating hijra identity in south India.* Chicago, IL: University of Chicago Press.

Reina, A. S., Maldonado, M. M., & Lohaman, B. J. (2013a) "He said they'd deport me": Factors influencing domestic violence help-seeking practices among Latina immigrants. *Journal of Interpersonal Violence, 29*(4), 593–615.

Reina, A. S., Maldonado, M. M., & Lohaman, B. J. (2013b). Undocumented Latina networks and responses to domestic violence in a new immigrant gateway: Toward a place-specific analysis. *Violence Against Women, 19,* 1472–1497.

Reuters News Agency (2014). Libya to compensate women raped during 2011 uprising. Retrieved from www.reuters.com

Richardson, V. E. (1999). Women and retirement. In J. D. Garner (Ed.), *Fundamentals of feminist gerontology* (pp. 49–66). New York, NY: Haworth Press.

Rinaldo, R. (2014). Pious and critical: Muslim women activists and the question of agency. *Gender & Society, 28*(6), 824–846.

Ringdal, N. J. (2004). *Love for sale: A world history of prostitution.* New York, NY: Grove Press.

Robertiello, G. & Terry, K. J. (2007). Can we profile sex offenders? A review of sex offender typologies. *Aggression and Violent Behavior, 12*(5), 508–518.

Rock, C. (1997). *Rock this!* New York, NY: Hyperion Books.

Rockler-Gladen, N. (2013). Against the objectification of females. *Blog article*. Retrieved from www.martyduren.com

Roessler, R. T., Neath, J., McMahon, B. T., & Rumrill, P. D. (2007). Workplace discrimination outcomes and their predictive factors for adults with multiple sclerosis. *Rehabilitation Counseling Bulletin, 50*(3), 139–152.

Rogers, T. N. R. (2002). Foreword to the Dover edition. In E. C. Stanton, *The Women's Bible*. Mineola, New York, NY: Dover.

Rohrbaugh, J. B. (2006). Domestic violence in same-gender relationships. *Family Court Review, 44*(2), 287–299.

Roiphe, K. (1994). *The morning after: Sex, fear and feminism*. Boston, MA: Little, Brown.

Rosario, M., Schrimshaw, E. W., Hunter, J., & Levy-Warren, A. (2009). The coming-out process of young lesbian and bisexual women: Are there butch/femme differences in sexual identity development?. *Archives of sexual behavior, 38*(1), 34–49.

Rosenbaum, J. E. (2009). Patient Teenagers? A comparison of the sexual behavior of virginity pledgers and matched nonpledgers. *Pediatrics, 123*(1), 110–120.

Roshanrawan, S. M. (2009). Passing-as-if: Model-minority subjectivity and women of color Identification. *Meridians: Feminism, Race, Transnationalism, 10*(1), 1–31.

Rossi, N. E. (2010). "Coming Out" stories of gay and lesbian young adults. *Journal of Homosexuality, 57*, 1174–1191.

Roughgarden, S. (2009). *Evolution's rainbow: Diversity, gender, and sexuality in nature and people*. Los Angeles, CA: UCLA Press.

Rousso, H. (2013). *Don't call me inspirational: A disabled feminist talks back*. Philadelphia, PA: Temple University Press.

Rowbotham, J. (1989). *Good girls make good wives: Guidance for girls in Victorian fiction*. New York, NY: Basil Blackwell.

Rozario, S. (2007). The dark side of micro-credit. Retrieved from *Open Democracy* website: www.opendemocracy.net

Rushworth, R. (1994). Mustn't grumble. In L. Keith (Ed.), *Mustn't grumble: Writing by disabled women* (pp. 38–40). London, UK: The Women's Press,

Russo, V. (1987). *The celluloid closet: Homosexuality in the movies*. New York, NY: Harper & Row.

Sachs, A. (2008). How not to look old: Author Charla Krupp. Retrieved from *Time Magazine* website: www.time.com

Saed, K. (2005). On the edge of belonging. In *Living Islam out loud: American Muslim women speak* (pp. 86–94). Boston, MA: Beacon Press.

Salih, S. (2001). Versions of virginity in late medieval England. Cambridge, UK: D.S. Brewer.

Samuels, E. J. (2003). My body, my closet: Invisible disability and the limits of coming-out discourse. *GLQ: A Journal of Lesbian and Gay Studies, 9*(1–2), 233–255.

Sanday, P. R. (2002). *Women in the center: Life in a modern matriarchy*. Ithaca, New York, NY: Cornell University Press.

Sanger, A. (2007). Eugenics, race, and Margaret Sanger revisited: Reproductive freedom for all? *Hypatia, 22*(2), 210–217.

Sanger, M. (1921). The eugenic value of birth control propaganda. *Birth Control Review, 5*(10), 1–10.

Sanger, M. (2004 reprint). *The autobiography of Margaret Sanger*. Mineola, New York, NY: Dover.

Saunders, J. P. (2011). *The art of whoring: Adventures in prostitution*. Self-published.

Savino, J. O. & Turvey, B. E. (2011). Sex trafficking: A culture of rape. In J. O. Savino, & B. E. Turvey (Eds.), *Rape investigation handbook* (2nd ed., pp. 57–84). Waltham, MA: Academic Press.

Saxton, M. (1987). The something that happened before I was born. In M. Saxton & F. Howe (Eds.), *With wings: An anthology of literature by and about women with disabilities* (pp. 51–55). New York, NY: Feminist Press.

Saxton, M. (2012). Barbara Waxman Fiduccia and disability feminism: Introduction. Paper for the Center for Women Policy Studies. Retrieved from www.centerwomenpolicy.org

Saxton, M., Curry, M. A., Powers, L. E., Maley, S., Eckels, K., & Gross, J. (2001). "Bring My Scooter So I Can Leave You" A study of disabled women handling abuse by personal assistance providers. *Violence Against Women, 7*(4), 393–417.

Sayu Bhojwani, S. (2011). Welcome mat and spiked gate: Two stories of immigrants in the United States. *Race/Ethnicity, 4*(3), 373–379.

Scharff, C. (2011). Disarticulating femin ism: Individualization, neoliberalism and the othering of 'Muslim women.' *European Journal of Women's Studies, 18*(2), 119–134.

Schlafly, P. (2009). The incidence of domestic violence is exaggerated. In M. Wilson (Ed.), *Domestic violence: Opposing viewpoints* (pp. 29–33). Detroit, MI: Greenhaven.

Schlafly, P. (2014). *Who killed the American family?* Washington, DC: WND Books.

Scott, C. L. & Philpott, D. (2014). *Sexual assault in the military: A guide for victims and families.* Lanham, MD: Rowman & Littlefield.

Scott-Maxwell, F. (1968). *Measure of my days: One woman's enduring, vivid celebration of life and aging.* New York, NY: Penguin.

Seacat J. D., Dougal S. C., Roy D. (2014). A daily diary assessment of female weight stigmatization. *Journal of Health Psychology*, Retrieved Mar 18, 2014, Number 1359105314525067.

Seguino, S. (2013). Toward gender justice: Confronting stratification and unequal power. *GÉNEROS-Multidisciplinary Journal of Gender Studies, 2*(1), 1–36.

Sethi, S. P. (1994). *Multinational corporations and the impact of public advocacy on corporate strategy: Nestle and the infant formula controversy.* Boston, MA: Kluwer Academic.

Selinger, E. (2008). Does microcredit "empower"? Reflections on the Grameen Bank debate. *Human Studies, 31*, 27–41.

Severy-Hoven, B. (2013). Master narratives and the wall painting of the house of the Vettii, Pompeii. In D. R. Gabaccio & M. J. Maynes (Eds.), *Gender history across epistemologies* (pp. 20–60). Hoboken, NJ: Wiley-Blackwell.

Shagar, L. K., Lai, A., & Raman, A. (2013). Prostitutes fake virginity to boost income. Retrieved from Star Online website: http://www.thestar.com.my/News

Shah, B. (2014). Women's bodies were the ultimate battleground of war-torn 2014. Retrieved from *Huffington Post* www.huffingtonpost.com

Shad, S. (1997). *Dragon ladies: Asian American feminists breathe fire.* Boston, MA: South End Press.

Shah, S. (1997). Introduction: Slaying the dragon lady. In S. Shah (Ed.), *Dragon ladies: Asian American feminists breathe fire* (pp. xii-xxi). Boston, MA: South End Press.

Shahid, H. A. & Horan, K. (2014). *Devotion and defiance: My journey in love, faith and politics.* New York, NY: W.W. Norton.

Shalit, W. (2004). *Return to modesty: Discovering the lost virtue.* New York, NY: Touchstone.

Shambaugh, R. (2008). *It's not a glass ceiling, it's a sticky floor: Free yourself from the hidden behaviors that sabotage your career.* New York, NY: McGraw Hill.

Shen, A. J. (2007). *A tiger's heart: The story of a modern Chinese woman.* New York, NY: Soho Press.

Shepela, S. T. & Levesque, L. L. (1998). Poisoned waters: Sexual harassment and the college climate. *Sex Roles, 38*(7/8), 589–611.

Sher, J. (2013). *Somebody's daughter: The hidden story of America's prostituted children and the battle to save them.* Chicago, IL: Chicago Review Press.

Sherr, L. (2014). Women have surgery to 'restore' virginity. Retrieved from *ABC News* website: www.abcnews.go.com/2020

Sherry, M. (2004). Overlaps and contradictions between queer theory and disability studies. *Disability & Society, 19*(7), 769–783.

Shields, S. (2009). Gender: An intersectionality perspective. *Sex Roles, 59*, 301–311.

Shilts, R. (1987). *And the band played on: Politics, people, and the AIDS epidemic.* New York, NY: St. Martin's Press.

Shorey, R. C., Brasfield, H., Febres, J., & Stuart, G. L. (2011). The association between impulsivity, trait anger, and the perpetration of intimate partner and general violence among women arrested for domestic violence. *Journal of Interpersonal Violence, 26*(13), 2681–2697.

Shreve, A. (1989). *Women together, women alone: The legacy of the consciousness-raising movement.* New York, NY: Fawcett Columbine.

Shumow, L. & Schmidt, J. A. (2014). *Enhancing adolescents' motivation for science: Research-based strategies for teaching male and female students*. Thousand Oaks, CA: Corwin.

Siddiqi, D. M. (2011). Transnational feminism and "local" realities: The imperiled Muslim woman and the production of (in)justice. *Journal of Women in the Middle East and the Islamic World, 9*, 76–96.

Siebers, T. (2004). Disability as masquerade. *Literature and Medicine, 23*,(1), 1–22.

Signore, C., Spong, C. Y., Krotoski, D., Shinowara, N. L., & Blackwell, S. C. (2011). Pregnancy in women with physical disabilities. *Obstetrics & Gynecology, 117*(4), 935–947.

Silva-Martinez, E. & Murty, S. (2011). Ethics and cultural competence in research with battered immigrant Latina women. *Journal of Ethnic and Cultural Diversity in Social Work, 20*(3), 223–239.

Simpson, M. (2009). Traveling soap operas, Brazil to Krygyzstan: Meaning-making and images of the "Muslim Woman." *Journal of International Women's Studies, 11*(1), 304–326.

Siraj, A. (2010). "Because I'm the man! I'm the head": British married Muslims and the patriarchal family structure. *Contemporary Islam, 4*, 195–214.

Siraj, A. (2012). "I don't want to taint the name of Islam": The influence of religion on the lives of Muslim lesbians. *Journal of Lesbian Studies, 16*(4), 449–467.

Sirleaf, E .J. (2009). *This child will be great: Memoir of a remarkable life by Africa's first woman president*. New York, NY: HarperCollins.

Sirleaf, E. J. (2011). A voice for freedom: Nobel lecture. Retrieved from Nobel Peace Prize website: www. nobelprize.org

Skerritt, A. J. (2011). *Ashamed to die: Science, denial, and the AIDS epidemic in the South*. Chicago: Lawrence Hill Books.

Skidmore, T. E., Smith, P. H., & Green, J. N. (2010). *Modern Latin America* (7th ed.) .New York, NY: Oxford University Press.

Slattery, A. J. & Smith, E. (2012). *African American families today; Myths and realities*. Lanham, MD: Rowman & Littlefield..

Smith, A. (2003). Not an Indian tradition: The sexual colonization of Native peoples. *Hypatia, 18*(2), 70–85.

Smith, B. (1998). *The truth that never hurts: Writings on race, gender, and freedom*. Rutgers, NJ: Rutgers University Press.

Smith, H. M. (2007). Psychological services needs of older women. *Psychological Services, 4*(4), 277–286.

Snyder, K. (2014). Why women leave tech: It's the culture, not because "math is hard." *Fortune Magazine*. Retrieved from www.fortune.com

Solinger, R. (2013). *Reproductive politics: What everyone needs to know*. New York, NY: Oxford University Press.

Sommer, M. H. (2000). *Sex, law, and society in late imperial China*. Stanford, CA: Stanford University Press.

Sommers, C. H. (2012). CDC study on sexual violence in the U.S. overstates the problem. Retrieved from *Washington Post* website: www.washingtonpost.com

Spar, D. L. (2013). *Wonder women: Sex, power, and the quest for perfection*. New York, NY: Sarah Crichton Books.

Spence, J. D. (1990). *The search for modern China*. New York, NY: W.W. Norton.

Spitzer, B. H. & Cupach, W. R. (2014). *The dark side of relationship pursuit: From attraction to obsession and stalking*. New York, NY: Routledge.

Stacey, D. (2015). *Griswold v. Connecticut* 1965. Retrieved from *About Health* website: http://contraception.about.com

Stanley, J. (2015). Fertility is not a "disease"! How extremists fundamentally misunderstand contraception. Retrieved from *Salon* website: www.salon.com.

Stansell, C. (2010). *The feminist promise: 1792 to the present*. New York, NY: The Modern Library.

Stanton, E. C. (1848). We now demand our right to vote. Retrieved from http://womenshistory. about.com/od/stantoneworks/fl/We-Now-Demand-Our-Right-to-Vote-1848.htm

Stanton, E. C. & Mott, L. (1848). Seneca falls declaration. Retrieved from http://womenshistory. about.com/od/suffrage1848/a/seneca_declartn.htm

Steele, V. (2001). *The corset: A cultural history* (Vol. 5). New Haven, CT: Yale University Press.

Stein, A. (1993). The year of the lustful lesbian. In A. Stein (Ed.), *Sisters, sexperts, queers: Beyond the lesbian nation* (pp. 13–34). New York, NY: Penguin.

Stevens, B. (2011). Politicizing sexual pleasure, Oppression and disability: Recognizing and undoing the impacts of ableism on sexual and reproductive health. Paper for Center for Women Policy Studies. Retrieved from www.centerwomenpolicy.org

Stevens, E. P. (1973). Machismo and marianismo. *Society, 10*(6), 57–67.

Stewart, J. (1987). The body's memory. In M. Saxton & F. Howe, F. (Eds.), *With wings: An anthology of literature by and about women with disabilities* (pp. 129–136). New York, NY: Feminist Press,

Stine, G. J. (2004). *AIDS update 2004.* San Francisco, CA: Pearson.

Stohr, G. & Winkler, M. A. (2015). Ruth Bader Ginsburg thinks Americans are ready for gay marriage. *Bloomberg Business.* Retrieved from www.bloomberg.com.

Stosny, S. (2008). Are you dating an abuser? Emotional abuse, verbal abuse: The early signs. *Psychology Today,* December 17. Retrieved from www.psychologytoday.com

Stoller, R. J. (1984). *Sex and gender: The development of masculinity and femininity.* London, UK: Karnac Books.

Stuart, D. M. (2009).The Violence Against Women Act is effective. In M. Wilson (Ed.), *Domestic violence: Opposing viewpoints* (pp. 104–112). Detroit, MI: Greenhaven Press.

Sue, D. W., Capodilupo, C. M., Torino, G. C., Bucceri, J. M., Holder, A., Nadal, K. L., & Esquilin, M. (2007). Racial microaggressions in everyday life: implications for clinical practice. *American psychologist, 62*(4), 271.

Sullivan, R. & Lee, K. (2008). Organizing immigrant women in America's sweatshops: Lessons from the Los Angeles Garment Worker Center. *Signs: Journal of Women in Culture and Society, 33*(3), 527–532.

Summers, C. H. (1994). *Who stole feminism?* New York, NY: Sentinel.

Sutin, A. R. & Terracciano, A. (2013). Perceived weight discrimination and obesity. *PLoS One, 8*(7), e70048.

Sutin, A. R., Stephan, Y., Carretta, H., & Terracciano, A. (2015). Perceived discrimination and physical, cognitive, and emotional health in older adulthood. *The American Journal of Geriatric Psychiatry, 23*(2), 171–179.

Szymanski, D. M. & Henning, S. L. (2007). The role of self-objectification in women's depression: A test of objectification theory. *Sex Roles, 56*(1–2), 45–53.

Takaki, R. (1998). *Strangers from a different shore: A history of Asian Americans,* (rev. ed.). Ebookit.com

Tanenbaum, L. (2000). *Slut: Growing up female with a bad reputation.* New York, NY: Harper Perennial.

Tannahill, R. (1980). *Sex in history.* New York, NY: Stein and Day.

Telesetsky, A. (1998). In the shadows and behind the veil: Women in Afghanistan under the Taliban rule. *Berkeley Women's Law Journal, 13,* 293–305.

Thiara, R. K., Hague, G., Bashall, R., & Harwin, N. (2012). *Disabled women and domestic violence: Responding to the experiences of survivors.* Jessica Kingsley Publishers.

Thomas, G. (2011). Michelle Bachelet's Liderazgo Femenino (Feminine Leadership). *International Feminist Journal of Politics, 13*(1), 63–82.

Thomas, W. H. (2004). *What are old people for? How elders will save the world.* Acton, MA: VanderWyk & Burnham.

Thornhill, R. & Palmer, C. T. (2000). *A natural history of rape: Biological bases of sexual coercion.* Cambridge, MA: The MIT Press.

Thornton, R. (1987). *American Indian holocaust and survival: A population history since 1492.* Norman, OK: University of Oklahoma Press.

Thorpe, H. (2009). *Just like us: The true story of four Mexican girls coming of age in America.* New York, NY: Scribner.

Thorpe, H. (2014). *Soldier girls: The battles of three women at home and at war.* New York, NY: Scribner.

Tjaden, P. & Thoennes, N. (2000). Full report of the prevalence, incidence, and consequence of violence against women. Retrieved from Department of Justice website: www.justice.gov. ovw/tribal-communities

Tiano, S. (1994). *Patriarchy on the line: Labor, gender, and ideology in the Mexican maquila industry.* Philadelphia: Temple University Press.

Tomiyama, A. J. & Mann, T. (2013). If shaming reduced obesity, there would be no fat people. *Hastings Center Report, 43*(3), 4–5.

Tone, A. (2001). *Devices and desires: A history of contraceptives in America.* New York, NY: Hill & Wang.

Track, S. (1995). We have to have ceremonies. In J. Katz (Ed.), *Messengers of the wind: Native American women tell their life stories* (pp. 21–32). New York, NY: Ballantine Books.

Trafzer, C. E. & Lorimer, M. (2014). Silencing California Indian genocide in social dtudies texts. *American Behavioral Scientist, 58*(1), 64–82.

Treasure, J. & Alexander, J. (2013). *Anorexia nervosa: A recovery guide for sufferers, families and friends* (2nd ed.). New York, NY: Routledge.

Trohlic, N. S. (2015). The U.S. female genital mutilation crisis. Retrieved from *Daily Beast* website: www.thedailybeast.com

Troost, H. (2008). Reclaiming touch: Rape culture, explicit verbal consent, and body sovereignty. In J. Friedman & J. Valenti (Eds.), *Yes means yes! Visions of female sexual power & a world without rape* (pp. 171–178). Berkeley, CA: Seal Press.

Tsouroufli, M. (2012). Breaking in and breaking out of medical school: feminist academic interrupted? *Equality, Diversity and Inclusion: An International Journal, 31*(5/6), 467–483.

Tula, M. T. (1994). *Hear my testimony.* Boston, MA: South End Press.

Turner, C. (2006). *Islam: The basics.* New York, NY: Routledge.

Turshen, M. (1999). The ecological crisis in Tanzania. In J. Silliman. & Y. King (Eds.), *Dangerous intersections: Feminist perspectives on population, environment, and development* (pp. 89–107). Boston, MA: South End Press,

Ukockis, G. (2015). Who pays for sex? A qualitative analysis of sex tourism. Presentation at End Slavery Cincinnati Conference, February 6, 2015.

UNAIDS (United Nations AIDS). (2012). Report on the global AIDS epidemic. Retrieved from website unaids.org.

UNAIDS (United Nations AIDS), UNFPA, & UNIFEM. (2004). Women and AIDS: Confronting the crisis. Retrieved from www.unfpa.org/sites/default/files/pub-pdf/women_aids

United Nations Security Council (2008). Resolution 1280. Retrieved from http://www.ohchr.org/en/newsevents/pages/rapeweaponwar.aspx

Valenti, J. (2007). *Full frontal feminism: A young woman's guide to why feminism matters.* Berkeley, CA: Seal Press.

Valenti, J. (2008). *He's a stud, she's a slut and 49 other double standards every woman should know.* Berkeley: Seal Press.

Valenti, J. (2010). *The purity myth: How America's obsession with virginity is hurting young women.* Berkeley, CA: Seal Press.

Valenti, J. (2014). The California shooting spree is proof that misogyny kills, *Business Insider,* businessinsider.com, May 26, 2014.

Vartanian, L. R., Thomas, M. A., & Vanman, E. J. (2013). Disgust, contempt, and anger and the stereotypes of obese people. *Eating and Weight Disorders, 18*(4), 377–382.

Venkataramini-Kothari, A. (2007). Understanding South Asian immigrant women's experience of intimate violence. In S. D. Dasgupta (Ed.), *Body evidence: Intimate violence against south Asian women in America* (pp. 11–23). New Brunswick, NJ: Rutgers University Press.

Wadud, A. (1999). *Qur'an and Woman: Rereading the Sacred Text from a Woman's Perspective* (pp. ix–x). Oxford, UK: Oxford University Press.

Wahls, Z. & Littlefield, B. (2011). *My two moms: Lessons of love, strength, and what makes a family.* New York, NY: Gotham Books.

Wahud, A. (2005). The Koran teaches that women have the same rights as men. In M. S. Yuan (Ed.), *Women in Islam* (pp. 9–13). Detroit, MI: Thomson Gale.

Waldman, A. & Levi, R. (2011). Inside this place, not of it: Narratives from women's prisons. Book excerpt retrieved from http://womenandprison.org/social-justice/view/excerpt

Walker, A. (2014). "I'm not a lesbian; I'm just a freak": A pilot study of the experiences of women in assumed-monogamous other-sex unions seeking secret same-sex encounters online, their negotiation of sexual desire, and meaning-making of sexual identity. *Sexuality & Culture, 18,* 911–935.

Walker, L. (1977). Who are the battered women? *Frontiers: A Journal of Women's Studies, 2*(1), 52–57.

Walker, R. (2007). Becoming the third wave. In E. Freedman (Ed.), *The essential feminist reader* (pp. 397–401). New York, NY: The Modern Library,

Wallace, M. (1980). *Black macho and the myth of the superwoman.* New York, NY: Warner Books.

Walley-Jean, J. C. (2009). Debunking the myth of the "angry black woman": An exploration of anger in young African American women. *Black Women, Gender & Families, 3*(2), 68–86.

Walters, M. (2002). The rights and wrongs of women: Mary Wollstonecraft, Harriet Martineau, Simone de Beauvoir. In M. Evans (Ed.), *Feminism and the enlightenment* (pp. 268–329). New York, NY: Routledge.

Walther, W. (1995). *Women in Islam: From medieval to modern times.* Princeton, NJ: Markus Wiener Publishers.

Walton, D. (2001). What's a leg got to do with it? In G. Kirk & M. Okazawa-Rey (Eds.), *Women's lives: Multicultural perspectives* (pp. 126–127). Mountain View, CA: Mayfield.

Walton, D. (2011). What's a leg got to do with it?: Black, female and disabled in America. Paper for Center for Women Policy Studies. Retrieved from www.centerwomenpolicy.org

Wang, Z. (1999). *Women in the Chinese enlightenment: Oral and textual histories.* Berkeley, CA: University of California Press.

Ward, R. & Howe, C. (2011). 'If I look old, I will be treated old': hair and later-life image dilemmas. *Ageing and Society, 31*(2), 288–307.

Warren, C. S. (2014). Body area dissatisfaction in white, black and Latina female college students in the USA: an examination of racially salient appearance areas and ethnic identity. *Ethnic and Racial Studies, 37*(3), 537–556.

Warshaw, R. (1994). *I never called it rape: The Ms. Report on recognizing, fighting and surviving date and acquaintance rape.* New York, NY: HarperPerennial.

Wasserstrom, J. N. (2013). *China in the 21st century: What everybody needs to know,* (2nd ed.). New York, NY: Oxford University Press.

Watkins, S. A., Rueda, M. & Rodriguez, M. (2001). *Introduction to feminism.* Cambridge, UK: Icon Books.

Watson, B. (2005). *Bread & Roses: Mills, migrants, and the struggle for the American dream.* New York, NY: Viking Press.

Watson, C. E. (2014). Witches, female priests and sacred manoeuvres: (De)stabilising gender and sexuality in a Cuban religion of African origin. In J. de Groot & S. Morgan (Eds.), *Sex, gender and the sacred: Reconfiguring religion in gender history* (pp. 31–50). Hoboken, NJ: Wiley.

Weise, J. (2011). The disability rights movement and the legacy of poets with disabilities. In J. Bartlett, S. Black, & M. Northen (Eds.), *Beauty is a verb: The new poetry of disability* (pp. 138–144). El Paso, TX: Cinco Puntas Press,

Weiss, E. (2003). *Family and friends' guide to domestic violence: How to listen, talk and take action when someone you care about is being abused.* Volcano, CA: Volcano Press.

Weiss, E. (2004). *Surviving domestic violence: Voices of women who broke free.* Volcano, CA: Volcano Press.

West, A. D. (2001). HIV/AIDS education for Latina inmates: The delimiting impact of culture on prevention efforts. *The Prison Journal, 81*(1), 20–41.

West, L. A. (1997). Introduction. In L. A. West (Ed.), *Feminist Nationalism* (pp. xi–xxxvi). New York, NY: Routledge.

Westbrook, L. & Schilt, K. (2013). Doing gender, determining gender: Transgender people gender panics, and the maintenance of the sex/gender/sexuality system. *Gender & Society, 28*(1), 32–57.

Whisman, V. (1993). Identity crises: Who is a lesbian, anyway? In A. Stein (Ed.), *Sisters, sexperts, queers: Beyond the lesbian nation* (pp. 47–60). New York, NY: Penguin .

White, T. R. & Hernandez, J. M. (2013). Muslim women and girls: Searching for democracy and self-expression. *Journal of International Women's Studies, 14*(3), 64–82.

Whitehorse, E. (1995). In my family, the women ran everything. In J. Katz (Ed.), *Messengers of the wing: Native American women tell their life stories* (pp. 55–65). New York, NY: Ballantine Books.

Whiting, J. B., Parker, T. G., & Houghtaling, A. W. (2014). Explanations of a violent relationship: The male perpetrator's perspective. *Journal of Family Violence, 29,* 277–286.

WHO (World Health Organization). 2014 Factsheet on FGM retrieved from www.who.int/mediacentre/factsheets/fs241/en/).

WHO (World Health Organization). HIV/AIDS Data and Analysis retrieved from www.who.int/hiv/topics/mtct/en/

Wild, K., Wiles, J. L., & Allen, R. E. (2013). Resilience: thoughts on the value of the concept for critical gerontology. *Ageing and Society, 33*(01), 137–158.

Wiles, J. L., Wild, K., Kerse, N., & Allen, R. E. (2012). Resilience from the point of view of older people: 'There's still life beyond a funny knee'. *Social Science & Medicine, 74*(3), 416–424.

Wilkins, J. (2011). *Straight talk about … date rape.* New York, NY: Crabtree.

Williams, B. (2015). Taraji P. Henson says her 20-year-old son was racially profiled so she found one way to help resolve it. Retrieved from *Huffington Post* website: www.huffingtonpost.com

Williams, L. (2000). *It's the little things: Everyday interactions that anger, annoy, and divide the races.* New York, NY: Harcourt.

Williams, L. S., Alvarez, S. D., & Andrade Hauck, K. S. (2002). My name is not Maria: Young Latinas seeking home in the heartland. *Social Problems, 49*(4), 563–584.

Williams, R. H. & Vashi, G. (2007). Hijab and American Muslim women: Creating the space for autonomous selves. *Sociology of Religion, 68*(3), 269–287.

Wilson, J. (2013). *The street politics of abortion: Speech, violence, and America's culture wars.* Stanford, CA: Stanford University Press.

Win, T. L. (2014). Women activists defy danger to protect the environment. Retrieved from *Thomas Reuters Foundation* website: www.trust.org.

Wiseman, R. (2009). *Queen bees and wannabes: Helping your daughter survive cliques, gossip, boyfriends, and the new realities of girl world.* New York, NY: Three Rivers Press.

Wolf, A. (2013). *The XX factor: How the rise of working women has created a far less equal world.* New York, NY: Random House.

Wolf, N. (1991). *The beauty myth: How images of beauty are used against women.* New York, NY: Anchor Books.

Wood, M. L. & Price, P. (1997). Machismo and marianismo: Implications for HIV/AIDS reduction and education. *American Journal of Health Studies, 13*(1), 44.

Worthen, M. G. F. (2012). An argument for separate analyses of attitudes toward lesbian, gay, bisexual men, bisexual women, MtF and FtM transgender individuals. *Sex Roles, 68,* 703–723.

Wozniak, D. F. & Allen, K. (2013). *Surviving domestic violence: A guide to healing your soul and building your future.* Avon, MA: Adams Media.

Wright, D. C. (2011). The history of China (2nd ed.). Santa Barbara, CA: Greenwood.

Xinran, X. (2002). *The good women of China: Hidden voices.* New York, NY: Pantheon Books.

Yates, A. (2013). *Compulsive exercise and the eating disorders: Toward an integrated theory of activity.* New York, NY: Brunner/Mazel.

Yen Mah, A. (1997). *Falling leaves: The memoir of an unwanted Chinese daughter.* New York, NY: Broadway Books.

Yihong, J. (2006). Rethinking the 'iron girls': Gender and labour during the Chinese cultural revolution. *Gender & History, 18*(3), 613–634.

Young, A. F. (2004). *Masquerade: The life and times of Deborah Sampson, continental soldier.* New York, NY: Vintage Books.

Young, I. M. (2009). Five faces of oppression. *Geographic thought: A praxis perspective,* 55–71.

Yousafzi, M. & Lamb, C. (2013). *I am Malala: The girl who stood up for education and was shot by the Taliban.* New York, NY: Little, Brown.

Yu, C. Y. (1989). The world of our grandmothers. In Asian Women's United of California (Ed.), *Making waves: An anthology of writings by and about Asian American women* (pp. 33–42). Boston, MA: Beacon Press.

Yuan, M. S. (2005). Introduction. In M. S. Yuan (Ed.), *Women in Islam* (pp. 5–8). Detroit, MI: Thomson Gale.

Yuval-Davis, N. (2006). Intersectionality and feminist politics. *European Journal of Women's Studies, 13*(3), 193–209.

Zevy, L. & Cavallaro, S. A. (1987). Invisibility, fantasy, and intimacy: Princess Charming is not a Prince. In Boston Lesbian Psychologies Collective (Eds.), *Lesbian psychologies: Explorations and challenges* (pp. 83–94). Urbana, IL: University of Illinois Press.

Zhang, N. (2001). In a world together yet apart: Urban and rural women coming of age in the seventies. In X. Zhong, W. Zheng, & B. Di (Eds). *Some of us: Chinese women growing up in the Mao era* (pp. 1–26). New Brunswick, NJ: Rutgers University Press.

Ziarek, E. P. (2008). Right to vote or right to revolt? Arendt and the British Suffrage militancy. *Differences, 19*(3), 1–27.

Zimmerman, M. A. (2013). Resiliency theory: A strengths-based approach to research and practice for adolescent health. *Health Education & Behavior, 40*(4), 381–383.

Zoya, Follain, J. & Chistofari, R. (2002). *Zoya's story: The Afghan woman's struggle for freedom.* New York, NY: William Morrow.

Index

First Wave Feminism 34–42, 45, 58
First Wife/Second Wife *see* China
FIV (Feline Immunodeficiency Virus)
Food deserts 104
Forced sterilization 277, 296, 326, 382
Foreign aid 320
Foot binding *see* China
Forty-year-old Virgin (The) 394
Fourth Wave feminism 7, 61
Francis, Don 405
Frankenstein 29
Free Love Movement 58
Freedom Trash Can 99
French Revolution 31, 309
Friedan, Betty 45–48, 52, 84, 213–214
Fundamentalism 8, 57, 341–342

Gadfly 419
Gandhi, Mohatma 423
Gay bashing *see* Homophobia
Gay cancer/gay plague *see* HIV/AIDS
Gay Liberation Front *see* Lesbians
Geisha girls *see* Sex Trade
Gender complementarity 10–11, 274
Gender Identity Disorder/Gender
    Dysphoria 64, 68–71
Gender imbalance 312–313, 383–384
Gender norms/rules xvi, xviii, 24, 49, 69, 72–74,
    76–78, 81–82, 107, 180, 238, 266, 414, 418
Gender stratification 174
Gender-based segregation 174
Geologic Society of London 13
Ghettoization 221–222
Gilbraith, Lillian 201
Gillibrand, Kirsten 177, 186
Ginsburg, Ruth Bader 80
Girls Gone Wild *see* Sex trade
Girly culture 16, 101–102
    Princess 76, 102
Glaser, Elizabeth 408
Global Gag Rule *see* Mexico City Policy
Glass ceiling 173, 264
Globalization 8, 185, 317–330, 361–362, 363,
    389, 397
Goffman, Erving 293
Gold digger 4, 9–10
Gold widows 322
Golden Lotus *see* China
Gore-Booth, Eva 81–82
Grameen Bank 327–328
Grandma Moses 214
Great Depression 42–43, 45
Great Leap Forward *see* China
Green Fuse movement 314

Griswold case 158
Guttmacher Institute 164
Gynocide *see* Witch hunts

HAART (Highly Active Anti-Retroviral
    Treatment) 404, 407
Hadith *see* Islam
Haley, Nikki 185
Hamasa 343–344
Han 261
Hangover (The) 18
Harlem 244
Harvard University 49, 183
Hashtag #yesallwomen 11
Hatch, Orrin 171
Henson, Taraji P. 256
Hermaphrodites *see* Intersexed persons
Hernandez v. Texas 232–233
Heterosexism 84, 87
Heterosexual 7, 71, 82, 84–85, 86, 87, 88, 94, 109,
    154, 169, 253, 407–408
Heterosexual privilege 87
Hice, Jody 11
Higher education 8, 33, 54, 197–203, 204, 240, 359
    Bluestocking 196
    MRS degree 196
    Sororities 102, 198
Hijab/Burqa see Islam
Hijra 71, 72
Hill, Anita 171
Hispanic *see* Latinas
HIV/AIDS 9, 238, 304, 391, 403–416
    Cultural norms 414–415
    Gay cancer/gay plague 406
    Gender aspects 409–410
    Prevention 78, 237–238, 411, 413, 415
    Retrovirus 405, 406
Homicide *see* DV/IPV
Homophobia
    Heterosexual/homosexual dichotomy 87
    Internalized 7, 88, 90
    Queerbashing 87
Hong Kong 267
Honor killings 153, 303, 310, 341, 349
Honorary males/men 24, 32, 358
Hormones 64–65, 68, 164, 213
Housewives 32, 52, 54–55, 223
Housing instability 221, 294
Howard University 256
HPV *see* Sexually Transmitted Infection
Human rights 52, 63, 166, 177, 251, 296, 303,
    304–306, 308, 310, 314, 327, 353, 355, 358,
    391, 420–422
Human Rights Watch 341

Nafisa of Egypt 336
NAFTA (North American Free Trade Agreement) 361
National Association of Colored Women (NACW) 40–41
National Association of Social Workers (NASW) 5, 85, 95, 239
National Coalition Against Domestic Violence (NCADV) 132, 143, 144
National Institute of Justice 126
National Network to End Domestic Violence (NNEDV) 143, 417
National Organization of Women (NOW) 52, 84–85, 165
Nationalism 308–309, 344
Nationalists in China *see* China
Native American stereotypes 278–280
Navajos 281
Nazis 81, 275, 357
Neoliberalism 185, 320, 324, 360, 362
Nepal 421
Nervous disorders 33
New York City, New York 38, 59, 83, 95, 116, 126, 153, 233, 267, 268
NGO (Non-governmental organization) 325, 330, 381, 421
Nicaragua 166
Nobel Peace Prize 327, 347, 420
Nongendered person 72
Nondisabled *see* Disabilties
Northampton, Massachusetts xvi
NOW *see* National Organization for Women
Nursing profession 5, 30, 95–96, 131, 139, 157, 180, 207, 216, 256, 325, 408, 410

Obama, Michelle 249–251
Obesity 17, 102–104, 253
Objectification 13–14, 59, 73, 100–101, 117, 138, 290, 395, 396, 419–420
Older women 208–218
    Poverty 182
    Successful aging 216–218
One child campaign *see* China
Oppression xvii, 14, 24, 35, 58, 59, 84, 90, 91, 117, 142, 198, 221–226, 277, 281, 293, 305, 309, 314–315, 340–341, 344, 348, 349, 355–356, 367, 378, 387, 389, 393, 417, 420–421
Oriental 260, 262, 268

Paglia, Camille 393
Pakistan 72, 326, 339, 348–350, 390–391
Palin, Sarah 185
Parental expectations *see* Asian American women
Parks, Rosa 119
Passing *see* Disabilities *and* Lesbians

Pathological altruism 206–208
    Burnout/Compassion fatigue 207–208
Pathologized heterosexuality 253
Patriarchy/patriarchal xvi, 10–11, 15, 23–24, 34, 84, 89, 90, 153, 158, 163, 169, 180, 202, 216, 223, 236, 247–248, 277, 307, 308–309, 314, 317, 333, 346, 353, 359, 360, 367, 373, 384, 393, 419
Paul, Alice 38, 55
Pay inequality *see* Unequal pay
Paycheck Fairness Act 184
Pearl Harbot 261
Peeping tom *see* voyeurism
People's Republic of China *see* China
Peron, Eva 356, 357
Peron, Juan 357
Peronist Women's Party 357
Person-in-Environment perspective xvii
Personhood Amendment 17
Pew Research Center 80, 205, 332
Phallocentric 81
Philippines 108
Physicians' Crusade 162
Picture bride 261
Pill (The) *see* Birth control
Pimp 253, 387–388, 392, 399, 400, 409
    Also see Sex Trafficking
Pink Triangle 81
Pinochet, Auguste 356–358
Planned Parenthood xv, 159
Plastic surgery *see* Beauty standard
Pocahantas 279–280
Polaris Project 392, 400
Polygyny/Polygamy 305, 337–338
Pompeii, Italy 72
Pornography *see* Sex Trade
Portugal 359
Postfeminist 59
Post-racist 244
Post-sexist 244
Post Traumatic Stress Disorder (PTSD) 141, 145
Pouissant, Alvin 247
Power and Control Wheel *see* DV/IPV
Pregnancy 3, 49, 155–158, 159, 161–168, 192, 214, 234, 296, 304, 305, 321, 326, 355, 371, 381–382, 400, 410
    Myths 151
Pretty Woman 387
Princess *see* Girly culture
Princeton University 49
Professional Beauty Association 212
Property rights 14, 35, 36, 48, 322
Prostitution *see* Sex Trade
Protection orders/Restraining orders *see* DV/IPV

Printed in Australia
AUHW011405271119
320555AU00008B/66

9 780190 239398